Learning Vocabulary in Another Language

THE CAMBRIDGE APPLIED LINGUISTICS SERIES

The authority on cutting-edge Applied Linguistics research

Series Editors 2007–present: Carol A. Chapelle and Susan Hunston
1988–2007: Michael H. Long and Jack C. Richards

For a complete list of titles please visit: www.cambridge.org/elt/cal

Recent titles in this series:

Learning Vocabulary in Another Language

Second Edition

I. S. P. Nation
Victoria University of Wellington

The first edition of this title was
published under the series editorship
of Michael H. Long and Jack C. Richards

CAMBRIDGE
UNIVERSITY PRESS

CAMBRIDGE
UNIVERSITY PRESS

University Printing House, Cambridge CB2 8BS, United Kingdom

Published in the United States of America by Cambridge University Press, New York

Cambridge University Press is part of the University of Cambridge.

It furthers the University's mission by disseminating knowledge in the pursuit of education, learning and research at the highest international levels of excellence.

www.cambridge.org
Information on this title: www.cambridge.org/9781107623026

First published 2001
Second edition 2013

A catalogue record for this publication is available from the British Library

Library of Congress Cataloguing in Publication data
Nation, I. S. P. Learning vocabulary in another language / I. S. P. Nation. – Second Edition.
    pages   cm. – (Cambridge applied linguistics)
ISBN 978-1-107-04547-7 (hardback) – ISBN 978-1-107-62302-6 (pb)
1. Vocabulary – Study and teaching.   2. Language and languages – Study and teaching.   I. Title.
P53.9.N29   2013
418.0071 – dc23   2013021172

ISBN   978-1-107-62302-6   Paperback
ISBN   978-1-107-04547-7   Hardback

Contents

Series editors' preface

Over ten years ago, when the first edition of *Learning Vocabulary in Another Language* was published, vocabulary learning was characterised by the then series editors as an area studied by only a few pioneers, Paul Nation being one of them. In part due to the tremendous impact of the first edition of Nation's book, today research and teaching of second language vocabulary learning is no longer the preoccupation of just a few. On the contrary, throughout applied linguistics, vocabulary, formulaic expressions, word patterns and lexical bundles are centre stage in the study of how learners develop the ability to make meaning. With the importance of the lexical dimension of language development recognised, the research basis for understanding vocabulary teaching and learning has grown to be substantial. A second edition of Paul Nation's seminal work was needed.

The second edition of *Learning Vocabulary in Another Language* possesses the same qualities that made the first edition so popular. It is organised around issues relevant to readers needing a solid understanding of vocabulary in order to improve practices in second language vocabulary teaching and assessment. For example, chapters outline the goals of vocabulary learning, teaching and explaining vocabulary, vocabulary and listening and speaking, as well as vocabulary and reading. The book presents and interprets a comprehensive pool of research on second language vocabulary acquisition, and in so doing it provides research-based recommendations for practice. Relevant research appears across the domains of linguistics, second language acquisition, assessment and technology; Nation has culled the pertinent findings to address important questions such as whether or not learners actually acquire new word meanings from context and how learners use dictionaries. The style of writing is direct and engaging for readers at a range of levels. The book begins with the basics (that is, knowing a word), and it builds to the real world challenges educators face, such as assessing vocabulary knowledge and use, and developing the vocabulary component of a language course.

We are very happy to welcome this new edition of *Learning Vocabulary in Another Language* to the Cambridge Applied Linguistics Series.

Carol A. Chapelle and Susan Hunston

Acknowledgements

The authors and publishers acknowledge the following sources of copyright material and are grateful for the permissions granted. While every effort has been made, it has not always been possible to identify the sources of all the material used, or to trace all copyright holders. If any omissions are brought to our notice, we will be happy to include the appropriate acknowledgements on reprinting.

Parts of Chapter 4 appeared in Joe, A., Nation, P. and Newton, J. (1996) Speaking activities and vocabulary learning. *English Teaching Forum* **34**, 1: 2–7; Parts of Chapter 5 appeared in Nation, I. S. P. (1997) The language learning benefits of extensive reading. *The Language Teacher* **21**, 5: 13–16; Parts of Chapter 8 appeared in Nation, I. S. P. (1982) Beginning to learn foreign vocabulary: A review of the research. *RELC Journal* **13**, 1: 14–36; Table on p. 488 taken from Nation/Webb (2011) Researching and Analyzing Vocabulary, 1E. Copyright © 2011 Heinle/ELT, a part of Cengage Learning, Inc., www.cengage.com/permissions. Reproduced by permission; Parts of Chapter 14 appeared in Nation, I. S. P. (1998) Helping learners take control of their vocabulary learning. *GRETA* **6**, 1: 9–18.

Introduction

This book is about the teaching and learning of vocabulary, but the teaching and learning of vocabulary is only a part of a language development programme. It is thus important that vocabulary teaching and learning is placed in its proper perspective.

Learning goals

Vocabulary learning is only one sub-goal of a range of goals that are important in the language classroom. The mnemonic LIST is a useful way of remembering these goals that are outlined in Table 0.1. L = Language, which includes vocabulary; I = Ideas, which cover content and subject matter knowledge as well as cultural knowledge; S = Skills; and T = Text or discourse, which covers the way sentences fit together to form larger units of language.

Although this book focuses on the vocabulary sub-goal of language, the other goals are not ignored. However, they are approached from the

Table 0.1 *Goals for language learning*

General goals	Specific goals
Language items	pronunciation
	vocabulary
	grammatical constructions
Ideas (content)	subject matter knowledge
	cultural knowledge
Skills	accuracy
	fluency
	strategies
	process skills or subskills
Text (discourse)	conversational discourse rules
	text schemata or topic type scales

viewpoint of vocabulary. There are chapters on vocabulary and the skills of listening, speaking, reading and writing. Discourse is looked at in Chapter 6 on specialised uses, and pronunciation, spelling and grammar are looked at in relation to vocabulary knowledge in Chapter 3.

The four strands

The approach taken in this book rests on the idea that a well-balanced language course should consist of four major strands (Nation, 2007; Nation and Yamamoto, 2011). These strands can appear in many different forms, but they should all be there in a well-designed course.

Firstly, there is the strand of learning from comprehensible meaning-focused input. This means that learners should have the opportunity to learn new language items through listening and reading activities where the main focus of attention is on the information in what they are listening to or reading. As we shall see in the following chapter, learning from meaning-focused input can best occur if learners are familiar with at least 98 per cent of the running words in the input they are focusing on. Put negatively, learning from meaning-focused input cannot occur if there are lots of unknown words.

The second strand of a course is the strand of meaning-focused output. Learners should have the chance to develop their knowledge of the language through speaking and writing activities where their main attention is focused on the information they are trying to convey. Speaking and writing are useful means of vocabulary development because they make the learners focus on words in ways they did not have to while listening and reading. Having to speak and write encourages learners to listen like a speaker and read like a writer. This different kind of attention is not the only contribution that speaking and writing activities can make to language development. From a vocabulary perspective, these productive activities can strengthen knowledge of previously met vocabulary.

The third strand of a course is one that has been subject to a lot of debate. This is the strand of language-focused learning, sometimes called form-focused instruction. There is growing evidence (Ellis, 2005; Williams, 2005) that language learning benefits if there is an appropriate amount of usefully focused deliberate teaching and learning of language items. From a vocabulary perspective, this means that a course should involve the direct teaching of vocabulary and the direct learning and study of vocabulary. As we shall see, there is a very large amount of research stretching back to the late 19th century which shows that the gradual cumulative process of learning a word can be given a strong boost by the direct study of certain features of the word.

The fourth strand of a course is the fluency development strand. In the activities which put this strand into action learners do not work with new language items. Instead, they become more and more fluent in using items they already know. A striking example of this can be found in the use of numbers. Learners can usually quickly learn numbers in a foreign language. But if they go into a post office and the clerk tells them how much the stamps they need are going to cost, they might not understand because the numbers were said too quickly for them. By doing a small amount of regular fluency practice with numbers (the teacher says the numbers, the learners write the figures), the learners will find that they can understand one-digit numbers said quickly (1, 7, 6, 9) although they have trouble with two-digit numbers said quickly (26, 89, 63, 42) or three-digit numbers (126, 749, 537, 628). A little further practice will make these longer numbers fluently available for comprehension. If a course does not have a strong fluency strand, then the learning done in the other three strands will not be readily available for normal use.

In a language course, these four strands should get roughly the same amount of time. That means that no more than 25 per cent of the learning time in and out of class should be given to the direct study of language items. No less than 25 per cent of the class time should be given to fluency development. If the four strands of a course are not equally represented in a particular course, then the design of the course needs to be looked at again.

These four strands need to be kept in mind while reading this book. Where recommendations are made for direct vocabulary learning, these should be seen as fitting into that 25 per cent of the course which is devoted to language-focused learning. Seventy-five per cent of the vocabulary development programme should involve the three meaning-focused strands of learning from input, learning from output and fluency development.

The four strands apply generally to a language course. In this book we will look at how vocabulary fits into each of these strands. It is worth stressing that the strands of meaning-focused input and output are only effective if the learners have sufficient vocabulary to make these strands truly meaning focused. If activities which are supposed to be meaning focused involve large amounts of unknown vocabulary, then they become language focused because much of the learners' attention is taken from the message to the unknown vocabulary. Similarly, fluency development activities need to involve little or no unknown vocabulary or other language items, otherwise they become part of the meaning input and output strands, or language-focused learning.

Main themes

A small number of major themes run through this book, and these are first dealt with in Chapters 2, 3 and 4. Firstly, there is the cost/benefit idea based on the results of word frequency studies. Its most important application is in the distinction between high-frequency and mid- and low-frequency vocabulary and the different ways in which teachers should deal with these types of vocabulary. The cost/benefit idea also applies to individual words in that the amount of attention given to an item should be roughly proportional to the chances of it being met or used again, that is, its frequency.

Secondly, there is the idea that learning a word is a cumulative process involving a range of aspects of knowledge. Learners thus need many different kinds of meetings with words in order to learn them fully. There is to date still little research on how vocabulary knowledge grows and how different kinds of encounters with words contribute to vocabulary knowledge. In this book, knowing a word is taken to include not only knowing the formal aspects of the word and knowing its meaning, but also being able to use the word.

Thirdly, there is the idea that teachers and learners should give careful consideration to how vocabulary is learned, in particular, the psychological conditions that are most likely to lead to effective learning. Because these conditions are influenced by the design of learning tasks, quite a lot of attention is given to the analysis and design of vocabulary-learning activities.

The audience for this book

This book is intended to be used by second and foreign language teachers. Although it is largely written from the viewpoint of a teacher of English, it could also be used by teachers of other languages.

This book is called *Learning Vocabulary in Another Language* partly in order to indicate that most of the suggestions apply to both second and foreign language learning. Generally the term **second language** will be used to apply to both second and foreign language learning. In the few places where a contrast is intended, this will be clear from the context.

The first and the second editions

"I've got the first edition. Is it worth buying the second edition?" – this is a question I expect to be asked, so here is my answer.

Yes. Most of the changes in the second edition are the result of a large amount of research which has appeared since the first edition was published in 2001. By my rough calculation, over 30 per cent of the research on vocabulary that has appeared in the last 110 years was published in the last eleven years. Teaching and learning vocabulary, particularly for foreign and second language learners, is no longer a neglected aspect of language learning. So, if you don't buy the second edition you will be out of date by eleven years and at least 30 per cent of the field. On a rough estimate, at least one-fifth of the book is new material.

There were also errors in the first edition, largely because of a lack of research on the relevant areas. Some of that research has now been done, much of it by my students, colleagues and friends, and a few people who fit two or all of those categories.

I am also pleased to note that my thinking has changed on some issues in the teaching and learning of vocabulary, largely as a result of research findings and my own experience and thinking. These include the idea of mid-frequency vocabulary, largely as a result of research on word lists and testing native speaker vocabulary size. I also now feel that I am beginning to understand what collocations are. I am also becoming more sceptical of the value of vocabulary teaching, largely because of its necessarily limited scope and limited effectiveness.

When working on this second edition, I often wondered if the field of teaching and learning vocabulary is now so vigorous and large that it is beyond the scope of any one book and certainly one person. If you have already bought this book, then I hope I am wrong and you have got your money's worth.

Changes in the second edition

One of the changes in Chapter 1 is because of Chung and Nation's (2003, 2004) research on technical vocabulary. In the first edition I got this completely wrong, saying that about five per cent of the running words in a technical text would be technical vocabulary. In fact research showed that it was closer to 20 to 30 per cent of the running words. The second major change in Chapter 1 is as a result of the development of the lower-frequency word family lists based on the British National Corpus. At the time of writing, these lists now go up to the 24th one-thousand word lists, and the development of these lists has meant that we can do much more detailed analysis of texts and their vocabulary demands, as well as develop more soundly based vocabulary size tests. This research has highlighted the idea of mid-frequency words (Schmitt and Schmitt, 2012). At the time of writing the first edition, Coxhead's (2000) work on the Academic Word List was just being completed. The research just made it into the first edition, but in this second edition it is given the additional attention it deserves.

Chapter 2, 'Knowing a word', includes recent research on the relationship between first language (L1) and second language (L2) vocabulary storage. Chapter 3 includes a description of Technique Feature Analysis first introduced in Nation and Webb (2011a). Chapter 4 on listening and speaking includes recent work on vocabulary learning through lectures and learning in interactive activities. Chapter 5 on reading and writing is largely reorganised, and there is much more on glossing because of the growth in research on electronic glossing. It also includes recent corpus and experimental work on text coverage as well as recent studies of learning from graded readers and reading fluency. Chapter 6, 'Specialised uses', now has critiques of the academic word list, recent work on technical vocabulary and a section on content-based vocabulary teaching. Chapter 7, 'Vocabulary-learning strategies', includes recent research on strategy training and strategy use. The research on strategy use is now becoming more rigorous with less dependence on questionnaires. Chapter 8 contains recent research on guessing. Chapter 9, 'Word parts', has only very few changes. The changes in Chapter 10 are largely due to the growth in electronic dictionaries. Chapter 11, 'Deliberate learning from word cards', includes recent research on whether expanded spacing is better than even spacing within a learning session. It also includes criteria for evaluating flashcard programmes (Nakata, 2011). It also includes what I consider to be the most significant recent research finding in the field of vocabulary learning, namely that rote learning results in both implicit and explicit knowledge (Elgort, 2011) and thus the learning/acquisition distinction is not relevant for vocabulary. Chapter 12 on finding and learning collocations is almost completely rewritten. For me this was the most unsatisfactory chapter in the first edition. I now feel I am beginning to see how the work on collocations fits together, largely by separating the types of criteria used to classify collocations into criteria of form, meaning, function and storage. I have kept a few small sections but have taken a new approach to the chapter. There has been a large amount of research on collocations and some of it is very innovative. However there is still a need for clear definitions of what kind of units are being investigated and following these definitions closely when doing the research. Chapter 13 on testing changes the table of test sensitivity to agree with Laufer and Goldstein's (2004) findings. There is now more on the Word Associates Test, and there is also recent research on vocabulary size, including (Biemiller, 2005) findings with

L1 learners and research on the *Vocabulary Size Test*. Chapter 14 on planning has very few changes.

There is now an international community of vocabulary researchers and I am grateful to them for the knowledge, support and encouragement they have given me in the preparation of this book and in my research and writing.

Since I wrote my first book, *Teaching and Learning Vocabulary* (Nation, 1990) and the first edition of this book, another generation of vocabulary researchers has appeared. Although this is still a relatively small group, it is made up of very productive researchers who have identified a range of useful research focuses and who persist in exploring and refining research in those chosen areas. It is also notable that recently two books focusing on the research methodology of vocabulary studies have appeared (Nation and Webb, 2011; Schmitt, 2010). Research on vocabulary is clearly alive and well.

I am very grateful to Norbert Schmitt, Pavel Szudarski, Suhad Sonbul and Laura Vilkaite for comments on a draft of this book. Their insightful comments led to significant improvements in the book.

References

Biemiller, A. (2005). Size and sequence in vocabulary development, in Hiebert, E. H. and Kamil, M. L. (eds.), *Teaching and Learning Vocabulary: Bringing Research into Practice*. Mahwah, NJ: Lawrence Erlbaum Associates, pp. 223–42.

Chung, T. M., & Nation, P. (2003). Technical vocabulary in specialised texts. *Reading in a Foreign Language*, **15**, 2, 103–16.

Chung, T. M., & Nation, P. (2004). Identifying technical vocabulary. *System*, **32**, 2, 251–63.

Coxhead, A. (2000). A new academic word list. *TESOL Quarterly*, **34**, 2, 213–38.

Elgort, I. (2011). Deliberate learning and vocabulary acquisition in a second language, *Language Learning*, **61**, 2, 367–413.

Ellis, R. (2005). Principles of instructed language learning, *System*, **33**, 209–24.

Laufer, B., & Goldstein, Z. (2004). Testing vocabulary knowledge: Size, strength, and computer adaptiveness. *Language Learning*, **54**, 3, 399–436.

Nakata, T. (2011). Computer-assisted second language vocabulary learning in a paired-associate paradigm: A critical investigation of flashcard software, *Computer Assisted Language Learning*, **24**, 1, 17–38.

Nation, I. S. P. (1990). *Teaching and Learning Vocabulary*. Boston: Heinle.

Nation, I. S. P. (2007). The four strands. *Innovation in Language Learning and Teaching*, **1**, 1, 1–12.

Nation, I. S. P. and Webb, S. (2011). *Researching and Analyzing Vocabulary*. Boston: Heinle Cengage Learning.

Nation, I. S. P. and Yamamoto, A. (2011). Applying the four strands to language learning, *International Journal of Innovation in English Language Teaching and Research*, **1**, 2, 1–15.

Schmitt, N. (2010). *Researching Vocabulary: A Vocabulary Research Manual*. Basingstoke: Palgrave Macmillan.

Schmitt, N. and Schmitt, D. (2012). A reassessment of frequency and vocabulary size in L2 vocabulary teaching. *Language Teaching*, doi:10.1017/S0261444812000018.

Williams, J. (2005). Form-focused instruction, in Hinkel, E. (ed.), *Handbook of Research in Second Language Teaching and Learning*. Mahwah, NJ: Lawrence Erlbaum Associates, pp. 671–91.

1   *The goals of vocabulary learning*

The idea behind this chapter is that it is helpful to use frequency and range of occurrence to distinguish several levels of vocabulary. Distinguishing these levels helps ensure that learners learn vocabulary in the most useful sequence and thus gain the most benefit from the vocabulary they learn. Making the high-frequency/mid-frequency/low-frequency distinction ensures that the teacher deals with vocabulary in the most efficient ways.

Counting words

There are several ways of counting words, that is, deciding what will be counted.

Tokens

One way is simply to count every word form in a spoken or written text and if the same word form occurs more than once, then each occurrence is counted. So, the sentence, *It is not easy to say it correctly*, would contain eight words, even though two of them are the same word form, *it*. Words which are counted in this way are called **tokens**, and sometimes **running words**. If we try to answer questions like 'How many words are there on a page or in a line?', 'How long is this book?', 'How fast can you read?' or 'How many words does the average person speak per minute?', then our unit of counting will be the token.

Types

We can count the words in the sentence *It is not easy to say it correctly* another way. When we see the same word occur again, we do not count it again. So the sentence of eight tokens consists of seven different words or **types**. We count words in this way if we want to answer questions like 'How large was Shakespeare's vocabulary?', 'How many words do you need to know to read this book?' or 'How many words does this dictionary contain?'

Lemmas

Counting *book* and *books* as two different words to be learned seems a bit strange. So, instead of counting different types as different words, closely related words could be counted as members of the same word or **lemma**. A lemma consists of a headword and its inflected forms and reduced forms (*n't*). Usually, all the items included under a lemma are all the same part of speech (Francis and Kučera, 1982). The English inflections consist of plural, third person singular present tense, past tense, past participle, *-ing*, comparative, superlative, possessive (Bauer and Nation, 1993). The Thorndike and Lorge (1944) frequency count used lemmas as the basis for counting, and the computerised count on the Brown corpus produced a lemmatised list (Francis and Kučera, 1982). In the Brown count the comparative and superlative forms were not included in the lemma, and the same form used as a different part of speech (*walk* as a noun, *walk* as a verb) are not in the same lemma. Variant spellings (*favor, favour*) are usually included as part of the same lemma when they are the same part of speech. Leech et al. (2001) used similar criteria in their count of the British National Corpus (http://ucrel.lancs.ac.uk/bncfreq).

Lying behind the use of lemmas as the unit of counting is the idea of **learning burden** (Swenson and West, 1934). The learning burden of an item is the amount of effort required to learn it. Once learners can use the inflectional system, the learning burden of *mends*, if the learner already knows *mend*, is negligible. One problem to be faced in forming lemmas is to decide what will be done with irregular forms such as *mice, is, brought, beaten* and *best*. The learning burden of these is clearly heavier than the learning burden of regular forms like *books, runs, talked, washed* and *fastest*. Should the irregular forms be counted as a part of the same lemma as their base word or should they be put into separate lemmas? Lemmas also separate closely related items, such as the adjective and noun uses of words like *original*, and the noun and verb uses of words like *display*. An additional problem with lemmas is to decide what is the headword of the lemma – the base form or the most frequent form? (Sinclair, 1991: 41–2).

Using the lemma as the unit of counting greatly reduces the number of units in a corpus. Bauer and Nation (1993) calculated that the 61,805 tagged types (or 45,957 untagged types) in the Brown corpus become 37,617 lemmas, which is a reduction of almost 40% (or 18% for untagged types). Nagy and Anderson (1984) estimated that 19,105 of the 86,741 types in the Carroll et al. (1971) corpus were regular inflections.

Word families

Lemmas are a step in the right direction when trying to represent learning burden in the counting of words. However, there are clearly other affixes which are used systematically and which greatly reduce the learning burden of derived words containing known base forms, for example *-ly*, *-ness* and *un-*. A **word family** consists of a headword, its inflected forms and its closely related derived forms.

The major problem in counting using word families as the unit is to decide what should be included in a word family and what should not. Learners' knowledge of the prefixes and suffixes develops as they gain more experience of the language. What might be a sensible word family for one learner may be beyond another learner's present level of proficiency. This means that it is usually necessary to set up a scale of word families, starting with the most elementary and transparent members and moving on to less obvious possibilities (Bauer and Nation, 1993). Ward and Chuenjundaeng (2009) warn that we need to be cautious in assuming that learners know the family members of word families. Their study of low-proficiency Thai university students showed that the students' ability to see the relationship between stems and derived forms was very limited. Neubacher and Clahsen (2009) found that less proficient non-native speakers of German were more influenced by the morphological structure involving regular affixes than high proficiency non-native speakers. Non-native speakers seemed more likely to store words as unanalysed wholes.

Which unit we use when counting will depend on our reason for counting. Whatever unit we use, we need to make sure it is the most suitable one for our purpose. We need to make this decision when working out how much vocabulary our learners need to know.

How much vocabulary do learners need to know?

Whether we are designing a language course or planning our own course of study, it is useful to be able to set learning goals that will allow us to use the language in the ways we want to. When we plan the vocabulary goals of a long-term course of study, we can look at three kinds of information to help decide how much vocabulary needs to be learned: the number of words in the language, the number of words known by native speakers, and the number of words needed to use the language.

How many words are there in the language?

The most ambitious goal is to know all of the language. This is very ambitious because native speakers of the language do not know all the vocabulary of the language. There are numerous specialist vocabularies, such as the vocabulary of nuclear physics or computational linguistics, which are known only by the small groups of people who specialise in these areas. Still, it is interesting to have some idea of how many words there are in a language. This is not an easy question to answer because there are numerous other questions which affect the way we answer it. They involve considerations like the following.

What do we count as a word? Do we count *book* and *books* as the same word? Do we count *green* (the colour) and *green* (a large grassed area) as the same word? Do we count people's names? Do we count the names of products like *Fab*, *Pepsi*, *Vegemite*, *Chevrolet*? One way to answer these questions and the major question 'How many words are there in English?' is to count the number of words in very large dictionaries. *Webster's Third New International Dictionary* is one of the largest non-historical dictionaries of English. It contains around 54,000 base word families excluding proper names (Goulden et al., 1990: 322–3). This is a very large number and is well beyond the goals of most first and second language learners. Another way is to look at very large collections of texts and see how many words occur in those texts. Nagy and Anderson (1984) projected from their analysis of part of the data from Carroll et al.'s (1971) *Word Frequency Book* that, excluding proper names, foreign words, formulae, numbers and non-words, there were between 54,000 and 88,500 different word families in printed school English, depending on what is included in a word family. The *Word Frequency Book* is based on a corpus of 5 million running words. An analysis of the British National Corpus using the Range program comes up with similar figures.

There are 272,782 word types in the British National Corpus that are not in the first 20,000 word family lists and the accompanying proper name, marginal words, transparent compounds and abbreviations lists. Almost half of the 272,782 different word families are proper nouns. Four per cent are foreign words and six per cent are low-frequency members of word families already in the 20 one-thousand-word lists. Ideally, these family members should be added to the families in the existing lists.

The new words not yet in the lists plus the 20,000 in the word lists total around 70,000 word families which is a figure within Nagy and

Anderson's (1984) estimates, and the number of words in most reasonably sized non-historical dictionaries.

A major reason for trying to see how many words there are in English is to set the boundaries for measures of learners' vocabulary size. Early studies of vocabulary size using faulty methodology (Diller, 1978; Seashore and Eckerson, 1940) reached estimates that were well beyond the number of words in the language.

How many words do native speakers know?

Instead of considering how many words there are in the language, a less ambitious way of setting vocabulary learning goals is to look at what native speakers of the language know. Unfortunately, research on measuring vocabulary size has generally been poorly done (Nation, 1993), and the results of the studies stretching back to the late nineteenth century are often wildly incorrect. We will look at the reasons for this in Chapter 13.

More reliable studies (Goulden et al., 1990; Zechmeister et al., 1995) suggest that educated adult native speakers of English know under 20,000 word families. These estimates are rather low because the counting unit is word families which have several derived family members, and proper nouns are not included in the count. A very rough rule of thumb would be that for each year of their early life, starting at the age of three and probably up to 25 years old or so, native speakers add on average 1,000 word families a year to their vocabulary (Biemiller and Slonim, 2001). Learning 1,000 word families a year is an ambitious goal for non-native speakers of English, especially those learning English as a foreign rather than second language. In one important respect however the learning burden of English words for learners of English as a foreign language is becoming easier. This is because a large number of English words exist as loanwords in the learner's first language. For example, Daulton (2008) estimates that about half of the first 3,000 words of English exist in Japanese in some form or other, and Japanese learners know the meanings of these loanwords. The existence of these loanwords makes the learning of their English forms easier.

We need to be careful when seeing native speakers' language proficiency as a goal for L2 learners. Mulder and Hulstijn (2011) looked at the Dutch language proficiency of native speakers of Dutch. They tested native speakers across a wide range of ages (18–76 years old) and with a wide range of educational backgrounds and in a wide range of professions. Lexical fluency and lexical memory span declined with age while lexical knowledge increased. High education and a high profession level positively affected lexical knowledge and lexical memory span. There was a large variability in native speakers' language knowledge and skills. This variability has also been noted in studies of the vocabulary size of young native speakers of English (Biemiller and Slonim, 2001). This variability raises the question of what type of native speakers we should use when comparing them with non-native speakers.

How much vocabulary do you need to use another language?

Studies of native speakers' vocabulary suggest that second language learners need to know very large numbers of words. While this may be useful in the long term, it is not an essential short-term goal. This is because studies of native speakers' vocabulary growth see all words as being of equal value to the learner. Frequency-based studies show very strikingly that this is not so, and that some words are much more useful than others (see Schmitt, 2008, for a very useful discussion of vocabulary-learning goals). Thus, another way of setting vocabulary-learning goals is to work out how many really useful words learners need to know.

Table 1.1 shows part of the results of a frequency count of just under 500 running words in the Ladybird version of the children's story, *The Three Little Pigs*. It contains 124 different word types.

The most frequent word is *the* which occurs 41 times in the book. Note the large proportion of words occurring only once and the very high frequency of the few most frequent words. Note also the quick drop in frequency of the items.

When we look at texts our learners may have to read and conversations that are like ones they may be involved in, we find that a relatively small amount of well-chosen words can allow learners to do a lot. An analysis of various kinds of texts using 1,000-word family lists made from the British National Corpus (Nation, 2006) shows that between 3,000 to 4,000 word families are needed to get 95% text coverage, and between 6,000 and 9,000 word families are needed to gain 98% coverage (see Table 1.2). A coverage of 98% is chosen as the goal because a small amount of research supports this figure (Hu and Nation, 2000; Schmitt et al., 2011; van Zeeland and Schmitt, 2012), and because this represents a manageable amount of unknown vocabulary. If 2% of the running words are not known, this equates to one word in 50, or one word in every five lines (assuming 10 words

Table 1.1 *An example of the results of a frequency count*

the	41	than	4	by	2	him	1
little	25	very	4	care	2	houses	1
pig	22	asked	3	chin	2	huff	1
house	17	carrying	3	day	2	knocked	1
a	16	eat	3	does	2	live	1
and	16	gave	3	huffed	2	long	1
said	14	give	3	let	2	mother	1
he	12	his	3	m	2	must	1
i	10	in	3	no	2	my	1
me	10	it	3	puffed	2	next	1
some	9	ll	3	strong	2	off	1
wolf	9	met	3	take	2	once	1
build	8	myself	3	then	2	one	1
t	8	not	3	time	2	puff	1
third	8	on	3	too	2	road	1
was	8	pigs	3	along	1	set	1
of	7	please	3	are	1	so	1
straw	7	pleased	3	ate	1	their	1
to	7	shall	3	blow	1	them	1
you	7	soon	3	but	1	there	1
man	6	stronger	3	came	1	took	1
second	6	that	3	chinny	1	up	1
catch	5	they	3	come	1	upon	1
first	5	three	3	door	1	us	1
for	5	want	3	down	1	walked	1
will	5	who	3	fell	1	we	1
bricks	4	with	3	go	1	went	1
built	4	won	3	grew	1	were	1
himself	4	yes	3	had	1	which	1
now	4	yours	3	hair	1	your	1
sticks	4	big	2	here	1	yourselves	1

per line), or six unknown words per 300-running word page, or around 1,200 unknown words in a 200-page book. There is research that shows that 95% coverage may be sufficient for spoken narrative texts (van Zeeland and Schmitt, 2012).

The figures in Table 1.2 assume that vocabulary is learned in the order of its frequency. That is, that the first 1,000 words are learned before the second 1,000 words, and the second 1,000 words are learned before the third 1,000 words, and so on. This is a reasonable assumption for the high- and mid-frequency levels of the language.

Table 1.2 *English vocabulary sizes needed to get 95% and 98% coverage (including proper nouns) of various kinds of texts (Nation, 2006)*

Texts	95% coverage	98% coverage	Proper nouns
Novels	4,000 word families	9,000 word families	1–2%
Newspapers	4,000 word families	8,000 word families	5–6%
Children's movies	4,000 word families	6,000 word families	1.5%
Spoken English	3,000 word families	7,000 word families	1.3%

Webb and Macalister (forthcoming) show that texts written for young native speakers (the very popular New Zealand School Journals) have the same vocabulary size demands as texts written for native-speaking adults. Predictably, graded readers provide a much more favourable vocabulary load.

Frequency-based word lists

We can usefully distinguish three kinds of vocabulary based on frequency levels. Let us look at a written academic text and examine the different frequency levels of vocabulary it contains. The text is from Neville Peat's (1987) *Forever the Forest. A West Coast Story* (Hodder and Stoughton, Auckland).

The vocabulary is divided into three groups according to frequency lists of word families. The high-frequency words (the most frequent 2,000 word families) are unmarked in the text, the mid-frequency words (7,000 word families from the 3rd to the 9th 1,000-word lists inclusive) are in *italics*, and the low-frequency words (10th 1,000-word list onward) are in **bold**.

> Sustained-*yield* management ought to be long-term government policy in *indigenous* forests *zoned* for production. The adoption of such a policy would represent a break through the boundary between a *pioneering*, extractive phase and an *era* in which the

timber industry adjusted to living with the forests in **perpetuity**. A forest sustained is a forest in which harvesting and *mortality* combined do not exceed *regeneration*. Naturally enough, faster-growing forests produce more *timber*, which is why attention would tend to swing from **podocarps** to *beech* forests regardless of the state of the **podocarp** resource. The colonists cannot be blamed for *plunging* in without thought to whether the resource had limits. They brought from *Britain* little experience or understanding of how to maintain forest structure and a *timber* supply for all time. Under *German* management it might have been different here. The *Germans* have practised the sustained approach since the seventeenth century when they faced a *timber* shortage as a result of a series of wars. In *New Zealand* in the latter part of the twentieth century, an anticipated shortage of the most valuable native *timber*, *rimu*, prompts a similar response – no more *contraction* of the *indigenous* forest and a balancing of yield with *increment* in selected areas.

This is not to say the idea is being *aired* here for the first time. Over a century ago the first *Conservator* of Forests proposed sustained harvesting. He was cried down. There were far too many trees left to bother about it. And yet in the *pastoral* context the dangers of **overgrazing** were appreciated early in the piece. *New Zealand geography* students are taught to this day how **overgrazing** causes the *degradation* of the soil and hillsides to slide away, and that with them can go the *viability* of hill-country sheep and cattle farming. That a forest could be **overgrazed** as easily was not widely accepted until much later – so late, in fact, that the *counter* to it, sustained-yield management, would be forced upon the industry and come as a shock to it. It is a simple enough concept on paper: balance harvest with growth and you have a natural *renewable* resource; forest products forever. Plus the social and economic benefits of regular work and income, a regular *timber* supply and relatively stable markets. Plus the environmental benefits that *accrue* from minimising the impact on soil and water qualities and wildlife.

In practice, however, sustainability depends on how well the dynamics of the forest are understood. And these vary from area to area according to forest make-up, soil *profile*, *altitude*, *climate* and factors which forest science may yet discover. *Ecology* is deep-felt.

High-frequency words

In the example text, high-frequency words, including the function words *in, for, the, of, a,* and so on, are not marked at all. Appendix 3 contains a complete list of English function words. The high-frequency words also include many content words: *government, forests, production, adoption, represent, boundary.* The classic list of high-frequency words is Michael West's (1953) *A General Service List of English Words,* which contains around 2,000 word families, although these are not solely frequency based. Almost 80% of the running words in this text are high-frequency words. Schmitt and Schmitt (2012) argue for having a 3,000-word family high-frequency vocabulary list. Such a number, plus proper nouns, transparent compounds and marginal words, typically provides 95% coverage of a text.

Mid-frequency words

The second group of words are the mid-frequency words. They include words like *zoned, pioneering, aired* and *pastoral,* and are marked in italics in the text. There are 6,000 to 7,000 of them (depending on how many high-frequency word families one assumes there are) and they range from the third 1,000 words to the ninth 1,000 words (note that the ninth 1,000 words start with the word family number 8,001 and end with word family number 9,000). Mid-frequency words include generally useful, moderately frequent words, including many that almost got into the high-frequency word list. The mid-frequency words are distinguished from the low-frequency words because, together with the high-frequency words, they represent the amount of vocabulary needed to deal with English without the need for outside support. They are also largely general-purpose vocabulary. Schmitt and Schmitt (2012) cover a good range of reasons for distinguishing mid-frequency vocabulary from low-frequency vocabulary. One important such reason is that it highlights this vocabulary and clearly sets it as a learning goal.

Low-frequency words

Only three word families in the text are not mid-frequency words but are low frequency, beyond the first 9,000 words of English: *perpetuity, overgraze* and *podocarp.* They are marked in bold. Low-frequency words make up about 1 per cent of the words in this text, and there are thousands of them in the language. By far the biggest group of words, they make up only a very small proportion of the running words.

These words consist of technical terms for various subject areas and words that we rarely meet in our use of the language. Mid-frequency readers (see Paul Nation's website, www.victoria.ac.nz/lals/staff/paul-nation.aspx) are designed to provide opportunities to incidentally learn mid-frequency words by lightening the vocabulary load of the text, and this is done primarily by replacing the low-frequency words with high- or mid-frequency words.

Specialised vocabulary

For certain kinds of text, particularly academic text, there may be shortcuts that learners can take by focusing on the vocabulary which is particularly important in such texts.

Academic words

Academic texts contain many words that are common in different kinds of academic texts, *policy, phase, adjusted, sustained*. Typically these words make up about 9% of the running words in the text. The best-known list of academic words is the Academic Word List (Coxhead, 2000). Appendix 1 contains the 570 headwords of this list. This small list of words is very important for anyone using English for Academic Purposes (see Chapter 6). In the text above they include the words *sustained, policy, extractive, phase, adjusted, exceed* and so on. Davies and Gardner have developed a useful academic vocabulary list that does not build on a particular high-frequency list (www.academicwords.info).

Technical words

The text above contains some words that are very closely related to the topic and subject area of the text. These words include *indigenous, regeneration, overgraze, podocarp, beech, rimu* (a New Zealand tree), *timber* and *forest*. These words are reasonably common in this topic area but are not so common elsewhere. As soon as we see them we know what topic is being dealt with. Technical words like these typically cover a large proportion of the running words in a text. They differ from subject area to subject area. If we look at technical dictionaries, such as dictionaries of economics, geography or electronics, we usually find about 1,000 entries in each dictionary. Technical words however can consist of high-frequency words, mid-frequency words and what in another text would be classified as low-frequency words. As we shall see in a later chapter, technical words can make up between 20% and 30% of the running words in a text. Words from the *Academic Word List* may also be technical words in some texts.

For academic purposes, learning the *Academic Word List* and the technical vocabulary of the relevant field is an efficient way for a second language learner to cope with the vocabulary of an academic text. Figure 1.1 provides data for an academic textbook where technical words have been distinguished from the other levels of words.

Figure 1.1 Coverage of academic text by the **General Service List**, *academic words, technical words and other vocabulary in an applied linguistics text*

In Figure 1.1, technical words have been taken out of the first 2,000 words (represented in this figure by the *General Service List*) and the *Academic Word List* (AWL) and this of course reduces their coverage to 68.5% and 6.9% respectively. As the divisions under 'Technical' in the figure show, the *General Service List* would otherwise cover 68.5% plus 9.2% (77.7%). 'Other' includes both mid- and low-frequency words. Note the large text coverage by the technical words (20.6%), and the relatively large coverage by the technical words from the first 2,000 and the *Academic Word List*.

Frequency levels in a large corpus

We have just looked at an example of a short text. Let us now look at a longer text. Table 1.3 gives figures for a collection of texts consisting of 100 million running words, namely the British National Corpus.

Each of the 20 word lists contains 1,000 word families. The proper nouns list contains over seventeen 1,000 word families, but does not include every proper noun in the British National Corpus. The compounds list contains transparent compounds like *forever, aftershave* and *ashtray* where the meaning of the compound is transparently related to the meaning of the parts. The marginal words list contains items like *er, ooh, aah, gosh, sshh* which are common in spoken language but are not dictionary entry words. Note the very fast drop in

Table 1.3 *Coverage of the British National Corpus by word family lists made from the corpus*

Lists	% coverage of tokens	% cumulative coverage of tokens including proper nouns, marginal words and transparent compounds
1st 1,000	77.96	81.14
2nd 1,000	8.10	89.24
3rd 1,000	4.36	93.60
4th 1,000	1.77	95.37
5th 1,000	1.04	96.41
6th 1,000	0.67	97.08
7th 1,000	0.45	97.53
8th 1,000	0.33	97.86
9th 1,000	0.22	98.08
10th 1,000	0.28	98.23
11th 1,000	0.15	98.38
12th 1,000	0.11	98.49
13th 1,000	0.09	98.58
14th 1,000	0.07	98.65
15th 1,000	0.06	98.71
16th 1,000	0.04	98.75
17th 1,000	0.04	98.79
18th 1,000	0.03	98.83
19th 1,000	0.02	98.85
20th 1,000	0.01	98.86
Proper nouns	2.57	
Marginal words	0.31	
Compounds	0.30	
Not in the lists	1.02	99.08

percentage of text coverage for the higher frequency lists. Also note in Column 3 that it takes around 4,000 word families plus proper nouns, marginal words and transparent compounds to get to 95% coverage and 9,000 word families to get to 98% coverage.

Looking at Column 2, we can see that there are 43 words per 1,000 running words from the 1,000 words at the third 1,000 level. From the 1,000 words at the ninth 1,000 level there will be around two words per 1,000 tokens, roughly around one word per 500-word page. From the 1,000 words at the twentieth 1,000 level, there will be one word in every 10,000 running words, or one in every 200 pages.

Table 1.4 *Coverage of the British National Corpus by high-, mid- and low-frequency words*

Type of vocabulary	% coverage
High-frequency (2,000 word families)	86%
Mid-frequency (7,000 word families)	9%
Low-frequency (tenth 1,000 word level onwards)	1–2%
Proper nouns, exclamations etc.	3–4%
Total	100%

Table 1.4 uses the figures in Table 1.3 to show the rough proportions of words at the high-, mid- and low-frequency word levels.

The figures in Table 1.4 are approximate and include the 1.02% of tokens indicated as *Not in the lists* in the last row of Table 1.3, which are distributed between the low-frequency words and the proper nouns and so on.

Figure 1.2 presents the data in Table 1.4 in a diagrammatic form. Proper nouns, exclamations and so on have been included with high-frequency words in the figure. The size of each of the sections indicates the proportion of the text taken up by each type of vocabulary.

There are some very important generalisations that can be drawn from Table 1.4 and the other information that we have looked at. We will look at these generalisations and at the questions they raise. Brief answers to the questions will be given here with little explanation, but the questions and their answers will be examined much more closely in later chapters.

High-frequency words

There is a small group of high-frequency words which are very impor-tant because these words cover a very large proportion of the running words in spoken and written texts and occur in all kinds of uses of the language.

How large is this group of words? The usual way of deciding how many words should be considered as high-frequency words is to look at the text coverage provided by successive frequency-ranked groups of the words (see Nation, 2001, for the effect of using a variety of criteria to decide on the boundary between high- and low-frequency words). The teacher or course designer then has to decide where the coverage gained by spending teaching time on these words is no longer worthwhile. The rapid drop in Table 1.4 shows that the group

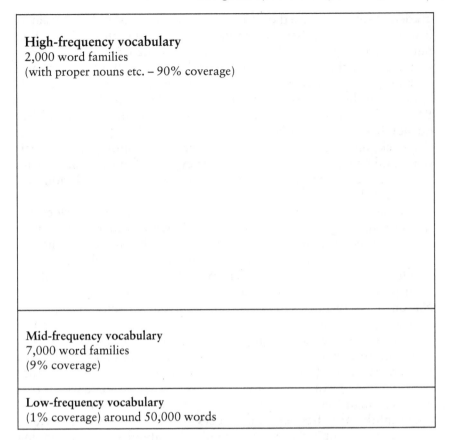

High-frequency vocabulary
2,000 word families
(with proper nouns etc. – 90% coverage)

Mid-frequency vocabulary
7,000 word families
(9% coverage)

Low-frequency vocabulary
(1% coverage) around 50,000 words

Figure 1.2 Coverage of the British National Corpus by high, mid- and low-frequency word family lists

of high-frequency words is relatively small. Schmitt and Schmitt (2012) suggest that 3,000 word families is a suitable size for the group of high-frequency words. In this book, we will stay with 2,000 but this has clearly become a matter of debate and will be affected by the reason for distinguishing high-frequency words from mid-frequency words.

What are the words in this group? The classic list of high-frequency words is Michael West's (1953) *A General Service List of English Words*, which contains around 2,000 word families. About 165 word families in this list are function words, such as *a*, *some*, *two*, *because* and *to* (see Appendix 3). The rest are content words, that is nouns, verbs, adjectives and adverbs. The older series of graded readers are based on this list. Because of its age and because it was made using other criteria besides frequency, this list is falling out of favour. The major problem with replacing it is the difficulty of making a list that is suitable for learners in the school system, and that takes account of both spoken and written language which is relevant to the learners using the lists. The first 2,000 words of the BNC/COCA lists on Paul Nation's website are also not solely frequency based but include complete lexical sets of numbers, days of the week, months and seasons. Research is continuing on the feasibility and construction of high-frequency word family lists. Making such a list is a much more difficult task than it seems (Nation and Webb, 2011: 131–55).

How stable are the high-frequency words? In other words, does one properly researched list of high-frequency words differ greatly from another? Frequency lists may disagree with each other about the frequency rank order of particular words but if the research is based on a well-designed corpus there is generally about 80% agreement about what particular words should be in the list of high-frequency words. Nation and Hwang's (1995) research on the *General Service List* showed quite a large overlap between the this and more recent frequency counts. Replacing some of the words in the *General Service List* with other words from a more recent frequency count resulted in an increase in coverage of only 1%. It is important to remember that the 2,000 high-frequency words of English consist of some words that have very high frequencies and some words that are frequent but are only slightly more frequent than others not in the list. The first 1,000 words cover about 74% and the second 1,000 about 4% of the running words in an applied linguistics academic text. When making a list of high-frequency words, both frequency and range must be considered. Range is measured by seeing how many different texts or subcorpora each particular word occurs in. A word with wide range occurs in many different texts or subcorpora.

How should teachers and learners deal with these words? The high-frequency words of the language are so important that considerable time should be spent on these words by both teachers and learners. The words are a small enough group to enable most of them to get attention over the span of a long-term English programme. They need to be met across the four strands of meaning-focused input, meaning-focused output, language-focused learning and fluency development. This attention thus should be in the form of incidental learning, direct teaching and direct learning, and there should be planned meetings with the words. The time spent on them is well justified by their frequency, coverage and range, and by the relative smallness of the group of words.

Table 14.4 lists some of the teaching and learning possibilities that will be explored in much more detail in other chapters of this book.

In general, high-frequency words are so important that anything that teachers and learners can do to make sure they are learned is worth doing.

It is sometimes argued that teachers should not do much about high-frequency vocabulary because:

1. high-frequency vocabulary occurs frequently and therefore repeated opportunities to meet these words will take care of learning, and
2. high-frequency vocabulary probably contains a lot of concrete words which are much easier to learn and retain than abstract words (see, for example, Sadoski, 2005).

However, high-frequency vocabulary does deserve some deliberate attention because:

1. it covers such a large proportion of connected spoken and written text that such text will be inaccessible until a reasonable amount of high-frequency vocabulary is known (Nation, 2006), so it needs to be learned as quickly as possible;
2. comprehension of text will suffer if learners cannot access high-frequency vocabulary with some degree of fluency (Perfetti and Hart, 2001; Rasinski, 2000); and
3. without knowledge of high-frequency vocabulary, learners will not be able to produce spoken or written text.

It needs to be noted that this argument is about the deliberate learning and teaching of vocabulary, and probably has most to do about the deliberate teaching of vocabulary. In a well-balanced course, just one-quarter of the time should be spent on deliberate study (Nation, 2007), and only a relatively small proportion of that one-quarter should involve deliberate teaching.

Mid-frequency words

There is a large group of generally useful words that occur rather infrequently, but frequently enough to be a sensible learning goal after the high-frequency and specialised vocabulary is known.

Because of the finding (Nation, 2006) that it takes around 6,000–9,000 words plus proper nouns to reach 98% coverage of the text, it is useful to distinguish mid-frequency and low-frequency words. These are largely distinguished on the basis of range, frequency and dispersion. Mid-frequency words consist of 7,000 word families from the third to the ninth 1,000, and low-frequency words are those from the tenth 1,000 onwards.

Let us consider the reasons and evidence for creating the category of mid-frequency words.

1. *Range and frequency*. In my work with the British National Corpus word families, I used the British National Corpus broken into 10 equally sized subcorpora, each of 10 million running words. It was around the tenth 1,000 word families that words with a range of 9 rather than 10 occurred. That is, they did not occur in every subcorpus. This indicates that at around this frequency level, less generally frequent words occur. This may be the point at which individual native speakers' vocabularies start to diverge according to their interests. It may be possible to gain evidence of this from data gained from the expanded version of the *Vocabulary Size Test*. For native speakers from about 13 years old, we should find comprehensive knowledge of the first 9,000 with less shared knowledge between native speakers from the tenth 1,000 onwards. The most frequent 9,000 words are likely to be of roughly equal value for dealing with spoken and written text.

2. *Coverage*. 9,000 word families plus proper nouns provide 98% coverage for novels. 8,000 word families plus proper nouns provide 98% for newspapers. The truly low-frequency words cover less than 2% of the running words.

3. *Familiarity*. Native-speaking teenagers and adults are likely to be largely familiar, at least receptively, with the first 9,000 word families. We would expect even non-literate native speakers to know the first 9,000 words of English reasonably well. High-proficiency non-native speakers, such as those doing doctoral study through the medium of English, are likely to be familiar with most of the first 9,000 word families.

4. *Learning goals*. A vocabulary consisting largely of high-frequency words is insufficient for unassisted reading of unsimplified text. It is important that learners continue to increase their vocabulary size in a systematic way at least until they gain good coverage of text. Around 3,000–4,000 words plus proper nouns provide 95% coverage of novels, newspapers and films (Nation, 2006; Webb and Rodgers, 2009a and 2009b). At least the third 1,000 to the fifth 1,000-word lists should be an explicit vocabulary-learning goal for non-native speakers who know the high-frequency words, and after that the sixth 1,000 to the ninth 1,000 words are the next rational goal. Nation (2009) looks at how much unsimplified text would need to be adapted to produce reading material that would

support these goals. Separating out mid-frequency vocabulary, providing word lists and researching the stability of such lists can raise the profile of such vocabulary and hopefully encourage the deliberate learning (not teaching) of such vocabulary and the production of helpful reading texts that focus on them and bridge the gap between current graded reader series and unsimplified texts (see Paul Nation's website for some free mid-frequency readers at three frequency levels).

What kinds of words are they? Some mid-frequency words are words that did not manage to get into the high-frequency list. It is important to remember that the boundary between high-frequency and mid-frequency vocabulary is an arbitrary one. Any of several hundred mid-frequency words could each be candidates for inclusion within the high-frequency words rather than within the mid-frequency words simply because their position on a ranked frequency list which takes account of range is dependent on the nature of the corpus the list is based on and the way it is divided into subcorpora. A different corpus would lead to a different ranking, particularly among the words on the boundary. This, however, should not be seen as a reason for large amounts of teaching time being spent on mid-frequency words at the 3,000- or 4,000- word level. Here are some words in the British National Corpus that fall just outside the high-frequency boundary: *nod, pupil, evolution, boast, glove, rod* and *entrepreneur.*

As Table 1.3 shows, each 1,000 level from the third 1,000 onwards provides steeply decreasing coverage of text – third 1,000 4.36%, fourth 1,000 1.77%, fifth 1,000 1.04%, sixth 1,000 0.67% and so on. Clearly, there is more value in learning the third 1,000 than in learning the fourth 1,000, and when the learners deliberately study mid-frequency words, they should largely be guided by frequency lists to make sure that the most useful mid-frequency words are learned first. Note that the text coverage of the third 1,000 words (4.36%) is almost half of the total text coverage of all the 7,000 mid-frequency words (8.84%).

How many mid-frequency words are there? The arbitrary figure for the number of mid-frequency words is 7,000 word families, from the third 1,000 to the ninth 1,000 inclusive. With the high-frequency words and proper nouns these provide 98% coverage of most kinds of text. On their own, they cover around 9% of the tokens of texts.

What should teachers and learners do about mid-frequency words? Teachers' and learners' aims differ with mid-frequency vocabulary. The teacher's aim is to train learners in the use of strategies to deal with such vocabulary. These strategies include guessing using context clues, deliberate learning using vocabulary cards or flashcard

Table 1.5 *The differing focuses of teachers' and learners' attention to high- and mid-frequency words*

	High-frequency words	Mid-frequency words
Attention to each word	Teacher and learners	Learners
Attention to strategies	Teacher and learners	Teacher and learners

programmes (Nakata, 2011), using word parts to help remember words and using dictionaries. When teachers spend time on low-frequency words in class, they should be using the low-frequency words as an excuse for working on those strategies. The learners' aim is to continue to increase their vocabulary. The strategies provide a means of doing this.

As Table 1.5 shows, learners should begin training in the strategies for dealing with vocabulary while they are learning the high-frequency words of the language. When learners know the high-frequency vocabulary and move to the study of mid-frequency words, the teacher does not spend substantial amounts of class time explaining and giving practice with vocabulary, but instead concentrates on expanding and refining the learners' control of vocabulary-learning and coping strategies. Learners however should continue to learn new words.

Low-frequency words

There is a very large group of words that occur very infrequently and cover only a small proportion of any text.

What are the low-frequency words and how many low-frequency words are there? Low-frequency words are those beyond the most frequent 9,000 words of English. There are tens of thousands of them.

What kinds of words are they? Many low-frequency words are proper names. Around 3% of the running words in the British National Corpus are words like *Carl, Johnson, Ohio* (see Table 1.3). The words in the proper nouns list cover 2.6% of the tokens, and about half of the words not in the lists are proper nouns. They make up a very large proportion of the word types in any large corpus (around 50%). In some texts, such as novels and newspapers, proper nouns are like technical words – they are of high frequency in particular texts but not in other texts, their meaning is closely related to the message of the text, and they could not be sensibly pre-taught because their use in the text reveals their meaning. Before you read a novel, you do not need to learn the characters' names.

'One person's technical vocabulary is another person's low-frequency word.' This ancient vocabulary proverb makes the point that, beyond the high- and mid-frequency words of the language, people's vocabulary grows partly as a result of their jobs, interests and specialisations. The technical vocabulary of our personal interests is important to us. To others, however, it is not important and from their point of view is just a collection of low-frequency words.

Some low-frequency words are simply low-frequency words. That is, they are words that almost every language user rarely uses. Here are some examples: *eponymous, gibbous, bifurcate, plummet* and *ploy*. They may represent a rarely expressed idea, they may be similar in meaning to a much more frequent word or phrase, they may be marked as being old-fashioned, very formal, belonging to a particular dialect, or vulgar, or they may be foreign words.

How many low-frequency words do learners need to know? When learners have a vocabulary size of 9,000 words and know the technical vocabulary of the subject areas they are involved in, it is useful for them to keep expanding their vocabulary. The more vocabulary that is known and the better it is known, the more effectively the language can be used. Adult native speakers have receptive vocabulary sizes of around 20,000 word families and learners who already know the mid-frequency words may want to see native speaker vocabulary size as a learning goal.

What should teachers and learners do about low-frequency words? Teachers should teach low-frequency words only when they are essential to the understanding of the text or when they are in a relevant technical vocabulary. Learners may choose to deliberately learn low-frequency words, but it is probably best to learn them largely incidentally through reading and listening. Reading is likely to provide greater opportunities for such learning because written texts typically make use of a larger vocabulary than spoken texts. Dictionary use can help in such learning, particularly where the low-frequency words are adjectives and there are few context clues to their meaning. Research also shows that incidental learning from listening is less than from reading (Brown et al., 2008). Here are some low-frequency words that I have recently looked up on my iPod while reading novels. I found it impossible to guess their meaning from context clues, largely I hope because of a lack of context clues – *adipose, afflatus, philter, cetacean, plangent, mephitis, prelapsarian*. I have yet to find an opportunity to use these in speaking or writing!

Specialised vocabulary

It is possible to make specialised vocabularies which provide good coverage for certain kinds of texts. These are a way of extending the high-frequency words for special purposes.

What special vocabularies are there? Special vocabularies are made by systematically restricting the range of topics or language uses investigated. It is thus possible to have special vocabularies for speaking, for reading academic texts, for reading newspapers, for reading children's stories or for letter writing. Technical vocabularies are also kinds of specialised vocabularies. Some specialised vocabularies are made by doing frequency counts using a specialised corpus. Some are made by experts in the field gathering what they consider to be relevant vocabulary.

There is a very important specialised vocabulary for second language learners intending to do academic study in English. This is the *Academic Word List* (see Appendix 1). It consists of 570 word families that are not in the most frequent 2,000 words of English but which occur reasonably frequently over a very wide range of academic texts. That means that the words in the academic vocabulary are useful for learners studying humanities, law, science or commerce. The list is not restricted to a specific discipline. The academic vocabulary has sometimes been called sub-technical vocabulary because it does not contain technical words but it contains rather formal vocabulary. The *Academic Word List* is drawn from words from the third 1,000 to the seventh 1,000, although in some frequency counts based on formal text, some *Academic Word List* words occur in the first 2,000.

Adding the academic vocabulary to the high-frequency words changes the coverage of academic text from 76.1% to 86.1%. Expressed another way, with a vocabulary of 2,000 words, approximately one word in every four will be unknown. With a vocabulary of 2,000 words plus the Academic Word List, approximately one word in every ten will be unknown. This is a very significant change. If, instead of learning the vocabulary of the Academic Word List, the learner had moved on to the third 1,000 most frequent words, instead of an additional 10% coverage there would only have been 4.3% coverage (see Table 1.3).

What kinds of words do they contain? The *Academic Word List* is reprinted in Appendix 1. Hirsh (2004) looked at why the same group of words frequently occur across a very wide range of academic texts. Sometimes a few of them are closely related to the topic and are in effect technical words in that text. Most however occur because they allow academic writers to do the things that academic writers want to do. That is, they allow writers to refer to others' work (*assume, establish, indicate, conclude, maintain*). They allow writers to work with data in academic ways (*analyse, assess, concept, definition, establish, categories, seek*). They also add formality and seriousness to what is being said, and in academic text and newspapers they do jobs that would otherwise be done by high-frequency words. We consider this issue again in Chapter 6.

Technical words contain a variety of types which range from words that do not usually occur in other subject areas (*cabotage, amortisation*) to those that are formally like high-frequency words but which may have specialised meanings (*chest, by-pass, arm* as used in anatomy). Chapter 6 on specialised vocabulary looks more fully at technical words.

How large are they? Research on technical vocabularies (Chung and Nation, 2003; Chung and Nation, 2004) shows that technical vocabulary makes up a very large proportion of the running words of a technical text. As we shall see in a later chapter, in Chung's study (Chung and Nation, 2004), around 20% of the running words in an applied linguistics text were technical words, and over 30% of the words in an anatomy text were technical words. Technical words are words that are closely associated with a particular subject area. Some technical words are not likely to be known by people who are not familiar with the subject area. Some technical words are high-frequency words, such as *cost, price, demand, supply* in economics, which still retain most of their generally known meaning. The size of the technical vocabulary will differ from one subject area to another. Subject areas like medicine or botany have very large technical vocabularies, well in excess of 6,000 words. Subject areas like applied linguistics or geography are likely to have smaller technical vocabularies. A rough guess from looking at dictionaries of technical vocabulary is that they are likely to contain between 1,000 and 2,000 words. If multiword units are also counted as technical words, like *gross national product*, this will then increase the size of technical vocabularies.

How can you make a special vocabulary? The *Academic Word List* was made by deciding on the high-frequency words of English and then examining a range of academic texts to find what words were not amongst the high-frequency words (the *General Service List*), but had wide range and reasonable frequency of occurrence. Range was important because the academic vocabulary is intended for general academic purposes.

One way of making a technical vocabulary is to compare the frequency of words in a specialised text with their frequency in a general corpus (Chung, 2003). Words which are proportionally much more frequent in the specialised text, or which occur only in the specialised text, are highly likely to be technical vocabulary.

What should teachers and learners do about specialised vocabulary? Where possible, specialised vocabulary should be treated like high-frequency vocabulary. That is, it should be taught and studied in a variety of complementary ways. The *Academic Word List* should be dealt with across the four strands of a course. Where the technical vocabulary is also high-frequency vocabulary, learners should be helped to see the connections and differences between the high-frequency meanings and the technical uses. For example, what is similar between a *cell wall* and other less specialised uses of *wall*? Where the technical vocabulary requires specialist knowledge of the field, teachers should train learners in strategies which will help them understand and remember the words. Much technical vocabulary will only make sense in the context of learning the specialised subject matter. Learning the meaning of the technical term *morpheme* needs to be done as a part of the study of linguistics, not before the linguistics course begins.

Zipf's law

The psycholinguist George Zipf (1935; 1949) is well known for his work on vocabulary (see Meara and Moller, 2006, for a review of one of his books), and is best known for what is now called **Zipf's law**. Zipf's law says that when we look at a ranked frequency list made from a text or a collection of texts, we can multiply the rank of the item by its frequency and always get the same answer (rank × frequency = a constant figure; see Sorrell, 2012, for a very clear description of Zipf's law). Table 1.6 shows how this works for every tenth word in George Orwell's novel *Animal Farm*.

Table 1.6 *Zipf's law applied to data from Animal Farm*

Word type	Rank	Frequency	Rank × frequency
he	10	324	3,240
farm	20	166	3,320
no	30	102	3,060
work	40	72	2,880
what	50	58	2,900
day	60	51	3,060

Note in Column 4 how the results from multiplying rank with frequency are all roughly the same, around 3,000.

If Zipf's law worked well, we could predict the frequency of any item in a frequency-ranked list if we knew the rank and frequency of a single item in the list. Zipf's law does not work with this degree of accuracy, but when we draw a curve from the application of Zipf's law, it shows us that in a text or collection of texts there will be a small number of words which occur very frequently and a very large number of words that occur infrequently. Zipf's law also allows us to predict how many word types will occur only once, twice, three times and so on in a text. Using the formula '1 divided by frequency times (frequency + 1), $-\dfrac{1}{f(f+1)}-$,' we can work out that half of the word types in a text will occur only once (frequency). Webb and Macalister (forthcoming) found that 42% of the mid-frequency and low-frequency word families in the New Zealand School Journals (written for children) occurred only once, and 47% of the mid-frequency and low-frequency words in a collection of newspaper and fiction texts occurred only once. If we are interested in words with a frequency of 2, the formula tells us that one-sixth will occur twice. Zipf's law describes a distribution that is not restricted to vocabulary, but applies to many natural occurrences, like the distribution of wealth and the effects of repetitions.

Even in very controlled texts, such as graded readers, Zipf's law still applies. So, it is not unusual to find lots of words occurring once in coursebooks written for learners of English and in simplified texts. Even well-designed coursebooks and graded readers will contain large numbers of words occurring only once or twice. The major effect of simplification is to remove words which are outside the word lists used to guide the simplification. This may have only a small effect on changing the range of word frequencies in the text. There is another implication of Zipf's law: Any text will contain a large number of words occurring only once or twice, and so if we wish to learn low-frequency words through meeting them in context, very large quantities of input are needed.

Zipf's law is not a rule that language producers follow. It simply describes the nature of vocabulary use. The common sense explanation of Zipf's law is that if we want to say different things we need to use some different words, but these different words will occur with common general-purpose words. It is useful to think of the extremes of this situation. If we wanted to stop Zipf's law working, we should write a text that uses exactly the same sentence which contains no repeated words over and over again. In this way, every word would have exactly the same frequency. At the other extreme, we could stop Zipf's law working by never repeating any word that we have said before. In this way, every word would have a frequency of one. If however we use language normally to speak about different things, then Zipf's law will apply. A part of the explanation of Zipf's law is that some words (function words) are essential no matter what you say, and these make up the bulk of the very high-frequency words. The most frequent 10 word types of English cover around 25% of the tokens. The most frequent 100 word types cover around 50% of the tokens. If we look at Table 1.1, we can see that important topic words (*little, pig, house*) are also likely to occur among the very frequent words, particularly if the text we are analysing is on a single topic or in a restricted topic area. In Murphey's (1992) frequency count of pop songs, which content word occurred among the most frequent ten words? Love.

So, the implications that we need to draw from Zipf's law are as follows.

1. A small number of high-frequency words will make up a very large proportion of the words in any text. Although some of these words will be function words, many of them will be content words, and it is worth learning these high-frequency words before going on to learn less frequent words.
2. A very large number of different words will make up a relatively small proportion of the tokens in a text. These words eventually need to be learned, but there are so many of them that learning them needs to be the responsibility of the learners rather than the teacher.
3. When analysing the vocabulary in a text, we can expect to see large numbers of words occurring only once or twice. That is the nature of language use. If we want to make texts accessible for learners of English, we should try to replace the low-frequency words that are outside the learners' current learning goals. There will still be many words that occur only once or twice in the text, but if these are known words or words that are currently worth learning, they will not be an overwhelming problem for the learners.
4. When reading texts where one of the goals is to incidentally learn new vocabulary, it is important to do large quantities of reading. By reading large quantities of texts on a variety of topics, learners can have a chance of getting enough repetitions to support the learning of mid-frequency vocabulary.

Zipf is also well known for another law, sometimes called the **law of least effort**. This law states that items which we use frequently tend to be short. Long and complex items tend to be less frequent. We can see this law at work in frequency counts, where most high-frequency words are short single-syllable words. In general, the longer a word is, the less frequent it is likely to be. Both of Zipf's laws also apply to grammar. Simple grammatical constructions are typically more frequent than longer or more complex related grammatical constructions, and the most frequent construction tends to be twice as frequent as the next one in the frequency list and three times as frequent as the third item in the list. A good example of this can be seen with constructions involving the word *too*, for example, *too hot, too hot to eat, too hot for me* and *too hot for me to eat*. If we draw a graph of the frequencies of these four constructions we get a rough Zipf curve.

In Chapter 5 we will look at vocabulary frequency profiles as a way of assessing productive use of written vocabulary. Edwards and Collins (2010) used Zipf's law and variations of it to evaluate the effectiveness of statistical modelling and lexical frequency profiles as ways of determining vocabulary size. Their plain language discussion of Zipf's law is particularly helpful for non-mathematicians to understand the patterned nature of word frequency distributions. Their findings support the use of lexical frequency profiles as a way of estimating the size of the homogeneous groups of learners, but they caution that lexical frequency profiles are less accurate for individuals and for groups of learners with large vocabulary sizes.

Testing vocabulary knowledge

In this chapter, a very important distinction has been made between high-frequency words, mid-frequency words and low-frequency words. This distinction has been made on the basis of the frequency, coverage and quantity of these words. The distinction is very important because teachers need to deal with these kinds of words in quite different ways, and teachers and learners need to ensure that the high-frequency words of the language are well known to them.

It is therefore important that teachers and learners know whether the high-frequency words have been learned. There are several tests available which will allow teachers and learners to see what is known and what needs to be learned.

The *Vocabulary Size Test* (Beglar, 2010; Nation and Beglar, 2007) is designed to measure a learner's total vocabulary size. There are some bilingual versions of the test available at Paul Nation's website. The learners' score on the test is multiplied by 100 to get their vocabulary size. It is useful to look at their vocabulary size in relation to the text coverage figures in Column 3 of Table 1.3. Someone with a vocabulary size of 3,000 words will have somewhere around 93.6% coverage of text, meaning that around 6% of the words in an unsimplified text will be unknown to them. That works out at about one unknown word in every 17 running words, or about 18 unknown words per 300-word page, quite a heavy vocabulary load.

The 1,000 word family levels in the test are used solely to make sure that there was no frequency bias in the sampling of the items. There are not enough items at any one 1,000-word frequency level (10 items, or 5 items in a reduced version) to give a reliable estimate of a learner's knowledge of that particular level. The test is solely intended to be a measure of total vocabulary size. That is why it is important for learners to sit all levels of the test and not just some of the earlier levels. There is also evidence from data gathered from Myq Larson's website (http://my.vocabularysize.com) that mixing items from different frequency levels results in better sustained attention to the test rather than having the learners go from easy high-frequency items to difficult low-frequency items.

The *Vocabulary Levels Test* (Nation, 1983; Schmitt et al., 2001) can be used to measure whether the high-frequency words have been learned, and where the learner is in the learning of academic and low-frequency vocabulary. There are also productive versions of the original form of the test (Laufer and Nation, 1995; Laufer and Nation, 1999; see also the freely available *Vocabulary Resource Booklet* on Paul Nation's website). See Read (1988) and Schmitt et al. (2001) for some research on this test. The test is designed to be quick to take, to be easy to mark and to be easy to interpret. It gives credit for partial knowledge of words. Its main purpose is to let teachers quickly find out whether learners need to be working on high-frequency or mid-frequency words, and roughly how much work needs to be done on these frequency bands. Before using the test, it is important to understand how it is designed and how to interpret the results. It differs from the *Vocabulary Size Test* not only in its format, but also in that it is a diagnostic test. It does not measure how many words someone knows but indicates whether learners need to be focusing on high-, academic or mid-frequency words. There are 1,000- and 2,000-level bilingual versions of the *Vocabulary Levels Test* in several languages (look in the Vocabulary Resource Booklet on Paul Nation's website). These are very useful for measuring how many of the high-frequency words are known.

In a very interesting and detailed analysis of the use of the *Vocabulary Levels Test* with his French-speaking learners, Cobb (2000) found that their performance on the *Vocabulary Levels Test* was largely a result of the ease with which they answered the items involving Graeco-Latin words (either the word itself and/or in the definition). The test was thus not measuring just learning of English, but was also measuring the learners' skill at making use of cognate relationships between French and English. Cobb then developed an L1-specific test which deliberately excluded cognates, based on the Productive *Vocabulary Levels Test* format. The results of this test correlated very highly (.9) with other proficiency measures, compared to a correlation of (.59) between the *Vocabulary Levels Test* and reading comprehension. Cobb suggests the new test was so effective because it measured actual learning, not guessing from cognates. Boyle (2009) found an appropriate balance of Germanic (33%) and Graeco-Latin words (66%) in the old *Vocabulary Levels Test*. However, unlike Cobb, Boyle found his Emirati students gained much higher scores on the Germanic words than on the Graeco-Latin words, and that some of the Graeco-Latin words that were known in the test were loanwords in the local Arab dialect of the United Arab Emirates. This lack of Graeco-Latin words could act as a barrier to successful academic reading.

Vocabulary tests like the *Vocabulary Size Test* and the *Vocabulary Levels Test*, which sample from frequency levels without concern for the L1 of the learners, will always involve a guessing from cognates effect (Nguyen and Nation, 2011). One solution is to do what Cobb did and remove such items from the tests. The problem is that then tests like the *Vocabulary Size Test* are no longer a measure of vocabulary size because significant portions of the vocabulary of the language are left out. As Cobb points out, when such tests are used, we have to realise that they are not just measuring learning but are also measuring learning burden in that cognates and loans are being answered correctly from L1–L2 parallels, not from learning. These parallels however do reflect ease of learning.

There is much more to vocabulary testing than simply testing if a learner can choose an appropriate meaning for a given word form, and we will look closely at testing in Chapter 13. However, for the purpose of helping a teacher decide what kind of vocabulary work learners need to do, the *Vocabulary Size Test* and the *Vocabulary Levels Test* are well proven, reliable and very practical tests.

Training learners in choosing which words to learn

Measuring vocabulary size is a useful step in deciding which words to learn. Barker (2007) makes a good case for training learners to take a systematic and principled approach to choosing the vocabulary they learn. He provides a very practical checklist that learners can use, noting that they are likely to feel a sense of empowerment when they find that the information they need is available through their own searching. This training should cover the following points.

1. *Sources of information about word frequency and lists of useful words*. These sources should include how to access the BNC/COCA lists, the *General Service List* (West, 1953) the Academic Word List (Coxhead, 2000) and the Academic Vocabulary List, how to use Tom Cobb's web-based version of the lexical frequency profiler (www.lextutor.ca), what dictionaries provide frequency information and how to interpret it, where word frequency lists can be found, and for the more adventurous and computer-literate learners how to make your own word frequency lists using, for example, the Frequency or Range programs available from Paul Nation's website.

2. *An understanding of the nature of word frequency*. This should relate particularly to Zipf's law which shows that from a word frequency perspective not all words are created equal, and that a relatively small number of words occur very frequently, and a very large number of words occur very infrequently. Using the Frequency program which comes with the Range program is a very effective way of bringing this message home (see also Tom Cobb's website, www.lextutor.ca). In relation to point 1 above, it is also useful for learners to realise that lists like the Academic Word List assume previous knowledge of the *General Service List*, and that usually it is best to know *General Service List* words before Academic Word List words.

3. *Practice in considering personal language needs*. The frequency level of words is a useful guide to the likely value they will give as a result of learning them. However, we all have special interests and what would be a low-frequency word for one person may be an essential word for another person. If you love a particular sport then the vocabulary of that activity is of great value to you. Barker (2007) also notes that some words are very attractive for a variety of reasons, and this attractiveness can make learning them a pleasant task. Learners may also feel gaps in their knowledge that they need to fill. When learning Japanese while living in Japan, I felt the need to be able to ask if it was all right to go into a certain part of a shrine or not. When our son started school as the only non-native speaker in the school, we taught him how to say *I want to go to the toilet* as that seemed to us as likely to be his most pressing language need on his first day at school.

Table 1.7 *A staged set of vocabulary-learning goals*

Language use	Number of words	Source of words
Survival vocabulary for foreign travel	120 words and phrases	Nation and Crabbe (1991)
Reading the easiest graded readers	100–400 word families	
Reading intermediate-level graded readers	1,000 word families	
Basic speaking skills	1,200 word families	West (1960: 38–40, 95–134: 'A minimum adequate vocabulary for speech')
Basic listening skills	3,000 word families	
Reading graded readers and using monolingual dictionaries	3,000 word families	*A General Service List of English Words* (West, 1953); BNC/COCA word family lists
Reading mid-frequency readers	4,000/6,000/8,000 word families	BNC/COCA word family lists
Reading unsimplified text with the help of a dictionary, and watching TV	3,000 words	BNC/COCA word family lists
Unassisted reading of unsimplified text	6,000–9,000 words	BNC/COCA word family lists

4. *The importance of knowing roughly how many words you know and what a reasonable learning goal should be in terms of number of words.* The my.vocabularysize.com website provides an easily used measure. Tom Cobb's website provides several computerised vocabulary tests that can provide quick results. Table 1.7 suggests several useful staged vocabulary goals that the results of these tests can be related to.

5. *Options for dealing with vocabulary.* When learners meet an unknown word, they can choose what to do about it. Learners should get some guided practice in applying these options. One way of doing this is to provide the learners with a list of actions and possible reasons for those actions. They then try to justify each of the actions by matching reasons to them. The same reason can be used to justify several actions.

Actions

1. Deal with the word quickly by ignoring it or guessing it from context.
2. Find the meaning and mark the word in the dictionary so that you know you have met it before if you look it up again.
3. Find the meaning and put the word on a word card to learn later.
4. Find a meaning and work on the word now.

Reasons

1. It is a high-frequency word.
2. It is a low-frequency word.
3. It is a useful technical term for me.
4. I think I have seen this word before.
5. I have never seen this word before.
6. I can easily guess the meaning of the word.
7. I can see how this word is related to an L1 or L2 word that I already know.
8. I need to use this word receptively or productively now.
9. This seems like a word I could use often.
10. This word is one that I feel like learning.

So, the first option, of dealing with the word quickly, could be justified using reasons 2, 5, 6, 7.

6. *Ease or difficulty in learning a particular word.* Sometimes a new word will be easy to learn because it contains word parts that the learner already knows. If the learning burden is light, then for only a little effort a new word can be learned. The word may also be easy to learn because it is a loan word or cognate in the learner's L1. Words that are easy to spell and easy to pronounce may also be easy to learn. Occasionally a word may be easy to learn because of the striking and memorable situation in which it was met. Learners can be given practice in recognising word parts and should be encouraged to deliberately learn the most frequent prefixes and suffixes (see Chapter 9). Looking at a list of words and deliberately considering which have known parts and which are loan words in the L1 may also be a useful consciousness-raising activity.

The six points that we have just covered involve deciding whether to learn a particular word or not. How this deliberate learning can be done is the subject of several chapters of this book, particularly learning from word cards, using mnemonic techniques like the keyword technique and word part analysis, and using a dictionary as a learning tool. Vocabulary learning also involves knowing what to learn about a word, and it also involves making sure that there will be repeated spaced opportunities to meet, use and learn more about the word. It also involves knowing the importance of learning from input and making use of what has been learned through output.

Most of the questions looked at in this chapter will be looked at again in later chapters.

References

Barker, D. (2007). A personalized approach to analyzing 'cost' and 'benefit' in vocabulary selection. *System, 35*, 523–33.

Bauer, L. and Nation, I. S. P. (1993). Word families. *International Journal of Lexicography, 6, 4*, 253–79.

Beglar, D. (2010). A Rasch-based validation of the Vocabulary Size Test. *Language Testing, 27, 1*, 101–18.

Biemiller, A. and Slonim, N. (2001). Estimating root word vocabulary growth in normative and advantaged populations: Evidence for a common sequence of vocabulary acquisition. *Journal of Educational Psychology, 93, 3*, 498–520.

Boyle, R. (2009). The legacy of diglossia in English vocabulary: What learners need to know. *Language Awareness, 18, 1*, 19–30.

Brown, R., Waring, R. and Donkaewbua, S. (2008). Incidental vocabulary acquisition from reading, reading-while-listening, and listening to stories. *Reading in a Foreign Language, 20, 2*, 136–63.

Carroll, J. B., Davies, P. and Richman, B. (1971). *The American Heritage Word Frequency Book*. New York: Houghton Mifflin, Boston American Heritage.

Chung, T. M. (2003). A corpus comparison approach for terminology extraction. *Terminology, 9, 2*, 221–45.

Chung, T. M. and Nation, P. (2003). Technical vocabulary in specialised texts. *Reading in a Foreign Language, 15, 2*, 103–16.

Chung, T. M., and Nation, P. (2004). Identifying technical vocabulary. *System, 32, 2*, 251–63.

Cobb, T. (2000). One size fits all? Francophone learners and English vocabulary tests. *Canadian Modern Language Review, 57, 2*, 295–324.

Coxhead, A. (2000). A new academic word list. *TESOL Quarterly, 34, 2*, 213–38.

Daulton, F. E. (2008). *Japan's Built-in Lexicon of English-based Loanwords*. Clevedon: Multilingual Matters.

Diller, K. C. (1978). *The Language Teaching Controversy*. Rowley, MA: Newbury House.

Edwards, R., and Collins, L. (2010). Lexical frequency profiles and Zipf's law. *Language Learning, 61, 1*, 1–30.

Francis, W. N. and Kučera, H. (1982). *Frequency Analysis of English Usage*. Boston: Houghton Mifflin Company.

Goulden, R., Nation, P. and Read, J. (1990). How large can a receptive vocabulary be? *Applied Linguistics, 11, 4*, 341–63.

Hirsh, D. (2004). *A functional representation of academic vocabulary*. Victoria University of Wellington, Wellington.

Hu, M. and Nation, I. S. P. (2000). Vocabulary density and reading comprehension. *Reading in a Foreign Language*, **13**, 1, 403–30.

Laufer, B. and Nation, P. (1995). Vocabulary size and use: Lexical richness in L2 written production. *Applied Linguistics*, **16**, 3, 307–22.

Laufer, B. and Nation, P. (1999). A vocabulary size test of controlled productive ability. *Language Testing*, **16**, 1, 36–55.

Leech, G., Rayson, P. and Wilson, A. (2001). *Word Frequencies in Written and Spoken English*. Harlow: Longman.

Meara, P. and Moller, A. (2006). Review of The Psycho-biology of Language by G. K. Zipf. *System*, **34**, 455–7.

Mulder, K. and Hulstijn, J. (2011). Linguistic skills of adult native speakers as a function of age and level of education. *Applied Linguistics*, **32**, 5, 475–94.

Murphey, T. (1992). The discourse of pop songs. *TESOL Quarterly*, **26**, 4, 770–74.

Nagy, W. E. and Anderson, R. C. (1984). How many words are there in printed school English? *Reading Research Quarterly*, **19**, 3, 304–30.

Nakata, T. (2011). Computer-assisted second language vocabulary learning in a paired-associate paradigm: A critical investigation of flashcard software. *Computer Assisted Language Learning*, **24**, 1, 17–38.

Nation, I. S. P. (1983). Testing and teaching vocabulary. *Guidelines*, **5**, 1, 12–25.

Nation, I. S. P. (1993). Using dictionaries to estimate vocabulary size: Essential, but rarely followed, procedures. *Language Testing*, **10**, 1, 27–40.

Nation, I. S. P. (2006). How large a vocabulary is needed for reading and listening? *Canadian Modern Language Review*, **63**, 1, 59–82.

Nation, I. S. P. (2007). The four strands. *Innovation in Language Learning and Teaching*, **1**, 1, 1–12.

Nation, I. S. P. (2009) New roles for L2 vocabulary? In Li Wei and Cook, V. (eds.), *Contemporary Applied Linguistics Volume 1: Language Teaching and Learning* Continuum, Chapter 5, pp. 99–116.

Nation, P. and Beglar, D. (2007). A vocabulary size test. *The Language Teacher*, **31**, 7, 9–13.

Nation, P. and Crabbe, D. (1991). A survival language learning syllabus for foreign travel. *System*, **19**, 3, 191–201.

Nation, I. S. P. and Hwang, K. (1995). Where would general service vocabulary stop and special purposes vocabulary begin? *System*, **23**, 1, 35–41.

Nation, I. S. P. and Webb, S. (2011). *Researching and Analyzing Vocabulary*. Boston: Heinle Cengage Learning.

Neubacher, K. and Clahsen, H. (2009). Decomposition of inflected words in a second language. *Studies in Second Language Acquisition*, **31**, 403–35.

Nguyen, L. T. C. and Nation, I. S. P. (2011). A bilingual vocabulary size test of English for Vietnamese learners. *RELC Journal*, **42**, 1, 86–99.

Perfetti, C. and Hart, L. (2001). The lexical basis of comprehension skill. In Gorfien, D. S. (ed.), *On the Consequences of Meaning Selection: Perspectives on Resolving Lexical Ambiguity*. Washington, DC: American Psychological Association, pp. 67–86.

Rasinski, T. V. (2000). Speed does matter in reading. *The Reading Teacher*, **54**, 2, 146–51.

Read, J. (1988). Measuring the vocabulary knowledge of second language learners. *RELC Journal*, **19**, 2, 12–25.

Sadoski, M. (2005). A dual coding view of vocabulary learning. *Reading & Writing Quarterly*, **21**, 221–38.

Schmitt, N. (2008). Teaching vocabulary. *Pearson Education handout*.

Schmitt, N., Jiang, X. and Grabe, W. (2011). The percentage of words known in a text and reading comprehension. *The Modern Language Journal*, **95**, 1, 26–43.

Schmitt, N. and Schmitt, D. (2012). A reassessment of frequency and vocabulary size in L2 vocabulary teaching. *Language Teaching*, doi:10.1017/S0261444812000018.

Schmitt, N., Schmitt, D. and Clapham, C. (2001). Developing and exploring the behaviour of two new versions of the Vocabulary Levels Test. *Language Testing*, **18**, 1, 55–88.

Seashore, R. H. and Eckerson, L. D. (1940). The measurement of individual differences in general English vocabularies. *Journal of Educational Psychology*, **31**, 14–38.

Sinclair, J. M. (1991). *Corpus, Concordance, Collocation*. Oxford: Oxford University Press.

Sorrell, C. J. (2012). Zipf's law and vocabulary. In Chapelle, C. A. (ed.), *Encyclopaedia of Applied Linguistics*. Oxford: Wiley-Blackwell.

Swenson, E. and West, M. P. (1934). On the counting of new words in textbooks for teaching foreign languages. *Bulletin of the Department of Educational Research, University of Toronto*, **1**.

Thorndike, E. L. and Lorge, I. (1944). *The Teacher's Word Book of 30,000 Words*. New York: Teachers College Columbia University.

van Zeeland, H. and Schmitt, N. (2012). Lexical coverage and L1 and L2 listening comprehension: The same or different from reading comprehension? *Applied Linguistics*, doi:10.1093/applin/ams074.

Ward, J. and Chuenjundaeng, J. (2009). Suffix knowledge: Acquisition and applications. *System*, **37**, 461–9.

Webb, S. and Macalister, J. (forthcoming). Is text written for children useful for L2 extensive reading? *TESOL Quarterly*.

Webb, S. and Rodgers, M. P. H. (2009a). The lexical coverage of movies. *Applied Linguistics*, **30**, 3, 407–27.

Webb, S. and Rodgers, M. P. H. (2009b). The vocabulary demands of television programs. *Language Learning*, **59**, 2, 335–66.

West, M. (1953). *A General Service List of English Words*. London: Longman, Green and Co.

West, M. (1960). *Teaching English in Difficult Circumstances*. London: Longman.

Zechmeister, E. B., Chronis, A. M., Cull, W. L., D'Anna, C. A. and Healy, N. A. (1995). Growth of a functionally important lexicon. *Journal of Reading Behavior*, **27**, 2, 201–12.

Zipf, G. (1949). *Human Behavior and the Principle of Least Effort: An Introduction to Human Ecology*. New York: Hafner.

Zipf, G. K. (1935). *The Psycho-Biology of Language*. Cambridge, MA: MIT Press.

2 *Knowing a word*

Words are not isolated units of the language, but fit into many related systems and levels. Because of this, there are many things to know about any particular word and there are many degrees of knowing. One of the major ideas explored in this chapter is the relationship and boundaries between learning individual items and learning systems of knowledge. For example, it is possible to learn to recognise the form of a word simply by memorising its form. It is also possible to learn to recognise the form of a regularly spelled word by learning the systematic sound–spelling correspondences involved in the language. Recognition of the word then involves the application of some of the spelling rules. The relationship between item knowledge and system knowledge is complex and there has been enormous debate about certain aspects of it, for example, as it affects young native speakers of English learning to read. For each of the aspects of what it means to know a word, we will look at the item–system possibilities. A second major idea explored in this chapter is what some see as the receptive–productive scale of knowledge and how it applies to each aspect of vocabulary knowledge.

The aims of this chapter are to examine what could be known about a word, to evaluate the relative importance of the various kinds of knowledge, to see how they are related to each other, and to broadly suggest how learners might gain this knowledge. The chapter also looks at the learning burden of words, that is, what needs to be learned for each word and what is predictable from previous knowledge.

Learning burden

The learning burden of a word is the amount of effort required to learn it. Different words have different learning burdens for learners with different language backgrounds. Each of the aspects of what it means to know a word can contribute to the learning burden of a word. The general principle of learning burden (Nation, 1990) is that the more a word represents patterns and knowledge that the learners are already familiar with, the lighter its learning burden. These patterns and knowledge can come from the first language, from knowledge of other languages, and from previous knowledge of the second language. So, if a word uses sounds that are in the first language, follows regular spelling patterns, is a loanword in the first language with roughly the same meaning and fits into roughly similar grammatical patterns as in the first language with similar collocations and constraints, then the learning burden will be very light. The word will not be difficult to learn. For learners whose first language is closely related to the second language, the learning burden of most words will be light. For learners whose first language is not related to the second language, the learning burden will be heavy. De Groot (2006) presents evidence which shows that learning burden affects learning. L2 words that most closely resembled L1 spelling patterns were easier to learn and were less likely to be forgotten. Learning L2 word forms is strongly affected by the orthographic nature of the learners' L1. From an L2 English perspective, learners within L1 using the same letters have an easier job than learners with a different alphabetic system (such as Korean) who have an easier job than learners whose L1 uses characters (Chinese) (Hamada and Koda, 2008).

Teachers can help reduce the learning burden of words by drawing attention to systematic patterns and analogies within the second language, and by pointing out connections between the second language and the first language.

Teachers should be able to quickly estimate the learning burden of words for each of the aspects involved in knowing a word, so that they can direct their teaching towards aspects that will need attention and towards aspects that will reveal underlying patterns so that later learning is easier.

Do L1 and L2 words share the same lexical store?

Research shows that particularly at low proficiency levels, L2 words are directly connected to their L1 equivalents (Jiang, 2002; Kroll et al. 2002; Kroll and Stewart, 1994). Whether words are learned with L1 translations or pictures does not affect connection to the L1, it happens regardless (Altarriba and Knickerbocker, 2011; Lotto and De Groot, 1998). However, even newly learned words can also access meaning directly without going through the L1 (Finkbeiner and Nicol, 2003).

In a fascinating series of experiments, Williams and Cheung (2011) show that when learning words from another language (L2 or L3) between-language connections are made for aspects of the meaning that are context independent, that is, they are part of the core concept of the word. However, aspects of meaning that are context dependent, such as collocates, are not transferred from the L1 but need to be learned through experience with the L2. They note that newly learned words rapidly access meaning, but do not necessarily inherit all of the semantic information related to the translations with which they were paired during learning. This finding does not agree with Webb's (2009) findings which found transfer from L1. The differences may have been a result of the different ways of testing.

Williams and Cheung's findings underline the importance of learning through the four strands which involve a balance between deliberate and incidental learning, but also a balance between concept-focused and associative learning. That is, between 'learning the words' and learning through meeting and using the word. Deliberately learning an L2→L1 connection is fine, but it is only one step towards knowing the word.

The Williams and Cheung (2011) studies provide strong cross-language support for Elgort's (2011) finding that deliberate learning directly results in implicit knowledge. Newly learned L2 or L3 words can act as primes for L1 words, showing that deliberately learned L2 or L3 words can be fluently accessed subconsciously and are integrated into the semantic system.

Wolter (2001) suggests that the L1 and L2 lexicons are basically structurally similar, and that differences are caused by differences in depth of knowledge of particular words and also in the number of words known (see also Zareva, 2007). Wolter (2006) has a very interesting discussion of L1→L2 lexical and conceptual relationships, suggesting that paradigmatic relationships may require little if any modification as a result of mismatches between L2 and L1, while syntagmatic relationships like collocations are more likely to require modification, although not necessarily if there are L1→L2 parallels. Webb's research (Webb, 2008) provides some support for this idea.

The receptive / productive distinction

This section looks at what is involved in making the receptive/productive distinction in order to examine some of the issues involved in the distinction.

The validity of the receptive/productive distinction in most cases depends on its resemblance to the distinction between the receptive skills of listening and reading, and the productive skills of speaking and writing (Crow, 1986; Palmer, 1921: 118). **Receptive** carries the idea that we receive language input from others through listening or reading and try to comprehend it. **Productive** carries the idea that we produce language forms by speaking and writing to convey messages to others. Like most terminology, the terms receptive and productive are not completely suitable because there are productive features in the receptive skills – when listening and reading we produce meaning. The terms **passive** (for listening and reading) and **active** (for speaking and writing) are sometimes used as synonyms for receptive and productive (Corson, 1995; Laufer, 1998; Meara, 1990) but some object to these terms as they do not see listening and reading as having some of the other characteristics which can be attached to the term passive. I will use the terms receptive and productive and, following Schmitt (2010: 86), will use the terms **meaning recognition** and **meaning recall** for receptive knowledge, and **form recognition** and **form recall** for productive knowledge where this makes things clearer.

Essentially, receptive vocabulary use involves perceiving the form of a word while listening or reading and retrieving its meaning. Productive vocabulary use involves wanting to express a meaning through speaking or writing and retrieving and producing the appropriate spoken or written word form. Melka Teichroew (1982) shows the inconsistent use of the terms receptive and productive in relation to test items and degrees of knowing a word, and considers that the distinction is arbitrary and would be more usefully treated as a scale of knowledge.

Although reception and production can be seen as being on a continuum, this is by no means the only way of viewing the distinction between receptive and productive. Meara (1990) sees the distinction between productive and receptive vocabulary as being the result of different types of association between words. Productive vocabulary can be activated by other words, because it has many incoming and outgoing links with other words. Receptive vocabulary consists of items which can only be activated by external stimuli. That is, they are activated by hearing or seeing their forms, but not through associational links to other words. Meara thus sees productive and receptive as not being on a cline but representing different kinds of associational knowledge. One criticism of this view might be that language use is not only associationally driven, but, more basically, is meaning driven. Being able to actively name an object using an L2 word can be externally stimulated by seeing the object without necessarily arousing links to other L2 words.

According to Corson (1995: 44–5) receptive vocabulary includes the productive vocabulary and three other kinds of vocabulary – words that are only partly known, low-frequency words not readily available for use, and words that are avoided in productive use. These three kinds of vocabulary overlap to some degree. Corson's description of productive and receptive vocabulary is strongly based on the idea of use and not solely on degrees of knowledge. Some receptive vocabulary may be very well known but never used and therefore never productive. Some people may be able to curse and swear but never do. Thus Corson occasionally uses the term **unmotivated** to refer to some of the receptive vocabulary.

Corson (1995: 179–80) argues that for some people the Graeco-Latin vocabulary of English may be receptive for several reasons. Firstly, Graeco-Latin words are generally low-frequency words and thus require more mental activation for use. Secondly, the morphological structure of Graeco-Latin words may be opaque for some learners, thus reducing the number of nodes or points of activation for each of these words. Thirdly, some learners because of their social background get little opportunity to become familiar with the rules of use of the words. Corson's (1995) idea of the lexical bar (barrier) is thus important for the receptive/productive distinction.

What the lexical bar represents is a gulf between the everyday meaning systems and the high status meaning systems created by the introduction of an academic culture of literacy. This is a barrier that everyone has to cross at some stage in their lives, if they are to become 'successful candidates' in conventional forms of education. (Corson, 1995: 180–81)

In short, the barrier is the result of lack of access to the academic meaning systems strongly reinforced by the morphological strangeness of Graeco-Latin words. For some learners much vocabulary remains at best receptive because of the lexical bar.

The scope of the receptive/productive distinction

The terms receptive and productive apply to a variety of kinds of language knowledge and use. When they are applied to vocabulary, these terms cover all the aspects of what is involved in knowing a word. Table 2.1 lists these aspects using a model which emphasises the parts. It is also possible to show the aspects of what is involved in knowing a word using a process model, which emphasises the relations between the parts. At the most general level, knowing a word involves form, meaning and use.

From the point of view of receptive knowledge and use, knowing the word *underdeveloped* involves:

- being able to recognise the word form when it is heard;
- being familiar with its written form so that it is recognised when it is met in reading;

Table 2.1 *What is involved in knowing a word*

Form	spoken	R	What does the word sound like?
		P	How is the word pronounced?
	written	R	What does the word look like?
		P	How is the word written and spelled?
	word parts	R	What parts are recognisable in this word?
		P	What word parts are needed to express the meaning?
Meaning	form and meaning	R	What meaning does this word form signal?
		P	What word form can be used to express this meaning?
	concept and referents	R	What is included in the concept?
		P	What items can the concept refer to?
	associations	R	What other words does this make us think of?
		P	What other words could we use instead of this one?
Use	grammatical functions	R	In what patterns does the word occur?
		P	In what patterns must we use this word?
	collocations	R	What words or types of words occur with this one?
		P	What words or types of words must we use with this one?
	constraints on use	R	Where, when, and how often would we expect to meet this word?
	(register, frequency …)	P	Where, when, and how often can we use this word?

Note: R = receptive knowledge, P = productive knowledge

- recognising that it is made up of the parts *under-*, *-develop-* and *-ed* and being able to relate these parts to its meaning;
- knowing that *underdeveloped* signals a particular meaning;
- knowing what the word means in the particular context in which it has just occurred;
- knowing the concept behind the word which will allow understanding in a variety of contexts;
- knowing that there are related words like *overdeveloped*, *backward* and *challenged;*
- being able to recognise that *underdeveloped* has been used correctly in the sentence in which occurs;
- being able to recognise that words such as *territories* and *areas* are typical collocations; and
- knowing that *underdeveloped* is not an uncommon word and is not a pejorative word.

From the point of view of productive knowledge and use, knowing the word *underdeveloped* involves:

- being able to say it with correct pronunciation including stress;
- being able to write it with correct spelling;
- being able to construct it using the right word parts in their appropriate forms;
- being able to produce the word to express the meaning 'underdeveloped';
- being able to produce the word in different contexts to express the range of meanings of *underdeveloped;*
- being able to produce synonyms and opposites for *underdeveloped;*
- being able to use the word correctly in an original sentence;
- being able to produce words that commonly occur with it; and
- being able to decide to use or not use the word to suit the degree of formality of the situation. (At present *developing* is more acceptable than *underdeveloped* which carries a slightly negative meaning.)

Table 2.1 and the accompanying example of *underdeveloped* give an indication of the range of aspects of receptive and productive knowledge and use. It should be clear from this that if we say a particular word is part of someone's receptive vocabulary, we are making a very general statement that includes many aspects of knowledge and use, and we are combining the skills of listening and reading. In general, it seems that receptive learning and use is easier than productive learning and use, but it is not clear *why* receptive use should be less difficult than productive. There are several possible explanations which are probably complementary rather than competing (Ellis and Beaton, 1993a: 548–9).

1. *The 'amount of knowledge' explanation.* Productive learning is more difficult because it requires extra learning of new spoken or written output patterns (see Crow, 1986, for a similar argument). This will be particularly noticeable for languages which use different writing systems from the first language and which use some different sounds or sound combinations. For receptive use, learners may only need to know a few distinctive features of the form of an item. For productive purposes, their knowledge of the word form has to be more precise. This is clearly seen in young children who can display good receptive knowledge of a word such as spaghetti, but can only very roughly approximate its spoken form productively: *stigli* or *parsghetti*.

   The form of items is more likely to influence difficulty than meaning is, because there is much more shared knowledge of meaning between two distinct languages than there is shared form. Words in two languages might not have precisely the same meaning but in most cases the overlap is much greater than the distinctions. Initially, then, knowledge of the word form is more likely to be the factor affecting difficulty than knowledge of meaning, and more precise knowledge of the word form is required for productive use, thus making productive learning more difficult than receptive learning.

   This amount of knowledge explanation also relates to contextual knowledge like collocation. Such knowledge requires a lot of exposure to the language. It is not essential for receptive use but necessary for production.

2. *The 'practice' explanation.* In normal language-learning conditions, receptive use generally gets more practice than productive use, and this may be an important factor in accounting for differences in receptive and productive vocabulary size, particularly in measures of total vocabulary size. There is some evidence that both receptive learning and productive learning require particular practice to be properly learned (DeKeyser and Sokalski, 1996). This argument goes against the one that says that productive knowledge includes all the knowledge necessary for receptive use. This degree of practice factor is easily controlled in experimental studies.

3. *The 'access' explanation.* Ellis and Beaton (1993a: 548–9) suggest that a new foreign language word in the early stages of learning has only one simple link to its L1 translation (the receptive direction):

The receptive direction

Foreign word $\longrightarrow$ L1 translation
kaki $\longrightarrow$ *leg*

The L1 word however has many competing associations (the productive direction) and thus productive recall is more difficult than receptive because there are many competing paths to choose from, and the ones within the L1 lexical system are likely to be stronger.

The productive direction

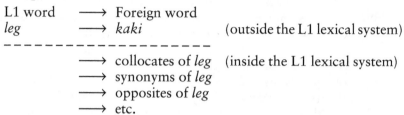

L1 word   ⟶ Foreign word
leg   ⟶ *kaki*   (outside the L1 lexical system)
- - - - - - - - - - - - - - - - - - - -
               ⟶ collocates of *leg*   (inside the L1 lexical system)
               ⟶ synonyms of *leg*
               ⟶ opposites of *leg*
               ⟶ etc.

The tip-of-the-tongue experiments (Brown and McNeill, 1966) provide some evidence of this.

4. *The 'motivation' explanation.* Learners are not motivated, for a variety of reasons including socio-cultural background, to use certain kinds of knowledge productively (Corson, 1995). Thus although some vocabulary may be well known and could be used productively, it is not used and remains in the learners' receptive vocabulary. Note that from this point of view, for some words the receptive/productive distinction is not a knowledge continuum but a distinction between motivated and unmotivated vocabulary. If a learner knows a word well enough to use it productively but never uses it productively, is it a part of that learner's productive vocabulary?

To truly compare the relative difficulty of receptive and productive learning, it is necessary to use test item types that are equivalent in all significant features affecting difficulty except the receptive/productive distinction. It also seems important, if the receptive/productive distinction is seen as a knowledge scale, that there be one scale for oral use (listening and speaking) and one for written use (reading and writing).

Waring (2002) points out that there is no simple match between a test format and the type of knowledge it is intended to measure. A multiple-choice recognition test, for example, may be designed to measure receptive vocabulary knowledge, but also measures other kinds of knowledge besides that, and does not measure some aspects that we would see as being an important part of receptive knowledge such as largely unassisted recall of meaning. Waring suggests that a self-report measure using a multi-state model may avoid many of the complications involved in more commonly used measures like translation, multiple-choice or completion tests. A **multi-state model** assumes that there is no linear order to the states and that knowledge of a word can change from one state to any of the others at different times. Waring's State Rating Task uses five categories:

A I understand this word and I know how to use it.	C I think I understand this word and I know how to use it.
B I understand this word but I don't know how to use it.	D I think I understand this word but I don't know how to use it.

E   I do not know this word.

These categories are not linear and the first four are based on understanding and use of the word. When doing the task, the learner assigns listed words to any one of the five categories by writing A, B, C, D or E next to the word. When trialling the State Rating Task, Waring found high correlations with scores on translation and sentence writing tests using the same words, and also on the receptive and productive *Vocabulary Levels Test*, and the Nelson Quickcheck test. High reliability was found on test/retest three days apart. Although the test is well researched and of great use to researchers, teachers will probably be reluctant to use a test that does not involve an actual demonstration of knowledge by, for example, choosing an answer, providing a translation or writing a word. It is however one of the 'purest measures' of receptive and productive knowledge. Its strong contribution to the receptive/productive debate is that it regards receptive/productive not as a continuum but as a set of states of knowledge.

Experimental comparisons of receptive and productive vocabulary

When comparing receptive and productive learning, the two test items (one to measure receptive learning and one to measure productive learning) should be both recognition items or both recall items (see Chapter 13). Some studies use a recognition item for measuring receptive knowledge (meaning recognition):

> *kaki* a. *book*
> b. *leg*
> c. *face*
> d. *fruit*

and a recall item for measuring productive knowledge (form recall):

Translate this word into Indonesian (the L2):

> *leg* _____

It is then impossible to tell how much the difference in scores is a result of the productive/receptive distinction or the recognition/recall distinction. Other confounding differences in test items may be the presence or absence of sentence context, oral and written presentation, and integration in and separation from a communicative task. Some studies, however, have avoided this problem of confounding variables.

Stoddard (1929) is one of the earliest foreign vocabulary-learning studies to directly compare receptive and productive learning and to test with equivalent test formats. Half of Stoddard's 328 English school-age subjects learned 50 French–English word pairs (receptive learning). The other half learned the same items as English–French word pairs (productive learning). Both groups sat the same recall test with half of the items tested receptively (meaning recall – see the French word, write the English translation) and half of the items tested productively (form recall – see the English word, write the French translation). Table 2.2 gives Stoddard's results.

Table 2.2 *Average scores for receptive and productive learning and testing of French vocabulary (Stoddard, 1929)*

	Receptive test (French–English) Max = 25	Productive test (English–French) Max = 25	Total Max = 50
Receptive learning (French–English) Group A	15.1	6.0	21.1
Productive learning (English–French) Group B	13.1	8.0	21.1
Total	28.2	14.0	

The conclusions to be drawn from Stoddard's data are:

1. *Receptive tests are easier than productive tests.* The score for the receptive test (28.2) was twice as high as that for the productive test (14.0).
2. *The type of test favours the type of learning.* Those who learned receptively got higher scores on the receptive test than those who learned productively (15.1 and 13.1). Those who learned productively got higher scores on the productive test than those who learned receptively (8.0 and 6.0).
3. *The effect of the type of test is greater than the effect of the type of learning.* Learners had similar scores (21.1) for both kinds of learning,

and the receptive learners' score on the receptive test (15.1) was much higher than the productive learners' score on the productive test (8.0).

Stoddard's (1929) study used simple comparison of raw scores, did not control for an order effect in testing (the receptive test always preceded the productive), and did not exercise deliberate control over the direction of learning to ensure that the receptive learning was indeed in the direction of French to English and that the productive learning was indeed in the other direction.

Like Stoddard, Webb (2009) used test formats involving L1→L2, L2→L1 translation. He compared the receptive and productive vocabulary knowledge of Japanese learners of English. The test formats differed only in the variable tested: receptive/productive knowledge. Test formats in other studies (Fan, 2000; Laufer, 1998; Morgan and Oberdeck, 1930; Waring, 1997) used formats that also differed on recognition and recall, thus making a pure receptive/productive comparison impossible. Although the words were sampled from a dictionary, bias was avoided (Nation, 1993) by using the frequency bands provided in the dictionary. The words were pilot tested to make sure that there would be no problems in scoring translations because of semantically related words. This adjustment meant that the test could not be a measure of total or actual vocabulary size, but allowed clearer comparison between receptive and productive knowledge. The tests were marked both strictly and leniently and the results of the two ways of marking were compared. As is consistent with other studies, receptive knowledge was larger than productive knowledge, but the difference was quite small (with lenient marking, productive knowledge was 93% of sensitive knowledge, and with strict marking 77%). This supports Laufer and Paribakht's (1998) claim that most EFL learners gain their vocabulary knowledge through deliberate learning and thus tend to have stronger knowledge of words than ESL learners with larger vocabularies. As word frequency dropped, so did the likelihood of knowing the words. The results showed that learners had at least partial productive knowledge of most of the words they learned receptively.

Waring (1997) performed an experiment somewhat similar to Stoddard's (1929) but with the same learners being tested on the same items receptively first and then productively. Waring also tested retention on the same day, the next day, one week after the learning and a month after the learning. The results, especially with delayed recall, were remarkably similar to Stoddard's, with the same three conclusions being confirmed. Waring also found that receptive learning took less time than productive learning, and that scores on productive tests were consistently at lower levels over time than scores on receptive tests, with very little being scored on the productive tests after three months. Waring (1997) also found extremely large individual differences in learning rate and amount recalled, with a very low correlation (0.29) between receptive and productive learning times, indicating that many learners are not proficient at both receptive and productive learning.

Is a combination of receptive and productive learning better than receptive or productive learning alone? Mondria and Wiersma (2004) investigated this question with Dutch secondary school learners of French. The learning and testing involved decontextualised L1→L2 word pairs, and the testing involved recall of L1 or L2 equivalents, both in an immediate post-test and a delayed post-test. For any one kind of knowledge, combined receptive and productive learning was not better than the learning targeted for a particular kind of knowledge (receptive learning for receptive knowledge, productive learning for productive knowledge).

These four experiments show the importance of the receptive/productive distinction, especially with test types. With test items that differ only on the receptive/productive dimension, receptive tests are much easier than productive tests. There is also a relationship between the way something is learned and the way it is tested but this is not nearly as strong as the effect of test type. If we make a very large and partly justified mental jump and equate testing with language use, then these experiments suggest the following things:

1. More time and repeated effort is needed to learn vocabulary for speaking and writing than is needed for listening and reading. All things being equal, receptive learning is easier than productive learning.
2. Generally it is more efficient to do receptive learning for receptive use, and productive learning for productive use. Combined receptive plus productive learning is not markedly better for any one kind of use (Mondria and Wiersma, 2004). However if both receptive and productive knowledge is needed, then it is better to do both receptive and productive learning. The simple overriding principle is 'Learn what you need to know'.
3. If productive use is needed, as in speaking and writing, there must be productive learning (form recall). This goes against the comprehensible input hypothesis in that it says that receptive learning is not always sufficient as a basis for productive use. It is still not clear if readiness for productive use can be reached by receptive 'overlearning', for example large quantities of reading or listening, or whether there must be 'pushed' output with learners being made to speak or write (Swain, 1985).

4. Learners will differ greatly in their skill at learning vocabulary and in their skill at learning vocabulary for different purposes. It is thus worthwhile checking the receptive and productive learning of learners, and providing training to help those who need it.

Griffin (1992) conducted a series of experiments on vocabulary learning focusing mainly on list learning and learning with a context sentence. Griffin's studies show that there are numerous factors such as proficiency, perceived goal and materials that can affect learning. Learning from lists is a complex activity and care needs to be taken in interpreting the results of such studies. Griffin found that receptive learning is easier than productive learning, learners score higher when the testing format matches the learning format, and that the associations formed are bi-directional (receptive learning can result in productive knowledge and vice versa). Griffin also found that most forgetting seems to occur soon after learning. Griffin tentatively concluded that, if learning is only to be done in one direction, then learning L1→L2 pairs (productive learning) may be more effective than L2→L1 (receptive learning). A major strength of Griffin's (1992) work is that he brings a strong background in psychology and in his review and discussion draws on areas of research not often considered in second language vocabulary learning.

Ellis and Beaton (1993a) investigated the productive learning of German vocabulary (English–German) under keyword and other conditions. The testing involved firstly receptive testing (see and hear the German word, type in the English translation) and subsequently productive testing (see the English word, type in the German translation). Receptive testing (German–English) gave significantly more correct responses (68%) than did English–German productive testing (53%) both by subjects and by words (Ellis and Beaton, 1993a: 541). This superiority for receptive testing occurred even though the experiment confounded direction of testing and order of the tests (receptive was always tested before productive) which could have boosted the productive scores (p. 548).

Webb (2005) found that if time-on-task is equal, receptive learning (reading three sentences) can result in better learning than productive learning (write your own sentence). In both treatments, the L1 translation of the target word was provided. The better learning may have been at least partly because some learners in the productive treatment did not have enough time to complete the task well and, more importantly, the receptive learners had more time than they needed and they used this for rote learning of the items. If time-on-task is not controlled for, then the longer productive tasks resulted in better learning on all the ten measures of learning used.

Webb (2009) compared receptive and productive learning of word pairs (L1→L2, L2→L1). Learning was measured using five receptive knowledge tests and five productive knowledge tests of orthography, syntax, grammatical function, association, and meaning and form. The words were learned in lists with learners covering either the L2 word form or the L1 translation when doing recall for learning. Those learning productively got higher scores on all the productive tests and on the receptive orthography test. Those learning receptively gained higher scores on the four other receptive tests. Both kinds of learning resulted in gains in all of the measured aspects of word knowledge. Not all differences were significant but that may have been because of a ceiling effect. Receptive learning alone is not enough if learners need productive knowledge, and in learning to recognise word forms, productive learning is particularly useful.

Shintani (2011), in a well-designed study that made a very welcome contribution to the unfortunately small number of EFL studies of very young learners (6 to 8-year-olds) learning English vocabulary, found that both receptive and productive learning resulted in substantial receptive and productive knowledge. As in other studies, receptive test scores were higher than productive test scores. However, the receptive learning group performed almost as well on the productive tests as the productive learning group. It is also noteworthy that on a delayed post-test five weeks after the treatment these young learners gained similar scores to those gained on the immediate post-test given one week after the treatment.

The receptive/productive distinction is a very important distinction in language testing and also in teaching and learning. It is reflected in the four strands in meaning-focused input and meaning-focused output strands, and when looking at what is involved in learning a word, it provides a useful way of separating related degrees of knowledge.

Aspects of knowing a word

The distinctions made in Table 2.1 are not just arbitrary conveniences. For example, drawing heavily on research in experimental psychology and language acquisition, Ellis (1994: 212) distinguishes the form-learning aspects of vocabulary learning (Ellis calls them Input/Output aspects) and the meaning aspects of vocabulary. This distinction is based primarily on the kind of learning best suited to the various aspects.

Ellis (1994: 212; 1995) argues for a dissociation between explicit and implicit learning where formal recognition and production rely on implicit learning, but the meaning and linking aspects rely on explicit, conscious processes.

Implicit learning involves attention to the stimulus but does not involve other conscious operations. It is strongly affected by repetition. Explicit learning is more conscious. The learner makes and tests hypotheses in a search for structure (Ellis, 1994: 214). Explicit learning can involve a search for rules, or applying given rules. It is strongly affected by the quality of the mental processing. What Ellis calls the **mediational** aspect is the mapping or linking of knowledge of the word form to knowledge of the meaning of the word.

What this means is that, especially for high-frequency words, teachers should explain the meaning of words, and learners should do exercises, look up dictionaries and think about the meanings. After brief attention to spelling and pronunciation, however, experience in meeting and producing the word form should be left to encounters in meaning-focused use.

Aitchison (1994: Chapter 15) sees children acquiring their first language vocabulary as performing three connected but different tasks: a labelling task, a packaging task and a network building task (p. 170). These correspond to the three divisions in the meaning section of Table 2.1 – connecting form and meaning, concept, and associations.

Table 2.3 provides a broad overview of the different kinds of knowledge and the most effective kinds of learning. It is important to note however that it is possible and helpful to approach the learning of word forms, for example, through explicit learning, but that essentially the most effective knowledge for this aspect of vocabulary is implicit and there must be suitable repeated opportunities for this kind of learning to occur.

The grammar and collocation aspects of use involve pattern recognition and production and thus are most effectively the goal of implicit learning (Ellis and Sinclair, 1996: 236–8). The constraints on vocabulary use are more closely related to meaning and would benefit more from explicit learning. That is, the teacher and learner should discuss where and when certain words should not be used. As Elgort's (2011) research shows, the link between kinds of learning and kinds of knowledge is not simple, and explicit learning can result in implicit as well as explicit knowledge, and implicit learning can result in implicit knowledge and some explicit knowledge.

Robinson (1989) argues for a 'rich' approach to vocabulary teaching and uses Canale and Swain's (1980) division of communicative competence into grammatical, sociolinguistic, discourse and strategic competence as a checklist for ensuring that all the dimensions of vocabulary knowledge and skill are covered. Robinson stresses the importance of ensuring learners have the skill of negotiating the meaning of words.

Table 2.3 *Kinds of vocabulary knowledge and the most effective kinds of learning*

Kinds of knowledge		Kinds of learning	Activities
Form		implicit learning involving noticing	repeated meetings as in repeated reading
Meaning		strong explicit learning	depth of processing through the use of images, elaboration, deliberate inferencing
Use	grammar collocation	implicit learning	repetition
	constraints on use	explicit learning	explicit guidance and feedback

Levelt's process model of language use

Table 2.1 lists the various aspects of what is involved in knowing a word without considering how these aspects are related to each other and how they are involved in normal language use. It is also of value for making decisions about the teaching and learning of vocabulary to see how the aspects of vocabulary knowledge fit into the process of language use. In order to do this we will look at Levelt's (1989; 1992) model of language use and its adaptations (Bierwisch and Schreuder, 1992; de Bot, 1992; de Bot et al., 1997). Figure 2.1 outlines Levelt's model.

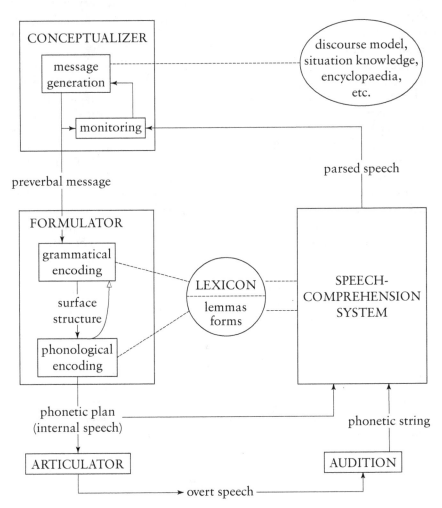

Figure 2.1 Levelt's model (1989: 9) of speech production

In this model we are most interested in the lexicon and so a brief description will be enough to outline the other parts of the model.

The conceptualiser is where the spoken message begins. The sub-processes involve intending to say something, choosing the necessary information, putting it in a roughly suitable order, and checking that it fits with what has been said before. In Figure 2.1 the square boxes represent processing components which make use of procedural knowledge. The two rounded components represent knowledge stores of declarative knowledge. Procedural knowledge is not accessible through introspection. Declarative knowledge is largely examinable through conscious thought and reflection. This is a very important distinction, because models of language acquisition see quite different roles for procedural and declarative knowledge in the development of second language proficiency.

The message fragments output of the conceptualiser is input for the formulator which changes the preverbal message into a phonetic plan. This change involves grammatically encoding the message and then phonologically encoding the message. In the grammatical encoding, information in the lemma part of the lexicon is accessed by procedures in the grammatical encoder. The most striking feature of this is that these procedures are 'lexically driven' (Levelt, 1989: 181). That is, that the grammar, morphology and phonology are determined by the particular words that are chosen. Levelt calls this the 'lexical hypothesis'. This idea fits very well with Sinclair's (1987) 'idiom principle' (see Chapter 9). In the phonological encoding, the form part of the lexicon is accessed by procedures in the phonological encoder. The output of the formulator is a phonetic plan. The articulator changes this plan into actual speaking.

From the point of view of speaking, the rest of the model is involved in self-monitoring. That is, listening to what is being produced, comprehending it and using it to adjust further production. De Bot et al. (1997) present an adaptation of Levelt's model to include both language production and language reception.

Let us now look more closely at the lexicon component in Levelt's model. We have already noted two very important points about it. Firstly, that the knowledge it contains is declarative. That is, it is con-sciously known and can be built up both through incidental learning and through formal study. Secondly, it is the choice of particular words that determines the grammar and phonology of the sentences and so grammar and other aspects are important components of what it means to know a word and this knowledge must be closely related to each particular word. This underlines the importance of meeting words in use as a way of developing vocabulary knowledge. It also shows how the decontextualised learning of vocabulary is not sufficient, although it may be useful, for 'knowing a word'.

Levelt (1989: 9, 188) divides the lexicon into two parts, one that contains lemmas and one that contains forms. The lemmas each consist of semantic and grammatical knowledge – that is, knowledge of the meaning components of a word and knowledge of the syntactic category (part of speech) of a word, its grammatical functions, and some other grammatical restrictions and marking that determine its use, such as person, number, tense and so on. It is possible that, in addition to meaning components, the lemma contains information about appropriateness, style and other constraints that make the lemma fit particular contexts well (p. 183). The information about the lemma is linked by what Levelt calls a pointer to the morpho-phonological form of the word. This simply means that meaning and form are linked in the lexical store.

The various bits of information about any particular word in the lexicon are related to each other not only because they are about the same word but also they are related in a more organised way that involves the processes of producing or receiving the word. Here is a typical speaking production sequence:

1. The conceptualiser produces a preverbal message consisting of information the speaker wishes to convey.
2. The formulator accesses the lexicon to find the lemma with the appropriate meaning components.
3. Some of these meaning components will be directly connected to particular grammatical features. Other grammatical components that are part of the lemma will be activated.
4. The meaning and grammar components of the lemma are linked to the morphological and phonological features of the word.
5. The appropriate morphological form is chosen or produced for the word to encode the meaning and grammatical function of the word.
6. The phonological features of the word are produced to match the morphological form of the word.
7. The articulator produces the word.

The steps crudely outlined above are very closely related to each other in a series of cause–effect sequences. For example, the link between Steps 2 and 3 in the case of the word *painter* is that the meaning of 'someone who paints' is related to a singular countable noun 'expressing the agentive of the action expressed by the verb stem'

(Levelt, 1989: 183). Step 4 links this explicitly to the form *painter*. At Step 5 the morphological form *paint + er* is chosen because the suffix *-er* connects to the agentive function of the word and is an affix producing a noun. At Step 6 the appropriate stress pattern can be chosen. The suffix *-er* does not alter the phonological form of the root *paint*.

All of the aspects of knowing a word described here are present in Table 2.1. The difference is however that in this process-based description using Levelt's (1989) model, the aspects are shown to be influencing each other.

Levelt (1989: 183) distinguishes between item relations **within** entries in the lexicon (the types of cause–effect relations for a single word we have just been looking at) and item relations **between** entries (different words). Levelt considers that inflections are items belonging to the same lexical entry. That is, they are related **within** an entry. Derivations, however, are different lexical entries.

Levelt classifies relations between entries into two kinds: **intrinsic** and **associative**. Intrinsic relationships are based on the four features of meaning, grammar, morphology and phonology. Words can also be related because they enter into semantic relations of antonymy, synonymy and so on, or being members of the same lexical set such as days of the week, or parts of the body. Words may be related because they are the same part of speech or fulfil the same grammatical function. Words can be morphologically related to each other through derivation by being members of the same word family. Words may also be related to each other because of their phonological form, that is, for example, they share the same initial sounds or final sounds.

It is generally true to say that when sets of words are being learned, the relations between these new entries in the lexicon can be a source of interference making the learning task more difficult. That is, learning opposites, morphologically similar words or phonologically similar words together can make learning much more difficult. When words are not learned in sets, the relations by analogy between new and known words can make learning easier. That is, if you already know several words with a certain consonant cluster, then learning a new one with the same initial cluster will be easier. Similarly, already knowing the word for 'a male relative older than your parents' will make the learning of the word for 'a male relative younger than your parents' easier. We will look at the effects of intrinsic relationships on learning in detail in a later chapter.

Associative relations (Levelt, 1989: 184) depend mainly on frequent collocations than on aspects of meaning. Examples include *green* and *grass*, *heat* and *light*, *thunder* and *lightning*. Associative and intrinsic relationships may overlap if intrinsically related items also often occur together. Associative relations carried over from the first language may help deepen the level of processing in the learning of second language words.

Schmitt and Meara (1997) suggest that morphology and associations are related in that when more members are included within a word family because of increasing control of the morphological system, there will be a greater range of potential associations, as each affixed form will tend to bring different associations.

Let us now look at the nine aspects of what is involved in knowing a word as shown in Table 2.1 to see what each aspect includes. Because some of these aspects, namely word parts, word meaning and collocations are covered in later chapters, these aspects will be only dealt with briefly here.

Spoken form

Knowing the spoken form of a word includes being able to recognise the word when it is heard and, at the other end of the receptive–productive scale, being able to produce the spoken form in order to express a meaning. Knowledge of the spoken form can be broken down into many parts. Research on the **tip-of-the-tongue** phenomenon (Brown and McNeill, 1966) reveals some of this knowledge. The tip-of-the-tongue phenomenon occurs when you cannot recall a known word and you search your brain for it. By looking at what information is produced, we can get some idea of how words are classified and stored in the brain. The formal similarities that occur between the target word form and the forms that the search tosses up include number of syllables, initial letter, final letter, syllabic stress and suffix.

Producing the spoken form of an English word includes being able to pronounce the sounds in the word as well as the degrees of stress of the appropriate syllables of the word if it contains more than one syllable.

Research on vocabulary difficulty indicates that an important factor affecting learning is the pronounceability of a word (Ellis and Beaton, 1993b; Higa, 1965; Rodgers, 1969). Pronounceability depends on the similarity between individual sounds and suprasegmentals like stress and tone in the first language and second language, the ways in which these sounds combine with each other (called **phonotactic grammaticality**; Scholes, 1966), and the relationship between the spelling and sound systems. Numerous contrastive analysis studies have shown that predicting the pronunciation difficulty of individual sounds is not a simple process (see, for example, Hammerly, 1982). Learning second language sounds that are only slightly different from first language sounds may be more difficult than learning some sounds that do not occur at all in the first language.

Each language allows certain combinations of sounds and does not allow others. The implicit learning of these patterns allows young native speakers of English to reliably distinguish between words which are permitted English words according to the patterns and those which are not. Treiman (1994), in a study based on word games, presents evidence that native speakers regard consonant clusters, particularly initial consonant clusters, as units and are reluctant to split them up when playing word games. Final consonant clusters may also be regarded as units rather than a string of phonemes but the rules under-lying their structure are more complex. The learning of these patterns however is one way in which the learning of a system makes the learn-ing of individual words easier. This may account for the greater ease in vocabulary learning as learners' proficiency in the second language develops.

Research by Gathercole and Baddeley (1989) indicates that an important factor influencing vocabulary learning is the ability of learn-ers to hold a word in their phonological short-term memory. A varia-ble influencing this for second language learners must be the learners' ability to 'chunk' the spoken form of a word into meaningful segments which in turn depends on L1 and L2 similarity and the learners' level of proficiency in L2. Papagno et al. (1991), in a series of experiments, compared several conditions for learning word pairs. Essentially three conditions were examined:

1. The learners associate word forms that are already familiar to them. For example, English speakers had to learn to associate the words in pairs like *roof – artist*. In this kind of learning the learners do not have to learn new forms. They simply have to associate known forms. Deliberately interfering with phonological memory did not have serious effects on this kind of learning, probably because the learners were using meaning-based associations to remember the pairs.

2. The learners associate word forms that consist of a known first language word and a foreign language word, but where the foreign language word resembles some other first language word, for example *throat – garlo*, where the Russian word *garlo* has some formal similarities with the English word *gargle*. Because the foreign words were 'meaningful' for the learners, deliberately interfering

with phonological short-term memory did not have serious effects on this kind of learning, largely because the learners were using meaning cues rather than phonological rehearsal to remember the new foreign language forms.

3. The learners associate word forms that consist of a known first language word and a foreign language word, but where the form of the foreign language word does not readily give rise to associations with known forms, for example *oak – sumu* (a Finnish word). Interfering with phonological short-term memory had serious effects on this kind of learning. This was probably because the learners needed to use phonological rehearsal to learn the new forms (the Finnish words) because the learners were not readily able to create meaningful associations with the new forms.

Papagno et al.'s (1991) piece of research is very important because it shows that learners need not be limited by the capacity of their short-term phonological memory. In previous research with native speakers (Gathercole and Baddeley, 1989), the size of individuals' short-term phonological memory was found to be a good predictor of their first language vocabulary learning (see Table 2.4). Service (1992), looking at foreign language vocabulary learning, found that young Finnish learners' skill at repeating nonsense words was the best predictor of their achievement in English in the following two years (see also Papagno et al., 1991: 332).

Papagno et al.'s research indicates that foreign language learners can overcome limitations on phonological memory and limitations created by foreign languages whose word forms are very different from those of their first language, by developing meaning-based association learning techniques, such as the keyword technique. That is, instead of solely relying on phonological repetition to make the form of a foreign word stick in the mind, the learners should be making connections between the shape of the foreign word and the shape of already known words either in their first language, the foreign language, or other languages they know. This idea fits neatly within the levels of processing hypothesis where the quantity of learning depends on the quality of the mental processing that occurs when the learning takes place. It also underlines the importance of helping learners to see that the shape of the foreign words they have to learn is not random but is patterned on underlying rules. That is, there is a phonotactic grammaticality underlying the spoken forms of the words. See Gupta and Tisdale (2009) for a different view.

The important influence of phonological short-term memory must not be underestimated. In a well-conducted rich experiment with

Table 2.4 *Age and the correlation of the non-word repetition test with vocabulary size for young native speakers (Gathercole and Baddeley, 1993)*

Age	Correlation
4	0.559
5	0.524
6	0.562
8	0.284

second language learners, Ellis and Beaton (1993a) looked at receptive and productive knowledge of foreign language (German) – first language (English) word pairs learned in various conditions, including keyword and repetition conditions. For productive learning (L1→L2) the similarity between the phonological patterns of the two languages was very important. The more pronounceable the foreign words were, the easier they were to learn. Pronunceability was not found to be so important for receptive learning (L2→L1). Learning using the keyword technique is most effective when the foreign word form is very easy to learn or when the form of the keyword closely resembles the form of the foreign word. When either of these two conditions does not apply, then repetition of the foreign word form to establish a secure memory for its form is a very important part of vocabulary learning.

Phonological awareness involves the realisation that spoken words are made up of separable sounds, and that separable sounds can go together to make a word. Phonological awareness is important because it is a prerequisite to understanding the alphabetic principle, that is, that letters can represent sounds. Understanding the alphabetic principle in turn is a very useful step towards reading using phonics (regular spelling–sound relationships). Hu (2008) found that young Chinese-speaking learners of English with poor phonological awareness were slower in learning new L2 words than children with good phonological awareness, and this effect persisted across several years. The explanation for this is that poor phonological awareness makes it difficult to form the well-established spoken representation of a word that is needed to make it stay in memory.

There seem to be different effects for phonologically based and mnemonically based strategies on long-term retention. Wang and Thomas (1992) found that although mnemonic keyword learning took less time and gave better results for immediate recall, on a long-term measure (one week later) rote repetition was superior. Part of the explanation for this is that learners using the mnemonic strategy did not choose their own keywords, but nevertheless it is clear that repetition of new word forms is a useful strategy, and sustained follow up of initial learning is essential for long-term memory.

Research (Gathercole and Baddeley, 1993: 49) also shows that for native speakers the size of the phonological short-term memory plays a less important role in vocabulary learning as learners get older. As shown in Table 2.4, the correlation between vocabulary size and non-word repetition skill decreases with age.

The decreasing size of the correlations suggests that the more words you know, the easier it is to learn new words because of the phonological features that the new words share with already known words. Research by Service (1992) with young Finnish learners of English shows that it is not age that is the likely cause of the reduction of the importance of phonological short-term memory but previous learning. The contribution of phonological short-term memory is probably most important when beginning to learn another language because there is often little other relevant knowledge to relate new forms to (Gathercole and Baddeley, 1993: 56).

Cheung (1996) found that for 12-year-old second language learners the capacity of their phonological short-term memory was a significant factor in learning for those with lower second language proficiency. Learners with higher proficiency may have been drawing more on long-term knowledge of the second language to support their learning (see also Hulme et al., 1991).

It is thus very important in vocabulary learning that learners rapidly develop knowledge and strategies that increase the efficiency of and reduce dependence on short-term phonological memory. Learners differ in the size of their short-term phonological memory and these differences in size can have marked effects on their long-term learning. The more they can use meaning-based means of learning word forms, such as the keyword approach, and the more they can support their short-term phonological memory through analogy with known words and familiarity with the underlying phonotactic patterns, the less their learning will be restricted by the size of their short-term phonological memory. Familiarity with underlying patterns can be achieved in several complementary ways. Firstly and most importantly, learners should quickly become familiar with a large number of words. Secondly, learners' attention can be deliberately drawn to the patterning of sounds in the second language. This can be done by grouping regularly spelled, similarly patterned words together, and by asking learners to distinguish real words from nonsense words which do not follow permissible sound combinations. Nation (2009: 151–9) presents a list of the most regular sound–spelling correspondences. Thirdly, words containing infrequent or unusual sequences of sound can be deliberately avoided in the early stages of language learning. Words which have a similar form to first language words will have a lighter learning burden than words containing unfamiliar sounds and unfamiliar combinations of sounds.

Written form

One aspect of gaining familiarity with the written form of words is spelling. As Brown and Ellis (1994) point out in the introduction to their excellent collection of articles about spelling, this has been a growth area for research. What is striking about the research on spelling is the way that it reflects the issues involved in other aspects of vocabulary and language knowledge. That is, the same questions arise. What are the roles of system knowledge and stored wholes? How do these different kinds of knowledge interact in the development of the skill? What are the roles of language use and direct study of language in the development of the spelling skill? How do the different aspects of vocabulary knowledge – spoken form, word building, grammar, collocations and meaning – affect each other?

The ability to spell is most strongly influenced by the way learners represent the phonological structure of the language. Studies of native speakers of English have shown strong effects on spelling from training in categorising words according to their sounds and matching these to letters and combinations of letters (Bradley and Huxford, 1994). The training in one of the studies involved 40 ten-minute training sessions but the positive effects persisted for years. Early training helps create a system that improves later learning and storage. Playing with rhymes can help in this awareness of phonological units and is an effective categorisation activity.

Comparison of the spelling of English speakers with speakers of other languages shows that the irregularity in the English spelling system creates difficulty for learners of English as a first language (Moseley, 1994).

Poor spelling can affect learners' writing in that they use strategies to hide their poor spelling. These include using limited vocabularies, favouring regularly spelled words and avoiding words that are hard to spell. Although there is no strong relationship between spelling and intelligence, readers may interpret poor spelling as a sign of lack of knowledge.

There is a strong link between spelling and reading. Some models suggest that changes in spelling strategy are related to changes in reading strategy. Skill at reading can influence skill at spelling and there is evidence that literacy can affect phonological representations.

Learners can represent the spoken forms of words in their memory in a variety of ways – as whole words, as onsets (the initial letter or letters) and rimes (the final part of a syllable), as letter names, and as phonemes. One way of representing a model of spelling is to see it as consisting of two routes: one accesses stored representations of whole words and the other constructs written forms from sound–spelling correspondences. It is generally considered that this model is too simplistic and that the two routes influence each other and the choice of routes depends on the type of processing demands.

The learning burden of the written form of words will be strongly affected by first and second language parallels (does the first language use the same writing system as the second language?), by the regularity of the second language writing system, and by the learners' knowledge of the spoken form of the second language vocabulary.

A training programme to improve spelling should involve:

1. Opportunities for substantial amounts of extensive reading at levels where fluency can improve, that is, with texts containing virtually no unknown vocabulary;
2. Practice in categorising and analysing words according to their spoken form. This can involve rhyming activities where learners put rhyming words into groups, think of rhymes for given words, listen to rhymes, and make simple poems. This should also involve activities for increasing phonological awareness. The most basic and useful of these are getting practice in putting sounds together to make words. For example, the teacher says (sounding out the letters) /t/ /e/ /n/, what word is that? When learners are good at this, they can take the teacher's role and break up words into their sounds.
3. Relating spoken forms to written forms at a variety of levels (the word level, the rime level, the syllable level and the phoneme level). Most attention should be given to regular patterns. It may be helpful to make mnemonic links using analogy, and to match motor movements (writing in the air, tracing, writing) to sound. This kind of activity should aim at developing understanding of the alphabetic principle, that letters can represent sounds.
4. Spaced repeated retrieval. The programme should involve short lessons preferably three or four times a week involving recall of previously practised words and patterns of sound–spelling correspondence.
5. Monitoring and feedback. Teachers should check that learners are making progress and should inform learners of their progress.

Regular checks could involve dictation, classifying words according to sound patterns and spelling patterns, and monitoring free written work.

6. Learners being trained in the use of learning strategies and the goals of those strategies and being encouraged to become independent in the application of the strategies. Strategies may include finding analogies, cover and recall, focusing on difficult parts, and setting regular learning goals. Learners should also apply the strategies to words that they see as important and problematical for them.

Schmitt (2000: 46–50) has a useful discussion of the importance of speed in word form recognition.

Word parts

The learning burden of words will be light if they are made of known parts, that is, affixes and stems that are already known from the first language or from other second language words. However, some affixes and stems change their form when they are joined together, for example, *in- + legal = illegal* and this can increase learning burden. We will look at this in more detail in Chapter 9.

Knowing a word can involve knowing that it is made up of affixes and a stem that can occur in other words. There is evidence that, for first language users of English, many low-frequency, regularly formed, complex words are rebuilt each time they are used. That is, a word like *unpleasantness* is not stored as a whole unanalysed item, but is reformed from *un-*, *pleasant*, and *-ness* each time it is used. This does not necessarily mean that the word is learned in this way. It may be that for some words their whole unanalysed form is learned initially, and it is later seen as fitting into a regular pattern and is then stored differently.

This way of dealing with complex words suggests that there are reasonably regular predictable patterns of word building. Bauer and Nation (1993) have attempted to organise these into a series of stages based on the criteria of frequency, regularity of form, regularity of meaning, and productivity. Lying behind this series of stages is the idea that learners' knowledge of word parts and word building changes as their proficiency develops.

It is thus also possible to argue that knowing a word involves knowing the members of its word family, and what are considered as members of the word family will increase as proficiency develops. For example, knowing the word *mend* can also involve knowing its forms, meanings and uses as *mends*, *mended* and *mending*. At a later stage of proficiency, knowing *mend* may also involve knowing *mender, mendable* and *unmendable*. There is research evidence to support the idea that word families are psychologically real, and that when we talk about knowing a word, we should really be talking about knowing a word family. Nagy et al. (1989) found that for native speakers the speed of recognition of a word was more predictable from the total frequency of its word family than from the frequency of the particular word form itself. Gardner (2007) has a very useful discussion of the problems in defining what a word is when carrying out corpus-based studies. Bogaards (2001) has an interesting discussion of the notion of a word, preferring for learning purposes to use 'lexical units' which may include multiword units and distinguish significant polysemic senses, so that *party* as in *rescue party* would be a different single word lexical unit from *party* in *Conservative Party*. We will look at word parts much more closely in Chapter 9.

There is value in explicitly drawing learners' attention to word parts. In particular, an important vocabulary-learning strategy is using word parts to help remember the meaning of a word. This strategy requires learners to know the most frequent and regular affixes well, to be able to recognise them in words, and to be able to re-express the meaning of the word using the meanings of its word parts. The learning burden of a word will depend on the degree to which it is made of already known word parts and the regularity with which these fit together.

Connecting form and meaning

Typically, learners think of knowing a word as knowing what the word sounds like (its spoken form) or looks like (its written form) and its meaning. But not only do learners need to know the form of a word and its meaning, they need to be able to connect the two. For example, a learner of English might be aware of the form *brunch*. The learner might also know that there is a concept for a single meal which takes the place of breakfast and lunch. The learner might also know that the form *brunch* is the appropriate form to communicate the concept of a meal combining breakfast and lunch. It is possible to know the form *brunch* and have no concept of its meaning. It is also possible to be familiar with the form and to have the appropriate concept but not to connect the two.

The strength of the connection between the form and its meaning will determine how readily the learner can retrieve the meaning when seeing or hearing the word form, and retrieve the word form when wishing to express the meaning. Baddeley (1990) suggests that each successful retrieval of the form or meaning strengthens the link between the two. It is thus very important that the learners not only see the form and meaning together initially, but have plenty of spaced repeated opportunities to make retrievals. This is looked at more closely in Chapter 11, which includes the use of word cards.

Making the form–meaning connection is easier if roughly the same form in the first language relates to roughly the same meaning. That is, the learning burden of making the form–meaning connection is light if the word being learned is a cognate or a loanword shared by the first language and the second language. For some languages, the presence of loanwords makes learning much easier.

Words that look like cognates with the L1 are treated as if they were cognates with the L1 meaning being assigned to them (Hall, 2002). Hall's study involved Spanish learners of English, but with the large numbers of loanwords being borrowed into languages which are completely unrelated to English, it is likely that this effect is not limited to closely related languages.

Daulton (1998) notes the enormous number of English loanwords in Japanese, up to 38% of the 2,000 most frequent words of English, and 26% within the University Word List. Daulton's study and other studies on Japanese indicate that the existence of loanwords helps the learning of English even in those cases where the learners need to extend the limited meaning that the loanword has in Japanese. Some examples of loanwords in Japanese are *paatii* (party), *piano* (piano), *booru* (bell), *Waarudo Shiriizu* (World Series). Unsurprisingly, several studies have found positive effects for learning cognates. Cognates in three languages are recognised faster than those in two languages that the learners know (Tonzar et al., 2009).

Another way of making the form–meaning connection easier is to put a first language link between the second language word form and the meaning. This is the basis of the keyword technique which is described more fully in Chapter 11. In the keyword technique, the foreign language word form is linked to a first language word which sounds like it and this is linked to the meaning by an image involving the meaning of the first language word and the meaning of the second language word. So, for a Thai learner to learn *cow*, the learner thinks of a Thai word that sounds like *cow*, for example *khâw* meaning 'rice', and then creates an image of a cow eating rice.

The form–meaning connection is easier to make if the sound or shape of the word form has a clear connection to the meaning. In New Zealand sign language many signs are to some degree iconic, that is, their shape and movement clearly relate to the meaning. The sign for *trophy* is represented by a movement like lifting a trophy. The

trophy
award
cup
prize

Both fists are held out at waist-level, some way apart, palms facing each other/up, blades down, and are moved up to chest level.
Hint: Raising a trophy cup by its handles.

USE: (Nc) Our team got a trophy for winning the tournament. Who will win the world cup? We won a gold cup. We also won the award for the best uniform. Who got the prize?

⊝△0 ▽₀↑‖   A C W

Dictionary of New Zealand Sign Language (Kennedy, 1997) includes short hints in many of its entries to draw readers' attention to these connections to make learning easier.

Webb (2007) compared the learning of words which had high-frequency L2 synonyms (*locomotive – train*) with the learning of words that did not (*lick*). Learning involved using L2–L1 word pairs and the testing involved 10 tests for each word covering a range of receptive and productive aspects of word knowledge including meaning in form, associations, orthography and grammar. In most aspects, the differences in learning were small either with a context sentence or without one. There were significant differences for para-digmatic association, syntagmatic association and orthography.

Concept and referents

A notable feature of words that is especially striking when words are looked up in a dictionary is that they have a lot of different meanings. This is particularly so for the high-frequency words. The dictionary entries for a single very high-frequency word may cover a page or more of a standard dictionary. When we look at the range of meanings which may be included for a single word, we may notice that some of the entries are quite different from each other. For example, for the word *bank*, we may find *the bank of a river* and *the national bank*. These words, which share the same form and part of speech, are sometimes derived from different sources, Old Norse and Latin. Words which have the same form but have completely unrelated meanings are called **homonyms** (the same written and spoken forms – *bank*, *bank*), **homographs** (the same written form but different spoken forms – *row*, *make a row* = loud noise) and **homophones** (the same spoken form but different written forms – *blue*, *blew*). These should be counted and learned as different words, preferably at different times.

Some of the entries for a particular word will show a clear relationship with each other. For example, *bear a heavy physical load* and *bear emotional distress*; *a person's head* and *the head of a school*. Should these different related uses be treated as the same word or as two or more different words? Nagy (1997) points out that there are two ways in which language users can deal with related meanings, and both ways are essential to normal language use.

1. The language user may have a permanent internal representation of each related meaning. This means that when the word form is met, the user has to select the appropriate sense of the word from those stored in the brain. This process can be called **sense selection**.
2. The language user has an underlying concept for a word that is appropriate for the range of meanings with which the word is used. For example, the word *fork* is best represented by a two-pronged shape which covers the range of uses of fork, the fork you can eat with, a fork in the road, forked lightning and so on. When the learner meets the word in use, the learner has to work out during the comprehension process what particular real world items the word is referring to. This process is called **reference specification**. For example, *John* is a masculine first name. If someone tells us *John will be here at 6pm*, we have to decide which particular John is being referred to.

Both of these processes, sense selection and reference specification, are normal features of language use. The interesting question is which process is the one that accounts for most of the allocation of meaning to a word? From a teaching and learning point of view, do learners have to learn and store multiple meanings for a word or do they need to have an underlying meaning which they use to work out particular meanings for a word when they use language? Should teachers be trying to show the underlying meaning between different uses of a word or should the teacher treat the different uses as different items to learn. Dictionaries try to distinguish several meanings of a word rather than show the common features running through various uses. For example, *root* is given the meanings (1) part of a plant which is normally in the soil; (2) part of a hair, tooth, tongue etc. which is like a root in position or function; (3) that from which something grows; (4) form of a word; (5) (*arith.*) quantity which multiplied by itself ....

For learning, words can be defined with reference to learners' first language or to English. For example, from the point of view of an Indonesian the word *fork* is several words: *garpu* (the fork we eat with), *pertigaan* or *simpang jalan* (the fork in the road), *cabang* (the fork in a tree; in Indonesian it is the same word as for 'branch').

However, from the point of view of the English language, *fork* is one word. It is possible to describe the meaning of *fork* so that this meaning includes most uses of the word. Defining a word by looking for the concept that runs through all its uses reduces the number of words to learn. Instead of having to learn three words represented by the form *fork*, by learning the underlying concept of *fork* the learners have only one item to learn. There are other reasons for approaching vocabulary learning from this point of view. One of the educational values of learning a foreign language is seeing how the foreign language divides up experience in a different way from the first language. From an Indonesian point of view, *fork* is defined mainly by its function – something to push food on to your spoon. From an English point of view, *fork* is defined by its shape. Treating meaning in English as if it were just a mirror of the first language hides this difference. Another reason for drawing attention to the underlying concept is that every occurrence of the word will act as a repetition of what was taught instead of as a different item. That is, each occurrence of the word will contain known features and will build on previous learning.

To decide if you are dealing with one word or more than one word, see if extra learning is required. Can *branch* (of a tree) be taught in such a way that *branch* (of a bank or business) requires no additional learning?

Ruhl (1989) argues that rather than follow dictionaries in seeing words as having multiple meanings, we should assume that each word has a single inherent lexical meaning. There are two major sources of meaning when we comprehend a word in context, (1) its inherent lexical meaning (what it means as an isolated word), and (2) the inferential meaning which we infer from other words in the immediate context and from our knowledge of the world. The lexical meaning may be very abstract. Where a word has more than one sense, we should assume that these senses are related to each other by general rules that apply to other words. These rules include the idea that words can have a range of senses from concrete to abstract and these differences in concreteness and abstractness are inferred from the context. Similarly, the direction of movement of a verb (up – down) and its speed and means of movement need not be part of the lexical meaning but may be inferred from context and our world knowledge.

Ruhl produces evidence to support his position by examining lots of examples of use and showing that the apparent variations in meaning can be accounted for by inferential meaning, and that a stable though abstract meaning for the word can be seen which runs through all senses of the word.

There is often a cultural dimension to the meaning and use of vocabulary, and teachers should help learners explore this. Spinelli and Siskin (1992: 313) suggest some useful guidelines:

1. Present and practice vocabulary within culturally authentic semantic fields and networks of relationships.
2. Present and practice vocabulary in ways that distinguish the native and target culture.
3. Use authentic visuals where native culture/target culture referents differ in form.
4. Present and practice a word's denotation and connotation (what we have termed concept and associations).
5. Present and practice vocabulary in ways that will reinforce appropriate behaviour in the target culture.

Care needs to be taken to ensure that interference is not encouraged in the early stages of learning a particular word. Some of the most striking cultural differences relate to food, family relationships and politeness behaviour.

Kellerman (1985) reports cases of U-shaped behaviour where Dutch learners of German initially accept correct Dutch-like idioms in German, then reject them, and then eventually accept them. Kellerman sees L1 playing an important role at stage 1 and stage 2. At stage 1, where the Dutch-like idiom in German is accepted, L1 is a source of support for learning. In stage 2, learners are developing awareness of differences between L1 and L2 and thus tend to be suspicious of similarities. At stage 3, as the Dutch learners have a more native-speaker-like command of German, L1 has a diminished effect and the idioms are accepted as German idioms. Levenston's (1990) data on advanced English learners' lack of acceptance of abstract uses of words like *cement* in *cement a relationship* may be a result of similar U-shaped behaviour with the learners being at stage 2.

Bogaards (2001) compared learning a new sense for a known word with learning a new word. Where there was a clear relationship between the old and new senses, new senses were easier to learn than new words. Learning unrelated senses for new words was as difficult as learning completely new words. Completely new words, however, were not well remembered on a three-week delayed post-test. Form rather than meaning is likely to be the major factor affecting difficulty, especially if the meanings are familiar L1 meanings. This finding provides support for getting learners to see the underlying core meaning of words. Unfortunately, the delayed post-test in Bogaards' study was different from the immediate post-test, so test format was confounded with time of administration.

Associations

In a fascinating paper, Miller and Fellbaum (1991) describe the semantic relationships between a very large number of English words. They show that it is necessary to distinguish between parts of speech to describe the organisational structure of the lexicon. The most pervasive and important relationship is synonymy, but nouns, adjectives and verbs each use preferred semantic relations and have their own kind of organisation. Understanding these relations is useful for explaining the meanings of words and for creating activities to enrich learners' understanding of words. Understanding how the lexicon might be organised is also useful for the creation of limited vocabularies for defining words and for the simplification of text. Miller and Fellbaum's goal is to model how the lexicon is organised so that we can better understand the nature of language, language knowledge and language use.

Nouns

Nouns can be organised into hierarchies represented by tree diagrams and these hierarchies can involve many levels. Here is one strand of a hierarchy:

animal
vertebrate
mammal
herbivore
perissodactyl
equid
horse
pony

Miller and Fellbaum (1991: 204–5) say that 26 unique beginning points are sufficient to begin tree diagrams that include every English noun. These beginning points are:

act, action, activity	food	process
animal, fauna	group, collection	quantity, amount
artefact	location, place	relation
attribute, property	motive	shape
body, corpus	natural object	society
cognition, ideation	natural phenomenon	state, condition
communication	person, human being	substance
event, happening	plant, flora	time
feeling emotion	possession, property	

The relationship between items in a hierarchy is called **hyponymy** (*tree* is the hypernym, *beech* is the hyponym). *Hypo-* means 'under' as in *hypodermic* – an injection *under* the skin. Three additional kinds of information are needed to distinguish between nouns: namely parts, attributes and functions. A house is a hyponym of building and it has certain parts (bedrooms, a kitchen) and a certain function (for people to live in). The whole–part relationship (house–kitchen) is called **meronymy** (*kitchen* is a meronym of the holonym *house*).

Adjectives

Predicative adjectives need to be distinguished from non-predicative adjectives. This is one of many instances of the connection between lexical organisation and syntactic behaviour. Non-predicative adjectives cannot be used after the verb *to be* as the predicate of a sentence (*The leader is former), are not gradable (*very previous), and cannot be made into nouns. Non-predicative adjectives are organised like nouns in hyponymic relationships. Predicative adjectives are basically organised into opposites (antonymy; see also Deese, 1965). There is meaning-based antonymy (*hot/cold*) and word form-based antonymy (*healthy/unhealthy*). Adverbs are organised like adjectives.

Verbs

A basic distinction needs to be made between verbs representing an event and those representing a state (a distinction which is also important in the grammatical behaviour of verbs). Verbs representing an event can be organised into shallow hierarchies. Miller and Fellbaum (1991: 215) suggest that there are 14 semantically distinct groups:

1. bodily care
2. bodily functions
3. change
4. cognition
5. communication
6. competition
7. consumption

8. contact
9. creation
10. motion
11. perception
12. possession
13. social interaction
14. weather

There tend to be a lot of items at one particular level of these shallow hierarchies.

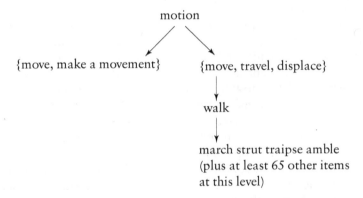

The hierarchical relationship for verbs is different from that for nouns. Miller and Fellbaum term it 'troponymy', and it expresses the idea that something is done in a particular manner. So, *to stroll* is 'to walk in a particular manner'. There is a variety of other relationships that Miller and Fellbaum call 'entailment', which basically means that engaging in one action involves engaging in the other. So, *snore* entails *sleep*, *win* entails *play*, and *stagger* entails *walk*. Antonymy can exist between the co-troponyms.

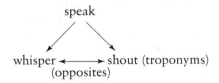

Cruse (1986) provides an exhaustive treatment of lexical relations.

The relationships described here (synonymy, hyponymy, meronymy, antonymy, troponymy and entailment) are very useful starting points for making classification activities with words that learners already know. Classification activities can involve distinguishing and grouping similar items in various ways, justifying the distinguishing and grouping by explaining the relationship, and using the relationship to produce or change text, such as suggesting cause–effect chains, expressing the opposite of a statement, making a generalisation from a particular piece of evidence, or restating something in a precise way (see Sokmen, 1992, for some examples). The grouping and distinguishing of items can make use of schematic aids like tree diagrams, Venn diagrams, flow diagrams and matrices.

Learners can be helped in explaining relationships by the teacher providing descriptive phrases to use including: *x is a part of y*; *x is a kind of y*; *x is y done in a certain way*; *x is the opposite of y*; *x is like y*; and *x involves y*.

Care needs to be taken in reading first language research because various meanings are given to terms like 'contextual' and 'association'. For Stahl and Fairbanks (1986: 74) 'contextual knowledge' is knowledge of a core concept and how it is realised in different contexts – what we have called knowing its referents. Stahl and Fairbanks (p. 75) also include 'associations' within knowing the meaning of a word but refer to an association between a new word and either a definition or a context as for example in rote learning – what we have referred to here as the form–meaning connection.

Yavuz (1963) and Yavuz and Bousfield (1969) found that even when a partly learned word had been forgotten, the connotative aspects of its translation were still retained.

Grammatical functions

In order to use a word it is necessary to know what part of speech it is and what grammatical patterns it can fit into. Many linguists now consider the lexicon to play an important, if not central, role in grammar. Sinclair's (1987) corpus-based research suggests that lexical choice, particularly of verbs, largely determines the grammatical construction of the rest of the sentence. Levelt's (1989) description of speech production discussed earlier in this chapter sees aspects of grammatical knowledge being included in the lexicon.

The grammatical learning burden of items depends on parallels between the second language and the first language, and the parallels in grammatical behaviour between words of related meaning. If a second language user takes the same grammatical patterns as its rough equivalent in the first language, then the learning burden will be light. If words of related meaning like *hate* and *like* take similar patterns, then the learning burden of one of them will be lighter because the previous learning of the other will act as a guide.

Collocations

Knowing a word involves knowing what words it typically occurs with. Is it more usual, for example, to say that we ate some *speedy food*, *quick food* or *fast food*? Pawley and Syder (1983) argue that the reason we can speak our first language fluently and choose word sequences that make us sound like native speakers is because we have stored large numbers of memorised sequences in our brain. Instead of constructing these each time we need to say something, we frequently draw on these ready-made sequences.

Collocations differ greatly in size (the number of words involved in the sequence), in type (function words collocating with content words, e.g. *look* and *at*; content words collocating with content words, e.g. *united* and *states*), in closeness of collocates (*expressed* their own honest *opinion*), and in the possible range of collocates (*commit* with *murder, a crime, hara kiri, suicide*...). We will look at these features and many other aspects in Chapter 12 on multiword units.

The availability of large corpora, cheap effective software and powerful computers has helped research on collocation considerably. The research however can only be done to a certain point by a computer, and then judgement and analysis must be used.

Research on collocations shows that there are patterns. An awareness of these patterns can reduce the learning burden of certain words. Where collocations are similar between the first and second language, the learning burden will be lighter.

Collocation is only one of a wide range of relationships that relate to the appropriate interpretation and productive use of vocabulary. Miller (1999) shows that a very important aspect of knowing a word is having a cognitive representation of the set of contexts in which a given word form can be used to express a given meaning. This contextual knowledge can involve situational context, topical context and local context. Collocation is largely local context information provided by words in the immediate neighbourhood of a word. Topical context information comes from knowledge of the topic that is being written or spoken about. Thus understanding the meaning of *ball* could at least partly depend on what topic is being dealt with, *dancing, football, golf* or *partying*. Situational information involves general knowledge and knowledge of the particular situation in which the communication occurs.

Constraints on use

Most words are not constrained in their use by sociolinguistic factors. Where there are constraints, the clues for constraints on use can come from the way the word is translated into the first language or from the context in which the word is used. In some languages there are very severe constraints on the terms used to refer to people, particularly in showing the relationship of the speaker to the person being referred to. Learners may anticipate this and be particularly cautious in this area when using a second language.

There are several factors that limit where and when certain words can be used. Failure to observe these can result in inappropriate use. One way of seeing the range of constraints on use of words and to gain information about constraints on particular words is to look at the 'style values' or usage labels in dictionaries (Cassidy, 1972; Hartmann, 1981). Hartmann notes the difficulty in consistently assigning words to the various categories. Cassidy observes that the labels 'low', 'barbarous' and 'corrupt' are no longer used, and suggests a set of scales which include *extent* (international–national–regional–local–individual); *quantity* (frequency); *currency* (out of use [obsolete]–going out of use [archaic]–in present stable use–of uncertain stability); *recency*, *restrictedness*, *level* (cultivated–general–uncultivated [illit.]); *register* (formal–informal [colloq.]–familiar); and *figuration* (literal–metaphoric [fig.]–extremely metaphoric).

The typical frequency of a word acts as a constraint on its use. If a teacher spends a lot of time on a word and overuses it, this affects the learners' use of the word. Overusing low-frequency words has a comical effect (*Salamanca Road bifurcates at the Terrace.*). If time is given to words according to their usefulness in English then this effect can be avoided. Learners may have difficulty with low-frequency words in knowing whether to use them productively or to prefer a more frequent word.

Constraints on use may differ across cultures. In Thai, names like *pig*, *fatty*, *shrimp* and *mouse* are common nicknames. They are less acceptable in English. Adjectives like *fat* and *old* have to be used with care in English when describing someone who is present. In some cultures to say someone is fat is a compliment indicating that they are well off and well cared for. To say someone is old carries with it ideas of wisdom and respect.

Most constraints on use are best dealt with by discussion and explicit cross-cultural comparison. The frequency constraint is best dealt with by familiarity with the language, although in the early stages of learning direct information about whether a word is commonly used or not, is helpful. Several dictionaries include frequency information. Native speakers' intuitions of word frequency are not very accurate (Schmitt and Dunham, 1999).

Item knowledge and system knowledge

In several aspects of what it means to know a word we have seen the choice that exists between attention given to the systems which lie behind vocabulary (the affixation system, the sound system, the spelling system, collocation, the grammatical system, lexical sets) and the unique behaviour of each word. This choice gives rise to several important questions.

What systematic aspects of vocabulary deserve explicit attention? N. Ellis (1995) argues for less explicit attention to formal features and more to meaning, relying largely on experience to build up knowledge of word forms. Ellis does not rule out the value of explicit attention to sound, spelling and grammar rules, but sees experience as being a strong essential component of learning. The cautious position adopted in this book is that both kinds of learning are useful. The teacher's skill lies in balancing the kinds of attention across the four strands of a course. Explicit attention to form and system should never occupy more than 25% of class time, but it should not be absent.

When should this attention to the systematic aspects of vocabulary knowledge be given: when the individual items are first met or after they have been at least partly learned? That is, should words be first learned as unanalysed wholes without careful concern for the other words they relate to, and later their place within word building systems, lexical fields and grammatical patterns can be explored? This would certainly parallel first language learning. Myles et al. (1998) present evidence to support this position in second language learning. There is no doubt that attention to form and rules must be supported and prepared for by experience with the items in use. In some cases this may involve memorisation of units that will later be analysed and in other cases it may involve learning a rule or pattern that is then subsequently practised and used.

There is undoubtedly a relationship between frequency of occurrence of individual items and the role of system knowledge in their use. That is, high-frequency items are used largely on the basis of particular experience with that item rather than on the application of rules. Very frequent derived forms, like *impossible* and *beautiful*, are stored and used as if they were base words rather than being reconstructed according to derivational rules each time they are used. We will look at this issue again in the chapter on collocation.

We have looked at a wide range of aspects involved in knowing a word and have looked at the evidence regarding how learners might gain this knowledge. In the following chapter, we draw on the range of aspects involved in knowing a word to see how direct teaching can contribute to developing this knowledge.

References

Aitchison, J. (1994). *Words in the Mind* (2nd ed.). Oxford: Blackwell.

Altarriba, J. and Knickerbocker, H. (2011). Acquiring second language vocabulary through the use of images and words. In Trofimovich, P. and McDonough, K. (eds.), *Applying Priming Methods to L2 Learning, Teaching and Research*: 1 (pp. 21–47). Amsterdam: John Benjamins.

Baddeley, A. (1990). *Human Memory*. London: Lawrence Erlbaum Associates.

Bauer, L. and Nation, I. S. P. (1993). Word families. *International Journal of Lexicography*, **6**, 4, 253–79.

Bierwisch, M. and Schreuder, R. (1992). From concepts to lexical items. *Cognition*, **41**, 23–60.

Bogaards, P. (2001). Lexical units and the learning of foreign language vocabulary. *Studies in Second Language Acquisition*, **23**, 321–43.

Bradley, L. and Huxford, L. (1994). Organising sound and letter patterns for spelling. In Brown, G. D. A. and Ellis, N. C. (eds.), *Handbook of Spelling*, (pp. 425–39), Chichester: John Wiley and Sons.

Brown, G. D. A. and Ellis, N. C. (1994). *Handbook of Spelling*. Chichester: John Wiley and Sons.

Brown, R. and McNeill, D. (1966). The "Tip of the Tongue" phenomenon. *Journal of Verbal Learning and Verbal Behavior*, **5**, 4, 325–37.

Canale, M. and Swain, M. (1980). Theoretical bases of communicative approaches to second language teaching and testing. *Applied Linguistics*, **1**, 1, 1–47.

Cassidy, F. G. (1972). Toward more objective labeling in dictionaries. In Alatis, J. E. (ed.), *Studies in Honor of Albert H. Marckwardt*, pp. 49–56, Washington: TESOL.

Cheung, H. (1996). Nonword span as a unique predictor of second-language vocabulary learning. *Developmental Psychology*, **32**, 5, 867–73.

Corson, D. J. (1995). *Using English Words*. Dordrecht: Kluwer Academic Publishers.

Crow, J. T. (1986). Receptive vocabulary acquisition for reading comprehension. *Modern Language Journal*, **70**, 3, 242–50.

Cruse, D. A. (1986). *Lexical Semantics*. Cambridge: Cambridge University Press.

Daulton, F. E. (1998). Japanese loanword cognates and the acquisition of English vocabulary. *The Language Teacher*, **22**, 1, 17–25.

de Bot, K. (1992). A bilingual production model: Levelt's speaking model adapted. *Applied Linguistics*, **13**, 1, 3–24.

de Bot, K., Paribakht, T. and Wesche, M. (1997). Towards a lexical processing model for the study of second language vocabulary acquisition: Evidence from ESL reading. *Studies in Second Language Acquisition*, **19**, 309–29.

de Groot, A. (2006). Effects of stimulus characteristics and background music on foreign language vocabulary learning and forgetting. *Language Learning*, 56, 3, 463–506.

Deese, J. (1965). *The Structure of Associations in Language and Thought.* Baltimore: The John Hopkins Press.

DeKeyser, R. M. and Sokalski, K. J. (1996). The differential roles of comprehension and production practice. *Language Learning*, 46, 4, 613–42.

Elgort, I. (2011). Deliberate learning and vocabulary acquisition in a second language. *Language Learning*, 61, 2, 367–413.

Ellis, N. C. (1994). Vocabulary acquisition: The implicit ins and outs of explicit cognitive mediation. In Ellis, N. C. (ed.), *Implicit and Explicit Learning of Languages* (pp. 211–82). London: Academic Press.

Ellis, N. C. (1995). Vocabulary acquisition: psychological perspectives and pedagogical implications. *The Language Teacher*, 19, 2, 12–16.

Ellis, N. C. and Beaton, A. (1993a). Factors affecting foreign language vocabulary: Imagery keyword mediators and phonological short-term memory. *Quarterly Journal of Experimental Psychology*, 46A, 3, 533–8.

Ellis, N. C. and Beaton, A. (1993b). Psycholinguistic determinants of foreign language vocabulary learning. *Language Learning*, 43, 4, 559–617.

Ellis, N. C. and Sinclair, S. G. (1996). Working memory in the acquisition of vocabulary and syntax: Putting language in good order. *Quarterly Journal of Experimental Psychology*, 49A, 1, 234–50.

Fan, M. (2000). How big is the gap and how to narrow it? An investigation into the active and passive vocabulary knowledge of L2 learners. *RELC Journal*, 31, 2, 105–19.

Finkbeiner, M. and Nicol, J. (2003). Semantic category effects in second language word learning. *Applied Psycholinguistics*, 24, 369–83.

Gardner, D. (2007). Validating the construct of "word" in applied corpus-based research: A critical survey. *Applied Linguistics*, 28, 2, 241–65.

Gathercole, S. E. and Baddeley, A. D. (1989). Evaluation of the role of phonological STM in the development of vocabulary in children: A longitudinal study. *Journal of Memory and Language*, 28, 200–213.

Gathercole, S. E. and Baddeley, A. D. (1993). *Working Memory and Language.* Hove: Lawrence Erlbaum Associates.

Griffin, G. F. (1992). *Aspects of the Psychology of Second Language Vocabulary List Learning.* University of Warwick.

Gupta, P. and Tisdale, J. (2009). Does phonological short-term memory causally determine vocabulary learning? Toward a computational resolution of the debate. *Journal of Memory and Language*, 61, 4, 481–502.

Hall, C. J. (2002). The automatic cognate form assumption: Evidence for the parasitic model of vocabulary development. *IRAL*, 40, 2, 69–87.

Hamada, M. and Koda, K. (2008). Influence of first language orthographic experience on second language decoding and word learning. *Language Learning*, 58, 1, 1–31.

Hammerly, H. (1982). Contrastive phonology and error analysis. *IRAL*, 20, 1, 17–32.

Hartmann, R. R. K. (1981). Style values: Linguistic approaches and lexicographical practice. *Applied Linguistics*, 2, 3, 263–73.

Higa, M. (1965). The psycholinguistic concept of 'difficulty' and the teaching of foreign language vocabulary. *Language Learning*, **15**, 3&4, 167–79.

Hu, C. F. (2008). Rare of acquiring and processing L2 color words in relation to L1 phonological awareness. *Modern Language Journal*, **92**, 1, 39–52.

Hulme, C., Maughan, S. and Brown, G. D. A. (1991). Memory for familiar and unfamiliar words: Evidence for a long-term memory contribution to short-term memory span. *Journal of Memory and Language*, **30**, 685–701.

Jiang, N. (2002). Form–meaning mapping in vocabulary acquisition in a second language. *Studies in Second Language Acquisition*, **24**, 617–37.

Kellerman, E. (1985). If at first you do succeed. In Gass, S. M. and Madden, C. G. (eds.), *Input in Second Language Acquisition* (pp. 345–53). Rowley, MA: Newbury House.

Kennedy, G. (ed.). (1997). *Dictionary of New Zealand Sign Language*. Auckland: Auckland University Press.

Kroll, J., Michael, E., Tokowicz, N. and Dufour, R. (2002). The development of lexical fluency in a second language. *Second Language Research*, **18**, 2, 137–71.

Kroll, J. F. and Stewart, E. (1994). Category interference in translation and picture naming: Evidence for asymmetric connections between bilingual memory representations. *Journal of Memory and Language*, **33**, 149–74.

Laufer, B. (1998). The development of passive and active vocabulary: Same or different? *Applied Linguistics*, **19**, 2, 255–71.

Laufer, B. and Paribakht, T. S. (1998). The relationship between passive and active vocabularies: Effects of language learning context. *Language Learning*, **48**, 3, 365–91.

Levelt, W. J. M. (1989). *Speaking: From Intention to Articulation*. Massachusetts: MIT Press.

Levelt, W. J. M. (1992). Accessing words in speech production: Stages, processes and representations. *Cognition*, **42**, 1–22.

Levenston, E. A. (1990). The acquisition of polysemic words with both literal and metaphorical meaning. *Paper delivered at AILA, Thessalonika*.

Lotto, L. and De Groot, A. (1998). Effects of learning method and word type on acquiring vocabulary in an unfamiliar language. *Language Learning*, **48**, 1, 31–69.

Meara, P. (1990). A note on passive vocabulary. *Second Language Research*, **6**, 2, 150–54.

Melka Teichroew, F. J. (1982). Receptive vs. productive vocabulary: A survey. *Interlanguage Studies Bulletin (Utrecht)*, **6**, 2, 5–33.

Miller, G. A. (1999). On knowing a word. *Annual Review of Psychology*, **50**, 1–19.

Miller, G. A. and Fellbaum, C. (1991). Semantic networks in English. *Cognition*, **41**, 197–229.

Mondria, J. A. and Wiersma, B. (2004). Receptive, productive, and receptive+productive L2 vocabulary learning: What difference does it make? In Bogaards, P. and Laufer, B. (eds.), *Vocabulary in a Second Language: Selection, Acquisition and Testing* (pp. 79–100). Amsterdam: John Benjamins.

Morgan, B. Q. and Oberdeck, L. M. (1930). Active and passive vocabulary. In Bagster-Collins, E. W. (ed.), *Studies in Modern Language Teaching*, **16** (pp. 213–21).

Moseley, D. (1994). From theory to practice: errors and trials. In Brown, G. D. A. and Ellis, N. C. (eds.), *Handbook of Spelling* (pp. 459–79). Chichester: John Wiley and Sons.

Myles, F., Hooper, J. and Mitchell, R. (1998). Rote or rule? Exploring the role of formulaic language in classroom foreign language learning. *Language Learning*, **48**, 3, 323–63.

Nagy, W. E. (1997). On the role of context in first- and second-language learning. In Schmitt, N. and McCarthy, M. (eds.), *Vocabulary: Description, Acquisition and Pedagogy* (pp. 64–83). Cambridge: Cambridge University Press.

Nagy, W. E., Anderson, R., Schommer, M., Scott, J. A. and Stallman, A. (1989). Morphological families in the internal lexicon. *Reading Research Quarterly*, **24**, 3, 263–82.

Nation, I. S. P. (1990). *Teaching and Learning Vocabulary*. Rowley, MA: Newbury House.

Nation, I. S. P. (1993). Using dictionaries to estimate vocabulary size: Essential, but rarely followed, procedures. *Language Testing*, **10**, 1, 27–40.

Nation, I. S. P. (2009). *Teaching ESL/EFL Reading and Writing*. New York: Routledge.

Palmer, H. E. (1921). *The Principles of Language Study*. London: George G. Harrap & Co.

Papagno, C., Valentine, T. and Baddeley, A. (1991). Phonological short-term memory and foreign-language vocabulary learning. *Journal of Memory and Language*, **30**, 331–47.

Pawley, A. and Syder, F. H. (1983). Two puzzles for linguistic theory: Nativelike selection and nativelike fluency. In Richards, J. C. and Schmidt, R. W. (eds.), *Language and Communication* (pp. 191–225). London: Longman.

Robinson, P. J. (1989). A rich view of lexical competence. *ELT Journal*, **43**, 4, 274–82.

Rodgers, T. S. (1969). On measuring vocabulary difficulty: An analysis of item variables in learning Russian-English vocabulary pairs. *IRAL*, **7**, 4, 327–43.

Ruhl, C. (1989). *On Monosemy: A Study in Linguistic Semantics*. Albany: State University of New York Press.

Schmitt, N. (2000). *Vocabulary in Language Teaching*. Cambridge: Cambridge University Press.

Schmitt, N. (2010). *Researching Vocabulary: A Vocabulary Research Manual*. Basingstoke: Palgrave Macmillan.

Schmitt, N. and Dunham, B. (1999). Exploring native and non-native intuitions of word frequency. *Second Language Research*, **14**, 4, 389–411.

Schmitt, N. and Meara, P. (1997). Researching vocabulary through a word knowledge framework: Word associations and verbal suffixes. *Studies in Second Language Acquisition*, **19**, 17–36.

Scholes, R. J. (1966). *Phonotactic Grammaticality*. The Hague: Mouton & Co.

Service, E. (1992). Phonology, working memory, and foreign language learning. *Quarterly Journal of Experimental Psychology*, **45A**, 1, 21–50.

Shintani, N. (2011). A comparative study of the effects of input-based and production-based instruction on vocabulary acquisition by young EFL learners. *Language Teaching Research*, **15**, 2, 137–58.

Sinclair, J. M. (1987). Collocation: a progress report. In Steele, R. and Threadgold, T. (eds.), *Language Topics: Essays in Honour of Michael Halliday* (pp. 319–31). Amsterdam: John Benjamins.

Sokmen, A. J. (1992). Students as vocabulary generators. *TESOL Journal*, **1**, 4, 16–18.

Spinelli, E. and Siskin, H. J. (1992). Selecting, presenting and practicing vocabulary in a culturally-authentic context. *Foreign Language Annals*, **25**, 4, 305–15.

Stahl, S. A. and Fairbanks, M. M. (1986). The effects of vocabulary instruction: A model-based meta-analysis. *Review of Educational Research*, **56**, 1, 72–110.

Stoddard, G. D. (1929). An experiment in verbal learning. *Journal of Educational Psychology*, **20**, 7, 452–45.

Swain, M. (1985). Communicative competence: some roles of comprehensible input and comprehensible output in its development. In Gass, S. M. and Madden, C. G. (eds.), *Input in Second Language Acquisition* (pp. 235–53). Rowley, MA: Newbury House.

Tonzar, C., Lotto, L. and Job, R. (2009). L2 vocabulary acquisition in children: Effects of learning method and cognate status. *Language Learning*, **59**, 3, 623–46.

Treiman, R. (1994). Sources of information used by beginning spellers. In Brown, G. D. A. and Ellis, N. C. (eds.), *Handbook of Spelling* (pp. 75–91). Chichester: John Wiley and Sons.

Wang, A. Y. and Thomas, M. H. (1992). The effect of imagery-based mnemonics on the long-term retention of Chinese characters. *Language Learning*, **42**, 3, 359–76.

Waring, R. (1997). A study of receptive and productive learning from word cards. *Studies in Foreign Languages and Literature* (Notre Dame Seishin University, Okayama), **21**, 1, 94–114.

Waring, R. (2002). Scales of vocabulary knowledge in second language vocabulary assessment. *Kiyo* (Occasional papers of Notre Dame Seishin University, Okayama), **26**, 1, 40–54.

Webb, S. (2005). Receptive and productive vocabulary learning: The effects of reading and writing on word knowledge. *Studies in Second Language Acquisition*, **27**, 33–52.

Webb, S. (2007). The effects of repetition on vocabulary knowledge. *Applied Linguistics*, **28**, 1, 46–65.

Webb, S. (2008). The effects of context on incidental vocabulary learning. *Reading in a Foreign Language*, **20**, 232–45.

Webb, S. (2009). The effects of receptive and productive learning of word pairs on vocabulary knowledge. *RELC Journal*, **40**, 3, 360–76.

Williams, J. N. and Cheung, A. (2011). Using priming to explore early word learning. In Trofimovich, P. and McDonough, K. (eds.), *Applying Priming Methods to L2 Learning, Teaching and Research: 1* (pp. 73–103). Amsterdam: John Benjamins.

Wolter, B. (2001). Comparing the L1 and L2 mental lexicon. *Studies in Second Language Acquisition*, **23**, 41–69.

Wolter, B. (2006). Lexical network structures and L2 vocabulary acquisition: The role of L1 lexical/conceptual knowledge. *Applied Linguistics*, **27**, 4, 741–7.

Yavuz, H. (1963). The retention of incidentally learned connotative responses. *Journal of Psychology*, **55**, 409–18.

Yavuz, H. and Bousfield, W. A. (1969). Recall of connotative meaning. *Psychological Reports*, **5**, 319–20.

Zareva, A. (2007). Structure of the second language mental lexicon: How does it compare to native speakers' organization? *Second Language Research*, **23**, 2, 123–53.

3 Teaching and explaining vocabulary

The main message of this chapter is that vocabulary teaching has only a limited role to play in the learning of vocabulary (about one-quarter of one of the four strands of a course), and teachers need to be careful not to overplay this role at the expense of the time available for the deliberate and incidental learning of vocabulary.

What is involved in vocabulary teaching and what role should teaching play?

Many first language researchers question the value of spending teaching time on particular words, especially using rich instruction. The arguments used against the direct teaching of vocabulary for first language learners include the following:

1. There are too many words to teach. Research on the vocabulary size of native speakers shows that, even by the most conservative estimates (D'Anna et al., 1991; Nation, 1993), native speakers know tens of thousands of word families. Direct teaching could only have a very trivial impact on such knowledge.
2. There is a lot to learn about each word (Nagy, 1997). Chapter 2 of this book outlined the various aspects of what is involved in knowing a word. Nagy challenges the idea of a word family, showing that for many complex and compound forms of words there is substantial extra learning required, and this increases the number of words to be learned.
3. To have an immediate effect on vocabulary knowledge, substantial time has to be spent on teaching each word. McKeown et al. (1985) had to spend at least 15 minutes per word to have a significant effect on language use. This means that not many words could be dealt with in this way in class time. However, McDaniel and Pressley (1989) found that with 30 seconds of concentrated learning time on

each word, subsequent comprehension of a reading text was significantly improved.

4. There are other ways of increasing vocabulary size which require less teacher effort and less classroom time, and which have numerous other benefits. These ways involve the incidental learning of vocabulary through meeting the words in reading and listening, and in using the words in speaking and writing. Although incidental learning is not as effective as direct deliberate learning for any particular word, there is so much more opportunity for incidental learning that it accounts for most of first language vocabulary learning.

5. There are also arguments about the effectiveness of teaching. Although aspects of vocabulary learning are affected by teaching in ways that grammatical learning is not, teaching is still an activity with very uncertain outcomes. File and Adams (2010), in a well-controlled second language experiment, compared words taught before a reading lesson (**isolated**), words taught during the reading lesson (**integrated**) and words met but not taught during the reading (**incidental**). Not surprisingly, words met incidentally showed little gain on an immediate vocabulary knowledge scale post-test. As well as not receiving explanation from the teacher, little time was spent on the words met incidentally. There was no significant difference between isolated and integrated words on both the immediate post-test and the two week delayed post-test. On the immediate post-test, out of a possible average gain of around 42 points, there was a gain of 20 points for the isolated treatment and 15 points for the integrated treatment, meaning that teaching had a 35% (15 out of 42) to 48% (20 out of 42) effect. On the delayed post-test, the gain was around 17%, indicating that the form of the given word was familiar but the meaning could not be recalled. The design of the study made it unlikely that the words were met again between the immediate and delayed post-tests which indicate that there is substantial forgetting over two weeks. The teaching of the 12 words and the reading took around 27 minutes for a 35% to 48% return (around five words).

All of these arguments are true and suggest caution in the use of substantial direct vocabulary instruction with native speakers of a language. There are however some important differences between native speakers and second language learners which allow for a greater but still cautiously applied role for direct vocabulary instruction for learners of vocabulary in another language. The major differences are as follows:

1. Native speakers of a language quickly learn the high-frequency words of the language. By the age of five, it is likely that native speakers of English have a vocabulary of around 3,000 to 4,000 word families. Non-native speakers beginning their study of English generally know very few English words. Because the high-frequency words of the language are so important for language use, and consist of a relatively small number of words (2,000–3,000), it is practical and feasible to directly teach a substantial number of them.

2. Native speakers have enormous opportunities to learn from input and to produce output. Foreign language learners and some second language learners do not have the same rich opportunities. Language courses try to increase these opportunities but they will still be only a fraction of what native speakers have access to. In addition, while native speakers receive input adjusted to their level of proficiency, it is difficult for foreign language learners to find this outside the classroom. Direct vocabulary learning is a way of trying to bridge the gap between second language learners' present proficiency level and the proficiency level needed to learn from unsimplified input.

3. Second language learners have less time for learning. They usually begin their study of the second language around the age of twelve and at the age of seventeen or eighteen may need to read unsimplified texts and compete with native speakers in an English-medium university. Direct vocabulary study is a way of speeding up the learning process.

There are three very important cautions which apply to the use of direct vocabulary instruction with learners of another language.

Firstly, the instruction should be directed towards the high-frequency words of the language. Where learners are going on to academic study this would also include the Academic Word List vocabulary. The benefits of knowing high-frequency vocabulary balance the time and effort required for direct vocabulary instruction. Secondly, direct vocabulary instruction is only one part of one of the four strands of a well-balanced course. It should thus occupy only a small proportion of the course time. Thirdly, direct instruction can deal effectively with some aspects of word knowledge and not very effectively with others which rely on quantity of experience and implicit rather than explicit knowledge.

Deliberate teaching fits into the language-focused learning strand of the four strands. A problem with the application of the four strands principle is that the language-focused learning strand is the one where there is the greatest number of different teaching techniques and where there are most likely to be newly devised techniques. It is also the strand where a diligent teacher can do the most preparation and where the widest range of published materials can be applied. In contrast, the message-focused meaning-focused input, meaning-focused output, and fluency development strands involve learners in making use of language through listening, speaking, reading and writing. It is also the strand where it seems that teaching can be most effective, because the strand involves a deliberate focus on a particular learning goal and can draw on a teacher's specialist linguistic knowledge. For these reasons, the time spent on the language-focused learning strand is typically much greater than it should be. If the meaning-focused input and meaning-focused output strands are well run, the teacher should have little work to do beyond monitoring what is going on. If the fluency strand is well run, the teacher's main job may be as a time-keeper. The language-focused learning strand however is where the teacher can truly teach, and this unfortunately can lead to too much time being spent on teacher-led language-focused learning.

A crucial factor in considering the role of direct teaching of vocabulary is the relationship between the knowledge gained from direct teaching and subsequent incidental learning through the meaning-focused and fluency strands of a course.

There is some evidence that as vocabulary size increases, depth of vocabulary knowledge also increases (Qian, 1999). One way of interpreting this finding is to say that increased contact with a language not only allows us to learn new words but also allows us to strengthen and enrich our knowledge of previously learned but only partially known words. If this is true, we could see direct teaching and also deliberate learning as providing a quick and effective boost in knowledge of the word (particularly of word form and meaning) with subsequent incidental learning filling in the many gaps in knowledge and use of that word.

This means that teachers should have very limited goals for vocabulary teaching, giving attention to only high-frequency words, focusing on only the most important aspects of knowing a word, and not spending much time on each word.

What are the features of good vocabulary-teaching techniques?

A vocabulary learning activity is used to reach a particular goal. A learning goal may be a Language goal (vocabulary, grammar), Ideas (the content such as cultural knowledge, safety information...), Skills (accuracy, fluency) and Text (discourse schemata, rhetorical devices, interaction routines). (The mnemonic LIST is a way of remembering these general goals.) In this book we are interested in the vocabulary-learning goal. When looking at teaching and learning activities, we can answer this question about the learning goal in a very general way by citing a vocabulary-learning goal. But we can also be more specific if we wish by considering all the aspects of what is involved in knowing a word (see Table 2.1) and deciding which of these is the learning goal of the activity (see Table 3.1). For example, is the learning goal to learn the spelling of some words, their pronunciation, or more commonly to recognise a word form and link it to its meaning? In general when looking at learning goals and analysing how a goal will be reached, it is simplest to consider only one learning goal at a time. Most activities however can achieve several learning goals. Let us look at some vocabulary activities to see what their specific vocabulary-learning goal might be.

Table 3.1 *The learning goals of some vocabulary activities*

Activity	Learning goals
Guessing from context	Word form, form–meaning link, collocates
	Learn a strategy
Keyword technique	Link form to meaning, word form
	Learn a strategy
Breaking words into parts	Link form to meaning, word form
	Learn a strategy
Split-information tasks with annotated pictures	Bring receptive vocabulary into productive use
'It's my word ...': Learners present words they have met	Teach word form, meaning and use
	Develop an awareness of what is involved in knowing a word

In order to reach a goal, the knowledge or information that makes up that goal needs to be available. The sources of information about a word, for example the word's meaning, can come from textual input such as a reading or listening text, or the context provided on a worksheet. It can come from a reference source such as a teacher or a dictionary, or it can come from the learners in a group who already know something about the word. Newton's (2013) study found that when learners discussed the meanings of words from the worksheet with each other, by far the majority of words discussed resulted in useful and accurate information being provided about the words. This is not surprising. Vocabulary tests of learners who have roughly the same proficiency level usually show a remarkable diversity of knowledge (Saragi et al., 1978). All learners usually know the higher-frequency words, and one or two learners but not all know many of the other words appropriate to their level of proficiency. In addition learners could use the context clues to work out meanings of the words that nobody knew before the activity. Table 2.1 in Chapter 2, which provides a list of what is involved in knowing a word, is useful for deciding what the goal of a vocabulary-learning activity might be.

Barcroft (2009) argues that because humans have limited processing capacity, focusing attention on one aspect of vocabulary knowledge necessarily means that other aspects of knowledge will receive less attention and therefore be poorly learned. For example, focusing on word meaning may mean that word form may be poorly learned.

Drawing on Morris et al.'s (1977) idea of transfer-appropriate processing, Barcroft sees his model of **type of processing resource allocation** (TOPRA) as an improvement on the levels of processing hypothesis. The level of processing hypothesis says that the depth with which words are processed determines how well they are retrieved. However, Barcroft says that thoughtful processing of the semantic aspect of words does not result in better learning of form. Essentially, Barcroft's model says that we learn what we focus on, and viewed in this way the levels of processing hypothesis could be applied to tasks which focus on some aspect of word knowledge. Presumably, a word–form-focused task involving thoughtful processing would have better results than a different form-focused task involving more superficial processing.

Hummel (2010) found that doing L1 and L2 sentence translation where the translation of the target word was provided resulted in useful learning but not as much as copying the L2 sentence where the translation of the target word was provided.

This finding may provide support for Barcroft's (2006) argument that we largely learn what we focus on. The translation task involved four kinds of activity:

1. The learner sees the L2 target word and its L1 translation.
2. The learner sees the L1 or L2 sentence.
3. The learner translates the L1 or L2 context through retrieval of the translations of the context words.
4. The learner writes the L2 or L1 sentence.

Whereas the copying task involved only two of these kinds of activity (1 and 4), the receptive word translation task only required at least the information in 1 above, so perhaps 2, 3 and perhaps 4 are distracting tasks.

If this conclusion is true, it provides further support for a minimal kind of deliberate word learning if recall of word meaning is the goal.

Large amounts of information may distract rather than enrich learning. If the language-focused learning strand is to have greatest effect, it may be most efficient to use simple well-focused tasks.

Barcroft's model and his related research have made a very important contribution to our understanding of vocabulary-learning activities and the importance of looking at the learning goals (and focuses) of particular activities.

Which vocabulary learning activities are the best ones?

One approach to evaluating vocabulary-teaching activities is to analyse them to see how well they set up conditions that research has shown are important for learning.

Laufer and Hulstijn (2001) investigated the effect of what they called **task involvement** on incidental vocabulary learning. They see involvement as being affected by three features in tasks. Their description of these features can be seen as an attempt to operationalise levels of processing in terms of the levels of processing hypothesis:

- *Need*. Need does not exist if the target vocabulary is not needed to complete the task. Need is moderate if the task requires the target vocabulary, and it is strong if the learner feels the need for the vocabulary. Need is the attitudinal component of involvement.
- *Search*. Search does not exist if the word forms and their meanings are supplied as a part of the task. Search is moderate if learners have to search for the meaning of the item (receptive), and strong if learners have to search for the form to express a meaning (productive).
- *Evaluation*. Evaluation involves deciding if a word choice is appropriate or not. Evaluation is moderate if the context is provided and is strong if the learner has to create a context. Choosing between subentries in a dictionary entry involves evaluation.

Involvement is affected by each of these features and they can occur in combination. Laufer and Hulstijn's research shows that the greater the involvement load, the more effective the learning.

Table 3.2 contains some tasks with an analysis of their involvement load (– = no involvement load, + = moderate involvement, ++ = strong involvement).

The **Involvement Load Hypothesis** has had the very beneficial effect of stimulating research on vocabulary-teaching activities and the conditions they create, and several published studies (Folse, 2006; Hulstijn and Laufer, 2001; Keating, 2008; Kim, 2008) have tested the hypothesis and pointed out what needs to be considered in such studies. Hulstijn and Laufer (2001) compared reading with glosses and

Table 3.2 *Tasks and amount of involvement for vocabulary learning*

Task	Need	Search	Evaluation
Reading with questions. Words glossed are not relevant to the task	–	–	–
Reading with questions. Words glossed are relevant to the task	+	–	–
Reading with questions. Needed words looked up	+	+	–
Read and fill in given words	+	–	+
Write sentences using given words	+	–	++
Writing a composition	++	++	++

multiple-choice questions (involvement load =1), reading with glosses and multiple-choice questions and blanks with words to fill in (IL=2), and writing a composition using given words (IL=3). Immediately after, and one or two weeks later, learners were given an L2→L1 word translation test. The results confirmed the Involvement Load Hypothesis.

Folse (2006) pointed out that Laufer and Hulstijn's tasks differed not only in involvement load but also in repetition and time-on-task. Folse compared one fill-in-the-blanks sheet (IL=4), three fill-in-the-blanks sheets (IL=4), and writing original sentences using given target works (IL=5). Testing involved a modified Vocabulary Knowledge Scale testing three levels of knowledge (don't know, translation, write a sentence). Folse controlled for time-on-task by doing a post hoc analysis of learners who used the same time for tasks 2 and 3. His results were contrary to the Involvement Load Hypothesis prediction, the three fill-in-the-blanks task scored higher (see Bruton and García-López, 2007, and Folse, 2007, for a response). Kim (2008) conducted a partial replication of Hulstijn and Laufer (2001) using their three tasks with a graphic organiser activity added to task 1 to equate time-on-task, measuring learning through the Vocabulary Knowledge Scale. The results on both the immediate and two week delayed post-tests confirmed the involvement load prediction. Kim (2008) also compared two tasks of similar involvement load, writing a composition and writing original sentences. Once again the prediction of the Involvement Load Hypothesis was confirmed as there were no significant differences between the two treatments. Keating (2008) also replicated Hulstijn and Laufer (2001) but used low-proficiency learners, and both receptive (L2→L1) and productive (L1→L2) vocabulary translation tests. His results generally confirmed the Involvement Load Hypothesis predictions. To control for time-on-task, Keating combined test results and time spent on each task to work out words learned per minute. When this was done, the effects of involvement load and the contrasts between the tasks largely disappeared. This method of controlling for time-on-task has its problems and as Keating suggests, we need to be cautious when considering the results.

The Involvement Load Hypothesis draws on the levels of processing theory. However, we need to be careful in applying it. The theme of Barcroft's research is that we learn what we focus on, and if we have to focus on aspects that are not closely related to the target knowledge that we want, then such a focus can have a negative effect on learning. Barcroft (2002) looked at the learning of Spanish (L2) words by native speakers of English, where there was a meaning focus (decide on the pleasantness of each word), a form focus (count the number of letters in each word), and a non-focused "do your best" focus. Free and cued recall in Spanish was better when learning involved a form focus rather than a meaning focus in learning. Free recall of the L1 meanings was better when there was a meaning focus on learning. Performance in the two focused conditions was not as good as in the "do your best" condition. Barcroft argues that we need to be careful when applying the levels of processing theory. Deeper processing does not result in better learning if the focus of attention is not appropriate. We need to consider what aspect of vocabulary knowledge we want to focus on when evaluating vocabulary-teaching activities. Barcroft's work also underlines the importance of having several measures of vocabulary learning when doing experimental research.

Nation and Webb (2011: 3–15, 18–24, 317–23) critique the Involvement Load Hypothesis. Their main concern is that its strength is also its weakness. That is, it provides a simple testable way of evaluating a teaching activity, but because it is simple, with only three categories, it does not include a lot of the factors that we know are important for vocabulary learning. They propose an expanded checklist called **Technique Feature Analysis** that includes the features of involvement load but adds factors such as awareness, negotiation, repetition, spacing of retrievals, creative use, interference and imaging (see Table 3.3). Nation and Webb (2011) present a detailed description of the categories plus analysed examples. A careful comparison of the two checklists, Involvement Load and Technique Feature Analysis, shows a reasonable amount of overlap between them, because although Technique Feature Analysis has 18 categories each with a score of 0 or 1, Involvement Load has three categories, each with a possible score of 0, 1 or 2. However, as Nation and Webb show (pp. 318–19), the two systems do not give the same ranking of activities, so they can readily be tested against each other.

Overall, the research on the Involvement Load Hypothesis has been very productive and has shown the value of such an analytical approach to evaluating teaching activities. The time-on-task issue is one that affects a large amount of research in the field and needs careful consideration (Nation and Webb, 2011: 273–5). There has been a clear lack of research on particular vocabulary-teaching techniques but there is now a growing number of very useful studies that fill this gap (see for example, File and Adams, 2010; Barcroft, 2004, 2006; Rott, 2005, 2007; Pulido, 2004, 2007; Webb, 2007a, 2008). We need to know more about the techniques we use.

Table 3.3 lists the criteria used in Technique Feature Analysis. Let us now look at the research which lies behind these criteria. The review

Table 3.3 *A checklist for Technique Feature Analysis*

Criteria	Scores	
Motivation		
Is there a clear vocabulary-learning goal?	0	1
Does the activity motivate learning?	0	1
Do learners select the words?	0	1
Noticing		
Does the activity focus attention on the target words?	0	1
Does the activity raise awareness of new vocabulary learning?	0	1
Does the activity involve negotiation?	0	1
Retrieval		
Does the activity involve retrieval of the word?	0	1
Is it productive retrieval?	0	1
Is it recall?	0	1
Are there multiple retrievals of each word?	0	1
Is there spacing between retrievals?	0	1
Creative use		
Does the activity involve creative use?	0	1
Is it productive?	0	1
Is there a marked change that involves the use of other words?	0	1
Retention		
Does the activity ensure successful linking of form and meaning?	0	1
Does the activity involve instantiation?	0	1
Does the activity involve imaging?	0	1
Does the activity avoid interference?	0	1
Maximum score		18

of the research will follow the same five major headings as in Table 3.3 – motivation, noticing, retrieval, creative use and retention.

What learning conditions help vocabulary learning?

Motivation

Motivation and interest are important enabling conditions for noticing. The choice of content can be a major factor stimulating interest. In his study of learning from listening, Elley (1989: 185) found quite different results from the same learners listening to two different stories. This seemed to have been due to the lack of involvement of learners in one of the stories because of its strangeness, lack of humour, low levels of action and conflict and so on. Without the engagement and aroused attention of learners, there can be little opportunity for other conditions favouring learning to take effect. Although there is no generally accepted theory of why interest is important and the factors that arouse interest, teachers need to watch their learners carefully and seek their opinions about what stories and topics they find interesting. There is some evidence (Bawcom, 1995) that teachers' views of what will be interesting do not match with what learners find interesting.

Interest can also be looked at from the word level. Elley (1989) asked teachers to rate vocabulary in a story according to its importance to the plot of the story that was read to the class (salience). This is a kind of measure of interest in relation to the story. There was a moderate correlation (.42) between the ratings of importance to the plot and vocabulary learning. This indicates that if teachers chose to write up or define words that figured centrally in the plot, the chances of them being learned would be higher than with words not so important for the plot.

Motivation may also be built into an activity. Crossword puzzles for example present an achievable challenge as do memory-based activities like the use of word cards.

There are three important general cognitive processes that may lead to a word being remembered. These include noticing (through formal instruction, negotiation, the need to comprehend or produce, awareness of inefficiencies), retrieval and creative (generative) use. These processes can be viewed as three steps with the later steps including the earlier steps. Schmitt (2008: 339) looked at a variety of factors affecting vocabulary learning, concluding that anything that increases the amount of exposure, use, time, or attention to vocabulary is likely to increase learning.

Noticing

The first cognitive process encouraging learning is noticing, that is giving attention to an item. This means that learners need to notice the word, and be aware of it as a useful language item (see Ellis, 1991; McLaughlin, 1990; Schmidt, 1990, for discussions of noticing). This noticing may be affected by several factors, including the salience of the word in the textual input or in the discussion of the text, previous contact that learners have had with the word, and learners' realisation that the word fills a gap in their knowledge of the language (Ellis, 1990; Schmidt and Frota, 1986). Noticing also occurs when learners look up a word in a dictionary, deliberately study a word, guess from context or have a word explained to them.

Noticing involves **decontextualisation**. Decontextualisation occurs when learners give attention to a language item as a part of the language rather than as a part of a message. That is, it temporarily becomes part of the language-focused learning strand of a course. This can occur in a variety of ways. Here are some examples:

- While listening or reading, the learner notices that a word is a new word, or thinks, 'I have seen that word before', or thinks, 'That word is used differently from the ways I have seen it used before'.
- The teacher draws attention to a word by writing it on the blackboard.
- Learners negotiate the meaning of a word with each other or with the teacher.
- The teacher explains a word for the learners by giving a definition, a synonym or a first language translation.

Notice that decontextualised here does not mean that the word does not occur in a sentence context. All the examples given above can occur, for example, with words that are in a story that the teacher is reading aloud to the class. Decontextualisation means that the word is removed from its message context to be focused on as a language item. The focus can be very brief or can be for a long time. It may be that most language learning necessarily involves some degree of decontextualisation. That is, in order to acquire the language, learners need to consciously see language items as parts of the language system rather than only as messages. The problem is in deciding how much of this kind of attention to give, what to direct it to, and when to give it. However, even if decontextualisation is not an essential element of language learning, there is evidence that it can certainly help learning. We will look at four kinds of decontextualisation: negotiation, defining, enhancement and raising word consciousness.

Negotiation

There is a growing number of studies which show that vocabulary items that are negotiated are more likely to be learned than words that are not negotiated (Ellis et al., 1994; Newton, 2013). This is not a surprising finding, but care needs to be taken in interpreting it. Ellis, et al. (1994) found that although negotiation helped learning, the negotiated task took much more time than the non-negotiated elaborated input task. In the Newton study, it was found that although negotiated items were more likely to be learned than non-negotiated items (68% to 54%), negotiation only accounted for about 17% of the vocabulary learning. This is probably because only a few items can be negotiated without interfering too much with the communication task. So, although negotiation really helps vocabulary learning, it is not the means by which most vocabulary is learned. It is thus important for teachers to draw on other complementary ways of decontextualising items to improve the quality of learning.

The negotiation studies have revealed another feature of learning through negotiation that is of significance to learning from input, namely learners observing negotiation learn vocabulary just as well as learners who do the actual negotiation (Ellis and Heimbach, 1997; Ellis et al., 1994; Newton, 2013; Stahl and Clark, 1987; Stahl and Vancil, 1986). This indicates that it is not the negotiation itself which is important but the learning conditions of noticing and gaining information that negotiation sets up. If learners are engaged in a task, then observing others negotiating is just as effective as doing the negotiation. This is good news for large-class, teacher-centred activities where there is not an opportunity for every learner to negotiate.

Newton (2013) found that all the instances of negotiation of meaning in the four tasks he studied involved negotiating items in the textual input. No vocabulary items that were introduced in the discussion and that were not in the textual input were negotiated. This indicates that teachers can have a major effect on determining what is noticed. We will look more closely at this in the vocabulary and speaking section in Chapter 4.

Definition

Some studies (Brett et al., 1996; Elley, 1989) show that vocabulary learning is increased if vocabulary items are briefly explained while learners are listening to a story. In Elley's (1989) study, such defining more than doubled the vocabulary gains. Some studies of reading similarly indicate that looking up words in a dictionary increases learning

(Knight, 1994), although this finding is not consistently supported in other studies (Hulstijn, 1993) (see Chapter 10).

This inconsistency may be at least partly explained by a finding by R. Ellis (1995) which indicated that simple definitions were the most effective. A simple definition is short and includes only a few defining characteristics of the word. This agrees with a study by Chaudron (1982) which found that more elaborate definitions tended to be confusing rather than helpful. Several studies of learning from lists or word cards (Nation, 1982) have shown that for many learners learning is faster if the meaning of the word is conveyed by a first language translation. First language translations are probably the simplest kind of definition in that they are short and draw directly on familiar experience.

Like negotiation, defining while telling a story is a form of decontextualisation, that is, focusing attention on words as words rather than as parts of a message. In order to increase incidental vocabulary learning while listening to a story, teachers can put target words on the blackboard as they occur, point to them on the blackboard as they recur, translate them, define them simply and encourage learners to negotiate their meaning with the teacher. Ellis and Heimbach (1997), working with young learners of English as a second language, found that a group negotiating with the teacher was more effective for vocabulary learning than when there was individual negotiation in one-to-one interaction with the teacher. A variant of storytelling may be for the teacher to read the story to a particular learner who is set up to negotiate with the teacher while the rest of the class are like eavesdroppers on the storytelling and negotiation. Ellis and He (1999) found learner-to-learner negotiation more effective for older learners (see Chapter 4).

Glossing either in hard-copy reading or with hypertext is a way of encouraging noticing as well as providing information. In some studies (Hulstijn, 1993; Watanabe, 1997) two choices are given (a right choice and a clearly wrong choice) to increase noticing (see Chapter 5).

Textual enhancement

Highlighted hyperlinks increase clicking to consult the glosses but do not slow down the reading, do not increase scores on the comprehension measure and do not increase vocabulary learning (De Ridder, 2002). Han et al. (2008) describe the methodological issues affecting research on textual enhancement of written input. Only two studies (Barcroft, 2002; Kim, 2006) have focused on vocabulary learning. Kim found little effect for textual enhancement, and Barcroft found mixed results including negative effects on unenhanced words, that is, unenhanced words tended to be ignored. Bishop (2004) found that non-highlighted words were looked up more often than non-highlighted formulaic sequences. Highlighted formulaic sequences were looked up much more frequently than non-highlighted formulaic sequences and more often than highlighted words. Looking up resulted in slightly higher text comprehension scores.

Word consciousness

Scott and Nagy (2004) argue for developing word consciousness with L1 learners, a move also strongly supported by Graves (2006). Word consciousness involves an interest in and an awareness of word parts, word order, word choice in different uses of the language (speech/writing; formal/informal, technical/non-technical), how words extend their meanings, underlying core meanings, and how words are learned. Learners can be encouraged to sharpen and expand their use and knowledge of words by analysing known members of a lexical set, for example words to describe hitting like *strike*, *beat*, *punch*, *slap* and so on. Other activities include classification activities according to semantic features such as *with a loud noise*, *deliberately* or *punishment* and so on, and word mapping and contextualisation activities. Word consciousness training and activities may also be of benefit to L2 learners. Strategy training is certainly a part of word consciousness, and L2 teachers can encourage word consciousness through giving brief lessons on the history of English, word parts and the nature of word meaning including polysemy and homonymy.

An argument against the decontextualisation of vocabulary is the teachability hypothesis (Pienemann, 1985) which basically argues that explicit teaching of language items will not be effective if learners are not at the right stage of language development. It is likely that much of vocabulary learning is not affected by developmental sequences and thus explicit teaching has the potential to directly contribute to implicit knowledge (Elgort, 2011; Ellis, 1990). The temporary decontextualisation of vocabulary items during a message-focused task like listening to a story is of major benefit to second language proficiency.

Teachers can have a direct influence on noticing in speaking and writing tasks by giving thought to where wanted vocabulary items are placed in the written input, and by some form of pre-teaching or 'consciousness raising' of wanted items before the activity. Teachers can use a range of attention-drawing techniques in listening and reading tasks to encourage noticing.

Retrieval

The second major process that may lead to a word being remembered is retrieval (Baddeley, 1990: 156). A word may initially be noticed and its meaning comprehended in the textual input to the task, or through teacher explanation or dictionary use. If that word is subsequently retrieved during the task then the memory of that word will be strengthened. Retrieval may be receptive or productive. Receptive retrieval involves perceiving the form and having to retrieve its meaning when the word is met in listening or reading. Productive retrieval involves wishing to communicate the meaning of the word and having to retrieve its spoken or written form as in speaking or writing. Retrieval does not occur if the form and its meaning are presented simultaneously to the learner. In the psychological literature, retrieval where the word or its meaning is recalled is called the **testing effect** because a retrieval is like a test (Pyc and Rawson, 2007).

Several studies (Elley, 1989; Stahl and Fairbanks, 1986) have shown the importance of repetition as a factor in incidental vocabulary learning. As Baddeley (1990: 156) suggests, it is not simply repetition which is important but the repeated opportunity to retrieve the item which is to be learned. When learners hear or see the form of the word, they need to retrieve what they know of its meaning. This retrieval is likely to be retrieval of ideas stored from previous meetings and retrieval of content and information from the present meeting. Baddeley (1990) suggests that each retrieval of a word strengthens the path linking the form and meaning and makes subsequent retrieval easier.

Vidal (2011) found that repetition was the major factor affecting learning from reading compared with the other factors of predictability from word form, type of elaboration and type of word (academic, low-frequency, technical). For reading, the greatest increase in learning occurred between two and three repetitions. For listening, the greatest increase occurred between five and six repetitions. Vidal found a moderate correlation between repetition and learning (.44).

Brown et al. (2008) found that words that were repeated more often had a greater chance of being learned. The data showed that many repetitions of the words (at least 20 and probably 50 or more times) will be needed for substantial learning. Webb (2007b) found gains over several aspects of knowing a word as a result of repetition, but at least ten repetitions and preferably more would be needed to develop rich knowledge of several aspects of a word. In Webb's study the words were met in isolated sentences of varying degrees of informativeness. The strength of his study was that learning was measured across ten different aspects of what is involved in knowing the word.

Webb (2007a) looked at the learning of words met in context once, three times, seven times and ten times. Knowledge of each word was tested on ten different tests (orthography, association, grammatical functions, syntax, and meaning and form, both receptively and productively). There were gains in knowledge on aspects of knowing a word and these gains increased as repetitions increased. Although there were substantial gains, ten repetitions were not sufficient to develop full knowledge of the words.

It is possible to calculate how much input, in terms of number of running words, a learner needs to get within a certain time in order for there to be an opportunity to meet a recently met word again before the memory of the previous meeting fades (Nation and Wang, 1999). If too much time has passed between the previous meeting and the present encounter with the word, then the present encounter is effectively not a repetition but is like a first encounter with the word. If however a memory of the previous meeting with the word remains, then the present encounter can add to and strengthen that memory. There are two major factors involved in such a calculation – the learner's vocabulary size and the length of time that memory of a meeting with a word lasts.

- *The learner's vocabulary size.* The more words a learner knows, the less frequently occurring are the next words they need to learn. For example, if we use figures from the Francis and Kučera (1982) frequency count, a learner who knows 1,000 different words would have to read or listen to 10,000 running words in order for a word at the 1,000-word level to be repeated. If the learner knew 2,000 different words, on average, they would have to read or listen to 20,000 running words for a word at the 2,000 level to be repeated. The larger the vocabulary size, the greater the quantity of language that needs to be processed in order to meet the words to be learned again.
- *The length of time that the memory of a meeting with a word lasts.* A repetition can only be effective if the repetition is seen by the learner to be a repetition. That is, there must be some memory of the previous meeting with the word. A critical factor then is the length of time that such a memory lasts. Delayed post-tests of vocabulary learning indicate that memory for words can last several weeks. Elley (1989) found the memory for the new words remained after three months. Elley's design however involved three repetitions of the stories and also incorporated some use of definitions. Brett et al. (1996) found that words were still remembered after six weeks. Their design used serialised stories with definitions. Ellis

et al. (1994) used two post-tests – one two days after the treatment, and one about a month later. A more sensitive delayed post-test about two-and-a-half months after the treatment was also used and showed that the learning was still retained. Bearing in mind that the treatments in the three studies allowed some repeated opportunities to meet the unknown words and also involved some deliberate focusing on the words through definition or negotiation, a conservative interpretation would be that we could reasonably expect learners to retain a memory for a meeting with a word at least a month later. This estimation of how long a memory for a word will remain must be very inexact as there are numerous factors affecting such a memory, including the quality of the meeting with a word, the number of meetings and the learning burden of the word.

There are of course other factors. McCafferty et al. (2001) suggest that the relevance of a word to a task, its salience, affects its learning, particularly if it is a word that learners have specifically asked about because of its obvious relevance to the task. However, with these cautions in mind, it is very useful to try to estimate how much listening and reading a learner would need to be doing per week in order for incidental receptive vocabulary learning to proceed in an effective way. This is looked at more closely in the section on simplification in Chapter 5, but on average learners would need to listen to stories at least three times a week for about fifteen minutes each time. They would need to read about one graded reader every two weeks (Nation, 1997; Nation and Wang, 1999). As we shall see in Chapter 11, retrievals need to be spaced rather than massed together.

An effective way to get repeated retrieval is to read the same story several times. With younger children this is not difficult to do and is welcomed by them. Older learners may not be so receptive to this. A second option is to serialise a long story, that is, to read a chapter at a time. There is a tendency in continuous stories for vocabulary to be repeated. Teachers could maximise this by briefly retelling what happened previously in the story before continuing with the next instalment.

The repeated readings or the serial instalments should not be too far apart. Listening to a story two or three times a week is likely to be more beneficial for learning than once a week. If the teacher notes up target vocabulary on the board as it occurs in the story, it is best to note it up just after it is heard rather than before. This will encourage retrieval rather than recognition.

Teachers can design retrieval into speaking activities by making it necessary for learners to reuse the words that occurred in the textual input. This can be done by making the task involve retelling of the textual input, by making the task involve a procedure whereby the same material has to be discussed or presented several times through a change in group membership as in the pyramid procedure (Jordan, 1990), or by making the solution to the task involve considerable discussion of the information provided in the textual input as in a problem-solving discussion. Linked skills activities where the same material is focused on three times, each time through a different skill of listening, speaking, reading and writing, are ideal for such retrieval.

In a strip story activity (Gibson, 1975) learners are each given a sentence to memorise from a paragraph. They then must tell their sentences to each other and decide whose sentence is first, second and so on. No writing is allowed. Because learners must memorise their sentences, they then have to retrieve them each time they tell them to the rest of the group. Memorisation thus ensures a form of retrieval.

Retrieval is thus easily built into activities and is most effective if the retrieval involves some change to what has been met before.

Creative use

The third major process that may lead to a word being remembered is creative use. In Joe (1995) the term generative use was used, but was used in a way that was not consistent with Wittrock's (1974) use of the term generation. In order to preserve this use of the term generation, the terms **creative use** or **creative processing** will be used in this book. These also have the advantage of being relatively transparent terms.

There are now an increasing number of studies which show that creative processing is an important factor in first and second language vocabulary learning. Creative processing occurs when previously met words are subsequently met or used in ways that differ from the previous meeting with the word. At its most striking, the new meeting with the word forces learners to reconceptualise their knowledge of that word. For example, if a learner has met the word *cement* used as a noun as in *We bought half a ton of cement*, and then meets *We cemented our relationship with a drink*, the learner will need to rethink the meaning and uses of *cement* and this will help firmly establish the memory of this word. Creative use is not restricted to metaphorical extension of word meaning and can apply to a range of variations from inflection through collocation and grammatical context to reference and meaning. Joe (1995) found that quality of knowledge as measured by three different tests of each word was closely related to the degree of creative use of each word in a retelling task. R. Ellis (1995) found that a factor he called 'range' was significantly related to vocabulary learning in a negotiated listening task. The task involved second language learners listening to directions and having to place items on a picture. Range referred to the number of separate directions (commands) that a word occurred in, and could be considered a kind of measure of creativeness. Stahl and Vancil (1986) found that discussion was a crucial factor in learning vocabulary from semantic mapping. The discussion presumably gave opportunity for the new vocabulary involved to appear in differing forms and contexts. Elley (1989) found that pictorial context for a word in a story was a significant factor in vocabulary learning from listening to stories. Although it is stretching the idea of creative use to make a picture a creative use of a word, the accompaniment of a text with a picture, like creative use, can lead to a form of mental elaboration that deepens or enriches the level of processing of a word (Baddeley, 1990: 160–77) and thus enhances learning. Our knowledge of the nature of creative use and the classification of uses into different degrees of creativity is still sketchy. Negotiation improves learning not only through decontextualisation but possibly also through the opportunity for creative use. During negotiation, a word is used in a variety of grammatical contexts, often in a variety of inflected or derived forms, and often with reference to a variety of instances. These can all be creative uses.

Creative processing can also be receptive or productive. In its receptive form it involves meeting a word which is used in new ways in listening or reading. In its productive form, it involves producing new ways of using the wanted vocabulary in new contexts (Wittrock, 1974, 1991). This means that a word is used creatively if it is used in speaking in a way which is different from its use in the textual input.

There are degrees of creative use. Creative use occurs, but is low, if the linguistic context for the word is only slightly different from the textual input:

chronic pain becomes *very chronic pain*

Creative use is high if the word is used in a substantially different way, perhaps indicating that the word has begun to be integrated into the learner's language system:

chronic pain becomes *chronic backache* or *chronic illness*

Joe (1995) found that degree of creation was closely related to amount of learning in retelling tasks. Newton (2013) found that negotiation of the meaning of a word greatly increased its chances of being learned. Negotiation of the meaning of a word will usually involve creative use of that word during the negotiation. The most striking receptive creative uses of vocabulary are those where meeting the word in a new context forces learners to reconceptualise the meaning that they previously had for that word.

In a well-controlled experiment, Hall (1991) looked at the effect of split information tasks on the learning of mathematics vocabulary, namely *parallel, diagonal, vertical, perimeter*. The experiment involved a comparison of split information pairs, teacher-fronted learning and individual study. All groups made gains in vocabulary learning, but the split information group made significantly more than the other groups. An analysis of the transcripts showed that there was a low correlation (.36) between total exposure to the words and learning, but that there was a high correlation (.93) between learning and the number of uses of the words not closely dependent on input. This means that having to produce the words in ways which are not just repetitions of the written exercise material results in superior learning.

Teachers can try to affect the quality of the mental processing of vocabulary while learners listen to input in the following ways.

Rather than read the same story several times, as in the Elley (1989) study, it may be better to use a longer story and present it part by part as a serial. As we have seen in the section on repeated retrieval, long texts provide an opportunity for the same vocabulary to recur. If this recurrence is in contexts which differ from those previously met in the story, then this creative use will contribute to learning. There have not been any published studies examining the degree of creative use of vocabulary in long texts such as simplified readers, but some unpublished studies done as projects for a Masters level course have shown that the recurrences of words that are the target words at a particular level of a graded reader series are overwhelmingly creative uses rather than verbatim repetitions of the word in the same context. Graded readers thus set up excellent conditions for vocabulary growth.

If the teacher is able to supplement the storytelling with pictures, by using blackboard drawings, an OHP or a blown-up book, then this will contribute positively to vocabulary learning by adding a visual effect.

If it is possible to provide simple contextual definitions of words, that is definitions using example sentences, then this could help learning if the example sentences differ from those in which the word occurs in the story. The contextual definition would then be a creative use of the word.

Teachers can encourage productive creative use by requiring retelling of the written input from a different focus, by distributing the information in a way that encourages negotiation, and by requiring learners to reconstruct what was in the text rather than just repeat it. Verspoor and Lowie's (2003) research suggests that a fruitful activity for establishing vocabulary is to give learners the core meaning of a word and then get them to guess the meaning of figurative senses in context. Such an activity might take this form.

bow = to bend over
He bowed to pressure and agreed. _____
I am sorry to bow out so late. _____

Much research needs to be done on how the design of activities can encourage creative use. It is likely that adding elements of role play, taking a different viewpoint, or the removal of the text during retelling can increase creative use and thus strengthen learning.

Retention

Vocabulary learning is strengthened if learners process words and their meanings both visually and linguistically. It is also helped if interference with related words (Tinkham, 1997), such as near synonyms, opposites or members of the same lexical set, is avoided.

Instantiation (Anderson et al., 1978) involves recalling or experiencing a particular instance or example of the meaning of a word. For example, we see an actual ball when we meet the word form *ball*. Notice that it is possible to learn vocabulary without instantiation. For example, when using word cards to make L2–L1 connections, it is possible to look at the L2 word and recall its L1 translation without thinking of a particular instance of the meaning. It may be that an important reason why using words in real-life situations helps learning is that each use involves instantiation. That is, each use is connected with a particular meaningful example.

Imaging differs from instantiation in that a deliberate visual image is created to help learning. The best-known application of imaging is the keyword technique (see Chapter 11) where a linking image is created to connect a word form with its meaning. Deconinck et al. (2010) describe an interesting procedure where learners are asked to evaluate how well a word form matches its meaning. That is, some people consider that the word *tiny* sounds like something small, whereas *enormous* sounds like something big. Evaluating form–meaning connections in this way had marked positive effects on learning.

The levels of processing hypothesis says that the more deeply and thoughtfully something is processed, the more likely it is to be retained. Difficulty has often been equated with depth of processing. That is, if something is difficult to interpret or remember, then this extra effort leads to deeper processing. We need to be cautious in applying this idea. There is evidence (de Groot, 2006) that words with low learning burden are easily learned and are also well retained. This is probably because they fit well into already existing systems of knowledge. Words with a heavy learning burden require extra attention and processing, and it could be useful to know if this extra attention results in better retention of these difficult words than more easily learned words. Deconinck (2012: 174) notes that we need to distinguish between the intrinsic difficulty of the material to be learned and the conditions under which it is learned. Easy material such as cognates are easily learned and retained well. Items which are learned under conditions involving thoughtful processing may also be retained well.

We have now looked at a very important range of conditions helping vocabulary learning. Let us now look at how we can use these conditions in teaching activities.

How can we apply technique analysis to improving learning?

We can apply our knowledge of what helps learning to the design and use of vocabulary-teaching activities. This is most easily done by using four questions that teachers should ask about any teaching or learning activity:

1. What is the learning goal of the activity?
2. What psychological conditions does the activity use to help reach the learning goal?
3. What should a teacher look for to see if the goal is likely to be reached?
4. What should a teacher do to make sure that the conditions occur?

Let us look at a vocabulary-teaching technique to see how these questions might be used.

The **What is it?** technique (Nation, 1978a) is a useful way of teaching new vocabulary, in particular becoming familiar with the spoken form of the word and linking it to its meaning. The teacher gradually communicates the meaning of a word by using it in context. When learners think they know what the word means, they raise their hands. After enough hands are raised, the teacher asks a learner for a translation or explanation of the meaning. The teacher's description might go like this. The word being taught is *precise*:

Sometimes it is important to make a precise measurement. Sometimes it is not important to be precise. Doctors need a lot of information to find the precise nature of a disease. If you tell me your precise age, you will tell me how old you are in years, months, and days! When you give someone precise instructions, the instructions must be accurate and complete ...

When using this technique several things are important. First, not too much information is given about the word at the beginning, so that learners have to listen attentively to the word in a range of contexts. Second, the teacher repeats the sentences wherever possible, by saying each sentence at least twice when it is first used and by going back over the previously said sentences. The teacher does not ask the first learners who raise their hands for the meaning of the word (a translation, a synonym or a definition), but keeps on describing until most of the class have raised their hands. If this technique is used properly, learners will have made a very good start to knowing the word *precise*. It is however easily possible to use the technique badly, by giving the meaning too quickly, by not repeating the sentences and by removing any challenge for attention. This is another way of saying that there are features in the effective use of the technique that encourage learning. These design features are the repetition of the word and its contexts, the presence of a variety of rich contexts, the order of the contexts with the least informative given first, and the need to give careful attention to the word and its contexts in order to be able to complete the activity by working out its meaning.

These design features set up conditions that research tells us are important for language acquisition. These conditions include having a positive attitude to the activity (helped by its puzzle-like nature), noticing the item several times, and thoughtfully processing its meaning. These conditions help reach the vocabulary-learning goal. It is therefore important that teachers are aware of the important features of techniques so that they know how to use techniques and what to look for when they are being used (Loschky and Bley-Vroman, 1993: 165).

When the technique is being used the teacher should be looking for signs that it might be achieving its learning goal. These signs include seeing if learners are interested and paying attention, seeing if they are trying to find an answer, and seeing if they do find the answer but not too soon.

Table 3.4 is an attempt to relate the conditions favouring vocabulary learning to the signs that they are occurring and the features of the activities that encourage them. As our knowledge of vocabulary learning increases, it may be possible to develop a more detailed table where the various aspects of vocabulary knowledge are related to different learning conditions and the design features of activities.

Table 3.4 *The conditions of learning, signs and features in activities with a vocabulary-learning goal*

Psychological conditions encouraging learning	Signs that the conditions are likely to be occurring	Design features of the activity that promote the conditions
Noticing a word	The learner consults a glossary. The learner pauses over the word. The learner negotiates the word.	Definition, glosses, highlighting Unknown words in salient positions
Retrieving a word	The learner pauses to recall a meaning. The learner does not need to consult a dictionary or gloss. The learner produces a previously unknown word.	Retelling spoken or written input
Using the word creatively	The learner produces a word in a new sentence context. Learners produce associations, causal links and so on.	Role play based on written input Retelling without the input text Brainstorming

How should we do direct vocabulary teaching?

Sometimes the reason for directly teaching a word is to remove a problem so that learners can continue with the main task of understanding a text or communicating a message. In these cases, a short clear explanation is needed. Often a translation, a quick definition in the form of a synonym, or a quickly drawn diagram will be enough. Here are some examples:

- *head* the top or most important part, e.g. head of your body, head of a match, head of the organisation (explained in the first language)
  This explanation is brief, is reinforced by examples, and focuses on the underlying meaning. Dictionaries have over twenty subentries for *head*. Most can be fitted into one underlying meaning.
- *comprehensive* includes all the necessary things together
  This explanation tries to include the meaning of the prefix com- (together) in the explanation. This definition should be related to the context in which the word occurred.
- *freight* goods carried
  This explanation is very brief because this is a mid-frequency word and does not deserve time. It could be given as a first language translation. It is enough to satisfy the learners and to allow the class to move on quickly.

Sometimes however, because the word is important, it may be appropriate to provide what Beck et al. (1987: 149) call **rich instruction** and McWilliam (1998) calls **rich scripting**. This involves giving elaborate attention to a word by going beyond the immediate demands of a particular context of occurrence. In general rich instruction is appropriate for high-frequency words and words for which the learner has special needs. The best time to provide rich instruction is when learners have already met the word several times and may be ready to make it part of their usable vocabulary. The aim of rich instruction is to establish the word as an accessible vocabulary item. Rich instruction involves (1) spending time on the word; (2) explicitly exploring several aspects of what is involved in knowing a word; and (3) involving learners in thoughtfully and actively processing the word. Rich instruction can be a teacher-led activity, it can be student led particularly when students report on words they have met and explored, it can be done as group work, or it can be done in individualised exercises.

Rich instruction must be used only with appropriate vocabulary, in conjunction with the other strands of the course, and with an appropriate allocation of time that does not take time away from the other strands. Baumann et al. (2007) describe a wide range of vocabulary-development activities for first language learners.

There are several ways of providing rich instruction:

- Learners examine a range of contexts and uses. For example, contexts containing the word are analysed to provide a definition or translation of the word. Learners look at concordances or dictionary entries for collocations. "Read with resources" at www.lextutor.ca provides multiple contexts for each word that is clicked.
- Learners do semantic mapping based on a text or based around a theme. Variations of semantic mapping can include using a word to think of cause–effect relationships between that word and other words, and thinking of specific examples or components of a more general word (Sokmen, 1992).
- Learners analyse the form and meaning of a word breaking it into word parts, isolating parts of its meaning and extensions of its meaning. The etymology of the word can be examined (Ilson, 1983).
- Several definition types are combined as in the 'What is it?' activity where learners listen to contextual definitions of a word and try to think of a second language synonym or a first language translation (Nation, 1990).
- A new word is placed in a lexical set with known words. This can involve the use of classification activities where learners put newly met words and known words into groups and perhaps grade or scale them in some way.
- Various aspects of what it means to know a word are looked at – spelling, pronunciation, word parts, meaning, grammatical use and collocations.

Direct vocabulary teaching can occur in a variety of situations – during formal vocabulary teaching, as incidental defining in lectures, story-telling or reading aloud to a class, and during deliberate teaching of content as in lectures, on-the-job instruction, and glossing or **lexical familiarisation** in academic reading. It can also occur as a part of intensive reading.

Strapp et al. (2011) looked at the effects of negative evidence (*That's wrong*, a correct recast) and positive evidence on L1 vocabulary learning. Negative evidence usually comes as a result of errors. Positive evidence involves exposure to correct examples but not as a part of correction. In their study, Strapp et al. defined negative evidence as being reactive, coming after an error, and positive evidence as coming before learner production. Research generally supports the effectiveness of negative evidence compared to positive evidence, possibly because of its explicit nature. Strapp et al. also found negative evidence to be more effective, indicating that teacher correction and peer correction have useful roles to play.

When considering what could be learned from the deliberate communication of information about a word, it is important to consider the following factors, which all relate to the idea that learning a word is a cumulative process (Swanborn and de Glopper, 1999). That is, except in the unusual circumstance where the various features of a second language word are very closely parallel to an equivalent item in the first language, we should expect knowledge of a word to be gradually built up as the result of numerous spaced meetings with the word. A word is not fully learned through one meeting with it, even if this meeting involves substantial deliberate teaching. This is because:

1. there are numerous things to know about a word, namely its form (spoken, written and its component affixes and stem), its meaning (underlying concept, particular instantiations and associations) and its use (collocations, grammatical patterns and constraints on its use).
2. there are several strands through which knowledge of a word needs to develop, namely through meeting in meaning-focused input, through direct study and teaching, through meaning-focused production, and through fluency development activities.
3. as we shall see, learners seem to be capable of dealing with only a limited amount of information at a time – too much confuses.

Because of this, we should expect only limited learning from single meetings with a word and should bear this in mind when we plan or carry out those meetings. This means that a small positive step forward in knowledge, such as being told the translation of a word, should not be criticised as being only a partial inadequate representation of the word, but should be seen as a useful step in the cumulative process of learning a particular word. Celik (2003) found the use of code switching to the L1 useful for clarifying the meaning of unknown L2 words, and found evidence for learning occurring from this clarification.

The way in which a word is defined can have a major effect on the learning that occurs. McKeown (1993) examined the effectiveness of dictionary definitions for young native speakers of English. She found that if definitions were revised so that they used simpler language, focused on the typical underlying meaning of the word and encouraged learners to consider the whole definition, then learners were more able to write typical sentences using the new word and to explain aspects of its meaning. Unhelpful definitions were too general or vague, consisted of disjointed parts, and used words whose typical meanings took learners off on the wrong track. The revised meanings that were more effective tended to be longer than the original dictionary definitions.

R. Ellis (1995) looked at the factors affecting vocabulary acquisition from oral input. In one treatment, the input was pre-modified, that is, the definitions and explanations were built into the text. In the other treatment, the input was interactionally modified, that is, the definitions and elaborations occurred as a result of student requests. In the interactionally modified input condition, it was found that the shorter the definition and the fewer defining characteristics it contained, the more likely acquisition was to occur. Ellis (1995: 426) interpreted this to mean that too much elaboration of word meaning results in capacity overload for learners with limited short-term memories. Short, direct definitions work the best in oral input. Ellis (p. 429) and (1994: 17) also suggests that too much information makes it difficult for a learner to identify what features are critical to the meaning of a word. This finding is supported by Chaudron's (1982) study of teachers' oral definitions. Chaudron suggests that over-elaborated definitions may make it difficult for learners to know if the same information is being repeated or if new information is being added, as in *the Japanese have this tremendous output and this tremendous productivity*. The learner may be unsure if *output* and *productivity* are synonyms or different pieces of information. Chaudron presents a substantial list of structures and semantic–cognitive relationships that can be used to classify the kinds of elaborations that teachers use to help learners with vocabulary.

Studies with native speaking children (Miller and Gildea, 1987; Scott and Nagy, 1997) and non-native speakers (Nesi and Meara, 1994) have found that learners often misinterpret dictionary definitions by focusing on just one part of a definition, for example:

intersect = divide (sth) by going across it

*We must intersect the river for arrive village (Nesi and Meara, 1994: 9)

Sometimes dictionary definitions encourage this.

There is no conflict between Ellis' (1995) and Chaudron's (1982) contention that shorter definitions are best and that elaboration may cause confusion, and McKeown's (1993) finding that clearer definitions tend to be longer than their less revealing counterparts. In essence all three researchers are saying that good definitions need to be specific, direct, unambiguous and simple. The 'Goldilocks principle' may apply here – not too much, not too little, but just right.

There are many ways of communicating word meanings.

- by performing actions;
- by showing objects;
- by showing pictures or diagrams;
- by defining in the first language (translation);
- by defining in the second language; and
- by providing language context clues.

When communicating the meaning of a word, the choice of the way of communicating meaning should be based on two considerations – the reason for explaining the meaning of the word, and the degree to which the way of explaining represents the wanted meaning for the word.

Let us now look briefly at the various ways of communicating the meanings of words.

Using actions, objects, pictures or diagrams

Real objects, pictures and so on are often seen as the most valid way of communicating the meaning of a word, but as Nation (1978b) points out, all ways of communicating meaning involve the changing of an idea into some observable form and all ways of communicating meaning are indirect, are likely to be misinterpreted, and may not convey the exact underlying concept of the word. An advantage of using actions, objects, pictures or diagrams is that learners see an instance of the meaning and this is likely to be remembered. If this way of communicating meaning is combined with a verbal definition then there is the chance that what Paivio calls 'dual encoding' will occur (Paivio and Desrochers, 1981). That is, the meaning is stored both linguistically and visually. Because objects and pictures often contain a lot of detail, it may be necessary to present several examples so that learners can determine the essential features of the concept or accompany the object or picture with focusing information. A picture is not necessarily worth a thousand words, but one which clearly represents the underlying concept of the word undoubtedly is. Lazarton (2004) looked at the role of gesture in unplanned vocabulary explanations by a teacher of English as a second language. Lazarton found that the majority of the explanations were accompanied by gestures (and sometimes demonstrations) that help explain the meaning of the words and in some cases were essential for understanding.

Translating

Translation is often criticised as being indirect, taking time away from the second language, and encouraging the idea that there is an exact equivalence between words in the first and second languages. These criticisms are all true but they all apply to most other ways of communicating meaning. For example, there is no exact equivalence between a second language word and its second language definition. Similarly, a real object may contain many features that are not common to all instances of the word it exemplifies. Pictures and demonstrations take time away from the second language in the same way that using the first language to communicate word meaning takes time away from the second language. Translation has the advantages of being quick, simple and easily understood. Its major disadvantage is that its use may encourage use of the first language that seriously reduces the time available for use of the second language. Hummel (2010) argues for viewing translation as an elaborative process that substantially enriches the connections for a newly translated L2 word. Altarriba and Knickerbocker (2011) found that learning translations resulted in faster response times than learning using black and white, and coloured pictures. However, many studies show a strong positive effect when the method of testing, for example using pictures or L1 translations, matches the method of learning (Lotto and De Groot, 1998).

Defining and providing examples in the second language

We will now look in greater detail at communicating meaning using the second language because this occurs very often in academic lectures and textbooks. Learners can benefit from practice in recognising and interpreting these definitions.

Flowerdew (1992) carried out a very careful analysis of the definitions used in 16 biology and chemistry lectures to non-native speakers of English. On average, there was a definition every 1 minute 55 seconds or about 20 definitions per lecture, showing that deliberate definition is a significant way of communicating meaning. The classic definition type, called a **formal definition**, consists of (a) a term (the word to be defined); (b) the class it fits into, and (c) its defining characteristic(s). Here are some examples from Flowerdew (1992) and Bramki and Williams (1984). The parts of the first few are numbered to mark (a) term, (b) class, and (c) defining characteristics.

1. (a) Consumer goods are those (b) commodities which (c) satisfy our wants directly.
2. (a) A middle zero is (b) a zero which (c) has no digits on each side.
3. Now (b) a photo that (c) we take through a microscope we call (a) a micrograph.

4. A way of defining a metal is by saying that it is an element that readily forms a cation.
5. A fully planned economy is one in which all the important means of production are publicly owned.
6. An activity which helps to satisfy want is defined as production.
7. One major objective of science is to develop theories. These are termed general statements or unifying principles which describe or explain the relationship between things we observe in the world around us.
8. Remember, I said ultra-structure is the fine structure within the cell.

Note that the order of the parts is not always **term** + **class** + **characteristic(s)**, that the class word may be a 'dummy', that is, a word that repeats the term (example 2) or a referential item (example 5), and that there are various formal signals of definition (bolding, italicising or quotation marks, indefinite noun groups, and *which* or *that*, *define* and *call* and so on.). **Semi-formal** definitions do not contain the class and so consist of only the term and the characteristic(s). Here are some examples:

9. You remember that we said that (1) compounds were (3) made from two or more different elements combined chemically.
10. So all living organisms were responding to stimuli/this we call responsiveness.
11. A stable electronic configuration is like the inert gases.

Flowerdew (1992) has a third major category of definition types called **substitution** where a word, word part, phrase or phrases with a similar meaning is used to define the term. This can be done using a synonym, paraphrase or derivation.

12. by fuse I mean join together
13. opaque ... you can't see through it
14. cytopharynx/cyto meaning cell ... and so cytopharynx just means the pharynx of a cell.

Flowerdew classifies the characteristic part of formal and semi-formal definitions according to the semantic categories of behaviour/process /function (example 4), composition/structure (example 9), location/ occurrence (example 8), and attribute/property (example 2).

A fourth minor category of definition types is the use of objects, photographs or diagrams.

Definition has a wide variety of forms, and learners may have difficulty in recognising some of them. Flowerdew (1992) found that about half of his definitions were clearly signalled, most frequently by the use of *call* (as in *we call*, *is called*, *called* etc.), and also by *mean(s)*, *or*, *known as*, *that is*, *defined*. Research is needed on second language learners' recognition and comprehension of definitions, and the learning that occurs from various types of definitions.

Definitions can be classified into two main types according to the role they play in the discourse in which they occur. **Embedded** definitions have the purpose of helping the listener or reader continue to comprehend the text. The words defined are generally not the focus of the information (Flowerdew, 1992: 209) of the text. Most of these are likely to be in the form of synonyms or paraphrase (see examples 12 and 13). Other definitions may play an important role in organising the discourse where a definition is used to introduce a subtopic that is then expanded on (understanding the technical terms is understanding the discipline).

Flick and Anderson (1980) compared native speakers' and non-native speakers' understanding of explicit and implicit definitions in academic reading material. They found that implicit definitions were more difficult to understand than explicit definitions. The difference in difficulty was similar for both native speakers and non-native speakers.

Bramki and Williams (1984) examined the first four chapters of an economics text. They noted the following features of the words that were intentionally defined in the text.

1. Almost all were nouns or nominal compounds.
2. Terms in titles, headings and subheadings were often later defined.
3. Sometimes there were typographic clues that a word was being defined, such as the use of italics or quotation marks.
4. Most defining occurred early in the corpus.
5. The defining was often done by a combination of devices.

Bramki and Williams (1984) found 136 examples in 17,802 running words – a rate of about once every 130 running words or two or three times per page. Table 3.5 lists the various types of lexical familiarisation they found.

Haynes and Baker (1993), in a comparison of native speakers and second language learners learning from lexical familiarisation, concluded that the major reason for second language learners' relatively poor performance was the presence of unknown vocabulary in the definitions provided in the text. Both native speakers and non-native speakers experienced some difficulty with familiar words that were used in narrower ways, mainly through not giving enough attention to the clues in the text.

Table 3.5 *Types and frequency of lexical familiarisation devices in an economics text*

Category	Frequency (%)	Examples	Common signals
Exemplification	44 (32%)	*Durable consumer goods* include such things as books, furniture, television sets, motor cars.	*such as, for example, is typified by*
Explanation	42 (31%)	*Saving* is the act of foregoing consumption.	Frequently unmarked, *i.e., means that*
Definition	35 (26%)	*Economics* is essentially a study of the ways in which man provides for his material well-being.	X is a Y which …
Stipulation	7 (5%)	'Land' in *Economics* is taken to mean … (a type of definition limited to a given situation).	B uses X to describe Y
Synonymy	5 (4%)	*Working capital* is sometimes called circulating capital.	
Non-verbal illustration	3 (2%)	A diagram	
	136 (100%)		

Richards and Taylor (1992) looked at the strategies used by intermediate and advanced learners of English as a second language and adult native speakers of English to produce written definitions of words. They found that the part of speech of the word influenced the type of definition chosen, and intermediate learners experienced difficulty in finding classifying (class) terms for analytic definitions. Richards and Taylor's (1992) list of definition types shows something of the range of possibilities available:

1. synonym   *beautiful* means *nice*
2. antonym   *young* means *not old*
3. analytic definition   An X is a Y which ...
4. taxonomic definition   *autumn* is a season
5. definition by exemplification   *furniture* – something like a chair, sofa, etc.
6. definition by function   *pen* – use it to write
7. grammatical definition   *worse* – comparison form of *bad*
8. definition by association   *danger* – lives have not been protected
9. definition by classification   *family* – a group of people

How should teachers (or writers) explain words?

Some of the guidelines presented here go beyond the research reviewed in this chapter to draw on points made in other chapters of this book.

1. *Provide clear, simple and brief explanations of meaning.* The research evidence clearly shows that particularly in the first meetings with a word, any explanation should not be complicated or elaborate. Learning a word is a cumulative process, so teachers need not be concerned about providing lots of information about a word when it is first met. What is important is to start the process of learning in a clear way without confusion. There are strong arguments for using learners' first language if this will provide a clear, simple and brief explanation (Lado et al., 1967; Laufer and Shmueli, 1997; Mishima, 1967). The various aspects involved in knowing a word can be built up over a series of meetings with the word. There is no need and clearly no advantage in trying to present these all at once. Elley's (1989) study of vocabulary learning from listening to stories showed that brief definitions had a strong effect on learning.
2. *Draw attention to the generalisable underlying meaning of a word.* If knowledge of a word accumulates over repeated meetings with the word, then learners must be able to see how one meeting relates to

the previous meetings. In providing an explanation of a word, the teacher should try to show what is common in the different uses of the word.

3. *Give repeated attention to words*. Knowledge of a word can only accumulate if learners meet the word many times. Repeated meetings can have the effects of strengthening and enriching previous knowledge. There is no need for a teacher to draw attention to a word every time it occurs, but particularly in the early stages of learning, drawing attention increases the chances that learners will notice it on later occasions. Teachers need to see the learning of particular words as a cumulative process. This means that they need to expect not to teach a word all in one meeting. They need to keep coming back to the word to help strengthen and enrich knowledge of the word.

4. *Help learners recognise definitions*. Definitions have certain forms (Bramki and Williams, 1984; Flowerdew, 1992) and may be signalled in various ways. Teachers can help learners by clearly signalling the definitions they provide, by testing learners to diagnose how well they can recognise and interpret definitions, and by providing training in recognising and interpreting definitions. A useful starting point for this is recognising definitions in written text. Bramki and Williams (1984) suggest that learners can be helped to develop skill in making use of lexical familiarisation firstly, by seeing marked-up text which indicates the word, the signal of lexical familiarisation and the definition – plenty of examples are needed at this stage; and secondly, by getting the student to then mark up some examples with the teacher gradually reducing the guidance given. Flowerdew (1992: 216) suggests that teachers and learners should discuss the various forms of definitions as they occur in context.

5. *Prioritise what should be explained about particular words*. There are many things to know about a word, and the different aspects of word knowledge enable different word use skills (Nist and Olejnik, 1995). Some of these aspects of knowledge can be usefully taught, some are best left to be learned through experience, and some may already be known through transfer from the first language or through patterns learned from other English words. When deliberately drawing attention to a word, it is worth considering the learning burden of that word and then deciding what aspect of the word most deserves attention. Most often it will be the meaning of the word, but other useful aspects may be its spelling or pronunciation, its collocates, the grammatical patterning or restrictions on its use through considerations of politeness, formality, dialect or medium.

6. *Help learners remember what is explained.* Understanding and remembering are related but different processes. The way in which a teacher explains a word can affect understanding or it can affect understanding and remembering. In order to help remembering, information needs to be processed thoughtfully and deeply. The quality of mental processing affects the quantity of learning. Teachers can help remembering by showing how the word parts (affixes and stem) relate to the meaning of the word, by helping learners think of a mnemonic keyword that is like the form of the new word, by putting the word in a striking visualisable context, by encouraging learners to retrieve the word form or meaning from their memory while not looking at the text, and by relating the word to previous knowledge such as previous experience or spelling, grammatical, or collocational patterns met before.

7. *Avoid interference from related words.* Words which are similar in form (Laufer, 1989) or meaning (Higa, 1963; Nation, 2000; Tinkham, 1993; Tinkham, 1997; Waring, 1997) are more difficult to learn together than they are to learn separately. When explaining and defining words, it is not helpful to draw attention to other unfamiliar or poorly established words of similar form or which are opposites, synonyms, free associates or members of the same lexical set such as parts of the body, fruit or articles of clothing. The similarity between related items makes it difficult for the learner to remember which was which. Confusion rather than useful learning is often the result. In the early stages of learning it is not helpful to use the opportunity to teach a word as the opportunity to teach other related words. Bolger and Zapata (2011) tested the learning of semantically related and unrelated words in story contexts, finding a slight learning advantage for semantically unrelated items. They suggested that the story context might have overcome much of the disadvantage caused by semantic relatedness. The small difference between the groups may also be at least partly attributed to the fact that the words in the unrelated passage consisted of four sets of related pairs.

How should teachers deal with words in intensive reading?

Teachers should deal with vocabulary in intensive reading in systematic and principled ways to make sure that learners get the most benefit from the time spent. There are two major decisions to be made for each unknown word when deciding how to deal with it.

- Should time be spent on it?
- How should the word be dealt with?

It is worth spending time on a word if the goal of the lesson is vocabulary learning and if the word is a high-frequency word, a useful topic word or a technical word, or contains useful word parts. It is also worth spending time on a word if it provides an opportunity to develop vocabulary-learning strategies like guessing from context and using word parts.

Let us now look briefly at a range of ways for dealing with words in intensive reading, examining the reasons why each particular way might be chosen. We will imagine that the words that we are considering giving attention to occur in a reading text.

1. *Pre-teach*. Pre-teaching usually needs to involve rich instruction and should only deal with a few words, probably five or six at the most. If too many words are focused on, they are likely to be forgotten or become confused with each other. Because pre-teaching takes quite a lot of time, it is best suited to high-frequency words and words that are important for the message of the text.

   Should words be taught before or during reading? Is it best to pre-teach words or teach them when they are met in the text? File and Adams (2010) found no significant difference for vocabulary learning, although there was a small non-significant advantage for pre-teaching. File and Adams suggest several reasons for the small vocabulary learning advantage for pre-teaching:

   ○ Pre-teaching involves a strong focus on vocabulary without the distraction of comprehension of the text.
   ○ Pre-teaching makes it clear that the goal is vocabulary learning not just text comprehension.
   ○ Pre-teaching involves two sets of meetings with the words – once during the pre-teaching and once during the actual reading of the text. The spacing between the meetings provides an opportunity for retrieval during the reading of the text.

   Because the vocabulary-learning differences between pre-teaching and teaching during reading are so small, it is not worth getting too concerned about this, and it is best to do what seems most useful and appropriate at the time for each word.

   From the perspective of text comprehension, vocabulary teaching during reading may interrupt comprehension of the text. However, the retrieval of the meaning of the pre-taught words may also be difficult during reading and thus interfere with comprehension.

2. *Replace the unknown word in the text before giving the text to the learners*. Some texts may need to be simplified before they are presented to learners. In general the low-frequency words that are not central to the meaning of the text need to be replaced.

Replacing or omitting words means that the teacher does not spend class time dealing with items that at present are of little value to the learners.

3. *Put the unknown word in a glossary.* This is best done with words that the teacher cannot afford to spend time on, particularly high-frequency words, but glossing need not be limited to these. Long (in Watanabe, 1997) argues that putting a word in a glossary gets repeated attention to the word if learners look it up. That is, they see the word in the text, they see it again in the glossary when they look it up, and then they see it again when they return to the text from the glossary. It could also be argued that between each of these three steps the word is being kept in short-term memory. Glossing could thus be a useful way of bringing words to learners' attention. Glossing helps learning (Watanabe, 1997; see Chapter 5 for more on glossing).

4. *Put the unknown word in an exercise after the text.* The words that are treated in this way need to be high-frequency words or words that have useful word parts. Exercises that come after a text take time to make and learners spend time doing them. The words need to be useful for the learners to justify this effort.

5. *Quickly give the meaning.* This can be done by quickly giving a first language translation, a second language synonym or brief definition, or quickly drawing a picture, pointing to an object, or making a gesture. This way of dealing with a word has the goal of avoiding spending time and moving on to more important items. It is best suited to low-frequency words that are important for the message of the text but which are unlikely to be needed again. Quick definitions help learning (Elley, 1989).

6. *Do nothing about the word.* This is suited to low-frequency words that are not important for the meaning of the text. It avoids drawing attention to items that, because of their low frequency, do not deserve class time.

7. *Help learners use context to guess, use a dictionary, or break the word into parts.* These ways of dealing with words are suited to high-frequency words because time is spent on them while using the strategies, but they are also suitable for low-frequency words that are easy to guess, have several meanings or contain useful parts. The time spent is justified by the increase in skill in these very important strategies.

8. *Spend time looking at the range of meanings and collocations of the word.* This is a rich instruction approach and, because of the time it takes, needs to be directed towards high-frequency words and other useful words.

What are the different kinds of vocabulary activities and procedures?

In Table 3.6 vocabulary activities are classified according to the various aspects of what is involved in knowing a word. Rich instruction would involve giving attention to several of these aspects for the same word. Below are descriptions and examples for each of the activities in Table 3.6.

Each aspect is the learning goal of the activity. Some of the activities could be classified under several aspects of what is involved in knowing a word.

Spoken form

Attention to the spoken form has the goals of getting learners to be able to recognise a word when they hear it, and to be able to pronounce a word correctly. Instruction is a useful way of beginning this process but, as N. Ellis (1995) argues, large amounts of meaning-focused use are necessary to develop fluency.

- *Pronouncing the words.* The teacher puts up words on the blackboard that learners have met during the week. The teacher pronounces them and learners repeat after the teacher. Then learners take turns pronouncing the words without the teacher's model and get feedback on their attempts.
- *Developing phonological awareness.* The teacher sounds out words, as in /p/ /e/ /n/, and learners say what word it is by saying its combined form /pen/. Other phonological awareness activities include finding rhymes, and deleting and adding sounds to a word to see what change occurs. Such activities are a very good way of preparing very young learners for reading.
- *Reading aloud.* The learners read aloud from a text and get feedback.

Written form

Although English has irregularities in its spelling system, there are patterns and rules which can guide learning (Nation, 2009: 151–9). Some learners may require particular attention to writing the letter shapes if their first language uses a different writing system from English.

- *Dictating words and sentences.* Learners write words and sentences that the teacher dictates to them. This can be easily marked if one learner writes on the blackboard. The teacher corrects this and the

Table 3.6 *A range of activities for vocabulary learning*

	spoken form	Pronouncing the words
		Developing phonological awareness
		Reading aloud
Form	written form	Dictating words and sentences
		Finding spelling rules
	word parts	Filling word part tables
		Cutting up complex words
		Building complex words
		Choosing a correct form
		Finding etymologies
	form–meaning connection	Using word cards
		Using the keyword technique
		Matching words and definitions
		Discussing the meanings of phrases
		Drawing and labelling pictures
		Peer teaching
		Solving riddles
		Answering True/False statements
		Reading with glosses
Meaning	concept and reference	Finding common meanings
		Choosing the right meaning
		Using semantic feature analysis
		Answering questions involving
		target words
		Playing at word detectives
	associations	Finding substitutes
		Explaining connections
		Making word maps
		Classifying words
		Finding opposites
		Suggesting causes or effects
		Suggesting associations
		Finding examples
	grammar	Matching sentence halves
		Putting words in order to make sentences
Use	collocates	Matching collocates
		Finding collocates
		Analysing and classifying collocates
	constraints on use	Identifying constraints
		Classifying constraints

other learners use it to correct their own work or their partner's work.

- *Finding spelling rules.* Learners work in groups with a list of words to see if they can find spelling rules.

Word parts

Chapter 9 on 'Word parts' describes the goals and knowledge required for this aspect of vocabulary learning. Attention to word parts allows learners to make full use of the word families they know, and also contributes to remembering new complex words.

- *Filling word part tables.* Learners work in pairs to complete tables like the following. Not all spaces can be filled. They check their work with another pair before the teacher provides the answers.

Noun	Verb	Adjective	Adverb
argument			
	evaluate		
		distinct	
			normally

- *Cutting up complex words.* Learners are given a list of words that they divide into parts. They can be asked to give the meaning of some of the parts.
- *Building complex words.* Learners are given word stems and make negatives from them, or make vague words (using *-ish, -y, -like*).
- *Choosing the correct form.* Learners are given sentences containing a blank and a word stem in brackets. They have to change the stem to the appropriate inflected or derived form to complete the sentence.

I went to the doctor for a _____ (consult).

- *Finding etymologies.* Learners look up etymologies in dictionaries to see how new words are related to those they already know.

Strengthening the form–meaning connection

This aspect of knowing a word tries to separate recognising the form and knowing a meaning from being able to connect a particular form to a particular meaning. Strengthening the form–meaning connection involves having to recall a meaning when seeing or hearing a particular word, or having to recall a spoken or written form when wanting to express a meaning.

- *Using word cards.* Learners use word cards to learn new vocabulary and receive training in how to use word cards. Chapter 11 looks closely at this strategy.
- *Using the keyword technique.* Learners get training and practice in the keyword technique (see Chapter 11).
- *Matching words and definitions.* Learners are given a list of definitions. Some could be in the form of synonyms, and learners must match them with a list of words they have met before. An alternative is to get them to find the words in a reading text to match the definitions.
- *Discussing the meaning of phrases.* Learners are given a list of phrases containing words they have already met before and have to decide on the meaning of the phrase.
- *Drawing and labelling pictures.* Learners read or listen to descriptions containing words they have recently met and draw or label pictures. Palmer (1982) describes a wide range of these information transfer activities.
- *Peer teaching.* Learners work in pairs. One learner has to teach the vocabulary in his or her list to the other learner. The learner who is the teacher has the word and a picture illustrating its meaning. Feeny (1976) found that those learners who acted as teachers learned almost as well as those who were being taught. Martin et al. (2002) suggest such teaching can occur in small groups and then to the whole class. Learners choose words that interest them and that they think would be useful for others (see also Mhone, 1988).
- *Solving riddles.* Riddles like the following can make the meaning of a word more memorable (Kundu, 1988; Sen, 1983).
  - When it is new it is full of holes. (*net*)
  - It has a head but cannot think. (*match*)
  - What is the longest word in the world? (*smiles* – because there is a mile between the first and last letters)
- *Answering True/False statements.* Learners respond to True/False statements that contain new vocabulary.
- *Reading with glosses.* Learners read texts with hard copy or hyperlink glosses.

Concept and reference

This aspect of word knowledge involves having a clear idea of the underlying meaning of a word that runs through its related uses, and also involves being aware of the range of particular uses it has, that is, what it can refer to. It is this knowledge which contributes to being able to understand a word when it is used in a new situation, and being able to use a word in creative ways.

• *Finding common meanings.* A useful technique for helping learners see the underlying concept or core meaning of a word is to see what is similar in different uses of the word. Dictionary entries and example sentences are useful sources for this activity.

  ○ He was *expelled* from school.
  ○ They were *expelled* from their villages.
  ○ The breath was *expelled* from her body.

Visser (1989) describes an easily made activity which helps learners see the core meaning of a word and put the word to use. Here is an example. Learners work in pairs or small groups.

1	2	3
Your *environment* consists of all the influences and circumstances around you.	The *environment* is the natural world.	Say what the similar ideas are in columns 1 and 2.
What are the features of a stimulating *environment*?	Describe three factors polluting the *environment*.	

Note that there is a task for learners to perform for each of the two uses of the word. Visser found that learners are usually successful in group tasks at seeing the common features in the uses. This can be made more certain by getting different groups to compare the core meanings they decided on.

• *Choosing the right meaning.* Learners are given a list of words in a reading text and have to choose the appropriate meaning from the dictionary. Instead of using a dictionary, the teacher can provide a set of possible meanings. All the meanings should be possible meanings for the word, but only one would fit in the context. For example, *They were scrubbing the flags in front of the house.* Here *flags* means 'flagstones'.

• *Using semantic feature analysis.* Numerous writers (Channell, 1981; Rudzka et al., 1981; Stieglitz, 1983; Stieglitz and Stieglitz, 1981) suggest that learners should fill in grids to refine their knowledge of related words. Overleaf is an example from Rudzka et al. (1981: 65).

	because unexpected	because difficult to believe	so as to cause confusion	so as to leave one helpless to act or think
surprise	✓			
astonish		✓		
amaze			✓	
astound				✓
flabbergast				✓

This type of activity has the potential for interference to occur between related items (Higa, 1963; Tinkham, 1993, 1997; Waring, 1997). It is important that this kind of activity is used when learners are already familiar with most of the items being compared and is thus used for revision.

- *Answering questions.* Learners are given questions to answer which contain words that they have recently met. The questions help them instantiate and apply the words (Winn, 1996).

  ○ When do you like to work with a *partner*?
  ○ Who would you call *darling*?

  The questions can relate to a reading passage.

- *Playing at word detectives.* Learners look for words they have already met in class and report back to the class about where they found them and the information they gathered about the word (Martin et al., 2002; Mhone, 1988). This activity is like McKeown et al.'s (1985) **extended rich instruction** where learners bring back evidence that they have seen or used a target word outside the classroom.

Associations

Knowing a range of associations for a word helps understand the full meaning of the word and helps recall the word form or its meaning in appropriate contexts. The associations of a word are to a large degree the result of the various meaning systems that the word fits into. These include, for example, synonyms, opposites, family members of the same general headword, words in a part–whole relationship, and superordinate and subordinate words.

- *Finding substitutes.* Learners choose words from a list to replace underlined words in a text.

- *Explaining connections.* Learners work in pairs or small groups to explain the connections between a group of related words:

    analyse   criteria   exclude   justify   classify

- *Making word maps.* Learners work in groups or with the teacher to make a semantic map based on a target word.
- *Classifying words.* Learners are given lists of words to classify into groups according to certain criteria, for example classifying words according to whether they have positive or negative connotations, or whether they are living or non-living. Dunbar (1992) suggests getting learners to classify the new vocabulary they are working on as a way of integrating vocabulary knowledge with subject matter knowledge. Such an activity is likely to lead to creative processing, particularly when learners explain and justify their classification. The examples Dunbar provides are in the form of tree diagrams.
- *Finding opposites.* Learners are given a list of words or words from a text and find opposites for the words.
- *Suggesting causes or effects.* Sokmen (1992), in an article rich in suggestions for vocabulary development, describes a useful activity where learners are given words or phrases which they then have to sort as causes or effects. They then have to think of causes to go with the effects or effects to go with causes. So, a phrase like *medical consultation* could get learners to think of the causes *illness, pain, tiredness* and the effects *medicine, hospital, reassurance* and so on.
- *Suggesting associations.* Learners are given four or five words. They work in small groups to list associates for those words. They then scramble the words and give them to another group who have to classify them under the same words. The two groups compare and discuss their classifications.
- *Finding examples.* The teacher provides learners with a list of categories like *food, household objects, numbers, jobs* and so on. Each learner chooses or is given one category. The learner then has to write as many words as possible under the category heading on a piece of paper. So, *food* should contain items like *bread, meat* and so on. Learners should write known words, not look up unknown words. After a set time, a learner passes their paper to the next learner who then tries to add words not already listed. The paper is passed on until all learners have their original sheet of paper back. The learner has to check the spelling with a dictionary and then these sheets become a class dictionary that is added to as new words are met (Woodward, 1985).

Grammar

Knowing a word involves knowing how to use it in sentences. There is continuing debate (Sinclair, 1991) about the relative roles of vocabulary and grammar in determining how words are used.

- *Matching sentence halves.* Learners are given sentence halves containing vocabulary they have met before and they have to match the halves to make complete sensible sentences.
- *Putting words in order to make sentences.* Learners put words in order to make sentences. They may need to supply some of the function words.

Collocation

More information about collocation is becoming available with the development of large corpora and the means of retrieving information from them. Knowing what words can occur with other words helps language use and contributes to the fluency with which language can be used. Chapter 12 looks in detail at collocation.

- *Matching collocates.* Learners are given lists of words to match. It may be possible to make several pairs with the same words (Brown, 1974).
- *Finding collocates.* Learners look in dictionaries, draw on their experience, use concordancers and use parallels with their first language to list collocates for given words.
- *Analysing and classifying collocates.* Learners group collocates to see if they share the same general meanings.

Constraints on use

Most words are not affected by constraints on use. That is, they are neutral regarding constraints like formal/informal, polite/impolite, child language/adult language, women's usage/men's usage, American/British, spoken/written. When these constraints do occur, it is usually important to be aware of them because they can affect the interpretation of the communication.

- *Identifying constraints.* Woodward (1988) suggests using codes like F for formal, I for informal, N for neutral, to put next to words to classify them on vocabulary posters in class.
- *Classifying constraints.* Learners are given lists of words they must classify according to a given constraint on use, for example American usage versus British usage.

Vocabulary teaching procedures

A procedure is a series of clearly defined steps leading to a learning goal. Teachers apply procedures to make sure that learners cover what needs to be covered in a task. From a vocabulary-learning perspective, procedures can be used to ensure that words are repeated and that various aspects of what is involved in knowing a word are covered. Here are some examples of such procedures.

Recycled words

Blake and Majors (1995) describe a five-step procedure involving: (1) pre-teaching of vocabulary; (2) oral reading of a text containing the vocabulary with discussion of the meaning of the text; (3) deliberate word study; (4) vocabulary puzzles, quizzes or tests; and finally (5) writing making use of the vocabulary. This procedure moves from receptive use to productive use with a focus on deliberate learning.

The second-hand cloze

This activity involves three steps: (1) learners read texts containing the target vocabulary; (2) they deliberately study the vocabulary; (3) learners are then given cloze passages which are summaries of the ones they originally read. In this step learners are helped to recall the target words by being given a list of L1 equivalents of the target words which they have to translate into the L2, and then use to fill the gaps in the cloze text. Laufer and Osimo (1991) tested the procedure experimentally and found superior learning for the words practised using the second-hand cloze procedure compared to the study of list translations. The second-hand cloze seems to have added a creative element to learning. Lee (2008) describes a variant of this where learners watch a video and then complete a rational cloze test based on the video with a list of words provided. Lee found substantial vocabulary learning from the activity.

The vocabulary interview

The nine headings in Table 3.6 can be used as a basis for learners to interview the teacher or each other about particular words. If learners interview each other, they should be aware of the nine aspects of knowing a word that the questions are based on and should have a chance to research their word. One of the goals of the interview procedure is to make learners aware of the aspects of knowing a word. Another goal is for them to learn new words.

Vocabulary notebooks

Vocabulary notebooks have been advocated as ways of enhancing vocabulary learning (Fowle, 2002; McCrostie, 2007; Schmitt and Schmitt, 1995). They involve entering substantial amounts of information about a word in a notebook usually in some organised way.

In a very revealing study, Walters and Bozkurt (2009) looked at the effect of keeping vocabulary notebooks on vocabulary knowledge as measured by a receptive vocabulary test, a controlled productive test and use in weekly writing. The vocabulary notebook group far outperformed the control group on these measures even though all the words occurred in both the treatment group and control group lessons. Many more vocabulary notebook words were learned than other unknown words that also appeared in the lessons. The most striking finding of this study is that without the sustained deliberate attention given to vocabulary notebook words, little other vocabulary was learned. Simply noting up words on the board and providing a meaning did not result in much vocabulary learning. The other striking finding is that even with the sustained deliberate attention needed for the vocabulary notebooks only about 40% of the vocabulary notebook words were learned receptively and 33% productively, clearly indicating that teaching does not equal learning. Learners saw the value of vocabulary notebooks, but because they were learners who were forced to study English for course requirements, they largely said that they would not continue to use them.

Deliberate learning from word cards may suffer the same fate with poorly motivated students. However, from word card learning we would expect a near-perfect rate of learning. The advantage that vocabulary notebooks may have over word card learning is the richness of the information entered into the notebooks (part of speech, translation, synonyms and antonyms, contexts, derived forms, collocations), and future research could look at this. The advantages of word card learning are its efficiency and its focus on knowing every word on the cards. Cards are easily and quickly made and take little class time. McCrostie (2007) found a wide variety of accuracy in the information entered into the notebooks indicating that if they are used learners need support and training in using them.

Rowland (2011) found some support for vocabulary notebooks among advanced learners, but they seemed to prefer them in a reduced rather than an elaborate form. Fowle (2002) found strong support for notebooks where English was taught as a foreign language within a school.

This section has looked at a wide range of vocabulary activities and procedures. They can all be evaluated using the Involvement Load

Hypothesis and Technique Feature Analysis (see Nation and Webb, 2011: 318–19, for numerous analysed examples). Teachers need to use the ones that work well but make sure that vocabulary teaching is in a good balance with the other strands of a course.

How can we develop learners' fluency?

Developing fluency is important because unless learners can quickly access their vocabulary knowledge, it is of little use to them. Because fluency development activities are meaning focused, they are typically done without any special attention to vocabulary.

Fluency involves learners making the best use of what they already know, so fluency activities need to meet the following conditions:

1. They involve only known language features. They thus involve working with easy material.
2. They involve pressure to go faster. This can occur because of time pressure, setting speed goals or repetition.
3. They involve large quantities of language use.
4. They are message focused. They involve learners using the language.

Nation (2009: Chapter 5) and Nation and Newton (2009: Chapter 9) describe a range of fluency development activities. It seems necessary to have fluency development activities across the four skills of listening, speaking, reading and writing.

Listening fluency

A listening corner is a place where learners can listen to tapes as part of self-access activities. The teacher makes a tape of a spoken version of writing that learners have already done. The writing could be done individually or as group compositions. In addition to learner compositions, learners can listen to recordings of what they have read before (in English or the first language), such as the reading texts from earlier sections of the coursebook.

Listening to stories is particularly suitable for learners who read well but whose listening skills are poor. The teacher chooses an interesting story, possibly a graded reader, and reads a chapter a day aloud to the learners. The learners just listen to the story and enjoy it. While reading the story the teacher sits next to the blackboard and writes any words or phrases that learners might not recognise in their spoken form. Any words learners have not met before may also be written, but the story should be chosen so that there are very few of these. During the reading of the first chapters the teacher may go fairly slowly and repeat some sentences. As learners become more familiar with the story, the speed increases and the repetitions decrease. Learner interest in this activity is very high and the daily story is usually looked forward to with the same excitement people have for television serials. If the pauses are a little bit longer than usual in telling the story, this allows learners to consider what has just been heard and to anticipate what may come next. It allows learners to listen to language at normal speed without getting lost. A list of prize-winning graded readers which are suitable for this activity can be found on the Extensive Reading Foundation website.

Speaking fluency

The 4/3/2 technique was devised by Maurice (1983). In this technique, learners work in pairs with one acting as the speaker and the other as the listener. The speaker talks for four minutes on a topic while the listener listens. Then the pairs change with each speaker giving the same information to a new partner in three minutes, followed by a further change and a two-minute talk. See Nation (1989), Arevart and Nation (1991) and de Jong and Perfetti (2011) for research on 4/3/2.

The best recording is a useful fluency activity involving a digital recorder. The learner speaks onto the recorder, talking about a previous experience or describing a picture or set of pictures. The learner listens to the recording noting any points where improvement could be made. Then the learner re-records the talk. This continues until the learner is happy with the recording. This technique can involve planning and encourages repetition through the setting of a quality-based goal.

Rehearsed talks involve learners using the pyramid procedure of preparing a talk individually, rehearsing it with a partner, practising it in a small group, and then presenting it to the whole class.

Reading

Speed reading and extensive reading of graded readers provide fluency improvement through the features of limited demands because of language control and quantity of processing (Nation, 2005). To be effective, speed-reading courses need to be written within a limited vocabulary so that learners can focus on the reading skill without having to tackle language difficulties. Speed-reading courses also have the added benefit of involving learners in keeping a running record of their speed and comprehension scores. Research on graded readers (Nation and Wang, 1999; Wodinsky and Nation, 1988) shows that reading only a few books at one level would provide learners with contact with almost all the words at that level. This shows that graded reading can provide a reliable basis for systematic coverage of vocabulary for fluency development.

Repeated reading is one approach to developing fluency in reading (Dowhower, 1989; Rasinski, 1989). Learners read the same text several times. There are several ways of doing this. One way is to set learners a new task to do each time so that each reading is for a different purpose. The tasks would become more demanding with each repetition. Another way is to set a time goal for reading the text, say, three minutes for a 500-word text. Learners reread the text until they can do it in the set time. An even simpler goal is to get learners to reread the text a set number of times. Research suggests that four or five times is most effective (Dowhower, 1989).

Writing

Continuous writing is an activity where learners are given a set time (usually 5–10 minutes) to write with the aim of producing a large quantity of writing within that time. Learners can record the number of words they wrote on a graph. The teacher responds to the writing not by correcting errors but by finding something positive in the content of the writing to comment on briefly.

Fluency development is particularly useful for developing knowledge of multiword units.

Should vocabulary-learning activities be matched to an individual's learning style?

Learning style is an individual's preferred way of learning. There are numerous lists of styles with the most basic classifications being concrete versus abstract, holistic versus analytic, and visual versus verbal, and there are more elaborate systems containing a wide range of styles (Cohen et al., 2006; Tight, 2010). Tight (2010) compared (1) matching the learning procedure to the preferred learning style; (2) mismatching the learning procedure to the style; and (3) mixed-style learning. The learning styles used were visual, auditory and tactile/kinaesthetic. The study used two vocabulary measures, productive recall (L1–L2 translation) and productive recognition (L1–L2 four-item multiple choice). For visual learners, the preferred learning style gave the best results. For other learners, mixed-style learning gave the best results. Visual learning involved seeing the objects either as real objects or pictures. Visual learning was also the preferred option in this study and also in surveys by other researchers. Although most learners have a style preference, matching learning to style does not have strong effects, but there is clearly value in providing a range of learning opportunities. This range of learning opportunities can be provided very effectively in computer-assisted vocabulary learning.

How can computer-assisted vocabulary learning help?

Computer-assisted vocabulary learning is dealt with in several places in this book: in Chapter 4 on listening and speaking when looking at vocabulary learning through interaction with others, when dealing with glossing in Chapter 5 on reading and writing, when looking at vocabulary flashcard programmes in Chapter 11 on learning from word cards, and in Chapter 10 on dictionary use. In this chapter, however, on teaching techniques, we look at six special characteristics of computer-assisted vocabulary learning which distinguish it from other ways of learning. Not all of these characteristics are unique to computer-assisted vocabulary learning, but computer-assisted vocabulary learning is an ideal way of putting them into practice. Under each characteristic, we look at relevant research. Before doing this it is important to make the point that while computer-assisted vocabulary learning is largely focused on the learning of vocabulary, the selection of vocabulary to learn is a critical feature. Too often, computer-assisted vocabulary-learning programs are developed by programmers and entrepreneurs with a good knowledge of computers, but little knowledge of vocabulary levels and principles of vocabulary selection and learning. It is very important that learners focus on the most useful vocabulary at the present stage of their learning. Fortunately there is a growing awareness of this.

Vocabulary content

Wordchip (van Elsen et al., 1991) draws on information from several frequency-based vocabulary lists to ensure that the vocabulary occurring in the activities will be generally useful to learners. Burling (1983) suggests that basic information on frequency level should be provided to learners so that they can decide whether to spend time on a particular word or not. Well-designed programs need to draw on frequency information and also need to have the flexibility for teachers and learners to play a part in choosing the vocabulary to focus on.

Another aspect of vocabulary content is the aspect that is focused on. Table 3.6 outlines the various kinds of knowledge involved in knowing a word. These include knowledge of the written and spoken forms of the word, knowledge of word parts and inflectionally and derivationally related words, knowledge of grammar, collocations, restrictions on use, and knowledge of meaning and associations.

Harrington (1994) describes a program, *CompLex*, that explicitly develops and monitors form-based and meaning-based links between words. For each word, the program can provide example sentences, related forms, a spoken form, synonyms, hyponyms (class–member), meronyms (part–whole), collocations, some grammatical information, and L1 and L2 meanings. The program keeps a record of the words a particular student knows and links are only made to other known items. The program is designed to complement courses and can be used in several ways. The learner can choose or supply words to go into the learner database (these are automatically checked against the program database). The learner can review and look up items. Harrington sees the strengths of *CompLex* as coming from the links it makes to many aspects of word knowledge, the restriction of these links to known vocabulary, and thus the opportunity for continual review through the activation of these links.

Computer-assisted vocabulary learning is quickly becoming a misnomer as programs are available on smartphone, iPod and iPad. Stockwell (2007) compared learners' preferences of learning through a mobile phone or a PC. Learners generally preferred the PC and used it much more for learning than the mobile phone. Problems with using the mobile phone were cost, noisy surroundings and the small screen. Its portability was an advantage.

Computer-assisted vocabulary learning has several advantages that distinguish it from other kinds of learning:

1. It can provide fast and easy access to a wide range of resources including other learners.
2. It can provide multimedia resources.
3. It can provide immediate feedback on success and progress.
4. It can monitor and control learning conditions making sure that optimal conditions are applied according to research findings.
5. It can adapt to the performance of the learner.
6. It can motivate and engage learners.

Let us now look at each of these in detail.

Computer-assisted vocabulary learning can provide fast and easy access to a wide range of resources including other learners. An important computer-based resource is a concordance. A concordance is a list of contexts exemplifying a word or word family. On Tom Cobb's website (www.lextutor.ca) there is a web-based concordancer. Laurence Anthony's website (www.antlab.sci.waseda.ac.jp/software.html) has a free downloadable concordancer called AntConc. They are both very easy to use. Here is an example of a concordance. Note that the search word can include various forms of the word:

1. under another name. Suddenly, Ntsiki   whispered   a warning. Biko stopped writing
2. here running in the hall. Excited voices   whispered.   A servant, partly dressed and
3. hand touched my shoulder. 'Smee?'   whispered   a voice that I recognised at once
4. Ntsiki. 'He was a great man, Ntsiki,' he   whispered.   'A man the world will always
5. But there was no reply. 'Mark?' I   whispered   again. I had been wrong, then.
6. 'I've never seen so much money before,'   whispered   Aku-nna, staring at Chike's
7. the white man's anger. After a lot of   whispering   among themselves,
8. think we had better rescue these,' she   whispered.   And they both gasped with
9. Then Wilson spoke, but no longer in a   whisper,   and I thought I heard my own
10. Then he began to speak. He spoke in a   whisper,   and his voice filled me with
11. about it. Now, I understood from the   whispers   around the table, that this was
12. and went to the door. 'Steve.' he   whispered   as he opened the door. Biko

Several writers and researchers recommend the use of concordances as a way of promoting vocabulary learning. The advantages of examining concordances are seen as being the following:

*   Learners meet vocabulary in real contexts. The information which these provide often differs from non-corpus-based descriptions.
*   Multiple contexts provide rich information on a variety of aspects of knowing a word, including collocates, grammatical patterns, word family members, related meanings and homonyms.
*   The use of concordances involves discovery learning, where learners are being challenged to actively construct generalisations and note patterns and exceptions.
*   Learners control their learning and learn investigative strategies.

To work effectively, however, learners need training in how to use concordances, and the data obtained from the concordances needs to be comprehensible to the learner. One way of overcoming the comprehensibility issue is for prepared 'dictionaries' of concordances to be used (Descamps, 1992). These dictionaries may already be partly organised, with the examples in a concordance for a particular word already grouped under headings.

Learners can perform a variety of activities with concordances:

- They can classify the items in a concordance into groups. Guidance, such as group headings, questions or a table to fill, may be already provided.
- They can make generalisations and rules based on the data.
- They can recall items when the contexts are presented with the concordance word deleted (Stevens, 1991).

Thurstun and Candlin (1998) provide examples of exercises. Schmitt (2000) also suggests activities that make use of a corpus and a concordancer.

Most concordance programs allow the user to determine the amount of context provided. The typical variations involve one line of context determined by what fills a line on a computer screen, a complete sentence, a complete paragraph, a set number of characters each side, or a set number of lines. Concordance programs may also allow sorting. This can be done by choosing the direction of the sort (to the left or to the right), or by sorting according to the way the user has tagged them. Concordance programs usually allow a limit to be placed on the number of contexts to be searched for.

Using concordances may initially require learners (and their teachers) to understand how a concordance is made and where the information comes from (Stevens, 1991). If learners are searching for their own concordances, then they need to understand how to use the wild card (usually marked by an asterisk *) to search for members of the word family. Learners also need to understand that some items are highly frequent while others are much less frequent. This helps them understand why some of their searches yield little data and others too much.

In the only experimental test of the value of concordances for learning, Cobb (1997) reported on an innovative program called *PET 200* which presents learners with example sentences drawn from a corpus. With several of these example sentences present, learners can (1) choose the meaning for the target word from a multiple-choice set of definitions; (2) identify a form to fit the example sentences where the target word has been replaced by a blank; (3) spell the target word after hearing its spoken form, and seeing contexts with a blank for the target word; (4) choose words from a list to fill blanks in texts; and (5) recall words to fill blanks in short contexts. The study involved pre- and post-testing with the Vocabulary Levels Test (Nation, 1990) and weekly quizzes involving spelling and gap filling in a text. When learners used the concordance information, their scores on the subsequent quizzes were higher than when they learned without the concordance information. Use of concordances seems to help learning especially where use in context is required. A feature of all activities in the program is that the level of mental processing required is deep and thoughtful.

Sun and Dong (2004) showed that the more support that is given to young learners (pre-task pronunciation and sentence-level translations during the task) the better their vocabulary learning.

Computer-assisted vocabulary learning can provide multimedia resources. Learning vocabulary through playing video games is only marginally computer-assisted vocabulary learning, but the characteristic that it does make extensive use of is the multimedia aspect. However, as deHaan et al. (2010) show, the cognitive load imposed by the multimedia and interaction can have negative effects on learning. In their study, they had one learner playing the video game and another learner observing. The vocabulary test (immediate and two weeks delayed) was a cloze test of the lyrics of the song that was the focus of the game. No choices were provided so recall of the words was required. Small spelling errors were accepted. The differences were enormous, with observers scoring 23.27 on the immediate post-test and players scoring 7.42 out of 41 (delayed post-test: observers 16.03; players 5.15). Some players were unable to recall any vocabulary. The percentage loss between the immediate and delayed post-tests was virtually the same for both groups (31%). Most of the target words were known on the pre-test (36 out of 41), so the study is more of an examination of recall rather than vocabulary learning. Nonetheless, the study has interesting implications for the use of video games for language learning.

Palmberg (1988) found that text-based computer games were an effective source of vocabulary learning. Some of the vocabulary in such games may not have relevance to the daily use of the language (*pirate, treasure, cutlass*) so adaptation may be needed to ensure that useful vocabulary goals are being met. Such programs may require dictionary access.

Coll (2002) looked at how access to support resources such as translation, transcripts and video-control tools can help incidental vocabulary learning from listening to chemistry videos. There was a control group in the study but it is not clear what they did. The effect of the treatment was small with an advantage for the computer group over the control of around six words on the blank-filling test with words provided and an advantage of one word on the sentence-writing test, and virtually equal gain scores on the receptive multiple-choice vocabulary cloze test.

There are astonishing websites like English Central with programs that provide video concordancing, allowing learners to see a range of video clips using a particular word.

Computer-assisted vocabulary learning can provide immediate feedback on success and progress. Groot (2000) reports on the program *CAVOCA* which uses increasingly informative sentence contexts, larger contexts and productive testing to quickly establish a large amount of vocabulary. An important feature of the program is the immediate informative feedback it gives. In comparison with non-computerised word-list learning, when the test favoured list learning (a receptive translation test), list learning did better. When the test favoured *CAVOCA* (a cloze test), *CAVOCA* did better. Groot argues that the contexts provided in the program result in better long-term retention than list learning, but that both kinds of learning are desirable.

Computer-assisted vocabulary learning can monitor and control learning conditions making sure that optimal conditions are applied according to research findings. Earlier in this chapter we looked at conditions for vocabulary learning, focusing on the conditions of noticing, retrieval and creative use. Computer-assisted vocabulary learning can set up these conditions very effectively. Noticing can be encouraged through the use of coloured, highlighted or flashing text. Retrieval can be encouraged through the use of delay and providing gradually increasing clues. Creative use is encouraged through meeting the vocabulary in a variety of contexts and in a variety of forms (spoken, written, pictorial).

Fox (1984) describes several programs that encourage retrieval of vocabulary with little textual context or with substantial textual context. Those with little textual context involve finding opposites, collocations and analogies. Those with substantial textual context involve restoring previously seen text or predicting the items needed to complete or continue a given text.

The Learning OS developed by Edunomics (cass@gol.com) has a set of vocabulary-learning programs which provide opportunity for spaced retrieval and which can make use of the learners' first language. The program keeps records of progress and provides useful feedback on the activities. A variety of exercise types allows for useful enrichment of the vocabulary items.

Research on the spacing of repetitions (see Chapter 4) indicates a useful role for computers in ensuring that the learner's effort is directed towards the vocabulary that most needs it. Some studies have looked at the effect on learning of giving learners control of the opportunity to repeat vocabulary or giving this control to the computer. Atkinson (1972) compared four repetition strategies:

1. Vocabulary is repeatedly presented in a random order.
2. Learners determine what vocabulary will occur in each trial.
3. The computer assumes that all items are of equal difficulty.
4. The computer assumes that all items are not of equal difficulty and provides repetition according to the learner's previous performance.

The best results as measured by a delayed post-test came from Condition 4, with Conditions 2 and 3 about equal and the random sequence the least effective. The differences in performance were large, with Condition 4 resulting in twice as much learning as the random-order condition.

In a somewhat similar study, van Bussel (1994: 72) found that learning style preference interacted with the type of sequence control.

Atkinson's (1972) study did not look at spaced repetition. Mondria and Mondria-de Vries's (1994) spacing suggestions for vocabulary cards can easily be applied to computer-assisted vocabulary learning and some programs have done this. See Chapter 11 on word cards for research on flashcard programs.

Computer-assisted vocabulary learning can adapt to the performance of the learner. Computer programs can store results and remember learners' performance. They can provide material at a level that is most suited to the learner's current level and can record where a learner needs to give further attention and provide for that.

Computer-assisted vocabulary learning can motivate and engage learners. Hubbard et al. (1986) looked at vocabulary learning through a CALL program which taught vocabulary using a short definition, an example sentence, and the opportunity to type in a keyword mnemonic. After a training session in using the program, the experimental group worked on the program independently for one hour a week in the computer laboratory. The results showed no correlation between vocabulary gains and gains on a reading test. When they looked back at the ways learners had used the program, Hubbard et al. found that the CALL program was accounting for only marginally more gains than what was happening outside the program. They also found that learners using the program were not using it effectively – they did not use the review lessons, they did not use the keyword mnemonic properly, and they did not use the practice tests. This was probably the result of low motivation and inadequate training. Clearly CALL is strongly dependent on engagement with the activities.

Qing and Kelly (2006) compared a group-administered versus individually monitored application of an elaborate CALL program called

Wufun. In general, scores on the individually monitored program were higher, indicating that computer-mediated instruction does not always keep motivation high. Their finding of higher learning gains on productive learning were an artefact of their calculation. In fact, if raw gains are divided by the number of words available for learning (not previously known) then receptive gains were higher which is in line with previous studies comparing receptive and productive knowledge. On average, learners gained around two to three words per hour.

Zapata and Sagarra (2007) compared online workbooks with paper workbooks for L2 vocabulary learning. After one semester there were no significant differences. After two semesters, the differences were significant but small (a 2.86 out of 30 difference between the two groups), in favour of the online groups. Online workbooks may be more motivating and provide repeated chances to learn. The strength of the study was the length of the treatments. The online workbooks provided immediate feedback while the paperwork book feedback came a week later.

Creating materials is likely to be much more involving than simply using materials. Nikolova (2002) compared learners reading with text, sound and picture annotations with learners who created their own annotations for the 20 target words. The test (immediate and one-month delay) was an L2→L1 word translation test. Although, without time being allowed for, the creating group performed better than the look-up group, the difference was still small (13 gain for the look-up group on the immediate post-test, and 15 gain for the creating group). The creating group however took over 2½ times as long (38 minutes) as the look-up group (15 minutes) to complete the activity. Clearly the look-up task was much more efficient.

So far, the research on computer-assisted vocabulary learning has not provided convincing and impressive results. This is likely to be the result of the newness of computer-assisted vocabulary learning and the need to develop programs that make the best use of the advantages it provides. It may also be that the more sophisticated programs are those that are commercially available because of the cost involved in developing them. It is more difficult to get permission to do research on such programs.

This chapter has looked at activities and procedures for teaching and learning vocabulary, including teaching techniques, ways of communicating meaning and computer-assisted vocabulary learning. These are all means of bringing conditions for learning into play. The quality of mental processing and the learning focuses set up by those learning conditions are what really matter. Teachers need to be able to examine the techniques they use and determine what goals they are trying to achieve, how they will achieve them and how they can adapt what they are doing if things are not going as planned.

References

Altarriba, J. and Knickerbocker, H. (2011). Acquiring second language vocabulary through the use of images and words. In Trofimovich, P. and McDonough, K. (eds.), *Applying Priming Methods to L2 Learning, Teaching and Research: 1* (pp. 21–47). Amsterdam: John Benjamins.

Anderson, R. C., Stevens, K. C., Shifrin, Z. and Osborn, J. (1978). Instantiation of word meanings in children. *Journal of Reading Behavior*, **10**, 2, 149–57.

Arevart, S. and Nation, I. S. P. (1991). Fluency improvement in a second language. *RELC Journal*, **22**, 1, 84–94.

Atkinson, R. C. (1972). Optimizing the learning of a second-language vocabulary. *Journal of Experimental Psychology*, **96**, 124–9.

Baddeley, A. (1990). *Human Memory*. London: Lawrence Erlbaum Associates.

Barcroft, J. (2002). Semantic and structural elaboration in L2 lexical acquisition. *Language Learning*, **52**, 2, 323–63.

Barcroft, J. (2004). Effects of sentence writing in second language lexical acquisition. *Second Language Research*, **20**, 4, 303–34.

Barcroft, J. (2006). Can writing a word detract from learning it? More negative effects of forced output during vocabulary learning. *Second Language Research*, **22**, 4, 487–97.

Barcroft, J. (2009). Effects of synonym generation on incidental and intentional L2 vocabulary learning during reading. *TESOL Quarterly*, **43**, 1, 79–103.

Baumann, J. F., Ware, D. and Edwards, E. C. (2007). "Bumping into spicy, tasty words that catch your tongue": A formative experiment on vocabulary instruction. *The Reading Teacher*, **61**, 2, 108–22.

Bawcom, L. (1995). Designing an advanced speaking course. *English Teaching Forum*, **33**, 1, 41–3.

Beck, I. L., McKeown, M. G. and Omanson, R. C. (1987). The effects and uses of diverse vocabulary instructional techniques. In McKeown, M. and Curtis, M. (eds.), *The Nature of Vocabulary Acquisition* (pp. 147–63). Mahwah, NJ: Lawrence Erlbaum Associates.

Bishop, H. (2004). The effect of typographic salience on the look up and comprehension of unknown formulaic sequences. In Schmitt, N. (ed.), *Formulaic Sequences*. Amsterdam: John Benjamins.

Blake, M. E. and Majors, P. L. (1995). Recycled words: Holistic instruction for LEP students. *Journal of Adolescent and Adult Literacy*, **39**, 2, 132–7.

Bolger, P. and Zapata, G. (2011). Semantic categories and context in L2 vocabulary learning. *Language Learning*, **61**, 2, 614–46.

Bramki, D. and Williams, R. C. (1984). Lexical familiarization in economics text, and its pedagogic implications in reading comprehension. *Reading in a Foreign Language*, **2**, 1, 169–81.

Brett, A., Rothlein, L. and Hurley, M. (1996). Vocabulary acquisition from listening to stories and explanations of target words. *Elementary School Journal*, **96**, 4, 415–22.

Brown, D. F. (1974). Advanced vocabulary teaching: The problem of collocation. *RELC Journal*, **5**, 2, 1–11.

Brown, R., Waring, R. and Donkaewbua, S. (2008). Incidental vocabulary acquisition from reading, reading-while-listening, and listening to stories. *Reading in a Foreign Language*, **20**, 2, 136–63.

Bruton, A. and García-López, M. (2007). Readers respond to K.S. Folse's "The effect of type of written exercise on L2 vocabulary retention". *TESOL Quarterly*, **41**, 1, 172–7.

Burling, R. (1983). A proposal for computer-assisted instruction in vocabulary. *System*, **11**, 2, 181–90.

Celik, M. (2003). Teaching vocabulary through code-mixing. *ELT Journal*, **57**, 4, 361–9.

Channell, J. (1981). Applying semantic theory to vocabulary teaching. *ELT Journal*, **35**, 2, 115–22.

Chaudron, C. (1982). Vocabulary elaboration in teachers' speech to L2 learners. *Studies in Second Language Acquisition*, **4**, 2, 170–80.

Cobb, T. (1997). Is there any measurable learning from hands-on concordancing? *System*, **25**, 3, 301–15.

Cohen, A. D., Oxford, R. L. and Chi, J. C. (2006). Learning style survey: Assessing your learning styles. In Cohen, S. A. and Weaver, S. J. (eds.), *Styles- and Strategy-based Instruction: A Teachers' Guide* (pp. 15–21). Minneapolis: Center for Advanced Research on Language Acquisition, University of Minnesota.

Coll, J. F. (2002). Richness of sematic encoding in a hypermedia-assisted instructional environment for ESP: Effects on incidental vocabulary retention among learners with low ability in the target language. *ReCALL*, **14**, 2, 263–84.

D'Anna, C. A., Zechmeister, E. B. and Hall, J. W. (1991). Toward a meaningful definition of vocabulary size. *Journal of Reading Behavior: A Journal of Literacy*, **23**, 1, 109–22.

de Groot, A. (2006). Effects of stimulus characteristics and background music on foreign language vocabulary learning and forgetting. *Language Learning*, **56**, 3, 463–506.

de Jong, N. and Perfetti, C. (2011). Fluency training in the ESL classroom: An experimental study of fluency development and proceduralization. *Language Learning*, **61**, 2, 533–68.

De Ridder, I. (2002). Visible or invisible links: Does the highlighting of hyperlinks affect incidental vocabulary learning, text comprehension, and the reading process? *Language Learning & Technology*, **6**, 1, 123–46.

Deconinck, J. (2012). *Fubbing foppotees and blandishing mattoids: Harnessing form–meaning motivation for the recall and retention of L2 lexis*. Vrije Universiteit Brussel, Brussels.

Deconinck, J., Boers, F. and Eyckmans, J. (2010). Helping learners engage with L2 words: The form–meaning fit. *AILA Review*, **23**, 95–114.

deHaan, J., Reed, W. M. and Kuwada, K. (2010). The effect of interactivity with a music video game on second language vocabulary recall. *Language Learning & Technology*, **14**, 2, 79–94.

Descamps, J. L. (1992). Towards classroom concordancing. In Arnaud, P. J. L. and Bejoint, H. (eds.), *Vocabulary and Applied Linguistics* (pp. 167–81). London: Macmillan.

Dowhower, S. L. (1989). Repeated reading: research into practice. *The Reading Teacher*, **42**, 502–7.

Dunbar, S. (1992). Developing vocabulary by integrating language and content. *TESL Canada Journal*, **9**, 2, 73–9.

Elgort, I. (2011). Deliberate learning and vocabulary acquisition in a second language. *Language Learning*, **61**, 2, 367–413.

Elley, W. B. (1989). Vocabulary acquisition from listening to stories. *Reading Research Quarterly*, **24**, 2, 174–87.

Ellis, N. C. (1995). Vocabulary acquisition: Psychological perspectives and pedagogical implications. *The Language Teacher*, **19**, 2, 12–16.

Ellis, R. (1990). *Instructed Second Language Acquisition*. Oxford: Basil Blackwell.

Ellis, R. (1991). The interaction hypothesis: A critical evaluation. In Sadtono, E. (ed.), *Language Acquisition and the Second/Foreign Language Classroom. RELC Anthology: Series 28* (pp. 179–211). Singapore: SEAMEO-RELC.

Ellis, R. (1994). Factors in the incidental acquisition of second language vocabulary from oral input: A review essay. *Applied Language Learning*, **5**, 1, 1–32.

Ellis, R. (1995). Modified oral input and the acquisition of word meanings. *Applied Linguistics*, **16**, 4, 409–41.

Ellis, R. and He, X. (1999). The roles of modified input and output in the incidental acquisition of word meanings. *Studies in Second Language Acquisition*, **21**, 285–301.

Ellis, R. and Heimbach, R. (1997). Bugs and birds: Children's acquisition of second language vocabulary through interaction. *System*, **25**, 2, 247–59.

Ellis, R., Tanaka, Y. and Yamazaki, A. (1994). Classroom interaction, comprehension and the acquisition of L2 word meanings. *Language Learning*, **44**, 3, 449–91.

Feeny, T. P. (1976). Vocabulary teaching as a means of vocabulary expansion. *Foreign Language Annals*, **9**, 5, 485–6.

File, K. and Adams, R. (2010). Should vocabulary instruction be integrated or isolated? *TESOL Quarterly*, **44**, 2, 222–49.

Flick, W. C. and Anderson, J. I. (1980). Rhetorical difficulty in scientific English: A study in reading comprehension. *TESOL Quarterly*, **14**, 3, 345–51.

Flowerdew, J. (1992). Definitions in science lectures. *Applied Linguistics*, **13**, 2, 202–21.

Folse, K. (2006). The effect of type of written exercise on L2 vocabulary retention. *TESOL Quarterly*, **40**, 2, 273–93.

Folse, K. (2007). The author replies. *TESOL Quarterly*, **41**, 1, 177–80.

Fowle, C. (2002). Vocabulary notebooks: Implementation and outcomes. *ELT Journal*, **56**, 4, 380–88.

Fox, J. (1984). Computer-assisted vocabulary learning. *ELT Journal*, **38**, 1, 27–33.

Francis, W. N. and Kučera, H. (1982). *Frequency Analysis of English Usage*. Boston: Houghton Mifflin Company.

Gibson, R. E. (1975). The strip story: A catalyst for communication. *TESOL Quarterly*, 9, 2, 149–54.

Graves, M. F. (2006). *The Vocabulary Book: Learning and Instruction*. Newark: International Reading Association.

Groot, P. J. M. (2000). Computer assisted second language vocabulary acquisition. *Language Learning & Technology*, 4, 1, 60–81.

Hall, S. J. (1991). *The Effect of Split Information Tasks on the Acquisition of Mathematics vocabulary*. Victoria University of Wellington, Wellington.

Han, Z., Park, E. S. and Combs, C. (2008). Textual enhancement of input: Issues and possibilities. *Applied Linguistics*, 29, 4, 597–618.

Harrington, M. (1994). CompLex: A tool for the development of L2 vocabulary knowledge. *Journal of Artificial Intelligence in Education*, 5, 4, 481–99.

Haynes, M. and Baker, I. (1993). American and Chinese readers learning from lexical familiarization in English text. In Huckin, T., Haynes, M. and Coady, J. (eds.), *Second Language Reading and Vocabulary* (pp. 130–52). Norwood, NJ: Ablex.

Higa, M. (1963). Interference effects of intralist word relationships in verbal learning. *Journal of Verbal Learning and Verbal Behavior*, 2, 170–75.

Hubbard, P., Coady, J., Graney, J., Mokhtari, K. and Magoto, J. (1986). Report on a pilot study of the relationship of high frequency vocabulary knowledge and reading proficiency in ESL readers. *Ohio University Papers in Linguistics and Language Teaching*, 8, 48–57.

Hulstijn, J. H. (1993). When do foreign-language readers look up the meaning of unfamiliar words? The influence of task and learner variables. *Modern Language Journal*, 77, 2, 139–47.

Hulstijn, J. and Laufer, B. (2001). Some empirical evidence for the involvement load hypothesis in vocabulary acquisition. *Language Learning*, 51, 3, 539–58.

Hummel, K. (2010). Translation and short-term vocabulary retention: Hindrance or help? *Language Teaching Research*, 14, 1, 61–74.

Ilson, R. (1983). Etymological information: Can it help our students? *ELT Journal*, 37, 1, 76–82.

Joe, A. (1995). Text-based tasks and incidental vocabulary learning. *Second Language Research*, 11, 2, 149–58.

Jordan, R. R. (1990). Pyramid discussions. *ELT Journal*, 44, 1, 46–54.

Keating, G. (2008). Task effectiveness and word learning in a second language: The involvement load hypothesis on trial. *Language Teaching Research*, 12, 3, 365–86.

Kim, Y. (2006). Effects of input elaboration on vocabulary acquisition through reading by Korean learners of English as a foreign language. *TESOL Quarterly*, 40, 2, 341–73.

Kim, Y. (2008). The contribution of collaborative and individual tasks to the acquisition of L2 vocabulary. *Modern Language Journal*, 92, 1, 114–30.

Knight, S. M. (1994). Dictionary use while reading: The effects on comprehension and vocabulary acquisition for students of different verbal abilities. *Modern Language Journal*, 78, 3, 285–99.

Kundu, M. (1988). Riddles in the ESL/EFL classroom: Teaching vocabulary and structure. *Modern English Teacher*, **15**, 3, 22–4.

Lado, R., Baldwin, B. and Lobo, F. (1967). *Massive Vocabulary Expansion in a Foreign Language Beyond the Basic Course: The Effects of Stimuli, Timing and Order of Presentation*. Washington, DC: U.S. Department of Health, Education, and Welfare.

Laufer, B. (1989). A factor of difficulty in vocabulary learning: Deceptive transparency. *AILA Review*, **6**, 10–20.

Laufer, B. and Hulstijn, J. (2001). Incidental vocabulary acquisition in a second language: The construct of task-induced involvement. *Applied Linguistics*, **22**, 1, 1–26.

Laufer, B. and Osimo, H. (1991). Facilitating long-term retention of vocabulary: The second-hand cloze. *System*, **19**, 3, 217–24.

Laufer, B. and Shmueli, K. (1997). Memorizing new words: Does teaching have anything to do with it? *RELC Journal*, **28**, 1, 89–108.

Lazarton, A. (2004). Gesture and speech in the vocabulary explanations of one ESL teacher: A microanalytic enquiry. *Language Learning*, **54**, 1, 79–117.

Lee, S. H. (2008). Beyond reading and proficiency assessment: The rational cloze procedure as stimulus for integrated reading, writing, and vocabulary instruction and teacher–student interaction. *System*, **36**, 4, 642–60.

Loschky, L. and Bley-Vroman, R. (1993). Grammar and task-based methodology. In Crookes, G. and Gass, S. (eds.), *Tasks and Language Learning* (pp. 122–67). Clevedon, Avon: Multilingual Matters.

Lotto, L. and De Groot, A. (1998). Effects of learning method and word type on acquiring vocabulary in an unfamiliar language. *Language Learning*, **48**, 1, 31–69.

Martin, M., Martin, S. and Wang, Y. (2002). The vocabulary self-collection strategy in the ESL classroom. *TESOL Journal*, **11**, 2, 34–5.

Maurice, K. (1983). The fluency workshop. *TESOL Newsletter*, **8**, 83.

McCafferty, S. G., Roebuck, R. F. and Wayland, R. P. (2001). Activity theory and the incidental learning of second -language vocabulary. *Language Awareness*, **10**, 4, 289–94.

McCrostie, J. (2007). Examining learner vocabulary notebooks. *ELT Journal*, **61**, 3, 246–55.

McDaniel, M. A. and Pressley, M. (1989). Keyword and context instruction of new vocabulary meanings: effects on text comprehension and memory. *Journal of Educational Psychology*, **81**, 2, 204–13.

McKeown, M. G. (1993). Creating effective definitions for young word learners. *Reading Research Quarterly*, **28**, 1, 17–31.

McKeown, M. G., Beck, I. L., Omanson, R. G. and Pople, M. T. (1985). Some effects of the nature and frequency of vocabulary instruction on the knowledge and use of words. *Reading Research Quarterly*, **20**, 5, 522–35.

McLaughlin, B. (1990). Restructuring. *Applied Linguistics*, **11**, 2, 113–28.

McWilliam, N. (1998). *What's in a Word? Vocabulary Development in Multilingual Classrooms*. Stoke on Trent: Trentham Books.

Mhone, Y. W. (1988). "...It's My Word, Teacher!" *English Teaching Forum*, **26**, 2, 48–51.

Miller, G. A. and Gildea, P. M. (1987). How children learn words. *Scientific American*, **257**, 3, 86–91.

Mishima, T. (1967). An experiment comparing five modalities of conveying meaning for the teaching of foreign language vocabulary. *Dissertation Abstracts*, **27**, 3030–31A.

Mondria, J. A. and Mondria-de Vries, S. (1994). Efficiently memorizing words with the help of word cards and "hand computer": Theory and applications. *System*, **22**, 1, 47–57.

Morris, C. D., Bransford, J. D. and Franks, J. J. (1977). Levels of processing versus transfer appropriate processing. *Journal of Verbal Learning and Verbal Behavior*, **16**, 519–33.

Nagy, W. E. (1997). On the role of context in first- and second-language learning. In Schmitt, N. and McCarthy, M. (eds.), *Vocabulary: Description, Acquisition and Pedagogy* (pp. 64–83). Cambridge: Cambridge University Press.

Nation, I. S. P. (1978a). 'What is it?': A multipurpose language teaching technique. *English Teaching Forum*, **16**, 3, 20–23, 32.

Nation, I. S. P. (1978b). Translation and the teaching of meaning: Some techniques. *ELT Journal*, **32**, 3, 171–5.

Nation, I. S. P. (1982). Beginning to learn foreign vocabulary: A review of the research. *RELC Journal*, **13**, 1, 14–36.

Nation, I. S. P. (1989). Improving speaking fluency. *System*, **17**, 3, 377–84.

Nation, I. S. P. (1990). *Teaching and Learning Vocabulary*. Rowley, MA: Newbury House.

Nation, I. S. P. (1993). Using dictionaries to estimate vocabulary size: Essential, but rarely followed, procedures. *Language Testing*, **10**, 1, 27–40.

Nation, I. S. P. (1997). The language learning benefits of extensive reading. *The Language Teacher*, **21**, 5, 13–16.

Nation, I. S. P. (2000). Learning vocabulary in lexical sets: Dangers and guidelines. *TESOL Journal*, **9**, 2, 6–10.

Nation, I. S. P. (2005). Reading faster. *Pasaa*, **30**, 21–37.

Nation, I. S. P. (2009). *Teaching ESL/EFL Reading and Writing*. New York: Routledge.

Nation, I. S. P. and Newton, J. (2009). *Teaching ESL/EFL Listening and Speaking*. New York: Routledge.

Nation, P. and Wang, K. (1999). Graded readers and vocabulary. *Reading in a Foreign Language*, **12**, 2, 355–80.

Nation, I. S. P. and Webb, S. (2011). *Researching and Analyzing Vocabulary*. Boston: Heinle Cengage Learning.

Nesi, H. and Meara, P. (1994). Patterns of misinterpretation in the productive use of EFL dictionary definitions. *System*, **22**, 1, 1–15.

Newton, J. (2013). Incidental vocabulary learning in classroom communication tasks. *Language Teaching Research*, **17**, 3, 164–87.

Nikolova, O. R. (2002). Effects of students' participation in authoring of multimedia materials on student acquisition of vocabulary. *Language Learning & Technology*, **6**, 1, 100–122.

Nist, S. L. and Olejnik, S. (1995). The role of context and dictionary definitions on varying levels of word knowledge. *Reading Research Quarterly*, **30**, 2, 172–93.

Paivio, A. and Desrochers, A. (1981). Mnemonic techniques in second-language learning. *Journal of Educational Psychology*, **73**, 6, 780–95.

Palmberg, R. (1988). Computer games and foreign-language learning. *ELT Journal*, **42**, 4, 247–51.

Palmer, D. M. (1982). Information transfer for listening and reading. *English Teaching Forum*, **20**, 1, 29–33.

Pienemann, M. (1985). Learnability and syllabus construction. In Hyltenstam, K. and Pienemann, M. (eds.), *Modelling and Assessing Second Language Development* (pp. 23–75). Clevedon: Multilingual Matters.

Pulido, D. (2004). The relationship between text comprehension and second language incidental vocabulary acquisition: A matter of topic familiarity? *Language Learning*, **54**, 3, 469–523.

Pulido, D. (2007). The effects of topic familiarity and passage sight vocabulary on L2 lexical inferencing and retention through reading. *Applied Linguistics*, **28**, 1, 66–86.

Pyc, M. A. and Rawson, K. A. (2007). Examining the efficiency of schedules of distributed retrieval practice. *Memory & Cognition*, **35**, 8, 1917–27.

Qian, D. (1999). Assessing the roles of depth and breadth of vocabulary knowledge in reading comprehension. *Canadian Modern Language Review*, **56**, 2, 282–307.

Qing, M. and Kelly, P. (2006). Computer assisted vocabulary learning: Design and evaluation. *Computer Assisted Language Learning*, **19**, 1, 15–45.

Rasinski, T. V. (1989). Fluency for everyone: Incorporating fluency instruction in the classroom. *The Reading Teacher*, **42**, 690–93.

Richards, J. C. and Taylor, A. (1992). Defining strategies in folk definitions. *Working Papers of the Department of English, City Polytechnic of Hong Kong*, **4**, 2, 1–8.

Rott, S. (2005). Processing glosses: A qualitative exploration of how form–meaning connections are established and strengthened. *Reading in a Foreign Language*, **17**, 2, 95–124.

Rott, S. (2007). The effect of frequency of input-enhancements on word learning and text comprehension. *Language Learning*, **57**, 2, 165–99.

Rowland, L. (2011). Lessons about learning: Comparing learner experiences with language research. *Language Teaching Research*, **15**, 2, 254–67.

Rudzka, B., Channell, J., Putseys, Y. and Ostyn, P. (1981). *The Words You Need*. London: Macmillan.

Saragi, T., Nation, I. S. P. and Meister, G. F. (1978). Vocabulary learning and reading. *System*, **6**, 2, 72–8.

Schmidt, R. W. (1990). The role of consciousness in second language learning. *Applied Linguistics*, **11**, 2, 129–58.

Schmidt, R. W. and Frota, S. (1986). Developing basic conversational ability in a second language: A case study of an adult learner of Portugese. In Day, R. (ed.), *Talking to Learn: Conversation in Second Language Acquisition* (pp. 237–326). Rowley, MA: Newbury House.

Schmitt, N. (2000). *Vocabulary in Language Teaching*. Cambridge: Cambridge University Press.

Schmitt, N. (2008). Teaching vocabulary. Pearson Education handout.

Schmitt, N. and Schmitt, D. (1995). Vocabulary notebooks: Theoretical underpinnings and practical suggestions. *ELT Journal*, **49**, 2, 133–43.

Scott, J. A. and Nagy, W. E. (1997). Understanding the definitions of unfamiliar verbs. *Reading Research Quarterly*, 32, 2, 184–200.

Scott, J. A. and Nagy, W. E. (2004). Developing word consciousness. In Baumann, J. F. and Kame'enui, E. J. (eds.), *Vocabulary Instruction: Research to Practice* (pp. 201–17). Guilford Press: New York.

Sen, A. L. (1983). Teaching vocabulary through riddles. *English Teaching Forum*, 21, 2, 12–17.

Sinclair, J. M. (1991). *Corpus, Concordance, Collocation*. Oxford: Oxford University Press.

Sokmen, A. J. (1992). Students as vocabulary generators. *TESOL Journal*, 1, 4, 16–18.

Stahl, S. A. and Clark, C. H. (1987). The effects of participatory expectations in classroom discussion on the learning of science vocabulary. *American Educational Research Journal*, 24, 4, 541–5.

Stahl, S. A. and Fairbanks, M. M. (1986). The effects of vocabulary instruction: A model-based meta-analysis. *Review of Educational Research*, 56, 1, 72–110.

Stahl, S. A. and Vancil, S. J. (1986). Discussion is what makes semantic maps work in vocabulary instruction. *The Reading Teacher*, 40, 1, 62–7.

Stevens, V. (1991). Classroom concordancing: Vocabulary materials derived from relevant, authentic text. *English for Specific Purposes*, 10, 35–46.

Stieglitz, E. L. (1983). A practical approach to vocabulary reinforcement. *ELT Journal*, 37, 1, 71–5.

Stieglitz, E. L. and Stieglitz, V. S. (1981). SAVOR the word to reinforce vocabulary in the content areas. *Journal of Reading*, 25, 1, 46–51.

Stockwell, G. (2007). Vocabulary on the move: Investigating an intelligent mobile phone-based vocabulary tutor. *Computer Assisted Language Learning*, 20, 4, 365–83.

Strapp, C. M., Helmick, A. L., Tonkovich, H. M. and Bleakney, D. M. (2011). Effects of negative and positive evidence on adult word learning. *Language Learning*, 61, 2, 506–32.

Sun, Y. and Dong, Q. (2004). An experiment on supporting children's English vocabulary learning in multimedia context. *Computer Assisted Language Learning*, 17, 2, 131–47.

Swanborn, M. S. L. and de Glopper, K. (1999). Incidental word learning while reading: A meta-analysis. *Review of Educational Research*, 69, 3, 261–85.

Thurstun, J. and Candlin, C. N. (1998). Concordancing and the teaching of the vocabulary of academic English. *English for Specific Purposes*, 17, 3, 267–80.

Tight, D. (2010). Perceptual learning style matching and L2 vocabulary acquisition. *Language Learning*, 60, 4, 792–833.

Tinkham, T. (1993). The effect of semantic clustering on the learning of second language vocabulary. *System*, 21, 3, 371–80.

Tinkham, T. (1997). The effects of semantic and thematic clustering on the learning of second language vocabulary. *Second Language Research*, 13, 2, 138–63.

van Bussel, F. J. J. (1994). Design rules for computer-aided learning of vocabulary items in a second language. *Computers in Human Behavior*, 10, 63–76.

van Elsen, E., van Deun, K. and Decoo, W. (1991). Wordchip: The application of external versatility to an English lexical CALL program. *System*, **19**, 4, 401–17.

Verspoor, M. and Lowie, W. (2003). Making sense of polysemous words. *Language Learning*, **53**, 3, 547–86.

Vidal, K. (2011). A comparison of the effects of reading and listening on incidental vocabulary acquisition. *Language Learning*, **61**, 1, 219–58.

Visser, A. (1989). Learning core meanings. *Guidelines*, **11**, 2, 10–17.

Walters, J. and Bozkurt, N. (2009). The effect of keeping vocabulary notebooks on vocabulary acquisition. *Language Teaching Research*, **13**, 4, 403–23.

Waring, R. (1997). The negative effects of learning words in semantic sets: A replication. *System*, **25**, 2, 261–74.

Watanabe, Y. (1997). Effects of single and multiple-choice glosses on incidental vocabulary learning. *JACET Bulletin*, **28**, 177–91.

Webb, S. (2007a). Learning word pairs and glossed sentences: The effects of a single context on vocabulary knowledge. *Language Teaching Research*, **11**, 1, 63–81.

Webb, S. (2007b). The effects of repetition on vocabulary knowledge. *Applied Linguistics*, **28**, 1, 46–65.

Webb, S. (2008). The effects of context on incidental vocabulary learning. *Reading in a Foreign Language*, **20**, 232–45.

Winn, S. (1996). Vocabulary revitalized. *TESOL Journal*, **5**, 4, 40.

Wittrock, M. C. (1974). Learning as a generative process. *Educational Psychologist*, **11**, 1, 87–95.

Wittrock, M. C. (1991). Generative teaching of comprehension. *Elementary School Journal*, **92**, 2, 169–84.

Wodinsky, M. and Nation, P. (1988). Learning from graded readers. *Reading in a Foreign Language*, **5**, 1, 155–61.

Woodward, T. (1985). From vocabulary review to classroom dictionary. *Modern English Teacher*, **12**, 4, 29.

Woodward, T. (1988). Vocabulary posters. *Modern English Teacher*, **15**, 3, 31–2.

Zapata, G. and Sagarra, N. (2007). CALL on hold: The delayed benefits of an online workbook on L2 vocabulary learning. *Computer Assisted Language Learning*, **20**, 2, 153–71.

4 Vocabulary and listening and speaking

This chapter looks at opportunities for vocabulary learning through the oral skills of listening and speaking. With careful thought and planning, listening and speaking can be important means of vocabulary growth.

What vocabulary knowledge is needed for listening?

Learning vocabulary through listening is one type of learning through meaning-focused input. Learners would need at least 95% coverage of the running words in the input in order to gain reasonable comprehension and to have reasonable success at guessing from context. Van Zeeland and Schmitt (In press) found that 95% coverage was adequate for listening to informal narratives. Staehr (2009) found 98% coverage was needed for academic listening. A coverage of 98% (one unknown word in every 50 words, or about two or three unknown words per minute) is not surprisingly better than less coverage (Bonk, 2000; Hu and Nation, 2000; Schmitt et al., 2011; van Zeeland and Schmitt, 2012). Studies of spoken language, especially colloquial spoken language used in informal situations, indicate that a vocabulary of around 3,000 word families is needed to provide around 95% coverage (Adolphs and Schmitt, 2003, 2004; Webb and Rodgers, 2009a, 2009b). Around 5,000–6,000 words are needed to get 98% coverage. More formal academic spoken language makes more use of the vocabulary in the Academic Word List, which provides around 4% coverage of university lectures. Typically, as vocabulary size increases, so does written comprehension (Schmitt et al., 2011).

Staehr (2009) found high correlations between performance on a listening test and a measure of vocabulary size (.7) and a measure of vocabulary depth (.65). The two vocabulary tests correlated highly with each other (.8) and together accounted for 51% of the variance in listening comprehension scores. Vocabulary knowledge is clearly an important aspect of listening. Vocabulary size is more important than knowledge of specific vocabulary. This is probably because vocabulary size is not just an indicator of how much vocabulary is known but is an indicator of reading proficiency, listening proficiency, and possibly a range of other factors like motivation, time spent learning English, experience in language use, skill at guessing from context, and so on.

Webb and Rodgers (2009a and b) found a vocabulary of around 6,000 word families was needed to gain 98% coverage of the words in movies and television programmes. Because of the support provided by visuals, they suggested that a vocabulary size of 3,000 words (providing 95% coverage) may be enough to cope with movies and television programmes. Learning rates are likely to be improved by repeated watching of the same movie. In a typical movie of about 110 minutes long, there could be around 139 new word families for learners who know 3,000 words, but this figure would vary depending on the length of the movie. Some movie genres they looked at had lighter vocabulary loads than others.

Van Zeeland and Schmitt (2012) looked at the lexical coverage needed for L1 and L2 learners to comprehend narrative listening text as measured by a 10-item multiple-choice test. Each story was listened to twice. As coverage increased (90%, 95%, 98%, 100%), so did comprehension. Van Zeeland and Schmitt argue that 95% coverage is adequate for a moderate level of comprehension and some learners can gain very good comprehension with this coverage.

Research on coverage generally supports the idea that the greater the coverage, the better the comprehension, although there is some as yet unpublished evidence that total vocabulary size may be a better predictor of comprehension. What coverage level and thus what vocabulary size is seen as being necessary for adequate comprehension will depend on how comprehension is conceptualised and operationalised by researchers and will also depend on the nature of the texts and the circumstances under which they are listened to.

The spoken/written distinction is the primary distinction affecting the type of vocabulary used, the occurrence of multiword units (Shin, 2009), and the nature of grammatical complexity (Biber and Conrad, 2009). Cummins (1986) attempted to incorporate the skills of L2 face-to-face communication and performance on L2 cognitive/academic tasks into a construct of 'language proficiency', in order to account for the relationship between language proficiency and academic achievement. Cummins used two continua as in Figure 4.1.

Informal speaking skills are in the top left section, usually being cognitively undemanding (dealing with familiar topics) and context

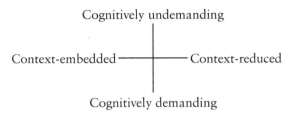

Figure 4.1 Cummins' framework of language proficiency

embedded (related to here and now). Academic discourse is in the bottom right being cognitively demanding (having a high information load) and context reduced (constructing its own mental reality).

Bonk (2000) used four short tape-recorded texts which were equated for total number of words, number of unique words, number of unique lexical words, number of syllables and duration of recording. They were all on similar topics of imaginary native customs. The texts deliberately differed from each other in the number of low-frequency words they contained. The learners listened to all four texts and wrote a recall protocol using either L1 or L2, as they preferred. These were scored on a four-point scale as a measure of comprehension of the texts. The same passages were then given as dictations with pauses between the phrases. The lexical words in the dictations were scored (minor spelling and grammatical errors were ignored) as a measure of the familiarity of the lexical items. That is, if a lexical word was adequately reproduced in the dictation by the learners, it was considered to be known. If not, it was considered by the researcher as unknown. Bonk found a significant but moderate correlation of .446 between comprehension (L1 or L2 recall) and amount of familiar lexis (dictation score). There was a significant difference between lexical recognition scores associated with good text recall and those associated with poor text recall. There were however many examples of 100% lexical scores associated with inferior comprehension. There was no clear lexical cut-off point for good comprehension, but lexical scores under 80% were unlikely to be matched with good comprehension. Function words make up around 44% of the running words in texts; 80% of the content words (80% of 56%) gives 45% coverage resulting on a total coverage of around 90%.

A vocabulary correlate of the cognitively demanding/context-reduced tasks would be the Academic Word List, that is, the subtechnical academic vocabulary common to a wide range of academic disciplines (Appendix 1). This contrasts with the prerequisite high-frequency general service vocabulary which would serve most communication needs in cognitively undemanding/context-embedded tasks. Cummins (1986: 156–7) considers that it takes immigrant students two years to gain face-to-face L2 communication skills, but between five and seven years to approach grade norms in L2 academic skills. From a vocabulary perspective, this means about two years to gain control of the 2,000 high-frequency general service words, and three to five years more to gain control of the academic vocabulary and other relevant mid-frequency and technical words. It is thus important to look at learners' proposed language use when deciding what vocabulary will be needed.

The True/False test in the free Vocabulary Resource Booklet on Paul Nation's website can be used to test listening vocabulary. The learners need to be able to see the relevant pictures when they are required. There are two forms of the test and the test items were graded according to the frequency of the tested words in West (1953). Details of the construction of the test can be found in Nation (1983). A vocabulary-based dictation test is described in Fountain and Nation (2000) and Nation (1990: 86–7). This test consists of five paragraphs with each successive paragraph containing words from a lower frequency level. Only the content words are scored when marking the test. There is a form of the test in Appendix 2.

Chang (2007) found that studying 25 relevant words before doing a listening comprehension test improved vocabulary knowledge as measured before the listening, but had no measurable effects on listening comprehension. Learners had different vocabulary preparation times and these resulted in scores of 76% (one-week preparation), 65% (one-day preparation) and 63% (30 minutes preparation) on the vocabulary test.

How can we provide vocabulary support for listening?

Vocabulary plays an important role in listening. Among ten problems related to listening comprehension, Goh (2000) included the four vocabulary-related problems of (1) learners do not recognise words they know; (2) learners cannot chunk the stream of speech; (3) learners are unable to form a mental representation of the words they hear; and (4) learners understand the words but not the message. Goh provides a substantial list of activities for improving listening comprehension which can be usefully balanced with graded message-focused practice and listening.

There are several ways of supporting listening by providing written input that is directly related to the listening task. These ways are very useful where learners have quite a large reading vocabulary but have had little opportunity to improve their listening skills.

Receptive information transfer

Receptive information transfer activities involve turning listening input into some diagrammatic form. Here is an example where learners have to fill in a timetable as they listen to two students talking to each other about their classes.

	Monday	Tuesday	Wednesday	Thursday	Friday
9–10			Mathematics		
10–11	Geography			English	
1–2		Art	Sport		
2–3			Sport		

Note that some of the places are already filled in. This helps learners check where they are on the task and provides helpful vocabulary that they will hear in the spoken description. It would also be possible to provide some of the written words underneath the table that have to be put in the appropriate place. Palmer (1982) has a very rich range of suggestions for the content of information transfer activities. Here are some of his categories.

- Maps and plans: streets, tours, architects plans, theatre seats, weather forecasts
- Grids and tables: passport details, polls, timetables, football results
- Diagrams and charts: family trees, weather records, pie graphs, flow charts
- Diaries and calendars: office holidays, appointments, hotel bookings
- Lists, forms, coupons: radio programmes, menus, diets, shopping lists, car rental forms

Using captions with videos

Syodorenko (2010) looked at the effects of same language captions and audio on watching videos. She found that captions had a positive effect on a written test of recognition of word forms, while the video plus audio group scored higher on an aural recognition test. The difference however was small, but modality of testing clearly needs to take into account the modality of learning. The group with a video, audio and captions learned more word meanings than the group without captions. Brown et al. (2008) found that listening only produced the lowest vocabulary-learning scores compared to reading only and reading while listening. Multiple-choice test vocabulary scores for listening were around nine out of 28 and remained largely unchanged on an immediate, one-week delayed, and three-months delayed post-test. Vocabulary translation test scores for listening averaged less than one out of 28. It seems there are reasonable amounts of vocabulary learning from listening but it is very much partial learning which would need reinforcement. Learners in the experiment liked reading while listening and it was strongly preferred over listening only.

Listening while reading

Learners can listen while they also read a written version of what they are listening to, and this can make a very good contribution to vocabulary learning (Brown, Waring, and Donkaewbua, 2008; Webb and Chang, 2012; Webb et al., 2013). Many graded readers are now accompanied by CDs and these can provide useful listening work. Repeated reading of short texts (around 300 words) while listening to a recording can result in substantial vocabulary learning. Webb and Chang (2012) compared repeated reading without listening with repeated reading with listening, and found that both treatments contributed to vocabulary learning as measured by a recall test, but repeated reading while listening resulted in much more vocabulary learning. Webb et al. (2013) found that listening while reading also contributed to the learning of collocations where they were repeated in the text.

Listening to stories

The teacher reads a story to the learners and writes important words on the blackboard as they occur in the story. During a ten-minute period about 20 to 30 words will be written on the board. While reading the story aloud the teacher should repeat sentences, and go at a speed that the learners can easily keep up with. This should be done two or three times a week for a few minutes each time in the same way as a serial occurs on television. Graded readers which are within the learners' vocabulary level are suitable. The Extensive Reading Foundation website is a useful source of prize-winning titles. Learners can also listen to stories that they have already read.

Quizzes

Quiz competitions can be a useful means of vocabulary expansion. The learners can be divided into teams and points given for correct answers. Manzo (1970) suggests that extra points can be given for a correct answer plus some extra detail. The teacher can prepare the questions so that useful vocabulary occurs in them.

What helps vocabulary learning from listening to stories?

There is a growing body of evidence (Brett et al., 1996; Elley, 1989) that learners can pick up new vocabulary as they are being read to. There are several conditions that make this learning more likely, and in this section we will look at how teachers can make sure that these conditions occur when they read aloud to their learners. The main conditions are interest in the content of the story, comprehension of the story, understanding of the unknown words and retrieval of the meaning of those not yet strongly established, decontextualisation of the target words, and thoughtful creative processing of the target vocabulary.

Interest

The most important condition to encourage learning relates to the choice of what is read, namely interest (Elley, 1989). Learners need to be interested in what they are listening to. Elley explained the differing amounts of vocabulary learning from two stories by the lack of involvement of the learners with one of the stories. Similarly, the vocabulary most likely to be learned was strongly related to the main ideas of the story. Teachers can help arouse learners' interest by choosing stories that learners are likely to be interested in, by presenting a story in serial form so that interest increases episode by episode, and by involving the learners in the story as in shared book reading where the teacher interacts with the learners about the story (Day and Bamford, 2004: 48–9).

Comprehension

Learners need to be able to understand the story. There are several sources of difficulty in learning vocabulary from listening to stories. At one level there is the vocabulary load of the story, that is, the density of unknown words. At another level there is the support provided by pictures and definitions. At yet another level there are the forms and meanings of the words themselves. Background knowledge, pictures and explanation can all make a story easier (Elley, 1989).

Difficulty also operates at the word level (Ellis, 1995; Higa, 1965). Ellis et al. (1994) found that shorter words were easier to learn than longer words. This suggests that when reading aloud to a class, it may be useful to break longer words into parts, if they are complex words, so that their formally simpler stems and affixes can be seen.

Repeated retrieval

Learners need to meet target vocabulary several times. The most effective way to get repeated retrieval is to read the same story several times. With younger children this is not difficult to do and is welcomed by them. Older learners may not be so receptive to this. A second option is to serialise a long story, that is, to read a chapter at a time. There is a tendency in continuous stories for vocabulary to be repeated, and certainly for a smaller number of different words to be used (Sutarsyah et al., 1994). Teachers could maximise repetition by briefly retelling what happened previously in the story before continuing with the next instalment. Much research still needs to be done on the effect of a continuous story on repetition. Brown et al. (2008) found that the more often a word was repeated the more likely it was to be retained. However, in their listening-only condition, the vocabulary retention scores were so low that the differences were not significant. They suggest however that very large numbers of repetitions would be needed to ensure vocabulary learning from listening – in the range of 50 to 100 repetitions.

The repeated readings or the serial instalments should not be too far apart. Listening to a story two or three times a week is likely to be more beneficial for learning than once a week. If the teacher writes up target vocabulary on the board as it occurs in the story, it is best to write it just after it is heard rather than before. This will encourage retrieval rather than recognition.

Decontextualisation

Learners need to focus on words not only as a part of the message but on the words themselves. This can be helped by noting words on the blackboard and by providing short definitions or translations of words. Elley (1989) and Brett et al. (1996) found that vocabulary learning is considerably increased if the teacher defines a word when it occurs in the story. This defining does two things. Firstly, it takes the word out of its message context and draws attention to it as a language item; that is, it decontextualises it. Secondly, it provides a meaning for the word. The most effective definitions are likely to be clearly marked as definitions, and are short and clear, possibly involving a first language translation. There is as yet no research on the effect of L1 translation on the learning of vocabulary through listening. Explaining vocabulary while L2 learners listen to a story helps vocabulary learning (Collins, 2005), especially if the explanation involves rich instruction.

In a series of experiments, Hulstijn (1992) compared incidental and intentional vocabulary learning, and compared inferring from context under several conditions with the meanings being provided. In incidental learning, the learners were not aware that they would be tested on the vocabulary they met, even though in some of Hulstijn's conditions synonyms or choices were provided, and for native speakers nonsense words were used. The incidental learning conditions resulted in very low learning scores, although it should be noted that Hulstijn's tests were quite demanding, involving receptive recall in one test and productive recall in another. Where learners were made aware that they would be tested on vocabulary knowledge, learning increased substantially and generally obliterated any differences between inferring and having meanings provided.

In the incidental learning conditions, having to infer the meaning of a word resulted in more learning than when the meaning was already provided in a gloss. However, Hulstijn noted that inferring often resulted in wrong inferences even when the inference was partly guided by the presence of multiple-choice answers. This condition should not be interpreted as a reason for discouraging inferring from context, because most native speakers' vocabulary learning occurs in this way (Nagy et al., 1985). It underlines the need for training learners in guessing from context and for complementing learning from context with more deliberate vocabulary-focused learning.

We have looked at the factors of interest, comprehension, repeated retrieval and decontextualisation. The final factor to examine is the role of deep processing in vocabulary learning through listening.

Creative processing

Learners need to meet new words in differing contexts that stretch their knowledge of the words. This stretching of knowledge will be helped by meeting the words in a range of linguistic contexts, in association with pictures (Elley, 1989), and in discussion and negotiation.

Teachers can try to affect the quality of the mental processing of vocabulary while learners listen to stories in the following ways.

Rather than read the same story several times, as in the Elley (1989) study, it may be better to use a longer story and present it part-by-part as a serial. Long texts provide an opportunity for the same vocabulary to recur. If this recurrence is in contexts which differ from those previously met in the story, then this creative use will contribute to learning. Except in deliberately repetitive stories, the re-occurrence of vocabulary in graded readers typically involves a different context for each repetition of a word. This is not deliberate but just a feature of the nature of language use.

If the teacher is able to supplement the storytelling with pictures, by using blackboard drawings, an OHP or a blown-up book, then this will contribute positively to vocabulary learning.

If it is possible to provide simple contextual definitions of words, that is, definitions using example sentences, then this could help learning, if the example sentences differ from those that the word occurs in in the story. The contextual definition would then be a creative use of the word.

Learning vocabulary from spoken input is an effective means of vocabulary expansion. The Elley (1989) and Brett et al. (1996) studies both examined long-term retention (three months, six weeks) and found that words were still retained.

The five factors considered here have been treated as separate factors, but they clearly interact with each other. Interest and comprehension are clearly related and we have seen how decontextualisation, repetition and deep processing affect each other. What is striking about the five factors is that they apply not only to incidental learning from spoken input but they also apply to more deliberate language-focused learning.

It should also be clear that we should not accept processes like negotiation and definition at their face value but need to see what conditions for learning they are setting up. By doing this we can distinguish between useful and not so useful instances of negotiation or definition, and we can see if the same conditions can be set up in other processes that draw attention to vocabulary.

Table 4.1 lists the five conditions and features that have been mentioned here. Using a variant of this table, it would be possible to rate a teacher's performance in reading a story aloud to a class, by giving points for each of the features listed in the table. The table suggests that some features, such as using interesting material, deserve more points than others, such as involving the learners. Some features, such as serialisation, however occur in several places on the table and this would need to be accounted for in an observation checklist. The assignment of features to useful, very good, and excellent is partly supported by research but is largely intuitive. It makes the point that research is a very useful guide in shaping our teaching activities but our intuitions and feelings as experienced teachers must also be recognised.

Table 4.1 *Conditions and features enhancing vocabulary learning from listening to stories*

Conditions	Features		
	1 useful	2 very good	3 excellent
Interest	Involve the listeners	Serialise	Use interesting material
Comprehension	Choose easy words to focus on	Control the pace Simplify	Choose easy material Use pictures
Repeated retrieval	Don't note up words on the board too soon Don't wait too long between readings	Serialise a long story Use related texts	Reread/retell the same stories
Decontextualisation	Put words on the blackboard Point to a word on the blackboard	Encourage negotiation	Define simply Translate
Deep processing	Use contextual definitions	Use pictures	Serialise Retell differently

How much vocabulary learning occurs through listening to lectures?

Academic reading and listening are means of vocabulary learning. Parry (1991) found that learners picked up new vocabulary from their academic reading, although surprisingly most of it was not technical vocabulary. This could have been because the technical words were defined in the text and were not seen as problematic. Each learner reading the same texts learned quite different vocabulary from the other learners in the study. Vidal (2003) however found that most new vocabulary learning through listening to lectures was technical vocabulary.

Vidal (2011) compared vocabulary learning from listening to lectures with vocabulary learning from reading academic texts, confirming Vidal's (2003) findings with lecture-listening input. Vidal found that the higher the proficiency level of the learners (as measured by TOEFL), the greater the vocabulary gains from listening and reading. As proficiency increased there was less difference between the listening and reading gains, but they were still rather different. The gains made by both the listening and reading groups were relatively small, but were still respectable. Although Vidal does not provide the raw figures for the different levels of vocabulary knowledge, it seems that for reading, out of 36 target words, 6.5 were learned well, 3.2 were partially known, and 9.7 were recognised as being seen in the texts. That is, there were gains on various levels for around 19 of the 36 words. For listening, the gains were 4.3 well known, 1.8 partially known, and 4.3 recognised as being heard in the lectures. Thus there were gains for over 10 of the 36 words. The test was a written test so this favoured the recognition scores for the reading group.

On the one-month delayed post-test, about half of the immediate gains were lost. For the highest proficiency students, there were no differences between listening and reading post-test scores, suggesting that vocabulary knowledge gained from listening may be a bit more stable than vocabulary knowledge gained from reading.

Smidt and Hegelheimer (2004) measured vocabulary learning from a computer-delivered mini-lecture. The vocabulary test was a partial dictation with the 20 target words missing. Learners gained an average of just under four words during the 15-minute lecture. The talking head lecture was accompanied by OHP and picture slides, and online dictionary access.

How much vocabulary learning occurs through interactive tasks?

When learners work with each other to complete a task, they often talk with each other about the language items they meet. Second language researchers call each instance of this discussion a **language-related episode**, although researchers may differ slightly on their precise definition of language-related episodes. Such episodes are important because they are overt signs that attention is being given to language features and this attention can result in learning. Such episodes help vocabulary learning.

There is evidence that in communicative tasks there is often a focus on vocabulary (Ellis et al., 2001; Williams, 1999). Language-related vocabulary episodes occur when learners ask each other or the teacher about the form and meaning of words. Here is an example from Newton (2013):

S3   and be fluent in two languages?
S1   pardon?
S2   huh?
S3   be fluent in two languages which have different written forms
S3   can can speak two languages

Such episodes help learning, because (a) they focus deliberate attention on unknown or partly known words; (b) they provide learners with information about these words; (c) they may provide repeated creative uses of the words; and (d) they may result in the learner producing the word. Research on language-related episodes typically shows that these episodes help comprehension (de la Fuente, 2002; Ellis et al., 1994; Loschky, 1994), short-term learning (de la Fuente, 2002; Ellis, 1995; Kim, 2008; Newton, 2013), and longer-term retention (de la Fuente, 2002; McDonough and Sunitham, 2009). Negotiation is one type of language-related episode, and other types include self-correction or the correction of others, talk about language, and discussion of aspects of language use (Swain and Lapkin, 1998). The McDonough and Sunitham study is included in this chapter because it involved synchronous interactive activity although it was through computer-mediated written communication. De la Fuente (2003) compared face-to-face negotiation of words with written computer-mediated interaction. Written computer-mediated interaction took almost twice as long, used shorter sentences, provided less repetition of the target words, and involved a greater likelihood of abandoning the negotiation than face-to-face interaction. Both treatments resulted in vocabulary learning, but the face-to-face group performed better on the productive oral vocabulary tests.

How often do vocabulary-related language-related episodes occur?

If language-related episodes are divided into vocabulary-related and grammar-related episodes, typically vocabulary-related episodes occur much more frequently, although the rate of occurrence of such episodes will depend on the difficulty of the material. McDonough and Sunitham (2009) found that 76% of their Thai learners' language-related episodes were vocabulary related. In 28 hours of transcript, there was a total of 300 such episodes, just over 10 per hour or roughly one every six minutes.

What do language-related episodes focus on?

Kim (2008) found that just over 50% of language-related episodes were focused on form (spelling or pronunciation). Newton (2013) found a strong effect for task-type, with split-information tasks involving labelling encouraging a focus on form rather than word meaning. In a study of classroom interaction, mainly between the teacher and learners, Alcón-Soler (2009) found a great deal of deliberate attention given to vocabulary (word meaning) (66.9% of the episodes) and only a small amount of attention to spelling (1.3%) and pronunciation (7.6%). This small amount of attention to word form may be because the learners were Spanish learners of English, and the interaction was largely between the learners and the teacher.

Are most vocabulary-related episodes successfully resolved?

When learners work with each other, do they give each other correct information about the meanings of words or their spelling when they are asked? Research shows that learners are generally good sources of language information. McDonough and Sunitham (2009) found that their rather low-proficiency Thai learners successfully resolved 70% of their language-related vocabulary episodes, left 25% unresolved and incorrectly resolved only 8% (the figures adding up to 103% may be the result of rounding the figures). Newton (2013) had similar findings. Kim (2008) found in his groups 53% resolved, 30% unresolved and 17% incorrectly resolved. In Kim's study, much fewer were resolved in individual work (39%) where learners thought aloud.

Do vocabulary-related episodes lead to retention?

Although learners can discuss the meaning or spelling of words when they meet them through listening or reading, this discussion need not necessarily lead to learning. In experimental studies learning is measured by a vocabulary test or tests which may occur immediately after the activity or several days or weeks later. The retention rates as measured by such tests depend on the sensitivity of the measures used and the amount of delay between the language-related episode and testing. Using specially made tests administered 7 to 12 days after the episodes, McDonough and Sunitham (2009) found 48% retention for successfully resolved episodes. A major problem with their study is that they did not distinguish receptive test items (L2→L1) from productive test items (L1→L2). They also did not relate the nature of the language-related episode discussion (whether it was on receptive or productive aspects of the target word) to the nature of the test. As we have seen in Chapter 2, productive tests are more difficult than receptive tests, and if the method of testing matches the method of learning, results will be higher. McDonough and Sunitham were not very satisfied with the learners 48% average score on the vocabulary tests, but this is quite a respectable score given that the tests were delayed tests, that they were recall not recognition tests, that they included productive as well as receptive items, and that they probably did not always match the method of learning to the method of testing. Memory for items in vocabulary-related language-related episodes was much higher than for grammar-related episodes.

Smith (2005) looked at pairs of learners communicating by writing through a computer chat program while they completed four 30-minute tasks. Smith only looked at negotiation episodes of 32 target words (eight per task) which had been pre-tested. There were 66 such language-focused episodes (8.6% of the possible items). The learners sat two immediate post-tests and two delayed post-tests (seven days) after each task. In terms of scores on all the post-tests there was no difference in effect between simple and complex negotiation, and between negotiation with no immediate or subsequent use (uptake) and negotiation with immediate or subsequent use. While negotiation and uptake can contribute to learning, learning can occur without uptake, just as learning can occur without negotiation. Unfortunately, Smith does not report the post-test scores for the words not negotiated. Although the Smith study focused on written communication, it is dealt with in this chapter because Kötter (2003) found that written computer-mediated interaction is viewed by its participants to be like speech rather than writing.

Is computer-mediated negotiation through writing better than spoken negotiation?

De la Fuente (2003) found roughly similar gains for oral interaction pairs and computer-mediated interaction pairs across four receptive and productive and oral and written vocabulary tests. Although most of these comparisons were not significant, there was a tendency for the oral group to learn more, possibly because the oral interaction was more extensive than the computer-mediated written interaction. However the computer-mediated interaction actually took twice as long. Computer-mediated interaction with a vocabulary focus helps vocabulary learning in much the same way that oral interaction does, but to a slightly lesser extent and with a greater expenditure of time.

Does the use of the L1 in vocabulary-related episodes help learning?

The L1 seems to be the language preference in learner-to-learner language-related episodes when learners share the same L1 (McDonough and Sunitham, 2009). The use of the L1 seems to be effective in resolving these episodes and in helping retention.

Do the active learners in language-related episodes learn more than those who ask or observe?

It is a common finding that there does not seem to be any difference in follow-up tests between learners who are active in negotiation and those just observe it. McDonough and Sunitham (2009) make the rather surprising finding that learners working in pairs seem to perform about the same on delayed post-tests for items that they had negotiated between themselves in the episodes, even though one of the learners was the source of the information. For 4% of the test items, only the learner who asked in the episode got the answer correct. The learner who provided the answer in the episode did not get it correct. For 23% of the test items, only the learner who provided the answer got the item correct. For 36% of the test items both got the item correct, and for 38% of the items both were incorrect even though one of them had provided the correct answer in a previous episode. This suggests problems with the test, although the test items resembled the context in which the episodes occurred.

DeHaan et al. (2010) found that learners observing players of a videogame recalled much more vocabulary than those actually playing (almost three times as much). They suggested this may have been because of the heavy cognitive load of actively playing the game.

There needs to be more research using multiple vocabulary measures comparing learners actively involved in language-related episodes with those simply observing. Multiple measures may reveal differences but it is likely that involved observation is at least as effective as overt participation.

Does most vocabulary learning in interactive activities occur through language-related episodes?

Language-related episodes are observable signs of learners giving deliberate attention to language features, and it is likely that such attention has a high chance of leading to learning. However, learning can occur through guessing from context clues and there may be no external signs that this is happening. In a study involving two groups of learners each doing four different tasks Newton (2001: 35) found that of the words learned, about one-fifth were learned through negotiation, and four-fifths were learned through guessing from context. Most vocabulary learning does not occur through negotiation, although if words are negotiated, they have a good chance (68% in Newton's study) of being learned. The reason that overall fewer words were learned through negotiation was because proportionally much fewer words were negotiated than guessed. In a truly communicative interaction we can probably only put up with a small amount of intrusive negotiation.

Kim (2008) compared pairs of learners doing a dicto-gloss with individual learners doing a dicto-gloss while thinking aloud. Although the number of language-related episodes per individual learner was the same, the pairs had more correctly resolved episodes and higher retention scores. Two heads are clearly better than one. In the pairs, 70% of the words discussed received a score of three or higher on the Vocabulary Knowledge Scale, indicating some knowledge of the meaning. The learners working individually gained such scores on only 35% of the words that they mentioned in their think-aloud episodes. Interaction makes a considerable difference.

Can learners be helped to deal with vocabulary in interactive activities?

Newton (2001) outlines a range of pre-task, during-task and post-task options for dealing with unfamiliar vocabulary. These include the pre-task activities of predicting based on given words, co-operative dictionary search and vocabulary studies. In-task options include the use of a glossary, an interactive glossary and encouragement to negotiate. After the task the learners can reflect on the vocabulary met during the task.

In several studies, Rod Ellis and his colleagues have looked at the role of unmodified input, premodified input and negotiation on vocabulary learning. The tasks used typically involved learners having to place small pictures of pieces of furniture or a utensil on a larger picture of an apartment or room. The different treatments usually involved the following kinds of input:

- *Baseline directions.* Typical native speaker instructions were used based on native speakers communicating with native speakers.
- *Premodified input.* Second language learners heard the baseline directions and negotiated the parts they did not understand with a native speaker. These interactions were recorded and used to prepare premodified directions. So when the task was performed there was no negotiation but the input had already been modified on the basis of negotiation with a different group of learners.
- *Interactionally modified input.* Learners negotiated the baseline directions with the teacher as the task was being done. To help learners, typical negotiating directions were put up on the blackboard, such as *What is a _____ ?*, and *Could you say it again?*.
- *Negotiated output.* Learners performed the task in pairs so that they and not the teacher provided the input.

Ellis et al. (1994) found that there were very large differences in the amount of time taken to perform the tasks, with the group getting interactionally modified input taking four and a half times the amount of time taken by the premodified group. There was also much greater repetition of target items for the interactionally modified group. Premodified input resulted in vocabulary learning but not as much as the interactionally modified input. Ellis (1995: 409) noted in an analysis of one of the studies reported in Ellis et al. (1994) that although more word meanings were learned from the interactionally modified input than from the premodified input, the rate of acquisition (in words per minute) was faster with the premodified input. Ellis and He (1999) controlled for the factor of time spent on the task, comparing premodified input, interactionally modified input and negotiated output. Learning occurred in all three treatments. They found that although the interactionally modified input group consistently scored higher than the premodified group, the differences were not statistically significant. The negotiated output group scored significantly higher than the other two groups. Ellis and He explain this better learning by learners working together in pairs in two complementary ways. Firstly, learners had more chance to produce the new words and thus process them more deeply. Secondly, the quality of the negotiation between non-native speaking learners was better than the negotiation between the teacher and learners. This quality differed in the comprehensibility of the definitions provided (learners used simpler words), the systematic approach to the task, and the one-to-one support provided by continual checking and feedback. Good negotiation works better than poor negotiation for vocabulary learning.

Ellis and Heimbach (1997) looked at young ESL children's negotiation and learning through negotiation. Children negotiated more when they were part of a group rather than when working one-to-one with a teacher. There was not a strong relationship between comprehension and acquisition of vocabulary, that is, vocabulary in sentences that were clearly understood was not necessarily learned.

De la Fuente (2002) compared premodified input, negotiated input and negotiated output while controlling for time on task, finding a superiority for negotiated over premodified input for comprehension, and receptive and productive vocabulary learning, and a superiority for negotiated output for productive learning.

There are important lessons from these studies that deserve repeating. Firstly, premodified input and negotiation both lead to vocabulary learning. Secondly, it is likely that the amount of learning from both of these kinds of input depends on the quality of the support for learning that each provides. That is, good simplification and glossing within a text is likely to lead to better learning than poor negotiation, and good negotiation will lead to better learning than poor simplification and glossing. Thirdly, premodification and negotiation are not in themselves conditions affecting learning, but they provide opportunities for conditions like retrieval, productive use, creative use and instantiation to occur.

Ellis and He's (1999) study did not control for repetition and creative use, factors which have been shown to be important for vocabulary learning. It would be interesting to see how controlling for these factors would affect the premodified/negotiated comparison of effects.

Teachers can encourage negotiation by ensuring that learners have the capability, willingness and opportunity to negotiate. Ellis and colleagues ensured capability by providing learners with a list of sentences that are useful in negotiating. Learners can be given practice in negotiating by setting negotiating as a goal and then modelling and providing practice in doing it. Learners can be made more willing to negotiate by using grouping arrangements where they feel comfortable asking for help (Ellis and Heimbach, 1997). These arrangements are likely to be with other learners of a similar proficiency level. The opportunity to negotiate can be provided by using split-information tasks, by designing in opinion gaps, by deliberately designing vocabulary gaps into tasks as in Woodeson's (1982) communicative crosswords, and by ensuring the written input to the task has some vocabulary that is not in the written input of others in the group.

An interesting finding in several of these studies was that the learners who observe the negotiation learn the negotiated vocabulary just as well as those actively involved in the negotiation.

Learning can occur through teacher–learner interaction with the teacher aiming to focus on vocabulary learning. Dobinson (2001) looked at learners' immediate recall of words that they had just met in a lesson and their performance on a matching vocabulary test two weeks and six weeks later. She also looked at how the recalled words had been dealt with in the lessons. Of all words recalled 92% had been mentioned by the teacher or learners during the lesson. Words recalled but not mentioned had occurred in a reading text or a written exercise. Of all the words recalled 75% had been repeated during the lesson. The number of repetitions did not match nicely with the number of learners recalling the words. Some of the words recalled by most people occurred only twice. Focusing on the word and turn-taking involving the words also clearly affected learning, but the quantity of such actions was once again not consistently related to the number of people who recalled the words. The average number of focuses per word was quite large, around 13 times. Similarly turn-taking averaged around 12 turns per word. Dobinson also found that learners who participated a lot did not necessarily learn more than those with less overt participation. In addition, large amounts of attention to a word tended to be counter-productive, resulting in fewer people recalling it. Learners clearly learned from classroom interaction and this learning was strongly helped by deliberate attention. Learning can also take place without such attention but perhaps not with the same degree of certainty. Almost half of the words recalled were recalled by only one learner.

Is there a special vocabulary of speaking?

Word frequency studies indicate that a much smaller vocabulary is needed for speaking than for writing (Nation, 2006). This difference, however, is probably also influenced by degree of formality and topics. We tend to write about more weighty matters than speak about them.

Pawley and Syder (1983) suggest that as well as vocabulary knowledge we need to have memorised large numbers of clauses and phrases which we can then easily retrieve and use. This allows us to speak in a fluent way sounding like native speakers because the words in the memorised chunks fit together well. This issue is looked at more deeply in Chapter 12 on multiword units.

Certainly, for the beginning stages of listening and speaking, it is important to work out a manageable list of items that should be learned to a high degree of spoken fluency. Nation and Crabbe (1991) did this for learners who had the goal of being able to use another language for short periods of travel or residence in another country. This 'survival' vocabulary consisted of around 120 items and included greetings, politeness formulas, numbers, ways of requesting food, accommodation, help and directions, ways of describing yourself, buying goods, and where necessary, bargaining. The words and phrases needed to do a limited set of things like this do not take very long to learn, but they need to be practised until they reach a high degree of fluency. This is particularly true of numbers and greetings. This basic survival vocabulary is freely available in several different languages in the Vocabulary Resource Booklet on Paul Nation's website.

Items in a basic spoken fluency list need to be practised as single items with learners having to retrieve the spoken forms while seeing the first language translation or some other way of representing the meaning. Then they need to be practised in flexible dialogues where there is some element of unpredictability. This can be done in small simulations and role plays.

There are several vocabulary items which are mainly used in spoken language and are unlikely to occur performing the same functions in written texts. Here is a list from Stenstrom (1990: 144) from the London-Lund corpus (see also McCarthy and Carter, 1997, for a comparison of spoken and written vocabulary and Shin, 2007, 2009, for a comparison of spoken and written multiword units).

- Apologies: *pardon, sorry, excuse me, I'm sorry, I beg your pardon*
- Smooth-overs: *don't worry, never mind*
- Hedges: *kind of, sort of, sort of thing*
- Expletives: *damn, gosh, hell, fuck off, good heavens, the hell, for goodness sake, good heavens above, bloody hell*
- Greetings: *hi, hello, good evening, good morning, Happy New Year, how are you, how do you do*
- Initiators: *anyway, however, now*
- Negative: *no*
- Orders: *give over, go on, shut up*
- Politeness markers: *please*
- Question tags: *is it, isn't it*
- Responses: *ah, fine, good, uhuh, OK, quite, really, right, sure, all right, fair enough, I'm sure, I see, that's good, that's it, that's right, that's true, very good*

- Softeners: *I mean, mind you, you know, you see, as you know, do you see*
- Thanks: *thanks, thank you*
- Well: *well*
- Exemplifiers: *say*
- Positives: *mhm, yeah, yes, yup*

There are several ways of looking at whether learners have enough vocabulary to carry out speaking tasks. The Vocabulary Size Test (see Paul Nation's website) is a useful starting point. If learners' receptive vocabulary is very small, their productive vocabulary is likely to be smaller. It would be useful to accompany this testing by doing the listening version of the 1,000 word level test (see the free Vocabulary Resource Booklet on Paul Nation's website) to make sure that the low score is the result of a small vocabulary and not a lack of reading skill.

Most tests of spoken English which involve rating scales contain a scale for rating the vocabulary component of speaking. This is useful as a way of increasing the reliability of a spoken test by increasing the number of points of assessment, but it would not be wise to try to isolate the vocabulary score from such a set of scales as a valid measure of vocabulary size.

A more focused way would be to do several small role plays based on 'survival' situations, then statements could be made about spoken vocabulary knowledge in terms of performance in certain situations, such as 'Has the vocabulary to go shopping' and so on.

How can learners develop fluency with spoken vocabulary?

Learners should become fluent with what they learn right from the early stages of language learning. The fluency development strand of a course is important at all stages of learning. At the early stages, learners should develop fluency with greetings, numbers, time, days of the week, *yes/no/OK/right*, time indicators like *today, yesterday, next week, last month*, some colours, and other items which could be used frequently. This fluency practice is best done with learners working in pairs with one learner acting as the teacher, but it can be done with the whole class as a teacher-led activity.

The first step is a listen-and-point activity. In this description we will use numbers as the focus of fluency development and assume that the teacher is working with just one learner. The learner has the numbers from 1 to 10 on a sheet in front of him.

1 2 3 4 5 6 7 8 9 10

The teacher says a number, for example *five*, and the learner points to 5. If learners are working in pairs, it may be necessary for the learner who is acting as the teacher to have a list of the numbers written in their full form, that is *one, two, three, four* .... The teacher keeps saying numbers, gradually increasing the speed, so that the learner is pushed to the limits of his or her fluency. If the learner points to the wrong number, the teacher says *No.* and says the number again. If the learner hesitates, the teacher waits until the learner points. The teacher can note which numbers are less fluently recognised by the learner and give these extra practice. Several minutes should be spent on this activity with the numbers being covered in a random order many times. This practises listening fluency.

The second step is for the learner to become the teacher so that speaking fluency is practised.

The third step also practises speaking fluency. The teacher points to a number, for example 5, and the learner says it.

Learners should reach a high level of fluency at step 1 before moving on to step 2. Fluency practice on the same items should be done on several different days so that there is opportunity for spaced retrieval.

For variety, and in a teacher-led activity with the whole class, learners can write the numbers as they hear them instead of pointing. So, the teacher says *five* and learners write 5.

Because this fluency practice is being done with lexical sets, it is very important that learners have had plenty of opportunity to learn words separately before they do the fluency practice. If the words are not well established, fluency practice could cause confusion and mixing up of the words and their meanings.

When the first language uses a different writing system from the second language, it is important to do fluency practice with the letters of the second language and their sounds. Table 4.2 lists examples where fluency practice can be given for beginners.

Items like apologies, greetings, responses, negatives and positives as listed in the section above on the special vocabulary of speaking can also be the focus of fluency activities.

It is a generally robust finding that pre-task planning results in increased fluency in a task (Ortega, 1999). More focused instructions about what to plan can result in improvements and complexity.

Suggestions for more advanced fluency practice can be found in Chapter 12.

Table 4.2 *Examples of vocabulary focus and activities for fluency practice*

Vocabulary	Sequence of difficulty	Chart to point to
Numbers	Single-digit numbers Double-digit numbers etc. Cardinal numbers Ordinal numbers	The numbers written as figures 1 2 3 4 5 6 7...
Days of the week	Days Days plus date, e.g. Monday the 3rd Days plus date plus month. e.g. Monday the third of August	First language words in order or a week cut from a first language calendar
Months of the year	As for days of the week	First language words in order or a twelve-months first language calendar
Time indicators: *today, tomorrow, last week, this month, next year*		A set of boxes with the middle one representing now, or a calendar.

How can a teacher use input to increase vocabulary knowledge?

As we will see in Chapter 5 on writing, it is not easy to bring learners' receptive vocabulary knowledge into productive use. The knowledge required for production is greater than the knowledge required for reception. An important way of helping learners gain control of this knowledge is for the teacher to enter into a dialogue with the learners encouraging them to produce vocabulary that the teacher models. One way of doing this is through semantic mapping.

Semantic mapping

Semantic mapping involves the teacher and the learners working together to build up on the blackboard a visual framework of connections between ideas like the map below.

There can be several starting points for semantic mapping. It can involve the recall of a previously read story, a recent current event, a film, a unit of study, or simply learners' general knowledge of a topic. Stahl and Vancil (1986) point out in their study of native speakers of English that it is the discussion which occurs during the building up of the semantic map that makes the activity contribute to vocabulary learning. The skill of the teacher is important in the way that the teacher enters into a dialogue with the learners and encourages them and supports them in participating in the dialogue.

In a semantic mapping activity aimed at increasing productive vocabulary, we would expect to see some of the following features:

1. The teacher encourages learners to produce vocabulary that can be put into the map. Rather than supplying the word forms for the learners, the teacher gives learners suggestions that will help them

retrieve the word from their receptive vocabulary. These suggestions can include paraphrases or first language translations of wanted items, and formal clues like the initial letters or sounds of the word.

2. The teacher asks learners to explain, justify and increase the connections between items in the semantic map. This has several learning goals. Firstly, it encourages repetition to help establish the vocabulary. Secondly, it encourages creative use by enriching associations with other items. Thirdly, it allows the teacher to help shape learners' production by rephrasing what they say. This helps them with grammatical and collocational aspects of the words. Fourthly, it helps learners explore the meaning of the relevant vocabulary.

3. The teacher goes back over what has already been put into the map, repeating the important vocabulary and reinforcing the connections. The teacher can encourage learners to participate in this revision.

4. The map is not the final outcome of the activity. After it has been completed, it is then used as a basis for talks or writing.

Gibbons' (1998) study of classroom interaction highlights ways in which the teacher can contribute to learners' language development by making their thinking and reporting more explicit through recasting what they say. The basis for the recasts is a dialogue between the teacher and the learners. It is not unusual to see the vocabulary of the teacher's recasts coming through in the learners' later speech and written reports.

Making decisions

This activity is described here as a representative of a range of similar problem-solving activities where the teacher can provide vocabulary input and encourage re-use of the vocabulary during the activity. The activity has four stages:

1. The teacher presents the topic which is expressed as an alternative question, for example, 'Should children continue to live with their parents after they finish school or should they should they leave home?' The teacher gives an example reason for each of the alternatives, for example, live with their parents because this saves money, and leave home because this encourages independence.

2. The learners form groups of about four people. Each group has to list reasons to support *one* side of the question. While learners do this, the teacher goes around the groups, providing needed vocabulary

and suggesting reasons that include useful vocabulary. The teacher gets learners to note down the vocabulary so that it will be used.

3. The groups of four now join together to make groups of eight. Each group of eight must be made up of a small group of four that prepared reasons for one side of the question and a small group of four that prepared reasons for the other side of the question. They must explain their reasons to each other and must reach a decision. They do not have to support their side of the question. They should deliberately try to use the vocabulary the teacher provided for them during the activity.

4. The groups of eight now report back their decision and reasons to the rest of the class, once again using the provided vocabulary.

How can a teacher use labeled diagrams to increase vocabulary knowledge?

Vocabulary support for speaking tasks can be provided by using labels on pictures and diagrams.

Information transfer activities

Palmer (1982) describes a wide range of information transfer activities which involve the learner turning a diagram, chart, table or form into written or spoken text. For example, a learner may have a map of a country with a route marked on it with various types of marking to indicate if the route represents travel by car, train, ship or plane. The learner describes the holiday route to another learner who marks it on his own map. The learner is helped in making the spoken description by the vocabulary used to label the diagram. Further help can be provided by giving the chance for preparation and practice. This can be done using an expert group/family group procedure. Two different information transfer tasks are prepared. All the learners who have one task get together to practise it. All the learners who have the other task get together and practice describing theirs. These are the expert groups. After this practice, the learners form pairs (family groups) with one learner from each half of the class. They then do the information transfer task.

Split-information tasks

Nation (1990) describes split-information tasks where learners decide if pictures are the same or different. The learner who begins describing the picture has labels on her picture. The other learner does not.

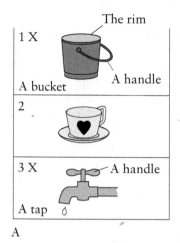

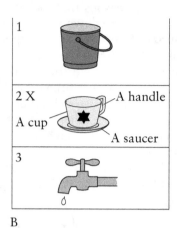

A   B

The set of pictures is made up so that the same labels occur on several different pictures and the same label will be on a picture where learner A starts speaking and on another picture where learner B starts speaking. This ensures that each learner makes both receptive and productive use of the words.

Hall (1992) used split-information tasks that focused on particular mathematics vocabulary including *diagonal* and *perimeter*. The same words appeared in a variety of tasks. Here is a sample task and the discussion that resulted from it. In a split information task each learner has unique, essential information. They must not show their pictures to each other.

A: Which is quicker?   B: Which is quicker?
    Your way or B's?   Your way or A's?

Here is a sample of the discussion that occurred during the task.

    A: Which is quicker? Your way or B's?
    B: Which is quicker? Your way or A's? Go!
    A: Which is quicker? Your way or B's?
    B: Which way does your way go?
    A: This way.
    B: No. Just say it. Go. Tell me.

A: It's going here.

B: How? How? It's how? My way cause its going diagonally. Mines

A: Why? Is it around the edge?

B: B's quicker. No. Hah. Put B.

A: I draw a line up there its B. It's a. A's a perimeter and the other diagonally. A is around.

B: Put B. Well put that. Say put that. Across diagonal. Not a perimeter.

A: B. What you got?

B: quicker.

How can a teacher use cooperative tasks to focus on vocabulary?

Cooperating activities are particularly effective in getting learners to explore a range of meanings that a word has and the range of elements of meaning it contains. Here are two examples of ranking activities. One focuses on the word *cancel* and the other on *instruction*.

- *Cancel*. Your team is supposed to play in a game on Saturday. List the reasons why the game might be cancelled. Rank them according to how likely they are to happen.

The vocabulary to be used can be included in the items to rank. The following example is based on the word *instruction* which occurred in a text in the phrase *reading instruction*.

- *Instruction*. You are about to begin studying at university for the first time. Before the university year begins you have a chance to receive instruction in a variety of skills. Rank them in order of value to you for university study.
  Instruction in writing assignments
  Instruction in taking lecture notes
  Instruction in using the library
  Instruction in organising and planning your time
  Instruction in making use of university clubs and facilities

The two examples are ranking activities, but problem solving activities, classification activities and brainstorming activities can also be used with a focus on a particular word.

Notice that the speaking activity can explore the meaning of the word or it can provide opportunities for the word to be repeated. Here are some more activities based on a reading text about an immigrant studying to become a nurse (*New Voices*, July 1997). The target word is italicised.

- Why do people become *refugees*? List as many causes as you can.
- Group these jobs according to the skills they *involve*: nurse, teacher, shop assistant, builder, computer programmer, factory worker, taxi driver.
- A group in your community has decided to *sponsor* a refugee family. List all the things that the sponsorship will involve.
- Using the text and your experience, list and group things you would need to do to become a *registered* nurse. Which one would you find the most difficult?

While the activities are being done, the teacher would look for the number of repetitions of the target word, the number of creative uses, and direct questions and statements about the meaning of the word.

Such activities which focus on a word are easy to make and can be very effective in helping learn the word. Learners should be told of the learning goal of the activity (Nation and Hamilton-Jenkins, 2000).

How can a teacher design activities to help incidental vocabulary learning?

Speaking tasks such as mini-lectures, ranking activities, split-information tasks, role play and problem-solving discussions are not usually thought of as having vocabulary-learning goals. One of the reasons is that it seems difficult to plan vocabulary learning as a part of a syllabus using activities that are largely productive, unpredictable and dependent on the people who happen to be in the discussion group.

However, such activities are a very useful means of vocabulary learning and a vocabulary-learning goal can be effectively designed into many speaking activities. It is also possible to plan what vocabulary is likely to be learned in particular activities. Although here the focus is on vocabulary learning, this may be an incidental goal in speaking activities. Speaking activities can achieve a range of goals and several may be achieved in the same activity.

Here is part of the transcript of a problem solving-discussion by three learners (S1, S2, S3) about redesigning a zoo (Newton, 1995; 2013). The task comes from Ur (1981).

S3:   ... All enclosures should be filled
S2:   Enclosures should be filled enclosure, do you know?
S1:   What means enclosure? Do you know?
S3:   Close ah—   should be filled
S2:   No I don't know enclos— enclosed
S1:   Filled what means fill? Oh oh all enclosed, I think that all enclosed that means enclosed

S2:   Fill
S3:   Filled, filled
S2:   Ohh
S1:   Every every area yes should be filled
S2:   Should be filled
S3:   Should be put put something inside
S1:   Yes because yes yes because you know two? the-
S2:   I see. No empty rooms ahh
S3:   No empty rooms yeah
S2:   Two is the empty I see
S1:   Yeah empty so we must fill it O.K.

The word *enclosures* comes from the typewritten handout that the learners are looking at. One of the points of information on this handout states, 'All the enclosures should be filled.' Learners S3 and S2 repeat the sentence from the handout and then S1 asks 'What means *enclosure?*' This then starts a discussion about the word. Notice that the form *enclosed* is also spoken although this does not appear on the handout at all.

What is clear from this example is that what is written on the handout has an effect on what is said during the discussion. In the example given above, it is also clear that the discussion involves the learners explaining the vocabulary to each other. The written input to the activity can play a major role in determining what is learned, if it includes vocabulary that is important for the speaking activity. Let us now look at vocabulary learning through a range of activities.

Retelling

As we shall see, retelling activities can take many forms. What is common to all of them is that learners read a text (usually about 100 to 200 words long), and retell it. From a vocabulary-learning point of view, the text provides new vocabulary and a context to help understand the vocabulary, and the retelling gives learners the chance to productively retrieve the vocabulary and ideally make creative use of it. Research by Joe (1998) indicates that the absence of the text during the retelling encourages creative use, but that having the text present during the retelling ensures that more of the target vocabulary is used in the retelling. As having the text present during retelling provides poor conditions for retrieval (the form which should be retrieved is already present in the text that the learner can look at), until further research is done on this technique, it is probably best not to have the text present during the retelling.

Other forms of retelling include '4/3/2' (Arevart and Nation, 1991; de Jong and Perfetti, 2011; Maurice, 1983) and 'Read and retell' (Simcock, 1993). 4/3/2 involves a learner giving the same talk to three different listeners one after the other, but with four minutes to give the first delivery of the talk, three minutes for the delivery of the same talk to the second listener, and two minutes for the third. The talk can be a retelling of a previously studied text. The repetition would not be expected to increase the range of creative use, but would provide opportunity for more fluent retrieval. De Jong and Perfetti (2011) showed that speaking fluency increased during the 4/3/2 task and transferred to speech about a new topic. De Jong and Perfetti explained the transfer as a result of proceduralisation because of repeated words and sentence structures during the tasks, but the effects must have gone deeper than particular words because transfer occurred even though there was little vocabulary overlap with the new topic.

Eller et al. (1988) observed native-speaking kindergarten children's vocabulary development on three separate occasions one day apart as they listened to and then retold the same picture book story. Eller et al. were able to show that the children's control of particular words increased from one listening and retelling to another. Although the study had some weaknesses, particularly in that the vocabulary observed was not pre-tested, this type of longitudinal process study has much potential in vocabulary acquisition research. The results of the study support the idea that knowledge of particular words gradually increases as the result of repeated encounters.

The Read and retell activity involves retelling of a written text, but the listener has a set of guiding questions to ask the reteller so that it seems like an interview. The design of the questions can encourage the use of the target vocabulary from the written text and ensure that all the important parts of the text are retold. Both the listener and the reteller study the text and the questions before the retelling, and they can rehearse the retelling to perform in front of others.

When observing retelling activities, the teacher would look for the use of the wanted vocabulary, particularly to see if it was in a salient enough position in the text to encourage its use in retelling, and to see if it was being used creatively in the retelling.

Role play

Role play activities can involve a written text on which the role play is based. It may involve written instructions to the role players. The 'Say it!' activity combines these features and is a simple introduction to role play. In the Say it! activity learners read a short text such as a newspaper report containing the wanted vocabulary. They can read it and discuss it together if they wish. Then they look at a grid containing short tasks for them to perform. The columns in the grid are labelled with the letters A, B and C, and the rows are numbered. The first learner in the group says the reference of a square, for example, B2, and the second learner in the group has to perform the task contained in the square B2. After that the second learner says a square reference and the third learner has to perform that task. This continues around the group. The same task may be performed more than once by different learners in the group.

Here is the newspaper report on which the following Say it! is based. Learners need to read the report carefully and discuss it before doing the Say it! activity.

CASTAWAYS SURVIVED ON SHARK'S BLOOD

Three fishermen who drifted on the Pacific for four months told yesterday how they drank shark's blood to survive.

The fishermen from Kiribati told their story through an interpreter in the American Samoa capital of Pago Pago after being rescued by the ship Sakaria.

Kautea Teaitoa, Veaieta Toanuea and Tebwai Aretana drifted 400 kilometres from home after their outboard motor failed on February 8.

They said four ships had refused to help them during their ordeal.

When they were picked up on June 4 they had eaten the last of a one-metre shark four days before and drunk all of its blood.

'I have not prayed so much in all my life,' Mr Aretana said.

	A	B	C
1	You are Kautea. Say what helped you survive.	You are Tebwai Aretana. How did you feel when the ships refused to help you?	You are a sailor on the Sakaria. What did you do to help the fishermen?
2	You are Tebwai. Explain why you were in the boat and what happened after it broke down.	You are Kautea. How did you feel when you caught the shark?	You are the captain. Explain why you stopped.
3	You are Veaieta. Explain what caused the problem.	You are the interpreter. Describe the feelings and appearance of the three men.	The journey was called an ordeal. Why was it an ordeal?

Notice that the tasks in each square are designed to encourage use of the wanted vocabulary and that they require the learners to reshape what was in the text to suit the viewpoint of the task. If the text is read, discussed, understood and then put away before doing the Say it! activity, then retrieval is encouraged. The role play nature of the tasks encourages creative use of the vocabulary.

Larger problem-solving role play activities can involve substantial written input that needs to be processed in a similar way (Nation, 1991). Learners need to read about the background to the problem, the problem, the constraints on the solution and their own roles.

Ranking

Newton (2013) found that shared tasks where learners all had equal access to the same information resulted in more negotiation of word meaning than split tasks where each learner had different information. Split tasks had more negotiation overall but most of this was not negotiation of word meaning. Vocabulary which is placed in the list of items to rank is most likely to be used in the activity, particularly if the items are difficult ones for the learners to agree upon. Words occurring in the description of the background and the instructions are less likely to be used and learned. Clearly the places where words occur on the worksheet have a major effect on whether they will be learned.

Other activities

There are numerous other speaking activities which make use of written input. These include split-information tasks (Nation, 1977), interview activities and information transfer activities (Palmer, 1982). Thoughtful design of the worksheets and careful observation of their use can maximise the opportunities for the incidental learning of useful vocabulary while the learners are involved in a meaning-focused speaking task.

Designing the worksheets

Let us look at a task to see how it would help vocabulary learning and consider how the task could be redesigned to create even more favourable opportunities for vocabulary learning. Learners work in groups to solve the following problem:

You have just seen one of your friends stealing things from a local shop. What will you do?

1. Inform the shop owner immediately.
2. Tell your friend to put it back.
3. Discuss it with your friend later to discourage him from doing it in the future.
4. Just ignore it.
5. Discuss it with your parents.

The following words in the written input are unknown to many of the learners: *local, inform, discourage, ignore*. *Inform* and *ignore* are important ideas in the text and the likelihood of them being noticed, discussed and used in the activity is quite high. *Local* and *discourage* may not get the same attention.

There are several important ways in which the activity could be improved for vocabulary learning. First, the numbers in front of the choices should be removed. If they are left there, then the learners will say things like *I think 4 is the best choice* instead of saying *I would just ignore it* which makes use of the target word *ignore*.

Second, the written input is quite short and does not contain a lot of useful new vocabulary. The written input thus needs to be increased in quantity and additional useful words to learn should be included. This can be done in several ways, by increasing the amount of description about each choice, by giving more description of the background to the task (more information about the friend and what was stolen, for example), or by adding more choices. Probably the most effective way will be to turn the activity into a role play. This would involve providing each player with a role card describing their role and goals, and adding descriptions of constraints to the activity (your friend's parents punish him severely for bad behaviour) (Nation, 1991).

Third, some changes could make more certain that the wanted vocabulary was used. The activity could be made into a ranking activity rather than a choosing activity. This might get more evenly spread discussion of the choices. Each learner in the group could be given responsibility for a different choice. They should make themselves very familiar with that choice and while they do not have to make it their first choice, they have to ensure that it gets sufficient discussion and consideration during the activity. It may be more effective to get them to memorise their option and then remove the written input.

Fourth, some changes could be made to give the wanted vocabulary the chance of being used often in the activity. These could include

Table 4.3 *Features to improve vocabulary learning from speaking tasks*

1 Make sure that the target vocabulary is in the written input to the task and occurs in the best place in the written input.
   Have plenty of written input.
   Make sure about 12 target words occur in the written input.
   Try to predict what parts of the written input are most likely to be used in the task and put wanted vocabulary there.

2 Design the task so that the written input needs to be used.
   Avoid the use of numbering in lists of items or choices.
   Use retelling, role play, problem-solving discussion based on the written input.
   Have a clear outcome to the task, such as ranking, choosing, problem solving, completion.

3 Get each learner in the group actively involved.
   Split the information.
   Assign jobs or roles.
   Keep the group size reasonably small (about four or five learners).
   Have learners of roughly equal proficiency in a group who feel comfortable negotiating with each other.

4 Ensure that the vocabulary is used in ways that encourage learning.
   Use tasks such as role play that require changing the context of the vocabulary.
   Use a procedure such as the pyramid procedure or reporting back to get the vocabulary reused.
   Remove the input so that recall is required, or after looking at the detailed sheet, use a reduced one for the task.
   After the task is completed, get the learners to reflect on what vocabulary they learned.

getting learners to report back to other groups on their decision and reasons for the decision, and moving through a pyramid procedure from pairs to fours to the whole class.

Table 4.3 lists changes that could be made to improve the vocabulary-learning potential of a communication activity.

The aim of all these changes to the activity is to increase the opportunities for vocabulary learning during the activity. The effectiveness of the changes may be seen by testing the vocabulary learning from the activity, or more informally by observing whether the learners are negotiating and using the wanted vocabulary during the activity.

An adapted activity

Here is an example of adaptations made to the shoplifting question.

The italicised words are the target words for learning. Note that the adapted version contains about twelve. Note also that there are now more choices and a lot of background information. You may wish to check the changes made against the list in Table 4.3.

You have a friend who comes from a poor family. One day when you were in a supermarket you saw your friend *conceal* a packet of sweets under his *jacket*. He thinks you did not see him steal them. You know that the *manager* of the supermarket is very *strict* about shoplifters and always calls the police and *prosecutes offenders*. You also believe that the shop has some kind of system for catching shoplifters. What will you do?

- *Inform* the manager immediately and ask him not to *prosecute* your friend.
- Tell your friend to return the sweets to the *shelves*.
- Discuss it with your friend later to *discourage* him from doing it in the future.
- Just *ignore* it.
- Discuss it with your parents.
- Ask your friend for half of the sweets.
- Leave the shop immediately so that you are not *connected* with your friend's actions.
- *Forcibly* take the sweets from your friend and put them back on the shelves.

Split information and expert groups

Split the choices between the members of the group taking two each. Form groups of the people with the same pairs of choices. In these expert groups discuss (1) what your choices mean; (2) the advantages; and (3) disadvantages of each choice. Then split into groups of four with a person from each expert group in the new group.

Alternatively, or additionally, the activity could be role played, with each learner taking a role (the friend's parents, a worker in the supermarket, the police, the person who stole the sweets, you). Or each person takes on a job while doing the activity.

- Encourage others to speak by asking, 'What do you think?', 'Do you agree?', 'Which one do you *favour*?'.
- Summarise what others have said beginning with phrases like, 'So you think that ...', or 'So we have decided that...'.

- *Deliberately* disagree with some of the group members by saying things like, 'No. That's not a good idea. I think ...', or 'I'm opposed to that. I think we should ...'.
- Keep the group working towards the answer by saying things like, 'Let's decide what we *definitely* won't do', or 'Let's decide on the best *solution*.'

Reporting back

After your group has decided on a course of action, prepare a list of reasons why you chose this one and why you did not choose the others. Report these reasons to the other groups.

Teachers who are serious about planning vocabulary learning should give careful attention to the design of speaking activities. Without compromising the communicative nature of spoken activities it is easily possible to increase the opportunity for planned vocabulary learning.

It is worthwhile noting that speaking activities do not always have to be carried out in the second language in order to help second language vocabulary learning. Knight (1996) found that although learners used the first language a lot, they were actually discussing unknown second language words. Lameta-Tufuga (1994) deliberately introduced a discussion activity in the first language about the task the learners were going to do. The discussion was used to get learners to clarify what they needed to know in order to do the task. After the discussion in the first language, learners did the writing task in the second language. Learners who were given the opportunity to discuss the task in their first language did better on the writing task than learners who discussed it in the second language. The transcripts of the first language discussion show that a lot of second language vocabulary and phrases are embedded in the first language discussion:

- *... um e pei o mea ei lalo e malo i le pressure ao mea ei luga e semi-fluid.* (It's like the things below are rigid due to pressure and those above are semi-fluid.)
- Because *o le* membrane, *magakua le* membrane *le* cell membrane *lea e allowiga le vai e alu mai leisi iku lea e kele ai le vai i le mea lea e kau leai se vai.* (Because of the membrane, remember the membrane, the cell membrane that allows water to move from one side with higher water concentration to where there is less water.)

This discussion gets attention to both the form and meaning aspects of important words in the text and places the English words in a rich, meaningful context.

In spite of the transitory nature of listening and speaking, it is possible to encourage vocabulary learning through these skills by increasing the opportunity for deliberate creative attention. While doing this, it is also important to make sure that the vocabulary demands of listening and speaking are not overwhelming, so that work in these skills can contribute to learning through meaning-focused attention and fluency development.

For native speakers, learning through listening and speaking accounts for most early vocabulary growth. Second language teachers need to ensure that the listening and speaking parts of their language program are substantial enough and supportive of vocabulary growth for their learners too.

References

Adolphs, S. and Schmitt, N. (2003). Lexical coverage of spoken discourse. *Applied Linguistics*, **24**, 4, 425–38.

Adolphs, S. and Schmitt, N. (2004). Vocabulary coverage according to spoken discourse context. In Bogaards, P. and Laufer, B. (eds.), *Vocabulary in a Second Language: Selection, Acquisition, and Testing* (pp. 39–49). Amsterdam: John Benjamins.

Alcón-Soler, E. (2009). Focus on form, learner uptake and subsequent lexical gains in learners' oral production. *IRAL*, **47**, 3/4, 347–65.

Arevart, S. and Nation, I. S. P. (1991). Fluency improvement in a second language. *RELC Journal*, **22**, 1, 84–94.

Biber, D. and Conrad, S. (2009). *Register, Genre, and Style*. Cambridge: Cambridge University Press.

Bonk, W. J. (2000). Second language lexical knowledge and listening comprehension. *International Journal of Listening*, **14**, 14–31.

Brett, A., Rothlein, L. and Hurley, M. (1996). Vocabulary acquisition from listening to stories and explanations of target words. *Elementary School Journal*, **96**, 4, 415–22.

Brown, R., Waring, R. and Donkaewbua, S. (2008). Incidental vocabulary acquisition from reading, reading-while-listening, and listening to stories. *Reading in a Foreign Language*, **20**, 2, 136–63.

Chang, A. C. (2007). The impact of vocabulary preparation on L2 listening comprehension, confidence and strategy use. *System*, **35**, 4, 534–50.

Collins, M. F. (2005). ESL preschoolers' English vocabulary acquisition from storybook reading. *Reading Research Quarterly*, **40**, 4, 406–8.

Cummins, J. (1986). Language proficiency and language achievement. In Cummins, J. and Swain, M. (eds.), *Bilingualism in Education* (pp. 138–61). London: Longman.

Day, R. R. and Bamford, J. (2004). *Extensive Reading Activities for Teaching Language*. Cambridge: Cambridge University Press.

de Jong, N. and Perfetti, C. (2011). Fluency training in the ESL classroom: An experimental study of fluency development and proceduralization. *Language Learning*, **61**, 2, 533–68.

de la Fuente, M. (2002). Negotiation and oral acquisition of L2 vocabulary. *Studies in Second Language Acquisition*, 24, 2, 81–112.

de la Fuente, M. J. (2003). Is SLA interactionist theory relevant to CALL? A study on the effects of computer-mediated interaction in L2 vocabulary acquisition. *Computer Assisted Language Learning*, 16, 1, 47–81.

deHaan, J., Reed, W. M. and Kuwada, K. (2010). The effect of interactivity with a music video game on second language vocabulary recall. *Language Learning and Technology*, 14, 2, 79–94.

Dobinson, T. (2001). Do learners learn from classroom interaction and does the teacher have a role to play? *Language Teaching Research*, 5, 3, 189–211.

Eller, R. G., Pappas, C. C. and Brown, E. (1988). The lexical development of kindergarteners: Learning from written context. *Journal of Reading Behavior*, 20, 1, 5–24.

Elley, W. B. (1989). Vocabulary acquisition from listening to stories. *Reading Research Quarterly*, 24, 2, 174–87.

Ellis, R. (1995). Modified oral input and the acquisition of word meanings. *Applied Linguistics*, 16, 4, 409–41.

Ellis, R., Basturkmen, H. and Loewen, S. (2001). Learner uptake in communicative ESL lessons. *Language Learning*, 51, 281–326.

Ellis, R. and He, X. (1999). The roles of modified input and output in the incidental acquisition of word meanings. *Studies in Second Language Acquisition*, 21, 285–301.

Ellis, R. and Heimbach, R. (1997). Bugs and birds: children's acquisition of second language vocabulary through interaction. *System*, 25, 2, 247–59.

Ellis, R., Tanaka, Y. and Yamazaki, A. (1994). Classroom interaction, comprehension and the acquisition of L2 word meanings. *Language Learning*, 44, 3, 449–491.

Fountain, R. L. and Nation, I. S. P. (2000). A vocabulary-based graded dictation test. *RELC Journal*, 31, 2, 29–44.

Gibbons, P. (1998). The centrality of talk. *Challenge in challenge*, QATESOL *Occasional Papers* 2, 33–52.

Goh, C. (2000). A cognitive perspective on language learners' listening comprehension problems. *System*, 28, 55–75.

Hall, S. J. (1992). Using split information tasks to learn Mathematics vocabulary. *Guidelines*, 14, 1, 72–7.

Higa, M. (1965). The psycholinguistic concept of 'difficulty' and the teaching of foreign language vocabulary. *Language Learning*, 15, 3&4, 167–79.

Hu, M. and Nation, I. S. P. (2000). Vocabulary density and reading comprehension. *Reading in a Foreign Language*, 13, 1, 403–30.

Hulstijn, J. H. (1992). Retention of inferred and given word meanings: Experiments in incidental vocabulary learning. In Arnaud, P. J. L. and Bejoint, H. (eds.), *Vocabulary and Applied Linguistics* (pp. 113–25). London: Macmillan.

Joe, A. (1998). What effects do text-based tasks promoting generation have on incidental vocabulary acquisition? *Applied Linguistics*, 19, 3, 357–77.

Kim, Y. (2008). The contribution of collaborative and individual tasks to the acquisition of L2 vocabulary. *Modern Language Journal*, 92, 1, 114–30.

Knight, T. (1996). Learning vocabulary through shared tasks. *The Language Teacher*, 20, 1, 24–9.

Kötter, M. (2003). Negotiation of meaning and codeswitching in online tandems. *Language Learning and Technology*, 7, 2, 145–72.

Lameta-Tufuga, E. U. (1994). *Using the Samoan Language for Academic Learning Tasks*. Victoria University of Wellington, Wellington.

Loschky, L. (1994). Comprehensible input and second language acquisition: What is the relationship? *Studies in Second Language Acquisition*, 16, 303–24.

Manzo, A. V. (1970). CAT: A game for extending vocabulary and knowledge of allusions. *Journal of Reading*, 13, 367–69.

Maurice, K. (1983). The fluency workshop. *TESOL Newsletter*, 8, 83.

McCarthy, M. and Carter, R. (1997). Written and spoken vocabulary. In Schmitt, N. and McCarthy, M. (eds.), *Vocabulary: Description, Acquisition and Pedagogy* (pp. 20–39). Cambridge: Cambridge University Press.

McDonough, K. and Sunitham, W. (2009). Collaborative dialogue between Thai EFL learners during self-access computer activities. *TESOL Quarterly*, 43, 2, 231–54.

Nagy, W. E., Herman, P. and Anderson, R. C. (1985). Learning words from context. *Reading Research Quarterly*, 20, 2, 233–53.

Nation, I. S. P. (1977). The combining arrangement: Some techniques. *Modern Language Journal*, 61, 3, 89–94.

Nation, I. S. P. (1983). Testing and teaching vocabulary. *Guidelines*, 5, 1, 12–25.

Nation, I. S. P. (1990). *Teaching and Learning Vocabulary*. Rowley, MA: Newbury House.

Nation, I. S. P. (1991). Managing group discussion: Problem-solving tasks. *Guidelines*, 13, 1, 1–10.

Nation, I. S. P. (2006). How large a vocabulary is needed for reading and listening? *Canadian Modern Language Review*, 63, 1, 59–82.

Nation, P. and Crabbe, D. (1991). A survival language learning syllabus for foreign travel. *System*, 19, 3, 191–201.

Nation, P. and Hamilton-Jenkins, A. (2000). Using communicative tasks to teach vocabulary. *Guidelines*, 22, 2, 15–19.

Newton, J. (1995). Task-based interaction and incidental vocabulary learning: A case study. *Second Language Research*, 11, 2, 159–77.

Newton, J. (2001). Options for vocabulary learning through communication tasks. *ELT Journal*, 55, 1, 30–37.

Newton, J. (2013). Incidental vocabulary learning in classroom communication tasks. *Language Teaching Research*, 17, 3, 164–87.

Ortega, L. (1999). Planning and focus on form in L2 oral performance. *SSLA*, 21, 1, 109–48.

Palmer, D. M. (1982). Information transfer for listening and reading. *English Teaching Forum*, 20, 1, 29–33.

Parry, K. (1991). Building a vocabulary through academic reading. *TESOL Quarterly*, 25, 4, 629–53.

Pawley, A. and Syder, F. H. (1983). Two puzzles for linguistic theory: Nativelike selection and nativelike fluency. In Richards, J. C. and Schmidt, R. W. (eds.), *Language and Communication* (pp. 191–225). London: Longman.

Schmitt, N., Jiang, X. and Grabe, W. (2011). The percentage of words known in a text and reading comprehension. *The Modern Language Journal*, **95**, 1, 26–43.

Shin, D. (2007). What English collocations would be unpredictable for Korean EFL learners? *Korean Journal of Applied Linguistics*, **23**, 2, 83–98.

Shin, D. (2009). *A Collocation Inventory for Beginners: Spoken Collocations of English*. Köln: LAP LAMBERT Academic Publishing.

Simcock, M. (1993). Developing productive vocabulary using the 'Ask and Answer' technique. *Guidelines*, **15**, 2, 1–7.

Smidt, E. and Hegelheimer, V. (2004). Effects of online academic lectures on ESL listening comprehension, incidental vocabulary acquisition, and strategy use. *Computer Assisted Language Learning*, **17**, 5, 517–56.

Smith, B. (2005). The relationship between negotiated interaction, learner uptake, and lexical acquisition in task-based computer-mediated communication. *TESOL Quarterly*, **39**, 1, 33–58.

Staehr, L. S. (2009). Vocabulary knowledge and advanced listening comprehension in English as a foreign language. *Studies in Second Language Acquisition*, **31**, 4, 577–607.

Stahl, S. A. and Vancil, S. J. (1986). Discussion is what makes semantic maps work in vocabulary instruction. *The Reading Teacher*, **40**, 1, 62–7.

Stenstrom, A. (1990). Lexical items peculiar to spoken discourse. In Svartvik, J. (ed.), *The London-Lund Corpus of Spoken English: Description and Research. Lund Studies in English 82* (pp. 137–75). Lund: Lund University Press.

Sutarsyah, C., Nation, P. and Kennedy, G. (1994). How useful is EAP vocabulary for ESP? A corpus based study. *RELC Journal*, **25**, 2, 34–50.

Swain, M. and Lapkin, S. (1998). Interaction and second language learning: Two adolescent French immersion students working together. *Modern Language Journal*, **82**, 320–37.

Syodorenko, T. (2010). Modality of input and vocabulary acquisition. *Language Learning & Technology*, **14**, 2, 50–73.

Ur, P. (1981). *Discussions that Work*. Cambridge: Cambridge University Press.

van Zeeland, H. and Schmitt, N. (2012). Lexical coverage and L1 and L2 listening comprehension: The same or different from reading comprehension? *Applied Linguistics*, doi:10.1093/applin/ams074.

Vidal, K. (2003). Academic listening: A source of vocabulary acquisition? *Applied Linguistics*, **24**, 1, 56–89.

Vidal, K. (2011). A comparison of the effects of reading and listening on incidental vocabulary acquisition. *Language Learning*, **61**, 1, 219–58.

Webb, S. and Chang, A. C.-S. (2012). Vocabulary learning through assisted and unassisted repeated reading. *Canadian Modern Language Review*, **68**, 3, 1–24.

Webb, S., Newton, J. and Chang, A. C.-S. (2013). Incidental learning of collocation. *Language Learning*, **63**, 1, 91–120.

Webb, S. and Rodgers, M. P. H. (2009a). The vocabulary demands of television programs. *Language Learning*, **59**, 2, 335–66.

Webb, S. and Rodgers, M. P. H. (2009b). The lexical coverage of movies. *Applied Linguistics*, **30**, 3, 407–27.

West, M. (1953). *A General Service List of English Words*. London: Longman, Green & Co.

Williams, J. (1999). Learner-generated attention to form. *Language Learning*, **51**, 303–46.

Woodeson, E. (1982). Communicative crosswords. *Modern English Teacher*, **10**, 2, 29–30.

5 Vocabulary and reading and writing

Reading and the four strands

When looking at language learning in general, or the learning of a particular skill like listening, speaking, reading or writing, it is useful to look at what can make up such a course across the four strands of meaning-focused input, meaning-focused output, language-focused learning and fluency development. About half the time in a reading course should be spent on meaning-focused input which should largely be done through extensive reading, although there are other meaning-focused reading activities which can contribute to this strand (Nation and Yamamoto, 2011). Reading can also contribute to meaning-focused output when learners talk about what they have read or write about what they have read. Meaning-focused output can contribute to reading, when learners gain background knowledge through speaking and writing which can make subsequent reading easier. There are also language-focused learning elements to improving the reading skill, as in intensive reading, the deliberate study of reading strategies, and the deliberate learning of vocabulary for reading. The fluency development strand has a major role to play in a reading course and this fluency development can occur through easy extensive reading, a focused speed reading course and activities like repeated reading. Fluency development should make up about one-quarter of the reading course.

In the reading section of this chapter, we look at how much vocabulary is needed to gain meaning-focused input through reading unsimplified material, how learners can increase their reading vocabulary, the value of reading unsimplified text and simplified text for vocabulary learning, and the value of reading simplified text for improving skill in reading.

How much vocabulary is needed for reading?

There has been a continuing interest in whether there is a language knowledge threshold which marks the boundary between not having enough language knowledge for successful language use and having enough language knowledge for successful use. There are at least two ways of defining what a threshold is. One way is to see a threshold as an all-or-nothing phenomenon. If a learner has not crossed the threshold, then adequate comprehension is not possible. If the learner has crossed the threshold, then, other things being equal, comprehension is possible for all learners. This is the strong view of a threshold and the one that corresponds to its traditional meaning.

Another way is to see a threshold as a probabilistic boundary. That is, if a learner has not crossed the threshold, the chances of comprehending adequately are low. If the learner has crossed the threshold, the chances are on the side of the learner gaining adequate comprehension, and the greater the distance over the threshold, the greater the comprehension. This is a considerably weakened definition of a threshold.

The major problems with the threshold idea relate to defining what is meant by comprehension and what other factors are affecting comprehension such as background knowledge and the nature of the low frequency vocabulary in the text.

Laufer and Sim (1985b) used comprehension questions and interviews with learners to determine a threshold score where learners could be said to be able to comprehend an English for Academic Purposes text in the First Certificate in English exam. Laufer (1989) then went a step further to see what percentage of word tokens (running words) needed to be understood in order to ensure 'reasonable' reading comprehension of the text. Laufer set reasonable comprehension as a score of 55% or more. Laufer found that the group that scored 95% and above on the vocabulary measure had a significantly higher number of successful readers (scores of 55% and above on the reading test) than those scoring below 95%. The 90% level did not result in significant differences between those above and below. A comparison of the 95% and above group with the 90–94% group revealed a significant difference in comprehension scores. In this study, Laufer does not justify the 55% threshold of comprehension (it does not agree with the 65–70% threshold determined in the Laufer and Sim, 1985a study) except to say it is the lowest passing grade in the Haifa University system. Laufer sees this as minimally acceptable comprehension.

It is necessary to understand why coverage of tokens is important: 80% coverage of a text means that one word in every five is unknown

Table 5.1 *The number of unfamiliar tokens per 100 tokens and the number of lines of text containing one unfamiliar word*

% text coverage	Number of unfamiliar tokens per 100 tokens	Number of text lines per 1 unfamiliar word
99	1	10
98	2	5
95	5	2
90	10	1
80	20	0.5

(about two words per line); 90% coverage means one in every ten words is unknown (about one word per line); and 95% coverage means one in every 20 is unknown (about one unknown word in every two lines) (see Table 5.1).

Hu and Nation (2000) compared the effect of four text coverages on reading comprehension of a fiction text. In the 100% text coverage, no words were unknown. In the 95% text coverage version, 5% of the running words were unknown (on average one unknown word in every 20). In the 90% version there was on average one unknown word in every ten running words, and in the 80% text coverage version there was one unknown word in every five running words. Hu and Nation found a predictable relationship between text coverage and comprehension, with comprehension improving as the text coverage by the known words increased. At the 95% coverage level, some learners gained adequate comprehension but most did not. At the 90% coverage level a smaller number gained adequate comprehension, and at the 80% level none did. Hu and Nation concluded that for largely unassisted reading for pleasure, learners would need to know around 98% of the running words in the text.

Hu and Nation's (2000) study suggests that the all-or-nothing threshold is around 80% vocabulary coverage for fiction text. No learner reading the text with this coverage achieved adequate comprehension. The probabilistic threshold is around 98%. With this coverage almost all learners have a chance of gaining adequate comprehension. If instead of adequate comprehension, a standard of minimally acceptable comprehension is applied (as Laufer did in her study), then 95% coverage is likely to be the probabilistic threshold.

Hu and Nation (2000) found a predictable relationship between percentage coverage of known words and comprehension. Most learners in this study needed 98% coverage to gain adequate comprehension of a fiction text. At 95% coverage, some gained adequate comprehension but most did not.

There are several weaknesses in the Hu and Nation study, and it may prove impossible to define adequate comprehension given the many purposes learners have for reading. Nevertheless, there has been continuing interest in the threshold of vocabulary knowledge needed for reading, particularly because this relates closely to vocabulary size. Unlike Hu and Nation, Schmitt et al. (2011) did not adapt the texts they used but had learners from a range of proficiency levels read them. The percentage coverage was determined by a vocabulary checklist test based on a sample of 50% of the words largely beyond the 1,000-word frequency level. Their conclusion was that the relationship between vocabulary coverage and comprehension was a linear one. That is, the more words that were understood, the better the text was comprehended. Higher coverage leads to higher comprehension. When deciding how much text coverage is need for comprehension, it is always worthwhile bearing in mind the commonsense explanation illustrated in Table 5.1. Essentially, this illustrates that the lower the density of unknown words, the greater the supporting context around the unknown words that do occur and therefore the greater the likelihood of being able to cope with the unknown word and with comprehension of the text. As a goal for learning and for the choice of suitable texts, 98% coverage is a sensible goal.

Text coverage of tokens is one way of determining the vocabulary load of a text. Another way is to see how many different words a learner would encounter when reading a particular text. A coverage of 2% of the tokens means that in an average novel (around 100,000 tokens long) there would be at least 700 different unknown word families beyond the ninth 1,000 level. This is a very heavy burden for anyone reading the novel. For this reason, the mid-frequency readers designed for learners with vocabulary sizes of 4,000, 6,000 or 8,000 word families (see Paul Nation's website) used the number of unknown word families rather than tokens as the goal when adapting the texts. This resulted in token coverages higher than 99%.

Using word family lists developed from the British National Corpus, Nation (2006) and Webb and Macalister (forthcoming) looked at the vocabulary sizes needed to gain 95% and 98% coverage of various kinds of texts. The word family was used as the unit of counting because such a study involves receptive knowledge and the assumption is that closely related members of a family are typically accessible when reading if one or more members of the family are known and the learners are familiar with the common word building devices of English. Table 5.2 (based on Nation, 2006) summarises the coverage figures.

Table 5.2 *Vocabulary sizes needed to get 95% and 98% coverage (including proper nouns) of various kinds of texts*

Texts	95% coverage	98% coverage	Proper nouns
Novels	4,000 word families	9,000 word families	1–2%
Newspapers	4,000 word families	8,000 word families	5–6%
Writing for children	4,000 word families	10,000 word families	3.5%
Children's movies	4,000 word families	6,000 word families	1.5%
Spoken English	3,000 word families	7,000 word families	1.3%

Table 5.2 shows that around 4,000 word families (which includes proper nouns) are needed to get 95% coverage of written text, and 3,000 word families for spoken text; 6,000–7,000 word families are needed for 98% coverage for spoken text and 8,000–10,000 for written text. It may be useful to call 95% coverage minimal coverage and 98% adequate coverage (Laufer and Ravenhorst-Kalovski, 2010).

In this book, the dividing line between meaning-focused input and language-focused learning will be 98% vocabulary coverage, although this dividing line must be seen as rather hazy and dependent on a variety of factors such as the amount of background knowledge a learner brings to a text, the relevance of the unknown words to the message of the text, the learner's reading skills, and the amount of support provided by pictures and other aids during the reading of the text.

Text register, for example, has marked effects on the type of vocabulary that occurs. Gardner (2004) conducted a corpus study of collections of theme-related and non-theme-related unsimplified expository and narrative texts typically used with upper elementary grade school native speakers. Narrative texts were found to use more words from an independently created high-frequency word list. Expository texts used more academic and theme-related vocabulary than narrative texts did. Text register also affects the occurrence of the same words across different texts, with texts in the same register being more likely to use the same vocabulary. A theme needs to be very tightly defined for there to be significant use of the same theme-related vocabulary between different texts in the same dramatic group.

Narratives are favourable texts for gaining control of the general service high-frequency words. However, because much of the vocabulary used in expository texts does not occur in narrative texts (and vice versa), it is important that learners read over a range of registers.

The evidence suggests that the probabilistic threshold is the one most supported by the research evidence. As yet unpublished studies suggest that overall vocabulary size rather than text coverage is the critical vocabulary factor in comprehension. The cause–effect relationships between vocabulary size and comprehension are probably complicated.

What role does vocabulary play in determining the readability of a text?

In his classic study of readability, Klare (1963) notes that the word is the most important unit in measuring readability and the characteristic most often measured is frequency.

However, the factors affecting the readability of a text obviously involve much more than the vocabulary. Chall (1958) points out that the vocabulary factor is an indicator of conceptual knowledge. Carrell (1987), in a very useful review of readability in ESL, considers a range of factors including motivation, prior knowledge, propositional density and rhetorical structure.

Readability formulas however focus on what is easily measurable and thus word length and sentence length are attractive measures. The Flesch Reading Ease Formula, for example, in its simplified version looks like this:

$$RE = .4(words/sentences) + 12(syllables/words) - 16$$

This means that with this formula the readability of a text is calculated by checking how long the sentences are (words/sentences) and how long the words are (syllables/words), with the idea that greater length of sentences and words equals greater difficulty.

Elley (1969) explored an easily applied measure of readability for reading material intended for native-speaking children, with very promising results. Elley used a graded frequency list based on writing done by children. The list consisted of eight levels. Readability measures were gained in the following way.

1. From each story or selection, take three passages each long enough to contain at least 20 nouns.
2. Using the graded word list, record the frequency level of all the nouns in the passage. That is, each noun appearing in the highest frequency level will receive a score of 1, those in the second highest level will receive a score of 2. Those not in the eight levels receives a score of 9.
   Use these rules:
   (a) Do not count people's names
   (b) Count lemmas not types or tokens
   (c) Count each lemma once only.

3. Add up the frequency level numbers and divide by the number of nouns.

Elley's measure performed better than a range of other readability measures. Elley's measure (or a variation of it) could be easily computerised, though the practicality of the measure is such that checking the nouns manually could take less time than typing the text or nouns into a computer.

Such readability measures however only consider the symptoms of some of the more important underlying factors affecting readability.

A danger of readability measures is that they may mislead their users into thinking that simply by adapting texts using the factors involved in readability formulas, texts can be made easier to read. This is not necessarily so. However, readability measures underline the importance of vocabulary knowledge in reading.

Brown (1998), in a substantial study carried out with Japanese university students, compared students' cloze scores on 50 passages with first language readability measures and linguistic characteristics of the texts. Brown found that the first language readability indices were only weakly related to the EFL students' scores on the cloze test and four of the linguistic characteristics (number of syllables per sentence, the average frequency of lexical items elsewhere in the passage, percentage of words with seven or more letters, and percentage of function words) when combined were more highly related to EFL difficulty. Greenfield (2004) found that only two measures (letters per word, and words per sentence) produced a correlation of 0.86 with cloze test scores.

Using data from the computational text analysis program Coh-Metrix, Crossley et al. (2008) found that three variables were much more successful than traditional measures in predicting cloze test scores. They were (1) written word frequency using data from an early version of the COBUILD corpus; (2) uniformity of sentence construction between adjacent sentences; and (3) content word overlap between adjacent sentences. Note that two of these measures are strongly vocabulary based. The three measures produced a multiple correlation of 0.93 and a corresponding $R2$ of 0.86 with the cloze test scores on the same passages (Crossley et al., 2008: 485). When we look at these measures closely, we can see that they reflect important features of good writing in graded readers and L1 children's books, namely the use of high-frequency vocabulary, and repetitive and clearly linked sentences.

Vocabulary clearly plays an important role in readability, but it does not make sense to apply first language measures to texts intended for L2 learners.

How much reading is needed for vocabulary development?

Cobb (2007) examines Krashen's (1985) claim that vocabulary learning from extensive reading is sufficient for requiring an adequate and substantial second language vocabulary. Although various studies of second language vocabulary learning from graded readers in extensive reading show only small amounts of vocabulary learning, both Cobb and Krashen agree in pointing out that such studies greatly underestimate the amount of vocabulary learning occurring through reading. This underestimation is largely a result of the insensitivity of the measures used, and in many studies, the use of only one measure of vocabulary knowledge. As Waring and Takaki (2003), Pigada and Schmitt (2006) and Webb (2005, 2008) have shown, multiple measures of different focuses and strengths show substantial amounts of vocabulary learning of different aspects of vocabulary knowledge, regardless of how the words were learned.

The most obvious argument for input alone being sufficient for vocabulary learning comes from first language learning. There is now good evidence that young native speakers of English learn around 1,000 word families a year so that five-year-olds have a vocabulary of around 3,000 words (Biemiller and Slonim, 2001), and 13-year-olds around 10,000 word families. It is likely that much of this learning comes from listening, but reading also plays an important role, particularly in accounting for the large range of vocabulary sizes among learners of the same age at upper primary and secondary school levels. Deliberate study of vocabulary is likely to account for only a very small part of this native speaker vocabulary growth. Native speakers get a large amount of spoken input and those turned on to reading may get a large amount of written input. It seems likely that children whose parents are not native speakers of English but who were born in an English-speaking country or arrive there at a young age (probably before the age of six or seven) are soon effectively native speakers of English from a vocabulary perspective. That is, their vocabulary size grows at the same rate as that of native speakers. So, can learners of English as a foreign language gain enough input to be able to learn the around 9,000 high-frequency and mid-frequency words needed to deal with unsimplified text? This does not mean that they have to have the same amount of input as native speakers, but it means that they have to have enough input to get sufficient repetition of the high- and mid-frequency words to ensure learning. Cobb (2007) argues that foreign language learners cannot feasibly get enough input to even meet enough words at the right level, let alone meet them with enough repetitions to learn them.

Using a sample of 10 words from each of the 1,000, 2,000 and 3,000 British National Corpus word family levels, Cobb (2007) looked at how often each of these 30 families occurred in sections of the around 170,000 tokens long Brown Corpus. His data showed that reading input of around 170,000 tokens is not sufficient to get enough repetitions (Cobb set the minimum of six repetitions which is rather low) to learn several of the second 1,000 and most of the third 1,000 words. A 300,000-word corpus of seven Jack London stories was also analysed, finding that 817 of the third 1000 words occurred and that only 469 are met six times or more. Cobb took 170,000 tokens and 300,000 tokens as large amounts of input for a foreign language learner. He equated 170,000 words to 100 newspaper pages, or six stories each the same length as *Alice in Wonderland*, or 17 academic articles.

McQuillan and Krashen (2008) responded to Cobb's analysis. Their first and most important point is that 170,000 or 300,000 tokens of input is a very pessimistic amount. Using data from Fraser (2007), they show that learners from a variety of L2 backgrounds read at rates from 83 words per minute to 206 words per minute. Studies by Chung and Nation (2006) and Tran (2012b) of learning from a speed reading course found rates higher than 200 words per minute by the end of the speed reading course for their EFL university students. McQuillan and Krashen chose the very conservative rate of 100 words per minute and worked out how many tokens could be read for a particular investment of time per day. So, reading for 60 minutes a day for one academic quarter (86.2 hours of reading) would result in the learner reading over 517,000 tokens. To calculate another way, if learners read for 25 minutes a day (only on weekdays) for 40 school weeks of the year at a rate of 100 words per minute, they would read 500,000 tokens. This is certainly a very manageable amount of reading. Note that this calculation and the resulting vocabulary learning from it assume the following things:

- Learners are reading material which is at the right level for them, preferably with 98% coverage of the tokens.
- Their reading rate is at least 100 words per minute. This is actually a slow reading rate.
- A minimum of six repetitions are needed for learning. This is likely to be an underestimate of the repetitions needed and it would be safer to require at least 10 and preferably 20 repetitions.

Cobb (2008) responded to McQuillan and Krashen's critique by pointing out that reading unsimplified text is very difficult for learners with vocabulary sizes of around 2,000 words and so a reading rate of

100 words per minute is too fast. This is now a different argument from that presented in Cobb (2007). It seems that Cobb and McQuillan and Krashen would not disagree that if the texts were at the right level for the learners so that they could read at a rate of at least 100 words per minute with no more than 2% of the running words outside the correct knowledge, it would not be unrealistic to achieve reasonably large amounts of reading input (from 500,000 to 1,000,000 tokens per year).

Thus, there are two major related issues involved in getting enough reading input. The first issue is that beyond the second 1,000-word level, it is hard to find enough material at the right level for learners at various vocabulary size levels (3,000 words, 4,000 words and so on) so that they can read with relative ease and enjoyment. The second major issue is that if we assume material is at the right level, how much would learners have to read to get enough repetitions to learn the new vocabulary they meet? Cobb and McQuillan and Krashen's basic disagreement is not as much a quantity disagreement as one related to the conditions for learning from input. McQuillan and Krashen assume reading under favourable vocabulary load conditions. Cobb assumes difficult vocabulary load conditions.

What if conditions were favourable? How much reading would learners have to do to learn vocabulary at the various 1,000 levels beyond the second 1,000? Table 5.3 shows data gained from differently sized corpora of novels.

Would learners be able to read the amounts shown in column 2 of Table 5.3 if the material were at the right level for them so that the target words would make up around 2% of the words in the text and the words beyond the target level were largely replaced? Table 5.4 converts the token figures into hours of reading per week. The calculation of the time in column 3 of Table 5.4 assumes that a learner reads at a speed of 200 words per minute five times a week for 40 weeks of the year. In column 4, the time is simply doubled for the slower reading speed of 100 wpm.

If a learner reads a total of 3 million tokens, then they would meet the first 10,000 words often enough to have a chance of learning them. However, Table 5.3 shows that if you see the learning of vocabulary through reading as a set of staged steps, then after learners know the first 2,000 words, the next step to learn the third 1,000 words would involve reading around an additional 300,000 tokens (Table 5.4, column 2, row 3). The next step, to learn the fourth 1,000 words, would require reading another half million tokens, and after that reading an additional 1 million tokens to learn the fifth 1,000 words.

Table 5.3 *Corpus sizes needed to gain an average of at least ten repetitions at each of nine 1,000 word levels using a corpus of novels*

1,000 word list level	Corpus size to get at least 10 repetitions at this 1,000 word level (repetitions)	Number of families met	Number of novels
2nd 1,000 families	171,411 (13.4)	805 of 2nd 1,000	2
3rd 1,000 families	300,219 (12.6)	830 of 3rd 1,000	3
4th 1,000 families	534,697 (12.6)	812 of 4th 1,000	6
5th 1,000 families	1,061,382 (13.7)	807 of 5th 1,000	9
6th 1,000 families	1,450,068 (13.1)	795 of 6th 1,000	13
7th 1,000 families	2,035,809 (13.7)	766 of 7th 1,000	16
8th 1,000 families	2,427,807 (14.1)	755 of 8th 1,000	20
9th 1,000 families	2,956,908 (12.0)	805 of 9th 1,000	25
10th 1,000 families	2,956,908 (9.8)	754 of 10th 1,000	25

Table 5.4 *Amount of reading in tokens and hours per week to meet the 1,000 word families around 10 times*

1,000 word list level	Amount to read (in tokens)	Hours per week @ 200 wpm	Hours per week @ 100 wpm
2nd 1,000	171,411	21 minutes	42 minutes
3rd 1,000	300,219	38 minutes	1 hour 16 minutes
4th 1,000	534,697	1 hour 5 minutes	2 hours 10 minutes
5th 1,000	1,061,382	2 hours 12 minutes	4 hours 24 minutes
6th 1,000	1,450,068	3 hours	6 hours
7th 1,000	2,035,809	4 hours 5 minutes	8 hours 10 minutes
8th 1,000	2,427,807	5 hours 3 minutes	10 hours 6 minutes
9th 1,000	2,956,908	6 hours 10 minutes	12 hours 20 minutes
10th 1,000	2,956,908	6 hours 10 minutes	12 hours 20 minutes

If we assume that each 1,000 word family step takes one year, then by the time the learners reached the sixth 1,000, they need to read one and a half million tokens in that year, and 2 million tokens in the next.

These are manageable amounts of reading. Thus, it is feasible to learn large amounts of vocabulary through reading, and the ready availability of graded readers for learning the first 3,000 word families, and mid-frequency readers for learning the fourth to ninth 1,000s means that reading material at the right level is available to support such learning.

Is input by itself all that is needed for vocabulary development?

The argument that comprehensible input is all that is needed for language growth is more complicated than it seems. It can be stated in several different ways, from the most extreme to the less extreme:

- Deliberate learning and learning from output do not help. Only input helps.
- Deliberate learning does not help. Learning from output helps but is not necessary.
- Deliberate learning and learning from output help, but they are not necessary.

From a vocabulary perspective, the extreme position, that deliberate learning and learning from output cannot help, and the second position that deliberate learning does not help, are not correct.

There is no doubt that meaning-focused input is essential for language learning, and that poorly focused and carried out language-focused learning is a waste of valuable learning time. It is also likely that production that learners are not ready for is not pleasurable and has negative effects on learning. Advocates of an input only position as the means of learning a language however need to consider the following questions.

Can the best kinds of meaning-focused output contribute to learning? Can the best kinds of language-focused learning speed up progress in receptive and productive language use by focusing on readily learned items? There is strong research evidence and commonsense evidence of positive answers to both of these questions.

- *Meaning-focused output.* Research on productive fluency activities like 4/3/2 (Arevart and Nation, 1991; de Jong and Perfetti, 2011; Nation, 1989) show that improvements in output fluency are accompanied by improvements in accuracy and complexity of language use. This is more than just a performance effect caused by a reduction in cognitive load.

Research on meaning-focused output activities shows that using newly met items in production enhances learning (Joe, 1995). The commonsense evidence is related to the time-on-task principle. You get better at speaking by doing lots of speaking, and you get better at writing by doing lots of writing. It would be foolish to expect improvement in either of these productive skills without practice in the skills.

- *Language-focused learning.* Research on deliberate vocabulary learning shows that such learning is highly efficient, resulting in initial learning of large amounts of vocabulary in a very short time. This learning is not only efficient but effective, in that such knowledge can be retained for a long time and involves the implicit knowledge which is essential for normal language use (Altarriba and Knickerbocker, 2011; Elgort, 2011). In addition, the evidence from studies on the effect of sleep on learning (Dumay and Gaskell, 2005, 2007) and priming studies (Elgort, 2011) shows that deliberately learned vocabulary is quickly integrated into the existing lexical system of the learners.

The commonsense evidence is that deliberately learned words, phrases and sentences can be used in message-focused language reception and production. Reading activities followed by deliberate attention to vocabulary result in better vocabulary knowledge (Sonbul and Schmitt, 2009).

Advocates of the importance of input could with some justification reject the idea of giving meaning-focused output the same allocation of time as meaning-focused input. They may want to see input far outweigh output. Under an equal time allocation however, the quantity of written input (in terms of total tokens) is highly likely to far outweigh the more slowly produced written output. Nonetheless, it may be more reasonable to see meaning-focused input and meaning-focused output as together making up 75% of the course time (meaning-focused input, meaning-focused output, fluency development) with a flexible allocation of time for input and output within that 75%.

The third position in favour of comprehensible input as the only source of learning needed says that other kinds of learning (deliberate learning and learning from output) help but are not necessary – learning from comprehensible input can do what other kinds of learning do. This position is harder to disprove. The major argument in favour of deliberate learning is that it can substantially speed up learning. The evidence from L1 learning and some L2 learning is that it is not necessary, particularly if L2 input at the right level is available. Where it is not available, deliberate learning may be essential in order for learners to achieve a vocabulary size which enables them to gain comprehensible input.

The evidence for output regarding vocabulary relates to the receptive/productive distinction. There is evidence that receptive learning contributes to productive knowledge (Webb, 2009). There is also evidence that productive learning has its greatest effect on productive knowledge (Webb, 2005, 2009), although this evidence relates to deliberate learning.

At the very least, learners who relied only on incidental learning would be slowing down their progress in moving towards reading unsimplified texts with ease. Deliberate learning of vocabulary can make a substantial contribution to vocabulary size and can provide the kind of vocabulary knowledge that is needed for reading.

How can learners increase their reading vocabulary?

Vocabulary learning can occur across the four strands of meaning-focused input (learning from listening and from reading), meaning-focused output (learning from speaking and from writing), language-focused learning (the deliberate study of vocabulary from word cards, from teaching and from vocabulary exercises) and fluency development. Learners need to draw on all these four opportunities for learning, and they are all looked at in detail in various parts of this book.

The research on learning second language vocabulary through reading is reviewed in Chapter 8 on guessing words from context. Generally, this research shows that small amounts of incidental vocabulary learning at a range of levels of strength of knowledge occur from reading. These small amounts can become big amounts if learners read large quantities of comprehensible text.

Experimental studies of extensive reading have used unsimplified texts written for young native speakers and simplified texts written for non-native speakers. Both of these kinds of texts provide favourable conditions for language learning, and their use has resulted in substantial learning. The experimental studies show that there are many benefits from extensive reading in quality of language use, language knowledge, and general academic success. To be effective an extensive reading program needs to involve large quantities of reading at an appropriate level.

The term **extensive reading** can have many meanings. In some cases, for example in China, extensive reading is used to refer to intensive reading of very long texts. In this book, however, extensive reading refers to the reading of large numbers of texts largely chosen by the learners where there are 5% or less unknown running words. It should aim to be a pleasurable activity with a focus on the quantity of enjoyable reading. The following list of principles which often characterise extensive reading is slightly adapted from Day and Bamford (2002). The order has been changed so that the principles are ranked with the most important principles coming first, and a two-strands principle (principle 5) has been added:

1. The reading material is easy.
2. Learners read as much as possible.
3. Reading is individual and silent.
4. Reading is its own reward.
5. The extensive reading course has a meaning-focused input strand and a fluency strand.
6. Reading speed is usually faster rather than slower.
7. A variety of reading material on a wide range of topics must be available.
8. Learners choose what they want to read.
9. The purpose of reading is usually related to pleasure, information and general understanding.
10. Teachers orient and guide their students.
11. The teacher is a role model of a reader.

(See Prowse, 2002, and Robb, 2002, for largely supportive critiques of Day and Bamford's principles.)

The idea that learners can develop their language knowledge through extensive reading is attractive for several reasons. Firstly, reading is essentially an individual activity and therefore learners of different proficiency levels could be learning at their own level without being locked into an inflexible class programme. Secondly, it allows learners to follow their interests in choosing what to read and thus increase their motivation for learning. Thirdly, it provides the opportunity for learning to occur outside the classroom. Fourthly, it provides the chance to gain large quantities of comprehensible input which is otherwise not easily available where English is taught as a foreign language. It is likely that the effects of extensive reading are more apparent in the short term on general reading skills than on language development (Yamashita, 2008).

A useful distinction is made between intensive reading and extensive reading. **Intensive reading** involves the close deliberate study of texts, usually short texts sometimes less than 100 words long, but often around 300–500 words long. Although the aim of intensive reading is to understand the text, the procedures involved direct a lot of attention to the vocabulary, grammar and discourse of the text. This deliberate attention to language features means that intensive reading fits within the strand of language-focused learning.

Research shows that reading accompanied by deliberate learning activities results in better vocabulary learning than reading by itself (Min, 2008; Paribakht and Wesche, 1993, 1996; Sonbul and Schmitt, 2009). Paribakht and Wesche (1993) attempted to equalise the time taken for the two treatments and to match the additional exercises for the reading-plus group with additional reading for the reading-only group, so that the result was not an effect of time on task.

Rather than compare reading with reading-plus activities, Laufer and Rozovski-Roitblat (2011) compared reading a text with the possibility of dictionary use with reading a text with accompanying vocabulary-focused activities, showing a very strong effect for the vocabulary-focused activities.

There have been several computer-based studies comparing deliberate vocabulary learning with learning from reading. This kind of study almost inevitably shows that the focused deliberate learning of vocabulary is more efficient than incidental vocabulary learning from reading (James, 1996; Tozcu and Coady, 2004). Deliberate vocabulary learning is better seen as a support for learning from reading, not a competitor. A combination of these two strands of learning is much more productive than relying on only one strand

Christensen et al. (2007) compared a computer-assisted rote-learning program (without sentence contexts) with a computer-based diglot reader (Burling, 1968, 1978), where an L1 text is gradually turned into an L2 text by progressively replacing L1 words with L2 words. By clicking on the L2 word in the text, the learner could hear it pronounced or see its L1 translation. The two programs gave similar results for vocabulary breadth and depth, but learners clearly preferred using the diglot program.

Unpublished studies of graded readers indicate that words at the current level of the reader (for example of Level 5 words in a Level 5 reader) largely occur in a variety of contexts, thus providing the opportunity for the useful learning condition of receptive creative retrieval to occur. In a diglot reader study, it would be useful to see what role having a connected text played in motivating students, compared to having a variety of isolated sentences in a rote-learning program. The fact that the learner is using language, as well as learning language when working with the diglot reader, may be a strongly motivating factor.

The experiments described above agree with other studies, largely comparing incidental and intentional learning (Hulstijn, 1988) which show more learning for a deliberate intentional focus on vocabulary.

Rather than compare reading input with reading plus activities, Brown et al. (2008) looked at the effect of the medium of the input. They tested vocabulary learning from three input modes: reading, reading-while-listening and listening. Predictably, scores on the receptive multiple-choice test were much higher than scores on the receptive translation tests. Reading-while-listening scores on the immediate multiple-choice test (average 13.31 out of 28) were similar to those on reading only (average 12.54), and listening-only scores were the lowest (8.2). A similar pattern was observed with the vocabulary translation test. The learners generally favoured the listening-while-reading mode while none favoured listening only. As several studies have found, the more frequently a word occurred, the more likely it was to be learned (Kweon and Kim, 2008; Laufer and Rozovski-Roitblat, 2011; Pellicer-Sanchez and Schmitt, 2010; Rott, 1999).

Brown et al. (2008) gave most emphasis to the low results on the three-month delayed translation post-test, but this greatly understates the learning that occurred. The multiple-choice vocabulary scores changed only slightly from the immediate test to the one-week delayed test to the three-months delayed test. Their point however is that for the most effective vocabulary growth, input has to occur in a sustained extensive reading programme and extensive listening programme. This provides the repetition needed for strong learning and the chance for words that were not initially picked up to be met again.

Brown et al.'s study used several measures of the same vocabulary and this provided a rich picture of vocabulary learning. Pellicer-Sanchez and Schmitt (2010) examined incidental L2 learning from an unsimplified text, *Things Fall Apart*, testing knowledge of spelling, word class, and recognition and recall of meaning. They found substantial amounts of vocabulary learning, with words occurring more than 10 times typically showing the most marked gains. Their study showed the importance of using multiple measures of vocabulary knowledge (see also Waring and Takaki, 2003; Pigada and Schmitt, 2006; Joe, 1995; Webb, 2008), and of using sensitive instruments to gain a richer view of vocabulary gains. Background knowledge did not 'moderate the relationship between comprehension and receptive retention of meaning' (Brown et al., 2008: 156).

Extensive reading involves reading large quantities of reasonably easy material with the focus on the meaning of the text. In general, extensive reading does not involve much additional language use besides filling out a brief book report form. From a vocabulary perspective, it is useful to distinguish two types of extensive reading: one which aims at vocabulary growth and one which aims at fluency development. For vocabulary growth, extensive reading texts should contain no more than 5%

unknown tokens (excluding proper nouns) and preferably no more than 2% to ensure that comprehension and guessing can occur, and no less than 1% or 2% to make sure that there is new vocabulary to learn. Texts which provide repetition of unknown vocabulary, that is, continuous texts on the same topic, would provide favourable conditions. If graded readers are used, learners should be reading at the level just beyond their present vocabulary knowledge. We will look at the vocabulary demands of unsimplified text and how learners can be supported in reading such text. We will also look in detail at the nature of graded or simplified material and how this material should be used in an extensive reading program.

We will also look briefly at fluency development. For fluency development, learners need to read texts that contain little or no unknown vocabulary. Unknown vocabulary slows down learners' reading and makes it more difficult for them to gain the smoothness and flow needed for pleasurable reading. If graded readers are used for fluency development, learners should be reading very easy texts at least one level below their present vocabulary knowledge.

Table 5.5 looks at the various kinds of reading that could make up a well-balanced reading course. Such a course would give most attention to meaning-focused reading through extensive reading, making sure that a proportion of this reading is focused on fluency development. There is also a role for intensive reading to direct the learner's attention to important language features and to deal with any language-based comprehension problems that they may encounter.

Table 5.5 *Types of reading and vocabulary coverage*

Type of reading	Learning goals	% vocabulary coverage
Intensive reading (about one-quarter of the reading course)	Developing language knowledge Developing strategy use	Less than 98% coverage
Extensive reading for language growth (about half of the reading course)	Incidental vocabulary learning Reading skills	98% coverage
Extensive reading for fluency development (about one-quarter of the reading course)	Reading quickly	99–100% coverage

The distinctions made in Table 5.5 are mainly for planning a reading or vocabulary programme to ensure that there is an appropriate range and balance of types of reading. If these rough distinctions are accepted along with their accompanying coverage figures, it is clear that if learners are to have meaning-focused input through reading, and fluency development through reading, at all stages of their proficiency development, then material written within a controlled vocabulary is an essential component of a reading course. To reinforce this idea, let us now look at the nature of unsimplified text.

Is reading unsimplified text a good way to help vocabulary growth?

Texts which are written primarily for native speakers to read typically make use of the full range of vocabulary available to the writer, and even texts which are written for young readers who are native speakers of English contain vocabulary which goes well beyond the first 5,000 words of English. A five-year-old native speaker of English has a vocabulary of several thousand words and books which are written for such readers make use of that vocabulary. Texts which are written within a controlled vocabulary for non-native speakers of English deliberately restrict the range of vocabulary used in the texts in order to match the vocabulary knowledge of the readers. This results in vocabulary control which is much more restricted than what would be used for young native speakers of English, and this makes it possible for learners of English to read texts with some degree of fluency and to gain enjoyment from them, even when they know less than a hundred words of English.

Let us consider a short text written for native speakers of English. The text is just 430 words long, and is called *Nana is in the plum tree*. It is written for children beginning to learn to read. The text contains 147 word families and 23 of these are not in the first 2,000 words of English. These include words like *nectar, buzzing, hissed, plum, swarm* and *zoom*. Clearly it is a story about bees, and the word *bees* is not in the first 2,000 words but occurs ten times in the story. Most of the other words in the story which are not in the first 2,000 words occur only once, and because of their close relationship to the topic are unlikely to be met again in the next story, or the next. The effect of simplification is not to get rid of these words that occur only once (in any text a very large proportion of the different words will occur only once regardless of whether the text is a simplified or an unsimplified text). Simplification makes sure that all the words in the text are useful words, not just for this story but for other stories as well, even if they only occur once in a particular text. If learners spent time learning the low-frequency words in a text without vocabulary control, this learning would be largely wasted because it would be a long time before they had a chance to meet or use these words again.

If the text is a much longer text, then the actual number of words occurring only once is of course much greater. Three texts are analysed in Table 5.6 – the Oxford Bookworms' version of *Dracula* (a Level 2 simplified text 7,957 running words long), the first 7,965 running words of the unsimplified original of *Dracula* which is of roughly the same length as the simplified version to control for the effects of text length, and the complete unsimplified original of *Dracula* (161,952 running words long). As Nation and Deweerdt (2001) have shown, the figures for the original Dracula are typical of other unsimplified novels.

Table 5.6 shows that for learners with a vocabulary of 2,000 words or less, the simplified text (98.6% coverage) would have one word outside the first 2,000 words in every seven lines. This provides a very supportive context for each unknown word. The short unsimplified text (91.3% coverage) and the original would have one word outside the first 2,000 in roughly every 1.2 lines. This is a very small context for the unknown words.

Table 5.6 *Conditions for comprehension and learning in a simplified version and the original version of Dracula*

Conditions	Simplified version	First 8,000 words of the original	Complete original
Percentage of words in first 2,000 plus proper nouns	98.6%	91.3%	92.8%
Total number of different word families	556	1,416	5,640
Word families not in first 2,000 excluding proper nouns	30 (5.4%)	530 (37.4%)	3,822 (67.8%)
Repetitions of word types not in first 2,000 excluding proper nouns	1x – 7 2x – 2 3x – 4	1x – 391 2x – 46 3x – 16	1x – 3,039 2x – 785 3x – 320

The density of unknown words is one measure of difficulty. A related measure is the actual number of different unknown words outside the first 2,000 and proper nouns. This affects difficulty because each new word is another item to guess or look up and if there are many of these, then good comprehension is difficult to achieve. Related to this are the repetitions of these unknown words. If a reasonable proportion of the coverage of the running words outside the first 2,000 is made up of repeated words then these have a very good chance of being learned and will quickly become known words that then add to the coverage of known words for the remainder of the text. The words *vampire*, *wolves*, *howl* and *coffin* are examples of repeated words outside the first 2,000 in *Dracula*. Table 5.6 shows that there are only 30 word families outside the first 2,000 and proper nouns in the simplified text, and several of these words are repeated many times. In the short unsimplified text on the other hand, 530 of the total 1,416 word families (37.4%) are not in the first 2,000. In the complete unsimplified version this rises to 67.8% of the word families. Moreover, 391 of these 530 word families occur only once in the text. This means that each one is potentially a comprehension and learning problem. Thus there are around 530 possible interruptions in the short unsimplified text and very, very few in the simplified text. These 'one-timers' make up a significant proportion of the total different words in the unsimplified text and this proportion increases with the length of the text. These one-timers require effort for comprehension and this effort is not repaid by the opportunity to meet them again when they would be less of a burden and would have a chance of being learned.

Even in the simplified text there are many words, particularly within the first 2,000 words, that occur only once in the text. However, because these words are from the most frequent 2,000 words of English, they are worth learning. It is a reasonable piece of advice to give to a learner of English that any word in a graded reader is worth learning. This piece of advice is certainly not true for an unsimplified text. Here are some of the uncommon words in the short unsimplified text from *Dracula*: *alacrity, aquiline, baying, crags, diligence* (a type of coach), *engendered, goitre, hospadars, oleander, polyglot*. Some of these words will eventually be useful additions to a broad and rich vocabulary, but there are thousands of more useful words to learn before these. It is thus not a good vocabulary-learning strategy to take an unsimplified text and carefully work through it learning every new word that is met in the text.

Simplification is a form of text adaptation like easification, elaboration and negotiation, and is an important tool in second language learning. It may be that the use of the term **simplification** with its implications of reducing text is unsuitable and some term like 'roughly tuning input' will get simplification the respectability it deserves. David Hill, at the first Extensive Reading World Congress in 2011 in

Kyoto, suggested the term 'ungraded texts' for authentic texts which are not simplified, thus placing the negative implication on authentic texts. Without simplification, the strands of meaning-focused input, meaning-focused output and fluency development become impossible for all except advanced learners.

We need to see simplification as one of a range of options for making text accessible. Each of the options – simplification, elaboration, easification, negotiation, intensive reading, glossing – has its own particular strengths and values. Rather than focusing on which one is the best, we need to look at what each has to offer and how each can be used to the best effect. Teachers need an expanded range of options not a reduced one.

Many of the criticisms of simplification are criticisms of bad simplification. We need to have standards of good simplification and praise those texts that exemplify them. The late Colin Mortimer used to draw the analogy between Shakespeare and the second language materials writer. Shakespeare wrote for a stage where there were no flashbacks, no voice-overs to reveal thought, little scenery and so on, and yet with all these restrictions created masterpieces. The second language materials writer is also working with severe limitations, but within these limitations it should also be possible to create small masterpieces. We need to see more of these masterpieces, and the annual graded reader competition organised by the Extensive Reading Foundation (www.erfoundation.org/erf) is a very good step towards encouraging this.

Will extensive reading of texts written for young native speakers make reading easier for non-native speakers?

The 'book flood' studies reviewed by Elley (1991) show striking increases made on measures of language use, language knowledge and academic performance. The studies of extensive reading that Elley was involved in are the most substantial in terms of length (12–36 months) and number of students (from over a hundred to several thousand). The book flood studies involved learners spending the greater part of their foreign language class time (four classes per week) reading books that interested them.

The measures of language use in Elley, and Elley and Mangubhai's (1981) studies included measures of oral language, reading comprehension and writing. An interesting finding in some of the studies was the improvement made in writing, which appeared most dramatically in the tests given two years after the beginning of the book flood. Elley and Mangubhai (1981: 23) suggest that this may have happened because learners' language knowledge had passed a threshold which was enough to allow them to produce their own ideas.

The improvements in reading, listening and oral language were equally striking but not so unexpected, because the 'shared book' approach used in one of the groups of classes involves learners in listening, reading and orally joining in with the reading of a story. The language knowledge measures included word recognition where learners have to read aloud a list of words, vocabulary knowledge and grammar. The vocabulary knowledge measures did not measure total vocabulary size or vocabulary growth. The measures of academic success involved the examinations used across the school system. Learners in the book flood groups also had a greater than normal success rate in these examinations. Although there were no formal measures of learners' attitudes to reading, informal observation and teacher reports indicated that book flood learners enjoyed reading.

These studies present compelling evidence of the improvements in second language acquisition that can be brought about by such programmes. Elley (1991: 378–9) attributes the success to five factors:

1. extensive input of meaningful print
2. incidental learning
3. the integration of oral and written activity
4. focus on meaning rather than form
5. high intrinsic motivation

The control groups in the studies were classes following a syllabus of language items that were presented one by one with substantial amounts of language-focused activity.

The books that were used in the experiments generally contained a lot of pictures and were not controlled according to a word list but were written appropriately for young native speakers (Elley and Mangubhai, 1981: 26). The books used were not graded readers but were ones that young native speakers of English would read. The children in the book flood studies were aged from 6 to 12 years old, and so the content matter of such books was appropriate.

Let us look at two books written without formal vocabulary control for young native speakers (*Dry Days for Climbing George* by Margaret Mahy, 1988; *The Three Little Pigs*) and compare them with a graded reader (*Indonesian Love Story*) written to fit into a prescribed vocabulary level. One of the texts, *The Three Little Pigs* in the Ladybird series, seems to have been used in the Fiji book flood study (Elley and Mangubhai, 1981: 26).

Table 5.7 *The percentage coverage (and cumulative coverage) of three texts by the high-frequency words of English, names and all the remaining words*

Books	1st 1,000	2nd 1,000	Names	Remaining words
Dry Days for Climbing George	76.8%	11.7% (88.5%)	5.1% (93.6%)	6.4% (100%)
The Three Little Pigs	78.1%	11.1% (89.2%)	7.5% (96.7%)	3.3% (100%)
Indonesian Love Story	82.7%	8.4% (91.1%)	7.9% (99%)	1.0% (100%)

Table 5.7 presents the vocabulary profile of the three texts showing the percentage of the running words in the 1,000 most frequent words according to West's (1953) *General Service List*, the words in the second 1,000 most frequent words, the names of characters and places, and the remaining words.

In *The Three Little Pigs* the words *pig, wolf* and *(Mr) Smith* make up the total of names. *Pig* is actually in the second 1,000 words but for comparison purposes it was counted as a name. Note that the names of the characters and places make up a large proportion of the words that are not in the first 2,000 words.

We can see from Table 5.7 that the graded reader *Indonesian Love Story* provides greater control with 99% of the words coming from the most frequent 2,000 words of English plus names, but the figures of 96.7% and 93.6% are still good coverage figures. In *The Three Little Pigs* just one word in every 30 will be outside the lists and in *Dry Days for Climbing George* one word in every 22. In addition, several of the words outside the lists were repeated several times (*huff, puff, chinny, chin*). Elley and Mangubhai's motivation for choosing books written for young native speakers was probably that these were much more attractively illustrated, and interesting for young readers. It also seems that in terms of vocabulary control such texts compare favourably with graded readers, although a lot of words outside the high-frequency words of the language will occur only once or twice in the texts and will therefore act as a barrier to easy reading.

However, lack of strict vocabulary control can be compensated for by repetition. Linse (2007) recommends using the many books written for young native speakers of English that use repetitive language as a way of telling the story. Although these do not have the same degree of vocabulary control as graded readers, the repetitive language and supportive illustrations make these engaging books very attractive to young second language learners and partly help overcome the vocabulary control issue.

A study of texts aimed at teenage native speakers of English however showed that such texts are not as accessible for non-native speakers as graded readers (Hirsh and Nation, 1992), although they required a slightly lower number of words than novels written for adults. Books in the *Sweet Valley High* series, for example, require a 6,000 word family vocabulary to reach 98% coverage.

We have seen that unsimplified text can place a very heavy vocabulary burden on second language readers. Unsimplified text has too many of its running words and its different words outside most second language learners' vocabulary knowledge, so that readers with a limited vocabulary meet an unknown word in every few running words. These unknown words make up a very large group of words, most of which occur only once in the text. A large number of texts would need to be read before many of them were met again. For learners of English with a vocabulary of less than 2,000 words, most unsimplified text is just too difficult and does not provide the conditions necessary for learning through meaning-focused input. Simplified texts, as in graded readers, can provide these conditions and are thus essential if there is to be a substantial meaning-focused input strand to a course. Struggling with difficult text can be a useful part of a course, but it is part of intensive reading.

Unsimplified texts do have important roles to play in language courses, and for most learners, being able to comprehend them represents a major goal of a language course. But the end is not always usefully the means. Good pedagogy involves helping learners reach their goals through suitably staged steps. In the beginning and intermediate stages of language learning, controlled texts are among the most suitable means of bringing the important strands of learning from meaning-focused input and fluency development into play. When learners' vocabulary size is large enough then unsimplified texts can fill these roles. At the beginning and intermediate stages, unsimplified text may have a role to play in intensive reading and strategy development in the language-focused learning strand of the course.

Learners of English are extremely fortunate in that there is this tremendous resource of thousands of graded readers at a variety of levels. This resource should be used as fully as possible and should not be rejected because the texts are not authentic unsimplified texts. To reject this resource is to effectively eliminate much of the essential strands of meaning-focused input and fluency development from language courses.

Later in this chapter, we look at the nature of graded readers and their use within an extensive reading programme. Now, however, let us look at how unsimplified material can be made more accessible for language learners whose vocabulary size is less than 6,000 or 7,000 words.

How can learners be supported when reading unsimplified text?

Some writers and teachers are uncomfortable with simplification, largely because they feel that the authenticity of the text is lost. This is a mistaken view as authenticity lies in the reader's response to the text not in the text itself (Widdowson, 1976). There are alternatives to simplification, but they are best regarded as complementary alternatives rather than substitutes.

In this section we look at a very wide range of ways of supporting the reading of unsimplified text. These include narrow reading, elaboration, easification, negotiation, intensive reading, pre-teaching, vocabulary exercises and glossing.

Narrow reading

Narrow reading involves reading within a very narrowly defined topic area so that the vocabulary that learners meet in the texts is limited because it relates to only one major topic. Research by Sutarsyah et al. (1994) shows that sticking to one topic area results in a substantial reduction of vocabulary load.

Narrow reading has been proposed as a way of making the reading task easier and helping learning (Gardner, 2004; Gardner, 2008; Hwang and Nation, 1989; Schmitt and Carter, 2000). For reducing vocabulary load and increasing repetitions however, the case for narrow reading (theme-based and author-based) is not overwhelming. Narrow reading may be more effective in increasing the amount of background knowledge that a learner brings to a text, thus aiding comprehension and as a result helping vocabulary learning. Narrow reading may also have motivational benefits as interest in the topic or love of an author's works grows. Min (2008) compared reading followed by vocabulary activities with narrow reading, where the repetitions of target words were roughly similar between the two treatments. The vocabulary activities created a more deliberate focus and resulted in more and stronger vocabulary learning. On the immediate post-test, 36.24 out of 50 words were learned in the reading with vocabulary activities treatment, and 24.64 were learned in the narrow reading treatment, showing that both contributed substantially to vocabulary learning, but that deliberate focus outweighed the effects of creative use alone. The treatments lasted a total of 10 hours over five weeks.

The reason for the only moderate vocabulary load and vocabulary repetition benefits of narrow reading is reflected in Zipf's law. Zipf's law describes the distribution and frequency of vocabulary in connected text. A small number of high-frequency words accounts for a very large proportion of the occurrences of tokens in the text. A very large number of words accounts for a very small proportion of the occurrences of tokens in the text. This happens for the following reasons. The function words of the language are needed in almost every sentence to fulfil the grammatical requirements of the language. These function words (around 176 word families) account for almost 50% of the running words of a text. Around 1,000 or so content words occur very frequently because they relate to things and ideas that are very common and largely unavoidable in our daily life. Whenever we want to talk or read or listen or write about ideas and things which are outside the most common, we need to use other words. Thus, narrow reading should increase the number of repeated words and decrease the number of words occurring only once or twice. The evidence shows that it does these things but only to a rather small degree. Narrow reading of unsimplified texts is by no means a substitute for reading simplified texts.

A further application of Zipf's law (Sorrell, 2012) also relates to the proportion of types in a text which occur only once in the text, or twice, or three times, and so on. Around 50% of the different words in a text occur only once, and about one-sixth of this number occur twice, and about one-twelfth of that number occur three times and so on. The only way we can avoid having words in a text that occur only once or twice is to keep repeating ourselves. Narrow reading does not reduce the number of one-timers.

However, narrow reading does reduce the total number of different words and thus makes the vocabulary load lighter (Sutarsyah et al., 1994). Getting advanced learners to do lots of reading within their subject matter areas and within their hobby interests where they also already have a lot of background knowledge is a good way of making unsimplified reading more manageable.

Elaboration

Elaborative modification of a text usually results in a text that is longer than the original. This is because an elaborative modification involves preserving as much of the original text as possible, and making its meaning more accessible to a second language learner by the addition of redundancy and a clearer signalling of the thematic structure (Parker and Chaudron, 1987). Redundancy is created by the addition of paraphrase, synonyms, optional syntactic markers, and the repetition of items to make coherence more apparent.

Advocates of elaborative modification (Long and Ross, 1993; Yano et al., 1994) have seen it as a replacement for simplification. They criticise simplification because it results in stilted text which is not cohesive, because native speakers do not normally simplify by controlling vocabulary and grammatical structure, and because it removes access to linguistic forms that learners need to develop their proficiency. These arguments are easily rebutted. While there are too many poor simplifications, there are many good ones too (see the Extensive Reading Foundation website). Simplification, especially of vocabulary, is a normal process, and the study of vocabulary frequency and coverage shows the enormous number of low-frequency items occurring only once in a text that makes reading unsimplified text for pleasure impossible for many learners.

Attempts to show that elaboration results in better comprehension than simplification have been largely unsuccessful (Parker and Chaudron, 1987; Long and Ross, 1993; Yano et al., 1994).

It is best to view elaboration as another way of making texts accessible for learners. Where it is important to retain as much of the original as possible, elaborative modification will be preferable to simplification. Where however large quantities of pleasurable reading are needed, simplification should be the preferred strategy.

Easification

Easification (Bhatia, 1983) involves making a text easy to read, not by changing the wording of the text, but by adding different kinds of support, such as diagrams, pictures, charts and tables, text summaries, glossaries, guiding questions and headings.

This support can be in the form of an accompanying sheet, or a computer-readable text with added support (see 'Reading with resources' on www.lextutor.ca), or an edited text.

Negotiation

Another way of making a reading text accessible is to read it with the help of others, negotiating the meaning of the text through discussion. Palincsar and Brown's (1986) interactive reading procedure is an example of this.

Ellis (1995) compared the effect of premodified input (simplification and elaboration) and interactionally modified input on vocabulary learning. Ellis's study involved spoken language, not reading. He found that although more word meanings were learned from the interactionally modified input, this was slow. Words were learned faster in premodified input. Over-elaboration of input reduced learning. Clearly each form of adaptation brings its own strengths and disadvantages. The teacher needs to match the form of adaptation of text to the learning goal and environmental constraints.

Paired reading is another form of negotiation in reading unsimplified texts. Two learners read the same text, helping each other when help is needed. As yet, this activity is largely unexplored.

Intensive reading and direct teaching

Commercially published reading courses usually include reading texts accompanied by a variety of exercises focusing on vocabulary, grammar, comprehension and discourse. There is considerable debate in the research on L1 reading about the value of deliberately spending time on vocabulary teaching, which includes direct teaching and vocabulary exercises. Nagy (1997) and his colleagues take the position that it is a waste of time teaching vocabulary. The two main supports for this position are firstly the large number of words in English, and secondly the large amounts of time needed to deliberately teach vocabulary. Because it takes such a long time to effectively teach a word, and because there are so many thousands of words, direct teaching at best can only account for a very, very small proportion of native speakers' vocabulary growth.

This is a strong argument and is well supported by L1 research. However, it does not apply quite so strongly to second language learners. There are two reasons for this. Firstly, there is the high-frequency/low-frequency distinction. Native speaking children beginning school already know close to 5,000 word families which include the high-frequency words. New vocabulary learning will largely be of the mid- and low-frequency words of the language. Non-native speakers however need to learn the high-frequency words. As we have seen, these make up a relatively small group of words which deserve time and attention. The arguments against direct teaching apply to mid- and low-frequency words.

The second reason in favour of some direct teaching for second language learners is that direct teaching can add to incidental learning of the same words and can raise learners' awareness of particular words so that they notice them when they meet them while reading. This consciousness-raising effect of teaching does not require much time to be spent on each word. The results are best seen from a long-term perspective of being one of the many meetings which will eventually lead to the word being well known.

It is important to see direct teaching as only one of a range of options for the deliberate learning of vocabulary. Deliberate learning using word cards is much more efficient and effective than most direct vocabulary teaching and vocabulary exercises if word card learning is carried out following the guidelines described in the Chapter 11.

Pre-teaching

If vocabulary is an important factor in reading and readability measures, then it is tempting to conclude that pre-teaching the vocabulary that will occur in a reading text should increase the readability of the text. This has been very difficult to show experimentally in first language studies. Tuinman and Brady (1974), for example, found that substantial pre-teaching of vocabulary resulted in little change in comprehension. Other studies (McKeown et al., 1985) have shown positive effects.

There have been several attempts to explain the inconsistent findings. One explanation is that vocabulary knowledge in itself is not the critical factor. Vocabulary knowledge is a symptom of wide reading, knowledge of the world and reading skill. Teaching vocabulary alone is ignoring the important world knowledge that lies behind it and which is critical for effective reading. Wixson (1986) points out methodological difficulties in measuring the effect of pre-teaching, particularly the importance of the pre-taught vocabulary for the message of the text, and the relationship between the pre-taught vocabulary and the comprehension measures. Graves (1986), in a substantial review of first language vocabulary learning and instruction, notes that several of the studies are poorly reported, so that it is difficult to evaluate the quality of the research. The well-reported and well-conducted studies show that pre-teaching vocabulary helps comprehension if the pre-teaching involves rich instruction. That is, the pre-teaching involves several meetings with the word, focuses on many aspects of what is involved in knowing a word including fluency of access to the word (Mezynski, 1983) and meeting the word in several sentence contexts (Stahl, 1990: 21), and gets the learners actively involved with processing the word.

Stahl and Fairbanks (1986), in a meta-analysis of first language studies of the effect of vocabulary teaching on comprehension, found a strong effect of vocabulary teaching on comprehension of passages containing taught words, and a slight effect of vocabulary teaching on comprehension of texts not designed to contain the target words.

In one of the few second language studies, Johnson (1982) found no significant differences in comprehension between learners who studied relevant vocabulary before reading, learners who had glosses available while reading, and learners who had no planned vocabulary support. The study of vocabulary before reading did not meet the criteria of rich instruction.

Pre-teaching vocabulary is time-consuming. In Alessi and Dwyer's (2008) study, it took a great deal of time. Hypertext glossing had more positive effects on comprehension and took half the time.

Vocabulary difficulty and pre-teaching of content do not seem to interact with each other for first language learners. Pre-teaching of background knowledge related to the content of a text does not compensate for unknown vocabulary in the text (Stahl et al., 1989). Vocabulary difficulty and prior knowledge affect different aspects of the reading process. Laufer (1992b) similarly found that academic ability as measured by a university entrance test did not compensate for lack of vocabulary in reading for second language learners.

Stahl et al. (1989) found that vocabulary difficulty affects literal comprehension of a text as measured by textually explicit questions, comprehension of central and supporting information, and exact cloze replacement of function words. That is, vocabulary knowledge affected the development of the microstructure of the text, background knowledge was helpful in grasping the macrostructure of the text.

It seems then that difficulty with vocabulary must be dealt with by vocabulary-focused means not by dealing with background knowledge. Because pre-teaching requires rich instruction and thus considerable time, it should focus on high-frequency words that will be useful for other texts as well. Stahl (1990: 17) suggests that pre-teaching an unimportant word may misdirect learners' reading of the text. In general, research on vocabulary instruction has shown that mixed methods which provide both contextual and definitional information are more effective both on reading comprehension and vocabulary learning than definitional methods (Stahl and Fairbanks, 1986). However, McDaniel and Pressley (1989) found that 30 seconds concentrated learning on each word had positive effects on the subsequent comprehension of a text.

Dealing with words in intensive reading

Table 5.8, from Nation (2004), lists the options for dealing with vocabulary in intensive reading. The decision about which option to choose needs to be based on the frequency level of the words focused on (whether they are high-frequency, mid-frequency or low-frequency

Table 5.8 *Dealing with vocabulary in intensive reading*

Ways of dealing with a word	Explanation
Pre-teach.	Before learners read the text the teacher spends some time explaining the meaning of some of the words and focusing on their form, meaning and use.
Replace it in the text before giving the text to the learners.	The text is simplified by replacing some of the unknown words with known synonyms or removing part of the text.
Put it in a glossary.	Some unknown words are listed with their meaning given in the L1 or the L2.
Put it in an exercise after the text.	Some unknown words are put in cloze, word building or other types of exercises after the text.
Quickly give the meaning.	The teacher gives a quick L1 translation or L2 explanation of the meaning of a word.
Do nothing about it.	The teacher passes over the word without saying anything about it.
Help learners use context to guess.	The teacher guides learners through a guessing strategy to work out the meaning of a word.
Help learners use a dictionary.	The teacher guides learners in using the dictionary to look up and learn about a word.
Break it into parts and explain.	The teacher helps learners practice a word analysis strategy relating the word's parts to the word's meaning.
Spend time looking at its range of meanings and collocations etc.	The teacher interrupts the reading to spend time explaining the meaning of a word and aspects of its form, meaning and use.

words), their importance for the message of the text, and the opportunities that each particular word provides for practising a strategy like guessing from context, using word parts, relating the unknown word to known loan words, or making use of a dictionary.

In general, mid-frequency and low-frequency words should be dealt with quickly (ignore, quickly give the meaning), or they should be occasionally used to practise a strategy. High-frequency words deserve class time and so can be pre-taught, have time spent on them during the reading, or be put in an exercise after the text. When high-frequency words are focused on to practice a strategy, this focus has the double benefit of spending time on a useful word and spending time on a useful strategy.

Intensive reading is part of the language-focused learning strand, and needs to share the vocabulary portion of this strand with learning from word cards, training in vocabulary strategy use and doing vocabulary exercises. This, in effect, means that intensive reading would make up a relatively small proportion of a language course (about one-sixteenth of the course time in a language course, and about one-eighth of the time in a reading course). Intensive reading is useful, even when it is conducted using grammar–translation methodology, but it needs to be balanced with other parts of the course (see Nation, 2009: Chapter 3) for a more detailed discussion of intensive reading.

Vocabulary exercises with reading texts

As suggested in Chapter 3, it is possible to analyse vocabulary-learning activities using criteria based on processes like noticing, retrieval, creative (or generative) use and imaging. This kind of analysis, called Technique Feature Analysis, is similar in purpose to the involvement load measure developed by Laufer and Hulstijn (2001), and can usefully be applied to the activities that are typically used with reading texts.

There are other ways of examining vocabulary activities. Paribakht and Wesche (1996) used Gass's (1988) five levels in learning from input to classify vocabulary exercises that accompany reading texts. This classification relates vocabulary exercises to the conditions under which learning might occur. Let us look at each of the five levels.

1. Gass's most basic level is called 'apperceived input' or noticing. There are several factors that can affect noticing, including repetition, salience and prior knowledge. Vocabulary exercises that make use of the noticing condition (selective attention) include listing words to notice at the beginning of the text, using highlighting in the text such as underlining, italics, bolding or the use of an asterisk. Glossing items may have a similar effect. The major effect is consciousness raising which will make the word more salient the next time it is met.
2. The next of Gass's (1988) levels is 'comprehended input'. This may be the first step towards receptive retrieval. Vocabulary activities at this level (recognition) involve matching words with first or second language synonyms, definitions or pictures.
3. Paribakht and Wesche's (1996) 'manipulation level' corresponds to Gass's 'intake'. Vocabulary activities at this level involve

morphological analysis of words resulting in forming words of different word classes by the addition of affixes.

4. The fourth level is called 'interpretation' (Paribakht and Wesche, 1996) or 'integration' (Gass, 1988) and involves activities like guessing from context, matching with collocates and synonyms, and finding the odd word out in a set.

5. The production level, which Gass calls 'output', involves recall of the target word form as in labelling activities, finding the form in the text to match with definitions given after the text, and answering questions requiring use of the target word.

It is also possible to classify such exercises according to the learning goal of the activity, that is, the aspect of vocabulary knowledge that the exercise contributes to. In Chapter 2 on what is involved in knowing a word these aspects have been described as *Form*: pronunciation, spelling, word parts; *Meaning*: concept, form-meaning connection, associations; and *Use*: grammar, collocations, constraints.

Glossing

Unknown words are sometimes glossed in texts for second language learners. A gloss is a brief definition or synonym, either in L1 or L2, which is provided with the text. Sometimes the words in the text are marked to show that they are glossed. Here is an example based on *Animal Farm:*

Glossing has certain attractions. Firstly, it allows texts to be used that may be too difficult for learners to read without glosses. This means that unsimplified and unadapted texts can be used. Secondly, glossing provides accurate meanings for words that might not be guessed correctly. This should help vocabulary learning and comprehension. Thirdly, glossing provides minimal interruption of the reading process, especially if the glosses appear near the words being glossed. Dictionary use is much more time consuming. Fourthly, glossing draws attention to words and thus may encourage learning.

small holes in the door of a hen-house	Mr Jones, of the Manor farm, had locked the hen-houses for the night, but was too drunk to remember to shut the *pop-holes. With the ring of light from his lantern dancing from side to
walked unsteadily	side, he *lurched across the yard, kicked off his boots at the back door, drew himself a last glass
room joined to the kitchen for washing dishes	of beer from the barrel in the *scullery, and made his way up to bed, where Mrs Jones was already snoring.

Research on glossing has focused on the effects of different types of glosses, and the effects of glossing on vocabulary learning and reading comprehension.

Types of glosses

Glosses can take many forms, particularly hard-copy glosses and electronic glosses. In this book we are concerned mainly with vocabulary, but electronic glosses can help word recognition through providing pronunciation, the meaning through the L1 and L2, visuals (Yanguas, 2009), another example sentence (Cheng and Good, 2009) or sentences (Gaskell and Cobb, 2004), grammatical information (Lomicka, 1998), and background content information (see Roby, 1999, for a taxonomy).

Are words best glossed in the learners' first language, that is using a translation, or in the second language? Are pictures the best way of glossing? Jacobs et al. (1994) found no difference between L1 and L2 glosses in their effect on comprehension and vocabulary learning. Learners were happy with L2 glosses as long as they could be easily understood. Ko (1995) found that L1 glosses resulted in better vocabulary learning but did not differ from L2 glosses in their effect on comprehension. Cheng and Good (2009) found L1 glosses the best for vocabulary learning. Ko (2005) found a positive effect for L2 glosses, but as Taylor (2006) points out, the test favoured L2 definitions. The first requirement of a gloss is that it should be understood. Chun and Payne (2004) found that looking up L1 glosses accounted for the greatest amount of look-ups (see also Bell and LeBlanc, 2000; Laufer and Hill, 2000; and Lomicka, 1998). Chun and Payne (2004) found that L1 definitions were preferred in lookups, and having look-up facilities helped those who really needed it. A look-up facility is clearly a useful resource.

Jones (2004) looked at computer-assisted vocabulary learning from listening to a text. Learners were able to access the meaning of some words either through pictures, L1 translations, or a combination of translations plus pictures. The multiple-choice post-tests included one based on picture choices, and one based on translations. Although the differences between the treatment groups were not statistically significant, learners who had access to pictures (pictures alone or pictures plus translations) did better on the picture test. Learners who had access to translations did better on the translation test. The same findings occurred for a translation recall test. Clearly, in such an experiment, testing has to be carefully considered to make sure that test format is not biasing the results. The study generally supports the idea of multimedia resources (pictures and translations) but the benefit of multimedia over single media was not statistically significant. Learners generally preferred translations to pictures.

Should the gloss suit the context in the text or should it require the learner to adapt it to the context? Research by Verspoor and Lowie (2003) supports the idea of having a core meaning gloss that needs to be adapted to what is in the text (see also Gettys et al., 2001).

Where should glosses occur? In hard-copy texts, the choices include (a) in the text directly after the glossed word; (b) in the margin on the same line as the glossed word; (c) at the bottom of the page containing the glossed word; and (d) at the end of the whole text. Watanabe (1997) found that glossing immediately after the glossed word did not work so well. Firstly, in the case of the gloss immediately after the word, learners have to realise that the following definition is in fact a definition and not new information. In some technical texts this is explicitly signalled by bolding or italicising defined words or by grammatically signalling the definition. Secondly, in the gloss conditions, the presence of the gloss (which included both the word form and its definition) drew learners' attention to the word and thus encouraged seeing the word as an item to learn and not just as a part of the message. Thirdly, because the gloss contained the word form, looking at the gloss gave another repetition of the word. Long (in Watanabe, 1997) suggests that this could involve three meetings with the word: (1) seeing it in the text; (2) seeing it in the gloss; and (3) looking back at it in the text to see how the meaning given in the gloss fits the context. In a study that looked at the effect of glossing on vocabulary learning and comprehension, Holley and King (1971) found no difference between glosses in the margin, at the foot of the page, and at the end of the text. Jacobs et al. (1994) found that learners expressed a clear preference for marginal glosses. It would seem best to follow this preference, particularly where vocabulary learning is one of the goals of glossing.

Should hypertext glosses be signalled? When words are glossed in an electronic medium, the glossed word may be highlighted to indicate that a gloss for the word is available. This is called textual enhancement. In many ways, the highlighting is like an invitation, and De Ridder (2002) found that compared to invisible (unhighlighted) links, highlighted text encouraged much more clicking. De Ridder's highlighting involved the use of colour (blue) and underlining. Highlighting did not affect vocabulary learning or comprehension. Bowles (2004) found that both hard-copy and electronic glossing greatly increased reported noticing of words. Rott (2007) found that bolding had no effect on vocabulary learning.

Should glosses involve learners in decision making? Hulstijn (1992) suggested that providing multiple-choice glosses where the choices were reasonably close in meaning to each other could result in more thoughtful processing of the vocabulary and thus improve vocabulary learning. Hulstijn found that choices did make a significant difference, but Watanabe (1997) did not find any difference. Hulstijn however suggests that choices are dangerous in that some learners made incorrect choices and thus upset learning. Rott et al. (2002) compared multiple-choice glossing (three choices plus *don't know*) with no glosses (the control group); a text reconstruction group that read one section of the text and then each individual tried to recall it in writing and went on to the next section using the same procedure; a group that had multiple-choice L1 glosses; and a group that had multiple-choice L1 glosses and recalled the text section by section.

The gloss group did better on vocabulary learning than the non-gloss groups on the immediate tests but not on the five-week delayed post-tests. The group that had glosses and did reconstruction was best of all on both immediate and delayed vocabulary tests. The gloss group also gained better comprehension than the non-gloss groups. Being given the meaning is surer than having to find it yourself.

Rott (2005) compared single translation glosses with multiple-choice translation glosses for four words, each occurring four times in the text. Vocabulary learning was measured by using the Vocabulary Knowledge Scale and a test like the multiple-choice translation glosses. Comprehension using text recall in L1 was also measured. The learners did think-alouds as they did the reading. Rott found that multiple-choice glosses performed better than single glosses in establishing stronger form–meaning connections (as measured by the Vocabulary Knowledge Scale responses and by a delayed post-test). The difficulty in generalising from the study was that each word appeared four times and the encounters after the first clearly added to the quality of processing. Most glossed words in a text are likely to be words occurring only once.

Multiple-choice glosses should include confirmation of the correct choice in order for them to have the best effect. Hulstijn (1993) found that many of his learners made incorrect choices on the multiple-choice glosses, and he saw this as a major disadvantage to the technique. However, electronically confirming a correct choice or indicating a wrong choice could overcome this problem.

Do learners like glosses? Cheng and Good (2009), Davis and Lyman-Hager (1997), Ko (2005) and Lenders (2008) found very positive attitudes towards glosses. Ko's learners favoured glosses in the margin.

With the ready availability of computer-based glossing, there is a need for research on the most effective ways of accessing and providing the gloss. There is a range of alternatives to simply having the gloss always present (as in the example from *Animal Farm* above) and these include clicking on the word to get the gloss and having to type the word to get the gloss which might help learning of the word form. Instead of a gloss, clicking may provide access to a complete dictionary entry which will involve the learner in choosing the correct sense.

How much glossing should there be in a text? In most of the experimental studies, somewhere around 5% to 2% of the running words were glossed. In a hard-copy text, assuming around 10 words per line, this is one gloss for every two to five lines. Certainly glossing two or more words per line using margin glosses would strongly affect the layout of the text. De Ridder (2002) used electronic glosses at a density of 5–6% with no apparent negative effects. There is probably a density where glossing becomes too disruptive and although we do not have experimental or observational data on this, it is best to assume that the highest density of glossing should be no more than 5%, and preferably around 3%, of the running words. A counter-argument is that if the density of unknown words is low, then the text is too easy and so there may be no need to consult glosses (Taylor, 2006).

We have looked at the research on glossing to see how this provides guidelines for adapting texts. There is another very important source of information to guide adaptation, namely vocabulary frequency and density data from actual texts. That is, if learners have a certain vocabulary size, how much adaptation of text is needed to make it more manageable? A useful rule would be to gloss mid-frequency words and replace low-frequency words (tenth 1,000 onwards). Because low-frequency words typically cover just over 1% of the running words, this replacement is not a major task (see Table 5.9).

Table 5.9 column 3 shows that the 1,133 low-frequency words in the text make up 1.52% of the running words. If these words were replaced, this would involve changing around four to five words per 300-word page. If learners knew the first 3,000 words of English (row 2 of the data in Table 5.9), 5.79% of the running words (about 17 per 300-word page) would need to be glossed. With a 5,000-word vocabulary, this drops to 2.26% of the running words (about seven per page). With a vocabulary size of 3,000–4,000 words, glossing seems a very feasible option for reading unsimplified text. While it

Table 5.9 *Coverage by mid-frequency words in a typical unsimplified text* (Lord Jim) *given various vocabulary sizes*

Words assumed known (cumulative % coverage)	Remaining mid-frequency (% coverage)	Low-frequency (% coverage)
2,000 (90.03%)	8.45%	1.52%
3,000 (92.69%)	5.79%	1.52%
4,000 (94.95%)	3.53%	1.52%
5,000 (96.22%)	2.26%	1.52%
6,000 (97.05%)	1.43%	1.52%
7,000 (97.64%)	0.84%	1.52%
8,000 (98.11%)	0.37%	1.52%
9,000 (98.48%)	0	1.52%

would be best to remove the low-frequency words, their low density and coverage make glossing them acceptable. It is the total number of these words, over 1,000 in the novel, that makes it desirable to remove them. Only a few of them have significant repetitions in *Lord Jim* – for example, *schooner, stockade, infernal, rajah*. The mid-frequency readers on Paul Nation's website are adapted by replacing the very low-frequency words and some of the mid-frequency words with no other changes.

Is reading with glosses in CALL better than reading with glosses in hard copy? With the fast growing popularity of electronic readers, this question may soon be irrelevant. However, to his surprise Lenders (2008) found that learners preferred hard-copy reading to reading on a computer screen. Bowles (2004) found no significant differences between hard-copy reading and electronic glossing for vocabulary learning or comprehension. Glossing is helpful regardless of the medium.

Glosses can have the goals of improving comprehension and helping vocabulary learning. In choosing amongst all the options, the goals of glossing need to be considered and balanced against firstly, the degree of interruption to reading and the time involved, and secondly, the wanted learning outcome, particularly comprehension or vocabulary learning.

In a meta-analysis of well-conducted L2 studies using computer-mediated glosses, Abraham (2008) found a medium effect size for glosses on comprehension of a text, and a large effect size for vocabulary learning on both immediate and delayed tests. The largest effect size was for intermediate learners whose vocabulary learning was measured by receptive multiple-choice tests.

Effects of glossing on vocabulary learning

Bowles (2004) notes that when reading, learners probably see glosses simply as aids to comprehension rather than as sources of vocabulary learning. However, most studies have found that glossing has a positive effect on vocabulary learning (Bowles, 2004; Hulstijn et al., 1996; Jacobs et al., 1994; Ko, 2005; Watanabe, 1997). Hulstijn (1992) found that although learners without glosses did not differ from learners with glosses on items correctly translated in the vocabulary post-test, the learners without glosses made many more incorrect translations. The lack of glosses led to incorrect guesses from context. In a carefully controlled study, Hulstijn et al. (1996) compared the effect of L1 marginal glosses, dictionary use, and no glosses or dictionary use on incidental learning of vocabulary from text. Learners in the dictionary group consulted the dictionary infrequently with the result that there was little difference in vocabulary learning between the dictionary group and the control group. However, the few words that were looked up had a good chance of being learned. The study also looked at the effect of frequency of occurrence in the text (one occurrence or three occurrences). Frequency was found to have a significant effect on learning especially for the group who had marginal glosses. Marginal glosses encouraged learning. Learners in the marginal gloss group made greater gains than the dictionary or non-gloss or dictionary group. Yanguas (2009) found no clear difference for text, picture, and text plus picture for vocabulary learning. Glosses were clearly superior to no glosses. Mehrpour and Rahimi (2010) also found positive effects for a glossary.

A study by Chun and Plass (1996) of incidental vocabulary learning from a reading text found text and picture annotations of looked-up words gave better short-term and delayed (two weeks) retention than text alone or text and video. The amount of incidental vocabulary learning was quite high compared with other studies that did not use multimedia.

Having a hyperlink to the gloss provides the opportunity for mental retrieval with feedback for words that are glossed more than once. That is, on the second or later meeting with the word, the reader has a chance to try to remember (retrieve) what its previous gloss was before confirming it by clicking on the hyperlink. It may be useful if the second or later retrievals of a gloss are signalled to the person clicking the gloss to make them aware that they have looked at this word before. Some learners make a pencil mark in their hard-copy dictionary when they look up the word, so that repeated look-ups show the need to learn that word deliberately.

Superscript glosses, where the unknown word has its definition written in smaller script above it, are another glossing option:

> lying comfortably
> At one end of the big barn, on a sort of raised platform, Major was already <u>ensconced</u> on his bed of straw...

Yeung (1999) compared superscript glosses above words with a list of words and glosses at the end of the short text. The glosses were written in the L2, English. Yeung found different effects for different levels of learners. For the younger secondary school L2 learners, superscript glosses improved comprehension, while the glosses at the end of the text improved vocabulary learning. For the older secondary school L2 learners, the effects were reversed with superscript glosses improving vocabulary learning and glosses at the end improving comprehension. Yeung explained this by suggesting that for the older learners, knowledge of the glossed words was not important for comprehension and thus having glosses in the text interfered with comprehension. Comprehension scores were very low in both the treatment and control groups effectively showing a floor effect, so the passage itself may have simply been too difficult. Yeung's study with younger secondary school learners suggest that the location of glosses does have an effect which may be one of signalling the kind of learning expected as well as providing the most suitable focused conditions for such learning – superscript for comprehension, listing for vocabulary learning.

Superscript glosses may be very efficient for comprehension, but may take attention away from the form of the word, and do not involve retrieval or thoughtful processing, although this remains to be researched.

Hulstijn et al. (1996) argued that glossing helps learning in that it makes sure an unknown word is not ignored, and this deliberate attention can mean that later unglossed occurrences of the word can build on the previous meetings.

The effects of glossing on comprehension

The effects of glossing on comprehension are mixed, although the weight of evidence is in favour (Bowles, 2004; Davis, 1989; Jacobs, 1994; Lomicka, 1998; Watanabe, 1997). The negative results on comprehension may be because the glossed words made up less than 5% of the running words and in most experiments less than 3% of the running words, allowing learners 95%–98% coverage of the unglossed parts of the text which is enough for adequate comprehension. Comprehension may be more likely to be affected by glossing if there are larger numbers of unknown glossed words so that the glosses allow learners to gain 98% coverage.

Davis (1989) found that glossing was more effective than pre-teaching vocabulary. Watanabe (1997) found a positive effect of gloss-ing on open-ended comprehension questions. Yanguas (2009) found that text plus picture glosses were better than text alone, or picture alone for comprehension. Ko (2005), Jacobs et al. (1994) and Cheng and Good (2009) found no effect for glossing on comprehension. Ko (2005) found small comprehension differences between no gloss, L1 gloss, and L2 gloss groups which, although the L2-control comparison was significant, were too small to be of pedagogical interest.

Do glosses make reading slower? Roby (1999) wisely suggests that in glossing studies, the effect of gloss consultation on reading times needs to be reported. In a study using hypertext, De Ridder (2002) found that increased clicking, which was encouraged by highlighted words, did not slow down reading compared to unhighlighted text. However, clicking did take around 5%–10% of the time on the reading and its accompanying task.

If glosses are used with the two goals of helping comprehension and helping vocabulary learning, there needs to be a balance between reducing disruption of reading and encouraging thoughtful process-ing. Several compromises are possible, but the following guidelines gain some support from research.

- Use glosses. Both online glosses and hard-copy margin glosses can help comprehension and vocabulary learning.
- For hard-copy materials use marginal glosses (Jacobs et al., 1994). For computerised materials use hyperlink glosses. Learners like these two forms of glossing (Jacobs et al., 1994; Ko, 2005), and both involve only a small level of disruption of the flow of reading and encourage thoughtful processing.
- Use L1 glosses for learners with a vocabulary of less than 2,000 words. It is not easy to write sensible L2 glosses using less than the 2,000 most common words of English. For more advanced learn-ers, either L1 or L2 glosses are fine, although L2 glosses are gener-ally preferred.
- Use simple glosses rather than multiple-choice glosses, particularly if the glossed words are repeated in the text. Simple glosses are easier to make, and are less disruptive. Multiple-choice glosses are not strongly supported by research (Hulstijn, 1992; Watanabe, 1997).
- Where possible, use glosses which draw on the underlying core meaning of the word. This encourages thoughtful processing. However, it may result in awkward glosses.

- Allow a range of information to be accessed through glosses – pronunciation, L1 translation, L2 definition, visuals, example sentences – but allow choice of what is accessed.
- Don't signal hyperlink glosses. Signalling increases clicking but does not lead to improved comprehension or vocabulary learning.
- Where possible replace the low-frequency words (tenth 1,000 onwards) and gloss the mid-frequency words. Low-frequency topic words may need to be kept in the text.

Do individual differences and reading purpose affect the type and amount of look-up? Chun and Payne (2004) found that size of working memory as measured by non-word repetition was related to the number of look-ups, with learners with lower memory span looking up more. It is also likely that learners with different visual and verbal operating preferences benefit from being able to follow these preferences (Plass et al., 2003). For some learners an overload of information may have negative effects (Chun and Plass, 1996). Grace (2000) found no difference between males and females in learning vocabulary using L1 translations in both immediate and delayed retention tests. The translations were not single word equivalents but were translations of the whole dialogue seen and heard on the computer screen.

The nature of the task also affects look-up behavior. Hulstijn (1993) found that the relevance (salience) of a word to a reading task increased look-up.

It is essential that glossing is related to the vocabulary size of the learners, so that glossing helps and allows sufficient comprehension (Rott et al., 2002).

We have now looked at the vocabulary load of unsimplified text, how unsimplified texts can help vocabulary learning, and a wide range of ways of providing vocabulary support for the reading of unsimplified text. We now look at simplified texts and extensive reading using such texts.

Is reading simplified texts a good way to help vocabulary growth?

Simplified texts making up a reading scheme are often are called graded readers. Graded readers are complete books that have been prepared so that they stay within a strictly limited vocabulary. They are typically divided into several vocabulary levels with accompanying grammatical controls. Table 5.10 shows the vocabulary grading scheme of the Oxford Bookworms series.

There are six levels in the series. To read the books at Level 1, a learner would need a vocabulary of around 400 word families. Some

Table 5.10 *The vocabulary levels in the Oxford Bookworms series*

Level	New words	Cumulative words	Length of the books
1	400	400	4,743–5,890
2	300	700	5,511–7,960
3	300	1,000	8,819–12,194
4	400	1,400	14,342–20,142
5	400	1,800	20,379–25,272
6	700	2,500	24,840–31,501

of the titles available at this level are *White Death*, *Mutiny on the Bounty*, *The Phantom of the Opera*, and *One Way Ticket*. The next level, Level 2, adds another 300 word families making a total of 700 words. All of the books at Level 2 are within this vocabulary. Some topic words not in the vocabulary and proper nouns are also allowed. Some of the titles are simplifications and abridgements of well-known works (*Sherlock Holmes Short Stories*, *Dracula*) while others are original pieces of writing specially written for the series. This has prompted some to call graded readers 'language learner literature' (Day and Bamford, 1998). The texts are not all fiction. The Oxford Bookworms Library has a black series which consists of fiction, a green series for younger readers, and a factfiles series of non-fiction titles.

Graded readers can contribute to a course in many ways. They can be a means of vocabulary expansion, that is, learners increase their vocabulary size by reading them. Because their vocabulary is controlled by the levels in the series, it is possible for elementary learners to read books where well over 95% of the vocabulary is already familiar to them. They can thus learn the remaining words through guessing from context or dictionary use under conditions which do not place a heavy learning burden on them.

Graded readers can be a means of establishing previously met vocabulary. This means that learners can enrich their knowledge of known vocabulary and increase the fluency with which the vocabulary is retrieved. Nation and Wang (1999) concluded that the graded reading scheme they studied was designed to reinforce and establish previously met vocabulary. This is probably the way most publishers regard graded readers. This fits with West's (1955: 69) view of graded readers as 'supplementary' readers, which serve to provide reading practice, enrich known vocabulary, and provide motivation to continue study through success in use. West deserves to be credited with creating the first series of graded readers with strict vocabulary control. West had designed a reading-based English course called the New Method English Course for his learners of English in Bengal. The course systematically taught vocabulary through a series of reading texts. West realised that it would be very useful at various places in the course for learners not to meet new words but to have a chance to establish the words they had already met. So, he wrote books, many of them adaptations of existing texts like *Robinson Crusoe*, and *Tales from the Greeks*, which did not use any new vocabulary but worked within the vocabulary that was taught in the English course. These were called the New Method Supplementary Readers because they were supplementary to his New Method Readers. Because his course had six levels, there were six levels of supplementary readers. These readers were widely used by teachers and learners including those who were not using his New Method Readers.

Now every major ELT publisher has their own series (and often more than one) of graded readers. These include Oxford Bookworms, Cambridge English Readers, Macmillan Readers, Scholastic Readers, Penguin Readers, Foundations Reading Library, and Heinemann Readers.

Graded readers can also play a role in the development of reading skills, particularly the development of reading fluency (Beglar et al., 2012).

There are now several excellent substantial reviews of graded readers (Bamford, 1984; Hill, 1997, 2001, 2008; Hill and Thomas, 1988a, 1988b, 1989; Thomas and Hill, 1993) mainly coming from the Edinburgh Project on Extensive Reading. They consider a wide range of factors including the attractiveness of the covers, the length of the texts, illustrations, degree of vocabulary and grammatical control, number of levels, accompanying exercises, subject matter, and interest.

There are several important questions that need to be answered when developing a simplified reading scheme and when using it, and research has begun to provide some answers to them. When publishers and editors design a graded reading scheme, these questions include determining the number of new words at each level, the size of the steps between each level, the lengths of the texts, the number of levels, and the vocabulary size covered by the last level in the series so that the next step to unsimplified reading is not a big step. When teachers and learners make use of graded readers, these questions include helping learners decide at what level they should begin reading, the number of books they should read at each level, and the number of books they should read within a certain time frame. They also include determining how to monitor progress in extensive reading, how to motivate learners to begin reading and keep on reading, and how to ensure that the learners actually do the reading. We will look at these questions in the following sections. See also the free booklets on extensive reading available from Compass Publishing (www.compasspub.com/english/customer/service_wherebuy.asp) and the Extensive Reading Foundation (www.erfoundation.org/ERF_Guide.pdf). Rob Waring's website (www.robwaring.org/er/) also has a very large number of useful resources and links.

What are the features of a good graded reading scheme?

What is the optimum proportion of unknown to known words in a graded reader?

At the beginning of this chapter, we looked at the optimum density of unknown words in a reading text in order for learners to gain reasonable comprehension of the text. The ideal unknown density was around 2%, meaning that 98% of the running words in the text should already be familiar to the learners. This is a density of around one unknown word in every 50, or one unknown word in every five lines of the text. This density figure comes from research on reading (Hu and Nation, 2000; Schmitt et al., 2011), but it is reassuring to note that in supplementary readers, West also considered that the ratio of unknown words to known should be one in fifty running words (1955: 21).

As Nation and Wang (1999) have shown, the number of target words at the beginning levels in a graded reading scheme needs to be fairly small at the high-frequency levels because each unknown target word will cover a reasonably high proportion of the running words in the text. As the levels move on to the less frequent words, the number of new words at each level should become larger because each target word will be less frequent and will thus cover a smaller proportion of the running words in the text.

What is the optimum spacing of vocabulary levels in a series?

Ideally the steps between the levels would allow a learner who has learned all the vocabulary at one level to read the next level within the desired proportion of known words. That is, when moving from one level to another having learned all the words at the previous level, the learner should have close to 98% coverage of the running words at the new level. Nation and Wang (1999) found that when learners move to a new level in their graded reading, it is likely that they will meet quite a high proportion of unknown words. At this point it would be wise to supplement the learning through reading with direct study of the new vocabulary, using word cards. This is best done as an individual activity with learners making their own cards and choosing the words from the books to put on the cards. Teachers can give useful advice and training in how to go about this learning. This may need to be done for only the first one or two books at a level. After that the density of unknown words will be light enough to allow more fluent reading.

Nation and Wang (1999) examined a corpus of 42 graded readers (seven readers at each of six levels in the same scheme). Ideally, in terms of percentage coverage of text, the levels in a graded reading scheme should be roughly equal. That is, when a learner moves from Level 2 readers to Level 3 readers, the new words at Level 3 should cover the same percentage of running words as the words at Level 2 did when the learner moved from Level 1 to Level 2. If this was so, then the vocabulary burden of each level would be equal in terms of assisting comprehension. Ideally, the percentage coverage of text by the newly introduced words should be 2% or less, because then the words from the previous levels and the proper nouns could cover 98% of the text, making comprehension and guessing from context easier (Laufer, 1992a; Liu and Nation, 1985).

Using the coverage data from their study, Nation and Wang suggested the following set of levels:

Level	Number of word families
1	500
2	700
3	1,000
4	1,500
5	2,000
6	3,000
7	5,000

These levels differ considerably from those used in most graded reading schemes, although some come very close to it. The stages are small at the earlier levels, and become very large at the later levels.

Another way of spacing the levels is to base them on a manageable set of words that could be learned within a set time. It is likely that the size of the levels is not as important as controlling the vocabulary in the readers so that no more than a small percentage of words are not covered by previous levels. *AntWordProfiler* provides a ready means of checking vocabulary level while writing or editing a graded reader.

Using performance on cloze tests taken from various levels of a set of graded readers, Cripwell and Foley (1984) investigated the effectiveness of the grading scheme used in those readers. They found that scores on the cloze tests decreased from level to level of the graded reader series indicating that the steps in the grading scheme resulted in a change in the difficulty of the texts. What was alarming in the study was the low level of reading proficiency of EFL learners even after four and five years of study.

What is the highest vocabulary level that a series of readers should reach?

Ideally, after the highest graded reader level, a learner should be able to move to friendly unsimplified texts and not face too large a proportion of unfamiliar words. Some series stop around the 2,000-word level, others go to the 3,000- and 5,000-word levels. Unfortunately, as Nation (2006) has shown, this is still several thousand words away from the vocabulary size required for 98% coverage of unsimplified text. Ideally, graded readers need to go up to at least the 6,000- or 7,000-word level, because an 8,000-word vocabulary is needed to gain 98% coverage of newspapers, and a 9,000-word vocabulary is needed to gain 98% coverage of novels. That is, graded readers should cover a lot of the mid-frequency words.

There used to be a graded reading scheme called the Bridge Series, published by Longman, which assumed knowledge of the first 3,000 words of English, replaced words beyond the 7,000-word level, and glossed words from the fourth to the seventh 1,000-word levels in a glossary at the back of the book.

Technical Note

In the Bridge Series words outside the commonest 7000 (in Thorndike and Lorge: The Teacher's Wordbook of 30,000 Words. Columbia University, 1944) have usually been replaced by commoner and more generally useful words. Words used which are outside the first 3,000 of the list are explained in a glossary and are so distributed throughout the book that they do not occur at a greater density than 25 per running 1,000 words.

(from the introduction to the Bridge Series edition of *Animal Farm*, 1945)

Unfortunately the books in this series are now out of print, but the idea was a very good one. At present, the grading schemes for published graded readers stop too far short of unsimplified text. The mid-frequency readers are an attempt to fill this gap; they are available free, at the 4,000-, 6,000- and 8,000-word levels.

Is vocabulary learning helped by indicating the new words at a level in a text?

New vocabulary can be indicated in the text by printing in bold letters and by providing glossaries. There is evidence from learning from listening (Elley, 1989) and from studies comparing incidental and intentional learning (Hulstijn, 2001) that drawing attention to new words can increase the chances of them being learned. Bramki and Williams' (1984) study of lexical familiarisation in academic text shows that many of the important new words that are defined in the text are written in bold or italics or in quotation marks to draw readers' attention to them. Research on vocabulary enhancement suggests that enhancements like bolding and italicisation may help the learning of form but not of meaning. Highlighting new words when they first appear may be helpful, but because enjoyment of reading is one of the main goals, the texts should not be marked up too much.

Is careful grammatical control necessary to produce readable readers?

A criticism often made of simplified texts is that the simplification of vocabulary results in more difficult grammar. Another criticism is that strict control of grammar results in unnatural, awkward text. Many of the simplified reader schemes control not only vocabulary but also grammar. The Longman Structural Reader Series, for example, had a detailed scheme of grammatical control. Readability studies place grammatical features well below vocabulary in determining the readability of a text. However, grammatical features can play a significant part in determining readability (Tweissi, 1998). Research is needed to determine how much grammatical control is needed to make readers accessible for second language learners. It may be that rough control of sentence length and complex sentences is sufficient. However, Shiotsu and Weir (2007), in a series of studies, compared the roles of syntactic knowledge and vocabulary knowledge in predicting reading comprehension performance, and found that syntactic knowledge made a greater contribution. Thus although vocabulary typically plays a major role in readability measures, such measures need to take greater account of syntax, and when teaching reading comprehension focus on syntax needs to be an important part of the teaching.

How can we design a good graded reading programme?

How can learners decide which book to choose to begin graded reading?

Unfortunately, each publisher uses a different scheme for grading their readers. The number and the size of steps in the schemes are not the same, and the total vocabulary aimed at is also different. However, there is quite a large overlap of the high-frequency words in the various schemes (Wan-a-rom, 2008). There is a test for the Cambridge English Readers series at http://cdextras.cambridge.org/Readers/RPT_last. swf. A possible way to decide where to begin reading is for learners to sit the Vocabulary Size Test to find out their total vocabulary size, and then to use this result to help them decide the appropriate level in a particular graded reading scheme (see Wan-a-rom, 2010, for further suggestions). The Vocabulary Size Test is available in various bilingual versions. Very low-proficiency learners could sit the 1,000 and perhaps the 2,000 bilingual levels of the Vocabulary Levels Test (available in the Vocabulary Resource Booklet from Paul Nation's website). A simpler way is just to choose a book and begin reading it. If there are too many unknown words on the first two or three pages then an easier book should be chosen. When making this decision, learners should be aware of the two strands that should exist within an extensive reading course, each with a different set of learning goals: (1) For the fluency development strand, the book chosen should not contain any or very many unknown words because the goal is to read the book as quickly as possible in order to develop reading speed. (2) For the meaning-focused input strand, the book should contain a few new words but not too many, so that reading is not burdensome and there is the opportunity to learn new vocabulary incidentally while reading, making use of the guessing from context strategy.

How many readers should be read at each level?

How many readers need to be read at each level in order to (a) meet all of the words at that level and (b) have a good chance of learning most of the words at that level? Wodinsky and Nation's (1988) study showed that reading two texts at the 1,100-word level resulted in meeting only 57% of the unfamiliar words at that level. Similarly, reading only two readers provided little repetition of the unfamiliar words. Only 56 out of the 350 available words occurred 10 times or more in the two readers studied.

Nation and Wang (1999) calculated that learners would need to read around five books at each level to meet most of the words introduced at that level and to meet many of them several times. They found that most repetitions occurred at later levels of the scheme, largely because the books are longer, so it was best not to stay too long at the early levels. By working their way through the levels of a scheme, learners would gain a very large number of repetitions of the words in the scheme, particularly the words at the earlier levels of the scheme. Nation and Wang found that about three quarters of the words in the graded reading scheme occurred at least ten times in their corpus of 42 readers (seven readers at each of six levels). This result is of course dependent on the length of the graded readers in the scheme (see Table 5.10). Kweon and Kim (2008) found strong evidence for the effect of repetition of words on learning in sustained extensive reading, with learning generally increasing with frequency and with no obvious frequency cut-off points. It is probably best to stick with the idea of about five readers per level to ensure repetition and the chance to meet most of the new words at that level.

How many readers should learners be reading within a set time at each level?

The idea behind this question is that learners need to get repetitions of vocabulary in order to help learning. There is a rough way of providing a guideline for deciding how much extensive reading learners at a particular level should be doing. The two factors determining the necessary amount of reading are (a) the frequency level of the learners' vocabulary, and (b) the length of time that the memory of a meeting with a word is retained. Using evidence from delayed post-tests from vocabulary research, it was decided that a gap of two weeks was about the longest time that could be safely allowed for retention.

Nation and Wang (1999) calculated that learners needed to read one book per week at the early levels and around two books per week at the later levels. The books in the study from the Oxford Bookworm Library were each several thousand words long (see Table 5.10) and so if shorter texts were read, more would need to be read within the two-week period.

How can teachers motivate learners to do extensive reading?

The best motivation comes from success in reading. Learners' motivation to read in an L2 can be influenced by their experience of reading in their L1 and their experience of reading in their L2. Takase (2007) however found in her study of Japanese high school students little relationship between learners' reading in their L1 and in their L2. The major factor affecting reading was intrinsic motivation to read in a particular language. Motivation to read in one language did not mean that motivation was high to read in the other language. Getting learners to do silent extensive reading in class is a good way to begin such reading because it forces learners to read and have a chance of experiencing success.

How can teachers monitor progress and make sure that learners are doing the reading?

There are numerous ways of monitoring reading. Learners need to keep a record of what they have read and their brief reaction to it, so that they can see how much they have read and the teacher can monitor the amount of reading they did. The simplest way to do this is to have a table like this on an A4 sheet of paper:

Title of the book	Series and level	Purpose	Date begun	Date finished	Comment on the book	Interest

In the column headed 'Purpose' the learner can indicate whether the book was read for fluency development or for normal reading. In the column headed 'Interest', the learner can give the book a ranking from 1 to 5 in terms of how interesting the book was for them. This gives the teacher some idea about which are the popular books and other learners can look at their friends' rankings to see what books they might want to read next (see Rob Waring's website, www.robwaring. org/er/ER_info/worksheets/worksheets.html, for other worksheets). Learners can also log on to a website that provides tests for each graded reader and keeps a record for the class that the teacher can access (http://moodlereader.org/index.html/). Day and Bamford (2004) also provide numerous suggestions for monitoring reading.

What does research show about the value of reading graded readers for vocabulary growth?

Since Waring and Takaki's (2003) classic study, we have had a much richer picture of vocabulary learning from second language reading. Their study involved learners reading only one graded reader and was not a study of long-term extensive reading. Waring and Takaki used three measures for each of the 25 words in their study, finding that from one reading of the text, learners scored 15.3 out of 25 on a word form recognition test, 10.6 on a receptive multiple-choice vocabulary test, and 4.6 on a word meaning recall translation test. The study showed that learning occurs at different degrees of knowledge and having only one measure of vocabulary learning would greatly under-estimate the amount of learning occurring (see Nation and Webb, 2011: 99–103, for a detailed critique of the study). Pulido (2004) carried out a similar study, but a two-day delay between the end of the reading and the tests, and the difficulty of the translation tests resulted in less encouraging results. She found however that comprehension and vocabulary learning were closely related. Some studies (Horst et al., 1998; Saragi et al., 1978; Zahar et al., 2001) have used only one measure of learning and the amount of learning shown depends heavily on the level of difficulty of that measure.

Pigada and Schmitt (2006) investigated a single learner doing one month of extensive reading, but tested three aspects of knowledge of each word – spelling, meaning and grammar. A score of 0, 1, or 2 was given for each word (both in the pre-tests and post-tests) and so it was possible to measure changes in knowledge for both initially unknown words and partially known words. In many ways it is more important to measure changes in partially known words because in any text at a suitable reading level for a learner, there are likely to be more partially known words than unknown words. Pigada and Schmitt found that extensive reading resulted in gains in all three types of knowledge, that repetition positively affected the amount of knowledge gained for the words, that knowledge of around two-thirds of the 133 target words was enhanced in some way, and that knowledge of the written form was more readily affected than meaning and grammatical knowledge. Horst (2005) also found gains for substantial proportions of the unknown words met in graded readers. Horst looked at extensive reading over six weeks and designed individualised vocabulary tests which matched the books that each learner actually read.

These innovations in research design – the use of multiple tests, the opportunity to learn from a substantial amount of reading input, and the testing of words actually met – have resulted in a much more valid and optimistic picture of vocabulary learning from extensive reading.

Brown (2009) has a list of very practical suggestions as to how coursebooks can encourage extensive reading. These include recom-mendations in the coursebooks for particular graded readers, includ-ing excerpts from graded readers in the coursebook, including a reading log in the coursebook for recording extensive reading, and providing discussion activities which draw on extensive reading.

There is no reason to doubt the finding that learners incidentally gain small amounts of vocabulary knowledge from each meaning-focused reading of an appropriate text. The most important finding is that this vocabulary learning is not an all-or-nothing piece of learning for any particular word, but that it is a gradual process of one meeting with a word adding to or strengthening the small amounts of knowledge gained from previous meetings. The implications of this finding are very important for managing extensive reading. Essentially, vocabulary learning from extensive reading is very fragile. If the small amount of learning of a word is not soon reinforced by another meeting, then that learning will be lost. It is thus critically important in an extensive reading programme that learners have the opportunity to keep meeting words that they have met before. This can be done in two ways: (1) by doing large amounts of extensive reading at suitable vocabulary levels so that there are repeated opportunities to meet wanted vocabulary, and (2) by complementing the extensive reading programme with the direct study of vocabulary. A well-balanced language programme has appropriate amounts of message-directed activity and language-focused activity.

Is extensive reading a good way to improve language proficiency?

So far in this chapter we have focused largely on reading as a way of encouraging vocabulary learning. Let us now look at the wider benefits of extensive reading, with particular attention on the effects of reading texts written with vocabulary control.

The research on extensive reading shows that there is a wide range of learning benefits from such activity. Experimental studies have shown that not only is there improvement in reading, but there are improvements in a range of language uses and areas of language knowledge. Although studies have focused on language improvement, it is clear that there are affective benefits as well. Success in reading and its associated skills, most notably writing, makes learners come to enjoy language learning and to value their study of English.

However the figures on repetition indicate that teachers need to be serious about extensive reading programmes particularly in ensuring that learners do large amounts of reading. The benefits of extensive reading do not come in the short term, and the substantial long-term benefits justify the high degree of commitment needed. Macalister (2008a) found learner support for the introduction of a daily 20 minutes of extensive reading in an English for Academic Purposes programme for low-proficiency learners. Learners chose their own books, read quietly and were encouraged to read two graded readers a week. Questionnaires, observation and interview data revealed a growing enthusiasm for reading during the programme (see also Tabata-Sandom and Macalister, 2009).

Will extensive reading of unsimplified texts help learning?

Several correlational studies looking at the effect of a variety of factors on L2 proficiency have shown the importance of extensive reading. Huang and van Naerssen (1987) found that reading outside class was the most significant predictor of oral communicative ability. Green and Oxford (1995), in a study of the effect of learning strategies on language proficiency, found that reading for pleasure was most strongly related to proficiency. Gradman and Hanania (1991) found that out-of-class reading was the most important direct contributor to TOEFL test performance. This study raised the important issue of causality through the use of the LISREL program for analysing the data. Gradman and Hanania found the strongest connection going from individual out-of-class reading to TOEFL results. They found that oral exposure, speaking and listening outside class and communicative oral use affected out-of-class reading.

It is clear from these studies that extensive reading can be a major factor in success in learning another language. It is likely that the relationship between extensive reading and language proficiency is changing and complex. Success in formal study may make reading more feasible. Success in reading may increase motivation for further study and reading. These correlational studies are supported by Pickard's (1996) survey of the out-of-class strategies used by a group of German learners of English in Germany, where extensive reading of newspapers, magazines and novels ranked very high on the list of strategies used for learning English. Use of reading and other input sources may be the only practical options for out-of-class language development for some learners.

In a study using SRA reading boxes, Robb and Susser (1989) found extensive reading of SRA material and readers written for American teenagers produced several results superior to a skills-focused reading course involving less reading. The extensive reading programme also gave learners more enjoyment both of reading and writing. The effects of extensive reading were thus both cognitive and affective.

Will reading simplified texts increase reading skill and language proficiency?

In two experiments, one conducted with second language learners in England for a maximum of 60 hours (Hafiz and Tudor, 1989; Tudor and Hafiz, 1989) and one with learners in Pakistan for a maximum of 90 hours (Hafiz and Tudor, 1990), Hafiz and Tudor looked at the effect of extensive reading of graded readers on learners' language use.

The study in England used standardised reading and writing measures and analyses of the students' writing, while the study in Pakistan used only analyses of students' writing. Even with these limited and indirect measures, improvement was seen, particularly in writing. There was no significant change in the vocabulary used in writing for the group in England, but this is not surprising as the vocabulary of the graded readers was probably far below learners' vocabulary level (Hafiz and Tudor, 1990: 36). There were some indications that the simplified syntax of the graded readers seemed to encourage learners to simplify the syntax in their own writing. All of Hafiz and Tudor's measures were of language use. It is likely that if they included more direct measures of vocabulary size, word recognition and English structures, as Elley and Mangubhai (1981) did, then there would be even more signs of improvement. Tsang (1996) also found very positive effects of simplified reading on learners' writing performance.

Can reading simplified texts increase reading fluency?

Beglar et al. (2012) found that the learners who made the most progress in the development of reading fluency over a year-long extensive reading programme were not those who read the most, but those who read the most simplified material. Learners who had read a lot of unsimplified material did not make the same fluency gains as learners who had read a lot of texts written at a level which was most suitable for them. The major requirement of a fluency development activity is that it is easy and does not contain unknown language features.

It is worth including a targeted speed reading course in an extensive reading programme. A speed reading course involves learners reading a timed text around 500 words, answering comprehension questions on the text, marking them on an answer sheet and then recording their time in words-per-minute and their comprehension score on graphs. This procedure is followed for around 20 texts over several weeks. Free speed reading courses are available at www.victoria.ac.nz/lals/staff/paul-nation.aspx and at Sonia Millett's website.

Research on speed reading courses (Bismoko and Nation, 1974; Chang, 2010; Chung and Nation, 2006; Cramer, 1975; Tran, 2012b) shows learners can make substantial increases in speed from such a course and can reach speeds close to those of native speakers. A relatively small investment of time (20 sessions of less than 10 minutes each) can result in good gains.

Macalister (2010) found that the gains in a speed reading course transferred to faster reading of a different kind of text (unsimplified) at the end of the speed reading course and several weeks later at the end of the language course. Learners who did not do a speed reading course also increased their reading speed during an intensive English course but not to the same degree as those in the same programme who did a speed reading course. Tran (2012b) made a similar finding. Macalister (2008b) also looked at the sustained effect of a speed reading course by comparing the speed at the end of a speed reading course with speed measured a few weeks later. Just under half of the learners continued to increase their speed between the end of the speed reading course and the later measure. About half of the learners showed a decrease in speed a few weeks after the end of a speed reading course (although even with that decrease the vast majority of learners increased their speed from the beginning of a speed reading course to the final delayed measure). Macalister suggests that this shows that factors in addition to the speed reading course contribute to reading speed increases, and that some of the increase in the course may be due to becoming familiar with the kinds of activities done in the speed reading course. To clarify this with an analogy, by doing press-ups you might increase your arm strength, but you also just may get good at doing press-ups. This suggests that speed reading courses need to be accompanied by extensive reading programmes that can support gains during the speed reading course and help maintain them when the speed reading course ends.

Macalister's learners made similar increases to those in Chung and Nation's (2006) study, with three or four learners making no increase. Later research by Chung showed that by giving some individual attention to learners who were identified through a lack of increase on the first few passages as not likely to make an increase, every learner made an increase by the end of the course. That is, learners not making an increase can be encouraged to make an increase by some motivating individual attention.

Tran (2012a) found that speed gains in a speed reading course transferred to texts outside the course including texts on the computer. Tran also found speed reading gains were accompanied by gains in oral reading rate and memory span as measured by repetition of sentences of increasing length.

Improvement in fluency in a speed reading course could be explained using Perfetti and Hart's (2002) Lexical Quality Hypothesis. That is, repeated retrievals of high-frequency vocabulary strengthen the orthographic, phonological and semantic representations of those words so that they can be processed quickly and more processing time can be given to comprehension. To support this argument we would need to show that a reasonable number of words occurred frequently enough in the texts to strengthen their quality of representation in readers' minds and that these words cover a substantial proportion of the text. An analysis of Quinn et al.'s (2007) speed reading course shows that if we look only at the texts in the course then there are 236 word types which occur with a frequency of 10 or more occurrences in the 20 texts. These 236 types cover 77.1% of the tokens in the texts. So just becoming fluent with these frequently repeated word types could make a significant impact on reading speed. If we take five repetitions as the threshold for developing fluency, then there are 412 types with a frequency of five or more occurrences and they cover 87.52% of the tokens in the course. If the comprehension questions are also considered as part of the speed reading input (although the comprehension questions are not answered under speeded conditions), then there are 313 word types occurring 10 times or more and they cover 83.49% of the tokens. There are 501 types occurring five times or more and they cover 91.24% of the running words.

These coverage figures are high because the speed reading texts are simplified texts written within a limited vocabulary of 1,000 words, but the same words would also be very frequent in unsimplified English.

Thus, a possible explanation for what happens to learners when they do a speed reading course is that they develop high-quality lexical representations for the very-high-frequency words of the language, and because these high-frequency words cover a large proportion of any text (well over 70%) they allow learners to process text more fluently and with improved comprehension.

We have looked at how vocabulary knowledge affects reading and how reading affects vocabulary growth. There is clearly a strong two-way relationship. We have also looked at unsimplified and simplified texts, making the points that the vocabulary load of unsimplified text is very heavy for beginning and intermediate learners, and simplified texts (graded readers) are needed if learners are to have meaning-focused input at all proficiency levels. An extensive reading programme with texts at the right levels for all learners is an essential component of a well-designed language course.

Vocabulary and writing

Reading and writing are skills that are not naturally acquired and thus deserve considerable attention in a language development program. Vocabulary knowledge plays a central role in both of these skills, and in this section we look at how vocabulary knowledge supports writing. Of all the four skills, however, writing is the one where we know the least about the relationship between the skill and vocabulary knowledge.

How much does vocabulary use affect the quality of writing?

Holistic assessments of ESL learners' writing generally relate well to some form of vocabulary analysis of the writing. Astika (1993) found, when using Jacobs et al.'s (1981) ESL composition scale, that the vocabulary section accounted for the largest amount of variance by far. Santos (1988) found that lexical errors were rated as the most serious in EFL students' writing by university professors.

Vocabulary choice is a strong indicator of whether the writer has adopted the conventions of the relevant discourse community. Corson (1997) argues that, for writers with academic purposes, it is essential to gain productive written control of the Graeco-Latin vocabulary of English in order to be recognised as a member of the academic writing community. Laufer's (1994) studies show that university students generally show progress in this area by an increase in the amount of academic vocabulary in their academic writing. Leki and Carson (1994) found that second language learners see lack of vocabulary as the major factor affecting the quality of their writing.

Comparisons between native speakers' and second language learners' writing show not surprisingly that native speakers use a much wider range of vocabulary (Harley and King, 1989; Linnarud, 1986).

Engber (1995) compared measures of lexical richness with teachers' ratings of composition quality, finding that counting the number of error-free content word lemmas gave the strongest correlation (.57) with the teachers' ratings. Engber's findings support Laufer and Nation's (1995) decision to exclude lexical errors from analysis of writing using the Lexical Frequency Profile.

Clearly vocabulary plays a significant role in the assessment of the quality of written work.

How can we measure the quality of vocabulary use in writing?

There are several ways of measuring the productive written vocabulary of a language learner (see Read, 2000: 197–209, for a very useful discussion of vocabulary measures in writing). One way is to measure it directly and overtly using a discrete-point vocabulary test. Laufer and Nation (1999) have developed and trialled such a test which is a productive parallel of the receptive vocabulary levels test (Nation, 1983). The test is divided into word frequency levels (2,000; 3,000; University Word List; 5,000 and 10,000) and uses a completion item type where the first few letters of the word are provided to cue the tested word. Here are some examples.

1. I'm glad we had this opp_____ to talk.
2. There are a doz_____ eggs in the basket.
3. Every working person must pay income t_____.
4. The pirates buried the trea_____ on a desert island.

Laufer and Nation (1995) found substantial and significant correlations between total scores on the productive levels test and the proportion of words at the 1,000 level (negatively correlated with total scores) and at the University Word List level and not in any of the lists in learners' written compositions. That is, the higher a learner's vocabulary size as measured by the productive levels test, the fewer words used at the 1,000-word level and the more used from the University Word List and low-frequency levels in their written work. This shows that appropriate vocabulary tests can reflect language use (Arnaud, 1984, 1992; Laufer and Goldstein, 2004; Laufer and Nation, 1995).

Another way to measure vocabulary size and growth in written work is to analyse the vocabulary of learners' written compositions. Numerous measures have been suggested for doing this, which include lexical variation (also known as the type/token ratio), lexical originality, lexical density, lexical sophistication and lexical quality. Laufer and Nation (1995) provide a critique of these measures showing that each contains inherent weaknesses. In all of these measures, including the Lexical Frequency Profile, it is important to keep text length constant (Richards and Malvern, 1997) as a change in text length will affect the measures. Laufer and Nation propose a new measure, the **Lexical Frequency Profile**, which avoids the weaknesses of the other measures. This measure, like the others mentioned above, requires the use of a computer to do the analysis. In essence, the Lexical Frequency Profile is an analysis of the percentage of word families at various frequency levels in a piece of written work. The frequency levels are determined by reference to frequency counts – the *General Service List of English Words* (West, 1953) and the *University Word List* (Xue and Nation, 1984) now replaced by the *Academic Word List* (Coxhead, 2000). The computer program which does the analysis is available free at www.victoria.ac.nz/lals/staff/paul-nation.aspx and is now called Range (previously VocabProfile). The proper nouns and severe lexical errors are removed from the compositions and they are typed into the computer and saved in plain text format. The Range program is run over the files to gather the data. Laufer (1994) has arranged the data in two ways. One way is as a full profile with the percentages of word families at the 1,000/2,000/UWL and other levels. The other way is to use a condensed profile. This can be of two types: the 'Beyond

2,000' measure (Laufer, 1995) which simply looks at the total percentage of word families not in the 1,000 and 2,000 levels, and a condensed measure for more advanced learners which looks at the percentage of word families not in the 1,000, 2,000 and UWL levels. The studies Laufer has been involved in have looked at learners who are in the early stages of university study. The Beyond 2,000 measure has been most effective here because significant changes occur in the proportion of words used from the University Word List. Table 5.11 contains some typical figures from Laufer's studies.

Table 5.11 *Lexical frequency profiles of the compositions of various native speaker and second language learner groups*

Learners	Percentage of word families in the first 2,000 words according to West (1953)	Percentage of word families beyond the first 2,000 words
18-year-old native speakers (Laufer, 1994)	75%	25%
Israeli university entrants (Laufer, 1994)	90%	10%
The same Israeli learners one semester later (Laufer, 1994)	87%	13%
ESL learners (Laufer and Paribakht, 1998)	88%	12%

Laufer has shown that:

1. The Lexical Frequency Profile of learners' writing changes as a result of continuing contact with English. The proportion of words used from the first 2,000 becomes less and the words from the *University Word List* and words not in the first 2,000 and University Word List increase.
2. The Lexical Variation measure (number of types $\times$ 100 $\div$ the number of tokens) does not change over one or two semesters' contact with English.
3. There is a relationship between vocabulary size as measured by direct testing and learners' Lexical Frequency Profiles (Laufer and Nation, 1995).
4. The Lexical Frequency Profile is similar between similar kinds of writing done by the same learners within a few days of each other. That is, it is a stable measure (Laufer and Nation, 1995).

Morris and Cobb (2004) tested the Lexical Frequency Profile as a measure of second language learners' proficiency. They found that there was a low to moderate significant correlation (around .35) with grades in some undergraduate TESL courses. The Lexical Frequency Profile proved to be a useful component for inclusion in a collection of language proficiency assessment measures for high proficiency non-native speakers.

Meara and Bell's (2001) *P_Lex* works in a similar manner to the lexical frequency profile, except that it examines each 10-word segment of a text for low-frequency words. Read and Nation (2006) found it to be a very effective measure in their study of learners' performance in the IELTS speaking module.

Another measure of lexical diversity is *D* which is said to deal with many of the problems encountered by other measures (Daller et al., 2003; Duran et al., 2004). This measure has now been used in numerous pieces of research with largely positive results. Duran et al. (2004) carried out a validation study using a program *vocd* which is now available from the CHILDES website. The program was developed to meet the following criteria which have not been well met in other attempts to devise a measure of lexical diversity:

- A measure of lexical diversity should consider the range of vocabulary, whether it is repeated, and the effect of text length.
- It should use all the data without having to trim texts and be able to deal with texts of different lengths.
- It should follow a consistent sampling method.

Texts need to be specially prepared for the program by getting rid of spelling inconsistencies, removing repeated words used in hesitations in spoken texts, tagging homographs, removing non-words, and removing regular inflections, so that regularly formed lemmas were counted as one word type. The minimum text length required is 50 tokens.

Ideally in comparison studies, the conditions under which the gathering of texts occurred should be similar (Yu, 2009) with no big contrast in the number of topics covered. This kind of control ensures that language differences and not other differences are being compared. With suitable controls, *D* has been shown to be effective for measuring the development of lexical diversity in both native speakers and non-native speakers (but see McCarthy and Jarvis, 2007, for cautions). Yu also suggests sensible cautions in the use of *D*, and indeed other single measures of quality of text production. However, Yu found positive relationships using *D* with the speaking and writing performance of test candidates, and with overall language proficiency.

Crossley, Salsbury, McNamara and colleagues used the computerised text analysis program *Coh-Metrix* (Graesser et al., 2004) to gather data which will predict human judgements of lexical proficiency in the production of spoken and written text. Crossley et al. (2011) investigated trained raters' scoring of the content words of informal speech and found that four factors – lexical diversity (as measured by D), word imageability, word familiarity, and word hypernymy (the use of more general rather than specific words) – predicted around 60% of the variance in the human judgements. Lexical diversity as measured by D was by far the strongest predictor. Thus, the wider the range of words that learners use, the better their speaking. Crossley et al. (2009) found evidence of growth in the hypernymic measure over time. That is, as they learned more, learners learned more abstract terms for the more specific words they already knew.

So far we have looked at the Productive Levels test, and richness measures including the Lexical Frequency Profile and D. Strictly speaking, these measures look at the kind of vocabulary used but do not truly look at quality, that is, how well the words are used. Computer-based identification of errors is still in its early stages of development and we are yet to see a computer-based measure of vocabulary quality of use.

A third way of measuring vocabulary use in writing is to use a rating scale that focuses on vocabulary. Jacobs et al. (1981) include a vocabulary scale as one of the five scales in their ESL composition profile. The vocabulary scale is worth a total of 20 points out of 100. The other scales are content (30 points), organisation (20 points), language use (grammar) (25 points), mechanics (spelling, punctuation etc.) (5 points). Table 5.12 (overleaf) lists the four levels in the vocabulary section of Jacobs et al.'s scale.

Research by Ruegg et al. (2011) suggests that raters may have difficulty in truly rating vocabulary as a separate factor, and in particular in distinguishing it from grammar.

A fourth way of looking at vocabulary in learners' writing is to look at lexical errors. Lexical errors are generally rated as being among the most serious errors in analyses of errors (Dordick, 1996; Santos, 1988).

In a very detailed analysis of lexical errors in foreign language writing by Spanish learners, Agustin Llach (2011) found:

- reductions in lexical error as learners progressed through their years of learning English;
- a strong effect of lexical errors on assessments of writing quality accounting for around one-third of the variance;
- a move from form-based errors to meaning-based errors as proficiency developed; and
- low but significant correlations between lexical errors in writing and measures of receptive vocabulary knowledge.

Table 5.12 *Jacobs et al.'s (1981) vocabulary scale from their ESL composition profile*

Points out of 20	Descriptors
20–18	Excellent to very good: • sophisticated range • effective word/idiom choice and usage • word form mastery • appropriate register
17–14	Good to average: • adequate range • occasional errors of word/idiom form, choice, usage *but meaning not obscured*
13–10	Fair to poor: • limited range • frequent errors of word/idiom form, choice, usage *meaning confused or obscured*
9–7	Very poor: • essentially translation • little knowledge of English vocabulary, idioms, word form • OR not enough to evaluate

At grade 4, almost two-thirds of the errors were spelling mistakes and at grade 6, just over half were misspellings. Agustin Llach's study includes a detailed analysis of a range of lexical error taxonomies.

Liu and Shaw (2001) compared the use of the word *make* in a corpus of the writing of Chinese learners of English with three native speaker corpora. They found a wide range of differences leading them to suggest that deliberate attention may need to be given to some aspects of particular words to avoid fossilisation.

How can we improve vocabulary use in writing?

Learners' written vocabulary can be increased by a general focus on vocabulary size and by a focus on particular words in productive vocabulary-focused activities. Zhou (2009) found that learners wanted to increase their vocabulary knowledge for writing but were uncertain about how to do it.

In two studies, Laufer (Laufer, 1998; Laufer and Paribakht, 1998) compared three measures of vocabulary size. The first, the Vocabulary Levels Test (Nation, 1983), is a measure of receptive knowledge and includes items like the following:

1. file
2. involve   _____ look closely
3. oblige   _____ stop doing something
4. peer   _____ cry out loudly in fear
5. quit
6. scream

The second measure, the Productive Levels Test (Laufer and Nation, 1999), described earlier in this chapter, involved form recall and is a measure of productive (Laufer calls it 'active') vocabulary knowledge.

1. He has a successful car____ as a lawyer.
2. The thieves threw ac_____ in his face and made him blind.
3. To improve the country's economy, the government decided on economic ref_____.

These two measures are discrete-point measures with a deliberate focus on vocabulary. They test the same words.

The third measure, the Lexical Frequency Profile (Laufer and Nation, 1995), involves computer analysis of learners' free writing and is a measure of vocabulary in use. The Lexical Frequency Profile looks at the proportion of correctly used different words which are outside the high-frequency words of the language (see Flinspach et al., 2009) for the beginnings of a similar measure for native speakers).

Laufer (1998) found a high correlation between the two discrete-point measures (.67–.78), a large increase in size over the period of a year on each of the two measures, but no correlation between these measures and learners' Lexical Frequency Profile (the size of their free productive vocabulary in use) and no change in the Lexical Frequency Profile over a year.

While it is possible to make significant changes in vocabulary knowledge, it is not easy to move this knowledge into productive use. Laufer suggests that one cause of this may have been a lack of encouragement and suitable activities. Laufer also suggests that perhaps the receptive and productive knowledge increases were not large enough to influence actual use. This last explanation is unlikely as the increases in her study were substantial.

Laufer and Paribakht (1998), in a study involving a wider range of learners and ESL and EFL learners, however, found significant and moderate correlations between the receptive and productive discrete-point measures and the Lexical Frequency Profile. They found that the development of active vocabulary was slower and less predictable than the development of passive vocabulary. Laufer and Goldstein (2004) found using discrete-point tests that scores on an active recall vocabulary test was much lower than scores on the other tests.

In all of the studies, learners' vocabulary size as measured on the receptive test was larger than vocabulary size as measured by the productive test. Meara and Fitzpatrick (2000) have developed the very efficient *Lex30* which gets learners to respond to isolated stimulus words with other words which are then scored according to their frequency levels in the language.

Increases in fluency in production with near-beginners are not necessarily accompanied by an increase in richness of vocabulary use as measured by the Range program (Horst and Collins, 2006). This perhaps indicates that learners are more likely to make better use of the words they know rather than take risks with vocabulary they are unsure about. Horst and Collins show that a variety of measures can be used to measure changes in quality of vocabulary use, such as proportion of cognate words and L2 lexical gaps filled with L1 words.

Laufer et al.'s experiments indicate that it is not an easy job to bring receptive vocabulary into productive use, particularly for low-frequency words. Rott et al. (2002) found that having learners do written recalls of the text section by section helped vocabulary learning for target words which were glossed in the input text. However, they often found higher-frequency synonyms being used in the recall rather than the target words – *tree* instead of *oak*, *animals* instead of *livestock* – indicating that learning the meaning was occurring before productive learning of the word form. Coxhead (2007) similarly found learners reluctant to produce words in writing that they had just met in the reading input text. Productive knowledge needs to be built up and is usually not immediately achieved. Muncie (2002) however found some evidence that when writing several drafts of a composition, learners tended to use more sophisticated words on their final draft. This suggests that some deliberate attention to the vocabulary of a piece of writing may encourage more risk-taking with words.

Lee and Muncie (2006) looked at the effect of an elaborate sequence of work leading up to a piece of writing based on the story of the Titanic. It involved watching a movie, doing a cloze exercise, reading a closely related text, doing a reading comprehension activity, doing the first draft of the writing, discussing vocabulary based on a writing frame, writing the second draft, and then getting feedback and correction. They found a large amount of the target words were produced in the writing and largely remaining in a delayed rewriting two weeks later. The amount of exposure to the words in the pre-writing tasks was substantial and most of it had a deliberate vocabulary focus. A writing task at the end of a unit of work, as for example in linked skills tasks, can help vocabulary become productive. These findings support an earlier study by Lee (2003).

Research with native speakers indicates that even when the focus is on particular words to be used for a particular writing task, considerable pre-teaching of an intensive kind is needed to establish words and bring them into free productive use. Duin and Graves (1987) examined the effects on vocabulary knowledge, use of vocabulary in writing, and writing performance of pre-teaching 13 words over a six-day period. The more the treatment was focused on writing, and was intensive and rich, the better the results.

There seem to be at least two important factors affecting productive vocabulary use. The first is knowledge. Productive knowledge of vocabulary requires more learning than receptive knowledge. There is plenty of evidence for this both from experimental studies of receptive and productive learning (see Chapter 3) and from measures of learners' receptive and productive vocabulary size. Table 2.1 outlines the additional kinds of knowledge needed for production through the receptive/productive division in each of the nine sections of the table.

The second factor affecting productive vocabulary use is motivation. The term **motivation** is used here in Corson's (1985) sense which includes the desire and opportunity to use a word. We may know vocabulary but, because the opportunity and wish to use a particular word does not arise, that word remains as part of our 'unmotivated' vocabulary. That is, it could be used but it is not.

Activities that try to move vocabulary into productive use need to take account of these two factors. Let us now look at a range of these activities, starting with those that involve a great deal of teacher control over the writing and moving to those that involve more learner choice.

Reading and sentence completion

There are several varieties of completion activities that can follow reading a text and use words that occur in the text. The completions can range from copying from the text to having to use the words with a different inflection or derivational affix, or to express an idea not in the text.

Dykstra et al. (1966) devised a guided composition course called *Ananse Tales* which involved learners in copying short texts and making small and then eventually larger changes to them. There were about 20 texts and each was followed by around three to five suggested changes. Each level of change was numbered to show its difficulty level. Dykstra had a list of 57 ways of altering the text starting from simply copying, then changing *the Spider* to *the Spiders* (with necessary changes in verb and pronoun agreement), to changing the tense, to adding relative clauses, and finally to adding a new paragraph to the end of the text. Here is an example.

Why the Hyena has Stripes (Part 1)

1 Ananse, the spider, and his neighbour, the hyena, decided to go to the river together. 2 There they met the King of the river who presented them with a gift of many fish. 3 Ananse and the hyena made a fire, and as Ananse cooked the fish, he threw them over his shoulder on to the river bank to cool. 4 However, the greedy hyena caught and ate all of them.

5 When Ananse turned to eat his fish, tears of anger filled his eyes. 6 The hyena asked the spider why he was weeping, but Ananse calmly replied that the smoke from the fire was in his eyes. 7 Nevertheless, he was already planning his revenge.

Level 1.   Copy.
Level 2.   Rewrite the entire passage changing the word *hyena* to *zebra* each time it appears.
Level 5.   Rewrite the entire passage changing *Ananse, the spider* to *the spiders*. (When either *Ananse* or *the spider* appears alone, change it to *the spiders*.) Remember to change both the verbs and pronouns whenever it is necessary to do so.
Level 21. Rewrite the entire passage supplying adjectives before the words *spider, hyena,* and *river* (sentence 1); *shoulder* (sentence 3); *eyes* (sentence 5); and *fire* (sentence 6).
Level 32. Rewrite the entire passage supplying your own verbal phrases at the beginning of the following sentences. Begin your phrase with the verb form given here: sentence 1 (having heard); sentence 3 (having agreed); sentence 6 (seeing).

Learners enjoyed these language-focused learning activities, because they had a high degree of success and they could see clear progress through the simpler changes to the greater ones. Because these activities involved a large degree of copying and making small alterations to an existing text, they were a good way of bringing receptive vocabulary into productive use.

Paraphrase

Learners read sentences that they then have to re-express using the target word which is provided for them. The teacher will need to model the use of the word first or provide some example sentences.

Everybody will be helped by the changes.

(*benefit*) _____

Translation

Learners translate sentences or short texts from their first language. The target vocabulary may be provided.

The second-hand cloze

Pre-reading and translation are usefully linked in the second-hand cloze (Laufer and Osimo, 1991). This technique involves learners placing previously taught words into gaps in a text which summarises the content of a previously studied text. The formal context for the words is new. Learners are guided by having a dictated list of first language meanings which will fill the gaps but which have to be translated into the appropriate second language word.

Dictionary use

Learners need to be trained in dictionary use so that they can readily find words that they need in their writing (see Chapter 10). Harvey and Yuill (1997) investigated the monolingual dictionary use of learners engaged in a writing task. They found that the most common reasons, in order of frequency, for using a dictionary were:

- to find the correct spelling (24.4%);
- to check on a meaning (18.3%);
- to see if the word exists (12.8%);
- to find a synonym (10.6%); and
- to check on the grammar (10.5%).

The length of an entry was seen as the major challenge in finding needed information about a word. Summers (1988) found that dictionary use, particularly attention to example sentences, was useful when writing sentences.

Reading like a writer

Teacher and learners work together through a reading text noting features of the text that typify that style of writing. From a vocabulary perspective these features can include the degree of formality of the vocabulary, the use of lexical chains, lexical cohesion through the use of related words, and signals of changes in the stages of the text. In Chapter 6 in the section on the roles vocabulary can play in discourse, we look at these features in more detail. The learners are encouraged to use some of the features in a writing task.

The dicto-comp and related activities

In the dicto-comp (Ilson, 1962), learners listen to a text and then write it from memory. They can be encouraged to use target words by:

- seeing the words on the board as the text is read and having them remain there;
- seeing the words on the board as the text is read, then having all except the first two letters of each word rubbed off; or
- having translations of the target words put on the blackboard.

Activities related to the dicto-comp (Nation, 1991) include dictation, delayed copying, the reproduction activity (read a text, put it away, write it from memory), and the dicto-gloss where learners work together to reconstruct a previously heard text.

Guided semantic mapping

Learners work with the teacher to develop a semantic map around a topic. The teacher deliberately introduces several target vocabulary items and puts them on the map as well as elaborating on them with the learners. Learners then use the semantic map to do a piece of writing. If the writing is done in small groups, a learner in the group can be given the responsibility of ensuring that the target words are used.

Using written input to affect vocabulary use in writing

In Chapter 4, we looked at how written input can be designed and used to affect vocabulary use in speaking. The same guidelines can be applied to encourage the use of particular vocabulary in writing. These guidelines include providing plenty of written input to the task, designing the task to make use of the written input and using recall, and adaptation of the input to encourage creative use.

Using speaking activities to affect vocabulary use in writing

Speaking activities designed to encourage the use of certain vocabulary (see Chapter 4) can be used as the first stage of a writing task.

Learners do the specially designed speaking task which encourages spoken productive use of the target vocabulary. Then they report back orally on the result of their speaking task to the class. Finally, they prepare a written report on the conclusions of the speaking task. If these linked-skills tasks have been well designed, the target vocabulary will occur in the speaking task, the oral reporting and the written report.

Issue logs

Each learner decides on an interesting topic and over a period of several weeks collects information on this topic from newspapers, radio and television news, books, magazines, interviews and so on. Each week the learner reports orally to a small group and every two weeks he or she makes a written report summarising the information gathered so far. The learner is told to deliberately try to incorporate into the written summaries new vocabulary which has been met in the information gathering for the topic. The final outcome is a comprehensive written report.

Word-focused fluency training

Most fluency activities involve the reception and production of large amounts of coherent text. Snellings et al. (2002) looked at the effect of training the retrieval of individual words. The four computer-based activities involved:

1. choosing one of two words to continue a phrase;
2. deciding which of two words in the sentence was not correct;
3. choosing one of three words as the right one within a sentence; and
4. translating an L1 word in an L2 sentence into the L2.

The activities focused on both receptive and productive access, and were done using known words with time pressure. The activities resulted in faster lexical decision times (deciding if an item was a non-word or a real word) and production of written translations of L1 words.

Email interaction

Email can be a source of vocabulary learning, especially if the learner is communicating with a more proficient user such as a native speaker. Sasaki and Takeuchi (2010) looked at Japanese students' email exchanges with a native speaker to see if they copied words that the native speaker used and if they remembered these words. They also looked at learning which occurred without copying. They found that of an average of 19.3 target words used by the native speaker, each learner on average learned 3.6 by copying (2.4 were copied but not learned) and 3.9 by observing native speaker use without using the words in the email exchange (9.4 were used by the native speaker but not learned). The results are like those of Newton's (2013) study of oral interaction and negotiation (see Chapter 4). Copying the words used by the native speaker had a 60% chance of leading to learning. Observing was less sure (a 30% chance of learning), but accounted for a bit more learning. During the email exchanges learners consulted dictionaries and other resources.

An interesting aspect of the six-week study was that there was target vocabulary arranged with the native speaker that was tested in the pre- and post-tests but was not actually used by the native speaker and not by any of the learners in any of the emails. They were just over 29 words. 3.6 of these words on average were learned, showing that they must have been learned from the learners on-going language study. The learners were interviewed about the words in the emails that they had learned and it was clear from this that meeting the words in the emails encouraged learners to notice them when they occurred elsewhere. We thus have to see the gains over the six-week period as only partly coming from observed or copied use in emails.

In this chapter, we have looked at vocabulary and the skills of reading and writing. In the next chapter, we look at the important role played by special purposes vocabulary, namely academic and technical vocabulary, in academic texts.

References

Abraham, L. B. (2008). Computer-mediated glosses in second language reading comprehension and vocabulary learning: A meta-analysis. *Computer Assisted Language Learning*, 21, 3, 199–226.

Agustin Llach, M. P. (2011). *Lexical Errors in foreign language writing*. Bristol: Multilingual Matters.

Alessi, S. and Dwyer, A. (2008). Vocabulary assistance before and during reading. *Reading in a Foreign Language*, 20, 2, 246–63.

Altarriba, J. and Knickerbocker, H. (2011). Acquiring second language vocabulary through the use of images and words. In Trofimovich, P. and McDonough, K. (eds.), *Applying Priming Methods to L2 Learning, Teaching and Research: 1* (pp. 21–47). Amsterdam: John Benjamins.

Arevart, S. and Nation, I. S. P. (1991). Fluency improvement in a second language. *RELC Journal*, 22, 1, 84–94.

Arnaud, P. J. L. (1984). A practical comparison of five types of vocabulary tests and an investigation into the nature of L2 lexical competence. *Paper read at 7th World Congress of Applied Linguistics, Brussels* (January 21).

Arnaud, P. J. L. (1992). Objective lexical and grammatical characteristics of L2 written compositions and the validity of separate-component tests. In Arnaud, P. J. L. and Bejoint, H. (eds.), *Vocabulary and Applied Linguistics* (pp. 133–45). London: Macmillan.

Astika, G. G. (1993). Analytical assessment of foreign students' writing. *RELC Journal*, 24, 1, 61–72.

Bamford, J. (1984). Extensive reading by means of graded readers. *Reading in a Foreign Language*, 2, 2, 218–60.

Beglar, D., Hunt, A. and Kite, Y. (2012). The effect of pleasure reading on Japanese university EFL learners' reading rates. *Language Learning*, 62, 3, 665–703.

Bell, F. L. and LeBlanc, L. B. (2000). The language of glosses in L2 reading on computer: Learners' preferences. *Hispania*, 83, 274–85.

Bhatia, V. K. (1983). Simplification v. easification: The case of legal texts. *Applied Linguistics*, 4, 1, 42–54.

Biemiller, A. and Slonim, N. (2001). Estimating root word vocabulary growth in normative and advantaged populations: Evidence for a common sequence of vocabulary acquisition. *Journal of Educational Psychology*, 93, 3, 498–520.

Bismoko, J. and Nation, I. S. P. (1974). English reading speed and the mother-tongue or national language. *RELC Journal*, 5, 1, 86–9.

Bowles, M. A. (2004). L2 glossing: To CALL or not to CALL. *Hispania*, 87, 3, 541–52.

Bramki, D. and Williams, R. C. (1984). Lexical familiarization in economics text, and its pedagogic implications in reading comprehension. *Reading in a Foreign Language*, 2, 1, 169–81.

Brown, D. (2009). Why and how textbooks should encourage extensive reading. *ELT Journal*, 63, 3, 238–45.

Brown, J. D. (1998). An EFL readability index. *JALT Journal*, 29, 2, 7–36.

Brown, R., Waring, R. and Donkaewbua, S. (2008). Incidental vocabulary acquisition from reading, reading-while-listening, and listening to stories. *Reading in a Foreign Language*, 20, 2, 136–63.

Burling, R. (1968). Some outlandish proposals for the teaching of foreign languages. *Language Learning*, 18, 1, 61–75.

Burling, R. (1978). An introductory course in reading French. *Language Learning*, 28, 1, 105–28.

Carrell, P. (1987). Readability in ESL. *Reading in a Foreign Language*, 4, 1, 21–40.

Chall, J. S. (1958). *Readability: An Appraisal of Research and Application*. Ohio State Bureau of Education Research Monographs.

Chang, A. C.-S. (2010). The effect of a timed reading activity on EFL learners: Speed, comprehension, and perceptions. *Reading in a Foreign Language*, 22, 2, 284–303.

Cheng, Y. H. and Good, R. L. (2009). L1 Glosses: Effects on the EFL learners' reading comprehension and vocabulary retention. *Reading in a Foreign Language*, 21, 2, 119–42.

Christensen, E., Merrill, P. and Yanchai, S. (2007). Second language vocabulary acquisition using a diglot reader or a computer-based drill and practice program. *Computer Assisted Language Learning*, 20, 1, 67–77.

Chun, D. and Payne, J. S. (2004). What makes students click: Working memory and look-up behavior. *System*, 32, 481–503.

Chun, D. M. and Plass, J. L. (1996). Effects of multimedia annotations on vocabulary acquisition. *Modern Language Journal*, 80, 2, 183–98.

Chung, M. and Nation, I. S. P. (2006). The effect of a speed reading course. *English Teaching*, 61, 4, 181–204.

Cobb, T. (2007). Computing the vocabulary demands of L2 reading. *Language Learning and Technology*, 11, 3, 38–63.

Cobb, T. (2008). Commentary: Response to McQuillan and Krashen. *Language Learning and Technology*, 12, 1, 109–14.

Corson, D. J. (1985). *The Lexical Bar*. Oxford: Pergamon Press.

Corson, D. J. (1997). The learning and use of academic English words. *Language Learning*, 47, 4, 671–718.

Coxhead, A. (2000). A new academic word list. *TESOL Quarterly*, 34, 2, 213–38.

Coxhead, A. (2007). Factors and aspects of knowledge affecting L2 word use in writing. In Davidson, P., Coombe, C., Lloyd, D. and Palfreyman, D. (eds.), *Teaching and Learning Vocabulary in Another Language* (pp. 331–42). Dubai: TESOL Arabia.

Cramer, S. (1975). Increasing reading speed in English or in the national language. *RELC Journal*, 6, 2, 19–23.

Cripwell, K. and Foley, J. (1984). The grading of extensive readers. *World Language English*, 3, 3, 168–73.

Crossley, S. A., Greenfield, J. and McNamara, D. S. (2008). Assessing text readability using cognitively based indices. *TESOL Quarterly*, 42, 3, 475–93.

Crossley, S., Salsbury, T. and McNamara, D. (2009). Measuring L2 lexical growth using hypernymic relationships. *Language Learning*, 59, 2, 307–34.

Crossley, S. A., Salsbury, T., McNamara, D. S. and Jarvis, S. (2011). What is lexical proficiency? Some answers from computational models of speech data. *TESOL Quarterly*, 45, 1, 182–93.

Daller, H., van Hout, R. and Treffers-Daller, J. (2003). Lexical richness in the spontaneous speech of bilinguals. *Applied Linguistics*, 24, 2, 197–222.

Davis, J. N. (1989). Facilitating effects of marginal glosses on foreign language reading. *Modern Language Journal*, 73, 1, 41–8.

Davis, J. N. and Lyman-Hager, M. A. (1997). Computers and L2 reading: Student performance, student attitudes. *Foreign Language Annals*, 30, 1, 58–72.

Day, R. R. and Bamford, J. (1998). *Extensive Reading in the Second Language Classroom*. Cambridge: Cambridge University Press.

Day, R. and Bamford, J. (2002). Top ten principles for teaching extensive reading. *Reading in a Foreign Language*, 14, 2, 136–41.

Day, R. R. and Bamford, J. (2004). *Extensive Reading Activities for Teaching Language*. Cambridge: Cambridge University Press.

de Jong, N. and Perfetti, C. (2011). Fluency training in the ESL classroom: An experimental study of fluency development and proceduralization. *Language Learning*, 61, 2, 533–68.

De Ridder, I. (2002). Visible or invisible links: does the highlighting of hyperlinks affect incidental vocabulary learning, text comprehension, and the reading process? *Language Learning & Technology*, 6, 1, 123–46.

Dordick, M. (1996). Testing for a hierarchy of the communicative interference value of ESL errors. *System*, 24, 3, 299–308.

Duin, A. H. and Graves, M. F. (1987). Intensive vocabulary instruction as a prewriting technique. *Reading Research Quarterly*, 22, 3, 311–30.

Dumay, N. and Gaskell, G. (2005). Do words go to sleep? Exploring consolidation of spoken forms through direct and indirect measures. *Behavioral and Brain Sciences*, 28, 69–70.

Dumay, N. and Gaskell, G. (2007). Sleep-associated changes in the mental representation of spoken words. *Psychological Science*, 18, 1, 35–9.

Duran, P., Malvern, D., Richards, B. and Chipere, N. (2004). Developmental trends in lexical diversity. *Applied Linguistics*, 25, 2, 220–42.

Dykstra, G., Port, R. and Port, A. (1966). *Ananse Tales*. New York: Teachers College Press, Columbia University.

Elgort, I. (2011). Deliberate learning and vocabulary acquisition in a second language. *Language Learning*, 61, 2, 367–413.

Elley, W. B. (1969). The assessment of readability by noun frequency counts. *Reading Research Quarterly*, 4, 3, 411–27.

Elley, W. B. (1989). Vocabulary acquisition from listening to stories. *Reading Research Quarterly*, 24, 2, 174–87.

Elley, W. B. (1991). Acquiring literacy in a second language: The effect of book-based programs. *Language Learning*, 41, 3, 375–411.

Elley, W. B. and Mangubhai, F. (1981). *The Impact of a Book Flood in Fiji Primary Schools*. Wellington: New Zealand Council for Educational Research.

Ellis, R. (1995). Modified oral input and the acquisition of word meanings. *Applied Linguistics*, 16, 4, 409–41.

Engber, C. A. (1995). The relationship of lexical proficiency to the quality of ESL compositions. *Journal of Second Language Writing*, 4, 2, 139–55.

Flinspach, S. L., Scott, J. A. and Vevea, J. L. (2009). Rare words in students' writing as a measure of vocabulary. In Jimenez, R. T., Risko, V. J., Rowe, D. W. and Hundley, M. (eds.), *59th Annual Yearbook of the National Reading Conference* (pp. 187–200). Oak Creek, WI: National Reading Conference.

Fraser, C. (2007). Reading rate in L1 Mandarin Chinese and L2 English across five reading tasks. *The Modern Language Journal*, 91, 3, 372–94.

Gardner, D. (2004). Vocabulary input through extensive reading: A comparison of words found in children's narrative and expository reading materials. *Applied Linguistics*, 25, 1, 1–37.

Gardner, D. (2008). Vocabulary recycling in children's authentic reading materials: A corpus-based investigation of narrow reading. *Reading in a Foreign Language*, 20, 1, 92–122.

Gaskell, D. and Cobb, T. (2004). Can learners use concordance feedback for writing errors? *System*, 32, 3, 301–19.

Gass, S. M. (1988). Second language vocabulary acquisition. *Annual Review of Applied Linguistics*, 9, 92–106.

Gettys, S., Imhof, L. A. and Kautz, J. O. (2001). Computer-assisted reading: The effect of glossing format on comprehension and vocabulary retention. *Foreign Language Annals*, **34**, 2, 91–106.

Grace, C. A. (2000). Gender differences: Vocabulary retention and access to translations for beginning language learners in CALL. *Modern Language Journal*, **84**, 2, 214–24.

Gradman, H. and Hanania, E. (1991). Language learning background factors and ESL proficiency. *Modern Language Journal*, **75**, 1, 39–51.

Graesser, A. C., McNamara, D. S., Louwerse, M. and Cai, Z. (2004). Coh-Metrix: Analysis of text on cohesion and language. *Behavior Research Methods, Instruments, & Computers*, **36**, 193–202.

Graves, M. F. (1986). Vocabulary learning and instruction. *Review of Research in Education*, **13**, 49–89.

Green, J. M. and Oxford, R. (1995). A closer look at learning strategies, L2 proficiency and gender. *TESOL Quarterly*, **29**, 2, 261–97.

Greenfield, J. (2004). Readability formulas for EFL. *JALT Journal*, **26**, 1, 5–24.

Hafiz, F. M. and Tudor, I. (1989). Extensive reading and the development of language skills. *ELT Journal*, **43**, 1, 4–13.

Hafiz, F. M. and Tudor, I. (1990). Graded readers as an input medium in L2 learning. *System*, **18**, 1, 31–42.

Harley, B. and King, M. L. (1989). Verb lexis in the written compositions of young L2 learners. *Studies in Second Language Acquisition*, **11**, 4, 415–36.

Harvey, K. and Yuill, D. (1997). A study of the use of a monolingual pedagogical dictionary by learners of English engaged in writing. *Applied Linguistics*, **18**, 3, 253–78.

Hill, D. R. (1997). Survey review: Graded readers. *ELT Journal*, **51**, 1, 57–81.

Hill, D. R. (2001). Graded readers. *ELT Journal*, **55**, 3, 300–324.

Hill, D. (2008). Graded readers in English. *ELT Journal*, **62**, 2, 184–204.

Hill, D. R. and Thomas, H. R. (1988a). Survey review: Graded readers (Part 1). *ELT Journal*, **42**, 1, 44–52.

Hill, D. R. and Thomas, H. R. (1988b). Survey review: Graded readers (Part 2). *ELT Journal*, **42**, 2, 124–36.

Hill, D. R. and Thomas, H. R. (1989). Seven series of graded readers. *ELT Journal*, **43**, 3, 221–31.

Hirsh, D. and Nation, P. (1992). What vocabulary size is needed to read unsimplified texts for pleasure? *Reading in a Foreign Language*, **8**, 2, 689–96.

Holley, F. M. and King, J. K. (1971). Vocabulary glosses in foreign language reading materials. *Language Learning*, **21**, 2, 213–19.

Horst, M. (2005). Learning L2 vocabulary through extensive reading: A measurement study. *Canadian Modern Language Review*, **61**, 3, 355–82.

Horst, M., Cobb, T. and Meara, P. (1998). Beyond a Clockwork Orange: Acquiring second language vocabulary through reading. *Reading in a Foreign Language*, **11**, 2, 207–23.

Horst, M. and Collins, L. (2006). From *faible* to strong: How does their vocabulary grow? *Canadian Modern Language Review*, **63**, 1.

Hu, M. and Nation, I. S. P. (2000). Vocabulary density and reading comprehension. *Reading in a Foreign Language*, **13**, 1, 403–30.

Huang, X.-H. and van Naerssen, M. (1987). Learning strategies for oral communication. *Applied Linguistics*, 8, 3, 287–307.

Hulstijn, J. H. (1988). Experiments with semi-artificial input in second language acquisition research. In Hammarberg, B. (ed.), *Language Learning and Learner Language. Papers from a conference held in Stockholm and Abo 17–18 October, 1988. Scandinavian Working Papers on Bilingualism* (pp. 28–40). Stockholm: Centre for Research on Bilingualism, University of Stockholm.

Hulstijn, J. H. (1992). Retention of inferred and given word meanings: Experiments in incidental vocabulary learning. In Arnaud, P. J. L. and Bejoint, H. (eds.), *Vocabulary and Applied Linguistics* (pp. 113–25). London: Macmillan.

Hulstijn, J. H. (1993). When do foreign-language readers look up the meaning of unfamiliar words? The influence of task and learner variables. *Modern Language Journal*, 77, 2, 139–47.

Hulstijn, J. H. (2001). Intentional and incidental second-language vocabulary learning: A reappraisal of elaboration, rehearsal and automaticity. In Robinson, P. (ed.), *Cognition and Second Language Instruction* (pp. 258–86). Cambridge: Cambridge University Press.

Hulstijn, J., Hollander, M. and Greidanus, T. (1996). Incidental vocabulary learning by advanced foreign language students: The influence of marginal glosses, dictionary use, and reoccurrence of unknown words. *Modern Language Journal*, 80, 3, 327–39.

Hwang, K. and Nation, P. (1989). Reducing the vocabulary load and encouraging vocabulary learning through reading newspapers. *Reading in a Foreign Language*, 6, 1, 323–35.

Ilson, R. (1962). The dicto-comp: A specialized technique for controlling speech and writing in language learning. *Language Learning*, 12, 4, 299–301.

Jacobs, G. M. (1994). What lurks in the margin: Use of vocabulary glosses as a strategy in second language reading. *Issues in Applied Linguistics*, 4, 1, 115–37.

Jacobs, G. M., Dufon, P. and Fong, C. H. (1994). L1 and L2 vocabulary glosses in L2 reading passages: Their effectiveness for increasing comprehension and vocabulary knowledge. *Journal of Research in Reading*, 17, 1, 19–28.

Jacobs, H. L., Zingraf, S. A., Wormuth, D. R., Hartfiel, V. F. and Hughey, J. B. (1981). *Testing ESL Composition: A Practical Approach*. Rowley, MA: Newbury House.

James, M. (1996). *Improving Second Language Reading Comprehension: A Computer-Assisted Vocabulary Development Approach*. University of Hawaii, Honolulu.

Joe, A. (1995). Text-based tasks and incidental vocabulary learning. *Second Language Research*, 11, 2, 149–58.

Johnson, P. (1982). Effects on reading comprehension of building background knowledge. *TESOL Quarterly*, 16, 4, 503–16.

Jones, L. (2004). Testing L2 recognition and recall using pictorial and written test items. *Language Learning & Technology*, 8, 3, 122–43.

Klare, G. R. (1963). *The Measurement of Readability*. Ames, Iowa: Iowa State University Press.

Ko, M. H. (1995). Glossing in incidental and intentional learning of foreign language vocabulary and reading. *University of Hawaii Working Papers in ESL*, **13**, 2, 49–94.

Ko, H. (2005). Glosses, comprehension, and strategy use. *Reading in a Foreign Language*, **17**, 2, 125–43.

Krashen, S. (1985). *The Input Hypothesis: Issues and Implications*. London: Longman.

Kweon, S. O. and Kim, H. R. (2008). Beyond raw frequency: Incidental vocabulary acquisition in extensive reading. *Reading in a Foreign Language*, **20**, 2, 191–215.

Laufer, B. (1989). What percentage of text-lexis is essential for comprehension? In Lauren, C. and Nordman, M. (eds.), *Special Language: From Humans Thinking to Thinking Machines* (pp. 126–32). Clevedon: Multilingual Matters.

Laufer, B. (1992a). Reading in a foreign language: How does L2 lexical knowledge interact with the reader's general academic ability? *Journal of Research in Reading*, **15**, 2, 95–103.

Laufer, B. (1992b). How much lexis is necessary for reading comprehension? In Arnaud, P. J. L. and Bejoint, H. (eds.), *Vocabulary and Applied Linguistics* (pp. 126–32). London: Macmillan.

Laufer, B. (1994). The lexical profile of second language writing: Does it change over time? *RELC Journal*, **25**, 2, 21–33.

Laufer, B. (1995). Beyond 2000: A measure of productive lexicon in a second language. In Eubank, L., Selinker, L. and Sharwood-Smith, M. (eds.), *The Current State of Interlanguage* (pp. 265–72). Amsterdam: John Benjamins.

Laufer, B. (1998). The development of passive and active vocabulary: Same or different? *Applied Linguistics*, **19**, 2, 255–71.

Laufer, B. and Goldstein, Z. (2004). Testing vocabulary knowledge: Size, strength, and computer adaptiveness. *Language Learning*, **54**, 3, 399–436.

Laufer, B. and Hill, M. (2000). What lexical information do L2 learners select in a CALL dictionary and how does it affect word retention? *Language Learning & Technology*, **3**, 2, 58–76.

Laufer, B. and Hulstijn, J. (2001). Incidental vocabulary acquisition in a second language: The construct of task-induced involvement. *Applied Linguistics*, **22**, 1, 1–26.

Laufer, B. and Nation, P. (1995). Vocabulary size and use: lexical richness in L2 written production. *Applied Linguistics*, **16**, 3, 307–22.

Laufer, B. and Nation, P. (1999). A vocabulary size test of controlled productive ability. *Language Testing*, **16**, 1, 36–55.

Laufer, B. and Osimo, H. (1991). Facilitating long-term retention of vocabulary: The second-hand cloze. *System*, **19**, 3, 217–24.

Laufer, B. and Paribakht, T. S. (1998). The relationship between passive and active vocabularies: Effects of language learning context. *Language Learning*, **48**, 3, 365–91.

Laufer, B. and Ravenhorst-Kalovski, G. C. (2010). Lexical threshold revisited: Lexical text coverage, learners' vocabulary size and reading comprehension. *Reading in a Foreign Language*, **22**, 1, 15–30.

Laufer, B. and Rozovski-Roitblat, B. (2011). Incidental vocabulary acquisition: The effects of task type, word occurrence and their combination. *Language Teaching Research*, **15**, 4, 391–411.

Laufer, B. and Sim, D. D. (1985a). Taking the easy way out: Non-use and misuse of clues in EFL reading. *English Teaching Forum*, **23**, 2, 7–10, 20.

Laufer, B. and Sim, D. D. (1985b). Measuring and explaining the reading threshold needed for English for academic purposes texts. *Foreign Language Annals*, **18**, 5, 405–11.

Lee, S. H. and Muncie, J. (2006). From receptive to productive: Improving ESL learners' use of vocabulary in a postreading composition task. *TESOL Quarterly*, **40**, 2, 295–320.

Lee, S. Y. (2003). ESL learners' vocabulary use in writing and the effects of explicit vocabulary instruction. *System*, **31**, 537–61.

Leki, I. and Carson, J. G. (1994). Students' perceptions of EAP writing instruction and writing needs across the disciplines. *TESOL Quarterly*, **28**, 1, 81–101.

Lenders, O. (2008). Electronic glossing: Is it worth the effort? *Computer Assisted Language Learning*, **21**, 5, 457–81.

Linnarud, M. (1986). *Lexis in Composition*. Lund: Lund Studies in English.

Linse, C. (2007). Predictable books in the children's EFL classroom. *ELT Journal*, **61**, 1, 46–54.

Liu, E. T. K. and Shaw, P. M. (2001). Investigating learner vocabulary: A possible approach to looking at EFL/ESL learners' qualitative knowledge of the word. *IRAL*, **39**, 3, 171–94.

Liu, N. and Nation, I. S. P. (1985). Factors affecting guessing vocabulary in context. *RELC Journal*, **16**, 1, 33–42.

Lomicka, L. L. (1998). "To gloss or not to gloss": An investigation of reading comprehension online. *Language Learning & Technology*, **1**, 2, 41–50.

Long, M. and Ross, S. (1993). Modifications that preserve language and content. In Tickoo, M. L. (ed.), *Simplification: Theory and Application RELC anthology series no. 31* (pp. 29–52). Singapore: SEAMEO-RELC.

Macalister, J. (2008a). Implementing extensive reading in an EAP programme. *ELT Journal*, **62**, 3, 248–56.

Macalister, J. (2008b). The effect of a speed reading course in an English as a second language environment. *TESOLANZ Journal*, **16**, 23–33.

Macalister, J. (2010). Speed reading courses and their effect on reading authentic texts: A preliminary investigation. *Reading in a Foreign Language*, **22**, 1, 104–16.

McCarthy, P. M. and Jarvis, S. (2007). vocd: A theoretical and empirical evaluation. *Language Testing*, **24**, 4, 459–88.

McDaniel, M. A. and Pressley, M. (1989). Keyword and context instruction of new vocabulary meanings: Effects on text comprehension and memory. *Journal of Educational Psychology*, **81**, 2, 204–13.

McKeown, M. G., Beck, I. L., Omanson, R. G. and Pople, M. T. (1985). Some effects of the nature and frequency of vocabulary instruction on the knowledge and use of words. *Reading Research Quarterly*, **20**, 5, 522–35.

McQuillan, J. and Krashen, S. (2008). Commentary: Can free reading take you all the way? A response to Cobb (2007). *Language Learning & Technology*, **12**, 1, 104–8.

Meara, P. and Bell, H. (2001). P_Lex: a simple and effective way of describing the lexical characteristics of short texts. *Prospect*, **16**, 3, 5–19.

Meara, P. and Fitzpatrick, T. (2000). Lex30: An improved method of assessing productive vocabulary in an L2. *System*, **28**, 1, 19–30.

Mehrpour, S. and Rahimi, M. (2010). The impact of general and specific vocabulary knowledge on reading and listening comprehension: A case of Iranian EFL learners. *System*, **38**, 292–300.

Mezynski, K. (1983). Issues concerning the acquisition of knowledge: Effects of vocabulary training on reading comprehension. *Review of Educational Research*, **53**, 2, 253–79.

Min, H. (2008). EFL vocabulary acquisition and retention: Reading plus vocabulary enhancement activities and narrow reading. *Language Learning*, **58**, 1, 73–115.

Morris, L. and Cobb, T. (2004). Vocabulary profiles as predictors of the academic performance of Teaching English as a Second Language trainees. *System*, **32**, 75–87.

Muncie, J. (2002). Process writing and vocabulary development: Comparing Lexical Frequency Profiles across drafts. *System*, **30**, 225–35.

Nagy, W. E. (1997). On the role of context in first- and second-language learning. In Schmitt, N. and McCarthy, M. (eds.), *Vocabulary: Description, Acquisition and Pedagogy* (pp. 64–83). Cambridge: Cambridge University Press.

Nation, I. S. P. (1983). Testing and teaching vocabulary. *Guidelines*, **5**, 1, 12–25.

Nation, I. S. P. (1989). Improving speaking fluency. *System*, **17**, 3, 377–84.

Nation, I. S. P. (1991). Dictation, dicto-comp and related techniques. *English Teaching Forum*, **29**, 4, 12–14.

Nation, I. S. P. (2004). Vocabulary learning and intensive reading. *EA Journal*, **21**, 2, 20–29.

Nation, I. S. P. (2006). How large a vocabulary is needed for reading and listening? *Canadian Modern Language Review*, **63**, 1, 59–82.

Nation, I. S. P. (2009). *Teaching ESL/EFL Reading and Writing*. New York: Routledge.

Nation, I. S. P. and Deweerdt, J. (2001). A defence of simplification. *Prospect*, **16**, 3, 55–67.

Nation, P. and Wang, K. (1999). Graded readers and vocabulary. *Reading in a Foreign Language*, **12**, 2, 355–80.

Nation, I. S. P. and Webb, S. (2011). *Researching and Analyzing Vocabulary*. Boston: Heinle Cengage Learning.

Nation, I. S. P. and Yamamoto, A. (2011). Applying the four strands to language learning. *International Journal of Innovation in English Language Teaching and Research*, **1**, 2, 1–15.

Newton, J. (2013). Incidental vocabulary learning in classroom communication tasks. *Language Teaching Research*, **17**, 3, 164–87.

Palincsar, A. S. and Brown, A. L. (1986). Interactive teaching to promote independent learning from text. *The Reading Teacher*, **40**, 771–7.

Paribakht, T. S. and Wesche, M. B. (1993). Reading comprehension and second language development in a comprehension-based ESL programme. *TESL Canada Journal*, **11**, 1, 9–27.

Paribakht, T. S. and Wesche, M. B. (1996). Enhancing vocabulary acquisition through reading: A hierarchy of text-related exercise types. *Canadian Modern Language Review*, **52**, 2, 155–78.

Parker, K. and Chaudron, C. (1987). The effects of linguistic simplifications and elaborative modifications on L2 comprehension. *University of Hawaii Working Papers in ESL*, **6**, 2, 107–33.

Pellicer-Sanchez, A. and Schmitt, N. (2010). Incidental vocabulary acquisition from an authentic novel: Do things fall apart? *Reading in a Foreign Language*, **22**, 1, 31–55.

Perfetti, C. A. and Hart, L. (2002). The lexical quality hypothesis. In Verhoeven, L., Elbro, C. and Reitsma, P. (eds.), *Precursors of Functional Literacy* (pp. 189–213). Amsterdam: John Benjamin.

Pickard, N. (1996). Out of class language learning strategies. *ELT Journal*, **50**, 2, 150–59.

Pigada, M. and Schmitt, N. (2006). Vocabulary acquisition from extensive reading: A case study. *Reading in a Foreign Language*, **18**, 1, 1–28.

Plass, J. L., Chun, D. M., Mayer, R. E. and Leutner, D. (2003). Cognitive load in reading a foreign language text with multimedia aids and the influence of verbal and spatial abilities. *Computers in Human Behavior*, **19**, 221–43.

Prowse, P. (2002). Top ten principles for teaching extensive reading: A response. *Reading in a Foreign Language*, **14**, 2, 142–5.

Pulido, D. (2004). The relationship between text comprehension and second language incidental vocabulary acquisition: A matter of topic familiarity? *Language Learning*, **54**, 3, 469–523.

Quinn, E., Nation, I. S. P. and Millett, S. (2007). *Asian and Pacific Speed Readings for ESL Learners*; available from studentnotes@vicbooks.co.nz

Read, J. (2000). *Assessing Vocabulary*. Cambridge: Cambridge University Press.

Read, J. A. S. and Nation, I. S. P. (2006). An investigation of the lexical dimension of the IELTS speaking test. *IELTS Research reports*, **6**, 207–31.

Richards, B. J. and Malvern, D. D. (1997). *Quantifying Lexical Diversity in the Study of Language Development*. Reading: University of Reading.

Robb, T. (2002). Extensive reading in the Asian context: An alternative view. *Reading in a Foreign Language*, **14**, 2, 146–7.

Robb, T. N. and Susser, B. (1989). Extensive reading vs skill building in an EFL context. *Reading in a Foreign Language*, **5**, 2, 239–51.

Roby, W. B. (1999). "What's in a gloss?" *Language Learning & Technology*, **2**, 2, 94–101.

Rott, S. (1999). The effect of exposure frequency on intermediate language learners' incidental vocabulary acquisition through reading. *Studies in Second Language Acquisition*, **21**, 1, 589–619.

Rott, S. (2005). Processing glosses: a qualitative exploration of how form–meaning connections are established and strengthened. *Reading in a Foreign Language*, **17**, 2, 95–124.

Rott, S. (2007). The effect of frequency of input-enhancements on word learning and text comprehension. *Language Learning*, **57**, 2, 165–99.

Rott, S., Williams, J. and Cameron, R. (2002). The effect of multiple-choice glosses and input-output cycles on lexical acquisition and retention. *Language Teaching Research*, **6**, 3, 183–222.

Ruegg, R., Fritz, E. and Holland, J. (2011). Rater sensitivity to qualities of lexis in writing. *TESOL Quarterly*, **45**, 1, 63–80.

Santos, T. (1988). Professors' reactions to the academic writing of nonnative-speaking students. *TESOL Quarterly*, **22**, 1, 69–90.

Saragi, T., Nation, I. S. P. and Meister, G. F. (1978). Vocabulary learning and reading. *System*, **6**, 2, 72–8.

Sasaki, A. and Takeuchi, O. (2010). EFL students' vocabulary learning in NS–NNS e-mail interactions: Do they learn new words by imitation? *ReCALL*, **22**, 1, 70–83.

Schmitt, N. and Carter, R. (2000). The lexical advantages of narrow reading for second language learners. *TESOL Journal*, **9**, 1, 4–9.

Schmitt, N., Jiang, X. and Grabe, W. (2011). The percentage of words known in a text and reading comprehension. *The Modern Language Journal*, **95**, 1, 26–43.

Shiotsu, T. and Weir, C. J. (2007). The relative significance of syntactic knowledge and vocabulary breadth in the prediction of reading comprehension test performance. *Language Testing*, **24**, 1, 99–128.

Snellings, P., van Gelderen, A. and de Glopper, K. (2002). Lexical retrieval: An aspect of fluent second language production that can be enhanced. *Language Learning*, **52**, 4, 723–54.

Sonbul, S. and Schmitt, N. (2009). Direct teaching of vocabulary: Is it worth the effort? *English Language Teaching Journal*, **64**, 3, 253–60.

Sorrell, C. J. (2012). Zipf's law and vocabulary. In Chapelle, C. A. (ed.), *Encyclopaedia of Applied Linguistics*. Oxford: Wiley-Blackwell.

Stahl, S. A. (1990). Beyond the instrumentalist hypothesis: Some relationships between word meanings and comprehension. *Technical Report No. 505 of the Center for the Study of Reading, University of Illinois at Urbana-Champaign*.

Stahl, S. A. and Fairbanks, M. M. (1986). The effects of vocabulary instruction: A model-based meta-analysis. *Review of Educational Research*, **56**, 1, 72–110.

Stahl, S. A., Jacobson, M. G., Davis, C. E. and Davis, R. L. (1989). Prior knowledge and difficult vocabulary in the comprehension of unfamiliar text. *Reading Research Quarterly*, **24**, 1, 27–43.

Summers, D. (1988). The role of dictionaries in language learning. In Carter, R. and McCarthy, M. (eds.), *Vocabulary and Language Teaching* (pp. 111–25). London: Longman.

Sutarsyah, C., Nation, P. and Kennedy, G. (1994). How useful is EAP vocabulary for ESP? A corpus based study. *RELC Journal*, **25**, 2, 34–50.

Tabata-Sandom, M. and Macalister, J. (2009). That "eureka" feeling": A case study of extensive reading in Japanese. *New Zealand Studies in Applied Linguistics*, **15**, 2, 41–60.

Takase, A. (2007). Japanese high school students' motivation for extensive L2 reading. *Reading in a Foreign Language*, **19**, 1, 1–18.

Taylor, A. (2006). Factors associated with glossing: Comments on Ko (2005). *Reading in a Foreign Language*, **18**, 1, 72–73.

Thomas, H. C. R. and Hill, D. R. (1993). Seventeen series of graded readers. *ELT Journal*, **47**, 3, 250–67.

Tozcu, A. and Coady, J. (2004). Successful learning of frequent vocabulary through CALL also benefits reading comprehension and speed. *Computer Assisted Language Learning*, **17**, 5, 473–95.

Tran, Y. T. N. (2012a). The effects of a speed reading course and speed transfer to other types of texts. *RELC Journal*, **43**, 1, 23–37.

Tran, Y. T. N. (2012b). *EFL Reading Fluency Development and its Effects*. Victoria University of Wellington, Wellington.

Tsang, W.-K. (1996). Comparing the effects of reading and writing on writing performance. *Applied Linguistics*, **17**, 2, 210–33.

Tudor, I. and Hafiz, F. (1989). Extensive reading as a means of input to L2 learning. *Journal of Research in Reading*, **12**, 2, 164–78.

Tuinman, J. J. and Brady, M. E. (1974). How does vocabulary account for variance on reading comprehension tests? A preliminary instructional analysis. In Nacke, P. (ed.), *Interaction: Reading and Practice for College-Adult Reading* (pp. 176–84). Clemson, SC: National Reading Conference.

Tweissi, A. I. (1998). The effects of the amount and type of simplification on foreign language reading comprehension. *Reading in a Foreign Language*, **11**, 2, 191–206.

Verspoor, M. and Lowie, W. (2003). Making sense of polysemous words. *Language Learning*, **53**, 3, 547–86.

Wan-a-rom, U. (2008). Comparing the vocabulary of different graded-reading schemes. *Reading in a Foreign Language*, **20**, 1, 43–69.

Wan-a-rom, U. (2010). Self-assessment of word knowledge with graded readers: A preliminary study. *Reading in a Foreign Language*, **22**, 2, 323–38.

Waring, R. and Takaki, M. (2003). At what rate do learners learn and retain new vocabulary from reading a graded reader? *Reading in a Foreign Language*, **15**, 2, 130–63.

Watanabe, Y. (1997). Input, intake and retention: Effects of increased processing on incidental learning of foreign vocabulary. *Studies in Second Language Acquisition*, **19**, 287–307.

Webb, S. (2005). Receptive and productive vocabulary learning: The effects of reading and writing on word knowledge. *Studies in Second Language Acquisition*, **27**, 33–52.

Webb, S. (2008). The effects of context on incidental vocabulary learning. *Reading in a Foreign Language*, **20**, 232–45.

Webb, S. (2009). The effects of receptive and productive learning of word pairs on vocabulary knowledge. *RELC Journal*, **40**, 3, 360–76.

Webb, S. and Macalister, J. (forthcoming). Is text written for children useful for L2 extensive reading? *TESOL Quarterly*.

West, M. (1953). *A General Service List of English Words*. London: Longman, Green & Co.

West, M. (1955). *Learning to Read a Foreign Language* (2nd ed.). London: Longman.

Widdowson, H. G. (1976). The authenticity of language data. In Fanselow, J. F. and Crymes, R. (eds.), *On TESOL '76* (pp. 261–70). Washington, D.C.: TESOL.

Wixson, K. K. (1986). Vocabulary instruction and children's comprehension of basal stories. *Reading Research Quarterly*, **21**, 3, 317–29.

Wodinsky, M. and Nation, P. (1988). Learning from graded readers. *Reading in a Foreign Language*, **5**, 1, 155–61.

Xue, G. and Nation, I. S. P. (1984). A university word list. *Language Learning and Communication*, **3**, 2, 215–29.

Yamashita, J. (2008). Extensive reading and development of different aspects of L2 proficiency. *System*, **36**, 4, 661–72.

Yanguas, I. (2009). Multimedia glosses and their effect on L2 text comprehension and vocabulary learning. *Language Learning & Technology*, **13**, 2, 48–67.

Yano, Y., Long, M. H. and Ross, S. (1994). The effects of simplified and elaborated texts on foreign language comprehension. *Language Learning*, **44**, 2, 189–219.

Yeung, A. S. (1999). Cognitive load and learner expertise: Split-attention and redundancy effects in reading comprehension tasks with vocabulary definitions. *Journal of Experimental Education*, **67**, 3, 197–217.

Yu, G. (2009). Lexical diversity in writing and speaking task performances. *Applied Linguistics*, **31**, 2, 236–59.

Zahar, R., Cobb, T. and Spada, N. (2001). Acquiring vocabulary through reading: Effects of frequency and contextual richness. *Canadian Modern Language Review*, **57**, 3, 541–72.

Zhou, A. A. (2009). What adult ESL learners say about improving grammar and vocabulary in their writing for academic purposes. *Language Awareness*, **18**, 1, 31–46.

6   *Specialised uses of vocabulary*

When learners have mastered the 2,000–3,000 high-frequency words of general usefulness in English, it is wise to direct vocabulary learning to more specialised areas, depending on the aims of the learners. First, it is possible to specialise by learning the shared vocabulary of several fields of study, for example academic vocabulary. Next the specialised vocabulary of one particular field or part of that field can be studied. Because many courses focus on learners who will do academic study in English, we will look first at academic vocabulary.

What is academic vocabulary?

Academic vocabulary is variously known as 'generally useful scientific vocabulary' (Barber, 1962), 'sub-technical vocabulary' (Anderson, 1980; Cowan, 1974; Yang, 1986), 'semi-technical vocabulary' (Farrell, 1990), 'specialised non-technical lexis' (Cohen et al., 1988), 'frame words' (Higgins, 1966), and 'academic vocabulary' (Coxhead, 2000; Martin, 1976). The division of the vocabulary of academic texts into three levels of general service, or basic vocabulary, sub-technical vocabulary and technical vocabulary, is a commonly made distinction (although it ignores mid-frequency and low-frequency vocabulary which has no technical or sub-technical features). Dresher (1934) made such a three-part distinction when looking at mathematics vocabulary for native speakers. Other writers have independently made a similar distinction. Typically, academic vocabulary lists include words like *accumulate*, *achieve*, *compound*, *complex* and *proportion* which are common in academic texts and not so common elsewhere.

Flood and West (1950) posed the question, 'How many words are needed to explain everything in science to someone who has little or no training in science?' They answered this question by compiling a dictionary for readers of popular science, and determining how large a defining vocabulary was needed. The resulting defining vocabulary numbered just under 2,000 words – 1,490 words which made up the defining vocabulary of the *New Method Dictionary* and 479 additional words needed for scientific terms. A revised version of this vocabulary can be found in an appendix to West's (1953) *General Service List* (GSL). 60 of the 479 words are scientific terms like *alkali, cell, nucleus* and *molecule*; 125 are semi-scientific terms like *absorb, bulb, image* and *revolve*; the remainder are non-scientific words. It seems that a well-selected vocabulary of 2,000–2,500 words could be used to write popular scientific English, defining needed terms as they occurred. Coxhead and Hirsh (2007) developed a 318-word family list aimed at the sciences which did not include words from the *General Service List* or the *Academic Word List* and covered four per cent of their science corpus.

Several studies have investigated the vocabulary needed for academic study. Two of these, Campion and Elley (1971) and Praninskas (1972), assumed that learners already know a high-frequency vocabulary and looked at academic texts to see what words that are not in a general service vocabulary occur frequently across a range of academic disciplines. Two other studies (Ghadessy, 1979; Lynn, 1973) looked at the words above which learners of English wrote translations in their academic texts. There were considerable overlaps between these four lists and they were combined into one list, the *University Word List*, by Xue and Nation (1984) (also in Nation, 1990). This combined list of academic vocabulary was designed so that it consists of words not in the *General Service List*, but which occur frequently over a range of academic texts. The *University Word List*, which contained over 800 word families, gave an 8.5% coverage of academic texts. Its low coverage of non-academic texts showed its specialised nature. It provided 3.9% coverage of newspapers, and 1.7% coverage of fiction (Hwang and Nation, 1989). The major problem with the list is that it combined four very different studies using different criteria and corpora, and thus words got into the list for a wide variety of reasons.

The *University Word List* has now been replaced by the *Academic Word List* (Coxhead, 2000). This list of 570 word families is based on a 3,500,000-token corpus of academic English which is divided into four groupings of Arts, Science, Law and Commerce, with each grouping consisting of seven sub-groupings, including psychology, mathematics, history and so on. Both range and frequency were used in choosing words for the list, with all word families in the list occurring in all four groupings and occurring at least 100 times in the total corpus. The frequency of each of the words in the list was compared with their frequency in a 3,500,000 corpus of novels. This was done to see which words in the list were truly academic words and which were general service words not in West's *GSL*. The list appears to provide slightly better coverage of academic text than the *UWL* even though it contains fewer words. The list is divided into nine sub-lists of 60 words and one of 30, each based on range and frequency criteria (see Appendix 1). Coxhead (2011) reports on the *Academic Word List* ten years after it was first published, noting that a lot of research and materials development have made use of the list.

Why is academic vocabulary important?

There are several reasons why academic vocabulary is considered to be important and a useful learning goal for learners of English for academic purposes.

First, academic vocabulary is common to a wide range of academic texts, and not so common in non-academic texts. One of the earliest studies to look at this (Barber, 1962) is typical of the many small-scale studies that followed it. Barber compared three academic texts ranging in length from 6,300 to 9,600 tokens. This was done before computers were available for such research and, although the corpus was small, the analysis was very time-consuming but very carefully done. The finding of academic words common to the texts influenced a lot of thinking about English for Specific Purposes. Several subsequent studies have confirmed that it is possible to create an academic vocabulary common to a range of academic writing (Campion and Elley, 1971; Coxhead, 2000; Hwang and Nation, 1989; Praninskas, 1972). There has been little research comparing the frequency of specific academic words in academic and non-academic texts (Cowan, 1974), but the studies that did (Coxhead, 2000) show a big contrast in frequency.

Second, academic vocabulary accounts for a substantial number of words in academic texts. There are two ways of measuring this: one, by looking at the number of tokens (coverage) academic vocabulary accounts for; and two, by looking at the number of types, lemmas or word families. Sutarsyah et al. (1994) found that academic vocabulary (the *University Word List*) accounted for 8.4% of the tokens in the Learned and Scientific sections (Section J) of the *LOB* and *Wellington Corpora*, and 8.7% of the tokens in an Economics text. Coxhead (2000) found that her *Academic Word List* covered 10% of the tokens in her 3,500,000 running word academic corpus and around 8.5% in an independent academic corpus. These are substantial percentages given that a general service third 1,000-word list would only cover around 4.3% of the same corpus, but would be drawing on 1,000 rather than 570 word families. The coverage of each of the sublists in Coxhead's *Academic Word List* shows how even the specially selected *Academic Word List* contains words with a wide range of frequencies.

Table 6.1 *Coverage of the Academic Word List*

Sublists and number of word families	% coverage	Number of tokens per 350-word page
1 60 words	3.6%	12.3 words per page
2 60	1.8%	6.0
3 60	1.2%	4.2
4 60	0.9%	3.2
5 60	0.8%	2.7
6 60	0.6%	2.4
7 60	0.5%	1.7
8 60	0.3%	1.3
9 60	0.2%	1.0
10 30	0.1%	0.5
Total 570 words	10.0%	35.1

Zipf's law applies even to specially created word lists. Table 6.1 shows that the first sublist contains 60 word families and covers 3.6% of the running words of each page of an academic text which is equivalent to 12.3 tokens per page. That is, on average, just over 12 words per page of an academic text will be made up of words from sublist 1. Around 35 tokens per page of most academic texts will be from the *Academic Word List*.

Third, academic vocabulary is generally not as well known as technical vocabulary. In a small-scale investigation of difficulties found by second language learners reading academic texts, Cohen et al. (1988) found that non-technical vocabulary like *essential, maintain* and *invariable* was more often unknown than technical vocabulary. Cohen et al. identified some problems with such vocabulary in addition to simply not knowing the words:

- It was sometimes used with a technical meaning and sometimes not, and learners were not always aware of this.
- Learners were often not aware of related terms being used to refer to the same thing. That is, they did not pick up instances of lexical cohesion through paraphrase.

Anderson (1980) also found that sub-technical terms were the words most often identified as unknown by her learners in academic texts. Many learners get low scores on the *Academic Word List* section of the *Vocabulary Levels Test*. In a study with native speakers of English, Cunningham and Moore (1993) found that the presence of academic vocabulary in questions made those questions more difficult to answer.

Ghadessy (1979) and Lynn (1973) looked at the words that learners wrote translations above in their university textbooks. A lot of the words in Lynn and Ghadessy's lists are academic rather than technical vocabulary.

Fourth, academic vocabulary is the kind of specialised vocabulary that an English teacher can usefully help learners with. This is in contrast to technical vocabulary where the teacher can often do little, mostly because of the teacher's lack of background knowledge of the subject, the need to learn technical vocabulary while learning the content matter of the technical field, and the mixture of specialist disciplines within the same group of English students. From this perspective, an academic vocabulary list represents an extension of the general service vocabulary for learners with academic purposes. That is, it is a list of words that deserves a lot of attention in a variety of ways across the four strands from both learners and teachers no matter what their specialist area of academic study.

Trimble (1985: 129–130) suggests that a difficulty with some academic vocabulary is that it takes on extended meanings in technical contexts, and in different technical contexts there may be quite different meanings. For example, *fast* means 'resistant to' in medicine, 'a hard stratum under poorly consolidated ground' in mining, and 'said of colours not affected by light, heat or damp' in paint technology. Wang and Nation (2004) however found that homography and homonymy were not major factors in the *Academic Word List*. Separating homographs resulted in only three words dropping out of the *Academic Word List* because neither of the meanings could meet the list's range and frequency criteria.

Hyland and Tse (2007), Chen and Ge (2007), Hyland (2008) and Martinez et al. (2009) criticise the *Academic Word List* as being too general because each discipline uses *Academic Word List* words with different relative frequencies, and with senses and collocations specific to that discipline. This is undoubtedly true for many words in the list, and it is important when learners develop their knowledge of the words in the *Academic Word List* that they do this (at least partly) by receptive and productive use within the disciplines they are studying and working in. Learners get the best language preparation for the field they are going to study by working with texts within that field. It does not follow from this however that there is no value in looking for items that are common across a range of disciplines. There are common features, especially where there are common communicative purposes and common modes of communication across the disciplines.

In spite of these criticisms, there are however values in having a general academic word list:

- For classes of learners studying in a wide variety of academic disciplines, it provides the most efficient focus for vocabulary learning after learners know the first 2,000 words. Even the relatively low 6% coverage of science text that Hyland and Tse (2007) found is higher than coverage by the much larger third 1,000 words.
- Although there are homographs and homonyms in the *Academic Word List*, these have only a minor effect on membership of the list. Although some words may have different senses in different disciplines, these senses relate to a common core meaning. Learning the core meaning or a sense of an *Academic Word List* word is an excellent step towards dealing with it in a different discipline. It also makes the word accessible in a range of disciplines and different contexts.
- Because the *Academic Word List* is to a large degree a marker of formal written language, it is also useful for reading formal non-academic texts such as newspapers. The *Academic Word List* provides around 4% coverage of newspapers, and all of the words in the *Academic Word List* occur in newspapers.
- Although some *Academic Word List* words can be technical words in the particular discipline (as can high-frequency and low-frequency words), the majority of *Academic Word List* words are not technical words, and as Lynn (1973), Ghadessy (1979), Cohen et al. (1988), and results from the *Vocabulary Levels Test* have shown, this pervasive academic vocabulary is often not well known and is a source of difficulty when dealing with academic texts.
- Academic vocabulary refers to what academics do. Hirsh (2004) used the 'review – methods – results – discussion' divisions of academic articles to show that particular academic words were to some degree associated with particular divisions of academic articles. Academic vocabulary is used to perform academic functions like reviewing, describing, interpreting, applying, surveying, summarising, evaluating and critiquing. It is thus useful when looking at particular academic texts to keep in mind the ways in which these texts represent the nature of academic texts in general.
- Academic vocabulary is largely not salient vocabulary in a text, and thus is not always well learned (Cohen et al., 1988). Some academic vocabulary will become technical vocabulary in certain texts and topic areas, just as some high-frequency words can become technical vocabulary (Chung and Nation, 2003). However, the academic vocabulary that stays as academic and non-technical vocabulary by

its very nature is typically vocabulary that does not have the close relationship to the topic of the text that technical vocabulary has. It thus may need explicit attention to ensure it is learned.

Hyland and Tse (2007) and Martinez et al. (2009) observe that the *Academic Word List* performs quite differently on different corpora. While this is necessarily true, different corpora talk about different things and this requires different vocabulary and different senses of words. The essential difference between the approach taken by Hyland and Tse (2007) and that taken by Coxhead (2000) is that Coxhead sees polysemy as something that learners take account of as they use language, whereas Hyland and Tse consider that polysemic uses need to be learned and stored as separate items.

Nagy (1997) calls these two ways of dealing with polysemy 'reference specification' and 'sense selection'. They are not mutually exclusive positions – reference specification involves adapting a known core meaning to a particular context during the processes of comprehension and language production, and sense selection involves retrieving an already stored sense to match a particular context. If we consider the evidence from the learning and use of prefixes and suffixes and from multiword units, it is likely that highly frequent senses are stored as separate units (sense selection) and less frequent senses are dealt with on-line (reference specification). Thus items dealt with initially by reference specification may eventually, through very frequent meetings, be dealt with by sense selection. Certainly it is important that items from the *Academic Word List* which are met in texts from a variety of disciplines and from newspapers and elsewhere would also be met in learners' disciplines of study, and knowledge of them would be enriched and stored in relation to those disciplines.

It is of course more efficient, but less flexible, to study such items only in those disciplines (Ward, 1999; 2009). This narrow focus may make it less easy to see the core meaning of academic words, but it reduces the amount of learning required.

The best solution is not to see core meaning and specific senses as being mutually exclusive choices, but to see both kinds of knowledge as being valuable. It is important to meet academic words in discipline-specific texts. It is also important to see what is specific and what is more general in academic words.

As Hirsh (2004) has shown that a major reason why there is an academic vocabulary is because it allows academics to do the same kinds of academic things in a range of different disciplines, for example, to evaluate previous research, describe a methodology for research, to present results and to discuss the results. It is important to know your own academic discipline, and it is also important to know what makes it similar to other academic disciplines.

How can you make an academic vocabulary list?

Academic vocabulary lists are usually made by analysing a corpus of academic English. This can be done in several ways. One way is to take an area of specialisation such as electronics (Farrell, 1990), medicine (Salager, 1983; 1984) or engineering (Ward, 1999; 2009) and classify the kinds of vocabulary found. Farrell (1990), drawing on Cowan (1974), defines semi-technical vocabulary as formal, context-independent words with a high frequency and/or wide range of occurrence across scientific disciplines, not usually found in basic general English courses. This definition seems to hedge on range ('and/or wide range') but Farrell's later discussion makes it clear that range is a critical part of the definition, although he did not seem to use it when constructing his own list. Farrell created a semi-technical list consisting of 467 types from Section J of the *LOB Corpus*, using his intuition to remove the general words. The J section of *LOB* contains around 160,000 running words (eighty 2,000-word texts).

Salager (1983) used a comparison of frequencies in the Kučera and Francis (1967) count with frequencies of words in a 100,000 running word corpus of medical English to divide the vocabulary of a medical corpus into three categories: Basic English, Fundamental Medical English, and Specialised Medical English. The Fundamental Medical English largely corresponds to the *Academic Word List* and includes items such as *evaluate, differ, presence, factor* and *serve*. Salager classified the Fundamental Medical English terms into functional and notional categories such as description of process, cause and effect, measurement, description of illness or injury, in order to see what role these words played in medical discourse. Salager's (1983) study is noteworthy because of its use of comparison between a specialised corpus and a diverse corpus to highlight specialised vocabulary, and its attempt to explore the role that sub-technical vocabulary plays in academic discourse.

Ward (1999) suggests that it is not necessary and perhaps not desirable to set up the three levels of general purpose vocabulary, academic vocabulary and specialised vocabulary for learners who have clear specialised goals right from the early stages of their study. Ward created a list of frequent words from an engineering corpus (without distinguishing general purpose, academic and specialised vocabulary) and then applied this list to an independent set of engineering texts. He found that a 2,000 word family vocabulary was sufficient to provide over 95% coverage of the texts. This was much better coverage than that provided by the 2,000 words of the *GSL* and the 836 words of the *UWL*. Early specialisation helps strip away items that are useful in less specialised uses of the language but which may not occur in the specialised texts (Ward, 2009).

Davies and Gardner (www.academicwords.info) used proportional frequency to find academic words. They looked for words that were at least 50% more frequent in an academic corpus than in a general corpus, and came up with a very useful list. Over 40% of their top 500 words are also in the *General Service List* which may be a result of the proportional frequency being too low. They claim that their list has twice the coverage of the *Academic Word List* which is not surprising because it not only includes 40% of the words in the *Academic Word List* but also includes a similar number of words from the general high-frequency words of the language. The website provides a wealth of resources for finding information about each word.

Another way of making an academic vocabulary list is to take a diverse academic corpus and see what words occur with wide range and reasonable frequency that are not part of the general service high-frequency vocabulary (Campion and Elley, 1971; Praninskas, 1972; Coxhead, 2000). Coxhead's (2000) count was based on a 3,500,000 running word collection of recent academic articles and books. It was divided into four main faculty divisions – humanities, science, commerce and law. Each faculty was divided into seven disciplines, such as History, Education and so on. Range and frequency criteria were used in describing what words would be in the academic word list. The list, which we have already met several times, is called the *Academic Word List*. It assumes knowledge of the *General Service List*. This is a potential weakness of this approach, because the quality and content of one depends to some degree on the quality of the other.

Yet another way to make an academic word list is to collect words that learners write first language translations above in their academic texts (Lynn, 1973; Ghadessy, 1979). Rather than use range and frequency as criteria, difficulty (or lack of knowledge) is used as the criterion. Given the very large proportion of Graeco-Latin words in the *Academic Word List* (over 90%), this kind of list may depend on the first language background of the learners involved in the study. For example, around 80% of the words in the *Academic Word List* are cognate with words in Spanish.

There tends to be substantial overlap between these types of lists (Xue and Nation, 1984), indicating that there is a general academic vocabulary which causes problems for second language learners.

How can you sequence the introduction of academic vocabulary?

Worthington and Nation (1996) examined the occurrence of academic vocabulary (the *University Word List*) in several series each consisting of 12 texts to see if the natural occurrence of such vocabulary in texts was sufficient for providing coverage of the whole list, and providing a suitably gradual introduction to the words by not having too many or too few new items from the list in each text. They found that there were several difficulties involved in using the natural occurrence of vocabulary in texts to determine the quantity and sequencing of vocabulary.

- An impossibly large number of texts would be needed to cover all of the vocabulary of the *University Word List*. If texts were used as a means of sequencing vocabulary, it would be possible to do this for only a part of the *UWL*. Other ways of meeting the remaining vocabulary would have to be devised. These might include adaptation of texts, learning from lists, using specially prepared exercises, or simply leaving it somewhat to chance by encouraging extensive reading. Because the *Academic Word List* is smaller, this may be not so big an issue.
- A very large amount of unfamiliar *UWL* vocabulary is met in the first three or four texts. This is far too much to be usefully dealt with in a few lessons and so there would need to be vocabulary-learning preparation before meeting these texts.

It is clear from the difficulties involved in using texts to sequence the introduction of vocabulary that there would need to be a three-step approach to sequencing:

1. First, learners would need a gradual introduction over about 10 texts to the high-frequency, wide-range 180 items in the *Academic Word List*. This could be done by judicious selection or partial simplification of academic texts. The glossing could be done outside the text by the addition of glossaries at the side of the page or at the end of the text (Jacobs, Dufon, and Fong, 1994), or a form of elaboration could be used where the words are explained in the text itself (Long and Ross, 1993) The partial simplification would involve the replacement or glossing of *Academic Word List* words that are not in the first 180 items, in addition to the replacement of some of the words that are not in the first 2,000 and *Academic Word List*. At this step the sequencing is based on frequency and range.

2. Second, about 15 or more unadapted texts could be used to cover a further 180 or so items resulting in coverage of about half of the *Academic Word List*. At this step the occurrence of vocabulary in texts determines the sequencing of the vocabulary.
3. Third, because the unknown academic vocabulary load of the texts would not be so heavy, learners could be encouraged to do large amounts of extensive reading of academic texts, both within their subject areas and outside these areas. This could be accompanied by decontextualised learning of *Academic Word List* words, and study through formal exercises such as those involving word parts. At this step both frequency and range information, and occurrence in texts are used independently of each other to determine the sequencing of the items to be learned.

The assumption behind this sequencing has been that the occurrence of vocabulary in texts is the initial opportunity to meet the words which would then need to be learned to some degree so that they were not unknown items when met in subsequent texts. It is not sufficient to assume that simply meeting the items in a text would be enough to ensure learning. This meeting would have to be accompanied or followed up by intensive study and opportunity for use, so that the knowledge of each item of vocabulary would be cumulatively enriched.

Ghadirian (2002) proposed analysing naturally occurring texts and then using the coverage figures to sequence the texts. Because words in the *Academic Word List* occur frequently in newspapers, but not as frequently as in academic texts, newspaper reading can be an easier introduction and support for meeting academic vocabulary in texts. Huang and Liou (2007) developed a more sophisticated version of Ghadirian's program that not only sequenced texts according to word lists, but also took account of the occurrence of target vocabulary in the texts, so that the sequencing of the texts depended on three criteria:

1. the highest number of familiar words;
2. the lowest number of target words; and
3. the highest number of target words already met in previous texts in the sequence.

Their computerised extensive reading program included highlighted target words, and provided glosses. The program tracked gloss lookups and found that learners seldom looked up the target words. This suggests that their use of the online extensive reading system was not done with a high degree of commitment. If we recalculate the data looking at the average gain score and the total represented by the sample, we find that learners made a gain of around 17% on the unknown target words, representing a gain of 23 words over sixteen 300-word texts. The *Vocabulary Knowledge Scale* scores for the words were also not very high on the scale.

What is the nature and role of academic vocabulary?

There have been attempts to study the role that academic vocabulary plays in an academic text. At one level the Latinate nature of the vocabulary adds a tone of formality and learnedness. It is this aspect that Corson (1985; 1997) describes in his work on the lexical bar. Some writers have also tried to examine the kinds of language functions and notions that the academic vocabulary represents. Strevens (1973) suggests a classification of concepts which are general to science and technology and which reflect and convey the philosophy and methodology of science.

Discrimination and description imply concepts of identity and difference, processes, states, changes of state, quantification;
Classification implies concepts of taxonomies and the co-occurrence of features;
Inter-relation implies concepts of causality, influence, and interaction;
Explanation implies concepts of evidence, intuition, hypothesis, experiment, models, theory; etc.

(Strevens, 1973: 226–227)

Martin (1976) classifies academic vocabulary into (1) the research process; (2) the vocabulary of analysis; and (3) the vocabulary of evaluation. These categories correspond to parts of a typical report of experimental research.

In a fascinating and insightful paper, Meyer (1990) suggests that there is a process of delexicalisation or grammaticisation going on in English where words which used to carry a full lexical meaning are now becoming more like function words. These include words like *affecting, barring, concerning, fact, process* and *matter* whose jobs in some other languages are done by function words or inflections. These words are becoming more grammatical and less lexical. Meyer classifies them into three major categories:

1. Vocabulary relating to the domain of the text and the linguistic acts performed in it. This includes words like *argue, examine, survey* and *recommendation* which tell us what the authors are doing in their texts and what they ascribe to other authors.

2. Vocabulary describing scientific activities. This includes words like *analyse, examine, survey* and *implementation*. They relate closely to the categories described by Strevens (1973).
3. Vocabulary referring to the subject matter of scientific activities. This includes technical vocabulary but is by no means restricted to that. Meyer describes three main groups as examples:
   - Lexical expression of tense, aspect, modality etc.: *current, present, recent, ability, impossibility, likely.*
   - Classification of states of affairs: *change, development, process, structure, quality.* Meyer notes that many of these words seem to be taking on the role of classifiers, that is, general words to characterise a group of related items or state of affairs. Classifiers can fulfil the functions of acting as shorthand anaphoric items, acting as a general term to be elaborated on later, and acting as a kind of proper name for something already defined.
   - Relations between states of affairs: this is a very diverse group. It can include quantitative changes: *expansion, increase, decline, reduction*; causal relations: *arising, affecting, contribute*; set inclusion: *include, comprise*; and many others.

The academic vocabulary of texts allows the writer to talk about scientific activities. Viewed from this perspective, academic vocabulary performs important roles in helping academics do what they need to do. The 'context-independent' vocabulary is an important tool of the writer in doing learned and scientific things.

How can you test academic vocabulary?

The *Vocabulary Levels Test* (Schmitt et al., 2001) contains a section based on the *Academic Word List*. If a learner intends doing academic study in English in upper secondary school or at university, then a score of at least 27 out of 30 is desirable. If a learner has a lower score then study of the items in the *Academic Word List* will be very useful. Academic vocabulary needs to be used productively as well as receptively so it is important to monitor learners' productive knowledge of these words. The *Productive Levels Tests* devised by Laufer and Nation (1999) and the *Lexical Frequency Profile* (Laufer and Nation, 1995) which measures the proportion of various types of words in learners' free writing are useful measures for this.

How can you learn academic vocabulary?

For learners studying English for academic purposes, academic vocabulary is a kind of high-frequency vocabulary and thus any time spent learning it is time well spent. It is therefore important to have lists of academic vocabulary to help in planning and assessing learning. The four major strands of a language course – meaning-focused input, language-focused learning, meaning-focused output and fluency development – should all be seen as opportunities for the development of academic vocabulary knowledge. Thus there should be listening and reading activities that encourage the learning of academic vocabulary. There should be language-focused activities such as direct teaching, learning from word cards, and word part analysis. Academic vocabulary is largely of Latin or Greek origin and so learners can use word part analysis to help learn the vocabulary. Farid (1985) uses a word part approach to words in the Praninskas (1972) list. Chapter 9 on word parts contains a variety of suggestions and exercise types.

Because academic vocabulary is useful in speaking and writing, learners need the opportunity to use it in meaning-focused output activities, that is in speaking and writing in academic contexts. Corson (1995: 149) argues that using academic (Graeco-Latin) vocabulary helps users by letting them put their knowledge on display. Productive use of academic vocabulary is an important component of academic success. This can be encouraged through the presentation of prepared formal talks, discussions based on texts, writing summaries and critical evaluations of articles, and reviewing the literature of a topic.

Being able to use words fluently is a part of vocabulary knowledge. Being able to access words quickly means that more processing time is available for concentrating on what to say rather than how to say it. Fluency is encouraged by repeated opportunity to work with texts that are within the learner's proficiency. One way that fluency can be encouraged is through the use of issue logs, an idea developed by Nikhat Shameem and Alison Hamilton-Jenkins at the English Language Institute at Victoria University of Wellington. Each learner chooses a topic to follow and to become an expert on over several weeks during a pre-university English course. These topics might be terrorism, aging, happiness, global warming or Thai politics. Each learner regularly finds and reads newspaper reports on their topic, listens to TV and radio news, searches the web, and writes a weekly summary of recent events related to their topic. They present a weekly oral report to members of their small group who discuss their report. Such activities involve the learners using the four skills of listening, speaking, reading and writing with repeated attention to the same topic area. They thus soon bring a lot of background knowledge to their reading and discussion – ideal conditions for fluency development.

Knowing academic vocabulary is a high-priority goal for learners who wish to do academic study in English. After gaining control of the

2,000 high-frequency words, learners need to then focus on academic vocabulary. Knowing the 2,000 high-frequency words and the *Academic Word List* will give close to 90% coverage of the running words in most academic texts. When this is supplemented by proper nouns and technical vocabulary, learners will approach the coverage needed for reading.

For second language learners who do not know the academic vocabulary of English, it is important to determine if they have gained academic skills and experience in their first language. If they have, then direct learning of the *Academic Word List* is one of a variety of useful ways to get control of this vocabulary. If however, second language learners of English have not done academic study in their first language, simply learning the academic vocabulary will not make up for this lack of experience. They need to learn the academic vocabulary as they develop skill and experience in dealing with the appropriate range of academic discourse.

What is technical vocabulary?

The motivation for distinguishing technical vocabulary from other vocabulary is similar to that for distinguishing the academic vocabulary from the general service words, that is, to distinguish a group of words that will be particularly useful for learners with specific goals in language use, such as reading academic texts in a particular discipline, writing technical reports, or participating in subject specific conferences. There are so many words that need to be learned that prioritising them is a very useful start.

Having distinguished such a group of words it is possible to see how they affect language-learning goals, particularly the number of words that need to be known to be able to cope effectively with language in use. The approach taken here is to use percentage of text coverage as an indicator of this. Having distinguished such a group of words it is also possible to examine how they would be learned and the role of teaching in the learning process.

How can you distinguish technical vocabulary from other vocabulary?

Technical vocabulary consists of words that are closely related to the content of a particular discipline. Typically this close meaning relationship results in the words being frequent within that discipline or being unique to that discipline. Words which also occur in other disciplines need not have a narrow technical meaning in a particular discipline but frequently they do.

Technical vocabulary can come from any of the three vocabulary levels. Some high-frequency words can be technical vocabulary in certain disciplines. For example, *arm*, *leg* and *neck* are technical words in the field of anatomy. *Language*, *word* and *comprehend* are technical words in applied linguistics. Some mid-frequency academic words can take on technical meanings in certain disciplines, and what may be low-frequency words in one discipline may be technical words in another.

It is important to realise in this definition of technical words that technical words need not have meanings that are different from their general use outside a particular discipline, and need not be word forms that are unique to a particular discipline. The essential characteristic they need to have is that they are closely related in meaning to the content of that particular discipline.

Research on technical vocabulary (Chung and Nation, 2003; 2004) has shown that technical vocabulary covers a large proportion of the tokens in a technical text, and this coverage is at the expense of the coverage of the high-frequency words, words from the *Academic Word List*, and mid-frequency words. Chung and Nation (2003) found that technical vocabulary made up 31.2% of the running words in an anatomy text and 20.6% of the running words in an applied linguistics text. These are very high coverage figures and include high-frequency words and academic words that are technical words in that particular discipline.

A technical vocabulary can also be quite large. Chung and Nation (2003) found 4,270 technical word types in the anatomy text they studied, and 835 word types in the applied linguistics text they studied. The applied linguistics text was relatively short and so the technical vocabulary of applied linguistics is likely to be considerably larger than 835 word types.

There are several ways of identifying technical words. The most valid way is to have experts in the field decide on the degree of relatedness of a particular word to the subject matter of the field. For this reason, technical dictionaries are an attractive way of identifying technical vocabulary. The problem with such dictionaries however is that the criteria that were used to determine inclusion in the dictionary are usually not clearly outlined, and the dictionary is often the work of a single person rather than a consensus among several experts within the field.

Chung (2003) trialled a corpus comparison method for identifying technical vocabulary. This involves setting up a general corpus made of a wide variety of popular and technical texts including newspapers, novels, academic texts and magazines. The frequency of words in this general corpus were compared with the frequency of words in a specialised technical corpus, and words that were much more frequent in the technical corpus or unique to that technical corpus were classified as technical words. In her study, Chung decided that a word needed to be at least 50 times more frequent in the technical corpus to be classified as a technical word. When she compared the resulting list with one arrived at by a specialist's decision using a rating scale, she found roughly 90% agreement.

This shows that the corpus comparison method is a reasonably robust way of quickly distinguishing technical vocabulary. The weaknesses of this method were with two kinds of words: general high-frequency words that were also technical words (*chest, bypass, trunk* in anatomy) – these did not show a strong contrasting frequency between the technical and general corpora; and the collocates of technical words (*anterior, posterior, superior* in anatomy) – these showed a strong contrast but were not rated as technical using the scale. For other ways of distinguishing words in a general and specialist corpus see Chujo and Utiyama (2006).

How can you learn technical vocabulary?

Several writers (Barber, 1962; Higgins, 1966; Cowan, 1974) consider that it is not the English teacher's job to teach technical words – the words are learned through study of the field. As we shall see later, the use of general service words and academic words as technical words (*resistance* in Electronics; *wall* as in 'cell wall' in Biology; *demand* in Economics) means that the English teacher may be able to make a useful contribution to helping learners with technical vocabulary. Strevens (1973: 228) points out that learners who know the scientific field may have little difficulty with technical words. A Humanities-trained teacher who does not know the technical field may have greater difficulty.

Godman and Payne (1981: 37) argue that a technical term only makes sense when other related terms are also known. This is perhaps another way of saying that knowing a technical word involves knowing the body of knowledge that it is part of. Flowerdew (1992: 208) notes that definitions in science lectures to non-native speakers occur systematically. The lecture may be organised around definitions of the key terms in that topic area. This discourse role of definitions underlines the point that knowing the technical vocabulary is very closely related to knowing the subject area.

Considering the large numbers of technical words that occur in specialised texts, language teachers can usefully prepare learners to deal with them. If we look at technical words from the learners' point of view, the following information is revealed. Unknown technical words usually cannot be ignored when reading because they are closely connected to the topic being discussed. They are also difficult to guess from context if the reader does not already have a good background in that technical area. For the same reason, looking the word up in a dictionary does not bring much satisfaction. Clearly, learning technical words is closely connected with learning the subject.

Although English teachers are not usually well equipped to work with technical texts and the technical vocabulary they contain, they can help learners get accustomed to the idea that different uses of words may have a shared underlying meaning. The 'wall' of a living cell shares important features with the 'wall' of a house. Visser (1989) devised the following kind of exercise to deal with this. Learners can work individually or in pairs on the exercises.

interpret / ɪntɜːrprɪt / verb	interpret / ɪntɜːrprɪt / verb	What is the core meaning of this word?
If you **interpret** something in a particular way, you decide that this is its meaning or significance. *Even so, the move was interpreted as a defeat for Mr Gorbachev ... The judge says that he has to interpret the law as it's been passed ... Both of them agree on what is in the poem, but not on how it should be interpreted.*	If you **interpret** what someone is saying, you translate it immediately into another language. *The woman spoke little English, so her husband came with her to interpret... Three interpreters looked over the text for about three or four hours and found that they could not interpret half of it.*	
How would you interpret the meaning of this sign? ▶	Interpret this sentence into your language: 'I really like chocolate cake.'	

These exercises are easy to make and as well as improving knowledge of particular words, they get learners used to the idea that words 'stretch' their meanings. The sample sentences come from the COBUILD dictionary.

Memory (1990), in a study of ninth- and 12th-grade native speakers, looked at whether technical vocabulary was best taught before, during or after reading and found no significant difference. Learning was tested by the recall of definitions. The argument for learning technical vocabulary during reading emphasises the importance of seeing how a technical term fits into a framework of knowledge. It may thus be more revealing to also test using semantic mapping or some other measure that looks at how knowledge of a technical term is integrated into a field of knowledge.

Learners should approach specialised vocabulary strategically, considering whether particular words are worth learning, and considering how they can be most efficiently learned. The main purpose in isolating an academic vocabulary or a technical vocabulary is to provide a sound basis for planning teaching and learning. By focusing attention on items that have been shown to be frequent, and in the case of academic vocabulary of wide range, learners and teachers can get the best return for their effort.

The research on special purposes vocabulary is encouraging, although much still remains to be done. It has been shown that it is possible to devise lists of specialised words which are small enough to be feasible learning goals and which provide enough coverage of specialised text to make them a very valuable part of a learner's vocabulary. Specialised vocabulary is affected by factors that influence the use of all vocabulary. We will now look at these factors.

What roles can vocabulary play in discourse?

So far in this book we have mainly looked at vocabulary as isolated words or in phrase and sentence contexts. But the main role of vocabulary is to convey messages in extended spoken and written texts. We will now look at the part played by vocabulary in discourse.

Vocabulary use in a text arises from the communicative purposes of the text. There are two related aspects to consider. First, vocabulary use signals and contributes to the uniqueness of the text, that is, what makes this text different from all other texts. Second, vocabulary use carries general discourse messages which are shared with other texts of similar types. Thus, when we examine what vocabulary use does in a text, we can look at the special features of the text, and we can also look at how these special features are examples of general language constraints and discourse requirements. We will look at the general discourse messages that vocabulary can carry and see how these can affect particular texts. Table 6.2 lists the communicative messages of vocabulary in a text, classified according to Halliday's (1994) three major divisions of field, tenor and mode.

Let us now look in more detail at each of the three sets of discourse functions.

Table 6.2 *The discourse functions of vocabulary*

The information content of the text

1. The vocabulary reflects the topic of the text through the frequent use of particular words.
2. The vocabulary shows the formality of the text through use of *Academic Word List* vocabulary and other Latinate vocabulary.
3. The vocabulary shows how technical the subject matter is through the use of technical vocabulary and deep taxonomies.
4. The vocabulary shows the writer's or speaker's ideological position (Fairclough, 2001), often through metaphor.

The relationship between the writer or speaker and the reader or listener

5. The vocabulary shows the power relationships and frequency of contact relationships between the writer and reader, or speaker and listener through the use of vocabulary over the range of colloquial, spoken vocabulary to very low-frequency, learned vocabulary.
6. The vocabulary shows the writer or speaker's attitude to the subject matter or to others through the use of vocabulary over the range of emotionally involved to uninvolved.
7. The vocabulary shows the writer's wish to make the text accessible or inaccessible to certain readers or the writer's wish to communicate with the already initiated (Corson, 1985) through the selection of vocabulary and through defining in the text.
8. The pronoun use shows the writer's stance with regard to the audience.

The organisation of the text

9. The vocabulary signals the rhetorical stages or semantic structure of the text (e.g. problem–solution) (McCarthy, 1991).
10. The vocabulary shows the most important sentences in terms of drawing the main topics together (Hoey, 1991).
11. The vocabulary shows the connections between parts of the text through lexical cohesion (Halliday and Hasan, 1976), and use of 'grammaticised' words (Meyer, 1990; Winter, 1978).

How is vocabulary related to the information content of a text?

Function words

It might be expected that because the function words of English are a small, largely closed group that their frequency would be constant across a range of texts. However, this turns out not to be so. Although it is possible to predict that a small number of function words will account for a significant proportion of the running words of a text, the particular nature of the text will determine how frequent each function word is and their relative frequency.

The approximately 270 function word types (176 word families) account for 43–44% of the running words in most texts (Francis and Kučera, 1982; Johansson and Hofland, 1989). The unusually high frequency of some function words in a text may indicate important features of the discourse. In the economics textbook used in the Sutarsyah et al. (1994) study, *you* had a frequency much higher than its frequency in the general academic corpus, because the writer typically addresses his message directly to the reader to involve the reader in the topic: 'You have just been named chief economic strategist for OPEC.' Newton and Kennedy (1996) found different occurrences of prepositions and conjunctions in split information tasks compared with shared information tasks.

Topic-related vocabulary

Goodman and Bird (1984) argue that there are two major kinds of word frequency studies, each giving quite different information. The most common kind of word frequency study examines a large range of texts to establish general service high-frequency words. A more neglected kind of frequency study looks at the frequency of words within a particular text. If we want to understand why particular kinds of words are used in texts and how they are used, we must study individual texts intensively. The frequency with which words occur in a text is a result of the characteristics of the particular text itself.

The most immediately striking finding when looking at a frequency-ranked list of the vocabulary in a text is the way that topic-related words occur among the very high-frequency words. A brief glance at the most frequent content words in the list is usually sufficient to determine what the text is about. The following list contains the most frequent content words from part of a well-known children's story, *The Three Little Pigs*.

little	25	*man*	6
pig	22	*catch*	5
house	17	*bricks*	4
said	14	*built*	4
wolf	9	*now*	4
build	8	*sticks*	4
straw	7		

Typically, the most frequent content words in a text occur with a frequency per 1,000 words that is very much higher than their frequency per 1,000 words in other texts or in a collection of different texts. Sutarsyah et al. (1994) found that a group of 34 words in an economics textbook were so frequent that they accounted for 10% (one word in every line) of the running words in the text. These words occurred with a frequency of up to 60 times the frequency with which they occurred in a more general corpus of similar size. Here are some of those words: *price, cost, demand, curve, firm, supply, quantity, margin, economy, income, produce, market, consume, labour, capital, total.*

Each text has its own topic vocabulary which occurs because of the message the text is trying to convey. The vocabulary gives the text part of its unique flavour. This has several important messages for language teaching. First, in the production of simplified material, it is important that any vocabulary-grading scheme used is flexible enough to allow the use of topic-related vocabulary that may not be in the lists used to guide the grading of the material. There can be rules regarding the repetition of these additional words to make sure that they have a chance of being learned and that they do not act as a burden to the reader. If a particular word occurs only once then it may be a burden but if it is repeated several times in the book then the initial learning effort is repaid by the opportunity to use that learning again when the word reoccurs. Most well-designed graded reader schemes have rules of this kind.

Second, when learners are being asked to speak or write on a topic, their language production is likely to be more apt if they are given the chance to meet relevant topic-related vocabulary before they produce. This can be done in a variety of ways – through topic-related reading, discussion, direct teaching or accompanying support materials.

Third, from a course design perspective, learners may need exposure to a range of topics if they are to develop a rich vocabulary. In the Sutarsyah et al. (1994) study of an economics text, only 548 of the second 1,000 words of the *General Service List* occurred, compared to 796 in the more general corpus.

Fourth, we have seen in Chapter 1 how different texts contain quite different amounts of academic vocabulary. This shows that the general topic of the text influences the type of vocabulary that occurs. In an unpublished study, Jenkins (1993) developed a vocabulary of children's books, and in a similar study Hwang (1989) found evidence of a newspaper vocabulary (see also Chung, 2009). It is thus possible to make useful word lists for a variety of focused uses of the language. Courses focusing on a limited range of text-types could benefit from the development of a specialised vocabulary.

Fifth, teachers need to be careful when focusing on vocabulary in intensive reading. The content words that occur most frequently in a particular text may not be useful words when learners face a different text. Teachers may need to give most attention to less frequent words in a particular text that are high-frequency words across a range of texts. Today's teaching needs to help tomorrow's tasks.

How is vocabulary related to the organisation of a text?

The frequency of occurrence of topic-related words is however only one aspect of their occurrence in a text. In an insightful book, Hoey (1991) shows that by examining the number of lexical links between sentences in a non-fiction text, it is possible to identify:

- the sentences which are central to the topic of the text (these also tend to provide a reasonable summary of the text);
- the sentences which are marginal to the topic of the text; and
- where a topic is introduced and ends.

These lexical links include repetitions of words (in either the same form or in inflected or derived forms), paraphrase of various kinds (which includes synonyms and hyponyms among other things), substitution (including pronouns) and ellipsis (Hoey, 1991: 83). Essentially, sentences which are central to the topic of the text have more lexical links to other sentences, that is, they share more commonly referring vocabulary with other sentences in the text. In terms of discourse analysis, a major strength of Hoey's lexically based analysis of relationships is that it shows relationships between sentences that may be separated by several intervening sentences. These links between sentences often occur with the topic-related words and they can form 'lexical chains'. They can occur within a text and between speakers in a conversation (McCarthy, 1991: 69).

Learners need to be able to see the links between the various forms of topic-related vocabulary. For example, they need to see that *biologist* and *scientist* are in fact referring to the same person in a particular text. For this reason, Hoey (1991: 241) suggests that topic-related words which form links should be given priority when glosses are provided to accompany a text. This would have the effect of helping the learner quickly make sense of the text, because the sentences central to the topic would be understood. It would also help unknown words be learned by clarifying their relationship with synonymous known items. In addition, links through synonymy and paraphrase not only show shared aspects of meaning, but also highlight differences. Each new link can be part of a developing enrichment (McCarthy, 1991: 66). The results of Hoey's study can be used to justify:

- non-linear note-taking from text;
- looking for lexical links for seeing the structure of the text;
- not needing to understand every sentence to get the important ideas in a text;
- the importance of stressing lexis as a prerequisite for reading;
- teachers focusing on word families and lexical sets; and
- writers making clear connections between related parts of their text using lexical repetition.

Discourse-organising vocabulary

McCarthy (1991: 78–84) and McCarthy and Carter (1994: 105), drawing on the work of Winter (1977; 1978) and Hoey (1983), show how certain words are strongly associated with certain patterns of information. These patterns involve stages in a piece of discourse such as (1) stating the problem, (2) suggesting solutions, and (3) evaluation of the solutions. Vocabulary like *problem, crisis, dilemma, issue* are associated with the problem stage, while vocabulary like *address* (v.), *justifiable, effective, manage*, and idioms are associated with the evaluation stage. McCarthy (1991) gives most attention to the problem / solution / evaluation and hypothetical / real patterns, but as McCarthy suggests, there are numerous other patterns whose parts may by signalled by the occurrence of certain vocabulary. These include:

1. the various topic types (Johns and Davies, 1983; Nation, 1993) such as description of physical structure and characteristics (what something is like), instruction (how to do something), state / situation (what happened) and process (what happens);
2. the various genres (Derewianka, 1990) such as narratives, arguments, instructions, information reports, recounts and explanations;
3. the classical rhetoric classifications such as argument, narrative, exposition and description; and
4. the various clause or conjunction relations (Halliday and Hasan, 1976; Hoey, 1983; Nation, 1984; Winter, 1977, 1978) such as cause and effect, contrast, exemplification, and inclusion, especially when they relate several sentences rather than just clauses within a sentence.

Some of this discourse-organising vocabulary consists of words that act a little like pronouns in that they refer back or forward in the text to another part of the text. These have been called 'anaphoric nouns'

(Francis, 1994) and more generally 'discourse-organising words' (McCarthy, 1991: 75). They include words like *question, issue, assumption, hypothesis, position, case* and *situation* when they refer to another piece of text. Here are some examples from one text (Parkin, 1990: 101)

- If the supply of a good falls, its price rises. But by how much? To answer this *question, ...*
- You are trying to decide whether to advise a cut in output to shift the supply curve and raise the price of oil. To make this *decision ...*
- Let us compare two possible (hypothetical) *scenarios* in the oil industry ...

Meyer (1990) sees this discourse-organising vocabulary as becoming to some degree 'delexicalised', that is, depending more for its meaning on what it does or refers to in the text than what it carries with it. When learners meet these words in texts they need to be sensitive to their many functions, which include referring to other parts of the text and signalling a stage in the discourse.

Ivanič (1991) calls these words 'carrier nouns' and typifies them as being countable, abstract nouns which are like pronouns in that they have a constant meaning and a variable context-dependent meaning. Ivanič (p. 108) notes that these nouns often play an important role in exam questions ('Describe three factors that ...') because they can be accompanied by a number but they do not give anything away about the content of the answer. Because these nouns are not topic specific, they are important candidates for a general academic vocabulary like the *Academic Word List*. Their strengths as discourse-organising vocabulary are that they have a referential function and variable meaning like pronouns and yet unlike pronouns can be modified by demonstrative pronouns, numbers and adjectives, can occur in various parts of a sentence, and have a significant constant meaning. Francis (1994) refers to the function of these nouns as **labelling**. They tell the reader what to expect when they occur before their realisation and they encapsulate and classify what has been said when they occur after their realisation. They thus play an important role in the organisation of discourse.

Winter (1977) notes that the relationships between clauses and sentences are largely unsignalled, but when they are signalled there are three kinds of vocabulary that do the signalling:

Vocabulary 1: subordinators like *after, although, as, at the same time as*
Vocabulary 2: sentence connectors like *accordingly, in addition, all the same, also*

Vocabulary 3:   lexical items like *achieve, affirm, alike, cause, compare, conclude, consequence, problem*

Winter argues that the third group, Vocabulary 3, although it consists of nouns, verbs and adjectives, has many of the characteristics of closed-class or function words. The words in this third group make up a small and fairly closed set, are to varying degrees 'delexicalised', and their meaning is realised by words occurring before or after them. Winter (1977: 20) lists 108 headwords for Vocabulary 3, and of these 92 can be seen as paraphrases of words in Vocabulary 1 and Vocabulary 2 (see Table 6.3):

Table 6.3 *Examples of different markers of the same clause relationship*

Vocabulary 1	Vocabulary 2	Vocabulary 3
though	*nevertheless*	*concede*
if, unless	*otherwise*	*condition*
so that	*for this purpose*	*purpose*
whereas	*however*	*contrast*

These 108 headwords are not the complete list as many of them can be expressed by synonyms, but the relationships they signal make up a closed set. Because these delexicalised words can play an important signalling role in clause relationships, they thus play an important signalling role in discourse structure.

Marco (1998) sees procedural vocabulary (lexical words which structure discourse and establish meaning relationships) as consisting of two main groups, procedural organising vocabulary and procedural defining vocabulary. Procedural organising vocabulary is involved in clause relations and the structure of schemata. Procedural defining vocabulary includes formal signals of the act of defining (*is defined as, means*) and signals within the act of defining, namely category words and descriptions of attributes which relate to the parts of the classical definition pattern. Teachers need to be sensitive to the discourse functions of these discourse organising words and draw attention to them in intensive reading.

How does vocabulary signal the relationship between the writer or speaker and reader or listener?

Corson (1997) presents arguments to support the view that use of academic vocabulary is taken as evidence of being in control of the academic meaning systems, and is thus essential to academic success.

Academic vocabulary is overwhelmingly Graeco-Latin, and is not easy to learn because words refer to abstract ideas, they are infrequent and their forms do not reveal their meaning. Thus learners need to have 'a rich acquaintance with the specialist areas of discourse in which they appear, as well as frequent and motivated contact with the words themselves' (Corson, 1997: 701). Corson argues that meeting words receptively is insufficient for using them well. They need to be used in motivated talk about text. Not all learners have access to this experience.

The amount of academic and technical vocabulary in a text is a sign of the specialised and academic nature of the text. Studies involving the *University Word List* and its replacement, the *Academic Word List*, have shown the very uneven spread of this vocabulary across different types of writing. It is uncommon in fiction (1.7% text coverage), moderately frequent in newspapers (3.9% text coverage) and very frequent in academic texts (8.5% text coverage). The frequent occurrence of this vocabulary is thus a sign of the formal academic nature of a text, or in Corson's (1997) terms, that the text is drawing on different meaning systems from those texts with little academic vocabulary.

Some work has been done on examining the way vocabulary reflects the academic meaning systems. One area of attention has been in the use of reporting verbs as in 'Barrington (1967) *states* that ...'. Thompson and Ye (1991) look at the way the very large range of reporting verbs in English reflect evaluation of the citations that they report. There have been attempts to relate the kind of academic vocabulary used to what academic discourse does, namely citing, evaluation, hypothesising, contrasting, relating and explaining (Strevens, 1973; Martin, 1976; Meyer, 1990).

The amount of technical vocabulary in a text and presence or absence of explanation of this vocabulary is a sign of the intended audience for the text. It is not always easy to decide what is a technical term, and there are degrees of 'technicalness'".

Words in discourse

Let us now look at a short piece of academic text to see how vocabulary occurs in the text and to pull together the points made about vocabulary so far in this chapter. The text is taken from *Macroeconomics* by (Parkin, 1990: 102–3). The words marked in bold occur with a very high frequency in this book but with a much lower frequency in other texts (Sutarsyah et al., 1994).

Chapter 5 Elasticity

OPEC's Dilemma

If the **supply** of a **good** falls, its **price** rises. But by how much? To answer this question, **you** will have to don a flowing caftan: **You** have just been named chief economic strategist for OPEC – the Organization of Petroleum Exporting Countries. **You** want to bring more money into OPEC. Would **you** restrict the **supply** of oil to raise **prices**? Or would **you produce** more oil? **You** know that a higher **price** will bring in more dollars per barrel, but lower **production** means that fewer barrels will be sold. Will the **price** rise high enough to offset the smaller **quantity** that OPEC will sell? As OPEC's economic strategist, **you** need to know about the **demand** for oil in great detail. For example, as the world **economy** grows, how will that growth translate into an increasing **demand** for oil? What about substitutes for oil? Will we discover inexpensive methods to convert coal and tar sands into usable fuel? Will nuclear energy become safe and cheap enough to compete with oil?

In this chapter, **you** will learn how to tackle questions such as the ones just posed. **You** will learn how we can measure in a precise way the responsiveness of the **quantities bought** and sold to changes in **prices** and other influences on **buyers** or sellers.

Price Elasticity of Demand

Let us begin by looking a bit more closely at **your** task as OPEC's economic strategist. **You** are trying to decide whether to advise a cut in **output** to shift the **supply curve** and raise the **price** of oil. To make this decision, **you** need to know how the **quantity** of oil **demanded** responds to a change in **price**. **You** also need some way to measure that response.

Two Possible Scenarios

To understand the importance of the responsiveness of the **quantity** of oil **demanded** to a change in its **price**, let us compare two possible (hypothetical) scenarios in the oil industry, shown in Fig. 5.1 In the two parts of the figure, the **supply curves** are identical, but the **demand curves** differ.

Focus first on the **supply curve** labelled $S0$ in each part of the figure. This **curve** represents the initial **supply**. Notice that $S0$ cuts the **demand curve** in both cases, at a **price** of $10 a barrel and a **quantity** traded of 40 **million** barrels a day.

Now suppose that **you** contemplate a cut in **supply** that shifts the **supply curve** from $S0$ to $S1$. In part (a), the new **supply curve** $S1$ cuts the **demand curve** Da at a **price** of $30 a barrel and a **quantity** traded of 23 **million** barrels a day. In part (b), the same shift in the **supply curve** results in the new **supply curve** cutting the **demand curve** Db at a **price** of $15 a barrel and a **quantity** traded of 15 **million** barrels a day.

(Parkin, 1990: 102–3)

Firstly, note the very frequent occurrence of the marked words. There are 34 words in the book in total in this group and these 34 word families account for 10% of the running words in the text. There is on average one in every line of Parkin's book.

Secondly, notice the part of the text where these words do not occur. This is where a range of examples is being presented. Examples help bring a message alive but they also impose a vocabulary load because they move outside the normal vocabulary of the text.

Thirdly, notice that one of these highly frequent words is a function word, *you*. This is the only function word in the list of 34 words. Notice that it is frequent because of the way the writer treats the relationship between himself and the reader. He directly addresses the reader, involving the reader in the text and directing the reader in a polite version of the imperative ('you will have to learn ...'). This relationship is reflected in the unusually high frequency of this word.

Let us now look at the lexical chains in the text. Notice the relationship between the lexical chains and the very high-frequency vocabulary. Here are two related chains.

1. *price rises*
   raise prices
   a higher price
   will the price rise high enough
   raise the price
   change in price

2. *supply of a good falls*
   restrict the supply
   lower production
   smaller quantity that OPEC will sell
   a cut in output
   shift in the supply curve

Notice that by the end of the text the discussion has moved from actions (restrict the supply) to abstract representation (shift in the supply curve), which is the point of the whole book, learning the principles behind economic activity.

Notice the variety of forms and uses to convey the same idea. Because this text is an introductory text, the writer is very aware of and friendly to the reader (*you*). As a result the vocabulary used is largely accessible and not highly technical. There are few words that have forms unique to the field of economics (*elasticity* perhaps). Most are slightly narrowed uses of common words: *price, supply, demand, margin*. The whole book has a vocabulary of only 5,438 word families indicating once more its role as an accessible, introductory text.

The example text contains some discourse-organising words – *question, decision, scenarios* – that could be related to the problem / solution / evaluation pattern. There are also several anaphoric nouns that are very clearly formally related to what they refer to: *production, growth, response*. This clear relationship reflects once more the writer's intention to keep the text accessible.

This section has tried to show that the vocabulary in a text does more than convey particular meanings. It plays an important part in making a text a cohesive, coherent text that conveys a range of different kinds of messages to the reader or listener.

How well does content-based learning support the learning of vocabulary?

Content-based learning is where learning of the subject matter of a discipline like Mathematics, General Science or Economics is deliberately accompanied by language learning, that is, a course involving content-based learning uses the learning of the subject matter as a way to support the learning of a second or foreign language. Some countries, like Malaysia, have deliberately taught content matter subjects in English in secondary school, so that learners can increase their mastery of English as well as learning the content matter of the subject. One of the main arguments behind content-based learning is that a focus on the subject matter will make the learning of English genuinely more communicative. Content-based learning is also known as 'English Through the Curriculum'.

Learning through the four strands applies to content-based learning in the same ways that it applies to other kinds of learning. Language learning can occur incidentally through meaning-focused input, meaning-focused output and fluency development. Language learning can occur deliberately through language-focused learning activities. A danger in content-based learning is that the strand of the language-focused learning may be neglected because of the strong focus on the content matter of the course. Content-based learning is ideally suited to the learning of vocabulary. There are several reasons for this:

1. Content-based learning typically focuses on one subject area. From the point of view of reading, this would be called narrow reading where reading is done of texts which are closely related to each other (Hwang and Nation, 1989; Schmitt and Carter, 2000). This narrow focus results in much less diversity of vocabulary than there

would be in a course where the topic of a lesson changes from day to day or week to week. Sutarsyah et al. (1994) found that a 300,000-word economics text contained only 5,438 word families compared to the 12,744 word families occurring in a corpus of similar length but which was made up of 150 different texts.

2. When content-based learning is done all within one subject area, then the technical vocabulary of that area will play a very important part in the vocabulary load of the texts. A lot of this technical vocabulary will be repeated making it easier to learn. Chung and Nation (2004) found that technical vocabulary can cover between 20% and 30% of the running words in a technical text. Technical vocabulary can include vocabulary that is unique to a particular subject area, but in many subject areas a lot of the technical vocabulary consists of words that also occur outside that subject area. Many of these words would be high frequency words or academic words.

3. Content-based learning allows learners to gradually build up knowledge of the subject area. If the course is reasonably well designed, then previous lessons will make subsequent lessons much easier to comprehend because learners will bring content matter knowledge from the previous lessons to what they are studying now. This will allow learners to process the material deeply and thoughtfully which will assist in the learning of the vocabulary in that lesson. This building up of knowledge is ideal for learning through the strands of meaning-focused input, meaning-focused output and fluency development.

4. When learners study a subject area they learn new ideas and how to apply these ideas. This application of ideas can result in creative use of the relevant vocabulary (Joe, 1998). Typically, studying a subject area involves the use of linked skills activities where, for example, learners read about a topic, discuss the topic and then write about it. Such activities involve recycling the same vocabulary usually in contexts which are slightly different from each other. This repetition and creative use is of great benefit for vocabulary learning.

Thus, content-based learning provides excellent opportunities for learners to experience a manageable vocabulary load, repeated occurrences of the vocabulary, the opportunity to work with it at least partly familiar content and the chance to meet vocabulary in a variety of contexts which will strengthen and enrich their knowledge of the vocabulary.

A danger in content-based courses is that the deliberate learning of vocabulary may be neglected because of the strong focus on the content matter (Langham, 2003). It is important in content-based courses that there is a well-thought-out language-focused learning strand which includes activities such as deliberate teaching of vocabulary, deliberate learning through word cards, intensive reading and helping learners to recognise signals of definition when they are met in spoken and written texts.

In content-based courses it is worthwhile thinking out how much time should be devoted to language-focused learning. This will differ from course to course because of the other subjects that learners will be studying at the same time and which may include language-focused subjects. It will also depend on the goals of the content-based course, particularly how important the content-based learning is in relation to the language learning which is expected to occur.

Harmon et al. (2005) provide nine very useful suggestions to help learners develop their vocabulary knowledge:

1. Provide opportunities to engage in independent reading.
2. Relate below-grade level trade books to content area topics.
3. Use contextual-based approaches.
4. Encourage independent learning by allowing students to self-select terms to be studied.
5. Teach key vocabulary explicitly.
6. Provide opportunities for multiple exposures to key terms.
7. Avoid drill and practice activities.
8. Emphasise word part analysis when teaching vocabulary.
9. Provide staff development training in effective vocabulary instruction.

Harmon et al. also caution that teachers should not solely rely on oral explanations of content material but should get learners to tackle problems through reading.

Graves (2006: 5) proposes four components for an effective vocabulary development program for first language learners:

1. Provide rich and varied language experiences.
2. Teach individual words.
3. Teach word-learning strategies.
4. Foster word consciousness.

Special purposes vocabulary is closely related to a particular subject area or range of subject areas. This means that it is of great value to learners studying in those subject areas and thus deserves attention. Once again, it is useful to maintain a balance of kinds of attention across the four strands of a course so that learners have the opportunity to benefit from the different focuses of each strand. From this perspective, special purposes vocabulary differs from other vocabulary not in the way it is treated, but in the fact that it is identified as particularly useful vocabulary and thus deserves attention.

References

Anderson, J. I. (1980). The lexical difficulties of English medical discourse for Egyptian students. *English for Specific Purposes (Oregon State University)*, 37, 4.

Barber, C. L. (1962). Some measurable characteristics of modern scientific prose. In Barber, C. L. et al. (eds.), *Contributions to English Syntax and Philology* (pp. 21–43). Göteburg: Acta Universitatis Gothoburgensis.

Campion, M. E. and Elley, W. B. (1971). *An Academic Vocabulary List*. Wellington: NZCER.

Chen, Q. and Ge, G. (2007). A corpus-based lexical study on frequency and distribution of Coxhead's AWL word families in medical research articles. *English for Specific Purposes*, 26, 502–14.

Chujo, K. and Utiyama, M. (2006). Selecting level-specific specialized vocabulary using statistical measures. *System*, 34, 255–69.

Chung, M. (2009). The Newspaper Word List: A specialised vocabulary for reading newspapers. *JALT Journal*, 31, 2, 159–82.

Chung, T. M. (2003). A corpus comparison approach for terminology extraction. *Terminology*, 9, 2, 221–45.

Chung, T. M. and Nation, P. (2003). Technical vocabulary in specialised texts. *Reading in a Foreign Language*, 15, 2, 103–16.

Chung, T. M. and Nation, P. (2004). Identifying technical vocabulary. *System*, 32, 2, 251–63.

Cohen, A. D., Glasman, H., Rosenbaum-Cohen, P. R., Ferrara, J. and Fine, J. (1988). Reading English for specialised purposes: Discourse analysis and the use of student informants. In Carrell, P., Devine, J. and Eskey, D. E. (eds.), *Interactive Approaches to Second Language Reading* (pp. 152–67). Cambridge: Cambridge University Press.

Corson, D. J. (1985). *The Lexical Bar*. Oxford: Pergamon Press.

Corson, D. J. (1995). *Using English Words*. Dordrecht: Kluwer Academic Publishers.

Corson, D. J. (1997). The learning and use of academic English words. *Language Learning*, 47, 4, 671–718.

Cowan, J. R. (1974). Lexical and syntactic research for the design of EFL reading materials. *TESOL Quarterly*, 8, 4, 389–400.

Coxhead, A. (2000). A new academic word list. *TESOL Quarterly*, 34, 2, 213–38.

Coxhead, A. (2011). The Academic Word List 10 years on: Research and teaching implications. *TESOL Quarterly*, 45, 2, 355–62.

Coxhead, A. and Hirsh, D. (2007). A pilot science-specific word list. *Revue Française de Linguistique Appliquée*, 12, 2, 65–78.

Cunningham, J. W. and Moore, D. W. (1993). The contribution of understanding academic vocabulary to answering comprehension questions. *Journal of Reading Behavior*, 25, 2, 171–80.

Derewianka, B. (1990). *Exploring How Texts Work*. Rozelle, N. S. W.: Primary English Teaching Association.

Dresher, R. (1934). Training in mathematics vocabulary. *Educational Research Bulletin*, **13**, 8, 201–4.

Fairclough, N. (2001). *Language and Power*. London: Longman.

Farid, A. (1985). *A Vocabulary Workbook*. Englewood Cliffs: Prentice Hall.

Farrell, P. (1990). *Vocabulary in ESP: A Lexical Analysis of the English of Electronics and a Study of Semi-technical Vocabulary* (Vol. CLCS Occasional Paper No. 25). Dublin: Trinity College.

Flood, W. E. and West, M. P. (1950). A limited vocabulary for scientific and technical ideas. *ELT Journal*, **4**, 4&5, 104–8 & 128–37.

Flowerdew, J. (1992). Definitions in science lectures. *Applied Linguistics*, **13**, 2, 202–21.

Francis, G. (1994). Labelling discourse: an aspect of nominal-group lexical cohesion. In Coulthard, M. (ed.), *Advances in Written Text Analysis* (pp. 83–101). London: Routledge.

Francis, W. N. and Kučera, H. (1982). *Frequency Analysis of English Usage*. Boston: Houghton Mifflin.

Ghadessy, M. (1979). Frequency counts, word lists, and materials preparation: A new approach. *English Teaching Forum*, **17**, 1, 24–7.

Ghadirian, S. (2002). Providing controlled exposure to target vocabulary through the screening and arranging of texts. *Language Learning & Technology*, **6**, 1, 147–64.

Godman, A. and Payne, E. M. F. (1981). A taxonomic approach to the lexis of science. In *English for Academic & Technical Purposes: Studies in Honor of Louis Trimble* (pp. 23–39). Rowley, MA: Newbury House.

Goodman, K. S. and Bird, L. B. (1984). On the wording of texts: A study on intra-text word frequency. *Research in the Teaching of English*, **18**, 119–45.

Graves, M. F. (2006). *The Vocabulary Book: Learning and Instruction*. Newark: International Reading Association.

Halliday, M. A. K. (1994). *An Introduction to Functional Grammar*. London: Edward Arnold.

Halliday, M. A. K. and Hasan, R. (1976). *Cohesion in English*. London: Longman.

Harmon, J. M., Hedrick, W. B. and Wood, K. D. (2005). Research on vocabulary instruction in the content areas: Implications for struggling readers. *Reading & Writing Quarterly*, **21**, 261–80.

Higgins, J. J. (1966). Hard facts. *ELT Journal*, **21**, 1, 55–60.

Hirsh, D. (2004). *A Functional Representation of Academic Vocabulary*. Victoria University of Wellington, Wellington.

Hoey, M. (1983). *On the Surface of Discourse*. London: Allen and Unwin.

Hoey, M. (1991). *Patterns of Lexis in Text*. Oxford: Oxford University Press.

Huang, H. T. and Liou, H. C. (2007). Vocabulary learning in an automated graded reading program. *Language Learning & Technology*, **11**, 3, 64–82.

Hwang, K. (1989). *Reading Newspapers for the Improvement of Vocabulary and Reading Skills*. Victoria University of Wellington, Wellington.

Hwang, K. and Nation, P. (1989). Reducing the vocabulary load and encouraging vocabulary learning through reading newspapers. *Reading in a Foreign Language*, **6**, 1, 323–35.

Hyland, K. (2008). The author replies. *TESOL Quarterly*, **42**, 1, 113–14.

Hyland, K. and Tse, P. (2007). Is there an "Academic Vocabulary"? *TESOL Quarterly*, **41**, 2, 235–53.

Ivanič, R. (1991). Nouns in search of a context: A study of nouns with both open- and closed-system characteristics. *IRAL*, **29**, 1, 93–114.

Jacobs, G. M., Dufon, P. and Fong, C. H. (1994). L1 and L2 vocabulary glosses in L2 reading passages: Their effectiveness for increasing comprehension and vocabulary knowledge. *Journal of Research in Reading*, **17**, 1, 19–28.

Jenkins, S. (1993). The vocabulary burden of controlled and uncontrolled reading materials used with beginning ESL readers. Victoria University of Wellington, Wellington.

Joe, A. (1998). What effects do text-based tasks promoting generation have on incidental vocabulary acquisition? *Applied Linguistics*, **19**, 3, 357–77.

Johansson, S. and Hofland, K. (1989). *Frequency Analysis of English Vocabulary and Grammar 1&2*. Oxford: Clarendon Press.

Johns, T. and Davies, F. (1983). Text as a vehicle for information: The classroom use of written texts in teaching reading in a foreign language. *Reading in a Foreign Language*, **1**, 1, 1–19.

Kučera, H. and Francis, W. N. (1967). *A Computational Analysis of Present-day American English*. Providence, RI: Brown University Press.

Langham, J. (2003). The effects of ESL-trained content-area teachers: Reducing middle-school students to incidental language learners. *Prospect*, **18**, 1, 14–26.

Laufer, B. and Nation, P. (1995). Vocabulary size and use: lexical richness in L2 written production. *Applied Linguistics*, **16**, 3, 307–22.

Laufer, B. and Nation, P. (1999). A vocabulary size test of controlled productive ability. *Language Testing*, **16**, 1, 36–55.

Long, M. and Ross, S. (1993). Modifications that preserve language and content. In Tickoo, M. L. (ed.), *Simplification: Theory and Application*. RELC anthology series no. 31 (pp. 29–52). Singapore: SEAMEO-RELC.

Lynn, R. W. (1973). Preparing word lists: A suggested method. *RELC Journal*, **4**, 1, 25–32.

Marco, M. J. L. (1998). Procedural vocabulary as a device to organise meaning and discourse. *Australian Review of Applied Linguistics*, **21**, 1, 57–70.

Martin, A. V. (1976). Teaching academic vocabulary to foreign graduate students. *TESOL Quarterly*, **10**, 1, 91–7.

Martinez, I. A., Beck, S. C. and Panza, C. B. (2009). Academic vocabulary in agriculture research articles: A corpus-based study. *English for Specific Purposes*, **28**, 183–98.

McCarthy, M. (1991). *Discourse Analysis for Language Teachers*. Cambridge: Cambridge University Press.

McCarthy, M. and Carter, R. (1994). *Language as Discourse*. London: Longman.

Memory, D. M. (1990). Teaching technical vocabulary: Before, during, or after the reading assignment? *Journal of Reading Behavior*, **22**, 1, 39–53.

Meyer, P. G. (1990). Non-technical vocabulary in technical language. Paper delivered at AILA congress in Thessalonica.

Nagy, W. E. (1997). On the role of context in first- and second-language learning. In Schmitt, N. and McCarthy, M. (eds.), *Vocabulary: Description, Acquisition and Pedagogy* (pp. 64–83). Cambridge: Cambridge University Press.

Nation, I. S. P. (1984). Understanding paragraphs. *Language Learning and Communication*, 3, 1, 61–8.

Nation, I. S. P. (1990). *Teaching and Learning Vocabulary*. Rowley, MA: Newbury House.

Nation, I. S. P. (1993). Predicting the content of texts. *TESOLANZ Journal*, 1, 37–46.

Newton, J. and Kennedy, G. (1996). Effects of communication tasks on the grammatical relations marked by second language learners. *System*, 24, 3, 309–22.

Parkin, M. (1990). *Macroeconomics*. Englewood Cliffs, NJ: Prentice Hall.

Praninskas, J. (1972). *American University Word List*. London: Longman.

Salager, F. (1983). The lexis of fundamental medical English: Classificatory framework and rhetorical function (a statistical approach). *Reading in a Foreign Language*, 1, 1, 54–64.

Salager, F. (1984). The English of medical literature research project. *English for Specific Purposes, Oregon State University*, 87, 5 July.

Schmitt, N. and Carter, R. (2000). The lexical advantages of narrow reading for second language learners. *TESOL Journal*, 9, 1, 4–9.

Schmitt, N., Schmitt, D. and Clapham, C. (2001). Developing and exploring the behaviour of two new versions of the Vocabulary Levels Test. *Language Testing*, 18, 1, 55–88.

Strevens, P. (1973). Technical, technological, and scientific English. *ELT Journal*, 27, 3, 223–34.

Sutarsyah, C., Nation, P. and Kennedy, G. (1994). How useful is EAP vocabulary for ESP? A corpus based study. *RELC Journal*, 25, 2, 34–50.

Thompson, G. and Ye, Y. (1991). Evaluation in the reporting verbs used in academic papers. *Applied Linguistics*, 12, 4, 365–82.

Trimble, L. (1985). *English for Science and Technology: A Discourse Approach*. Cambridge: Cambridge University Press.

Visser, A. (1989). Learning core meanings. *Guidelines*, 11, 2, 10–17.

Wang, M.-t. K. and Nation, P. (2004). Word meaning in academic English: Homography in the Academic Word List. *Applied Linguistics*, 25, 3, 291–314.

Ward, J. (1999). How large a vocabulary do EAP Engineering students need? *Reading in a Foreign Language*, 12, 2, 309–23.

Ward, J. (2009). A basic engineering English word list for less proficient foundation engineering undergraduates. *English for Specific Purposes*, 28, 170–82.

West, M. (1953). *A General Service List of English Words*. London: Longman, Green & Co.

Winter, E. O. (1977). A clause-relational approach to English texts: A study of some predictive lexical items in written discourse. *Instructional Science*, 6, 1, 1–92.

Winter, E. O. (1978). A look at the role of certain words in information structure. In Jones, K. P. and Horsnell, V. (eds.), *Informatics 3* (pp. 85–97). London: Aslib.

Worthington, D. and Nation, P. (1996). Using texts to sequence the introduction of new vocabulary in an EAP course. *RELC Journal*, 27, 2, 1–11.

Xue, G. and Nation, I. S. P. (1984). A university word list. *Language Learning and Communication*, 3, 2, 215–29.

Yang, H. (1986). A new technique for identifying scientific/technical terms and describing science texts. *Literary and Linguistic Computing*, 1, 2, 93–103.

7 *Vocabulary-learning strategies*

Vocabulary-learning strategies are a part of language-learning strategies which in turn are a part of general learning strategies. In general, the findings of research on vocabulary-learning strategies agree with studies of more general language-learning strategy use. Schmitt (1997) provides a very useful overview of the rise in importance of strategy use in second language learning, noting that it grew out of an interest in learners' active role in the learning process.

It is not easy to arrive at a definition of what a strategy is, but to deserve attention from a teacher, a strategy would need to:

1. involve choice, that is, there are several strategies to choose from and one choice could be not to use the strategy;
2. be complex, that is, there are several steps to learn;
3. require knowledge and benefit from training; and
4. increase the efficiency and effectiveness of vocabulary learning and vocabulary use.

There are numerous strategies which have these features. Learners not only need to know about these strategies, but need to have skill in using them.

What vocabulary learning strategies are there?

Gu (2003a) provides an excellent review of research on a wide range of strategies for vocabulary learning, making the point that 'the choice, use, and effectiveness of vocabulary learning strategies depend on the task, the learner, and the learning context' (p. 1). Gu's review covers the task-dependent strategies of learning from context, dictionary use, vocabulary notetaking, rote rehearsal, encoding (the processing), word formation, semantic networks and vocabulary in use. Gu also covers person-dependent strategies, particularly those affected by skill at learning, learning style, holistic versus analytic, and gender. Gu's (2003b) case studies of two very successful learners nicely illustrate that there are personal and learning context aspects of strategy choice and use. Although the two learners were deliberately chosen for their contrasting personal learning styles, they shared several important approaches to learning which are a reflection of Chinese culture – a focus on memorisation and intentional learning, persistence, and a very pragmatic approach to learning.

There have been a few attempts to develop a taxonomy of vocabulary-learning strategies, usually as a part of a piece of research into learners' strategy use. Schmitt (1997) developed an extensive taxonomy organised around Oxford's (1990) social, memory, cognitive and metacognitive categories. Gu and Johnson (1996) also developed a substantial list divided into beliefs about vocabulary learning, metacognitive regulation, guessing strategies, dictionary strategies, note-taking strategies, memory strategies (rehearsal), memory strategies (encoding) and activation strategies. Zhang and Li (2011) used factor analysis to arrive at a six-part classification of vocabulary strategies, of which the three major headings were cognitive, metacognitive and affective.

Williams (1985) identifies five potentially trainable strategies for working out the meaning of unfamiliar words in written text. These include inferring from context, identifying lexical familiarisation, unchaining nominal compounds, synonym search and word analysis. Williams suggests that these should become the focus of deliberate, intensive teaching. What is interesting in several of these, particularly in lexical familiarisation and unchaining nominal compounds, is how they involve reinterpreting *known* words. That is, a known word like *snap* (to break) may be used in the phrase *snap election*. Thus, they offer a different kind of challenge to a second language learner who might not know any meaning for the words than for a native speaker who has to extend the reference of known words.

The following taxonomy tries to separate aspects of vocabulary knowledge (what is involved in knowing a word) from sources of vocabulary knowledge, and learning processes. The taxonomy is best viewed as a matrix with the aspects of what is involved in knowing a word listed along one side, and the sources and processes along the other. Let us look at a few examples to make this clear. One of the sources of information about a word is the contexts in which it occurs, for example in a reading text. The context can be a source of information for the various aspects of what is involved in knowing a word – its written form, its spoken form, its word parts, its meaning, what it refers to, its grammar, its collocations and constraints on its use. Similarly, the learning process of retrieval can be used to establish the written form of the word, its spoken form, its word parts and so on. Table 7.1 lists the major divisions of the taxonomy.

Table 7.1 *A taxonomy of kinds of vocabulary-learning strategies*

General class of strategies	Types of strategies
Planning: choosing what to focus on and when to focus on it	Choosing words Choosing the aspects of word knowledge Choosing strategies Planning repetition and spending time
Sources: finding information about words	Analysing words Using context Consulting a reference source in L1 or L2 Using parallels in L1 and L2
Processes: establishing knowledge	Noticing Retrieving Generating (creative use)
Skill in use: enriching knowledge	Gaining in coping with input through listening and speaking Gaining in coping with output through reading and writing Developing fluency across the four skills

The commitment to devote time to learning and to create and exploit opportunities for learning is an extremely important factor that affects all these classes of strategies. Tseng et al. (2006: 81) argue that it is important to look behind particular strategies and their use to investigate learners' capacity for self-regulation, namely the ability to put creative effort into trying to improve their own learning. This improvement can come through controlling commitment, concentration and action, boredom, stress, and the learning environment. They then show how a questionnaire instrument focusing on these factors to measure self-regulation in vocabulary learning can be developed. Following on from this research, Tseng and Schmitt (2008), in an insightful analysis, related motivation to stages in vocabulary learning, distinguishing quantitative and qualitative aspects of vocabulary strategy use, that is, how often and how many strategies are used, and how appropriately and well strategies are used. Their analysis shows that both the quantity and quality dimensions are dependent on self-regulation and motivation. Self-motivation, an essential component of autonomy, is central to continued effective vocabulary learning. Tseng and Schmitt's study provides a very useful broad view of vocabulary strategies. Let us now look more closely at the types of strategies in Table 7.1.

Planning vocabulary learning

The strategies in this category involve deciding on where to focus attention, how to focus the attention and how often to give attention to the item.

Choosing words. In Chapter 1 we briefly looked at the various frequency levels of vocabulary (high-frequency, mid-frequency, low-frequency levels), specialised lists (academic and technical), and the different returns for learning effort. Learners should know what their vocabulary goals are and should choose what vocabulary to focus on in terms of these goals. Gu and Johnson's (1996) study noted that this evaluative selective attention was a noted characteristic of successful learners. It is important that learners have access to lists of high-frequency, mid-frequency and academic words and are able to obtain frequency information from dictionaries. Learners should have a clear strategy for deciding what vocabulary to focus on and where to find this vocabulary (Barker, 2007).

Choosing aspects of word knowledge to focus on. In Chapter 2 we looked at what is involved in knowing a word. Learners need to be aware of these aspects of word knowledge. Most often the main concern will be recognising the word form and knowing the meaning of the word, but the need to use a word in speaking or writing will require attention to other aspects of knowing a word.

Choosing strategies. One of Gu and Johnson's (1996) and Kojic-Sabo and Lightbown's (1999) most successful groups of learners were those who actively drew on a wide range of vocabulary-learning strategies. Their least successful group used a much more limited range. Successful strategy users need a strategy for controlling their strategy use. This involves choosing the most appropriate strategy from a range of known options and deciding how to pursue the strategy and when to switch to another strategy. For example, consulting a dictionary could be followed by the use of word cards to establish knowledge of the word.

Planning repetition. Most vocabulary learning requires repeated attention to the item. One of the most important strategies to encourage remembering is the use of increasingly spaced retrieval (Baddeley, 1990; Pimsleur, 1967). This can involve an informal schedule for returning to previously studied items on word cards and the recycling of old material, or it can involve a more organised review system using a computer or a filing system (Mondria and Mondria-de Vries, 1994). We looked at the role of repetition in more detail in Chapter 3.

Sources: Finding information about words

In order to cope with new vocabulary when it occurs and to learn unfamiliar vocabulary, learners have to be able to get information about the vocabulary. This information can involve all of the aspects involved in knowing a word. It can come from the word form itself, from the context in which the word occurs, from a reference source, or from drawing on analogies and connections with other languages.

Analysing word parts. Because a large proportion of English words are derived from French, Latin or Greek, they are made up of word parts – affixes and stems. Being familiar with the common word parts can provide a useful basis for seeing connections between related words, checking guesses from context, strengthening form–meaning connections, and in some cases working out the meaning of a word. We will look at word parts more closely in Chapter 9.

Using context. Gu and Johnson (1996) subdivide the strategy of using context into the various kinds of cues that a learner could draw on, including background knowledge and linguistic cues. Guessing from context is examined in detail later in Chapter 8 where it is recommended that learners should be encouraged to draw on a range of cues.

Consulting a reference source. A variety of reference sources are available for gaining information about vocabulary. They can be subdivided into formal sources usually in a written form (dictionaries of various kinds, glossaries, lists, concordances) and more spontaneous sources, usually oral, such as asking teachers, native speakers or other learners for information. We examined negotiating unknown vocabulary in Chapter 4 on listening and speaking, and looked at the effects of glossing in Chapter 5. Chapter 8 will examine various strategies for dictionary use.

Using parallels with other languages. The learning burden of a word depends on how much its various aspects are similar to patterns and items that the learner already knows from previous study of the second language, from the first language or from other languages. These parallels can occur with all aspects of knowing a word and are most striking with cognate words. Swan (1997) provides a wide range of examples of helpful and unhelpful relationships between the first and second language. He also presents several versions of the **equivalence hypothesis** that second language learners might use when drawing on L1 patterns to use in L2, for example:

- Foreign words look different from mother tongue words but work in the same way (semantically and grammatically).
- Regard everything as the same unless you have a good reason not to.

More sophisticated versions of learners' equivalence hypotheses take account of linguistic and cultural distance. Kellerman's (1985) research shows that learners move towards being more cautious about using first language patterns in the second language as they learn more about the second language.

Processes: Establishing vocabulary knowledge

The third major set of strategies involves ways of remembering vocabulary and making it available for use. The major categories used here relate to the conditions for vocabulary learning described in Chapter 3 – noticing, retrieving, creative use. These conditions can apply to all aspects of vocabulary knowledge, and are ordered here from the least to the most effective, with creative use being the most effective for learning.

Noticing. Noticing involves seeing the word as an item to be learned. The strategies at this level include putting the word in a vocabulary notebook or list, putting the word on to a word card, orally repeating the word and visually repeating the word. These strategies tend to be largely recording strategies, but they are a very useful first step towards deeper processing of words.

Retrieving. Retrieval involves recall of previously met items. Each retrieval strengthens the connection between the cue and the retrieved knowledge. Receptively the cue may be the written or spoken form of the word and the retrieved information may be its meaning or use. Productively, the cue is the meaning or use and the retrieved information is the word form. There are thus many kinds of retrieval: receptive/productive, oral/visual, overt/covert, in context/decontextualised. Retrieval can occur across the four skills of listening, speaking, reading and writing. It involves recalling knowledge in the same form in which it was originally stored.

It is important for learners to realise that there is a substantial qualitative difference between:

1. studying words in lists and notebooks where the form and meaning and use of the word are all on display and need not be retrieved, and
2. retrieving previously met information where only a cue is present (such as the word form) and the other information has to be recalled by the learner.

Retrieval strategies (Type 2) are superior to noticing (Type 1) strategies. If learners keep vocabulary notebooks, they should become familiar with ways of covering up part of the entry so that they are encouraged to retrieve that information.

Creative use. Like retrieving, this group of strategies to establish vocabulary knowledge includes many kinds of creative use: receptive/productive, oral/visual, overt/covert, in context/decontextualised. From an instructional viewpoint, creative use involves 'rich instruction'. Creative use strategies include attaching new aspects of knowledge to what is known through instantiation (visualising examples of the word), word analysis, semantic mapping, and using scales and grids. It also includes rule-based creative use by creating contexts, collocations and sentences containing the word, mnemonic strategies like the keyword technique, and meeting and using the word in new contexts across the four skills of listening, speaking, reading and writing.

The three major categories of vocabulary strategies – planning, finding information, establishing knowledge – include a wide range of strategies of different complexity. In this and the following chapters, we will look at these in more detail.

Skill in use: Enriching knowledge

Skill in use comes from the three meaning-focused strands of a course. Learners need to know how to get large amounts of input through extensive reading at the right level and through repeated listening to recordings and watching movies. They also need to know how to gain comprehensible input from others in interactive situations. They need to take opportunities to produce language, drawing on what they have already studied or dealt with as input. In addition, learners need to know how to make listening, speaking, reading and writing easy so that they can develop fluency across the four skills of a course. Nation and Yamamoto (2011) show how this can be done by someone learning a language without the help of a teacher.

How can we train learners in strategy choice and use?

Most vocabulary-learning strategies can be applied to a wide range of vocabulary and are useful at all stages of vocabulary learning. They also allow learners to take control of learning away from the teacher, allowing the teacher to concentrate on other things.

Learners differ in their use of strategies. Studies of guessing from context indicate that female learners are more likely to guess and use other strategies than male learners (Zoubir-Shaw and Oxford, 1995).

Research also shows that learners differ greatly in the skill with which they use strategies.

It is therefore important to make training in strategy use a planned part of a vocabulary development programme. Such planning involves:

- deciding which strategies to give attention to;
- deciding how much time to spend on training learners in strategy use;
- working out a syllabus for each strategy that covers the required knowledge and provides plenty of opportunity for increasingly independent practice; and
- monitoring and providing feedback on learners' control of the strategies.

For each of the strategies, like guessing from context, using word parts, dictionary use and direct learning, learners need to spend a total of at least four or five hours per strategy spread over several weeks. There is little research to guide teachers in deciding how much time to spend on strategy training, but it is certainly not sufficient to demonstrate and explain a strategy to learners and then leave the rest to them. Learners need to understand the goal of each strategy and the conditions under which it works well. They need to gain the knowledge which is needed to use the strategy, and they need enough practice to feel comfortable and proficient in using the strategy. This all takes time, but it is repaid by the continuing gains that the learners get from being able to use the strategy well.

It has been argued at several places in this book that strategies are particularly useful for dealing with the mid-frequency and low-frequency words of a language. There are so many mid- and low-frequency words that teachers cannot possibly teach them all. Learners need to keep learning them, however, and strategies provide the essential means for doing so. No matter how much a learner knows, there will always still be words that are unknown and strategy use provides a way of coping with these unknown words.

Teachers need to understand and rehearse the arguments for giving time to strategy training. This is because they need to convince learners of the value of working on strategies and they may need to convince other teachers, too.

There are many options to choose from when designing a mini-syllabus for strategy development. The following list includes most of these options. Teachers need to choose from these and sequence them in a suitable way:

- The teacher models the strategy for the learners.
- The steps in the strategy are practised separately.

- Learners apply the strategy in pairs supporting each other.
- Learners report back on the application of the steps in the strategy.
- Learners report on their difficulties and successes in using the strategy when they use it outside class time.
- Teachers systematically test learners on strategy use and give them feedback.
- Learners consult the teacher on their use of the strategy, seeking advice where necessary.

Porte (1988) suggests that learners should be encouraged to examine the effectiveness of their vocabulary-coping strategies. This can be done by working through activities like guessing from context to see what learners do and what options are available.

How well do learners use strategies?

The effectiveness of a particular strategy can be evaluated by comparing learning using one strategy with using another strategy. Usually the other strategy is simply: 'Use your own way of learning'. Studies of more general strategy use can observe learners in several ways.

Studies can gather information about what learners say they usually do. This information is usually gathered through written questionnaires or oral interviews. Written questionnaires are easy to administer to large groups of people, but the data gathered is retrospective and may be not a true reflection of what actually happens when a learner tackles a word.

Studies can gather information about what learners are able to do. This information is usually gathered by getting learners to perform learning tasks, perhaps getting them to speak aloud while doing them, and observing them closely while they do the task. The learners are aware that they are being observed and may be aware of what the observer is investigating. Such data gathering is time consuming and the observation can influence the learners' performance, encouraging them to do things they do not normally do.

Studies can gather information about what learners say they did. This information is gathered by getting learners to perform a task under normal conditions; when they have finished they are asked to think back and describe what they did and what they were thinking about. This recall could be cued by a videotape of the task performance. It is time consuming to gather such data although written recall could be used. If a questionnaire is preceded by a relevant learning task, then this may increase the validity of the questionnaire as the learners can reflect on very recent experience when answering it. The retrospection however might not be a true reflection of what actually happened.

Studies can gather information about what learners actually do. This information has to be gathered while the learners are unaware of being observed or unaware of the goal of the observation. The difficulty with such data gathering is that it can only look for external signs of what is happening and thus could require high degrees of interpretation by the observer.

These four ways of data gathering differ in reliability, validity and practicality, with the more practical and reliable ways tending to be less valid in gaining information about normal behaviour. It is not surprising, given the difficulties mentioned above, that most large-scale strategy studies use questionnaires.

Studies relating questionnaire-reported strategy use with achievement as measured by a test of vocabulary size or a more general proficiency measure typically show greater achievement for learners who use (a) a lot of strategies; (b) a wide range of different strategies; and (c) use them often (Ahmed, 1989; Fan, 2003; Gu and Johnson, 1996; Kim, 2009; Kojic-Sabo and Lightbown, 1999; Lawson and Hogben, 1996). The most successful learners tend to be the ones who devote time to their study, independently seek learning opportunities and make good use of resources, especially of dictionaries.

Ahmed (1989) used observation of learners doing think-aloud tasks and a structured interview to gather data on Sudanese learners' vocabulary-learning strategies. The learners were divided into good learners and underachieving learners, as determined by school officials on the basis of school records and subjective assessment. Cluster analysis was then done on the data to see how these two groups of learners performed. The clusterings clearly distinguished good and underachieving learners, and also showed different patterns of strategy use at different levels of the school system. The good learners saw other learners as a resource for vocabulary knowledge. One cluster, predominantly of good learners, made full use of monolingual dictionaries, using them as a source of many kinds of information. Another high-achieving cluster made good use of bilingual dictionaries. Generally, the underachieving learners used a smaller range of strategies than the good learners. The underachievers tended to avoid active practice.

Gu and Johnson (1996) used a questionnaire to investigate advanced learners' use of English vocabulary-learning strategies. They then correlated this information with the learners' scores on tests of vocabulary size and general English proficiency to see the statistical relationships between reported strategy use and measures of English proficiency and vocabulary size. Gu and Johnson used their data in two ways: firstly, to see what strategies correlated well with previous learning, and secondly, to see what clusters of strategies different learners used and what types of learners they were.

There were small but significant positive correlations between vocabulary size and self-initiation strategies – seeking out personally relevant and interesting vocabulary (0.35); activation strategies – deliberately using the vocabulary that had been studied (0.31); selective attention – knowing which words to give attention to (0.24); dictionary look up strategies (0.24); semantic encoding – creating semantic associations and networks (0.24); extended dictionary strategies – looking at examples of use in the dictionary (0.23); and meaning-oriented note-taking strategies – writing down meanings and synonyms (0.23). Visual repetition – memorising spelling and writing the word repeatedly – (−0.2) correlated negatively with vocabulary size.

Generally, memorisation and attention to form strategies did not correlate positively or well with vocabulary size and proficiency. Vocabulary size and general English proficiency correlated reasonably highly with each other (0.53) and many of the same factors that correlated significantly with vocabulary size also correlated with proficiency at roughly the same order of magnitude. Kojic-Sabo and Lightbown (1999) found a correlation of .86 between vocabulary size and cloze test scores. Overall students' beliefs about vocabulary and their strategies explained only about 20% of the variance in either vocabulary size or English proficiency (Gu and Johnson, 1996: 660). Tseng and Schmitt (2008) found that what mattered was not which strategies were used or how many were used, but what was important was how *well* they were chosen and used.

Gu and Johnson distinguished five different types of learners by looking at the clustering of the various beliefs and strategies they examined. The types are listed here in order of their scores on the proficiency and vocabulary size measures:

1. *Readers.* These were the best students and a very small group. They believed in learning through natural exposure, as in reading, and careful study but not memorisation. They sought words that *they* considered to be useful and dealt with words in context.
2. *Active strategy users.* These were the next best students in terms of vocabulary size and proficiency. They were hard working and highly motivated. They used a variety of strategies to learn the words they considered important. These included natural exposure, memorisation, dictionary use, guessing and so on. They generally used strategies more than other learners.

These first two groups (readers and active strategy users) accounted for less than 11% of the learners in the study.

3. *Non-encoders*
4. *Encoders*

These two groups were very similar to each other in that they made average use of the various strategies. The only difference between them was that the encoders used more deliberate memorisation strategies like association, imagery, visualising the form of a word and breaking the word into parts. These two groups accounted for 87% of the learners.

5. *Passive strategy users.* This group accounted for less than 2% of the learners and was the least successful. They strongly believed in memorisation, but were well below other learners in their use of strategies. They were the reverse image of the active strategy users.

Some caution needs to be shown in interpreting the Gu and Johnson (1996) study. Firstly, it is based on self-report questionnaire data. What learners say they do does not always represent what they actually do. Qian (2004) surveyed second language learners about the strategies they used when they met an unknown word when reading, and about the kind of information they used when guessing from context. This was followed up by asking a subsample of the questionnaire respondents to take part in an experiment which involved reading a text, marking the unknown words, guessing their meanings and then being interviewed individually about how they guessed each unknown word. The ranking of sources of knowledge for guessing in the questionnaire bore little relationship to the ranking revealed in the interview: local clues (syntagmatic cues, morphological knowledge) predominated in the interview while top-down clues (global meaning, world knowledge) predominated in the questionnaire. Clearly, questionnaire data on strategy use has to be viewed with some scepticism and at least confirmed by some other method of investigation.

Secondly, there is no way in the study of determining how well learners used the strategies they said they used. There is plenty of evidence from other research that learners use strategies like guessing from context, memorisation and the keyword technique badly. Learners usually need considerable training in the keyword technique before they can use it comfortably and well. Thirdly, the data gained depends on the selection, classification, grouping and labelling of the various substrategies. Gu and Johnson (1996: 673–679) list all the questions they used and these should be looked at when examining the results. Some of Gu and Johnson's questions grouped under the same heading may draw on opposing rather than complementary features and have not been given a reversed value. For example in the section on 'Guessing strategies: Using background knowledge/wider context', use of topic knowledge is listed with lexical familiarisation and wider context. Haastrup (1989) suggests that using topic knowledge may result in good guessing but little vocabulary learning, while using language cues (lexical familiarisation, wider context) will help vocabulary learning. Similarly, using lists and cards are grouped together, although they may draw on different kinds of memory processes. Fourthly, the questionnaire was very long – 108 items plus personal data – and a fatigue factor may have accounted for 87% of the learners clustering around the average scores. However, this is a substantial and comprehensive study with important messages for teachers and learners.

- Some of the strongest correlations in the study involved learners making decisions about what vocabulary was important for them. Relating learning to personal needs and goals is at the centre of taking responsibility for learning.
- Memorisation is only useful if it is one of a wide range of actively used strategies. It should not be the major means of learning. This fits well with the viewpoint taken in this book that vocabulary learning should be balanced across the four strands of learning from meaning-focused input, direct learning, learning from output and fluency development. Memorisation is one part of the direct learning strand.
- There is a very wide range of strategy options for a language to draw on, and learners draw on these with varied success and skill. Learners could benefit from being made aware of these strategies, how to use them well and how to choose between them.

Lawson and Hogben (1996) got learners to think aloud while they learned twelve new words in another language. Thus, this investigation looked at what learners can do, rather than at what they say they do. Lawson and Hogben also measured how well each word was learned and correlated strategy use with recall of the word's meaning. Their findings are largely supported by other strategy studies:

1. The learners who recalled more words used a greater range of strategies and used strategies more often than those learners who recalled fewer words. This seems to be a robust finding of strategy studies.
2. In general, elaboration strategies are more effective than repetition and word feature analysis strategies.
3. Repetition strategies were the most frequently used strategies. Simple rehearsal was effective but other repetition strategies were not.

Instead of using a questionnaire, Lawson and Hogben's (1996) study not only gathered data about what learners could do, but also to a degree gathered data on how well the strategies were applied. Only three of the 15 students used a special mnemonic strategy.

Kojic-Sabo and Lightbown (1999) included a group of EFL learners in northern Yugoslavia and a group of ESL learners in Canada of roughly similar age and proficiency. There were similarities between the two groups, and the differences could be related to their learning environment, for example the lack of review procedures by ESL learners. The two most important factors were: time spent on learning outside the classroom, and initiative and independence of learning. Kojic-Sabo and Lightbown cautioned that not all strategies are generally useful for all learners and that quality of strategy use may be a critical factor.

Fan (2003) used a vocabulary test following the format of the *Vocabulary Levels Test* and a vocabulary-learning strategies questionnaire to explore the relationship between declared strategy use and L2 vocabulary proficiency. University-entry learners were asked to rate both how often they used a strategy and how useful they thought it was for them. The most frequently used strategies involved guessing, making use of known words and dictionary strategies. The keyword and other mnemonic techniques were not well known and were rarely used. Frequency of use and usefulness were not strongly related. Part of the reason for this is that strategies like guessing, which are relatively easily applied, do not always give good results. More time-consuming strategies like dictionary use can give good results but require time, effort and interruption to language use. Learners scoring high on the vocabulary test were more likely to use planning strategies and used opportunities to encounter new words both inside and outside of class. As found in other studies, proficient learners used more strategies and used strategies more often than less proficient learners.

Barcroft (2009) had learners do a vocabulary-learning task and then self-report in writing on what they had done. This has the advantage that the reporting does not interfere with or influence the learning, and is based on very recent performance. The task involved native speakers of English doing word–picture learning with Spanish as the L2. The words seem to have been chosen to avoid cognates. As found in other studies (Ahmed, 1989; Gu and Johnson, 1996), there were significant but low correlations between scores on the vocabulary tests and the number of strategies reported to have been used. The most frequent strategies were L2–picture association, L1–L2 association, L2–L1 translation and repetition. The highest vocabulary test scores were from the small number of learners reporting mnemonic techniques. The most commonly used strategies were effective but not as effective as the lesser used visualisation, mnemonic, oral rote rehearsal and retrieval strategies. Clearly, strategy training in memory-enhancing techniques could have useful effects.

Schmitt (1997) used a questionnaire to survey learners' reported strategy use and how useful they rated each strategy. The ratings for helpfulness were almost always higher than the amount of use, perhaps indicating that learners were aware of the value of an organised approach to vocabulary but do not organise themselves well. The study revealed a strong preference for bilingual dictionaries and a focus on word form to consolidate learning. Some of the consolidation strategies that learners rated highly (written repetition, oral repetition) did not correlate well with proficiency or vocabulary size in Gu and Johnson's (1996) study. This indicates learners could benefit from advice on strategy choice and use. Schmitt also compared Japanese learners' strategy use at four different age levels. He found that there was a trend away from a focus on form-based memorisation towards more meaning-based processing through the age groups.

Sanaoui (1995) conducted a series of intensive longitudinal case studies investigating the approaches to vocabulary learning taken by learners of French as a second language. She saw her subjects fitting into two major categories: those who used a structured approach to their learning and those who used an unstructured approach. In essence, some learners planned and organised the way they approached vocabulary learning. They took control of the learning rather than relying on what the language course provided. They used their own initiative in regularly creating opportunities for vocabulary learning by listening to the radio, watching videotapes, speaking with friends, making tapes for use while jogging or driving, reading and doing self-study. They kept systematic records of their vocabulary learning by using notebooks and lists. They reviewed what they had done several times a week and took their notebooks with them for review during spare moments. They deliberately sought out opportunities to use the items they had learned.

Learners who followed an unstructured approach, meanwhile, relied mainly on the course material. If they made lists, they did not review them and occasionally lost them. Their attention to vocabulary outside class tended to be opportunistic rather than planned. It seems that learners who organised their vocabulary learning made better progress than those who did not.

Leeke and Shaw (2000) found that only about one-third of post-graduate L2 learners of English studying for a degree in England kept any kind of written record of vocabulary or phrases, and most of these records involved L2 translations of vocabulary from specialist or other reading. Very few used word cards. A major reason for not keeping any systematic record may have been that these learners had now reached a reasonably high degree of proficiency and did not think that the effort of keeping a record would be repaid by the learning resulting from it. This was probably a realistic decision and has parallels with native speakers typically not keeping any record of new vocabulary met. Now that vocabulary size measures are available, it would be interesting to see if there is a relationship between vocabulary size and record keeping.

Nation and Moir (2008) examined the vocabulary-learning behaviours of ten adult learners of English who were all committed, conscientious and hard-working learners of English and spent several hours a week outside class working on vocabulary. Only one, the effective learner, showed a high level of responsibility for his learning and an awareness of what was involved in learning vocabulary.

The less effective learners:

- spent more time on vocabulary learning outside class than the effective learner;
- selected the words to learn from class texts rather than from a range of sources of interest and value to them;
- selected words simply because they were unknown rather than considering frequency, area of specialisation (i.e. academic or non-academic vocabulary), personal goals or previous meetings with the words;
- were aware that the words they selected were of limited use to them;
- focused on the meaning of the words in copied sentences rather than also exploring the range of collocations and uses, and creating their own sentences;
- used rote learning rather than strategies they were taught, such as the keyword strategy, word cards and trying to use the words in conversation;
- limited their learning to the short-term goals of the weekly test rather than focusing on their long-term goals;
- did not revise the words any more after the weekly test;
- knew that they were not learning efficiently but did not alter their selection of words or learning procedures;
- did not feel very satisfied with their vocabulary learning; and
- did not retain many of the words they studied.

The effective learner:

- chose words that he already partially knew but needed to improve;
- chose words from a wide range of sources;
- chose words from sources that were very relevant to him;
- explored multiple senses of a word and was strongly aware that being familiar with one sense may not be enough; and
- made an effort to use the words he learned.

Moir and Nation saw the causes of the poor approaches to vocabulary learning as follows:

1. a poor awareness of what is involved in learning a language;
2. limited control of language-learning strategies;
3. trying to meet the perceived expectations of the teacher;
4. the influence of the weekly tests; and
5. the carry-over of perceptions, expectations and strategies from previous learning experience.

Moir and Nation concluded that learners need a strong metacognitive understanding of the nature and purpose of the learning task, an awareness of a range of appropriate strategies and a clear understanding of their own needs. It is also clear that teachers and tests play a critical role in directly and indirectly shaping approaches to learning.

In general, the strategy studies show that there is value in being able to use a wide range of strategies and that many learners are restricted to too narrow a range. Strategy training may have a very useful role to play in second language vocabulary development, but research is needed on the effectiveness of specific strategy training.

What are the effects of training learners in strategy use?

Training may help low-proficiency learners in several ways. Mizumoto and Takeuchi (2009) looked at the effect of training learners in vocabulary-learning strategies, and found positive effects for learners with initial low levels of strategy use. Although the study lasted 10 weeks, each week involved instruction in a different strategy and it may have been better to have repeated instruction of fewer strategies, particularly the more complicated mnemonic strategies which learners found difficult to use. There was some evidence that strategy training which confirmed the use of strategies learners were already using was also valuable, and that strategy training had positive effects on motivation.

Some strategy training, such as making use of word parts or using word cards, involves new knowledge, such as learning the meanings of stems or prefixes, or learning memorisation and revision procedures.

It would be useful in research to separate this kind of content learning from actual strategy use to see where training affects strategy use.

Procedures that integrate strategies

Several writers (Kramsch, 1979; McComish, 1990; Mhone, 1988) describe procedures for getting learners to select their own vocabulary for learning, record it, learn it, share it with others, and be monitored and assessed on their learning. These procedures also relate to the use of vocabulary notebooks (Schmitt and Schmitt, 1995) in that they aim at learners taking responsibility for their own learning and developing the necessary skills to do this.

Let us look closely at Kramsch's (1979) procedure and consider and expand on the options available at each point.

1. *Selecting the words.* The learners are told that they need to learn five words a day – three chosen by them and two chosen by the teacher. Kramsch suggests that the learners look for vocabulary they can readily use in talking or writing, and words that are easily adaptable to any context. The learners need to develop a feeling for which words are low frequency and which are more useful. Now learners can more readily gain information about which words are particularly useful by consulting the frequency markings in the later editions of the *COBUILD Dictionary* or the Longman *Dictionary of Contemporary English,* or by consulting word lists such as those by West (1953) or Hindmarsh (1980). Kramsch points out that sometimes a word is chosen for aesthetic reasons, because it sounds nice, because it represents an unusual concept or because it has personal associations. McKenzie (1990) and Carroll and Mordaunt (1991) suggest that learners should choose words that are 'semi-familiar' to them, that is, words that are partly known and that they can imagine themselves using in the future. This is largely to help receptive vocabulary become productive.

   Robinson (1989) argues that more attention should be given to getting learners to use the high-frequency, non-context-dependent vocabulary that can be used to paraphrase and define. This allows learners to cope with breakdowns in communication and to more effectively engage in the negotiation of meaning.

2. *Recording the words and monitoring the recording.* Kramsch suggests writing the words on index cards along with a synonym, antonym or translation, and an example sentence. The way the word is recorded will have a strong effect on how it is learned. The teacher can check the cards to ensure that the words are useful and that the information recorded such as the context sentence is

correct. Carroll and Mordaunt (1991) also suggest noting definitions, etymology, the sentence the word occurred in, a sentence
created by the student, and synonyms and antonyms. Schmitt and
Schmitt (1995) suggest elaborating the information over a period of
time by listing derivatives, collocates, mnemonic cues and stylistic
information. McComish's (1990) word spider is a way of helping
learners remember the various types of information to look for, and
largely corresponds to the various aspects of what is involved in
knowing a word. It is important however not to overdo this recording, because noting words for deliberate learning is only one stage
in the learning of words and the expectations should not be too
high from such learning (see the section on vocabulary notebooks
in Chapter 3).

3. *Learning the words.* If words are recorded on small cards with the
word on one side and its translation on the back, then learners can
be instructed in the best ways to apply rote learning procedures.
Similarly, creative procedures like the keyword technique and
mental elaboration through self-created contexts, cause–effect
chains (Sokmen, 1992) and situational links can be used. Learners
need to be aware of the ways they can enhance learning and the
principles which lie behind the techniques.

4. *Sharing with others.* Learners should regularly present a word or a
few words to others by writing it on the board, defining it and
saying where they met it, why it is worth learning, how they
remembered it, and giving some example sentences containing it.
Learners get a boost when they find that others add the word to
their own store of items to learn. The class can question the pre-
senter about the word and make suggestions for learning. This is
also a useful opportunity for the teacher to provide comments.
Such presentations can only deal with a very small number of
words but they can be very useful in reinforcing what is known
about a word and how it can be learned, and in developing an
enthusiasm for vocabulary.

5. *Assessing and monitoring learning.* Kramsch suggests the following
procedure for testing learning: learners work in pairs or small
groups and exchange sets of cards. Each learner is tested on five
words by his or her partner. The learner has to define the tested
word and give a sample sentence containing it, and points are then
awarded. This testing provides another opportunity for sharing
words. Another way is for learners to supply the teacher with a list
of, say 20, words each week. The teacher makes a brief note next to
ten of the words. If the teacher writes *der.* after a word, the learner
has to write three derived forms of the word. If the teacher writes

coll., the learner has to provide three collocates. If the teacher writes *sent.*, the learner has to write a sentence using the word.

6. *Recycling the vocabulary.* Learners are encouraged to indicate in their writing, by using an asterisk, the words they have used from their cards. They are also encouraged to make conscious and deliberate efforts to use what they have learned. To a very small degree this can be done through classroom games and activities, but primarily it depends on each learner's initiative. Recycling also occurs when learners engage in the strands of meaning-focused input, meaning-focused output and fluency development. Finding opportunities to do this is indicative of a good language learner (Nation and Yamamoto, 2011).

Schmitt and Schmitt's (1995) description of the principles lying behind vocabulary notebooks and the ways in which they can be used is an excellent guide for teachers wishing to develop a strategy programme.

Research on vocabulary-learning strategies shows that there is value in knowing a range of strategies and having the capacity to use them. There are learning processes, for example retrieval, creative use, the use of mnemonic devices and the use of dictionaries, which are strongly supported by research and leaners benefit from training in their use. Such training however needs to occur over a reasonable period of time and involve repeated attention and practice with each strategy. In the following chapters we will look at some of the strategies in more detail.

References

Ahmed, M. O. (1989). Vocabulary learning strategies. In Meara, P. (ed.), *Beyond Words* (pp. 3–14). London: BAAL/CILT.

Baddeley, A. (1990). *Human Memory*. London: Lawrence Erlbaum Associates.

Barcroft, J. (2009). Strategies and performance in intentional L2 vocabulary learning. *Language Awareness*, 18, 1, 74–89.

Barker, D. (2007). A personalized approach to analyzing 'cost' and 'benefit' in vocabulary selection. *System*, 35, 523–33.

Carroll, M. C. and Mordaunt, O. G. (1991). The frontier method of vocabulary practice. *TESOL Journal*, 1, 1, 23–6.

Fan, M. (2003). Frequency of use, perceived usefulness, and actual usefulness of second language vocabulary strategies: A study of Hong Kong learners. *Modern Language Journal*, 87, 2, 222–41.

Gu, Y. P. (2003a). Vocabulary learning in a second language: Person, task, context, and strategies. *TESL-EJ*, 7, 2, 1–31.

Gu, Y. P. (2003b). Fine brush and freehand: The vocabulary-learning art of two successful Chinese learners. *TESOL Quarterly*, 37, 1, 73–104.

Gu, Y. and Johnson, R. K. (1996). Vocabulary learning strategies and language learning outcomes. *Language Learning*, **46**, 4, 643–79.

Haastrup, K. (1989). *Lexical Inferencing Procedures*, vols. 1 & 2. Copenhagen: Handelshojskolen i Kobenhavn.

Hindmarsh, R. (1980). *Cambridge English Lexicon*. Cambridge: Cambridge University Press.

Kellerman, E. (1985). If at first you do succeed. In Gass, S. M. and Madden, C. G. (eds.), *Input in Second Language Acquisition* (pp. 345–53). Rowley, MA: Newbury House.

Kim, E. J. (2009). *A Study on the Vocabulary Learning Strategies of Korean University Students*. Hankuk University of Foreign Studies, Seoul.

Kojic-Sabo, I. and Lightbown, P. (1999). Students' approaches to vocabulary learning and their relationship to success. *Modern Language Journal*, **83**, 2, 176–92.

Kramsch, C. J. (1979). Word watching: Learning vocabulary becomes a hobby. *Foreign Language Annals*, **12**, 2, 153–8.

Lawson, M. J. and Hogben, D. (1996). The vocabulary-learning strategies of foreign-language students. *Language Learning*, **46**, 1, 101–35.

Leeke, P. and Shaw, P. (2000). Learners' independent records of vocabulary. *System*, **28**, 2, 271–89.

McComish, J. (1990). The word spider: A technique for academic vocabulary learning in curriculum areas. *Guidelines*, **12**, 1, 26–36.

McKenzie, M. (1990). Letting lexis come from the learner: A word in the hand is worth two in the bush. *English Teaching Forum*, **28**, 1, 13–16.

Mhone, Y. W. (1988). "... It's My Word, Teacher!" *English Teaching Forum*, **26**, 2, 48–51.

Mizumoto, A. and Takeuchi, O. (2009). Examining the effectiveness of explicit instruction of vocabulary learning strategies with Japanese EFL students. *Language Teaching Research*, **13**, 4, 425–49.

Mondria, J. A. and Mondria-de Vries, S. (1994). Efficiently memorizing words with the help of word cards and "hand computer": Theory and applications. *System*, **22**, 1, 47–57.

Nation, I. S. P. and Moir, J. (2008). Vocabulary learning and the good language learner. In Griffiths, C. (ed.), *Lessons from Good Language Learners* (pp. 159–73). Cambridge: Cambridge University Press.

Nation, I. S. P. and Yamamoto, A. (2011). Applying the four strands to language learning. *International Journal of Innovation in English Language Teaching and Research*, **1**, 2, 1–15.

Oxford, R. (1990). *Language Learning Strategies: What Every Teacher Should Know*. New York: Newbury House/Harper and Row.

Pimsleur, P. (1967). A memory schedule. *Modern Language Journal*, **51**, 2, 73–5.

Porte, G. (1988). Poor language learners and their strategies for dealing with new vocabulary. *ELT Journal*, **42**, 3, 167–72.

Qian, D. (2004). Second language lexical inferencing: Preferences, perceptions, and practices. In Bogaards, P. and Laufer, B. (eds.), *Vocabulary in a Second Language: Selection, Acquisition, and Testing* (pp. 155–69). Amsterdam: John Benjamins.

Robinson, P. J. (1989). Procedural vocabulary and language learning. *Journal of Pragmatics*, **13**, 523–46.

Sanaoui, R. (1995). Adult learners' approaches to learning vocabulary in second languages. *Modern Language Journal*, **79**, 1, 15–28.

Schmitt, N. (1997). Vocabulary learning strategies. In Schmitt, N. and McCarthy, M. (eds.), *Vocabulary: Description, Acquisition and Pedagogy* (pp. 199–227). Cambridge: Cambridge University Press.

Schmitt, N. and Schmitt, D. (1995). Vocabulary notebooks: Theoretical underpinnings and practical suggestions. *ELT Journal*, **49**, 2, 133–43.

Sokmen, A. J. (1992). Students as vocabulary generators. *TESOL Journal*, **1**, 4, 16–18.

Swan, M. (1997). The influence of the mother tongue on second language vocabulary acquisition and use. In Schmitt, N. and McCarthy, M. (eds.), *Vocabulary: Description, Acquisition and Pedagogy* (pp. 156–80). Cambridge: Cambridge University Press.

Tseng, W.-T., Dornyei, Z. and Schmitt, N. (2006). A new approach to assessing strategic learning: The case of self-regulation in vocabulary acquisition. *Applied Linguistics*, **27**, 1, 78–102.

Tseng, W. and Schmitt, N. (2008). Toward a model of motivated vocabulary learning: A structural equation modeling approach. *Language Learning*, **58**, 2, 357–400.

West, M. (1953). *A General Service List of English Words*. London: Longman, Green & Co.

Williams, R. (1985). Teaching vocabulary recognition strategies in ESP reading. *ESP Journal*, **4**, 2, 121–31.

Zhang, B. and Li, C. (2011). Classification of L2 vocabulary learning strategies: Evidence from exploratory and confirmatory factor analysis. *RELC Journal*, **42**, 2, 141–54.

Zoubir-Shaw, S. and Oxford, R. (1995). Gender differences in language strategy use in university-level introductory French classes. In Klee, C. A. (ed.), *Faces in a Crowd: The Individual Learner in Multisection Courses* (pp. 181–213). Boston: Heinle.

8   *Learning words from context*

Incidental learning from context is the most important of all the sources of vocabulary learning. This is particularly true for native speakers learning their first language. It should also be true for second language learners, but many do not experience the conditions that are needed for this kind of learning to occur. A major goal of this chapter is to look at these conditions and see how they can be established. We will look at how successful learners can be at guessing from context, how much and what kind of learning can occur from this guessing, and the kinds of clues available for guessing. We will then look at how learners can be helped to become skilful at guessing from context.

Which is best: intentional or incidental learning?

Learning vocabulary from context is often seen as something opposed to the direct intentional learning and teaching of vocabulary (Kelly, 1990). This is an unfortunate viewpoint and the position taken in this book is that they are complementary activities, each one enhancing the learning that comes from the other. A well-balanced language-learning programme has an appropriate range of opportunities to learn from message-focused activities and from direct study of language items, with direct study of language items occupying no more than a quarter of the total learning programme.

In this chapter, learning from context is taken to mean the incidental learning of vocabulary from reading or listening to normal language use while the main focus of learners' attention is on the message of the text. The texts may be short or long. Learning from context thus includes learning from extensive reading, learning from taking part in conversations, and learning from listening to stories, films, television or the radio.

In this chapter, learning from context does not include deliberately learning words and their definitions or translations even if these words are presented in isolated sentence contexts (see, for example, Gipe and Arnold, 1979). This kind of learning is looked at in Chapter 11.

Context sentences and phrases are valuable aids in intentional, language-focused vocabulary learning, and part of the confusion behind the argument about learning from context versus learning from lists stems from seeing the difference as relying on the presence or absence of context, rather than the distinction made in this chapter between message-focused, incidental learning and language-focused intentional learning. As we shall see, however, this distinction between incidental and intentional is not easy to maintain, particularly if we accept that most learning involves conscious attention.

Hulstijn (2003) argues that the terms 'intentional' (learners are aware that they will be tested on particular items) and 'incidental' (learners are not aware of a later test) are not particularly relevant to studies of vocabulary learning. What is more important is the quality of the mental processing that takes place during learning.

Although learning vocabulary from context should be largely incidental learning, there should be a deliberate, intentional focus on developing the skills and strategies needed to carry out such learning. Because of the importance of guessing from context, it is worthwhile for both teachers and learners to spend time working on guessing strategies.

In a very carefully designed study, Mondria (2003) compared inferring only with inferring and verifying on a two week delayed L2→L1 translation test, finding that learning occurred in both methods, but inferring and verifying resulted in higher scores. When these were compared with inferring plus verifying plus memorising, Mondria found 6% retention for inferring, a further 9% as a result of verifying (being told the right answer), and a further 32% as a result of a chance to memorise. Thus, all steps resulted in some level of retention, with deliberate learning predictably having the strongest effect. The opportunity to infer with subsequent memorisation did not result in a significantly higher retention score than simply being given the meaning and the chance to memorise. That is, inferring does not add greater depth of processing that is reflected in a higher retention score. Students spent 27% more time on the inferring method compared to the meaning-given method with no extra gain in retention.

The meaning-given method (memorisation without inferring) resulted in a score eight times higher than the inferring score. The meaning-given method took 1.7 times longer, showing that it is not only much more effective in terms of retention, but also more efficient in terms of time. Mondria's calculation of the achievement rate was that the meaning-given method had a learning rate of .32 words per minute, while inferring had a learning rate of .06 words per minute.

In the meaning-inferred method, where guesses were verified or corrected, correctly inferred words were retained better than incorrectly inferred words.

How are reading and vocabulary growth related to each other?

Perfetti and Hart's (2002) Lexical Quality Hypothesis sees word knowledge as central to skilled L1 reading. Good knowledge of words involves strong knowledge of the spelling, pronunciation and meaning aspects of knowing a word. This however is not necessarily a call for teachers to teach more about words, but largely to ensure that learners have large amounts of experience using language, particularly in reading.

The simplest causal circle is that learners with good vocabulary knowledge and skills achieve better comprehension of text. Better comprehension of text allows learners to process more input (do more reading). Increased practice in processing input develops good vocabulary knowledge and skills (Perfetti and Hart, 2001):

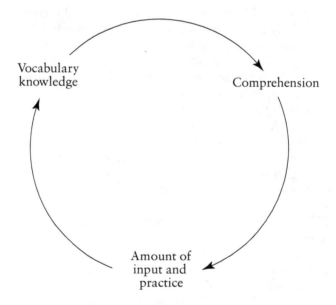

In a later paper, Perfetti (2010) elaborated on what were good vocabulary knowledge and skills, namely skill at decoding and skill at accessing word meaning. If we add skill at inferring from context and vocabulary size to these, we have a more elaborate causal circle.

Learners with good skills at inferring from context develop larger vocabulary sizes. A large vocabulary size supports decoding skills and skill at accessing word meaning. These four aspects of vocabulary skills enable learners to achieve better comprehension of text. Better comprehension of text allows learners to process more input. Increased input and practice in processing input allows more inferring from context.

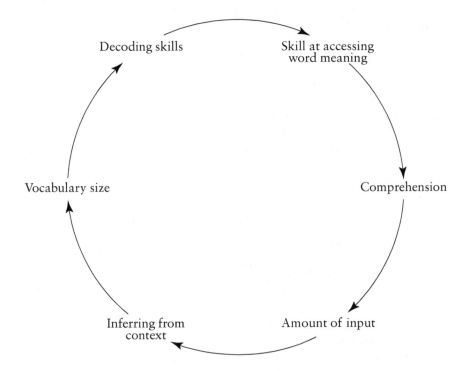

Like most models, this one also simplifies, and it ignores or assumes important factors like motivation, knowledge of the world and oral language growth. It also arranges the parts in a linear unidirectional fashion, and things are more complicated than that. Nonetheless, the skills, knowledge and experience that it includes are essential for vocabulary growth through reading, and there is research support for the parts of the model.

Van Daalen-Kapteijns et al. (2001) examined the L1 inferring skills of high and low verbal ability 11–12-year-olds. They found that the differences between the high and low verbal ability children were ones of degree of skill rather than the absence of a skill – all children are capable of inferring from context, some just do it better than others.

The circle is also relevant to L2 learners. Pulido and Hambrick (2008) provide evidence that L2 language use (both input and output) influences vocabulary growth, which in turn influences comprehension which in turn influences vocabulary growth. This provides strong support for making sure that learners experience quantity of input and output at the right levels.

What proportion of unknown words can be guessed from context?

To see what the chances are for successful guessing, we need to look at guessing from context which occurs under both realistic and favourable conditions. Firstly, we need to look at guessing where learners already know a large proportion of the words in the text. This is necessary for learners to be able to use the clues for guessing the unknown words. It is likely that at least 95% of the running words need to be already familiar to the learners for this to happen (Liu and Nation, 1985). A coverage of 95% means that there is one unknown word in every 20 running words, or one in every two lines. This is still a heavy load of unknown vocabulary and densities like 1 in 50 (98% coverage) are probably optimal. Studies which use higher densities of unknown words, for example 1 in every 10 running words, have shown little successful guessing, and set up conditions that make successful guessing unlikely (Bensoussan and Laufer, 1984; Laufer and Sim, 1985a). A critical factor in successful guessing is the learners' vocabulary size, because this will affect the density of unknown words in a text and how well the words making up the context are known (Qian, 1999). For second language learners, getting the optimal ratio of unknown to known running words may involve using simplified or adapted texts.

Secondly, the estimates of guessing need to be based on the actual words not known by each learner. This means that the choice of words to be examined needs to take account of actual learner knowledge, and not rely on teacher intuition or the unsystematic choice of words from a text. If the choice of words was carried out properly, then more readily generalisable statements about the percentage of text coverage and chances of guessing, or vocabulary size and the chances of guessing could be made. Schatz and Baldwin (1986) argue that most experiments on success in guessing from context are flawed because they use a mixture of high-frequency and low-frequency words most of which are already known to the learners. To truly test the availability of context clues, experimenters would need to focus on unknown words at the appropriate frequency level for the learners being tested. Schatz and Baldwin worked with native speakers aged between 16 and 17.

They found no significant difference between learners who had context to help them guess and learners who were tested on words in isolation. Schatz and Baldwin's tests were multiple choice and asked learners to provide a definition. The forms of the tests and the ways in which they were marked did not give credit for partial knowledge (see Nation and Webb, 2011: 83–7, for a critique of Schatz and Baldwin).

Thirdly, learner skill is a critical factor in guessing. Gibbons (1940), Cook et al. (1963) and many other studies have found a wide variation in the ability of learners to guess from context. From an optimistic viewpoint, if some learners can guess large numbers of words successfully, then potentially most learners can if they develop the skill. Studies of guessing should thus report performances of the best guessers as well as averages.

Fourthly, learners must be given credit for guesses that are not 100% correct but which make a small but positive contribution to knowledge of the meaning of the word. Learning by guessing from context is a cumulative procedure by which learners gradually develop their knowledge of words. It is likely, at least for some words, that the initial meetings with a word in context simply give rise to a vague knowledge of the form of the word and the awareness that it is unfamiliar and thus should get some attention next time it occurs. Beck et al. (1983), in an article subtitled 'All contexts are not created equal', argue that there is a range of helpfulness in natural text contexts for unknown words. They range from misdirective contexts where learners are likely to infer the opposite meaning, through non-directive contexts where no help is given, to general contexts where general aspects of word meaning are inferable, and ending with directive contexts which could lead learners to a specific, correct meaning for a word. Beck et al. are probably correct in saying not all contexts are equally informative, but by seeing the goal of one meeting as a specific correct meaning, they underestimate what can be learned from context. For instance, here is their example of a misdirective context (the least helpful in the scale) for the word *grudgingly*:

Sandra had won the dance contest and the audience's cheers brought her to the stage for an encore. 'Every step she takes is so perfect and graceful,' Ginny said *grudgingly*, as she watched Sandra dance.

There is useful partial information available from this context. First, there is the form of the word. Second, it has clear affixes and a stem form. Third, it functions as an adverb. Fourth, it can relate to the way people say things. Knowing these bits of information is still a long way from knowing the word, but they are initial, useful steps in the right direction.

Fifth, in discussions of learning from context, it is important to distinguish guessing from natural contexts on the one hand from deliberate learning with specially constructed or chosen contexts on the other hand.

Most studies of guessing from context do not take account of all of these five factors and thus tend to give misleading results.

With these five cautions in mind, let us now look at the results of studies of second language learners' guessing from context. Seibert (1945) found high rates of success (around 70%) in intensive guessing with learners who knew French guessing Spanish words in context. The similarities between these two closely related languages clearly helped the guessing. Bensoussan and Laufer's (1984) learners worked on a difficult text – around 12% of the running words were unknown to the learners, who were able to guess only a small percentage (13%) of the unknown words. Bensoussan and Laufer estimated that clues were not available for around 40% of the words that they considered to be problem words for the learners in the text.

Parry's (1991) longitudinal study of four adult learners guessing from context supports earlier non-native speaker studies in showing reasonable success in guessing from context with a range of 12% to 33% of guesses classified as correct, and a range of 51% to 69% of guesses either partly correct or correct. Most words found to be unknown were not particularly subject matter related but were in the register of formal expository prose. Horst et al. (1998) found gains of around 22%. Knight (1994) found that second language learners learned words from context while reading, on average 6% of the unknown words on an immediate translation test and 27% on an immediate multiple-choice test (corrected for guessing). Comparable scores were found on a delayed test two weeks later. The twelve unknown words in each of the tests occurred at a density of approximately one unknown word in 20 running words, meaning that the known words gave approximately 95% coverage of the text.

The findings from the few reasonably well-conducted studies of guessing by non-native speakers have not had impressive results. This may be partly due to poor design, but it is also the effect of the cumulative nature of such learning involving only small gains per meeting for most words.

'What proportion of unknown words can be guessed from context?' is probably not the right question. Rather, it should be 'Is it possible to use context to keep adding small amounts of information about words that are not yet fully known?' The answer to this question is clearly 'Yes' (Fukkink et al., 2001). It is likely that almost every context can do this for almost every word, but this has not yet been investigated experimentally.

How much vocabulary is learned from context?

There are several important factors to keep clear when trying to answer this question. First, it is important to distinguish working out the meaning of a word from context and remembering the meaning of a word worked out from context. Second, it is important to see learning as involving even small increases in knowledge of a word. Learning from context is a cumulative process where meaning and knowledge of form are gradually enriched and strengthened. Tests of learning from context need to be sensitive to small amounts of learning (Nagy et al., 1985). Third, it is important to see if the contexts and conditions for learning are typical of normal reading. Nagy et al. (1987) note that several studies use specially created contexts, combine contexts and definitions, or replace known words with nonsense words. These kinds of studies may provide useful information about the nature of learning from context but they cannot be used to estimate how much learning occurs from normal reading.

When learners who have apparently forgotten a lot of a previously known L2 are asked to relearn words, they do better on those words than on learning words that they have never met before (de Bot and Stoessel, 2000; Hansen et al., 2002). This speedier relearning shows that some subconscious memory for words can still exist even when they cannot register on a recall test. Relearning is thus a sensitive test of vocabulary knowledge and is capable of revealing knowledge that other less sensitive tests cannot pick up. As may be expected, ease of relearning is related to the length of time since the L2 was first learned, and the present level of proficiency in the L2.

Studies with young native speakers of English using text which has not been specially modified (Nagy et al., 1985; Nagy et al., 1987; Shu et al., 1995) have found that there is a chance of an unfamiliar item being learned to some degree from one exposure of between 1 in 10 or 1 in 20 respectively. The chance of learning in the experiments depended partly on how soon learning was measured after the reading occurred. Nagy et al. (1985) tested vocabulary learning 15 minutes after the reading and got a 1 in 10 rate. Nagy et al. (1987) tested vocabulary learning six days after the reading and got a 1 in 20 rate. A meta-analysis of 20 studies involving native speakers (Swanborn and de Glopper, 1999) confirmed these findings with students incidentally learning an average of 15% of the unknown words they met while reading. In all of these studies, the unknown words made up 3% or less of the running words. Smaller proportions of unknown words typically resulted in more learning. As we shall see later, quantity of reading with the opportunity for previously met items to recur within a certain time may be an important factor in learning from context. Even with rich specially constructed contexts, up to ten repetitions and some pre-teaching, learning is still low (Jenkins et al., 1984).

There are several things that can happen to an item met in context.

- It is guessed correctly to some degree and at least partially learned. This may happen to 5–10% of the words.
- It is guessed correctly to some degree but nothing about it is learned. This probably happens to many words.
- It is guessed incorrectly.
- It is not focused on, possibly because it is not important for the wanted message in the text. This does not exclude the possibility of small amounts of learning occurring.

Studies with second language learners have generally not been as carefully conducted as the studies with native speakers (Day et al., 1991; Dupuy and Krashen, 1993; Pitts et al., 1989; Saragi et al., 1978). Horst et al. (1998), however, in a study using a long text (a graded reader) and two kinds of vocabulary tests, found that about one in five of the unknown words were learned to some degree. In terms of actual words, this averaged about five words.

The higher gains in the Horst et al. study come partly from the effect of the length of the text, the use of a simplified reader where the unknown words do not occur too densely, and the conceptual knowledge that learners bring from their first language. Nagy et al. (1987) found that a major factor affecting learning from context was whether the word represented an unfamiliar concept. Shefelbine (1990) similarly found a greater difficulty for new concepts. In his study, however, the chances of learning vocabulary from natural contexts were higher than other studies because there was a deliberate focus on guessing vocabulary.

The incidental vocabulary learning from context in all these experiments is small, not only in the likelihood of words being learned but also in the actual number of items learned. This low rate has to be balanced against other considerations:

1. Incidental vocabulary learning is only one of the various kinds of learning that can occur when learners read. Not only can learners begin to learn new words and enrich known ones, they can improve grammatical knowledge, become more familiar with text structure, improve reading skills, learn new information and learn that reading can be an enjoyable activity.
2. Small gains become large gains if learners do large quantities of reading. If learners read thousands or millions of running words

per year, then considerable vocabulary learning is possible. Nagy (1997: 75) estimates that if a learner reads a million running words of text a year, and if two per cent of these words were unknown, this would amount to 20,000 unknown words per year. If one in twenty of these were learned, the annual gain would be 1,000 words a year. One million running words is roughly equivalent to three or four undergraduate textbooks (Sutarsyah et al., 1994), or ten to twelve novels, or 25 complete *Newsweek* magazines (Kennedy, 1987), or 65 graded readers of various levels (Nation and Wang, 1999).

3. Learning rates can be increased considerably by some deliberate attention to vocabulary (Elley, 1989; Hulstijn, 1992).

There are several implications to be drawn from the findings on the rate of vocabulary learning from context. First, it is important that learners do large quantities of interesting reading, large quantities for second language learners meaning something like a graded reader of a suitable level every week. Second, second language learners should not rely solely on incidental vocabulary learning from context. There needs to be judicious attention to decontextualised learning to supplement and be supplemented by learning from context. Direct vocabulary learning and incidental learning are complementary activities.

The low amount of learning from normal incidental guessing from context could be a benefit rather than a cause for concern. A single context generally provides an inadequate source of information about a word. It is particularly difficult to distinguish between core aspects of the meaning and those peculiar to the particular context. It may thus be good that learners do not quickly decide on a meaning and remember it well. Van Daalen-Kapteijns and Elshout-Mohr (1981) found that high ability students remained flexible in the meanings they attached to unfamiliar words so that they were ready to make later revisions if they proved necessary. The small, gradual increments of learning a word from context under normal conditions of incidental learning encourage a flexible approach to finally determining the meaning and make it unlikely that an initial, strong but wrong interpretation will be made and maintained.

It has been argued (Haastrup, 1989: 319–20) that words are likely to be remembered better if there was some difficulty in interpreting them. This hypothesis is based on studies by Jacoby et al. (1979) and Cairns et al. (1981) and which suggest that decision-making difficulty results in a more distinctive memory trace. Cairns et al. suggest that items met in highly predictable contexts may be easily processed but have low saliency in memory. This means that if learners read texts that they bring a lot of world knowledge to, they may be able to easily cope with unknown words but retain little memory for these words; that is, guessing will be easy but learning of vocabulary will be poor. If on the other hand learners have to rely heavily on linguistic bottom-up interpretation of the context and have to puzzle over the interpretation, guessing may be more laborious but learning of vocabulary may be greater. Research by Pulido (2003; 2007) with second language learners does not support this idea. Pulido (2009) found positive effects on guessing for L2 reading proficiency and background knowledge.

Fraser (1999) found more vocabulary was retained from inferring from context when:

- the inferring was followed up by consulting a dictionary (this almost doubled retention). Dictionary use makes an important contribution to vocabulary growth, and learners can benefit from training in dictionary use.
- first-language-based word identification was used, that is, learners retrieved an L1 synonym for the unknown word. Finding an L2 synonym was also effective but not as effective for retention as an L1 synonym, and creating a paraphrase for the meaning was the least effective for retention. This supports previous studies showing that a simple expression of word meaning is most effective for learning.
- learners remembered that they had seen the word before but they could not recall its meaning. This shows that vocabulary learning is best regarded as a cumulative process with subsequent meetings building on previous meetings, even though previous meetings only resulted in very small amounts of learning.

Fraser found a very wide range of individual differences in retention.

Paribakht (2005) found that words which had a clear L1 equivalent were easier to guess from context than L2 words which did not have a corresponding L1 word. Similarly, L2 words without a corresponding L1 word tended to be less well known. Examples of such words in English without corresponding Farsi words are *metropolitan, prognosis, intuitively, monogamy* and *clone*. Such words have to be expressed by phrases or definitions in Farsi.

What can be learned from context?

A critical factor in guessing from context is what is being learned. At the simplest level, the unknown word may represent a familiar concept and so the new label for that familiar concept is being learned. If the concept is an unfamiliar one, then both the concept and the label need to be learned. There is plenty of experimental evidence to show the difficulty in learning new concepts (Nagy et al., 1987). Although the word form and its meaning are among the most important things to know about a word, there are many other kinds of information that can be learned from context that are important in the receptive and productive use of the word. These are outlined in Chapter 2 and include the part of speech of the word, its collocates, the things it can refer to, and the various forms the word can take. These different kinds of information are all closely related to each other and come together to enrich a learner's knowledge of a word. The range of collocates that a word has helps specify its meaning. The grammatical patterns a word takes are closely related to its collocates. The affixes a word can take may affect its grammatical functions, its meaning and its range of collocates.

Fukkink et al. (2001) used measures for their experimental study of young L1 learners which considered the number of correct attributes of the word in the learners' guess, the presence of a false attribute and the degree of contextualisation of the guess. This rich analysis is an attempt to capture the incremental and multi-componential nature of the development of word knowledge.

Anderson and his colleagues (Anderson and Ortony, 1975; Halff et al., 1976; Anderson et al., 1978; Anderson and Shifrin, 1980) make the point that in language comprehension readers and listeners use their knowledge of the world and the analysis of the linguistic context to create particular instantiations of the words and phrases they comprehend. That is, they think of detailed particular instances guided by the words they read or hear and their knowledge of the world. So, when they see the sentence, *The golfer kicked the ball*, they think of a particular kind of ball, most likely a golf ball. When they see the sentence, *The baby kicked the ball*, their instantiation of *ball* will be different. The same applies to their instantiations of *kicked*. Word meanings are context sensitive.

The point of Anderson and his colleagues' investigations into instantiation is that knowing a fixed core meaning for a word is not sufficient for language use. People have a range of meaning representations for each word which they draw on with the help of context when they comprehend. Instantiation is usually necessary for full comprehension.

One very important value of context in learning vocabulary is that a variety of contexts will evoke a variety of enriching instantiations. Paired-associated learning is not likely to do this. Each paired-associate repetition is likely to strengthen but not enrich.

There is L1 experimental evidence to show that providing a sentence context, or several contexts, as well as a definition when learning words helps learning. Gipe and Arnold (1979) found contexts and definition to be superior to synonym or short definition, a classification task, or using the dictionary. Nist and Olejnik (1995) found that when learners saw the word in context and then looked at a definition, the context helped their performance on a multiple-choice test which required them to choose a correct example of use of the word.

An example of *aberration* would be:
a   having a glass of cold milk with freshly baked cookies
b   going to bed every night at exactly the same time
c   a 16-year-old who didn't want her own brand new car
d   an infant who woke up every four hours to eat

Prince (1996) looked at weak and advanced learners learning from context. The learning from context condition involved specially constructed sentences but did not provide an accompanying translation or definition; learners had to use the context to discover the meaning of the word. In the translation condition, learners saw an L1 word and its L2 translation. Learning was tested in two ways: by translation of isolated words and by filling a blank in a sentence. The sentences were not the same as those that acted as context during learning from context. Learning from translations resulted in higher scores than learning from context for both weak and advanced learners, and overall, learners found the translation test easier than the sentence completion test. Those in the advanced group who learned through context however did slightly better in the sentence completion test than in the translation test. Prince interprets this as indicating that this group were better able to transfer their knowledge to new applications. The weak group outperformed the advanced group where no transfer of learning was required, that is, where learning by translation was tested by translation.

Webb (2007; 2008) however found that having a context sentence during learning provided little if any advantage when many aspects of word knowledge were tested for each deliberately learned word. Learners were able to draw on analogy, world knowledge and commonsense when demonstrating their knowledge of the words.

What clues does a context provide and how effective are they?

The major motivation for analysing and classifying the various kinds of context clues is to provide a checklist for training learners in the skill in guessing from context. If teachers have a well-established list to work from, then they can be systematic and consistent in the way they draw learners' attention to clues and train them in recognising and using the clues. Furthermore, if the relative frequency and effectiveness of the various clues have been established, then it is possible to design a well-graded programme of work covering the range of clues.

Haastrup (1985; 1987; 1989) used think-aloud introspection and retrospection to study L2 learners' inferencing procedures to see what knowledge sources they used and how they combined knowledge from various sources. Haastrup classified the knowledge sources using Carton's (1971) three categories (which are not mutually exclusive):

- interlingual: cues based on L1, loan words in L1 or knowledge of other languages
- intralingual: cues based on knowledge of English
- contextual: cues based on the text or informants' knowledge of the world

The most careful and systematic attempt to come up with a system of clues for native speakers was carried out by Ames (1966). Ames used texts with every 50th word (provided the word was a content word) replaced by a nonsense word. Native speaking doctoral students introspected while they guessed each word. Ames's study has the strengths of systematically sampling content words and using several readers' performance. Its major weakness is that the majority of the words being guessed were already very well known to the students. That is, even though the words were replaced by nonsense words, they represented known concepts in familiar collocations. In spite of this weakness, this study provides a very useful survey of available clues.

Rankin and Overholser (1969) used Ames's (1966) classification system of contextual clues and devised test items to test the effectiveness of each type of clue. They found a wide range of effectiveness of the various clues but a highly consistent rank order of difficulty among grade levels and reading levels. Learners' reading ability was a good predictor of the ability to use each of the types of clues.

Care needs to be taken in using Ames's system as the names for some of the categories, for example 'language experience', and 'tone, setting, mood', do not clearly reflect the types of clues included. Ames provides plenty of examples in his article.

Table 8.1 (overleaf) lists Ames's categories with the rankings of effectiveness obtained by Rankin and Overholser (1969). There are other ways of classifying context clues. Sternberg and Powell (1983) use eight functional categories which describe the type of information conveyed rather than the devices used to convey the information. Sternberg and Powell's categories are temporal, spatial, stative

Table 8.1 Ames's (1966) categories of context clues with Rankin and Overholser's (1969) rankings of effectiveness in providing correct responses

Ames's category	Example	Number of items in Ames's study	% correct in Rankin and Overholser
Words in series	sonnets and *plays* of William Shakespeare	31	69
Modifying phrases	*slashed* her repeatedly with a knife	31	62
Familiar expressions	expectation was written all over their *faces*	26	61
Cause and effect	He reads not for fun but to make his conversation less *boring*.	10	59
Association	All the little boys wore short *pants*.	19	59
Referral clues	Sweden 15.3 etc. These *statistics* carry an unpleasant message.	13	55
Synonym clues	it provokes, and she *provokes* controversy	36	52
Definition or description	some looked alive, though no *blood* flowed beneath the skin	22	51
Preposition	He sped along a *freeway*.	20	50
Question and answer	Now, what about *writing* …?	9	43
Comparison or contrast	Will it be a blessing or a *bane*?	37	39
Main idea and detail	I soon found a *practical* use for it. I put orange juice inside it.	17	30
Non-restrictive clauses	24 hours – *hardly* a significant period of time	9	26

(physical properties), functional, value (worth or desirability), causal/enablement, class membership and equivalence. The italicised word is the word to be guessed, and which was replaced with a non-sense word in Ames's study.

Ames (1966) and Sternberg and Powell (1983) describe clues in the linguistic context of the unknown word. A variety of other factors can affect guessing from context. Artley (1943) includes typographical aids such as the use of italics, quotation marks or bolding; word elements such as the stems and affixes of words; and pictures and diagrams. Artley calls most of the kinds of clues described by Ames 'structural clues'.

In addition to these clues, there are what Jenkins and Dixon (1983) and others call 'mediating variables'. These mediate between the learners and the information in the text, strengthening or weakening the chances of guessing and learning from context. They include the following:

1. *Number of occurrences.* The more often an unknown word occurs the greater the chance of guessing and learning it (Horst et al., 1998; Stahl and Fairbanks, 1986).
2. *Proximity of recurrence.* The closer the repetitions the more likely will the clues from each occurrence be able to be integrated.
3. *Variability of contexts.* The more different the contexts in which a word recurs the greater the range of clues available.
4. *Presence of relevant clues.* Some contexts have useful clues, some do not.
5. *Proximity of relevant clues.* The nearer the clues are to the unknown word, the more likely they are to be used (Carnine et al., 1984).
6. *Number of relevant clues.* The more clues there are, the easier the guessing.
7. *Explicitness of relevant clues* (Carnine et al., 1984). A clearly signalled synonym within context helps learning.
8. *Density of unknown words.* If many unknown words are close to each other, the harder they will be to guess. Horst et al. (1998) found that successful guessing related to second language learners' vocabulary size. This is at least partly because the greater the learners' vocabulary size, the greater the number of known words in the surrounding context.
9. *Importance of the unknown word to understanding the text.* The more needed a word is, the more likely a learner will put effort into the guessing.

10. *Prior knowledge of the topic.* Real world knowledge can play a vital part in guessing. Learners who already have a topic-related script or schema can use this to help guessing.
11. *Familiarity of the concept.* If the concept is already known, guessing is easier (Nagy et al., 1987). If the concept is strange and unusual, guessing is difficult (Daneman and Green, 1986).
12. *Familiarity of the referents.* If the ideas in the clues are familiar to learners, guessing is easier (Jenkins and Dixon, 1983: 251–2).
13. *Concrete vs. abstract referents.* If the ideas in the clues are not abstract, then guessing is easier. Fukkink et al. (2001) found that unknown concrete words were easier for very young learners, but were equally difficult to abstract words for older learners.
14. *Amount of polysemy.* If the word is not polysemous, then guessing is easier (Saemen, 1970).

Studies of guessing from context have shown that there are high correlations between guessing skills and vocabulary knowledge, reading skill (Herman et al., 1987), reading comprehension and verbal IQ (Hafner, 1967). This suggests that an alternative to a direct focus on guessing skills would be a more general focus on improving reading skills. This more general focus is supported by the diversity of context clues that learners need to be able to draw on. There are so many clues that could be specifically taught and these appear in such a variety of forms that such a focus may be bewildering and demotivating. A more general reading skills focus may be more effective. However, if there are specific aspects to guessing that are not included in general reading proficiency, then a focus on guessing could be an effective way of getting competent readers to gain more vocabulary knowledge from context.

On evidence from the study of cloze tests (Chihara et al., 1977; Leys et al., 1983; Rye, 1985), it seems that most of the clues for guessing word meanings from context will come in the immediate context, that is, within the same sentence as the unknown word. Attempts to show that cloze items are affected by constraints across sentence boundaries have had mixed results (Rye, 1985). At most, it seems that context clues from other sentences are likely to account for much less than 10% of the available clues. Cziko (1978) suggests that sensitivity to discourse clues develops after sensitivity to syntactic clues in second language learners.

What are the causes of poor guessing?

Frantzen (2003) did a very interesting and detailed investigation of the causes of incorrect guessing. The amount of information available about a word in a particular context is clearly a factor affecting guessing.

Webb (2008) looked at learning words from three contexts for each word. The contexts were rated for the amount of information each provided about the unknown word. Learners were tested with four tests covering recognition/recall, and form/meaning. Predictably, there was more learning of both form and meaning from the more informative contexts. As is consistent with other studies, multiple-choice recognition tests gave higher scores than recall tests. The difference between more and less informative contexts on the form scores (both recall and recognition) were small and not statistically significant, although the small differences favoured informative contexts.

A major difficulty faced when guessing words from context is the form of the word to be guessed. Laufer and Sim (1985a), Bensoussan and Laufer (1984) and Nassaji (2003) found that second language learners made many responses based on known words that had some formal resemblance to the unknown word. Sometimes, these incorrect form-based guesses resulted in learners reshaping the grammatical context to fit their incorrect guess.

Laufer and Sim (1985a) looked at the errors that learners made in trying to interpret a difficult unsimplified text, and described the faulty approaches that learners took to interpreting the text. Step 1 was to interpret the meanings of the words, often relying on formal similarity to known words. Step 2 involved adding textual and extratextual knowledge. Step 3 involved imposing a sentence structure on the parts of the text to fit with the lexical clues and knowledge of the world gained from Steps 1 and 2. This approach resulted in considerable misinterpretation of the text. Laufer and Sim (1985a) argue that guessing from context should not be focused on until learners have a sufficiently large vocabulary to support such guessing.

Saemen (1970), in a study of young native speakers, found that uncommonly known meanings of polysemous words were harder to guess from context when the real word form was used compared with the use of a nonsense word – the known form led learners towards a known but inappropriate meaning. Fraser (1999: 239) suggests that although word form clues can be misleading, it may be impossible to train learners to hold off using such clues because they are accessed in a such a fast, automatic manner.

Marks et al. (1974) found that if young native speakers read a story containing familiar words and then read the same story again but this time with some unfamiliar words replacing some of the familiar words, they learned some of these unfamiliar words. The establishment of the familiar context on the first reading seemed to make it easier to learn the unfamiliar words on the later reading. This finding provides a degree of support for what some call 'diglot readers', where an L1 text gradually has its words replaced by L2 words until eventually it turns into an L2 text (Burling, 1968; 1983).

An important factor affecting guessing from context is the similarity between the learners' first and second languages. Palmberg (1988) found that young Swedish speakers were able to comprehend much of a specially prepared English text even though they knew almost no English. This can be a dangerous strategy, however, and in general it seems best to let context guide the guess rather than form.

Neuman and Koskinen (1992) looked at the effect of captioned television, television alone, simultaneous listening and reading, and reading alone on the learning of unknown vocabulary from context for ESL learners. They found the captioned television condition to be superior to the other conditions, and also evidence of a 'Matthew effect' (the rich get richer and the poor get poorer), in this case with learners of higher English proficiency learning more words.

Li (1988) compared second language learners' guessing from context in repeated contrived contexts through listening and reading, and found greater successful guessing from reading. Brown et al. (2008) found much less vocabulary learning on immediate post-tests from listening (multiple-choice 8.2 out of 28, translation 0.56) than from reading only (multiple-choice 12.54, translation 4.10) and reading while listening (13.31, 4.10).

The standard used to measure success at guessing is often too high and translation tests involving recall are among the toughest. When scoring recall tests credit is often not given for partial knowledge. Frantzen (2003), for example, sees *rope, something like a rope or chain, fastener* as incorrect guesses for *wire* in a context where the wire fastens the lid of the container. These guesses however show elements of meaning that make at least a small contribution to knowledge of *wire*.

Do different learners approach guessing in the same way?

We have looked at variables affecting guessing which are a result of the word itself and the context in which it appears. We have also looked at 'mediating' variables which are related to the context such as the number of times the word is repeated and distance between the clues and the word to be guessed. There are also variables that relate to the person doing the guessing. There is evidence that there are different ways of approaching the guessing task (van Daalen-Kapteijns and Elshout-Mohr, 1981) and different ability, knowledge and skills that learners bring to the guessing task.

There are several studies that examine second language learners' approaches to guessing from context (Arden-Close, 1993; Bensoussan and Laufer, 1984; Haastrup, 1989; Haynes and Baker, 1993; Homburg and Spaan, 1982; Huckin and Bloch, 1993; Laufer and Sim, 1985b; McKeown, 1985; Morrison, 1996; Nassaji, 2003; Parry, 1991; van Parreren and Schouten-van Parreren, 1981; Walker, 1983). In general, a good guesser uses a variety of clues, checks various types of clues against each other, does not let the form of the word play too large a part, and does not arrive at a guess prematurely. Proficiency in L2 is a major factor in successful guessing.

We need to be careful in interpreting the results of such studies because it is clear that the procedures used to investigate the guessing process influence what happens. At the very least, the investigative procedures of introspection or writing down the cues used substantially increase the amount of time that a reader would normally spend on guessing a word from context. In addition, the investigative procedures change it from being incidental learning to become an intentional, problem-solving activity, and often encourage definite guesses instead of allowing incremental learning. These studies show that there are substantial clues in the context that are available to the sensitive reader. The studies also show that not all readers can make good use of these clues.

Van Daalen-Kapteijns and Elshout-Mohr (1981) compared high verbal and low verbal native speakers' performance on a deliberately focused guessing-from-context task. High and low verbal learners were distinguished by measures that looked at quantity of word knowledge. High verbal learners tended to use an analytic strategy, choosing an initial model of the word meaning and transforming additional information to fill out and refine the initial model. The transforming (reshaping) part of the process was seen as being a critical feature of the analytic process. Low verbal learners also set up an initial model but tended to remember the various additional cues discovered from other contexts with little or no reworking or transformation of the initial model. Any final summing up of a definition then tended to rely on memory for the model and additional clues and required a weighing up of the various bits of information at that point.

Van Daalen-Kapteijns and Elshout-Mohr also found differences between high and low verbal learners in the quality of the form of the definition that they arrived at as a result of guessing. Low verbal learners tended to use a less standard form of definition compared to the succinct classic form of superordinate plus essential defining features. This same difference was also found when the high and low verbal learners were asked to define common words that were well known to them. The study shows that learners may approach guessing in different ways and this may result in qualitatively different outcomes. Although the study does not discuss this, it may be that there is a causative connection between the approach taken to guessing and vocabulary size.

Shefelbine (1990) found that native speakers with higher levels of general vocabulary were able to guess more words than learners with lower levels. This vocabulary size difference was both quantitative (lower vocabulary students knew fewer words) and qualitative (they knew some words less well than the higher vocabulary students). Lower vocabulary size means that (a) there are more words to guess; (b) there is less comprehensible context to support the guesses; and (c) learners bring less background knowledge to the texts they read.

Daneman and Green (1986) argue that learners' success in guessing from context will vary according to the size of their working memory. Working memory can be measured by getting learners to perform a reading span test. In this test learners are given increasingly longer sets of sentences to read aloud and at the end of each set they try to recall the last word of each sentence in the set. Their reading span is the maximum number of sentences they can read aloud while still being able to recall all of the last words in the sentences. The size of working memory and success in guessing from context are related because guessing from context involves integrating the information from successively met context clues (p. 8). If these clues are no longer available in memory then guessing will be poor. As well as finding a significant correlation (.69) between reading span and success at guessing from context, Daneman and Green found a significant correlation (.58) between skill at guessing and vocabulary knowledge. Sternberg and Powell (1983) found a similar correlation and argued that a vocabulary test measures past acquisition from context, while a learning-from-context task measures present acquisition.

Daneman and Green (1986) suggest that the capacity of working memory will vary according to how efficient a learner is in using the specific processes which are needed in the task they are working on. An optimistic view would be that training in these processes would increase the amount of information that could be held in working memory. Training in the processes needed for guessing from context could increase the space available in working memory for effective application of this skill.

Churchill (2007) has a fascinating account of how his knowledge of a particular Japanese word developed through the varied experiential context in which he met the word, highlighting the trial and error nature of such learning.

Arden-Close (1993) examined the guessing-from-context strategies of second language learners of different proficiency levels by getting learners to write their thoughts while they guessed. He found that even proficient learners were distracted by the form of the unknown words (*contamination = contain, spas = space*). Arden-Close used three kinds of texts – texts with words underlined, texts with words left out, and texts containing nonsense words. In both the underlined and nonsense word texts, the forms of the words tended to distract the learners. In the blank-filling texts, there was a higher success rate, presumably because only context and not word form clues could be used. Learners' guessing was limited by their knowledge of English but where they could bring background features to bear they could make good use of it and made more successful guesses. The lowest proficiency students often gave the meaning of neighbouring words as the guess for the unknown word. Arden-Close's analysis shows the complexity of the guessing skill and the close relationship it has with general language proficiency and reading proficiency. While training is likely to improve skill at guessing, it is unlikely to adequately compensate for low language proficiency.

Nassaji (2003) found that drawing on world knowledge and morphological knowledge had the highest degree of success and were the commonest sources used. While discourse knowledge was not commonly used, its success rate was relatively high. Nassaji's success rates, combining successful and partially successful, were around 50%. Nassaji (2004) also found a relationship between success at guessing and depth of vocabulary knowledge, thus underlining the importance of lexical knowledge in comprehension and related skills.

How can learners be trained to guess from context?

Meta-analyses of L1 studies in training in guessing from context have found that training results in better guessing (Fukkink and de Glopper, 1998; Kuhn and Stahl, 1998), although there was no clear consensus on what kind of training is the most effective.

Methods of training learners to guess can be classified into three major types (see Walters, 2004, for a very substantial critical review):

1. general strategy training, which can be as simple as a general principle such as look for clues, or as complicated as a series of steps as in Clarke and Nation (1980);
2. context clue instruction where learners are alerted to a range of useful context clues such as explicit textual definitions, synonyms, positives, and various other conjunction type relationships (Ames, 1966; Buikema and Graves, 1993); and
3. practice and feedback with cloze exercises.

Walters (2006) compared these three methods with second language learners using six hours of training for each method (three two-hour sessions). All three groups improved while the control group did not. The strategy group made the biggest increase, but the small number of subjects (around 12 in each group) and the very large standard deviations meant that the differences between the training groups were not significant. There were also increases in comprehension scores as a result of training in guessing. Clearly, training in guessing is worthwhile and deserves a reasonable investment of time and effort, not just a few sessions but small sustained attention to guessing (Hafner, 1965; Jenkins et al., 1989).

The most important ways in which teachers can help learners improve learning from context are:

1. by helping them find and choose reading and listening material of appropriate difficulty;
2. by encouraging them to read a lot and helping them gain a lot of comprehensible spoken input;
3. by improving their reading skills so that they read fluently and with good comprehension; and
4. by providing training in guessing from context, including training in a particular strategy which encompasses giving attention to various clues, and providing substantial focused guessing practice.

These ways are ranked in order of importance with the most important first. The reason for this ranking is that guessing from context seems to be a subskill of reading and seems to draw heavily on other reading skills. Good guessers are good readers (McKeown, 1985). The four ways described above can be more generally described as a matching of learner and text approach, a quantity approach, a general skill approach, and a particular skill approach. Nassaji (2006: 388) usefully sees lexical inferencing as a variety of more general inferencing, with the implication that isolating lexical inferencing from other language-related inferencing is to some degree misrepresenting what happens when learners read.

It may be that training in guessing helps vocabulary learning simply because it encourages learners to give deliberate thoughtful attention to vocabulary items – that is, it develops word consciousness (Scott and Nagy, 2004).

Does drawing attention to words help learning from context?

There is some evidence that a combination of attention-drawing activities, such as presenting words to learners before reading (Jenkins et al., 1984) and defining words as they occur in context (Elley, 1989) increases the amount of vocabulary learning. Swanborn and de Glopper

(1999), in a meta-analysis of 20 studies of learning from context, found that the nature of the vocabulary pre-test affected the amount of words learned. Laufer and Hill (2000) suggest that having words highlighted in their computerised text probably increased dictionary look-up and therefore learning. Drawing attention to words increases the chance of them being learned. It is important to distinguish between the effects of these kinds of activity on vocabulary learning and on comprehension of the text. Jenkins et al. (1984), studying young native speakers of English, found no direct effect of pre-teaching on comprehension, but there was a marked effect on the learning of the words from context.

Attention-drawing could be done in the following ways (several of these methods have been tested in experimental studies, but many have not):

1. Drawing attention to the word
   pre-testing
   pre-teaching
   seeing a list before reading
   highlighting (colour, bold, italics) in the text
   having a list while reading

2. Providing access to the meaning
   glossing
   teacher defining through pre-teaching
   teacher defining while listening to the text
   hypertext look-up
   dictionary look-up

3. Motivating attention to the word
   warning of a test
   providing follow-up exercises
   noting contexts while reading (e.g. filling in a notebook)

Do glossing and dictionary use help vocabulary learning?

There is now considerable evidence that when learners' attention is drawn towards unfamiliar words and there is a clear indication of their meaning, vocabulary learning is much greater than when learners read without deliberately focusing on new vocabulary.

Nist and Olejnik (1995) examined the procedure of meeting a word in context and then looking up its meaning in the dictionary. Four different kinds of tests were used to measure the learning of each word. They found that there was no interaction between the meeting in context and the looking up of the word, and that the quality of the dictionary definition determined the quality of learning. Nist and Olejnik argue that dictionaries can be substantial contributors to the process of vocabulary learning. Hulstijn's (1993) study of inferencing and dictionary look-up behaviour found that learners who were good at inferring preferred to confirm their guesses by consulting a dictionary. Learners differed greatly in their skill at inferring. There was a modest correlation (.50) between inferring ability and overall vocabulary size.

Watanabe (1997) compared three forms of vocabulary glossing in texts on second language learners' vocabulary learning. The three forms of glossing were: (1) inserting a brief explanation of the word in the text immediately after the word (Bramki and Williams, 1984, call this 'lexical familiarization'); (2) glossing the word in the margin '[crib = baby's bed]'; and (3) providing two-choice glosses in the margin. Hulstijn (1992) has suggested that multiple-choice glosses supplement contextual information, encourage mental effort by having to choose, and avoid incorrect inferences by providing a meaning. Glossing appeared to improve comprehension. The two conditions involving glosses in the margin of the text resulted in higher scores in the immediate and delayed post-tests compared to providing the meaning in the text and having no glosses or meaning provided in the text. Learning from the single-gloss treatment was higher than the multiple-choice gloss treatment in all post-tests but not significantly so. The slightly lower scores for multiple choice may have come from learners making the wrong choice. Glossing almost doubled the learning (17 words) compared to learning from the text with no glosses or lexical familiarisation (10 words).

Mondria and Wit-de Boer (1991) used specially constructed, isolated sentences to investigate second language learners' learning from context. The experience involved three stages: (1) a guessing stage where the context sentences were shown and learners guessed the translation of the target words; (2) a learning stage where learners saw the correct translations of the target words and had to learn them; and (3) a testing stage where learners saw the words in new non-informative contexts and had to translate them. It seems that the testing stage immediately followed the learning stage. Mondria and Wit-de Boer found no relationship between success at guessing and retention. It is likely that the learning stage overwhelmed the effects of guessing.

What formats should be used for testing or practising guessing?

Researchers have used a variety of formats for testing or practising guessing. These range from fixed deletion cloze procedure where the missing item is a blank, to unaltered texts where learners guess words with the real word form present.

There are several factors that need to be considered when deciding on a format for guessing:

The effect of the word form. Several studies (Bensoussan and Laufer, 1984; Laufer and Sim, 1985a; Nassaji, 2003) have shown that learners are often influenced by the actual form of the word. If the word resembles a known word, the form may lead them to a wrong guess. If the form contains familiar parts, then these may be used to guide the guess. One of the most difficult things to learn when becoming proficient at guessing is to let the context rather than the form guide the guess. Formats which use a blank remove this distraction. This may be useful at the early stages of developing a guessing strategy but it is important at some stage that learners get practice in suspending form-based guesses while they use the context to guess. When learners' guessing skill is tested, it is useful to see if they have control of this aspect of the strategy. It may also be useful to see if learners can deal with homographs when a different member is known.

Previous knowledge of the word to be guessed. When testing the guessing skill, it is necessary to be sure that learners do not already know the word that is to be guessed. One way of solving this problem is to replace the words to be guessed with nonsense words. This then means that any answer is truly a guess. Leaving blanks also achieves this purpose. However, there are several context clues that are available for known words that are not available for unknown words. These clues make guessing easier and not representative of guessing truly unknown words. For example, there are Ames's (1966) clues of familiar expressions (collocations), as in: *Who spends one evening a week* thacing *the fat with the boys?* Because the collocation is known, the word is easily guessed, but if *chewing the fat* was not known before, then it would not be guessable.

There are thus two kinds of previous knowledge to consider: the knowledge of the form itself, and the collocational, grammatical knowledge. Using nonsense words deals with the problem of knowledge of the form but it does not deal with the other kinds of knowledge. The validity of Ames's study is thus severely compromised by not taking account of this kind of knowledge. Nation and Webb (2011: 265–268) look more closely at the use of nonsense words in research.

The density of unknown words and the size of the context. An important factor affecting success at guessing is the ratio of known words to unknown words. Liu and Nation (1985) suggest that a ratio of one unknown to 24 known words is needed for successful guessing. That is, at least 95% of the words in the text must be familiar to the reader. If the density of unknown words is too great then learners do not have a chance to show their guessing skill.

Guessing could be tested or practised with isolated sentences or with continuous text. As we have seen, it seems that only a small proportion of the clues needed for guessing occur outside the sentence containing the unknown word. It thus may be acceptable for practicality reasons to practise or test some guessing in isolated sentences. However, at some stage in a learner's development of the guessing strategy it is important that the few clues from the wider context are given attention.

The types of words that are guessed. Words that represent unfamiliar concepts are more difficult to guess than words that represent known concepts (Nagy et al., 1987). It is likely, especially for second language learners, that the majority of words to be guessed represent known concepts. However, some, especially technical words, will also require learners to develop new concepts. Second language learners in their later meetings with words in context will also need to see distinctions between the L2 word and the nearest L1 equivalent. When testing the guessing skill it is thus important to see if learners are able to deal with unfamiliar concepts.

The different parts of speech are not equally represented at the various frequency levels. There tend to be more nouns among the lower frequency words, for example. If a true measure of the learners' guessing skill is needed, it is important that the kinds of words to be guessed represent the kinds of words that a learner with a given vocabulary size would need to guess. A strength of Ames's (1966) study was that he tried to get a representative sample of words to guess by using a cloze procedure. Unfortunately he did not take the vocabulary size of his learners into account and so did not restrict his sample to words outside their level of vocabulary knowledge.

It should be clear from the discussion of these four factors affecting guessing from context that the validity of a practice or testing format for guessing from context would be enhanced if: (a) the actual word form appeared in the context; (b) learners did not already know the word; (c) there was a low density of unknown words; (d) the unknown words were in a continuous text; and (e) the unknown words were typical of those a learner of that vocabulary size would meet. This is the ideal and for a variety of reasons, many of them related to pedagogical, reliability and practicality issues, other formats have been used. Table 8.2 lists the possibilities.

When practising and testing guessing from context it may be effective to draw on a variety of formats to focus attention on particular aspects of the guessing skill.

Table 8.2 *Features of formats for*
testing or practising guessing

1. Word form
   a. a blank space instead of the word
   b. a nonsense word
   c. a real word
2. Selection of words and contexts
   a. real randomly sampled contexts
   b. real selected contexts
   c. contrived contexts
3. Size and relationship of contexts
   a. isolated sentence contexts
   b. isolated paragraph contexts
   c. continuous text contexts

Dunmore (1989) reviewed exercise types in five different coursebooks for practising guessing from context and found four major exercise types:

- matching a given synonym with a word in the text;
- filling a blank with a suitable word;
- providing words before reading and then seeing if the learner can use context to find the meanings of the words; and
- developing awareness of text features that could help guessing.

Dunmore is critical of the various exercise types because they tend to test rather than train guessing, and encourage a belief that synonyms are sufficient to express the meanings of unknown words. This last criticism may be a little harsh as finding a first language translation or a second language synonym may be a reasonable first approximation of the meaning of a word.

What are the steps in the guessing-from-context strategy?

There is no one procedure for guessing from context, but most procedures draw on the same kinds of clues. Some procedures work towards the guess in an inductive approach. Others work out deductively from the guess, justifying the guess. A deductive approach is more suited to younger learners who will be less analytical in their approach and to advanced learners who are familiar with the various clues and wish to concentrate on developing fluency in guessing. An inductive approach, such as that described by Clarke and Nation (1980) is useful for making learners aware of the range of clues available and for developing the subskills that may be needed to make use of the clues. The aim of all guessing procedures is to help learners become fluent and skillful at guessing from context so that the guessing does not interrupt the normal flow of reading too much.

Let us look first at Clarke and Nation's (1980) five-step procedure. Further discussion of it can be found in (Nation, 1990) and Nation and Coady (1988).

Step 1.   Decide on the part of speech of the unknown word.
Step 2.   Look at the immediate context of the word, simplifying it grammatically if necessary.
Step 3.   Look at the wider context of the word, that is, the relationship with adjoining sentences or clauses.
Step 4.   Guess.
Step 5.   Check the guess.
             Is the guess the same part of speech as the unknown word?
             Substitute the guess for the unknown word. Does it fit comfortably into the context?
             Break the unknown word into parts. Does the meaning of the parts support the guess?
             Look up the word in the dictionary.

This procedure is strongly based on language clues and does not draw on background content knowledge. Linguistic clues will be present in every context, background clues will not. This procedure aims at being as generalisable as possible.

The procedure moves from a narrow focus on the word in Step 1 to a broader view in Step 3. Van Parreren and Schouten-van Parreren (1981) suggest that there are various levels of information with the grammar level being lower than the meaning level. The higher meaning level can only be used if the lower grammar level does not cause problems. Making a guess involves choosing the appropriate level at which to seek information and moving to another level if this proves to be the wrong one (p. 240).

Step 1 in Clarke and Nation's procedure encourages the learner to focus on the unknown word and ensures that the right word is focused on. Note that word-part analysis does *not* occur at this step. Arriving at a correct guess from word-part analysis is less sure than using context clues. Getting learners to delay using word-part clues is the most difficult thing to learn when developing skills in guessing from context.

Step 2 looks at the immediate context, that is, the clause containing the unknown word. This source of information will contain most of

the clues needed to guess most words correctly. Sometimes the immediate context is difficult to interpret because it is in the form of a
passive with a missing agent, because the subject and verb are separated by a relative clause or through nominalisation, or pronouns are
present which need to be interpreted. Learners can practise clarifying
the immediate context by unpacking nominalisations, turning the
passive construction into an active one, and by interpreting reference
words. There is an exercise called 'What does what?' which gives this
practice. Here is an example of the exercise applied to a text. The exercise is very easy to prepare.

The teacher chooses an appropriate text, preferably with line
numbers. The teacher then writes the line number and word and learners have to ask 'What does what?' about the word. In the example
below, the 'What does what?' questions have been added to clarify the
procedure. Usually learners will have to make the questions themselves. More information on 'What does what?' can be found in
Nation (1979; 2009: 39–43).

We live in a style that most of our grandparents could not even have *imag-
ined*. Medicine has cured diseases that *terrified* them. Most of us live in
better and more spacious homes. We eat more, we grow taller, we are even
born larger than they were. Our parents are amazed at the matter-of-fact
way we handle computers. We casually use *products* – microwave ovens,
graphite tennis rackets, digital watches – that did not *exist* in their youth.
Economic growth has made us richer than our parents and grandparents.
But economic *growth* and technical change, and the wealth they *bestow*,
have not *liberated* us from scarcity. Why not? Why, despite our immense
wealth, do we still have to face costs? (Parkin, 1990: Chapter 3)

Who imagines what?
What terrifies who?
Who produces what?
What did not exist?
What grows?
What bestows what?
What liberates who?

Step 3 involves looking at the wider context. A conjunction relationship activity can be used to practise this part of the procedure. In this
activity, the learners have to see what joining word can be put between
the clause containing the unknown word and the adjoining clauses.
Sometimes the relationship will already be marked by a conjunction,
adverbial or some other sign of the relationship, but these will still
have to be interpreted. Learners can be helped with this by having a list
of prototypical conjunction relationship markers like those in the left-
hand column of Table 8.3 (overleaf). The learners may need to become

Table 8.3 *Conjunction relationships and their meaning*

Relationship and prototypical marker	Other markers	The meaning of the relationship between the clauses
Inclusion *and*	*furthermore, also, in addition, similarly …*	The classes joined together are in a list and share similar information.
Contrast *but*	*however, although, nevertheless, yet …*	The clauses are in contrast to each other. One may be negative and the other positive. They may contain opposing information.
Time sequence *then*	*next, after, before, when, first …*	The clauses are steps in a sequence of events. They might not be in the order in which they happened.
Cause–effect *because*	*thus, so, since, as a result, so that, in order to, if …*	One clause is the cause and the other is the effect.
Exemplification and amplification *for example*	*e.g., such as, for instance …*	The following clause is an example of the preceding more general statement, or the following clauses describe the general statement in more detail.
Alternative *or*	*nor, alternatively …*	The clauses are choices and they will share similar information.
Restatement *in other words*	*that is (to say), namely …*	The following clause has the same meaning as the preceding clause.
Summary *in short*	*to sum up, in a word …*	The following clause summarises what has gone before.
Exclusion *instead*	*rather than, on the contrary …*	The following clause excludes what has just been said. That is, it has the opposite meaning.

familiar with the kinds of information that each of these markers provides, which is outlined in the right-hand column of the table, and they need to know the range of words that signal these relationships (see Nation, 1979; 1984; 1990: Appendix 6; and Halliday and Hasan, 1976, for further information on conjunction relationships).

Learners can practise this step by interpreting the relationship between pairs of sentences in a text. This is usefully done by learners working in pairs or small groups initially.

Step 4 is the guess – the moment of truth. When this is done as a class activity, the teacher can award percentage points for the guesses with 100% (or 110%) for a fully correct guess, 90% for a very good guess, 80% for a guess that comes close to the meaning, and so on. This is not the last step.

Step 5 involves checking the guess to see if it is on the right track. Comparing the part of speech of the guess with the part of speech decided on at Step 1 makes sure that the learner is focusing on the unknown word. Sometimes incorrect guesses are simply the meaning of an adjoining word. The second way of checking, substitution, makes sure that the context has been considered, because the word will not fit if it has not been considered. The third way of checking involves word part analysis. We will look at this in detail in Chapter 9. It comes at this stage to make sure that the learner does not twist the interpretation of the context on the basis of what the word looks like. Laufer's (1988) and Laufer-Dvorkin's (1991) study of synforms shows that this is a very common problem. The learner analyses the word parts and sees if the meaning of the parts relates to the guess. If they do, the learner can feel happy. Looking up the word in a dictionary is the last way of checking. It should be easy to choose the appropriate meaning from the dictionary if several meanings are listed there, because the guess will have given a good indication of which one to choose.

The deductive procedure (see, for example, Bruton and Samuda, 1981), involves the following steps:

Step 1. Guess the meaning of the word.
Step 2. Justify the guess using a variety of clues.
Step 3. Readjust the guess if necessary.

The advantage of this procedure is that it places the guess at the forefront of the activity and allows for intuition to play a part. It also works well as a group and class activity. Whichever approach learners tend to favour, they need not follow a rigid procedure when guessing but they should be aware of the range of possible clues and should have the skills to draw on them.

How should we plan the training of learners in the strategy of guessing from context?

Guessing from context is a complex activity drawing on a range of skills and types of knowledge. It is worth bearing in mind that it is a subskill of reading and listening and depends heavily on learners' ability to read and listen with a good level of proficiency. Learning a complex guessing strategy will not adequately compensate for poor reading or listening skills and low proficiency. Developing these reading and listening skills is the first priority.

When learners are given training in guessing from context, they should work with texts where at least 95% of the running words are familiar to them. This will allow them to have access to the clues that are there. In addition, the words chosen for guessing should be able to be guessed. Not all words have enough clues; adjectives are usually difficult to guess because they enter into few relationships with other words, while nouns and verbs are usually easier.

Training in guessing should be given plenty of time. In a pre-university course, it could be practised three or four times a week for about ten minutes each time for at least six weeks, and preferably longer. The aim of the practice is to get learners guessing quickly without having to deliberately go through all the steps. Fraser (1999) found that making learners familiar with the strategies of 'ignore, consult (a dictionary) and infer', involving about eight hours of instruction, resulted in a decrease in the amount of ignoring and an increase in the amount of inferring. The success rates were over 70% for consulting a dictionary and inferring from context if partially correct inferences were included. A further eight hours of instruction on linguistic context clues may have helped maintain the success rate of inferring, especially for inferring where learners created a paraphrase for the meaning of the unknown word.

Involving the class working together with the teacher, in groups, pairs and then individually, training can focus on the subskills: determining part of speech; doing 'What does what?'; interpreting conjunction relationships; and doing word part analysis. Training should also involve going through all the steps, gradually getting faster and faster. The teacher can model the procedure first, gradually handing over control to the learners. Learners can report on guessing that they did in their outside reading and listening and others can comment on their attempts. There can be regular guessing from context tests using isolated sentences and corrected texts. Learner improvement on these tests can be recorded as a means of increasing motivation.

Teachers should be able to justify the time and effort spent on the guessing strategy to themselves, their learners and other teachers. These justifications could include:

- the value of the strategy for high-frequency, mid-frequency and low-frequency words;
- the fact that the strategy accounts for most vocabulary learning by native speakers;
- the enormous number of words that can be dealt with and perhaps learned through this strategy;
- the effectiveness of the strategy;
- the benefits of the strategy in contributing to reading and listening comprehension;
- the fact that learners differ widely in their control of this skill, and training can narrow these differences; and
- the need for this skill in dictionary use.

Teachers should also be able to look critically at the various activities suggested for improving guessing (Dunmore, 1989; Honeyfield, 1977; Walters, 2004). Yosuke Sasao (http://ysasaojp.info) has developed a test of the guessing skill that can be used diagnostically and to measure improvement in guessing.

In any list of vocabulary-learning strategies, guessing from context would have to come at the top of the list. Although it has the disadvantages of being a form of incidental learning (and therefore less certain) and of not always being successful (because of lack of clues), it is still the most important way that language users can increase their vocabulary. It deserves teaching time and learning time. A well-planned vocabulary development programme gives spaced, repeated attention to this most important strategy.

In the following chapters we will look at the strategies of using word parts, using dictionaries and using word cards.

References

Ames, W. S. (1966). The development of a classification scheme of contextual aids. *Reading Research Quarterly*, 2, 1, 57–82.

Anderson, R. C. and Ortony, A. (1975). On putting apples into bottles: A problem of polysemy. *Cognitive Psychology*, 7, 167–80.

Anderson, R. C. and Shifrin, Z. (1980). The meaning of words in context. In Spiro, R. J., Bruce, B. C. and Brewer, W. F. (eds.), *Theoretical Issues in Reading Comprehension* (pp. 330–48). Mahwah, NJ: Lawrence Erlbaum Associates.

Anderson, R. C., Stevens, K. C., Shifrin, Z. and Osborn, J. (1978). Instantiation of word meanings in children. *Journal of Reading Behavior*, 10, 2, 149–57.

Arden-Close, C. (1993). NNS readers' strategies for inferring the meanings of unknown words. *Reading in a Foreign Language*, 9, 2, 867–93.

Artley, A. S. (1943). Teaching word-meaning through context. *Elementary English Review*, 20, 1, 68–74.

Beck, I. L., McKeown, M. G. and McCaslin, E. S. (1983). Vocabulary: All contexts are not created equal. *Elementary School Journal*, 83, 3, 177–81.

Bensoussan, M. and Laufer, B. (1984). Lexical guessing in context in EFL reading comprehension. *Journal of Research in Reading*, 7, 1, 15–32.

Bramki, D. and Williams, R. C. (1984). Lexical familiarization in economics text, and its pedagogic implications in reading comprehension. *Reading in a Foreign Language*, 2, 1, 169–81.

Brown, R., Waring, R. and Donkaewbua, S. (2008). Incidental vocabulary acquisition from reading, reading-while-listening, and listening to stories. *Reading in a Foreign Language*, 20, 2, 136–63.

Bruton, A. and Samuda, V. (1981). Guessing words. *Modern English Teacher*, 8, 3, 18–21.

Buikema, J. L. and Graves, M. F. (1993). Teaching students to use context cues to infer word meanings. *Journal of Reading*, 36, 6, 450–57.

Burling, R. (1968). Some outlandish proposals for the teaching of foreign languages. *Language Learning*, 18, 1, 61–75.

Burling, R. (1983). A proposal for computer-assisted instruction in vocabulary. *System*, 11, 2, 181–70.

Cairns, H. S., Cowart, W. and Jablon, A. D. (1981). Effects of prior context upon the integration of lexical information during sentence processing. *Journal of Verbal Learning and Verbal Behavior*, 20, 445–53.

Carnine, D., Kameenui, E. J. and Coyle, G. (1984). Utilization of contextual information in determining the meaning of unfamiliar words. *Reading Research Quarterly*, 19, 2, 188–204.

Carton, A. S. (1971). Inferencing: a process in using and learning language. In Pimsleur, P. and Quinn, T. (eds.), *The Psychology of Second Language Learning* (pp. 45–58). Cambridge: Cambridge University Press.

Chihara, T., Oller, J., Weaver, K. and Chavez-Oller, M. A. (1977). Are cloze items sensitive to discourse constraints? *Language Learning*, 27, 63–73.

Churchill, E. (2007). A dynamic systems account of learning a word: From ecology to form relations. *Applied Linguistics*, 29, 3, 339–58.

Clarke, D. F. and Nation, I. S. P. (1980). Guessing the meanings of words from context: Strategy and techniques. *System*, 8, 3, 211–20.

Cook, J. M., Heim, A. W. and Watts, K. P. (1963). The word-in-context: A new type of verbal reasoning test. *British Journal of Psychology*, 54, 3, 227–37.

Cziko, G. A. (1978). Differences in first- and second-language reading: The use of syntactic, semantic and discourse constraints. *Canadian Modern Language Review*, 34, 473–89.

Daneman, M. and Green, I. (1986). Individual differences in comprehending and producing words in context. *Journal of Memory and Language*, 25, 1–18.

Day, R. R., Omura, C. and Hiramatsu, M. (1991). Incidental EFL vocabulary learning and reading. *Reading in a Foreign Language*, 7, 2, 541–51.

de Bot, K. and Stoessel, S. (2000). In search of yesterday's words: Reactivating a long-forgotten language. *Applied Linguistics*, 21, 3, 333–53.

Dunmore, D. (1989). Using contextual clues to infer word meaning: an evaluation of current exercise types. *Reading in a Foreign Language*, 6, 1, 337–47.

Dupuy, B. and Krashen, S. D. (1993). Incidental vocabulary acquisition in French as a foreign language. *Applied Language Learning*, 4, 1&2, 55–63.

Elley, W. B. (1989). Vocabulary acquisition from listening to stories. *Reading Research Quarterly*, 24, 2, 174–87.

Frantzen, D. (2003). Factors affecting how second language Spanish students derive meaning from context. *Modern Language Journal*, 87, 168–99.

Fraser, C. A. (1999). Lexical processing strategy use and vocabulary learning through reading. *Studies in Second Language Acquisition*, 21, 225–41.

Fukkink, R., Blok, H. and de Glopper, K. (2001). Deriving word meaning from written context: A multicomponential skill. *Language Learning*, 51, 3, 477–96.

Fukkink, R. G. and de Glopper, K. (1998). Effects of instruction in deriving word meaning from context: A meta-analysis. *Review of Educational Research*, 68, 4, 450–69.

Gibbons, H. (1940). The ability of college freshmen to construct the meaning of a strange word from the context in which it appears. *Journal of Experimental Education*, 9, 1, 29–33.

Gipe, J. P. and Arnold, R. D. (1979). Teaching vocabulary through familiar associations and contexts. *Journal of Reading Behavior*, 11, 3, 282–5.

Haastrup, K. (1985). Lexical inferencing: A study of procedures in reception. *Scandinavian Working Papers on Bilingualism*, 5, 63–87.

Haastrup, K. (1987). Using thinking aloud and retrospection to uncover learners' lexical inferencing procedures. In Faerch, C. and Kasper, G. (eds.), *Introspection in Second Language Research* (pp. 197–212). Clevedon: Multilingual Matters.

Haastrup, K. (1989). *Lexical Inferencing Procedures*, vols 1 & 2. Copenhagen: Handelshojskolen i Kobenhavn.

Hafner, L. E. (1965). A one-month experiment in teaching context aids in fifth grade. *Journal of Educational Research*, 58, 10, 472–4.

Hafner, L. E. (1967). Using context to determine meanings in high school and college. *Journal of Reading*, 10, 7, 491–8.

Halff, H. M., Ortony, A. and Anderson, R. C. (1976). A context-sensitive representation of word meanings. *Memory and Cognition*, 4, 4, 378–83.

Halliday, M. A. K. and Hasan, R. (1976). *Cohesion in English*. London: Longman.

Hansen, L., Umeda, Y. and McKinney, M. (2002). Savings in the relearning of second language vocabulary: The effects of time and proficiency. *Language Learning*, 52, 4, 653–78.

Haynes, M. and Baker, I. (1993). American and Chinese readers learning from lexical familiarization in English text. In Huckin, T., Haynes, M. and Coady, J. (eds.), *Second Language Reading and Vocabulary* (pp. 130–52). Norwood, NJ: Ablex.

Herman, P., Anderson, R. C., Pearson, P. D. and Nagy, W. E. (1987). Incidental acquisition of word meaning from expositions with varied text features. *Reading Research Quarterly*, 22, 3, 263–84.

Homburg, T. J. and Spaan, M. C. (1982). ESL reading proficiency assessment: Testing strategies. In Hines, M. and Rutherford, W. (eds.), *On TESOL '81* (pp. 25–33). Washington: TESOL.

Honeyfield, J. (1977). Word frequency and the importance of context in vocabulary learning. *RELC Journal*, 8, 2, 35–42.

Horst, M., Cobb, T. and Meara, P. (1998). Beyond a Clockwork Orange: Acquiring second language vocabulary through reading. *Reading in a Foreign Language*, 11, 2, 207–23.

Huckin, T. and Bloch, J. (1993). Strategies for inferring word meanings: A cognitive model. In Huckin, T., Haynes, M. and Coady, J. (eds.), *Second Language Reading and Vocabulary* (pp. 153–78). Norwood, NJ: Ablex.

Hulstijn, J. (2003). Incidental and intentional learning. In Doughty, C. and Long, M. (eds.), *Handbook of Second Language Acquisition* (pp. 349–81). Oxford: Blackwell.

Hulstijn, J. H. (1992). Retention of inferred and given word meanings: Experiments in incidental vocabulary learning. In Arnaud, P. J. L. and Bejoint, H. (eds.), *Vocabulary and Applied Linguistics* (pp. 113–25). London: Macmillan.

Hulstijn, J. H. (1993). When do foreign-language readers look up the meaning of unfamiliar words? The influence of task and learner variables. *Modern Language Journal*, 77, 2, 139–47.

Jacoby, L. L., Craik, F. J. M. and Begg, J. (1979). Effects of decision difficulty on recognition and recall. *Journal of Verbal Learning and Verbal Behavior*, 18, 585–600.

Jenkins, J. R. and Dixon, R. (1983). Vocabulary learning. *Contemporary Educational Psychology*, 8, 237–60.

Jenkins, J. R., Matlock, B. and Slocum, T. A. (1989). Two approaches to vocabulary instruction: The teaching of individual word meanings and practice in deriving word meanings from context. *Reading Research Quarterly*, 24, 2, 215–35.

Jenkins, J. R., Stein, M. L. and Wysocki, K. (1984). Learning vocabulary through reading. *American Educational Research Journal*, 21, 4, 767–87.

Kelly, P. (1990). Guessing: no substitute for systematic learning of lexis. *System*, 18, 2, 199–208.

Kennedy, G. (1987). Expressing temporal frequency in academic English. *TESOL Quarterly*, 21, 1, 69–86.

Knight, S. M. (1994). Dictionary use while reading: The effects on comprehension and vocabulary acquisition for students of different verbal abilities. *Modern Language Journal*, 78, 3, 285–99.

Kuhn, M. R. and Stahl, S. A. (1998). Teaching children to learn word meanings from context. *Journal of Literacy Research*, 30, 1, 119–38.

Laufer, B. (1988). The concept of 'synforms' (similar lexical forms) in vocabulary acquisition. *Language and Education*, 2, 2, 113–32.

Laufer, B. and Hill, M. (2000). What lexical information do L2 learners select in a CALL dictionary and how does it affect word retention? *Language Learning &Technology*, 3, 2, 58–76.

Laufer, B. and Sim, D. D. (1985a). Taking the easy way out: non-use and misuse of clues in EFL reading. *English Teaching Forum*, 23, 2, 7–10, 20.

Laufer, B. and Sim, D. D. (1985b). Measuring and explaining the reading threshold needed for English for academic purposes texts. *Foreign Language Annals*, **18**, 5, 405–11.

Laufer-Dvorkin, B. (1991). *Similar Lexical Forms in Interlanguage*. Tübingen: Gunter Narr Verlag.

Leys, M., Fielding, L., Herman, P. and Pearson, P. D. (1983). Does cloze measure intersentence comprehension? A modified replication of Shanahan, Kamil, and Tobin. In Niles, J. A. and Harris, L. A. (eds.), *New Enquiries in Reading* (pp. 111–14). Rochester, NY: National Reading Conference.

Li, X. (1988). Effects of contextual cues on inferring and remembering meanings. *Applied Linguistics*, **9**, 4, 402–13.

Liu, N. and Nation, I. S. P. (1985). Factors affecting guessing vocabulary in context. *RELC Journal*, **16**, 1, 33–42.

Marks, C. B., Doctorow, M. J. and Wittrock, M. C. (1974). Word frequency and reading comprehension. *Journal of Educational Research*, **67**, 259–62.

McKeown, M. G. (1985). The acquisition of word meaning from context by children of high and low ability. *Reading Research Quarterly*, **20**, 4, 482–96.

Mondria, J. A. (2003). The effects of inferring, verifying and memorising on the retention of L2 word meanings. *Studies in Second Language Acquisition*, **25**, 4, 473–99.

Mondria, J. A. and Wit-de Boer, M. (1991). The effects of contextual richness on the guessability and the retention of words in a foreign language. *Applied Linguistics*, **12**, 3, 249–67.

Morrison, L. (1996). Talking about words: A study of French as a second language learners' lexical inferencing procedures. *Canadian Modern Language Journal*, **53**, 1, 41–75.

Nagy, W. E. (1997). On the role of context in first- and second-language learning. In Schmitt, N. and McCarthy, M. (eds.), *Vocabulary: Description, Acquisition and Pedagogy* (pp. 64–83). Cambridge: Cambridge University Press.

Nagy, W. E., Anderson, R. C. and Herman, P. A. (1987). Learning word meanings from context during normal reading. *American Educational Research Journal*, **24**, 2, 237–70.

Nagy, W. E., Herman, P. and Anderson, R. C. (1985). Learning words from context. *Reading Research Quarterly*, **20**, 2, 233–53.

Nassaji, H. (2003). L2 vocabulary learning from context: Strategies, knowledge sources, and their relationship with success in L2 lexical inferencing. *TESOL Quarterly*, **37**, 4, 645–70.

Nassaji, H. (2006). The relationship between depth of vocabulary knowledge and L2 learners' lexical inferencing strategy use and success. *Canadian Modern Language Review*, **90**, 3, 387–401.

Nation, I. S. P. (1979). The curse of the comprehension question: Some alternatives. *Guidelines: RELC Journal Supplement*, **2**, 85–103.

Nation, I. S. P. (1984). Understanding paragraphs. *Language Learning and Communication*, **3**, 1, 61–8.

Nation, I. S. P. (1990). *Teaching and Learning Vocabulary*. Rowley, MA: Newbury House.

Nation, I. S. P. (2009). *Teaching ESL/EFL Reading and Writing*. New York: Routledge.

Nation, I. S. P. and Coady, J. (1988). Vocabulary and reading. In Carter, R. and McCarthy, M. (eds.), *Vocabulary and Language Teaching* (pp. 97–110). London: Longman.

Nation, I. S. P. and Webb, S. (2011). *Researching and Analyzing Vocabulary*. Boston: Heinle Cengage Learning.

Nation, P. and Wang, K. (1999). Graded readers and vocabulary. *Reading in a Foreign Language*, 12, 2, 355–80.

Neuman, S. B. and Koskinen, P. (1992). Captioned television as comprehensible input: Effects of incidental word learning from context for language minority students. *Reading Research Quarterly*, 27, 1, 95–106.

Nist, S. L. and Olejnik, S. (1995). The role of context and dictionary definitions on varying levels of word knowledge. *Reading Research Quarterly*, 30, 2, 172–93.

Palmberg, R. (1988). On lexical inferencing and language distance. *Journal of Pragmatics*, 12, 207–14.

Paribakht, S. (2005). The influence of first language lexicalization on second language lexical inferencing: A study of Farsi-speaking learners of English as a foreign language. *Language Learning*, 55, 4, 701–48.

Parkin, M. (1990). *Macroeconomics*. Boston, MA: Addison-Wesley.

Parry, K. (1991). Building a vocabulary through academic reading. *TESOL Quarterly*, 25, 4, 629–53.

Perfetti, C. (2010). Decoding, vocabulary, and comprehension. In McKeown, M. G. and Kucan, L. (eds.), *Bringing Reading Research to Life* (pp. 291–303). New York: Guilford Press.

Perfetti, C. and Hart, L. (2001). The lexical basis of comprehension skill. In Gorfien, D. S. (ed.), *On the Consequences of Meaning Selection: Perspectives on Resolving Lexical Ambiguity* (pp. 67–86). Washington, D.C.: American Psychological Association.

Perfetti, C. A. and Hart, L. (2002). The lexical quality hypothesis. In Verhoeven, L., Elbro, C. and Reitsma, P. (eds.), *Precursors of Functional Literacy* (pp. 189–213). Amsterdam: John Benjamin.

Pitts, M., White, H. and Krashen, S. (1989). Acquiring second language vocabulary through reading: A replication of the Clockwork Orange study using second language acquirers. *Reading in a Foreign Language*, 5, 2, 271–5.

Prince, P. (1996). Second language vocabulary learning: The role of context versus translations as a function of proficiency. *Modern Language Journal*, 80, 4, 478–93.

Pulido, D. (2003). Modelling the role of second language proficiency and topic familiarity in second language incidental vocabulary acquisition. *Language Learning*, 53, 2, 233–84.

Pulido, D. (2007). The effects of topic familiarity and passage sight vocabulary on L2 lexical inferencing and retention through reading. *Applied Linguistics*, 28, 1, 66–86.

Pulido, D. (2009). How involved are American L2 learners of Spanish in lexical input processing tasks during reading? *Studies in Second Language Acquisition*, 31, 31–58.

Pulido, D. and Hambrick, D. Z. (2008). The *virtuous* circle: Modeling individual differences in L2 reading and vocabulary development. *Reading in a Foreign Language*, **20**, 2, 164–90.

Qian, D. (1999). Assessing the roles of depth and breadth of vocabulary knowledge in reading comprehension. *Canadian Modern Language Review*, **56**, 2, 282–307.

Rankin, E. F. and Overholser, B. M. (1969). Reaction of intermediate grade children to contextual clues. *Journal of Reading Behavior*, **1**, 3, 50–73.

Rye, J. (1985). Are cloze items sensitive to constraints across sentences? A review. *Journal of Research in Reading (UKRA)*, **8**, 2, 94–105.

Saemen, R. A. (1970). *Effects of commonly known meanings on determining obscure meanings of multiple-meaning words in context*. Retrieved from the Office of Education (DHEW), Washington, DC.

Saragi, T., Nation, I. S. P. and Meister, G. F. (1978). Vocabulary learning and reading, *System*, **6**, 2, 72–8.

Schatz, E. K. and Baldwin, R. S. (1986). Context clues are unreliable predictors of word meaning. *Reading Research Quarterly*, **21**, 4, 439–53.

Scott, J. A. and Nagy, W. E. (2004). Developing word consciousness. In Baumann, J. F. and Kame'enui, E. J. (eds.), *Vocabulary Instruction: Research to Practice* (pp. 201–17). Guilford Press: New York.

Seibert, L. C. (1945). A study of the practice of guessing word meanings from a context. *Modern Language Journal*, **29**, 4, 296–323.

Shefelbine, J. L. (1990). Student factors related to variability in learning word meanings from context. *Journal of Reading Behavior*, **22**, 1, 71–97.

Shu, H., Anderson, R. C. and Zhang, Z. (1995). Incidental learning of word meanings while reading: A Chinese and American cross-cultural study. *Reading Research Quarterly*, **30**, 1, 76–95.

Stahl, S. A. and Fairbanks, M. M. (1986). The effects of vocabulary instruction: A model-based meta-analysis. *Review of Educational Research*, **56**, 1, 72–110.

Sternberg, R. J. and Powell, J. S. (1983). Comprehending verbal comprehension. *American Psychologist*, **38**, 878–93.

Sutarsyah, C., Nation, P. and Kennedy, G. (1994). How useful is EAP vocabulary for ESP? A corpus based study. *RELC Journal*, **25**, 2, 34–50.

Swanborn, M. S. L. and de Glopper, K. (1999). Incidental word learning while reading: A meta-analysis. *Review of Educational Research*, **69**, 3, 261–85.

van Daalen-Kapteijns, M., Elshout-Mohr, M. and de Glopper, K. (2001). Deriving the meaning of unknown words from multiple contexts. *Language Learning*, **51**, 1, 145–81.

van Daalen-Kapteijns, M. M. and Elshout-Mohr, M. (1981). The acquisition of word meanings as a cognitive learning process. *Journal of Verbal Learning and Verbal Behavior*, **20**, 386–99.

van Parreren, C. F. and Schouten-van Parreren, M. (1981). Contextual guessing: A trainable reader strategy. *System*, **9**, 3, 235–41.

Walker, L. J. (1983). Word identification strategies in reading a foreign language. *Foreign Language Annals*, **16**, 4, 293–9.

Walters, J. (2004). Teaching the use of context to infer meaning: A longitudinal survey of L1 and L2 vocabulary research. *Language Teaching*, **37**, 243–52.

Walters, J. (2006). Methods of teaching inferring meaning from context. *RELC Journal*, **37**, 2, 176–90.

Watanabe, Y. (1997). Input, intake and retention: Effects of increased processing on incidental learning of foreign vocabulary. *Studies in Second Language Acquisition*, **19**, 287–307.

Webb, S. (2007). The effects of repetition on vocabulary knowledge. *Applied Linguistics*, **28**, 1, 46–65.

Webb, S. (2008). The effects of context on incidental vocabulary learning. *Reading in a Foreign Language*, **20**, 232–45.

9　Word parts

Most of the content words of English can change their form by adding prefixes or suffixes. These affixes are typically divided into two types – inflectional and derivational. The inflectional affixes in English are all suffixes. They include *-s* (plural), *-ed*, *-ing*, *-s* (3rd person singular), *-s* (possessive), *-er* (comparative), *-est* (superlative). Unlike most derivational suffixes, inflections do not change the part of speech of the word or word group they are attached to, and are added after a derivational suffix if the word has one.

Derivational affixes in English include prefixes and suffixes. Most of the derivational suffixes and a few prefixes change the part of speech of the word they are added to – for example, *happy* (adjective)/*happiness* (noun); *able* (adjective)/*enable* (verb). Some of the affixes, especially prefixes, also alter the meaning of the word in a substantial way – for example, *judge*/*prejudge*; *happy*/*unhappy*; *care*/*careless*. Words which contain affixes are sometimes called complex words.

There are two kinds of word stems, those which can stand as a word in their own right – *help*/*helpless* – and are called free forms, and those which cannot stand as a word in their own right without an affix (bound forms) *-clude* as in *preclude, include*. In general, bound stems are best learned as mnemonic items for particular words, that is, if you know that *-clude* means 'close' this may help you remember the meaning of *exclude* and perhaps *include*.

Researchers on the vocabulary growth of native speakers of English usually distinguish three main ways in which a learner's vocabulary increases: through being taught or deliberately learning new words, through learning new words by meeting them in context, and through recognising and building new words by gaining control of the prefixes and suffixes and other word-building devices. In this chapter we look at the extent to which word building affects vocabulary size, the psychological reality of the relationship between inflected and derived words and their stem form, and the teaching and learning options for gaining control of English word-building processes.

There are two related but distinguishable reasons for focusing on word parts. Firstly, prefixes and stems can work as mnemonic devices to help learners remember new words by relating them to the meanings of the known parts they contain. Secondly, knowledge of prefixes and suffixes can help learners see the relationship between word family members where one or more of the members is already known. This is especially useful for suffixes that are still productive, that is, that are still used to create new word family members (Ford et al., 2010). These two reasons could be called between-family knowledge and within-family knowledge.

Sadoski (2005: 229–230) suggests that word parts can make abstract words seem more concrete and therefore be easier to learn. For instance, knowing that *speculate* contains *-spec-* meaning 'to see' (as in *spectacles*) may make the more abstract word *speculate* seem that bit more concrete.

Is it worthwhile learning word parts?

One way to look at the value of learning word parts is to approach it in the same way we have approached the learning of vocabulary, that is, from the point of view of cost/benefit analysis. Is the effort of learning word parts repaid by the opportunity to meet and make use of these parts?

There are numerous studies of English affixes. Some have attempted to calculate the proportion of English words originating from Latin, Greek, Anglo-Saxon, Celtic and other sources (Bird, 1987; Bird, 1990; Grinstead, 1924; Roberts, 1965). Their studies relate to affixation because a large proportion of the words coming from Latin or Greek make use of affixes. Other studies (Nagy and Anderson, 1984; White et al., 1989) look at the proportion of words with affixes in a particular corpus. Other studies again (Bauer and Nation, 1993; Becker et al., 1980; Bock, 1948; Harwood and Wright, 1956; Stauffer, 1942) give the frequency of particular affixes within a corpus. They all confirm the frequent, widespread occurrence of derivational affixes. White et al.'s (1989) study of the four prefixes *un-*, *re-*, *in-* and *dis-* found that approximately 60% of the words with those prefixes could be understood from knowing the commonest meaning of the base word. Allowing for help from context and knowledge of the less common meanings of the prefixes, approximately 80% of prefixed words could be understood.

Where do English words come from?

Bird (1987; 1990), after a careful and detailed analysis of the 7,476 word type entries in the ranked vocabulary list of items with a frequency of 10 per million and above in the LOB corpus (Johansson and Hofland, 1989), concluded that 97% of these words were derived from approximately 2,000 roots. He found, as Roberts (1965) did, that the most frequent 1,000 words of English contain around 570 words of Germanic origin, but thereafter the Germanic words drop to around 360 per thousand. The words derived from French and Latin make up 36% of the first 1,000 and thereafter rise to about 51% (see Table 9.1).

Some of these parts that Bird (1987) analysed have a form that does not change in different words, such as *-ness*. Many of the others require considerable imagination and effort to see a connection, for example, CAP(UT) = 'head', which occurs in *capital, cap, cape, escape, cattle, chapel, chief, achieve*. Bird's figures roughly parallel the findings of Roberts (1965) and Grinstead (1924) with words of Germanic origin predominating in the first 1,000 and Italic and Hellenic words predominating from the second 1,000 onwards, averaging around 60% of English vocabulary.

Table 9.1 *Sources of the most frequent 7,476 words of English (from Bird, 1987)*

	1st 100	1st 1,000	2nd 1,000	from then on
Germanic	97%	57%	39%	36%
Italic	3%	36%	51%	51%
Hellenic	0	4%	4%	7%
Others	0	3%	6%	6%

How many words fit into a word family?

Nagy and Anderson's (1984) study of the word families in a section of the list based on the *American Heritage* corpus (Carroll et al., 1971) is a classic of its kind. Their goal was to see how many word families the sample contained, and by extrapolation all printed school English. To find this they classified the formally related words in their sample into word families using a scale of meaning relatedness. In doing the classification, they carefully distinguished the different types of word family members. Table 9.2 presents some of their data for types involving affixes.

Table 9.2 shows that 21.9% (roughly one-fifth) of the different types in a written text are inflected and 12.8% (roughly one-eighth) have a derivational affix.

Table 9.2 *Percentage of inflected and derived types in a corpus of texts*

Suffixation	7.6%
Prefixation	4.0%
Derived proper names	1.2%
Total derived forms	12.8%
Regular inflections	16.9%
Irregular inflections	0.3%
Inflections with proper names	4.7%
Total inflections	21.9%

Table 9.3 *The base and affixed members of a typical word family*

Word type	Inclusive definition	Only closely related items	Examples 1.	2.
Base word	1.00	1.00	*think*	*sure*
Regular inflections	1.90	1.16	*thinks, thinking*	*surer, surest*
Irregular inflections	0.70	0.20	*thought*	
Transparent derivatives	2.57	1.57	*thinker, unthinking*	*surely, ensure*
Less transparent derivatives	1.65		*unthinkable*	*surety, assure*
Other minor variations	1.46	0.89	*t'ink*	*Sure*
Total types in a family	7.64	4.66		

Table 9.3 shows how affixation affects the membership of a typical word family.

'Other minor variations' includes alternate spellings and pronunciations, capitalisation, truncations and abbreviations. Table 9.3 gives figures for the average number of affixed members of a word family. Column 2 uses an inclusive flexible definition of what can be in a family including less transparent derivatives such as *visual/visualise*, *percent/percentile*, *fend/fender*. Column 3 is more exclusive, allowing only very transparently related family members. The figures for each category of word type in the two columns differ because in Column 3 for 'Only closely related items', the less transparent derivatives would be considered as base words with their own set of family members, and thus the total number of word families is much greater for the same number of types, and the average is smaller. For each base form there are on average between 1.5 and 4 derived forms, depending on whether the inclusive or more restrictive definition of a family is used.

Table 9.4 *Word family sizes and different family frequency levels*

Word family frequency level	Number of family members	Average members per family
1st 1,000	6,838	6.8
2nd 1,000	6,367	6.4
3rd 1,000	5,871	5.9
4th 1,000	4,854	4.9
5th 1,000	4,302	4.3
6th 1,000	4,095	4.1
7th 1,000	3,681	3.7
8th 1,000	3,417	3.4
9th 1,000	3,188	3.2
10th 1,000	2,998	3.0
11th 1,000	2,926	2.9
12th 1,000	2,746	2.8
13th 1,000	2,436	2.4
14th 1,000	2,293	2.3
15th 1,000	2,280	2.3
16th 1,000	2,074	2.1
17th 1,000	2,071	2.1
18th 1,000	1,924	1.9
19th 1,000	1,847	1.9
20th 1,000	1,810	1.8

The number of words in a word family is very strongly related to family frequency. The more members a family contains, the more frequent it is likely to be. Table 9.4 has data from the word family lists that accompany the *Range* program on Paul Nation's website (www. victoria.ac.nz/lals/staff/paul-nation.aspx). At each level there are exactly 1,000 families. Note the quick drop in the number of words per family as we move from the high-frequency words to the mid-frequency words, and that by the time we get to the 10th 1,000 words, each family has an average of just three members. The average comprises all the family members including the headword.

The evidence of the origins of English words and analysis of word forms in a corpus show that word parts are a very common and important aspect of English vocabulary.

What are the most useful prefixes and suffixes?

Thorndike's (1941) study of 90 English suffixes, like many subsequent studies, made use of his studies of word frequency. For each suffix, Thorndike indicates how many words it occurs in – in total, and at what word frequency levels. He also provides a score representing the likelihood that a 16-year-old American child would recognise the particular suffix in various words, and a score for indicating how easy it would be to understand the whole word from knowing its parts. He also lists the various meanings of the suffix showing the number of words where it has that meaning. Thorndike's monograph is a rich source of information about the value of the various suffixes and their particular uses in written English. Thorndike also makes recommendations for the teaching of the individual suffixes.

Bauer and Nation (1993) set up seven levels of affixes based on the criteria of frequency (the number of words in which the affix occurs), regularity (how much the written or spoken form of the stem or affix changes as a result of affixation), productivity (the likelihood of the affix being used to form new words), and predictability (the number and relative frequency of the different meanings of the affix).

Thorndike's study considered not only the number of words with a particular affix but also the frequency of each affixed word. Thorndike did not consider productivity. A comparison of Thorndike's figures with Bauer and Nation's levels shows a high degree of agreement. Bauer and Nation's levels 2 to 6 only include affixed forms where the stem can exist as an independent word (a free form). For example, *pretty* as in *prettyish* is a free form, but *-ceipt* as in *receipt* is a bound form, not a free form, because *ceipt* cannot exist as an independent word.

The frequency studies of Stauffer (1942), Bock (1948), Harwood and Wright (1956), Becker et al. (1980) simply examine the frequency of the affixes with no consideration of different meanings, predictability, regularity or productivity. They show that a small number of affixes occur very frequently and account for a very high percentage of affix use. Stauffer (1942), for example, found that the 15 most common of the 61 prefixes he studied accounted for 82% of the total number of prefixed words in Thorndike's (1932) *Teacher's Word Book of 20,000 words*.

These studies all show that there is a relatively small group of very useful accessible affixes that learners could be introduced to at appropriate levels of their language development. Table 9.5 contains a recommended list divided into stages. Stage 1 can be used with low intermediate learners.

Table 9.5 *A sequenced list of derivational affixes for learners of English*

Stage 1

-able, -er, -ish, -less, -ly, -ness, -th, -y, non-, un- (all with restricted uses)

Stage 2

-al, -ation, -ess, -ful, -ism, -ist, -ity, -ize, -ment, -ous, in- (all with restricted uses)

Stage 3

-age (leakage), -al (arrival), -ally (idiotically), -an (American), -ance (clearance), -ant (consultant), -ary (revolutionary), -atory (confirmatory), -dom (kingdom; officialdom), -eer (black marketeer), -en (wooden), -en (widen), -ence (emergence), -ent (absorbent), -ery (bakery; trickery), -ese (Japanese; officialese), -esque (picturesque), -ette (usherette; roomette), -hood (childhood), -i (Israeli), -ian (phonetician; Johnsonian), -ite (Paisleyite; also chemical meaning), -let (coverlet), -ling (duckling), -ly (leisurely), -most (topmost), -ory (contradictory), -ship (studentship), -ward (homeward), -ways (crossways), -wise (endwise; discussion-wise), anti- (anti-inflation), ante- (anteroom), arch- (archbishop), bi- (biplane), circum- (circumnavigate), counter- (counter-attack), en- (encage; enslave), ex- (ex-president), fore- (forename), hyper- (hyperactive), inter- (inter-African, interweave), mid- (mid-week), mis- (misfit), neo- (neo-colonialism), post- (post-date), pro- (pro-British), semi- (semi-automatic), sub- (subclassify; subterranean), un- (untie; unburden).

Stage 4

-able, -ee, -ic, -ify, -ion, -ist, -ition, -ive, -th, -y, pre-, re-

Stage 5

-ar (circular), -ate (compassionate; captivate; electorate), -et (packet, casket), -some (troublesome), -ure (departure, exposure), ab-, ad-, com-, de-, dis-, ex- ('out'), in- ('in'), ob-, per-, pro- ('in front of'), trans-

---

The first four stages are based on levels 3 to 6 of Bauer and Nation (1993). Stage 5 is based on Stauffer (1942), Bock (1948) and Harwood and Wright (1956) who all analysed the Thorndike lists. Teachers may wish to be selective at the later stages of the table as the items are a mixture of high-frequency irregular items and low-frequency items. Thorndike (1941: 59), for example, recommends that the best way to learn what -some means is to learn the meanings of 20 or more words made with it. Similarly with -ure, Thorndike recommends that learners simply spend five minutes looking at a list of words ending in -ure.

There is no evidence to show that the stages in this list represent the order in which learners acquire a knowledge of affixes. There is also

no reason to expect that there is an invariant order in which they are acquired. The list however indicates an order for teaching and learning that will give the best return for learning effort.

Mochizuki and Aizawa (2000) and Schmitt and Meara (1997) found a clear relationship between vocabulary size and the number of affixes known. The scores for knowledge of individual affixes bear little relationship to the order of affixes in Bauer and Nation's (1993) scale. Mochizuki and Aizawa suggest knowledge of affixes depends on a variety of factors, and the criteria in Bauer and Nation cover only a few of these.

Schmitt and Zimmermann (2002) looked at productive knowledge of derivational suffixes, finding that their learners knew about two out of four of the derivatives per family. The data from the study generally supports the idea that at least for productive purposes, derived forms largely need to be learned as individual items rather than be produced according to morphologically based rules.

Do language users see words as being made of parts?

There has been continuing experimentation on whether native speakers of English and other languages treat words which contain prefixes and suffixes as set units or whether they reconstruct these complex words each time they use them by adding affixes to the stem. That is, do we store and retrieve *government* as a single form, or do we make it out of *govern* plus *-ment* each time we use it? This question is not a simple one because there are many variables that can influence the way language users store and retrieve words, and many ways in which words can be stored. Marslen-Wilson et al. (1994) list the important variables which include: the particular language involved; whether spoken or written use is investigated; whether prefixes or suffixes are being considered; whether inflectional or derivational affixes are considered; whether the affix and stem combinations are semantically transparent (the meaning of the whole equals the sum of the parts); and whether the forms of the parts are easily recognisable in their spoken or written forms.

There are several kinds of evidence that indicate that at least for lower-frequency, regularly formed, semantically transparent suffixed words, and possibly for some other kinds of complex words, they are recomposed each time they are used. Nagy et al. (1989) investigated whether the speed with which a word is recognised depends on the frequency of the word form alone or whether it depends on the combined frequency of the members of the word family. For example, does the speed at which a learner recognises the word *argue* depend only on the frequency of *argue* or does it depend on the combined frequency of *argue*, *argues*, *arguing*, *argument* and so on? If the speed of recognition depends on the combined frequency of members of the word family, then this is evidence that morphological relationships between words are represented in the lexicon. To make sure that it really was morphological relationships and not simply similar spelling, Nagy et al. also checked to see if the recognition of a word like *fee* was influenced by the frequency of formally similar words like *feet*, *feel*, *feed* which share some of the same letters but which are not morphologically related. Nagy et al. found that both inflected and derivational relationships significantly affected speed of recognition, while similar spelling did not. This suggests that inflected and derived forms are stored under the same entry or are linked to each other in the mental lexicon. This underlines the importance of making learners aware of morphological relationships and of considering words to be members of word families when teaching or testing.

Several factors affect the speed with which L1 readers access a word with a derivational affix during reading. These include: the frequency of the derived word form; the frequency of the base word; the total frequency of the word family containing the word; the number of members in the word family; the degree of regularity and transparency of the derived word; and the productivity of the affix in the derived word (Carlisle and Katz, 2006; Ford et al., 2010). These can be classified into morphological factors and experience factors. In the Carlisle and Katz study, the experience factors – frequency of the derived word form and number of words in the word family – accounted for the greater proportion of the variants. 'This result might indicate that facility of reading derived forms is most heavily influenced by exposure to derived words in print but is also influenced by awareness of the morphemic composition of words' (Carlisle and Katz, 2006: 686). This conclusion fits well with the Schmitt and Zimmermann (2002) L2 study. In order to increase learners' control of derivational affixes, we need to get them to read a lot and to provide some instruction in the most useful affixes.

Several researchers point out that there are differences between what etymological, linguistic and synchronic analysis reveal as being word parts, and what language users actually operate with as they construct complex words. A young native speaker of English, who is half-Thai and half-Caucasian, at the age of five told me he was 'half-Buddhess, half-Goddess'. Most native speakers do not realise that the words *rank* and *arrange*, are etymologically related, and that *tree*, *true* and *truth* are etymologically related. Although *business* is regularly related to *busy*, and *organisation* to *organ*, few native speakers would realise the connection.

Interpretation of interview data on vocabulary knowledge in Anglin (1993) suggests that derivational affixes may be learned without conscious knowledge. In their descriptions of derived words, 6-, 8-, and 10-year-old children rarely explicitly described derived words in terms of their root and affix. 'Children more often figure out an inflected or derived word by isolating its corresponding root word, identifying its meaning, and then casting the whole inflected or derived word appropriately into an illustrative sentence' (Anglin, 1993: 145).

In this typical example from Anglin (1993: 96), I is the interviewer and C is the child.

I. The next word is *unbribable*. What does the word *unbribable* mean?
C. Um … people try to bribe you and sometimes like they try to … say somebody had like $2,500.00 maybe and someone … say their friend who never cared for them or something … they would give you flowers and chocolates and they would say, 'I want to be your friend,' and all that, but they're just trying to bribe you. But *unbribable*, they won't do it, they just, you won't fall for it anymore. Like you won't get bribed; you'll be unbribable. You'll say no.
I. OK. Can you tell me anything more about the word *unbribable*?
C. Like I'm probably unbribable because I don't let anybody bribe me or anything to take my toys and money or something away. So I wouldn't let them do it to me. I'd just say like, 'I can't. I'm unbribable.'

There is also plenty of evidence (Nagy et al., 1993) that native speakers' use and awareness of morphological relationships develops from the very early stages of language use to at least when they are in their teenage years. Table 9.6 opposite lists the language factors that affect the likelihood of learners noticing and using word parts.

Let us look at some examples to make Table 9.6 clearer.

1. *-ness* as in *slowness* is an affix that meets many of the criteria in Table 9.6.

   • It appears in many words (*happiness, sadness, tenseness*). There are 307 different word types with this affix in the *LOB Corpus*.
   • It has a high frequency. Some of the word types containing *-ness* are very frequent.
   • *-ness* is still used to make new words, such as *deadness*. It is very productive.
   • It is generally but not always added to adjectives to make nouns. It has a high but not perfect regularity of function.
   • Words made with *-ness* are semantically transparent. Thorndike (1941) says that the meaning 'the quality, state, or condition of being x' accounts for about 95% of its uses and 'x behaviour', as in *brusqueness* and *kindness*, accounts for the rest.

Table 9.6 *Factors affecting the ease of perceiving and using word parts (technical terms are given in brackets)*

USE	The affix appears in many words.	(frequency)
	The affix appears in frequent words.	
	The affix continues to be used to form new words.	(productivity)
	The affixed word is the same form class as the base.	
	The affix attaches to a base of known form class and produces a word of known form class.	(regularity of function)
MEANING	The meanings of the stem and affix are closely related to the meaning of the complex word.	(semantic transparency)
	The affix has only one meaning or one very common meaning.	(predictability)
	The affix has both a semantic and grammatical meaning.	
FORM	The base is a complete word in its own right.	(a free form)
	This combination of letters only occurs as an affix.	
	The spoken form of the base does not change when the affix is added.	(regularity of the spoken base)
	The spoken form of the affix does not change when the affix is added.	(regularity of the spoken affix)
	The written form of the base does not change when the affix is added.	(regularity of the written base)
	The written form of the affix does not change when the affix is added.	(regularity of the written affix)

Note: Neutral affixes have a high degree of regularity. Non-neutral affixes are less regular.

- It has high predictability. Exceptions are *witness*, *business* and *(Your) Highness*.
- *-ness* does not add more than its syntactic meaning. *-ful* as in *cupful* or *un-* as in *unhappy*, on the other hand, add a clear semantic meaning.
- *-ness* is only added to free forms. If we take *-ness* away, the remaining base is always a word in its own right.
- The word *lioness* has a final *ness* which is not the affix *-ness*. This instance is unlikely to cause confusion.
- *-ness* is very regular in both spoken and written forms and with reference to both affix and base. The spelling rule 'y' becomes 'i', as in *happy – happiness*, applies. It is a neutral suffix.

2. In contrast to -ness, the suffix -ee as in *appointee* and *payee* has less systematic patterning. The *LOB Corpus* has 25 examples. None are of high frequency. It is occasionally used to form new words, so is still productive. -ee makes nouns usually from a verb base.
   - *-ee* has several meanings and the most regular pattern 'one who is x-ed' as in *payee* only accounts for a small number of its uses. Unpredictable examples include *bargee*, *absentee*, *goatee*, *bootee*, *committee* and so on.

McCutchen et al. (2009) present evidence that shows that fifth- and eighth-grade L1 learners are sensitive to the morphology of words. The levels devised by Bauer and Nation (1993) are an attempt to indicate for teachers staged sets of affixes that may be easily accessible to learners.

What are the most useful word stems?

The stems of complex words may be bound or free forms. Free forms can occur as words with no affixes. Bound forms can only occur with a prefix or a suffix. Advanced learners of English can usefully study small numbers of bound stems. One way of checking whether these stems are worth learning is to try to make substitution tables around them. If the stem can combine with many affixes to make a large number of words, it deserves attention. Here are some examples. In Table 9.7 opposite, for the word stem *port*, we can make the following words: *export, exportable, exporter, exportation*, and so on. Other useful stems include *fer (refer, prefer), form (deform, reform), ject (reject, injection), pos (oppose, propose), plic (complicated, applicable), scrib (scribble, subscribe), spect (inspect, spectacles), sta (circumstance, constant)* and *tract (tractor, subtract)*.

If learners have special purposes for learning English, it is worth investigating if there are affixes and stems which are important in their areas of specialisation. Students of Medicine, Botany and Zoology, for example, will find that there are affixes and stems that can give them access to many technical words in their fields.

Wei (2012) used a set of criteria based on meaning similarity, and spoken and written form similarity to find words in the third to tenth 1,000 words of English (mid-frequency words) that could be more easily learned by relating them through shared stems to words in the first 2,000 words of English. A learning hint was written for each related pair. Around 2,000 accessible low-frequency words were found – Table 9.8 on p. 402 presents several examples:

The mid-frequency word *certify* shares the same stem (*cert* meaning 'certain or sure') as the high-frequency word *certain*. Thus knowing *certain* can help with learning *certify* and other related words such as *certitude* and *certificate*. Note that in the first two examples the high- and lower frequency words are not etymologically related. For the vast majority of words, however, there was an etymological relationship. These hints would be a very useful addition to learner dictionaries. Table 9.9 lists the most useful stems.

Table 9.9 on p. 403 shows that the stem *posit*, or *pos*, is very useful because it is used in 21 different word families within the first 10,000 word families of English. These include *impose, compose, repose, deposit* and so on (see also Wei and Nation, 2013).

Table 9.7 *Word stems and affixes*

-PORT- *to carry*

ex-		[0]
im-		-able
trans-		-er
		-ation

[0]		[0]
re-	port	-able
sup-		-er

de-		[0]
		-ation

sup-		-ive

[Other useful words with *port*: *important*, *insupportable*]

-STRUCT- *to build*

con-		[0]
de-		-ion
in-		-ive
ob-		
	struct	
[0]		
re-		-ure

-VERS- *to turn*

a-		
ad-		
con-		
ob-		-e
per-		
re-		

a-		
con-	vers	-ive
sub-		-ion

di-		
extra-		
in-		-ion
intro-		
per-		
retro-		

Table 9.8 *Related high- and mid-frequency words and their meaning link*

High-frequency word	Mid-frequency word	Form and meaning link	Learning hint
certain	*certify*	cert = certain	to say that one is certain about something
arrange	*array*	arra(nge)	an ordered arrangement of people or things
provide	*proviso*	provi(d)	a condition provided in a legal document
force	*fort*	for(t) = strength	a strong building
video	*evident*	vide = see	easily seen

What knowledge is required for learners to use word parts?

To make use of word parts learners need to know several things. For receptive use, they have to be able to recognise that a particular complex word, such as *unhappiness*, is made up of parts, and that these parts can occur in other words, such as un*pleasant*, happi*ly* and *sad*ness. Tyler and Nagy (1989) call this 'relational knowledge'. Learners also need to know what the parts mean. In addition, they need to be able to see how the meanings of the stem and affix combine to make a new but related meaning. In the case of most suffixes this is largely syntactic, but particularly with prefixes, the affix can contribute significantly to the meaning of the complex word. An important extension of this to help learning is for learners to be able to see how the meaning of the parts relates to the dictionary meaning of a new word. This then allows the parts to act as mnemonic devices for the meaning.

For productive use, the learner needs a more detailed awareness of the formal changes to the stem and the affix that can occur when they are combined to form a complex word. These formal changes can affect the pronunciation: *flirt/flirtation* (stress change), *quantity/quantify*, *describe/description*. They may also affect the written form: *sacrilege/sacrilegious*, *legal/illegal*. Some changes in the written form are covered by regular spelling rules. Also for productive use the learner needs to be aware which form class of stem can take certain affixes. For example, *-ly* can be added to adjectives but not to nouns. Tyler and Nagy (1989) call this 'distributional knowledge'.

Table 9.9 *The most productive word stems (Wei, 2012)*

Rank	Stem forms	Meaning of the stems	Number of accessed words
1	*-posit-, -pos-*	put	21
2	*-spec(t)-, -spic-, -scope*	look	21
3	*-vers-, -vert-*	turn	19
4	*-ceive-, -cept-*	take	16
5	*-super-*	above	15
6	*-vent-, -ven-*	come	15
7	*-sens-, -sent-*	sense (feel)	15
8	*-sta-, -stan-, -stat-*	stand	14
9	*-nam-, -nom-, -nym-*	name	14
10	*-mit-, -mis-*	send	13
11	*-mid-, -med(i)-*	middle	13
12	*-pris-, -pre-*	take	13
13	*-vis-*	visit (see)	12
14	*-tract-*	draw	12
15	*-gen-*	produce	11
16	*-form-*	form	11
17	*-graph-*	write	11
18	*-sign-*	sign	10
19	*-cess-*	go	10
20	*-ord(i)-*	say	10
21	*-dict-, -dicate*	say	10

Before looking at activities to develop each of these kinds of knowledge, it is worth considering some general principles. Firstly, it is probably most efficient to begin to deal with word parts after learners have already learned a substantial number of complex words as unanalysed wholes. These can act as familiar items to attach their new knowledge of word parts to. Secondly, it is important to see the development of knowledge of word parts as being a long-term process. Basing it on a 'mini-syllabus' such as the levels described by Bauer and Nation (1993) is a useful way of systematically sequencing the teaching. Thirdly, as with all vocabulary learning, there is the danger of interference between items if formally or functionally similar items are focused on at the same time. It is probably wise to deal with one affix at a time as the opportunity arises, rather than having intensive word-building sessions where a range of new affixes is introduced. Fourthly, the use of word parts in understanding and producing words is essentially a creative activity. Anglin (1993) and others call it 'morphological problem solving'. Learners should therefore be encouraged to see the regular form and meaning patterns that lie behind the use of many word parts, and to take risks. Fifthly, there are large numbers of stems and affixes but some are much more useful than others. When giving attention to stems and affixes some thought should be given to their frequency, so that the learning and teaching effort is well repaid by many opportunities for use. Finally, it needs to be realised that many complex words are not based on regular, frequent patterns and are best learned as unanalysed wholes. Part of the learners' and teacher's skill is being able to recognise when this is the case.

L1 studies have shown that guessing from context and morphological analysis instruction can yield short-term effects, but even twelve 50-minute lessons over four weeks was not enough to yield delayed transfer effects (Baumann et al., 2002). It is likely that more extended teaching is needed.

What word-building skills should the teacher monitor and test?

There are four aspects of word building knowledge that are worth monitoring by a teacher. This can be done in a rather informal way through classroom tests sometimes with the learners contributing items. It can be done more formally through carefully designed tests that will be used with different classes and by different teachers. The four aspects are listed in order of importance.

Learners need to be able to recognise word parts in words.

1. Learners are given words that they break up:

unhappiness   *un*/happi/*ness*

Learners' knowledge of the meaning of the parts can also be tested by asking them to label the affixes.

not ← *un*/happi/*ness* → noun

This test is simple to make, a little time-consuming to mark, and requires learners to have explicit knowledge of the tested items. It is a good classroom test.

2. Learners group words according to their parts. Carroll (1940) developed the following item type for formal testing of learners' skill in recognising parts and identifying their meaning. Carroll's test contained 36 items like the following:

☐ 1. ready   ☐ 1. writing
☐ 2. read
☐ 3. regression   ☐ 2. back, again
☐ 4. region
☐ 5. repeat   ☐ 3. true
☐ 6. return
☐ 7. rectangle   ☐ 4. very

The instructions are as follows:

In the LEFT-HAND column of each problem there are several words which have some common element of meaning. This common element of meaning is represented by groups of letters in the words. But the group of letters which is found in each word *does not have the same meaning in all of them.* You are to find all the words in which the group of letters has the *same* meaning. Place a cross (X) in the box to the left of all the words which have that common element of meaning. In the RIGHT-HAND column of the problems are four words or phrases, *only one* of which is the English equivalent or meaning of the language unit common to the words you have just marked. Place a cross in the box to the left of the correct word or phrase.

Carroll (1940) found correlations higher than 0.9 between the learners' scores on choosing the correct examples in the left hand column and choosing the right meaning in the right hand columns of the items.

Learners need to be able to recognise what the affixes mean and do

There are two approaches to testing this, one which requires explicit knowledge and one which does not.

1. The learners are given a list of word parts and have to write their meaning or function. For example:

> *-ness*   _____
> *-less*   _____
> *re-*   _____

These parts could be presented in words:
> happi*ness*   _____
> care*less*   _____
> *re*consider   _____

To make the test a little easier and to make marking easier, choices could be provided.

Copy the appropriate meaning from the answers next to each word.
> happi*ness*   _____
> care*less*   _____
> *re*consider   _____
> etc.

Answers: again, makes a noun, down, without, makes a verb etc.

2. Tyler and Nagy (1989) devised the following item type to avoid the need for explicit knowledge:

> You can _____ the effect by turning off the lights.
> intensify, intensification, intensity, intensive

To avoid the effect of previous knowledge of the whole word forms, in one version they used nonsense stems.

> I wish Dr. Who would just _____ and get it over with.
> transumpation, transumpative, transumpate, transumpatic

In a later study Nagy et al. (1993) developed another item type to avoid the weaknesses they saw in the previous items (that is, the possibility of knowing the whole unanalysed form *intensify*, and the distracting effect of nonsense words ('How can I choose if I don't know what the word means?').

> Which sentence uses the word *powderise* correctly?
> a. First they had to find a *powderise* rock.
> b. First they had to *powderise* find the rock.
> c. First they had to find a *powderise* for the rock.
> d. First they had to find a way to *powderise* the rock.

Teachers may feel that this item type is undesirable for normal classroom use because of the effort required to prepare such items and the predominance of incorrect examples over correct ones. For Nagy et al.'s controlled experimental study however it worked well.

Learners need to be aware of the changes of written and spoken forms that occur when an affix is added to a word

1. The simplest way to test the written form is to give spelling dictation. That is, the teacher says words like *unhappiness* and the learners write them.
2. The teacher gives the learners a list of stems + affixes which the learners must combine:

    happy + *-ness* = _____
3. For some learners, the explicit testing of a spelling rule may be useful, for example 'What happens when you add a suffix beginning with a vowel to a word ending in y?'

    Change the *y* to *i* and add the suffix.

Learners need to know which classes of stems can take certain affixes

Tyler and Nagy (1989) tested this aspect of productive word building knowledge by giving the learners a list of items consisting of well-formed and ill-formed items that the learners had to respond to by indicating 'Yes' or 'No'. All the stems were known items.

tameness	_____
repeatise	_____
harshful	_____
flattish	_____
centreless	_____

In the above examples *repeatise* and *harshful* should be responded to with 'No' because *-ise* is not added to verbs, and *-ful* is not added to adjectives.

The following test can be used to see if learners are aware of morphological relationships between words they already know (McCutchen et al., 2009).

sad. We were all aware of her _____.

develop. There are several signs of _____.

If Corson's (1985) idea of the lexical bar is correct, learners may be reluctant to use derived forms wherever a simpler form is available. This avoidance could be picked up by researchers by counting the number of derived forms in learners speech or writing and comparing this with equivalent native speaker use. This is an unresearched area.

What is the word part strategy for remembering new words?

The word part strategy for learning new complex words involves two steps:

1. *Break the unknown word into parts.* This step requires learners to be able to recognise prefixes and suffixes when they occur in words.
2. *Relate the meaning of the word parts to the meaning of the word.* This step requires learners to know the meanings of the common word parts. This step also requires learners to be able to re-express the dictionary definition of a word to include the meaning of its prefix, and if possible its stem and suffix.

Here are some examples. The underlined words represent the meaning of the affix. Note how the dictionary definition does not usually give the meaning of the affixes.

Word	Dictionary definition	Reworded definition
unaccountable	does not seem to have any sensible explanation	not able to be explained
reshuffle	reorganisation of people or things, esp. jobs	change people or jobs again
community	people who live in a particular place or area	people who live together in a place
disperse	scatter	go away in many different directions
exhaust	drain the energy	make the energy go out
incessant	continual	not stopping

There are several ways of learning the meanings of prefixes and suffixes and becoming familiar with their forms. Basically, however, learners should deliberately learn the meanings of the most common prefixes and suffixes. The learning procedure can be the same as the deliberate learning of words using word cards as described in Chapter 11. The list given in Table 9.5 provides a useful set of items to learn. Time should be provided in class where necessary to make sure they are learned and simple tests should be given to monitor and encourage the learning.

After some affixes have been learned, there are various game-like activities that can be used to help establish the knowledge. These include 'word-making and word-taking' (Fountain, 1979), Bingo-type games (Bernbrock, 1980) and analysis activities (Nation, 1994: 182–90). Word-making and word-taking involves learners trying to combine cards with affixes and stems to make words. Analysis activities involve learners in breaking words into parts, grouping words with similar parts, and matching parts and meanings.

Learners can also teach each other prefixes and suffixes in pair work. One learner is the teacher and has a list of words with their prefixes and meanings of the prefixes listed. Table 9.10 is based on level 5 of Bauer and Nation (1993).

The learner of the pair folds the paper so s/he can only see the list of meanings. The 'teacher' says a word, says its prefix and then waits for the learner to find the meaning. The 'teacher' gives the learner three chances at finding the meaning in his list and then gives the answer.

Table 9.10 *A list of prefixes for a pair learning activity*

Prefix	Meaning	Example word
fore-	before	*forename*
bi-	two	*biplane*
en-	forms a verb	*encage; enslave*
ex-	former	*ex-president*
mis-	wrongly	*misfit*
pro-	in favour of	*pro-British*
semi-	half	*semi-automatic*
counter-	against	*counter-attack*
hyper-	above, over	*hyperactive*
inter-	between, among	*inter-African; interweave*
arch-	chief	*archbishop*
mid-	middle	*midweek*
neo-	new	*neo-colonialism*
post-	later, after	*post-date*
anti-	against	*anti-inflation*
un-	reversal of action	*untie; unburden*
sub-	under	*subclassify; subterranean*

The 'teacher' then moves on to the next word. However, just before a new word on the list is presented all the previous ones are tested again. This revision is more important than the initial testing.

Teachers should model the analysis of words and re-expressing word meanings as much as possible. This strategy of re-expressing word meanings is essentially an application of the keyword technique. The affixes or stem act as the keywords and the re-expressing of the meaning represents the combined imaging of the meaning of the keyword and the meaning of the target word.

The justification for spending time helping learners gain control of the word part strategy is that it can help the learning of thousands of English words. The strategy is useful for high-frequency, mid-frequency and low-frequency words, and is especially useful for academic and technical vocabulary.

It takes time to learn the important prefixes and suffixes and to learn to re-express meanings. A well-developed vocabulary development programme makes sure that this time is provided and planned for.

Some writers (Ilson, 1983; Pierson, 1989) suggest that learners should get information about the derivations of words – what languages they came from to English, and the form and meaning changes that occurred to them when they were adopted as English words. Pierson (1989) notes that this information is especially meaningful to Chinese learners in that they are aware of the etymology of the Chinese written characters and appreciate seeing a similar process of change in English words. An interest in etymology requires learners to have access to a dictionary that provides this information. Unfortunately learners' dictionaries do not provide simple versions of etymological information. Ilson (1983) suggests that there are four kinds of etymological information: (1) listing origins and cognates; (2) breaking words into their parts; (3) describing the processes by which particular words are formed *(brunch = breakfast + lunch)*; and (4) explaining the procedures in the development of particular words. The value of etymology for learners of English is that it is an interesting subject in its own right, but more importantly can help make some words more memorable, that is, it can help learning.

The study of cognates and loan words may be useful for some learners, especially where there are significant changes to the form of words after they have been borrowed. Daulton (2008) notes that although Japanese contains a large number of English loan words, the move to a syllabic spelling system has brought about striking formal changes. This means that there is a need for the deliberate pointing out of relationships.

The word-building systems of English are very important ways of enabling learners to make the most effective use of the stem forms they know. It is thus important to check that learners have the knowledge to make use of these systems and that, where appropriate, they are making use of that knowledge.

We have looked at the importance of prefixes, bases and suffixes for the learning of vocabulary. Using the information we have looked at so far, teachers should be able to (1) decide which affixes their learners should know; (2) test to see if their learners know them; and (3) design a range of activities to help them learn the affixes. Teachers should also be aware of the range of factors which cause difficulty in recognising and using word parts.

Using word parts to help remember new words is one of the major vocabulary learning strategies. It deserves time and repeated attention because it can involve such a large proportion of English vocabulary.

References

Anglin, J. M. (1993). Vocabulary development: a morphological analysis. *Monographs of the Society for Research in Child Development*, Serial No. 238, 58, 10, 1–165.

Bauer, L. and Nation, I. S. P. (1993). Word families. *International Journal of Lexicography*, 6, 4, 253–79.

Baumann, J. F., Edwards, E. C., Font, G., Tereshinski, C. A., Kame'enui, E. J. and Olejnik, S. (2002). Teaching morphemic and contextual analysis to fifth-grade students. *Reading Research Quarterly*, 37, 2, 150–73.

Becker, W. C., Dixon, R. and Anderson-Inman, L. (1980). *Morphographic and Root Word Analysis of 26,000 High Frequency Words: Follow Through Project*. Eugene, OR: University of Oregon.

Bernbrock, C. (1980). Stemgo: Aa word-stems game. *English Teaching Forum*, 18, 3, 45–6.

Bird, N. (1987). Words, lemmas and frequency lists: Old problems and new challenges (Parts 1 & 2). *Al-manakh*, 6, 2, 42–50.

Bird, N. (1990). *A First Handbook of the Roots of English*. Hong Kong: Lapine Education and Language Services Ltd.

Bock, C. (1948). Prefixes and suffixes. *Classical Journal*, 44, 132–3.

Carlisle, J. F. and Katz, L. A. (2006). Effects of word and morpheme familiarity on reading of derived words. *Reading and Writing*, 19, 669–93.

Carroll, J. B. (1940). Knowledge of English roots and affixes as related to vocabulary and Latin study. *Journal of Educational Research*, 34, 2, 102–11.

Carroll, J. B., Davies, P. and Richman, B. (1971). *The American Heritage Word Frequency Book*. New York: Houghton Mifflin, Boston American Heritage.

Corson, D. J. (1985). *The Lexical Bar*. Oxford: Pergamon Press.

Daulton, F. E. (2008). *Japan's Built-in Lexicon of English-based Loanwords*. Clevedon: Multilingual Matters.

Ford, M. A., Davis, M. H. and Marslen-Wilson, W. D. (2010). Derivational morphology and base morpheme frequency. *Journal of Memory and Language*, **63**, 117–30.

Fountain, R. L. (1979). Word making and word taking: A game to motivate language learning. *RELC Journal: Guidelines*, **1**, 76–80.

Grinstead, W. J. (1924). On the sources of the English vocabulary. *Teachers College Record*, **26**, 32–46.

Harwood, F. W. and Wright, A. M. (1956). Statistical study of English word formation. *Language*, **32**, 260–73.

Ilson, R. (1983). Etymological information: can it help our students? *ELT Journal*, **37**, 1, 76–82.

Johansson, S. and Hofland, K. (1989). *Frequency Analysis of English Vocabulary and Grammar 1 & 2*. Oxford: Clarendon Press.

Marslen-Wilson, W., Tyler, L., Waksler, R. and Older, L. (1994). Morphology and meaning in the English mental lexicon. *Psychological Review*, **101**, 1, 3–33.

McCutchen, D., Logan, B. and Biangardi-Orpe, U. (2009). Making meaning: Children's sensitivity to morphological information during word reading. *Reading Research Quarterly*, **44**, 4, 360–76.

Mochizuki, M. and Aizawa, K. (2000). An affix acquisition order for EFL learners: An exploratory study. *System*, **28**, 291–304.

Nagy, W. E., Anderson, R., Schommer, M., Scott , J. A. and Stallman, A. (1989). Morphological families in the internal lexicon. *Reading Research Quarterly*, **24**, 3, 263–82.

Nagy, W. E. and Anderson, R. C. (1984). How many words are there in printed school English? *Reading Research Quarterly*, **19**, 3, 304–30.

Nagy, W. E., Diakidoy, I. N. and Anderson, R. C. (1993). The acquisition of morphology: Learning the contribution of suffixes to the meanings of derivatives. *Journal of Reading Behavior*, **25**, 2, 155–69.

Nation, I. S. P. (ed.). (1994). *New Ways in Teaching Vocabulary*. Alexandria, VA: TESOL.

Pierson, H. (1989). Using etymology in the classroom. *ELT Journal*, **43**, 1, 57–63.

Roberts, A. H. (1965). *A Statistical Linguistic Analysis of American English*. The Hague: Mouton & Co.

Sadoski, M. (2005). A dual coding view of vocabulary learning. *Reading & Writing Quarterly*, **21**, 221–38.

Schmitt, N. and Meara, P. (1997). Researching vocabulary through a word knowledge framework: Word associations and verbal suffixes. *Studies in Second Language Acquisition*, **19**, 17–36.

Schmitt, N. and Zimmerman, C. (2002). Derivative word forms: What do learners know? *TESOL Quarterly*, **36**, 2, 145–71.

Stauffer, R. G. (1942). A study of prefixes in the Thorndike list to establish a list of prefixes that should be taught in the elementary school. *Journal of Educational Research*, **35**, 6, 453–8.

Thorndike, E. L. (1932). *Teacher's Word Book of 20,000 Words*. New York: Teachers College Columbia.

Thorndike, E. L. (1941). *The Teaching of English Suffixes*. New York: Teachers College, Columbia University.

Tyler, A. and Nagy, W. (1989). The acquisition of English derivational morphology. *Journal of Memory and Language*, **28**, 649–67.

Wei, Z. (2012). *Word Roots in English: Learning English Words through Form and Meaning Similarity*. Victoria University of Wellington, Wellington.

Wei, Z. and Nation, P. (2013). The word part technique: A very useful vocabulary teaching technique. *Modern English Teacher*, **22**, 1, 12–16.

White, T. G., Power, M. A. and White, S. (1989). Morphological analysis: Implications for teaching and understanding vocabulary growth. *Reading Research Quarterly*, **24**, 3, 283–304.

10 *Using dictionaries*

Dictionaries can be used for a wide range of purposes. Scholfield (1982b; 1997) has consistently distinguished between the different requirements and strategies for dictionaries which are to be used for comprehension (listening and reading) and dictionaries which are to be used for production (speaking and writing). As well as being sources of information, dictionaries can also be aids to learning (Nation, 1989). The following list covers most purposes for dictionary use:

Comprehension (decoding)

- Look up unknown words met while listening, reading or translating.
- Confirm the meanings of partly known words.
- Confirm guesses from context.

Production (encoding)

- Look up unknown words needed to speak, write, or translate.
- Look up the spelling, pronunciation, meaning, grammar, constraints on use, collocations, inflections and derived forms of partly known words needed to speak, write or translate.
- Confirm the spelling etc. of known words.
- Check that a word exists.
- Find a different word to use instead of a known one.
- Correct an error.

Learning

- Choose unknown words to learn.
- Enrich knowledge of partly known words, including etymology.

In the following sections we will look at these various purposes in more detail.

414

Do learners use dictionaries well?

Studies of second language learners' dictionary use have involved questionnaires (Bejoint, 1981; Tomaszczyk, 1979), analysis of filmed recordings (Ard, 1982), observing dictionary use (Atkins and Varantola, 1997) and filling out flowcharts immediately after dictionary use (Harvey and Yuill, 1997).

Harvey and Yuill (1997) looked at learners' use of a monolingual dictionary (*Collins COBUILD English Language Dictionary*) while writing. Because a monolingual dictionary alone was used, this study was largely restricted to learners looking up words that they already partly knew, or that they thought might exist in a similar form to their first language. Of the look-ups, however, 10.6% were done to find a synonym to replace a known second language word.

Table 10.1 lists the reasons for looking up words and gives the percentage of successful searches.

A notable finding of the study was the number of times that the example sentences were used to get information on meaning, grammar and register. The study also indicated that learners made little use of the grammatical coding scheme in the dictionary. Bejoint (1981) also found that learners said that they did not give much attention to the various coding schemes. Generally for these learners the degree of success in their dictionary use was quite high.

The Atkins and Varantola (1997) study examined users (who were largely very advanced and lexicographically sophisticated users of English) performing a translation task. They had access to both bilingual and monolingual dictionaries. The vast majority of look-ups were to find or check on an L2 translation. Success rates were higher in bilingual dictionaries and in L2–L1 translation. Gonzalez (1999) found a success rate of 80% for choosing the appropriate sense of a word.

Prichard (2008), in a computer-based reading study that allowed electronic dictionary look-up, found that most learners were sensibly selective in the words they looked up, typically choosing words that were important for the text they were reading and ignoring unknown words that were not related to main points in the text. About one-third of his 34-learner group used the dictionary excessively, in that they looked up very low-frequency words not related to main points. A future addition to this very interesting study would be to explore learners' motivations for such look-ups.

Most studies of learners' dictionary use have involved advanced and sophisticated learners. This is partly unavoidable because a reasonable level of proficiency is needed to use a monolingual dictionary. There is

Table 10.1 *Reasons for and degree of success in looking up words in COBUILD during a writing activity (based on Harvey and Yuill, 1997)*

Reason for searching for the word	% of total look-ups	% success of the search
to check on spelling	24.4%	92.8%
to confirm the meaning	18.3%	87.1%
to see if the word exists	12.8%	77.0%
to find a synonym to use instead of the known word	10.6%	63.9%
to find out about the grammar of the word	10.5%	90.2%
to check on the constraints or register of the word	9.3%	92.1%
to find collocations	8.2%	78.6%
to find a correctly inflected form	5.9%	100.0%

a noted lack of studies on less proficient learners and on the effects of training on dictionary use.

Do dictionaries help learners understand and produce text?

In a study by Luppescu and Day (1993), learners who used a dictionary took almost twice as long to read the passage as learners who did not use a dictionary. Electronic look-up however typically takes much less time than hard-copy look-up (Loucky, 2002; Roby, 1999).

Knight (1994) suggests that Bensoussan et al.'s (1984) finding of dictionary use not having any effect on comprehension may have occurred because the learners in their study were all high proficiency learners. Knight found no difference in comprehension scores with or without dictionaries for her high verbal ability group. Knight's low verbal ability learners' comprehension benefited from dictionary use. Their scores with dictionary access were close to the high verbal ability group who also had dictionary access. Without dictionary access, relying only on guessing from context, the difference between the high and low verbal ability groups was greater. The dictionary use group took longer to do the reading. A study of the amount of dictionary use suggested that high ability learners may have been using the dictionary when they did not need to. Hulstijn (1993) made a similar finding.

Others (Aust et al., 1993; Roby, 1999) found no measurable effect on comprehension for dictionary look-up.

Hulstijn (1993) found a very wide range of amount of dictionary consultation between individuals. Learners were generally strategic with the words they looked up, giving most attention to those words that were most relevant to the reading comprehension task that they were set, and ignoring words which were not relevant to the task. Words that could be easily inferred were looked up almost as much as words that were difficult to infer. Learners do not seem to have great faith in their inferring skills.

Generally dictionary use takes time and some learners may spend more time on dictionary use than they need to. This may be a result of the tasks that were used in the experiments and learners' awareness that they were involved in an experiment. Dictionary use helps learning and comprehension, and is particularly useful for learners who do not cope well with guessing from context.

Does dictionary look-up help with vocabulary learning?

Dictionaries can help learners with understanding and producing text, and with vocabulary learning. Luppescu and Day (1993) looked at the effect of bilingual dictionary use on vocabulary learning while reading. Students using a dictionary gained higher scores on a vocabulary test given immediately after the reading than students who did not use a dictionary. However, some items in the vocabulary test were answered incorrectly by more learners who used a dictionary than those who did not. This seemed to occur for words where there were many alternative meanings given in the dictionaries. This suggests that learners' dictionary searches were not very skilful.

Some studies of dictionary use have used texts and dictionaries on the computer. This means that each look-up can be electronically recorded (Knight, 1994; Hulstijn, 1993). In a carefully designed experiment with learners of Spanish as a second language, Knight (1994) found that learners who had access to a dictionary learned more words in both immediate and delayed (two weeks later) tests than learners who had no access to a dictionary.

The availability of electronic dictionaries (Loucky, 2002) means that tracking of learners' look-up behaviour is now an important source of data in vocabulary-learning studies involving dictionary use. Laufer and Hill (2000) used online dictionary look-up to track whether learners accessed L1, L2, L1 and L2, the sound of the words, information about the root of the word, or other information. They found a wide variety of look-up preferences and marked differences between Israeli and Hong Kong learners regarding the time spent on look-up, with Hong Kong learners spending almost twice as much time (for overall better learning results) than Israeli learners. On an immediate post-test of receptive vocabulary knowledge, the Israeli group scored 33.3% and the Hong Kong group 62%. Laufer and Hill suggest that the chance to choose what kind of information was accessed was a factor in the high learning rates.

Dictionary look-up generally helps vocabulary retention (Hulstijn et al., 1996; Knight, 1994; Laufer and Hill, 2000; Peters, 2007) and being able to access a variety of information including visuals is usually beneficial (Al-Seghayer, 2001; Chun and Plass, 1996; Laufer and Hill, 2000). Peters (2007) looked at the effect of the importance of the word in the text (actually needed to answer an accompanying comprehension task) and of warning of a following vocabulary test on vocabulary learning from reading. Her findings support those of Hulstijn (1993), namely that there was substantially more look-up of words that were needed to answer the comprehension task than there was of less relevant words. She also found that the warning of a vocabulary test had a small but positive effect on the number of look-ups. Each word was tested in four ways, and with both delayed and immediate tests. Once again text relevance (presence in the comprehension task) had a much stronger effect than warning of the vocabulary test. Peters' finding, particularly on the effect of accompanying comprehension questions, shows that through the design of accompanying activities vocabulary look-up and learning can be strongly affected. The amount of vocabulary learning in the study was affected by meeting the words in the text, looking them up in the dictionary and processing them in the comprehension task. Learners did not have to write the words in the comprehension task.

If dictionaries are used during a writing or L1–L2 translation task, there is a chance for vocabulary learning to occur. Bruton (2007) had Spanish learners of English at a secondary school perform teacher-led collaborative translation. English words that none of the learners could supply were looked up in an accompanying glossary (in effect, dictionary entries). Of the 10 words looked up by the whole class, 5.4 on average were correctly recalled when the same passage was retranslated as a test a week later. Because the marking criteria for the words demanded full correctness (no spelling errors or replacements by synonyms were allowed), the figure underestimates vocabulary learning. It is also likely that there is a further underestimation, as Bruton points out, because words not known by some but known by others on the initial translation were not considered in the calculation of learning. The collaborative translation class took 35 minutes, so the vocabulary return is a good one for the limited time involved.

What skills are needed to use a dictionary?

Several researchers (Neubach and Cohen, 1988; Scholfield, 1982b) have noted the complex nature of dictionary use. These skills differ according to whether the dictionary is used in conjunction with listening and reading (receptive use), or with speaking and writing (productive use). In the following sections the skills are described as steps in a strategy (see Scholfield, 1982b, for a detailed description of a similar strategy).

What skills are needed for receptive use?

Receptive use of a dictionary largely involves looking up the meaning of a word that has been met while reading or listening. The following steps make up a strategy that can be the basis for learner training. As each step is described, the skills needed at each step are spelled out, tests of these skills are suggested, and suggestions for training learners in the skills are provided.

The four steps in the strategy for looking up the meanings of words in a dictionary for comprehension (decoding) purposes are:

1. Get information from the context where the word occurred.
2. Find the dictionary entry.
3. Choose the most suitable sub-entry.
4. Relate the meaning to the context and decide if it fits.

Step 1. *Get information from the context where the word occurred.* The skills needed for this step include (1) deciding on the part of speech of the word to be looked up; (2) deciding if the word is an inflected or derived form that can be reduced to a base form; (3) guessing the general meaning of the word; and (4) deciding if the word is worth looking up by considering its relevance to the task and its general usefulness.

Each of these skills can be tested directly. Training in finding the part of speech can be done by intuitively classifying words in context into part of speech, or by following some rules that guide the classification. To gain skill in breaking words into parts learners can just practice doing so with feedback and guidance or they can learn the commonest affixes. Clarke and Nation (1980) suggest a way of training learners in guessing from context (see Chapter 8).

Step 2. *Find the dictionary entry.* The skills needed for this include (1) knowing the order of the letters of the alphabet (some dictionaries do not follow a strictly alphabetic order); (2) knowing the dictionary symbols for the different parts of speech; and (3) knowing alternative places to search, such as separate entries, sub-entries, word groups, derived forms, variant spellings and appendixes.

Each of these skills can be tested separately by getting learners to say the alphabet, interpret dictionary symbols and describe different places to search. The combined skills can be tested by doing timed searches. Learners can be prepared for this step by practising saying the alphabet, studying and being taught about the various symbols used in the dictionary with some practice in using them, observing skilled dictionary users searching for a word, and analysing dictionary entries and classifying their parts. There is a helpful split-information activity which can be used for gaining familiarity with the types of information that may be found in a dictionary entry.

Each learner has one of the following sentences to memorise. After memorising, each learner returns the piece of paper containing the sentence to the teacher. Then, without any writing, learners put the sentences in order so that the description of a typical dictionary entry is correct. Here are the sentences:

a. The phonetic variations can then be shown. For example /klever/.
b. Next, the entry gives the part of speech of the word. For example, noun, verb, adjective.
c. The meaning of the word is the next part of the dictionary entry.
d. Frequently the entry shows how the word is used in a sentence. This is to help you use the word more easily.
e. The entry for each word has its parts arranged in a certain order.
f. Then the entry can show variant spellings of the word, e.g. colour/ color.
g. Then the entry can have the information as to whether or not the word, if it is a noun, is countable or uncountable.
h. This may be accompanied by the year or century in which the word was first used in English.
i. The dictionary entry can have the derivation (what language the word comes from). For example *sahib* IndE and EPak.
j. The phonetic guide to the pronunciation of the word follows. For example /klevə/.
k. The actual spelling of the word is first in the entry.

Step 3. *Choose the right sub-entry.* Once the correct entry has been found there may be a need to choose between different meanings and uses listed within that entry. In order to make this choice, the information gained in Step 1 from the context in which the word occurred will need to be used. This may involve quick scanning of all or most of the sub-entries to make sure that the most appropriate sub-entry is chosen. There are useful tests of this skill which can also be used for practice. In a text, the teacher chooses words that have several different meanings or related meanings. For example, the context may say 'He was scrubbing the *flags* in front of his house.' The learner then has to find the most suitable entry, in this case that *flags* stands for *flagstones*. Learners can get guided practice in choosing between sub-entries through group discussion and systematic elimination of the inappropriate sub-entries. When they meet such words in context, learners can predict whether it is likely to be a common meaning or an uncommon meaning, because this will give some indication of how far in an entry they may need to search.

Step 4. *Relate the meaning to the context and decide if it fits.* This step involves adapting the meaning found in the dictionary to the context of the word in the text. In many cases this will not be a big change. In a few cases some narrowing or stretching of the meaning may be necessary. Another skill at this step is evaluating the success of the search, that is, does the meaning found fit nicely with the message of the text? There are two ways of testing whether learners have completed this step well: One way is to measure comprehension of the text with a focus on the parts containing the unknown words. Another way is to get learners to do self-evaluation of their search. Training at this step can involve making use of definitions and the example sentences in the dictionary to interpret words in context. Training can also involve paraphrasing the original contexts with the meaning of the unknown words added.

These steps seem complicated, but in practice learners may be able to follow them quite successfully. Before getting too far into a strategy-training programme, it is important to check that learners do need practice and training, and to check what aspects of the strategy need attention. A technique used by some learners is to mark each entry they look up in the dictionary each time they look it up. This helps them realise if they are looking up the same items more than once and can provide an incentive for some deliberate learning of particular items.

What skills are needed for productive use?

Using a dictionary for productive use is sometimes called using a dictionary for encoding, that is, turning ideas into language. It involves finding word forms to express messages. Bilingual dictionaries which go from the first language to the second language are an efficient way of doing this. Some writers suggest using a combination of bilingual and monolingual dictionaries for this purpose in order to get the best value from both types (Scholfield, 1982a; Stein, 1988).

It is possible to devise a strategy for using a dictionary for productive use. Scholfield (1981) describes a similar strategy for the correction of errors in written work.

Step 1. *Find the wanted word form.* The skills needed to do this include: bilingual dictionary use; using a dictionary like the *Longman Language Activator*; or using synonyms, opposites or related words in a monolingual dictionary. Using a monolingual dictionary requires considerable search skills and a reasonable proficiency level in the second language. The following steps assume that if the word is looked up in a bilingual dictionary, there may be a need to also look it up in a monolingual dictionary to gain more detailed information to allow productive use of the word.

Step 2. *Check that there are no unwanted constraints on the use of the word.* This step involves the skills of interpreting the dictionary's style labels and codes. These labels include indications about whether the word is in current use or archaic, whether it is formal or colloquial, whether it is only used in the United States or the UK, whether it is impolite and so on. Several writers have indicated the inconsistency with which dictionaries signal this information (Hartmann, 1981). Teachers can train learners in the interpretation of these labels through explanation and through practice in interpreting them.

Step 3. *Work out the grammar and collocations of the word.* Some of this information can come from the example sentences. Research on dictionary use indicates that learners are more likely to make use of the example sentences than they are to try to interpret grammatical coding schemes. This indicates that practice and training would be of great value in this particular skill of dictionary use. Generally the more detailed information given by a coding scheme, the more difficult it is to interpret. However, this grammatical information can be of great use in written and spoken production. Not only is it necessary to be able to interpret the codes (e.g. N COUNT), it is necessary to be able to apply this information – for example 'N COUNT means that it can be plural, and a singular form must have *a*, *the*, or a similar word in front of it'. Summers (1988) found that dictionary use helped in writing sentences, particularly where the dictionary provided example sentences.

Step 4. *Check the spelling or pronunciation of the word before using it.* In most learners' dictionaries the working out of the pronunciation requires reading phonetic script. This is a skill requiring considerable practice.

Dictionary use, as in the two strategies described here, is one of the four major options for learners to deal with unknown vocabulary. It is an essential complement to the other strategies of inferring from context, using word cards, and using word parts. Because the strategy of dictionary use provides access to so many words and to so much information about them, it deserves a considerable amount of class-room time. Teachers should be willing to spend up to an hour a week over several weeks checking that learners have control of these strate-gies and training learners in their use.

To put the dictionary use strategies into practice, it is necessary to have access to a good dictionary. The next section looks at what choices of dictionary types are available and how teachers and learn-ers can judge which ones they should own.

What dictionaries are the best?

There are three major kinds of learners' dictionaries in terms of the languages they use: monolingual, bilingual and bilingualised. Monolingual dictionaries are written all in one language. So, an English monolingual dictionary has an English headword, an English definition and all the examples and other information in English. Second language learners using a monolingual dictionary thus need to be able to interpret definitions and other information in the second language. Here is an example entry from the *Longman Dictionary of Contemporary English*. W2 indicates that the word is in the second 1,000 most frequent words in written English.

in.creas.ing.ly /in_kriːsiŋli/ *adv* more and more all the time [+adj/   W2
adv]: *The classes at the college have become increasingly full over
the past five years.* [sentence adverb]: *Increasingly, it is the
industrial power of Japan and South East Asia that dominates
world markets.*

In some monolingual dictionaries for learners of English the defini-tions are written within a controlled vocabulary of 2,000–3,000 words. Other learner dictionaries have a policy of making the defini-tions simple but not being limited by a fixed defining vocabulary. Learners seem to prefer dictionaries written in a controlled vocabulary (MacFarquhar and Richards, 1983).

Cumming et al. (1994) compared the effect of phrasal definitions, sentence definitions, phrasal definitions with an example sentence and sentence definitions with an example sentence. No difference was found on a production measure (write a sentence using the word) and a comprehension measure (which of six sentences using the word are correct?). Students indicated a clear preference for having examples with definitions and they favoured the sentence definition format.

In general monolingual learners' dictionaries contain much more information about each word than bilingual dictionaries do, and some teachers recommend that bilingual dictionaries be used in conjunction with monolingual dictionaries for writing and speaking.

Bilingual dictionaries use two languages. The headword and the examples are in one language and the meaning is in another language. Sometimes the example sentences are also provided in two languages. So, a bilingual dictionary for a French learner of English would have the headword in English, a French translation of the word to provide the meaning, example sentences in English with perhaps a French translation of those sentences. Another section of the dictionary might go the other way (for speaking or writing), with the headword in French and then English words that could be used to convey that meaning. Here is an example entry from the *Collins German Dictionary* (Terrell et al., 1991).

Nachprägen *vt sep* (*nachträglich prägen*) to mint *or* strike some more; (*fälschen*) to forge. **es wurden 200 Stück nachgeprägt** a further 200 copies were struck.

Bilingual dictionaries are often criticised. It is said that they encourage the use of translation (which is thought to be counter-productive in the language classroom), that they encourage the idea that words in the second language are equivalent in meaning to words in the first language (a one-to-one relationship), and that they provide little information on how words are used. These criticisms are misguided and unfair, and they also ignore the advantages of bilingual dictionaries (Thompson, 1987). Firstly, a more balanced view needs to be taken of the role of translation in the language classroom. As a way of communicating meaning, the first language has several advantages. However, care needs to be taken that there are a lot of chances for second language use, and second language use at a fluent level. Secondly, as Nation (1978) points out, translation as a way of communicating meaning is in general no better or worse than other ways. It would be just as misleading for a second language learner to believe that words in a second language are equivalent in meaning to their dictionary definitions as to believe that they are equivalent to their first language translation. Thirdly, while many bilingual dictionaries contain little information about each word, they can be seen as a complement, rather than a competitor, to monolingual dictionaries. Moreover, some bilingual dictionaries provide substantial information about each word.

The major advantages of bilingual dictionaries are (1) that they provide meanings in a very accessible way, and (2) that they can be bi-directional: English–first language, first language–English. Most monolingual dictionaries use a controlled vocabulary in their definitions. However, a learner has to know this vocabulary and has to be able to cope with the grammatical difficulties of the explanation. Numerous research studies (Lado et al., 1967; Laufer and Shmueli, 1997) have shown that vocabulary learning is much more effective learning L2–L1 pairs than learning L2–L2 definition pairs. There is also plenty of evidence that shows the difficulties native speakers (McKeown, 1993) and non-native speakers (Nesi and Meara, 1994) have in understanding definitions.

Dictionaries can be used for both receptive and productive use. Bilingual dictionaries which go from the first language to the second language provide easy access to vocabulary for productive use. This access is not easily provided in monolingual dictionaries. If bilingual and monolingual dictionaries are used to complement each other for productive purposes, then the best qualities of both can be used.

Bilingualised dictionaries contain the information that is in a monolingual dictionary plus a translation of the headword.

Electronic dictionaries

Electronic dictionaries have revolutionised dictionary look-up and research on dictionary look-up. The quality of dictionaries available electronically is very high and in many cases they are essentially the same dictionaries as those available in printed form. The variety of information available through electronic dictionary look-up typically exceeds that available in hard-copy look-up in several ways: (1) the actual spoken form (rather than phonetic script) is available; (2) there may be both L1 and L2 meanings; (3) there may be more visuals including video (see the brilliant example of the *Dictionary of New Zealand Sign Language*, Kennedy, 1997); and (4) instead of a few examples, mini-concordances may be available. Added to this additional information is the relative ease of access either through clicking or typing the first letters of the word, and the greater portability of the means of access through cell phones, iPods, iPads and electronic readers. The golden age of dictionaries is by no means past.

Li (2010) compared hard-copy reading accompanied by dictionary reference with computer-mediated reading accompanied by electronic dictionary access. The computer group performed better on vocabulary learning measures but the differences between the two treatments were not large, although significant.

Research on electronic dictionary look-up is easily tracked and timed (see Hill and Laufer, 2003, for a good example), allowing detailed analysis of what learners actually did and how long they spend doing it. When dictionaries are coupled with other learning tasks, we have very interesting opportunities for research.

Reading and dictionary use

Reading accompanied by a word-focused task results in better vocabulary retention than reading by itself. This is probably because of the deliberate attention given to words during the task and the amount of thoughtful processing involved in the task (Hill and Laufer, 2003; Laufer, 2001; Laufer and Hulstijn, 2001; Rott et al., 2002; Rott and Williams, 2003; Wesche and Paribakht, 2000).

Dictionary look-up is a word-focused task, and Hill and Laufer (2003) compared three types of task that were done with the text present and electronic dictionary look-up available:

1. answering message-focused comprehension questions that require knowledge of particular target words;
2. answering word-focused multiple-choice questions that required the right meaning of an isolated word form to be selected; and
3. answering word-focused multiple-choice questions that require the selection of the right words to express a given meaning.

Learning was measured using a receptive word meaning recall test allowing the use of the L1 or L2. Time-on-task was measured and virtually the same time was spent on each task. The third task, productive multiple-choice, produced the best results. The second and third tasks produced the greatest amount of dictionary look-up activity. The explicitly word-focused tasks produced more dictionary use and better learning than the more implicitly word-focused task.

Hill and Laufer (2003) make the point that the critical time factor is not time-on-task but time spent on the target item – we learn what we focus on. Hill and Laufer's first task, interpreting the word in context, is in several ways typical of what should occur during reading and should involve more thoughtful processing in the sense of figuring out that the unknown word in their sentence was critical to answering the question and then looking it up. But, Hill and Laufer suggest that the indirect nature of the activity may have made learners more satisfied with a superficial understanding (partly reflected by the fewer clicks for dictionary access). The more message-focused the activity, the less the explicit attention to vocabulary, and the less the vocabulary learning. All these tasks however resulted in vocabulary learning, with average scores for the tasks ranging from 5 out of 12 (42%) to 8.5 out of 12 (72%). This study confirms that dictionary access is likely to lead to learning and the amount of learning will depend on the reason for consulting the dictionary.

How can we evaluate dictionaries?

Which of these three types – monolingual, bilingual, bilingualised – is the best? Which particular dictionary is the best one to buy? There are several ways of answering these questions. One way is to examine and compare the kinds of information that dictionaries provide. A second way is to see what learners prefer and actually use. A third way is to look at the effects of use of the different types of dictionary on comprehension of text, language production, or understanding dictionary entries.

The kinds of information in dictionaries

One way of surveying the kinds of information that dictionaries provide is to relate it to what is involved in knowing a word (see Chapter 2). Discussion of these various types of information can be found in the numerous reviews of particular dictionaries (for example, Bauer, 1980; 1981; Benson, 1995; Hartmann, 1982), comparative reviews of dictionaries (Bogaards, 1996; Herbst, 1996; see also the *International Journal of Lexicography*, 1989, vol 2, No 1, for several comparative reviews) and general discussions of learners' dictionaries (Bejoint, 1981; Hartmann, 1992; Tickoo, 1987).

Table 10.2 overleaf relates the various kinds of information in dictionaries to what is involved in knowing a word. The table does not include some types of information which occur in some dictionaries, particularly information about 'false friends' and common errors which can help learners, and the table does not deal with the way in which the various bits of information are structured and signalled in dictionaries.

The learner can benefit not only from the type of information in the dictionary but also from the way it is presented. Baxter (1980) argues that using a monolingual dictionary makes learners realise that meaning can be conveyed by a definition as well as by a single word. This provides learners with the basis for a strategy in their spoken English – using a paraphrase-based definition for making up for gaps in their productive vocabulary. Marco (1999) describes the various functions of this procedural vocabulary: having to cope with L2 enhances learning of the defining vocabulary. Bilingual dictionaries,

Table 10.2 *Dictionary information and what is involved in knowing a word*

Form	spoken	R	
		P	pronunciation, alternate pronunciations
	written	R	
		P	spelling, hyphenation (syllabification)
	word parts	R	etymology
		P	inflections, derived forms
Meaning	form and meaning	R	derived forms, etymology, examples
		P	
	concept and referents	R	meanings, illustrations
		P	examples
	associations	R	examples
		P	synonyms, opposites, superordinates
Use	grammatical functions	R	
		P	grammatical patterns, examples
	collocations	R	
		P	collocations, examples
	constraints on use (register, frequency ...)	R	
		P	frequency, register, style, etc. (see Hartmann, 1981)

Note: in Column 3 R = receptive knowledge, P = productive knowledge

on the other hand, encourage the idea that a meaning should be expressed through a single appropriate word. They discourage the use of paraphrase.

Laufer (1992) compared example sentences made by lexicographers with those chosen from a corpus. She found that lexicographers' examples were better for comprehension, and similar to corpus-based examples for production. Her study also suggested that understanding corpus-based examples required a larger vocabulary size. Laufer (1993) found that examples alone did not provide as much help for comprehension as a definition. A definition plus examples gave greater help than either of these sources alone.

When evaluating dictionaries, considering the kinds of information presented in dictionaries and the ways in which the information is organised and presented, it is important to distinguish the goals of dictionary use: comprehension, production and learning. It is also useful right at the beginning to consider a few preliminary practical issues like the following:

- How much can learners afford to pay for a dictionary?
- Is the physical size of a dictionary an important consideration? Do learners have to carry it around? Does it have to be a pocket-sized dictionary?
- Are learners of a high enough level of proficiency to be able to understand definitions in a second language? Usually this requires a vocabulary of 2,000 words or more.

Choosing a dictionary for comprehension. Using a dictionary for comprehension or decoding involves using the dictionary to look up the meanings of words which have been met in reading or listening. Such a dictionary should have the features described in Table 10.3 overleaf. The features are ranked in order of their importance, with the most important first. This list of features is very short (see, for example, reviews by Bogaards, 1996, and Herbst, 1996) for a very detailed consideration of an extensive range of features). This short list is intended to cover the most important features, to be able to be applied reasonably quickly, and to not require great skill or background knowledge in application. Judgements based on the application of this list could be very usefully supplemented by reading more detailed reviews, especially comparative reviews of the dictionaries.

Choosing a dictionary for production. Table 10.2 lists the features that could occur in a substantial dictionary aimed at production. Table 10.4 on p. 431 indicates what a teacher or learner should look for when choosing a dictionary aimed at providing information for speaking and writing.

The first criterion, finding a word, may not be satisfied very well by most monolingual dictionaries. The *Longman Language Activator* attempts to provide access to unknown forms solely through the second language. It has been criticised as being a little complex to use (Benson, 1995). However, as most learners would benefit from training in dictionary use, it is reasonable to provide training in the use of more complex dictionaries if they provide the types of advantages the *Activator* provides.

Learners' preferences

Surveys of learners' preferences and use indicate that bilingual dictionaries are the preferred option for most learners (see Laufer and Kimmel, 1997, for a review; also Atkins and Varantola, 1997). Baxter's (1980) survey of his Japanese university students showed that overwhelmingly the students used bilingual rather than monolingual dictionaries.

Table 10.3 *Features and ways of checking the features of a learners' dictionary to be used to look up word meanings*

Features	Tests
1. The dictionary should contain lots of words and word groups.	<ul><li>See how many words the introduction says it contains.</li><li>Count 10 pages at random calculating how many words per page there are and multiply by the total number of pages in the dictionary.</li><li>Look up words in the low frequency levels of the British National Corpus lists.</li><li>Look up some useful word groups.</li></ul>
2. The meanings should be easy to understand.	<ul><li>Look in the introduction to see if the dictionary uses a limited defining vocabulary.</li><li>Look at entries for ten words to see if the meanings are easy to understand, and to see if first language translations are provided.</li></ul>
3. Derived words and word groups should be easy to find.	<ul><li>Look to see if derived forms especially irregularly spelled ones are listed separately.</li><li>Look to see if important idioms are entered under each of their parts.</li></ul>
4. The meanings should be easy to find.	<ul><li>Look at some entries to see if the most common meanings are listed first.</li><li>Look at some entries to see if different parts of speech get separate entries or clear sub-entries.</li></ul>
5. There should be examples and collocations to guide the search and confirm that the appropriate meaning has been found.	<ul><li>Look at some entries to see how many examples are given. Are the examples easy to understand?</li><li>Look at some entries to see if collocations are provided.</li></ul>

Table 10.4 *Features and ways of checking the features of a learners' dictionary to be used for writing or speaking*

Features	Tests
1. There should be ways of finding the appropriate word.	• See if the dictionary is bilingual. • See if the dictionary provides ways of accessing the word through thesaurus-like keywords (as in the *Longman Language Activator*). • See if the dictionary provides opposites, synonyms, superordinates and other related words as a part of an entry.
2. The dictionary should provide information about constraints on use of the word.	• See if the dictionary contains frequency information. • See if the dictionary contains codes telling if the word is formal, colloquial, rude or old fashioned. • Look in the introduction to see the range of codes used.
3. The dictionary should provide plenty of understandable example sentences as models for use.	• Count how many examples are provided for each word and different uses of a word. • Check if each of the examples for an entry is different enough to provide different kinds of information for use.
4. The dictionary should contain easily understood information about the grammar and collocations of the word.	• Look in the introduction to see the range of information provided. The minimum should be part of speech, count/non-count for nouns, and verbs should have their patterns indicated. • See how easy it is to understand the information provided.
5. The dictionary should show the spelling of inflected and derived forms.	• See if the entry for the base form provides access to the inflected and derived forms. • See if alternative spellings are provided.
6. The dictionary should show how the word is pronounced.	• See if the pronunciation of the word is indicated. • Decide if the pronunciation guide is easy to use.

Several studies of vocabulary-learning strategies have found dictionary use (Gu and Johnson, 1996), and particularly bilingual dictionary use (Kim, 2009), to be a preferred strategy.

Dictionaries and language use

In a study of bilingualised dictionaries, Laufer and Kimmel (1997) found that some learners used only the translation in the dictionary entry for all words, others used the monolingual definition, others varied for different words between using the translation or monolingual definition, and others used both. Laufer and Kimmel argue that, because people use the dictionary information in such a range of different ways, the bilingualised dictionary is preferable because it allows for such varied use.

Laufer and Hadar (1997) found that bilingualised dictionaries generally gave better results than bilingual and monolingual dictionaries on comprehension and production tests. The more skilled users were, the better they performed with the monolingual dictionary. However, the bilingualised dictionary users still achieved better results.

Dictionary use and learning

In this volume we are covering two major themes:

1. Learning any particular word is a cumulative process. We cannot expect that a word will be learned in one meeting and so need to see each meeting as a small contribution to learning.
2. Learning a word occurs across a range of different learning conditions. The position taken in this book is that those conditions should involve roughly equal proportions of the four strands of meaning-focused input, language-focused learning, meaning-focused output and fluency development. These strands provide partly overlapping, partly differing kinds of knowledge.

We can apply these two ideas to the role of dictionaries in language learning. Dictionary use is a kind of language-focused learning: the deliberate and explicit study of words. It is thus only one of a range of sources of information about words. Dictionary makers and their critics set very high standards for dictionary production. This is admirable and worth keeping to, because it will improve the information available in dictionaries. Learners, however, will only gain a small amount of information from any one dictionary look-up. This information may usefully add to what is already known and may be added to in later meetings with the word in a variety of ways, including further dictionary use. Expectations of what will be learned about words from dictionary use should not be too high, and so teachers and learners should make efforts to see that this knowledge is added to through other encounters with the word.

References

Al-Seghayer, K. (2001). The effect of multimedia annotation modes on L2 vocabulary acquisition: A comparative study. *Language Learning & Technology*, **5**, 1, 202–32.

Ard, J. (1982). The use of bilingual dictionaries by EFL students while writing. *ITL: Review of Applied Linguistics*, **58**, 1–27.

Atkins, B. T. S. and Varantola, K. (1997). Monitoring dictionary use. *International Journal of Lexicography*, **10**, 1, 1–45.

Aust, R., Kelly, M. and Roby, W. (1993). The use of hyper-reference and conventional dictionaries. *Educational Technology Research and Development*, **41**, 4, 63–73.

Bauer, L. (1980). Review of The Longman Dictionary of Contemporary English. *RELC Journal*, **11**, 1, 104–9.

Bauer, L. (1981). Review of Chambers Universal Dictionary. *RELC Journal*, **12**, 2, 100–103.

Baxter, J. (1980). The dictionary and vocabulary behaviour: A single word or a handful? *TESOL Quarterly*, **14**, 3, 325–36.

Bejoint, H. (1981). The foreign student's use of monolingual English dictionaries: A study of language needs and reference skills. *Applied Linguistics*, **2**, 3, 207–22.

Benson, M. (1995). Review of Longman Language Activator. *System*, **23**, 2, 253–5.

Bensoussan, M., Sim, D. and Weiss, R. (1984). The effect of dictionary usage on EFL test performance compared with student and teacher attitudes and expectations. *Reading in a Foreign Language*, **2**, 2, 262–76.

Bogaards, P. (1996). Dictionaries for learners of English. *International Journal of Lexicography*, **9**, 4, 277–320.

Bruton, A. (2007). Vocabulary learning from dictionary reference in collaborative EFL translational writing. *System*, **35**, 353–67.

Chun, D. M. and Plass, J. L. (1996). Effects of multimedia annotations on vocabulary acquisition. *Modern Language Journal*, **80**, 2, 183–98.

Clarke, D. F. and Nation, I. S. P. (1980). Guessing the meanings of words from context: Strategy and techniques. *System*, **8**, 3, 211–20.

Cumming, G., Cropp, S. and Sussex, R. (1994). On-line lexical resources for language learners: Assessment of some approaches to word definition. *System*, **22**, 3, 369–77.

Gonzalez, O. (1999). Building vocabulary: Dictionary consultation and the ESL student. *Journal of Adolescent and Adult Literacy*, **43**, 3, 264–70.

Gu, Y. and Johnson, R. K. (1996). Vocabulary learning strategies and language learning outcomes. *Language Learning*, **46**, 4, 643–79.

Hartmann, R. R. K. (1981). Style values: Linguistic approaches and lexicographical practice. *Applied Linguistics*, **2**, 3, 263–73.

Hartmann, R. R. K. (1982). Reviews of Chambers dictionaries. *System*, **10**, 1, 85–6.

Hartmann, R. R. K. (1992). Lexicography, with particular reference to English learners' dictionaries. *Language Teaching*, **25**, 3, 151–9.

Harvey, K. and Yuill, D. (1997). A study of the use of a monolingual pedagogical dictionary by learners of English engaged in writing. *Applied Linguistics*, **18**, 3, 253–78.

Herbst, T. (1996). On the way to the perfect learners' dictionary: A first comparison of OALD5, LDOCE3, COBUILD2 and CIDE. *International Journal of Lexicography*, **9**, 4, 321–7.

Hill, M. and Laufer, B. (2003). Type of task, time-on-task and electronic dictionaries in incidental vocabulary acquisition. *IRAL*, **41**, 2, 87–106.

Hulstijn, J., Hollander, M. and Greidanus, T. (1996). Incidental vocabulary learning by advanced foreign language students: The influence of marginal glosses, dictionary use, and reoccurrence of unknown words. *Modern Language Journal*, **80**, 3, 327–39.

Hulstijn, J. H. (1993). When do foreign-language readers look up the meaning of unfamiliar words? The influence of task and learner variables. *Modern Language Journal*, **77**, 2, 139–47.

Kennedy, G. (ed.). (1997). *Dictionary of New Zealand Sign Language*. Auckland: Auckland University Press.

Kim, E. J. (2009). *A Study on the Vocabulary Learning Strategies of Korean University Students*. Hankuk University of Foreign Studies, Seoul.

Knight, S. M. (1994). Dictionary use while reading: The effects on comprehension and vocabulary acquisition for students of different verbal abilities. *Modern Language Journal*, **78**, 3, 285–99.

Lado, R., Baldwin, B. and Lobo, F. (1967). *Massive Vocabulary Expansion in a Foreign Language Beyond the Basic Course: The Effects of Stimuli, Timing and Order of Presentation*. Washington, DC: U.S. Department of Health, Education, and Welfare.

Laufer, B. (1992). Corpus-based versus lexicographer examples in comprehension and production of new words. *EURALEX '92 Proceedings*, 71–6.

Laufer, B. (1993). The effect of dictionary definitions and examples on the use and comprehension of new L2 words. *Cahiers de Lexicologie*, **63**, 131–42.

Laufer, B. (2001). Reading, word-focused activities and incidental vocabulary acquisition in a second language. *Prospect*, **16**, 3, 44–54.

Laufer, B. and Hadar, L. (1997). Assessing the effectiveness of monolingual, bilingual and "bilingualised" dictionaries in the comprehension and production of new words. *Modern Language Journal*, **81**, 2, 189–96.

Laufer, B. and Hill, M. (2000). What lexical information do L2 learners select in a CALL dictionary and how does it affect word retention? *Language Learning & Technology*, **3**, 2, 58–76.

Laufer, B. and Hulstijn, J. (2001). Incidental vocabulary acquisition in a second language: The construct of task-induced involvement. *Applied Linguistics*, **22**, 1, 1–26.

Laufer, B. and Kimmel, M. (1997). Bilingualised dictionaries: How learners really use them. *System*, 25, 3, 361–9.

Laufer, B. and Shmueli, K. (1997). Memorizing new words: Does teaching have anything to do with it? *RELC Journal*, 28, 1, 89–108.

Li, J. (2010). Learning vocabulary via computer-assisted scaffolding for text processing. *Computer Assisted Language Learning*, 23, 3, 253–75.

Loucky, J. P. (2002). Improving access to target vocabulary using computerized bilingual dictionaries. *ReCALL*, 14, 2, 295–314.

Luppescu, S. and Day, R. R. (1993). Reading, dictionaries and vocabulary learning. *Language Learning*, 43, 2, 263–87.

MacFarquhar, P. D. and Richards, J. C. (1983). On dictionaries and definitions. *RELC Journal*, 14, 1, 111–24.

Marco, M. J. L. (1999). Procedural vocabulary: Lexical signalling of conceptual relations in discourse. *Applied Linguistics*, 20, 1, 1–21.

McKeown, M. G. (1993). Creating effective definitions for young word learners. *Reading Research Quarterly*, 28, 1, 17–31.

Nation, I. S. P. (1978). Translation and the teaching of meaning: Some techniques. *ELT Journal*, 32, 3, 171–5.

Nation, I. S. P. (1989). Dictionaries and language learning. In Tickoo, M. L. (ed.), *Learners' Dictionaries: State of the Art RELC Anthology Series No. 23* (pp. 65–71). Singapore: SEAMEO Regional Language Centre.

Nesi, H. and Meara, P. (1994). Patterns of misinterpretation in the productive use of EFL dictionary definitions. *System*, 22, 1, 1–15.

Neubach, A. and Cohen, A. (1988). Processing strategies and problems encountered in the use of dictionaries. *Dictionaries: Journal of the Dictionary Society of North America*, 10, 1–19.

Peters, E. (2007). Manipulating L2 learners' online dictionary use and its effect on L2 word retention. *Language Learning & Technology*, 11, 2, 36–58.

Prichard, C. (2008). Evaluating L2 readers' vocabulary strategies and dictionary use. *Reading in a Foreign Language*, 20, 2, 216–31.

Roby, W. B. (1999). "What's in a gloss?" *Language Learning & Technology*, 2, 2, 94–101.

Rott, S. and Williams, J. (2003). Making form-meaning connections while reading: a qualitative analysis of word processing. *Reading in a Foreign Language*, 15, 1, 45–75.

Rott, S., Williams, J. and Cameron, R. (2002). The effect of multiple-choice glosses and input-output cycles on lexical acquisition and retention. *Language Teaching Research*, 6, 3, 183–222.

Scholfield, P. J. (1981). Writing, vocabulary errors and the dictionary. *Guidelines*, 6, 31–40.

Scholfield, P. J. (1982a). The role of bilingual dictionaries in ESL/EFL: A positive view. *Guidelines*, 4, 1, 84–98.

Scholfield, P. J. (1982b). Using the English dictionary for comprehension. *TESOL Quarterly*, 16, 2, 185–94.

Scholfield, P. J. (1997). Vocabulary reference works in foreign language learning. In Schmitt, N. and McCarthy, M. (eds.), *Vocabulary: Description, Acquisition and Pedagogy* (pp. 279–302). Cambridge: Cambridge University Press.

Stein, G. (1988). ELT dictionaries, the teacher and the student. *JALT Journal*, **11**, 1, 36–45.

Summers, D. (1988). The role of dictionaries in language learning. In Carter, R. and McCarthy, M. (eds.), *Vocabulary and Language Teaching* (pp. 111–25). London: Longman.

Terrell, P., Schnorr, V., Morris, W. V. A. and Breitsprecher, R. (1991). *Collins German Dictionary* (2nd ed.). Glasgow: Collins.

Thompson, G. (1987). Using bilingual dictionaries. *ELT Journal*, **41**, 4, 282–6.

Tickoo, M. L. (1987). New dictionaries and the ESL teacher. *Guidelines*, **9**, 2, 57–67.

Tomaszczyk, J. (1979). Dictionaries: Users and uses. *Glottodidactica*, **12**, 103–19.

Wesche, M. B. and Paribakht, T. S. (2000). Reading-based exercises in second language vocabulary learning. *Modern Language Journal*, **84**, 2, 196–213.

11 Deliberate learning from word cards

This chapter is based on the idea that research has shown the deliberate learning of vocabulary to be such an efficient and effective way of learning that, in terms of speed of vocabulary growth, a course which includes both incidental learning from message-focused activities and deliberate learning will be much better than one that relies only on incidental learning. Deliberately learning vocabulary before it is met in message-focused activities means that such activities will be less difficult to do. Deliberately learning vocabulary after it has been met in a message-focused activity means that deliberate learning will be more meaningful and motivated.

The term 'learning from word cards' will be used to describe the formation of associations between a foreign language word form (written or spoken) and its meaning (often in the form of a first language translation, although it could be a second language definition or a picture or a real object, for example). This term has been deliberately chosen to connect this kind of learning with a strategy and to avoid the confusion of other terms such as 'list learning' (Griffin and Harley, 1996), 'paired associate learning' (Carroll, 1963; Higa, 1965), and 'learning word pairs' (Nation, 1982). As we shall see, list learning is not a desirable strategy if the order of the items in the list cannot easily be changed. Paired associates, referring to the association between form and meaning, is not a very transparent term, and word pairs wrongly implies that the meaning has to be expressed as a single word.

In the simplest form of learning from word cards, a learner writes a foreign word on one side of a small, easily carried card and its first language translation on the other. The learner goes through a set of cards looking at the foreign word and trying to retrieve its meaning. If it cannot be retrieved, the learner turns the card over and looks at the translation.

There are now many flashcard programs available (Nakata, 2011) which apply good principles and effectively exploit the strengths of computer-assisted vocabulary learning. We will look at these later in this chapter.

Is learning from word cards a useful activity?

Many teachers and writers about vocabulary learning see the direct study of vocabulary not immediately connected to a particular text as being opposed to learning from context (Judd, 1978; Oxford and Crookall, 1990; Turner, 1983) and thus dismiss it as a learning activity. Oxford and Crookall's (1990: 9–10) biased definition of decontextualising techniques provides the basic reasons for this dismissal of learning from word cards:

Decontextualising techniques are those that remove the word as completely as possible from any communicative context that might help the learner remember and that might provide some notion as to how the word is actually used as a part of the language.

This comment involves two criticisms:

1. Learning from word cards is not good for remembering.
2. Learning from word cards does not help with use of the word.

Two further criticisms are raised against deliberate learning:

3. Learning from word cards only provides explicit knowledge which is not the kind of knowledge needed for fluent use.
4. Deliberate learning can only deal with a small number of the words which need to be learned.

Before looking at each of these criticisms, it is necessary to make the point that the use of word cards does not exclude the possibility of putting a sample sentence or collocations on the card. Oxford and Crookall (1990) and others, however, would still regard this as decontextualised learning and thus undesirable because the word is not in a 'communicative' context, that is, it is not being used for a communicative purpose.

Is word card learning efficient?

The first criticism is that the lack of a context makes learning difficult. Judd (1978: 73) comments that words taught in isolation are generally not remembered. There is evidence that the presence of a sentence context can help with making the word form–word meaning association (Laufer and Shmueli, 1997), but there is also an enormous amount of evidence that shows that even without a sentence context large numbers of words can be learned in a short time and can be retained for a very long time.

Teachers and course designers greatly underestimate learners' capacity for the initial learning of foreign vocabulary. Thorndike (1908) found that his adult learners could average about 34 German–English word pairs per hour (1,030 words in 30 hours). The least efficient of his learners averaged nine per hour (380 words in 42 hours) and the most efficient 58 per hour (1,046 words in 18 hours). After 42 days more than 60% of the words were still retained. Webb (1962) gained even more spectacular results in a continuous six-hour learning session. Like Thorndike, Webb found a wide variation of achievement among learners. Some learners mastered only 33 lists of six English–Russian pairs (198 words) in six hours, an average of 33 word pairs per hour. Other learners mastered 111 lists (666 words) in under four hours, an average of about 166 words per hour. Both Thorndike and Webb found no decrease in learning capacity as the learning progressed. Webb found that after five hours of continuous learning, learning and recall were not less than in the first hour of learning. In fact, there was an increase in learning capacity as the experiment progressed. Thorndike (1908), and also Anderson and Jordan (1928), comparing tests covering several weeks, noticed that the fast learners still retained a greater percentage of words than the slower learners. That is, fast learners are not fast forgetters. De Groot (2006) similarly found that words learned quickly were not forgotten quickly. Speed of learning is largely affected by factors like concreteness or imageability of the word, pronunceability and cognates or loanwords status. These factors make some words easier to learn and also help them stay longer in memory. What is clear from these and similar studies is that there is a very wide range of skill in deliberate learning. It is not clear whether training reduces this range and to what degree it involves factors like the size of working memory.

The data on the number of repetitions required for learning is just as surprising. Lado et al. (1967) found that college students who had completed at least six credits of college Spanish achieved recognition scores averaging 95% and recall scores averaging 65% after meeting each word pair once in a 100-word list. The word pairs were infrequent Spanish words with English translations accompanied by pictures. Crothers and Suppes (1967) found that after seven repetitions of 108 Russian–English word pairs almost all of the learners had mastered all of the words. After six repetitions of 216 word pairs most learners had learned at least 80% of the words. Learning rates also tended to increase as the experiments progressed, thus showing the existence of a 'learning to learn' effect. In their study of indirect vocabulary learning in context, Saragi et al. (1978) found that on average the number of encounters required for most learners to recognise the meaning of a word was around sixteen. In this experiment the learners did not know that they would be tested on the new vocabulary and did not consciously study it while reading.

Does the learning gained from using word cards remain in learners' memory?

Studies of very long-term memory show that the results of deliberate learning persist over several years (Bahrick, 1984a&b; Bahrick and Phelps, 1987). Beaton et al. (1995) studied a learner who had learned a 350-word Italian vocabulary using the keyword technique ten years previously but who had not had any opportunity to use the knowledge (the trip to Italy did not happen!). Ten years later it was found he remembered 35% of the test words with spelling fully correct and over 50% with minor spelling errors. After looking at the vocabulary list for 10 minutes, recall increased to 65% (fully accurate) and 76% (some minor spelling errors). After one and a half hours' revision, recall was near to 100%. Thorndike (1908) found good retention well over a month later.

There is thus plenty of evidence that, for the simple word form–word meaning aspect of vocabulary learning, direct learning from word cards is an efficient activity. However, critics of such learning say that this learning has little to do with language use, which is the second major criticism of learning from word cards.

Is learning in context better?

'Learning in context' can mean several things. In this section we look at how seeing or hearing a word in at least a sentence context can provide useful information about it. The term is also used to refer to the kind of learning that occurs, that is, words met in context while reading or listening can be picked up incidentally and thus perhaps more readily become a part of our implicit knowledge. As we shall see in this chapter – and as we saw in Chapter 5 on learning through extensive reading –, learning words incidentally is not the only way vocabulary can enter implicit knowledge; it results in small amounts of learning and thus requires enormous amounts of reading and listening to be effective on its own.

In Chapter 2 we have looked at what is involved in knowing a word. In its simplest form, learning from word cards helps with learning the written form of the word, learning the concept of the word and making the connection between the form and the meaning. These are three of the nine aspects involved in knowing a word. Learning from word cards can also give a little knowledge of the grammar of the word, particularly its part of speech, its spoken form and perhaps one or two of its collocations.

There are still many aspects of knowing a word that are not effectively covered by learning from word cards, especially constraints on use of the word, the full range of collocations and grammatical patterns in which it occurs, the variety of referents and related meanings the word can have and its various morphological forms. Table 11.1 lists the aspects of knowing a word, indicating which ones are most helped by learning from word cards, which ones are partly helped and which are poorly dealt with by this strategy. Note that word cards can be used for both receptive and productive learning.

A similar table could be designed for incidental vocabulary learning from context where a different range of aspects would be marked. The point of this kind of analysis is to show that any one way of dealing with vocabulary is not effective in helping learners gain control of all aspects of word knowledge. It is necessary to see learning from context and learning from word cards as complementary ways of learning which are partly overlapping and reinforcing and which also give rise to some different kinds of knowledge. The strength of learning from word cards is that it is focused, efficient and certain. The strength of learning from context is that it places words in contexts of use, so that the conditions of learning closely resemble the conditions under which the words will need to be used. Webb (2007) found no significant difference on ten different vocabulary measures between learning a decontextualised word and its translation and learning a word and its translation with a sentence context. Webb (2009) found that receptive and productive decontextualised learning resulted in more than learning of form and meaning: it also resulted in substantial gains in knowledge of syntax, grammatical function and association. When words are learned deliberately, even without a sentence context or larger context, they are integrated into existing knowledge systems.

Part of the criticism that learning from word cards does not help with the use of the word relates to the nature of word meaning. Some writers take the position that the meaning of words comes from the context in which it occurs. Contexts, not dictionaries, determine meaning (Burroughs, 1982: 54). Firth (1957), however, saw collocation as only one kind of meaning. A similar position is taken in this book, that is, learners need to know a generalised underlying concept for a word and also need to know the particular uses and range of referents of this underlying concept. Learning from word cards is a very effective way of

Table 11.1 *Aspects of word knowledge dealt with by learning from word cards*

Form	spoken	R	✔
		P	
	written .	R	✔✔
		P	✔✔
	word parts	R	
		P	
Meaning	form and meaning	R	✔✔
		P	✔✔
	concept and referents	R	✔
		P	
	associations	R	
		P	
Use	grammatical functions	R	✔
		P	✔
	collocations	R	✔
		P	✔
	constraints on use (register, frequency ...)	R	
		P	

Notes: In Column 3 – R = receptive knowledge, P = productive knowledge
In Column 4 – ✔✔ = well dealt with, ✔ = partly dealt with

learning the underlying concept. Meeting words in context makes learners aware of how this concept changes to suit particular contexts and the range of contexts in which the word can be used.

So far, we have looked at two important criticisms of learning from word cards. The first, that word cards are not good for remembering, is simply wrong; the research shows otherwise. The second, that word cards do not help with the use of words is partly correct, but it regards such learning as an alternative to learning through meeting words in context when these two kinds of learning are not alternatives, but complementary. Both are needed. Learning the formal features of a word, its meaning and connecting the form to the meaning are very useful prerequisites to using a word. As well as learning through the use-based strands of meaning-focused input, meaning-focused output and fluency development, there is considerable benefit in also learning through language-focused learning of which learning from word cards is one strategy.

Does word card learning provide the knowledge needed for normal language use?

Vocabulary which has been deliberately learned out of context 'is stored and accessed in a manner that is similar to existing L1 and L2 lexical knowledge' (Elgort, 2011: 399), that is, deliberately learned vocabulary can be accessed subconsciously and fluently, and is typically integrated into the semantic system of the learners. To show this, Elgort carried out three psycholinguistic priming studies where vocabulary that had been deliberately learned was used as the primes. Thus, Krashen's (1985) distinction between acquisition and learning, which says that deliberately learned material is not available for normal language use, is not relevant to vocabulary knowledge. Elgort's results show that deliberate vocabulary learning is not only efficient (you can learn a lot of words) but effective (it provides useable knowledge). In terms of our knowledge of the theory of vocabulary learning, Elgort's study provides the most important advance in the last 20 years because it provides the very important link between deliberate learning and implicit knowledge. Deliberately learned vocabulary becomes both explicit and implicit knowledge.

Can deliberate learning result in enough words being learned?

There is a fourth criticism of the direct study of vocabulary, mainly put forward by first language researchers (Anderson and Nagy, 1992). Although this criticism focuses mainly on the teaching of vocabulary, it has had the effect of discouraging the teaching of strategies for direct vocabulary learning. The argument is that there are so many thousands of words in the language and it takes so much time to effectively learn a word that direct study is an inefficient procedure for vocabulary growth. Learners are better off concentrating on increasing their reading because their long-term vocabulary growth will be greater by incidental learning from context.

This criticism is largely correct for native speakers of English who begin school already knowing several thousand words. Biemiller and Boote (2006) argue strongly for teaching vocabulary to primary grade native speakers. They argue that this is feasible in terms of amount of words taught and learned (Biemiller, 2005; Biemiller, 2010; Biemiller & Slonim, 2001), teaching between 10 and 20 words a week would result in increases of around 400 words per year. This teaching is necessary to deal with a large individual differences in vocabulary size in primary grade children. The differences also exist in secondary grade children, possibly to a larger degree. A small vocabulary size is likely to have very severe effects on reading and learning through reading. Biemiller and Boote found learning rates of around 40% of the words that were taught. Repeated reading of texts was found to be a very useful contributor to vocabulary learning.

The inefficiency criticism is certainly not true for non-native speakers of English who do not know the high-frequency words of the language, or who need to quickly increase their knowledge of low frequency words. There are two reasons why the criticism is not correct for non-native speakers. Firstly, all words in English are not equally valuable; higher-frequency words are much more useful than low-frequency words. There is a very good return for the time and learning effort spent on high-frequency words, and mid-frequency words are generally more useful than low-frequency words. Secondly, learning from word cards can be a way of quickly raising learners' awareness of particular words so that when they meet these words in reading and listening they will be noticed and more easily learned. That is, direct learning is a very useful complement to learning from context, and just one step in the cumulative learning of a word.

In general, the critics of direct vocabulary learning need to take a broader view of what is involved in knowing a word and how vocabulary can be learned.

The values of direct learning of vocabulary are: (1) it is efficient in terms of return for time and effort; (2) it allows learners to consciously focus on an aspect of word knowledge that is not easily gained from context or dictionary use; (3) it allows learners to control the repetition and processing of the vocabulary to make learning secure; and (4) it provides the kind of knowledge (implicit knowledge) needed for normal language use.

There are also studies comparing incidental learning with intentional learning, which invariably show that deliberate, intentional learning results in much more learning in a set time than incidental learning. We will look at these studies later in this chapter. There is no doubt that for certain kinds of knowledge direct learning is highly efficient and enduring.

Ellis (1995) argues that learning word meaning and linking the word form to the meaning is especially suited to explicit conscious learning. One reason why this might be so is that learners can make use of deliberate mnemonic strategies like the keyword technique.

The use of word cards provides an opportunity for learners to focus on the underlying concept of a word that runs through its various related uses. This has several values. Firstly, it reduces the number of words to be learned. If a learner can see *kiss* as in *kiss someone's lips* and *kiss* as in *The wind kissed his face* as being essentially the same word even though they might be translated by different words in the first language, then there are fewer words to learn. Dictionaries do not encourage this view, rightly preferring to separate as many different uses as possible in order to make it easier for the reader to find the meaning for a particular context. For example, the entry for *knee* in *Collins COBUILD English Language Dictionary* has the following divisions:

1.1. The place where your leg bends
1.2. The place around or above your knee when you sit
2. The knee in a piece of clothing
3. To be on your knees
4. To bring a person or country to their knees

All of these uses share a clear common meaning and learners should be aware of this. Learners can do this analysis of underlying meaning as a way of preparing their word cards.

Secondly, looking at the underlying meaning of a word has an educational value. It demonstrates to learners that there is not a one-to-one correspondence between a word in the second language and the first language word. It shows learners that different languages categorise the world in different ways. Deliberate attention to concepts can also reveal the metaphors that users of the second language accept as a normal part of their view of the world (Lakoff and Johnson, 1980).

What is the most effective way of learning from word cards?

Learning from word cards is a way of quickly increasing vocabulary size through focused intentional learning. The strategy is one that many learners already use but often their use is not as effective as it could be. The design of the strategy draws heavily on research on paired associate learning, mnemonic techniques and vocabulary learning. In a later section of this chapter, we will look at how learners can be trained in the use of the strategy. Let us now look at the steps in the strategy. The three major steps involve choosing the words to learn, making word cards, and using the cards. Each of these steps involves the application of research-based principles. Table 11.2 lists the steps and principles. The application of these principles and the research evidence for them are described in detail.

Table 11.2 *Steps and principles involved in the word card strategy*

1. Choosing words to learn	• Learn useful words. • Avoid interference.
2. Making word cards	• Put the word or phrase on one side and the meaning on the other to encourage retrieval. • Use L1 translations. • Also use pictures where possible. • Keep the cards simple. • Suit the number of words in the pack to the difficulty of the words.
3. Using the word cards	• Use retrieval. • Space the repetitions, particularly the first one. • Learn receptively, then productively. • Start with small packs (or blocks) of words and increase the size as learning becomes easier. • Keep changing the order of the words in the pack. • Put known words aside and concentrate on the difficult words. • Say the words aloud or to yourself. • Put the word or phrase in a sentence or with some collocations. • Process the word deeply and thoughtfully using the mnemonic techniques of word parts or the keyword technique where feasible and necessary.

Choosing words to learn

The first step is to choose suitable words to learn.

Learn useful words. Priority should be given to high-frequency words and to words that clearly fulfil language use needs.

Avoid interference. Words that are formally similar to each other, or that belong to the same lexical set, or which are near synonyms, opposites or free associates should not be learned together (Erten and Tekin, 2008; Higa, 1963; Papathanasiou, 2009; Tinkham, 1993, 1997; Waring, 1997b). If the difficulty of learning semantically related words together (50% to 100% more difficult than unrelated words) is compared with the size of the effect of other variables, it can be seen how strong the interference effect is. De Groot (2006) found that regular spelling increased receptive learning by around 19% in the early stages of learning the words, imageability by around 16% and L1 frequency by around 7%.

Making word cards

The second step is to prepare the word cards. Small cards (around 5 × 4 cm) should be used so that they can easily be carried around.

Put the word on one side and the meaning on the other to encourage retrieval. The word or phrase to be learned is written on one side of the card and its meaning on the other. The word can be written in a sentence context instead of as a single item if this makes learning easier. Retrieval helps learning, although Barcroft (2007) did not find a strong effect (about 10% better than seeing the word form and its associated picture together). It is best to see the word and its meaning together initially (Royer, 1973) as this then allows successful retrieval on the next repetition. Making the word cards can thus be a major contributor to learning, and it is not unusual for a large proportion of the items in a pack of 50 words to be correctly retrieved immediately after making the cards.

Use first language translations. Research shows (Lado et al., 1967; Laufer and Shmueli, 1997; Mishima, 1967) that learning is generally better if the meaning is written in the learners' first language. This is probably because the meaning can be easily understood and the first language meaning already has many rich associations for the learner. Laufer and Shmueli (1997) found that L1 glosses are superior to L2 glosses in both short-term and long-term (five weeks) retention and irrespective of whether the words are learned in lists, sentences or texts.

One of the criticisms made of bilingual dictionaries, learning from lists and learning from word cards is that the use of the first language encourages learners to think that there is a one-to-one correspondence between the words in the second language and the first language. Learners need to be shown that this is not so, and looking for underlying meanings is a good way of doing so. Learners also need to be shown that there is not a one-to-one correspondence between a second language word and a second language definition, and between a second language word and a picture. The representation of meaning is a very inexact process and learners should be aware of this.

Hummel (2010) argues for viewing translation as an elaborative process that substantially enriches the connections for a newly translated L2 word. Hummel found that doing L1 to L2 sentence translation where the translation of the target word was provided resulted in useful learning but not as much as copying the L2 sentence where the translation of the target word was provided. This finding may provide support for Barcroft's (2006) argument that we largely learn what we focus on. The translation task involved four kinds of activity:

1. The learner sees the L2 target word and its L1 translation.
2. The learner sees the L1 or L2 sentence.
3. The learner translates the L1 or L2 context through retrieval of the translations of the context words.
4. The learner writes the L2 or L1 sentence.

Whereas the copying task involved only two of these kinds of activity (1 and 4), the receptive word translation task only required at least the information in 1 above, so perhaps 2, 3 and perhaps 4 are distracting tasks.

If this conclusion is true, it provides further support for a minimal kind of word learning if recall of word meaning is the goal. Large amounts of information may distract rather than enrich learning. If the language-focused learning strand is to have greatest effect, it may be most efficient to use simple well-focused tasks.

Use pictures where possible. In some cases the meaning of a word will be best expressed by a diagram or picture. Experiments involving pictures as a means of learning productive vocabulary indicate that questions like 'Which are more efficient, pictures or translations?' are not appropriate. Pictures and translations have different effects and so should be regarded as complementary sources of meaning rather than alternatives. Thus, for receptive learning, Lado et al. (1967) found that simultaneous presentation of both a written and spoken translation *accompanied* by a corresponding picture was superior to other arrangements and alternatives. Experiments by Kopstein and Roshal (1954) and Deno (1968), while favouring pictures over translations, noted the differing effects of pictures and translations under various learning and teaching conditions. Deno concluded that in his experiment pictures were not encoded in the same way as words (p. 206). Webber (1978) similarly found a superior effect for pictures. For older learners (Chen, 1990; Lotto and De Groot, 1998; Tonzar et al., 2009) L1 translations tend to work best; for young learners learning with pictures resulted in faster responses. The finding of a positive effect for pictures challenges models of L2 storage which see the L1 as a mediating link for lower proficiency learners.

A further argument for regarding pictures and translations as complementary is that different learners prefer different sources of meaning. Kellogg and Howe (1971) compared pictures and translations for learning Spanish words. They concluded that learning was significantly faster with pictures than with written words (p. 92). This however did not apply to all learners: 25 out of 82 learners learned faster with words than with pictures. So, although on average picture stimuli gave better results than words, a significantly large group within the class learned better from words. A teacher would achieve better results for all learners by providing both words and pictures rather than by providing the form favoured by the majority.

Not all words are picturable, but for those that are, the actual drawing of the picture on the card could improve memory. A suitable picture is an instantiation of the word and this may result in a deeper type of processing than a first language translation which does not encourage the learner to imagine a real instance of the meaning of the word.

Keep the cards simple. Other kinds of information like collocates, etymology, constraints and grammatical pattern could be put on the word card, but it is best to see learning from word cards as only one step in the cumulative process in learning a word and thus not to expect too much from this one kind of learning.

Suit the number of words in a pack to the difficulty of the words. In a series of experiments, Crothers and Suppes (1967) investigated the effect on learning of the number of Russian–English word pairs in a list. If, for example, learners are required to learn 300 foreign word pairs, is it better for the learners to study 100 of them several times first, then study the second 100 several times, and then the third 100, or is it better for the learners to try to learn all the 300 word pairs as one list? When 300 words are learned as one list, learners go through the whole 300 words once, then start at the beginning of the list again and continue going through until all the words are known. Crothers and Suppes studied the following list sizes: 18, 36, 72, 100, 108, 216 and 300 word pairs.

When difficulty was low, it was more efficient to use the largest sized group of words. When difficulty was high, then the smallest sized group of words was the best. Difficulty here has several meanings. Difficulty is high when there is limited time for learning and learners have no control over the time they can spend on each item. Difficulty is high when learners must recall and not just recognise the new words. Difficulty is high when the words themselves are difficult because, for example, they are difficult to pronounce and their English translations are adjectives, adverbs or verbs, rather than nouns (see Rodgers, 1969; Higa, 1965).

Kornell (2009) found that learning with a large group of words (around 20) was more effective on a test the following day than learning four small groups of words (five per group). Although it has been thought that increasingly spaced retrieval within a learning session is better than equally spaced retrieval, current evidence shows that equal spacing is at least as good as expanding spacing: the more influential factor is the length of the spaces. The longer the spacing between retrievals, that is, the number of other words that occur before the same word re-occurs in the learning session, the better it is for long-term retention (Karpicke and Bauernschmidt, 2011). Nakata (2008) found computer-based spacing of words to be better for long-term learning than word cards and lists. Note that the spacing schedule in these experiments relates to how many other words occur between each retrieval of each particular word in one study session. The spacing in the experimental research does not involve the spacing between study sessions. Nonetheless, it is likely that the spacing between sessions need not follow a strict schedule as long as the sessions are spaced.

It is worth stressing the importance of retrieval. As Karpicke and Blunt (2011: 772) note, because each active retrieval changes memory, the act of reconstructing knowledge must be considered essential to the process of learning. Retrieval is probably particularly important in learning when using word cards because such learning has very limited learning goals: to learn the spoken and written word forms, and to learn the form–meaning connection. In a study of learning ideas from text (not vocabulary learning), Karpicke and Blunt found that retrieval practice (read–retrieve–read again–retrieve) was substantially more effective than elaborative learning using concept mapping. This finding might also apply to word card learning in that elaborative learning might take attention away from its narrow learning goals. Richness of vocabulary knowledge may be best developed through message-focused language use in reading, listening, writing and speaking which is an essential complement to language-focused learning using word cards.

Retrieval can only occur if items have already been memorised, so typically in experiments on word pair learning, there is a learning phase where the items are studied and tested, and then there is a retrieval phase. If we apply this to the study of word cards, then it is useful to begin with an intensive learning session where words that are easily retrieved are put aside so that the unknown items can be focused on. The later sessions can be done with reasonably sized packs of cards (30 or more) using spaced retrieval within a learning session.

Using the cards

The quality of learning from word cards will depend on the way they are used.

Use retrieval. Writing the word on one side and its meaning on the other allows the learner to be able to retrieve the meaning of the word from memory. Having to retrieve the meaning results in far superior learning to seeing the word and its meaning at the same time (Baddeley, 1990; Landauer and Bjork, 1978). This is one reason why cards are better as a means of learning than vocabulary lists and vocabulary notebooks. In lists and notebooks, the word form and its meaning are usually both visible together. If lists and notebooks are to be used to help learning, then the meaning needs to be covered up so that learners have the chance to retrieve the item from memory. Retrieval is sometimes called 'the testing effect' because each retrieval is like a small test (Karpicke and Roediger, 2007).

If there is a delay between the presentation of a word form and its meaning, learners have an opportunity to make an effort to guess or recall the meaning, and presumably this extra effort will result in faster and longer-retained learning. However, the guessing can only be successful if the foreign word form gives a good clue to its meaning, either because the foreign and native words are cognates or because the word form and its translation have previously been seen together. Experimental evidence shows that simultaneous presentation of a word form and its meaning is best for the first encounter and, thereafter, delayed presentation (retrieval plus feedback) is best because there is then the possibility of effort leading to successful recall.

In an experiment by Royer (1973) learners saw each foreign word and its English translation simultaneously on the first trial and guessed by attempting to recall on subsequent trials. The group who were studying under the recalling procedure learned significantly more correct responses on a test given immediately after the learning sessions. Successful recall increases the chances that something will be remembered. Retrieving rather then simply seeing the item again seems to strengthen the retrieval route (Baddeley, 1990: 156).

Learners need to know the importance of retrieval and how to make it a part of the whole range of their learning activities. Meeting words in listening and reading texts provides an opportunity for retrieval as does using words in speaking and writing. Teachers should tolerate and allow for delays in retrieving vocabulary in the strands of meaning-focused input and meaning-focused output because the retrievals are contributing to learning. The combination of spaced repetition with retrieval is the basis of a strategy that Baddeley considers is easy to use and widely applicable (Baddeley, 1990: 158).

Space the repetitions. Repetition is essential for vocabulary learning because there is so much to know about each word that one meeting is not sufficient to gain this information, and because vocabulary items must not only be known they must be known well so that they can be fluently accessed. Repetition thus adds to the quality of knowledge and also to the quantity or strength of this knowledge.

There has been a great deal of research on how items should be repeated and much of this is relevant to learning vocabulary in another language. A very robust finding in memory research in general

(Baddeley, 1990; Kornell, 2009) and second language vocabulary learning research in particular (Bloom and Shuell, 1981; Dempster, 1987) is that spaced repetition results in more secure learning than massed repetition. Massed repetition involves spending a continuous period of time, say 15 minutes, giving repeated attention to a word. Spaced repetition involves spreading the repetitions across a long period of time, but not spending more time in total on the study of the words. For example, the words might be studied for three minutes now, another three minutes a few hours later, three minutes a day later, three minutes two days later and finally three minutes a week later. The total study time is fifteen minutes, but it is spread across ten or more days. This spaced repetition results in learning that will be remembered for a long period of time. The repetitions can be spaced at increasingly larger intervals, or can be evenly spaced. Recent research shows that within a learning session evenly spaced repetitions (fixed interval) are at least as effective as increasingly spaced repetitions (Pyc and Rawson, 2007). Interestingly, Kornell (2009) found that learners taking part in a massed or spaced study believed after the study that massed repetition had been more effective than spaced repetition even though their results later revealed that spaced was better. Kornell explained this as the mistaken belief that short-term performance equals long-term learning.

Spacing can refer to two learning conditions: (1) it can refer to different learning sessions that are separated from each other by being at different (spaced) times or on different days (between-session spacing); and (2) it can also refer to the number of words in a group of words for study. A group of five words provides a four-word spacing between chances to retrieve the same word. A group of 20 words provides greater spacing with 19 words between retrievals of the same word (within session spacing).

Karpicke and Roediger (2007) show that the critical spacing factor in enhancing delayed recall is the spacing between first presentation and the first retrieval attempt. This factor seems to account for most of the difference between evenly spaced and expanding retrievals. It means that when using word cards, it is better to go through all the items in a pack initially instead of spending time on each item. Karpicke and Roediger's experiments used five-item spacings, but Pyc and Rawson (2007) successfully used 23-item spacings, so packs of cards of 20 or so items may be effective. It also seems desirable not to go through the cards immediately after making them, but to wait for a few minutes.

An explanation of the positive effect of a delayed first retrieval is that it ensures that recall is not from short-term (primary) memory, but from long-term memory. This explanation may also partly explain why massed learning is not nearly as effective as spaced learning. Retrieval immediately after initial learning is more like massed learning than spaced learning, even if it is part of a spaced learning schedule.

Seibert (1927), Anderson and Jordan (1928) and Seibert (1930) investigated retention over periods of up to eight weeks. Most forgetting occurs immediately after initial learning and then, as time passes, the rate of forgetting becomes slower. For example, Anderson and Jordan measured recall immediately after learning, after one week, after three weeks and after eight weeks. The percentages of material retained were 66%, 48%, 39% and 37% respectively. This indicates that the repetition of new items should occur very soon after they are first studied, before too much forgetting occurs. After this the repetitions can be spaced further apart. Griffin (1992) also found that most forgetting seems to occur soon after learning.

Spacing learning sessions for words allows integration of the new learning within already existing knowledge systems. Lindsay and Gaskell (2010) review research that shows that there are important qualitative changes in the lexical knowledge of newly learned words that are not caused by further meetings with the words but by changes in the way the word is stored. These changes are helped by sleep and by spaced learning sessions. Until this change in storage occurs, newly learned words are functionally separate from the established lexicon. This evidence underlines the importance of delayed post-tests in vocabulary learning research, particularly where what is being measured relates to integration with other words. The time delay should be around 24 hours. Lindsay and Gaskell explain this delayed effect by proposing that we have two learning systems in the brain that depend on each other: (1) a slow learning network and (2) a rapid learning system, the Complementary Learning Systems account of learning and memory (Davis and Gaskell, 2009; McClelland et al., 1995). While this research is still in its infancy, it provides strong support for spacing between vocabulary learning sessions.

Bahrick (1984a&b) and Bahrick and Phelps (1987) examined the recall of second language vocabulary items after very long periods of non-use, from 8 to 50 years. They found that the nature of the original learning influenced recall. Items which were initially easy to learn and which were given widely spaced practice (intervals of 30 days) were most likely to be retained over many years. The memory curves showed a decelerating drop for the first three to six years and then little change up to 25 to 30 years after which there was further decline. Bahrick and Phelps' research supports the well-established finding of the superiority of spaced over massed practice.

Pimsleur (1967) proposed a memory schedule to act as a guide for the size of the spaces between the repetitions. Pimsleur's suggestion, based on research evidence, is that the space between each repetition should become larger, with the initial repetitions being closer together and the later repetitions much further apart. There is no particular reason why the spacing between the repetitions is a matter of precise measurement, but it is interesting to look at Pimsleur's scale as a rough guide for the type of spacing suggested. The scale is exponential, so if the first interval was five seconds, then the next interval should be $5^2 = 25$ seconds, the next $5^3 = 125$ seconds, and the next $5^4 = 625$ seconds (about 10 minutes) and so on. Table 11.3 on p. 455 applies to the calculation across 11 repetitions.

The general principle which lies behind the spacing is that the older a piece of learning is, the slower the forgetting. This means two things. Firstly, after a piece of learning, the forgetting is initially very fast and then slows down. Secondly, on the second repetition a piece of learning is older than it was on the first repetition and so the forgetting on the second repetition will be slower than it was. On the third repetition the forgetting will be even slower. This means that if we arbitrarily set an 80% probability of recall as the point at which a repetition is needed, then the time between the repetitions will need to become longer and longer. The right probability of recall level is one where the learner has forgotten enough to feel that the repetition is worthwhile attending to and yet not forgotten too much so that there is still a good chance of recalling and thereby strengthening the form–meaning connection.

There are several possible explanations of the positive effect of spacing:

1. People feel that they need to pay more attention to words in spaced conditions because words are considered to be less well known than in massed conditions. That is, massing words leads to a partly false sense of better knowledge of the items and thus less effort (see Kornell, 2009: 1311).
2. Spaced items are a bit more difficult to recall, so there is more to learn on a subsequent repetition than with massed items. Spacing allows time for the forgetting, so retrieving can have a more substantial learning effect. This differs from the first explanation in that it is not an allocation of effort but a quality of learning effect. The general principle is that successful but difficult retrievals are better for memory than successful but easy retrievals (Karpicke and Roediger, 2007: 706; Pyc and Rawson, 2009: 444). Karpicke and Roediger argue that the difficulty of early retrievals is most important and that is why evenly spaced retrievals are better for long-term memory than expanding retrievals. Landauer and Bjork

Table 11.3 *Pimsleur's memory schedule*

Repetition	1	2	3	4	5	6	7	8	9	10	11
Time spacing before the next repetition	5 secs	25 secs	2 mins	10 mins	1 hour	5 hours	1 day	5 days	25 days	4 months	2 years

(1978: 631) suggest that retrieval may be more effective than simultaneously seeing the word and its meaning because retrieval involves greater effort, or because retrieval is more similar to the performance required during normal use. The evidence against this explanation is that easily learned words are often regular and predictable in form, meaning and use, and thus fit well into existing knowledge and are thus easily retained (de Groot, 2006).

3. Spacing provides situational context variability, whereas massed learning is done in the same context (see Pyc and Rawson, 2009: 445).

4. Baddeley (1990: 154–5) speculates that, because long-term learning depends on physical changes in the brain, spacing repetitions allows time for the regeneration of neurochemical substances that make these changes. Massed learning does not allow enough time for these substances to regenerate and thus they cannot continue to make the physical changes needed for learning. This explanation is still a matter for debate and investigation.

Mondria and Mondria-de Vries (1994) describe the 'hand computer' as a way of organising and focusing repetition. The hand computer is simply a box divided into five sections, with the second section larger than the first, the third larger than the second and so on. The words to be learned are put on cards and initially go into Section 1. When a word is known it is put into Section 2. When Section 2 fills up the words in Section 2 are reviewed (this is called 'preventive maintenance') and those that are still known go into Section 3 and those not recalled go back to Section 1. The same procedure continues for Sections 3, 4 and 5, with words not recalled going back to Section 1. This procedure can be easily computerised and is a part of well-designed flashcard programs (Nakata, 2011).

Learning from repetition not only depends on the spacing of the repetitions but also on the nature of the repetition.

So far, we have looked at repetition as repetition of the same material, that is, the repetition contributes mainly to strength of knowledge. However, repetition can extend and enrich previous meetings. Table 11.4 outlines some of the possibilities.

There are many degrees of creative use depending on the closeness of the relationship of the meaning to be instantiated to the previously met concept or instantiation.

Learning from word cards will usually involve repetition of the same material because the cards themselves do not change from one repetition to another. However, learners can change the way they process the cards by thinking of new sentences containing the word,

Table 11.4 *Types of repetition of word meaning*

Type of processing	Type of repetition
Noticing	Seeing the same word form and simultaneously presented meaning again
Retrieval	Recalling the same meaning several times
Creative use	Recalling the meaning in different contexts requiring a different instantiation of the meaning

applying new mnemonic techniques, thinking of new instantiations of the word and imagining contexts of use.

When words are met in reading and listening or used in speaking and writing, the newness of the context will influence learning, that is, if the words occur in new sentence contexts in the reading text, learning will be helped. Similarly, having to use the word to say new things will add to learning (Joe, 1995).

The types of repetition are related to the goal of learning. McKeown et al. (1985: 533) found that if simple definitional learning was the goal then more repetitions were better than fewer, but the fewer repetitions (four encounters) achieved respectable results. If dealing with the word in context was needed, then the repetitions needed to enrich the knowledge of words. This enrichment was even more critical when fluency of access was required.

Stahl and Fairbanks (1986: 97), in a meta-analysis of vocabulary studies, found somewhat similar results with repetition of the same forms, meanings and contexts having strong effects on measures of meaning recall. It seemed however that more elaborative repetition had stronger effects on passage comprehension measures than repetition of the same information.

Repetition is only one of a number of factors affecting vocabulary learning and the correlations between repetitions and learning generally are only moderate. For example, Saragi et al. (1978) found a correlation of about .45 indicating that repetition accounted for around 20% of the factors involved in learning. It is thus not easy to fix on a particular number of repetitions needed for learning to occur. It is likely that repetition has a stronger effect in deliberate learning.

Kachroo (1962) found that words repeated seven times or more in his coursebook were known by most learners. Crothers and Suppes (1967) found that most items in their vocabulary-learning experiments were learned after six or seven repetitions. Tinkham (1993), like many other researchers, found that learners differed greatly in the time and number of repetitions required for learning: most learners required five to seven repetitions for the learning of a group of six paired associates, but a few required over 20 repetitions.

Learn receptively, then productively. It is best to first learn words receptively (see the word – recall the meaning), and then productively (see the meaning – recall the word form). There are two factors to consider here: the difficulty of the learning, and the way the learning will be used. Receptive learning is usually easier than productive learning (but see Stoddard, 1929; Griffin and Harley, 1996; Waring, 1997a), that is, it is usually easier to learn to recall a meaning for a given word form than it is to recall a word form for a given meaning. In the early stages of learning a language it is quite difficult to remember vocabulary because there is not much other knowledge of the second language for the vocabulary to fit into. It is thus better to learn vocabulary receptively first and then productively later. Learning productively means turning over the pack of word cards, looking at the meaning and trying to recall the second language word.

Numerous experiments have also shown that recall is better if the direction of learning (receptive or productive) matches the direction of testing, that is, receptive learning favours receptive testing, productive learning favours productive testing. This testing or use effect is much stronger than the learning effect (Griffin and Harley, 1996; Mondria and Wiersma, 2004; Stoddard, 1929; Waring, 1997a). This means that if words are to be learned for listening or reading (receptive use), then receptive learning is best. If words are to be learned for speaking or writing (productive use), then productive learning is best. If both receptive and productive use is needed, then vocabulary should be learned in both ways. Griffin and Harley suggest that if, for motivational or time reasons, only one direction of learning is possible then learning productively (see the meaning, recall the second language word) is probably the best. All the relevant experiments show that the learning is bi-directional, that is, by learning productively, some receptive knowledge is also developed, and vice versa.

Start with small packs (or blocks) of words and increase the size as learning becomes easier. There is still debate about how many words to study at one time. If the pack of word cards is large (around 50 cards), then there is good spacing between repetitions of the same item and spacing helps learning. However, small packs of cards (say around 10 to 20) have high success rates and so more successful retrievals contribute to better learning (Barcroft, 2007; Pyc and Rawson, 2007, 2009). The best compromise seems to be to use smaller packs when beginning to learn a language or a set of items, and larger packs when the words seem easier to learn.

Keep changing the order of the cards in the pack and give more repetitions to difficult words. Learning words from cards involves making connections, particularly between the word form and its meaning. However, when several words are learned at the same time then other associations may be made between the different words and some of these associations do not help learning. Learning related words together can make learning more difficult because the words interfere with each other. Learning words in a set order can result in serial learning where one word helps recall of the next word in the list. If lists are being learned to be recalled and used as lists, then serial learning is a useful thing. For vocabulary learning, however, serial learning is not useful because each word needs to be recalled independently of others without having to go through a series of words. The way to avoid serial learning is to keep changing the order of the words in the pack.

The order of the words in a list has other effects on learning. In general, items at the beginning of the list and at the end of the list are learned better than items in the middle. These are called the primacy and recency effects (Baddeley, 1990: 52). Putting difficult words near the beginning is also a way of ensuring that they get more attention.

Pyc and Rawson (2007) compared a drop-out schedule (where learned items were put aside and the more difficult items were focused on) with a conventional schedule (where each item got equal attention). The drop-out schedule was more efficient. So, it is a good idea to allocate more repetitions to the difficult items and less to the easy ones (see also Atkinson, 1972).

Say the words aloud or to yourself. Ellis (1997) presents evidence to show that putting items into the phonological loop is a major way in which they pass into long-term memory. According to Seibert (1927) silent rote repetition of vocabulary lists is not the most efficient way of learning. If foreign vocabulary is to be learned for productive purposes, that is, learners are required to produce the foreign words, then saying the words aloud brings faster learning with better retention. Seibert found that the result obtained by studying aloud was in every case far better than the results obtained by studying aloud with written recall and by studying silently. Seibert also measured the time required for relearning after two, 10 and 42 days and found that 42 days learning aloud produced a better result than the other two ways. Gershman (1970) also found that writing had no significant effect on learning. Thomas and Dieter (1987) found that practising the written form of words improved knowledge of the written form but did not contribute significantly to strengthening the word form–word meaning connection.

Put the word in a phrase or sentence or with some collocates. While there are numerous studies that examine the effect of context on vocabulary learning (Dempster, 1987; Gipe and Arnold, 1979; Griffin, 1992; Grinstead, 1915; Laufer and Shmueli, 1997; Morgan and Bailey, 1943; Morgan and Foltz, 1944; Pickering, 1982; Seibert, 1930), they differ so greatly from each other in method, quality of design and quality of reporting that it is impossible to regard them as either supporting or contradicting each other in addressing the question 'Does context help vocabulary learning?'

If we put aside the poorly reported and poorly conducted studies and take only those studies that (1) defined *context* as the target word being in a sentence context, (2) did not involve guessing, but provided a gloss of the target word (either in the first language, second language, or both), and (3) compared learning with the sentence context with paired associate learning, we are left with only five studies: Dempster, 1987; Griffin, 1992; Laufer and Shmueli, 1997; Seibert, 1930; and Webb, 2007.

Laufer and Shmueli (1997) compared words in isolation, words in a sentence, words in a text, and words in an elaborated text. All four treatments involved learners having access to the word form plus a gloss of the word. The sentence and list presentations were superior in both short-term and long-term retention. Laufer and Shmueli explain this superiority as being one of focus, with list and sentence presentations providing a more direct focus on the words themselves. Laufer and Shmueli tested learning by using a multiple-choice test with only English (L2) synonyms and definitions. There were no other tests looking for other aspects of knowledge that may have particularly favoured learning in a sentence context. Such a measure, for example getting learners to suggest collocates, may have shown the sentence context condition to be even more favourable for learning.

Seibert (1930) compared productive learning of paired associates (English–French), words in a sentence context with a gloss in brackets after the word 'On met *le mors* (bit) dans la bouche du cheval', and a mixture of paired associates and context. Learning was tested by first asking learners to translate the isolated first language word with the foreign language, and then getting them to translate the first language word given in the original foreign language sentence context into the foreign language. Tests were carried out at intervals of 50 minutes, two days, ten days and 40 days. Paired associate learning gave higher scores than the mixed approach and the sentence context approach. No statistical procedures were used beyond finding the mean, the standard deviation and the standard deviation divided by the square root of the mean, and it is likely that the differences between the results of the treatments may not have been significant.

Griffin (1992) examined the effect of a context sentence on learning and testing. He saw the major issue in the use of context sentences as one of transfer. 'What is in question here is the ability of a word learned in a list of word-pairs to cue an appropriate response in a dissimilar test condition' (p. 50). Griffin found that for some learners list learning may make transfer to productive use less effective. For others, however, list learning was highly effective. The provision of a sentence context can enhance learning because more information is provided about the word and if learners can and do use this effectively, learning will be enhanced. Learners however have to have the ability and motivation to use this information. Griffin found that where the test involved recalling a first language translation for a second language word, there was no advantage for learning in a context. The provision of a context sentence can have positive advantages for learners who can make use of it.

Dempster (1987) found no helpful effects for the use of definition plus sentence contexts compared with definition alone when measured by (a) a definition recall test; (b) sentence completion involving recall of the form of the word; and (c) writing a sentence using the word. What Dempster's results show is that the presentation of the word in multiple contexts does not improve definition recall. Context, however, may contribute to other aspects of word knowledge such as knowledge of the range of possible referents and collocational knowledge. Multiple varied contexts (Joe, 1998) may strengthen knowledge of the meaning of a word but this would require several measures of word knowledge for each word to determine the strength of the effect.

Webb (2007) used 10 different tests for each word in order to compare the effectiveness in learning of decontextualised word-pairs (word plus L1 translation) with the same word pairs plus a sentence context. Ten tests were used to measure different aspects of receptive and productive word knowledge (orthography, form–meaning connection, grammatical function, paradigmatic associations and syntagmatic associations). No significant difference was found between the decontextualised and sentence context treatments. This may have been because learners were drawing on semantic, grammatical and associational knowledge from the first language.

The few well-conducted relevant studies do not show a striking superiority of sentence context over isolated word but, because a sentence context can provide extra information and little effort is required to add a sentence context to word cards, it is probably advisable to use such contexts on cards wherever possible.

Wang and Thomas (1995) compared the effect of the keyword technique and the 'semantic context' strategy which involves seeing the word in a context sentence. Although the keyword technique gave superior learning as measured by immediate testing, the memory for the words learned by the keyword technique deteriorated more quickly so that after a two-day delay, the sentence context strategy learning was equal to or better than the keyword learning. The results of the keyword technique seem to be fragile over time.

Process the word deeply and thoughtfully. Ellis (1995) distinguishes between learning the form of a word (what he calls 'the input/output specifications') and linking that knowledge of the form to a meaning. Drawing on research evidence from memory research and second language learning, he proposes that learning to recognise and produce the spoken and written forms of words in a fluent way is primarily an implicit learning process. That is, it depends on practice and use. Explicit knowledge can guide this learning 'but essentially we learn to drive by driving itself, just as we learn to spell on the job of spelling or speak by speaking' (Ellis, 1995: 16). Linking this knowledge of word forms to meaning, however, is a strongly explicit process which benefits from the use of memory tricks, thoughtful processing, deliberate analysis and elaboration, and conscious connections to previous knowledge. Although these ideas have been around for hundreds of years, it was Craik and Lockhart's (1972) 'levels-of processing-theory' which brought them into recent prominence.

Experiments investigating the recall of familiar non-foreign words (Craik and Lockhart, 1972; Craik and Tulving, 1975) indicate that words which do not receive full attention and are analysed only at a superficial level do not stay long in the memory. On the other hand, words that are fully analysed and are enriched by associations or images stay longer in the memory. Craik and Tulving consider (1975: 290) that what the learners do while studying words is more important than how motivated they are, how hard they work, how much time they spend and the number of repetitions of each word. These findings cannot be totally applied to foreign vocabulary learning. Foreign vocabulary learning requires repetition even if only because one occurrence of a word will not contain enough information for a learner to master the word. Also recalling an already known form is a simpler task than learning an unfamiliar word form and connecting it to a given meaning. However, Craik and Lockhart's (1972) theory of the importance of the kind of operations or processing carried out on an item does receive support from experiments on the 'keyword' technique.

The **keyword technique** is primarily a way of making a strong link between the form of an unknown word and its meaning. It involves two steps after the learner has met the unknown word and has found or been provided with its meaning. The first step is to think of a first language word (the keyword) which sounds like the beginning or all of the unknown word. The second step is for the learner to think of a visual image where the meaning of the unknown word and the meaning of the keyword are combined. Here is an example.

If an Indonesian learner wants to learn the English word *pin*, the learner could use the key word *pintu* which is the Indonesian word for 'door'. The learner then thinks of an image involving a door and a pin.

The technique is more clearly seen as a four-part process. Here are some examples.

1.		2.		3.		4.
unknown word	➜	first language keyword	➜	a mental image combining the meaning of the unknown word and the meaning of the keyword	➜	meaning of the unknown word

The keywords have been chosen from a variety of languages including English. Bird and Jacobs (1999) suggest that for languages with very limited syllable structure like Chinese, it may also be useful to choose keywords not only from the first language but from known words in the second language.

Step 2 provides a word form link between the unknown word and the keyword. Step 3 provides a meaning link between the keyword and the meaning of the unknown word. The unknown word prompts recall of the keyword because of its formal similarity to the keyword. The keyword prompts recall of the image combining the keyword meaning and the meaning of the unknown word. This image prompts

1.		2.		3.		4.
fund	→	*fun* (Thai) meaning 'teeth'	→	a fund of money being eaten by a set of teeth	→	a supply of money for a special purpose
candid	→	*can* (English) meaning 'container'	→	a can with a label which honestly shows its contents	→	honest and truthful
core	→	*hor* (Serbo-Croat) meaning 'choir'	→	a choir standing on the core of an apple	→	the most important or central part

recall of the meaning of the unknown word and completes the set of links between the form of the unknown word and its meaning. Thus the whole sequence provides a link from the form of the unknown word to its meaning.

Instead of an image at Step 3, some experimenters (Pressley et al., 1980b) have used a sentence which describes what the image might be, for example, 'There is a *pin* in the *pintu*.' The keyword technique can be used with ready-made keywords and images as in the examples above. This is generally recommended for younger learners and seems to work as well as self-created keywords and images (Hall, 1988; see Gruneberg and Pascoe, 1996, for a discussion of this). Some researchers (Fuentes, 1976; Ott et al., 1973) found that learners in the control group were spontaneously using keyword-like techniques.

There has been considerable research on the keyword technique. It has been found that the technique works with:

1. learners of differing achievement (Levin et al., 1992; McDaniel and Pressley, 1984) although learners with low aptitude may find it more difficult to use the technique (McGivern and Levin, 1983)
2. learners at a variety of grade levels including very young children (Pressley et al., 1981)
3. elderly learners (Gruneberg and Pascoe, 1996)
4. educationally disadvantaged learners

The technique has been used with a wide range of languages: English speakers learning English words; English speakers learning Spanish, Russian, German, Tagalog, Chinese, Hebrew, French, Italian, Greek and Latin; Dutch speakers learning Spanish; and Arabic speakers learning English.

The keyword technique can be used in L1 or L2 learning, for learning the gender of words (Desrochers et al., 1989; Desrochers et al., 1991), and with learners working in pairs or individually (Levin et al., 1992). When it is used for L1 learning, the unknown word is an L1 word and the keyword is usually a higher frequency L1 word, for example, *cat* could be the keyword for *catkin*.

The experiments evaluating the keyword technique have compared it with:

- rote learning;
- use of pictures (Levin et al., 1982);
- thinking of images or examples of the meaning, or instantiation (Pressley et al., 1982);
- context – the unknown word is placed in sentence contexts and the meaning of the word is provided (Brown and Perry, 1991; Moore and Surber, 1992);
- added synonyms – the meaning is accompanied by other known synonyms (Pressley et al., 1982); and
- guessing from context (McDaniel and Pressley, 1984).

The keyword technique has been shown in these studies to usually perform better than any of these other methods and at least as well as them.

The keyword technique has positive effects on both immediate retention and long-term retention (one week to ten years). This finding is not consistent as there are a few studies which suggest that long-term retention is not good with the keyword technique (Wang and Thomas, 1992, 1995; Wang et al., 1993) and so such learning may need to be closely followed by some additional meetings with the words. The case study described by Beaton et al. (1995) shows that even after ten years without opportunity for use, some memory for words learned by the keyword technique remains. Without any revision 35% of the words were remembered with correct spelling and 50% correct or with some small spelling errors. After ten minutes spent looking at the vocabulary list around 75% were recalled correctly or with minor errors and after one and a half hours' revision almost 100% of the 350 words were recalled correctly. This relearning is a very sensitive test of retained knowledge.

The effect of the keyword technique is not limited to receptive recall of a synonym. Studies have shown it be effective for recall of definitions (Avila and Sadoski, 1996; Levin et al., 1992); in sentence completion tasks (Avila and Sadoski, 1996); in story comprehension (Avila and Sadoski, 1996; McDaniel and Pressley, 1984; Pressley et al., 1981); in writing sentences using the words studied (McDaniel and

Pressley, 1984); and in productive recall (Gruneberg and Pascoe, 1996; Pressley et al., 1980a). The keyword needs to overlap a lot in form with the unknown word for productive recall to be successful (Ellis and Beaton, 1993) and repetition may be more effective. Learners find using the keyword technique an enjoyable activity (Gruneberg and Sykes, 1991) and can achieve large amounts of learning with it (Gruneberg, 1992: 180; Gruneberg and Jacobs, 1991) with some learners learning 400 words in 12 contact hours and 600 words in four days. It is unlikely that these rates could be sustained but they represent very useful initial achievements.

To be effective, learners need extended training with the keyword technique. Hall (1988) spent a total of three hours over a period of four weeks training learners in the use of the keyword technique and even this was probably not enough time. As with all the major vocabulary-learning strategies, learners need to be brought to a level of skill and confidence where they find it just as easy to use the strategy as not use it. If their grasp of the strategy is unsure, then they will rarely use it. A fault with many of the experimental studies of the keyword technique is that training seems to have been very short or is not described clearly in the reports.

Several studies show that the keyword technique works well on some words (usually where keywords are easy to find) and not so well on others (Hall, 1988). It would be interesting to see if extended training in the keyword technique results in ease of use with most unknown words or if there are still problems finding keywords for many words and with some languages whose syllable structure differs greatly from the first language. Gruneberg's *Linkword* books (1987) provide keywords for a wide range of vocabulary indicating that the only limit on finding a key word could be the learner's imagination. In the books learners are encouraged to spend about 10 seconds thinking of the image so that there really is visualisation.

Barcroft et al. (2011) used a priming study to compare the nature of access to word meanings of words learned by the keyword technique with that of words learned by rote rehearsal. When the keyword was used as a prime, those who had learned by rote rehearsal had faster access to the meaning than those who had learned using a keyword. The interpretation of this finding is that accessing words learned by the keyword technique involves additional semantic processing which hinders access. The keyword technique uses additional links compared to the normal form–meaning connection, and while these make the item memorable, the path from form to meaning is more complicated. Because Barcroft et al. found no difference between keyword and rote rehearsal in amount of learning, they argue that we should not use a technique which provides lower quality access for no great advantage. The compromise position is that there is a very large amount of evidence to show that the keyword technique helps words stick in the memory, and so it should just be used for words that proved to be difficult to retain using normal word card retrieval procedures, that is, the keyword technique should not be used as the standard learning procedure, but should be used as a problem-solving last resort for words that keep slipping away.

Although there has been discussion of possible shortcomings of the keyword technique (see, for example, Sagarra and Alba, 2006: 230–31), the overwhelming evidence is strongly in favour of the technique for both immediate recall and long-term recall, and for use with a wide variety of languages. No vocabulary-learning technique has been so extensively investigated with largely similar positive results. Although there have been some improvements in research methodology to control for the effects of testing on learning and to correctly monitor the treatments, the results have confirmed the findings of Pressley's (1977) classic study and Ellis and Beaton's (1993) analysis that it is the attention to both form and meaning, as well as the linking visual image, that make the keyword technique work.

It is important not to see the keyword technique as a magic technique, but as one that applies important learning principles that can also be applied in other techniques. These principles include: the levels-of-processing principle – the more deeply and thoughtfully something is processed, the better it will be retained; the focus-of-attention principle – we learn what we focus on; the deliberate-attention principle – deliberate learning results in quick, secure learning; and the dual-encoding principle – having both linguistic and visual associations for a word helps retention.

A very useful direction for future research would be to move on from the keyword technique and explore how these principles and others work in other commonly used vocabulary learning techniques and activities.

Does difficulty in learning result in better retention? This all depends on the source of the difficulty.

1. De Groot and Keijzer (2000) found that words that are easy to learn are better retained. This is probably because the learning burden of the words was low and thus they fitted well into learners' previous knowledge. Vocabulary which was difficult to learn was not better retained, probably because the factors affecting difficulty also worked against retention.

2. Schneider et al. (2002) found that a difficult learning *process* results in better retention (productive versus receptive), but this confounds the amount of knowledge required with the difficulty of the learning process.
3. Tinkham (1993; 1997) found that a difficult learning process (keeping interfering items distinct) resulted in worse learning, but unfortunately Tinkham did not have a delayed retention test to see if this learning also resulted in poor long-term retention.

The best learning occurs when there is a strong deliberate focus on what needs to be learned for the subsequent test or use. We carry associations from learning with us and if these associations are relevant for later use, then they will have a positive effect. If they are negative (as in Tinkham's studies) then they will continue to cause problems.

Is flashcard software useful for vocabulary learning?

Computer programming allows very efficient tracing of repetitions, responses and spacing of words, and is thus ideally suited to applying the findings of research on memory and word card learning. Nakata (2011) did a detailed and comprehensive evaluation of flashcard programs, using a carefully justified set of evaluation criteria based on research findings. Here are his criteria. Each criterion can usually be justified by reference to research studies in paired-associate learning or vocabulary learning:

Flashcard creation and editing

1. *Flashcard creation.* Can learners create their own flashcards?
2. *Multilingual support.* Can the target words and their translations be created in any language?
3. *Multi-word units.* Can flashcards be created for multi-word units as well as single words?
4. *Types of information.* Can various kinds of information be added to flashcards besides the word meanings (e.g., parts of speech, contexts or audios)?
5. *Support for data entry.* Does the software support data entry by automatically supplying information about lexical items such as meaning, parts of speech or contexts from an internal database or external resources?
6. *Flashcard set.* Does the software allow learners to create their own sets of flashcards?

Learning

7. *Presentation mode.* Does the software have a presentation mode, where new items are introduced and learners familiarise themselves with them?
8. *Retrieval mode.* Does the software have a retrieval mode which asks learners to recall or choose the L2 word form or its meaning?
9. *Receptive recall.* Does the software ask learners to produce the meanings of target words?
10. *Receptive recognition.* Does the software ask learners to choose the meanings of target words?
11. *Productive recall.* Does the software ask learners to produce the target word forms corresponding to the meanings provided?
12. *Productive recognition.* Does the software ask learners to choose the target word forms corresponding to the meanings provided?
13. *Increasing retrieval effort.* For a given item, does the software arrange exercises in order of increasing difficulty?
14. *Generative (creative) use.* Does the software encourage generative use of words, where learners encounter or use previously met words in novel contexts?
15. *Block size.* Can the number of words studied in one learning session be controlled and altered?
16. *Adaptive sequencing.* Does the software change the sequencing of items based on learners' previous performance on individual items?
17. *Expanded rehearsal.* Does the software help implement expanded rehearsal, where the intervals between study trials are gradually increased as learning proceeds?

The criteria were best applied at the time of review in 2010 by *iKnow!*, a free web-based program (http://smart.fm/tour). What many programs lack is the chance to get the effect of creative use through seeing several different example sentences, the use of a variety of retrieval types (receptive/productive, recognition/recall) and support for data entry including frequency data. Overall, the flashcard programs are very good and as Tom Cobb (www.lextutor.ca) has often noted, computer-assisted language learning and vocabulary learning is an ideal marriage.

How can we train learners in the use of word cards?

The research reviewed in this chapter has shown that there is value in learning vocabulary using word cards. This learning, however, must be seen as part of a broader programme involving other kinds of direct learning as well as the strands of meaning-focused input, meaning-focused output and fluency development. The research also shows that there are ways of maximising learning and learners need to know about these and know how to make use of them in their learning. Some of Griffin's (1992) studies suggest the importance of informing learners about how to go about learning, so that factors like transfer of learning, serial position in a list and item difficulty are taken into account to suit the language-learning goal.

- Learners should know about the importance of retrieval in learning and how word cards encourage this by not allowing the word form and meaning to be seen simultaneously. They should know about receptive retrieval and productive retrieval.
- Learners should know the value of repeating and spacing learning and to include long-term review in their learning.
- Learners should know what information to include on their word cards, particularly a sentence context or some useful collocations.
- Learners should know what words to choose to put on their cards, giving particular attention to high-frequency words.
- Learners should know what to do with each word, rehearsing its spoken form and using mnemonic techniques like the keyword technique whenever a word is difficult to remember.
- Learners should keep changing the order of the cards, avoiding serial learning and putting more difficult items at the beginning of the pack so that they get more attention. They should re-form packs, taking out words that are now known and including new items.
- Learners should use small packs of cards in the early stages of learning and use bigger packs when the learning is easier.
- Learners should be aware of interference effects between semantically and formally related words and avoid including such related items in the same pack.
- Learners should make deliberate efforts to transfer the learning from word cards to meaning-focused language use.
- Learners should know how to monitor and reflect on their own learning, and adapt their learning procedures on the basis of this reflection.

Some of these points are easy to learn and require only a little explanation and discussion. Others, like the use of mnemonic devices, choosing words to go on the cards, avoiding interference and transferring knowledge, require much more time and attention. This training can involve:

1. understanding what should be done; this can be tested by quizzes;
2. observing and hearing about others' learning experiences and discussing strengths and weaknesses of what was observed;

3. performing learning tasks using word cards and reporting and reflecting on the experience; and
4. monitoring and training others in the use of word cards.

This training requires planning and a suitable allocation of time. The principle of spaced retrieval should be applied to the training procedure and teachers should plan a mini-syllabus spread over several weeks to train learners in the effective use of word cards. Teachers should be able to justify to themselves and to others the value of spending time training learners in the use of word cards. These justifications could include the following points:

- The word card strategy can be applied to both high-frequency and low-frequency words. It is a widely applicable strategy.
- Direct deliberate learning is faster and stronger than incidental learning.
- Direct learning can help incidental learning by raising consciousness of particular words and providing knowledge that can be enriched and strengthened through incidental meaning-focused learning.
- Learners differ greatly in their skill at direct learning. Training is likely to reduce these differences.
- Learners spontaneously do direct learning but they do not always do it efficiently. Training can increase their efficiency.
- Deliberate learning creates both implicit and explicit knowledge.

Learning using word cards should not be seen as an alternative to other kinds of learning. It should be seen as a useful and effective complement and simply one part of a well-balanced vocabulary-learning programme.

References

Anderson, J. P. and Jordan, A. M. (1928). Learning and retention of Latin words and phrases. *Journal of Educational Psychology*, **19**, 485–96.

Anderson, R. C. and Nagy, W. E. (1992). The vocabulary conundrum. *American Educator*, **16**, 4, 14–18; 44–47.

Atkinson, R. C. (1972). Optimizing the learning of a second-language vocabulary. *Journal of Experimental Psychology*, **96**, 124–9.

Avila, E. and Sadoski, M. (1996). Exploring new applications of the keyword method to acquire English vocabulary. *Language Learning*, **46**, 3, 379–95.

Baddeley, A. (1990). *Human Memory*. London: Lawrence Erlbaum Associates.

Bahrick, H. (1984a). Fifty years of second language attrition: Implications for programmatic research. *Modern Language Journal*, **68**, 2, 105–18.

Bahrick, H. P. (1984b). Semantic memory content in permastore: Fifty years of memory for Spanish learned in school. *Journal of Experimental Psychology: General*, **113**, 1, 1–37.

Bahrick, H. P. and Phelps, E. (1987). Retention of Spanish vocabulary over 8 years. *Journal of Experimental Psychology: Learning, Memory and Cognition*, **13**, 2, 344–9.

Barcroft, J. (2006). Can writing a word detract from learning it? More negative effects of forced output during vocabulary learning. *Second Language Research*, **22**, 4, 487–97.

Barcroft, J. (2007). Effects of opportunities for word retrieval during second language vocabulary learning. *Language Learning*, **57**, 1, 35–56.

Barcroft, J., Sommers, M. S. and Sunderman, G. (2011). Some costs of fooling mother nature: A priming study on the Keyword Method and the quality of developing L2 lexical representations. In Trofimovich, P. and McDonouhgh, K. (eds.), *Applying Priming Methods to L2 Learning, Teaching and Research: 1* (pp. 49–72). Amsterdam: John Benjamins.

Beaton, A., Gruneberg, M. and Ellis, N. (1995). Retention of foreign vocabulary using the keyword method: A ten-year follow-up. *Second Language Research*, **11**, 2, 112–20.

Biemiller, A. (2005). Size and sequence in vocabulary development. In Hiebert, E. H. and Kamil, M. L. (eds.), *Teaching and Learning Vocabulary: Bringing Research into Practice* (pp. 223–42). Mahawh, NJ: Lawrence Erlbaum Associates.

Biemiller, A. (2010). *Words Worth Teaching: Closing the Vocabulary Gap*. Colombus: McGraw-Hill.

Biemiller, A. and Boote, C. (2006). An effective method for building meaning vocabulary in the primary grades. *Journal of Educational Psychology*, **98**, 1, 44–62.

Biemiller, A. and Slonim, N. (2001). Estimating root word vocabulary growth in normative and advantaged populations: Evidence for a common sequence of vocabulary acquisition. *Journal of Educational Psychology*, **93**, 3, 498–520.

Bird, S. A. and Jacobs, G. M. (1999). An examination of the keyword method: How effective is it for native speakers of Chinese? *Asian Journal of English Language Teaching*, **9**, 75–97.

Bloom, K. C. and Shuell, T. J. (1981). Effects of massed and distributed practice on the learning and retention of second-language vocabulary. *Journal of Educational Research*, **74**, 4, 245–8.

Brown, T. S. and Perry, F. L. (1991). A comparison of three learning strategies for ESL vocabulary acquisition. *TESOL Quarterly*, **25**, 4, 655–70.

Burroughs, R. S. (1982). Vocabulary study and context, or how I learned to stop worrying about word lists. *English Journal*, **71**, 53–5.

Carroll, J. B. (1963). Research on teaching foreign languages. In Gage, N. L. (ed.), *Handbook of Research on Teaching* (pp. 1060–1100). Chicago: Rand McNally.

Chen, H. C. (1990). Lexical processing in a non-native language: Effects of language proficiency and learning strategy. *Memory and Cognition*, **18**, 3, 279–88.

Craik, F. I. M. and Lockhart, R. S. (1972). Levels of processing: A framework for memory research. *Journal of Verbal Learning and Verbal Behavior*, **11**, 671–84.

Craik, F. I. M. and Tulving, E. (1975). Depth of processing and the retention of words in episodic memory. *Journal of Experimental Psychology*, **104**, 268–94.

Crothers, E. and Suppes, P. (1967). *Experiments in Second-Language Learning*. New York: Academic Press.

Davis, M. H. and Gaskell, M. G. (2009). A complementary learning systems account of word learning: Neural and behavioral evidence. *Philosophical Transactions of the Royal Society B: Biological Sciences*, **364**, 3773–800.

de Groot, A. (2006). Effects of stimulus characteristics and background music on foreign language vocabulary learning and forgetting. *Language Learning*, **56**, 3, 463–506.

de Groot, A. M. B. and Keijzer, R. (2000). What is hard to learn is easy to forget: The roles of word concreteness, cognate status, and word frequency in foreign-language vocabulary learning. *Language Learning*, **50**, 1, 1–56.

Dempster, F. N. (1987). Effects of variable encoding and spaced presentation on vocabulary learning. *Journal of Educational Psychology*, **79**, 2, 162–70.

Deno, S. L. (1968). Effects of words and pictures as stimuli in learning language equivalents. *Journal of Educational Psychology*, **59**, 202–6.

Desrochers, A., Gelinas, C. and Wieland, L. D. (1989). An application of the mnemonic keyword method to the acquisition of German nouns and their grammatical gender. *Journal of Educational Psychology*, **81**, 1, 25–32.

Desrochers, A., Wieland, L. D. and Cot, M. (1991). Instructional effects in the use of the mnemonic keyword method for learning German nouns and their grammatical gender. *Applied Cognitive Psychology*, **5**, 19–36.

Elgort, I. (2011). Deliberate learning and vocabulary acquisition in a second language. *Language Learning*, **61**, 2, 367–413.

Ellis, N. C. (1995). Vocabulary acquisition: Psychological perspectives and pedagogical implications. *The Language Teacher*, **19**, 2, 12–16.

Ellis, N. C. (1997). Vocabulary acquisition, word structure, collocation, word-class, and meaning. In Schmitt, N. and McCarthy, M. (eds.), *Vocabulary: Description, Acquisition and Pedagogy* (pp. 122–39). Cambridge: Cambridge University Press.

Ellis, N. C. and Beaton, A. (1993). Factors affecting foreign language vocabulary: Imagery keyword mediators and phonological short-term memory. *Quarterly Journal of Experimental Psychology*, **46A**, 3, 533–58.

Erten, I. H. and Tekin, M. (2008). Effects on vocabulary acquisition of presenting new words in semantic sets versus semantically unrelated sets. *System*, **36**, 407–22.

Firth, J. R. (1957). *Papers in Linguistics*. London: Oxford University Press.

Fuentes, E. J. (1976). An investigation into the use of imagery and generativity in learning a foreign language vocabulary. *Dissertation Abstracts International*, 37, 2694A.

Gershman, S. J. (1970). Foreign language vocabulary learning under seven conditions. *Dissertation Abstracts International*, **31**, 3690B.

Gipe, J. P. and Arnold, R. D. (1979). Teaching vocabulary through familiar associations and contexts. *Journal of Reading Behavior*, **11**, 3, 282–5.

Griffin, G. F. (1992). *Aspects of the Psychology of Second Language Vocabulary List Learning*. University of Warwick.

Griffin, G. F. and Harley, T. A. (1996). List learning of second language vocabulary. *Applied Psycholinguistics*, **17**, 443–60.

Grinstead, W. J. (1915). An experiment in the learning of foreign words. *Journal of Educational Psychology*, **6**, 242–5.

Gruneberg, M. M. (1987). *Italian: Linkword Language System*. London: Corgi Books.

Gruneberg, M. M. (1992). The practical application of memory aids. In Gruneberg, M. and Morris, P. (eds.), *Aspects of Memory* vol. 1 (pp. 168–95). London: Routledge.

Gruneberg, M. M. and Jacobs, G. C. (1991). In defence of Linkword. *Language Learning Journal*, **3**, 25–9.

Gruneberg, M. M. and Pascoe, K. (1996). The effectiveness of the keyword method for receptive and productive foreign vocabulary learning in the elderly. *Contemporary Educational Psychology*, **21**, 102–9.

Gruneberg, M. M. and Sykes, R. (1991). Individual differences and attitudes to the keyword method of foreign language learning. *Language Learning Journal*, **4**, 60–62.

Hall, J. W. (1988). On the utility of the keyword mnemonic for vocabulary learning. *Journal of Educational Psychology*, **80**, 4, 554–562.

Higa, M. (1963). Interference effects of intralist word relationships in verbal learning. *Journal of Verbal Learning and Verbal Behavior*, **2**, 170–75.

Higa, M. (1965). The psycholinguistic concept of 'difficulty' and the teaching of foreign language vocabulary. *Language Learning*, **15**, 3&4, 167–79.

Hummel, K. (2010). Translation and short-term vocabulary retention: Hindrance or help? *Language Teaching Research*, **14**, 1, 61–74.

Joe, A. (1995). Text-based tasks and incidental vocabulary learning. *Second Language Research*, **11**, 2, 149–58.

Joe, A. (1998). What effects do text-based tasks promoting generation have on incidental vocabulary acquisition? *Applied Linguistics*, **19**, 3, 357–77.

Judd, E. L. (1978). Vocabulary teaching and TESOL: A need for re-evaluation of existing assumptions. *TESOL Quarterly*, **12**, 1, 71–6.

Kachroo, J. N. (1962). Report on an investigation into the teaching of vocabulary in the first year of English. *Bulletin of the Central Institute of English*, **2**, 67–72.

Karpicke, J. D. and Bauernschmidt, A. (2011). Spaced retrieval: Absolute spacing enhances learning regardless of relative spacing. *Journal of Experimental Psychology: Learning. Memory and Cognition*, **37**, 5, 1250–57.

Karpicke, J. D. and Blunt, J. R. (2011). Retrieval practice produces more learning than elaborative studying with concept mapping. *Science*, **331**, 772–5.

Karpicke, J. D. and Roediger, H. L. (2007). Expanding retrieval practice promotes short-term retention, but equally spaced retrieval enhances long-term retention. *Journal of Experimental Psychology: Learning, Memory and Cognition*, **33**, 4, 704–19.

Kellogg, G. S. and Howe, M. J. A. (1971). Using words and pictures in foreign language learning. *Alberta Journal of Educational Research*, 17, 89–94.

Kopstein, F. F. and Roshal, S. M. (1954). Learning foreign vocabulary from pictures vs. words. *American Psychologist*, 9, 407–8.

Kornell, N. (2009). Optimising learning using flashcards: Spacing is more effective than cramming. *Applied Cognitive Psychology*, 23, 1297–1317.

Krashen, S. (1985). *The Input Hypothesis: Issues and Implications*. London: Longman.

Lado, R., Baldwin, B. and Lobo, F. (1967). *Massive Vocabulary Expansion in a Foreign Language Beyond the Basic Course: The Effects of Stimuli, Timing and Order of Presentation*. Washington, DC: U.S. Department of Health, Education, and Welfare.

Lakoff, G. and Johnson, M. (1980). *Metaphors We Live By*. Chicago: University of Chicago Press.

Landauer, T. K. and Bjork, R. A. (1978). Optimum rehearsal patterns and name learning. In Gruneberg, M. M., Morris P. E. and Sykes, R. N. (eds.), *Practical Aspects of Memory* (pp. 625–32). London: Academic Press.

Laufer, B. and Shmueli, K. (1997). Memorizing new words: Does teaching have anything to do with it? *RELC Journal*, 28, 1, 89–108.

Levin, J. R., Levin, M. E., Glasman, L. D. and Nordwall, M. B. (1992). Mnemonic vocabulary instruction: Additional effectiveness evidence. *Contemporary Educational Psychology*, 17, 156–74.

Levin, J. R., McCormick, C. B., Miller, G. E., Berry, J. K. and Pressley, M. (1982). Mnemonic versus nonmnemonic vocabulary-learning strategies for children. *American Educational Research Journal*, 19, 1, 121–36.

Lindsay, S. and Gaskell, M. G. (2010). A complementary systems account of word learning in L1 and L2. *Language Learning*, 60, Supp 2, 45–63.

Lotto, L. and De Groot, A. (1998). Effects of learning method and word type on acquiring vocabulary in an unfamiliar language. *Language Learning*, 48, 1, 31–69.

McClelland, J. L., McNaughton, B. L. and O'Reilly, R. C. (1995). Why are there complementary learning-systems in the hippocampus and neocortex? *Psychological Review*, 102, 419–57.

McDaniel, M. A. and Pressley, M. (1984). Putting the keyword method in context. *Journal of Educational Psychology*, 76, 598–609.

McGivern, J. E. and Levin, J. R. (1983). The keyword method and children's vocabulary learning: An interaction with vocabulary knowledge. *Contemporary Educational Psychology*, 8, 46–54.

McKeown, M. G., Beck, I. L., Omanson, R. G. and Pople, M. T. (1985). Some effects of the nature and frequency of vocabulary instruction on the knowledge and use of words. *Reading Research Quarterly*, 20, 5, 522–35.

Mishima, T. (1967). An experiment comparing five modalities of conveying meaning for the teaching of foreign language vocabulary. *Dissertation Abstracts*, 27, 3030–31A.

Mondria, J. A. and Mondria-de Vries, S. (1994). Efficiently memorizing words with the help of word cards and "hand computer": Theory and applications. *System*, 22, 1, 47–57.

Mondria, J. A. and Wiersma, B. (2004). Receptive, productive, and receptive + productive L2 vocabulary learning: What difference does it make? In Bogaards, P. and Laufer, B. (eds.), *Vocabulary in a Second Language: Selection, Acquisition, and Testing* (pp. 79–100). Amsterdam: John Benjamins.

Moore, J. C. and Surber, J. R. (1992). Effects of context and keyword methods on second language vocabulary acquisition. *Contemporary Educational Psychology*, 17, 286–92.

Morgan, C. L. and Bailey, W. L. (1943). The effect of context on learning a vocabulary. *Journal of Educational Psychology*, 34, 561–5.

Morgan, C. L. and Foltz, M. C. (1944). The effect of context on learning a French vocabulary. *Journal of Educational Research*, 38, 213–16.

Nakata, T. (2008). English vocabulary learning with word lists, word cards and computers: Implications from cognitive psychology research for optimal spaced learning. *ReCALL*, 20, 1, 3–20.

Nakata, T. (2011). Computer-assisted second language vocabulary learning in a paired-associate paradigm: A critical investigation of flashcard software. *Computer Assisted Language Learning*, 24, 1, 17–38.

Nation, I. S. P. (1982). Beginning to learn foreign vocabulary: A review of the research. *RELC Journal*, 13, 1, 14–36.

Ott, C. E., Butler, D. C., Blake, R. S. and Ball, J. P. (1973). The effect of interactive-image elaboration on the acquisition of foreign language vocabulary. *Language Learning*, 23, 2, 197–206.

Oxford, R. and Crookall, D. (1990). Vocabulary learning: A critical analysis of techniques. *TESL Canada Journal*, 7, 2, 9–30.

Papathanasiou, E. (2009). An investigation of two ways of presenting vocabulary. *ELT Journal*, 63, 4, 313–22.

Pickering, M. (1982). Context-free and context-dependent vocabulary learning: An experiment. *System*, 10, 1, 79–83.

Pimsleur, P. (1967). A memory schedule. *Modern Language Journal*, 51, 2, 73–5.

Pressley, M. (1977). Children's use of the keyword method to learn simple Spanish vocabulary words. *Journal of Educational Psychology*, 69, 5, 465–72.

Pressley, M., Levin, J., Hall, J., Miller, G. and Berry, J. K. (1980a). The keyword method and foreign word acquisition. *Journal of Experimental Psychology: Human Learning and Memory*, 5, 22–9.

Pressley, M., Levin, J., Kuiper, N., Bryant, S. and Michener, S. (1982). Mnemonic versus nonmnemonic vocabulary-learning strategies: Additional comparisons. *Journal of Educational Psychology*, 74, 693–707.

Pressley, M., Levin, J. R. and McCormick, C. B. (1980b). Young children's learning of foreign language vocabulary: A sentence variation of the keyword method. *Contemporary Educational Psychology*, 5, 22–9.

Pressley, M., Levin, J. R. and Miller, G. E. (1981). The keyword method and children's learning of foreign vocabulary with abstract meanings. *Canadian Journal of Psychology*, 35, 283–7.

Pressley, M., Samuel, J., Hershey, M., Bishop, S. and Dickinson, D. (1981). Use of a mnemonic technique to teach young children foreign language vocabulary. *Contemporary Educational Psychology*, 6, 110–16.

Pyc, M. A. and Rawson, K. A. (2007). Examining the efficiency of schedules of distributed retrieval practice. *Memory & Cognition*, 35, 8, 1917–27.

Pyc, M. A. and Rawson, K. A. (2009). Testing the retrieval hypothesis: Does greater difficulty correctly recalling information lead to higher levels of memory? *Journal of Memory and Language*, 60, 437–47.

Rodgers, T. S. (1969). On measuring vocabulary difficulty: An analysis of item variables in learning Russian-English vocabulary pairs. *IRAL*, 7, 4, 327–43.

Royer, J. M. (1973). Memory effects for test-like-events during acquisition of foreign language vocabulary. *Psychological Reports*, 32, 195–8.

Sagarra, N. and Alba, M. (2006). The key is in the keyword: L2 vocabulary learning methods with beginning learners of Spanish. *Modern Language Journal*, 90, 2, 228–43.

Saragi, T., Nation, I. S. P. and Meister, G. F. (1978). Vocabulary learning and reading. *System*, 6, 2, 72–8.

Schneider, V. J., Healy, A. F. and Bourne, L. E. (2002). What is learned under difficult conditions is hard to forget: Contextual interference effects in foreign vocabulary acquisition, retention, and transfer. *Journal of Memory and Language*, 46, 418–40.

Seibert, L. C. (1927). An experiment in learning French vocabulary. *Journal of Educational Psychology*, 18, 294–309.

Seibert, L. C. (1930). An experiment on the relative efficiency of studying French vocabulary in associated pairs versus studying French vocabulary in context. *Journal of Educational Psychology*, 21, 297–314.

Stahl, S. A. and Fairbanks, M. M. (1986). The effects of vocabulary instruction: A model-based meta-analysis. *Review of Educational Research*, 56, 1, 72–110.

Stoddard, G. D. (1929). An experiment in verbal learning. *Journal of Educational Psychology*, 20, 7, 452–7.

Thomas, M. H. and Dieter, J. N. (1987). The positive effects of writing practice on integration of foreign words in memory. *Journal of Educational Psychology*, 79, 3, 249–53.

Thorndike, E. L. (1908). Memory for paired associates. *Psychological Review*, 15, 122–38.

Tinkham, T. (1993). The effect of semantic clustering on the learning of second language vocabulary. *System*, 21, 3, 371–80.

Tinkham, T. (1997). The effects of semantic and thematic clustering on the learning of second language vocabulary. *Second Language Research*, 13, 2, 138–63.

Tonzar, C., Lotto, L. and Job, R. (2009). L2 vocabulary acquisition in children: Effects of learning method and cognate status. *Language Learning*, 59, 3, 623–46.

Turner, G. (1983). Teaching French vocabulary: A training study. *Educational Review*, 35, 1, 81–8.

Wang, A. Y. and Thomas, M. H. (1992). The effect of imagery-based mnemonics on the long-term retention of Chinese characters. *Language Learning*, 42, 3, 359–76.

Wang, A. Y. and Thomas, M. H. (1995). Effect of keywords on long-term retention: Help or hindrance? *Journal of Educational Psychology*, 87, 3, 468–75.

Wang, A. Y., Thomas, M. H., Inzana, C. M. and Primicerio, L. J. (1993). Long-term retention under conditions of intentional learning and the keyword mnemonic. *Bulletin of the Psychonomic Society*, **31**, 6, 545–7.

Waring, R. (1997a). A comparison of the receptive and productive vocabulary sizes of some second language learners. *Immaculata (Notre Dame Seishin University, Okayama)*, **1**, 53–68.

Waring, R. (1997b). The negative effects of learning words in semantic sets: A replication. *System*, **25**, 2, 261–74.

Webb, S. (2007). Learning word pairs and glossed sentences: The effects of a single context on vocabulary knowledge. *Language Teaching Research*, **11**, 1, 63–81.

Webb, S. (2009). The effects of receptive and productive learning of word pairs on vocabulary knowledge. *RELC Journal*, **40**, 3, 360–76.

Webb, W. B. (1962). The effects of prolonged learning on learning. *Journal of Verbal Learning and Verbal Behavior*, **1**, 173–82.

Webber, N. E. (1978). Pictures and words as stimuli in learning foreign language responses. *The Journal of Psychology*, **98**, 57–63.

12 Finding and learning multiword units

What are multiword units?

There are four major kinds of multiword units: (1) A multiword unit can be a group of words that commonly occur together, like 'take a chance'; (2) it can be a group of words where the meaning of the phrase is not obvious from the meaning of the parts, as with 'by and large' or 'be taken in' (be tricked); (3) it can simply refer to all the combinations of a particular word or type of word and its accompanying words whether they are highly frequent, strongly associated, or not; and (4) it can refer to word groups that are intuitively seen as being formulaic sequences, that is, items stored as single choices (see Durrant and Schmitt, 2009: 159, for an excellent discussion of these four types).

These different kinds of multiword units are based on a variety of criteria – frequency of co-occurrence, compositionality (do the parts make the whole?), form and storage, and so it is not too surprising that there is a large and growing list of terms to cover multiword units. Wray (2000) lists around 50 terms including composites, conventionalised forms, idiomatic phrases, routine formulae, phrasal expressions, and stock utterances, just to describe formulaic sequences, and there are at least as many again to describe multiword units more generally (lexical bundles, collocations, phrasal units, multiword units). The large number of terms reflects the different purposes for looking at multiword units, and the fragmented nature of research in this area. Walker (2011) suggests that the definition of what is a multiword unit affects what appears in learners' dictionaries. A major issue in research on multiword units is the need to set clear criteria and, where possible, develop standard terminology to describe the different types of multiword units.

The theme of this chapter and a recurring theme in this book is that the characteristics of language items and their use should play a major role in determining how they are learned and taught, and how they are investigated.

Multiword units have the following characteristics:

1. Most multiword units are variable in nature, despite having what Sinclair (2004a) calls a typical 'canonical' form. This means they may change their word order, may change the words that occur in them in addition to the main collocates, and may change the morphological form of their collocates.
2. In all multiword units, the individual words that it is made up of are not arbitrarily combined, but come together in ways that are consistent with their typical grammatical and semantic use outside any particular multiword unit.
3. Some multiword units are more than the sum of their parts, and although the meanings of the parts contribute to the whole, there is more to be known about the whole multiword unit.
4. Many multiword units are probably stored as single choices (Sinclair, 2004b; Siyanova-Chanturia et al., 2011), but this storage does not necessarily mean that they are unanalysed (see 2 above) or are of fixed or invariable form (see 1 above).
5. Just as single words are used for a communicative purpose, multiword units also have communicative purposes. This communicative purpose is an important part of what is involved in knowing the multiword unit.

Because of these characteristics, the following points are important when teaching and learning multiword units:

- It is important to learn the main parts of the multiword unit and to eventually experience how they can be varied and what other changes can occur in the multiword unit.
- It is helpful to see how the meanings of the parts contribute to make the meaning of the whole.
- It is valuable to gain fluency in recognising and accessing multiword units.
- It is best to focus on coherent, well-formed units, to see how they are used in context, and to understand their effect.

Similarly, the following points are important when investigating multiword units for the purposes of teaching and learning:

- It is important to take account of variability when searching for instances of multiword units.
- It will be useful to relate the occurrence of the words in the multiword unit to their uses in other contexts.

- It is important to note their frequency, transparency and variability.
- It may be appropriate to include the criterion of grammatical well-formedness, and to note the communicative functions of the multi-word units.

Why are multiword units important?

Sinclair and others (Cheng et al., 2008; Lewis, 1993; Sinclair, 2004a; Stubbs, 2009) present very convincing evidence that words need to be learned in their typical multiword units, largely because their most common senses are not what we would intuitively expect (the most common sense of *see* is 'understand' not 'see visually') and their frequent multiword units reveal this. In addition, learning words in multiword units is helpful because for many words there is a typical pattern in which they occur. As Stubbs (2009: 120) puts it, 'there is little point in knowing the word *ebb*, without knowing its phraseology', that is, it often occurs with *low* and 'the collocation *at*-LOW-*ebb* is typically used to talk about people's morale and spirits, which are at a lower ebb than some time in the past' (p. 121).

Sinclair (2004a: 280–81) puts it even more strongly, namely that the meaning of a word includes its relevant patterning, that is, the collocations and colligations in which it occurs along with its semantic preference and semantic prosody. 'The lexical item is best described maximally, not minimally' (p. 281). A minimal description would be a description of the meaning of an individual word without any description of its use.

This, however, should not be seen as a choice between learning the meanings of either individual words or multiword units. Both kinds of learning are important and valuable. All multiword units except the few core idioms are to some degree compositional, that is, the meaning of the parts contribute substantially to the meaning of the whole. Consider for example these items from Martinez and Schmitt (2012): *a few, rather than, be likely to, the following, last night, look for* and *be expected to*. This compositionality is not arbitrary (Liu, 2010; Walker, 2011) and understanding the meaning of the parts makes learning and retaining the meaning of the multiword unit easier (Boers and Lindstromberg, 2009; Bogaards, 2001). There is thus a two-way value for learning by analysing multiword units – the multiword units will be easier to learn, and the meaning and use of the words in them will also be better understood.

Any multiword unit or multiword unit pattern will typically involve one sense of the word, and it is important when learning vocabulary to see beyond that sense to the core meaning of the word, that is, the meaning that runs through all its senses. This allows a learner to cope receptively with not only the most common multiword units involving the word, but also its numerous less frequent uses.

When considering maintaining a balance between attention to individual words and attention to multiword units, it is important to see such learning occurring across the four strands, that is, at least three-quarters of the learning opportunities should come from meeting and using items in communicative contexts, and one-quarter should come from giving deliberate attention to lexical items. Deliberate teaching and learning should give attention to both individual words and multiword units, and more information about the phrasal nature of words which can be used to guide their deliberate teaching and learning will clearly be desirable and very useful. However, as for individual words, most learning opportunities for multiword units will occur through receptive and productive use.

There are several strong and well-supported reasons why knowledge of multiword units is an important part of language use. These relate to the nature of language knowledge, the nature of language and the nature of language use.

Nature of language knowledge

Wray (2002; 2004) presents a large amount of evidence to show that proficient users of the language make use of what she calls formulaic sequences – multiword units that may be stored as whole units. Wray calls them 'morpheme equivalent units' because they are used in much the same way as single words. These formulaic sequences need not be unanalysed and it is possible for all the words in the sequence to be known and used individually in other uses. The same 'linguistic material is stored in bundles of different sizes' (Wray, 2008: 12). Analysis occurs only when there is some need for it.

A variety of factors influence the number of formulaic sequences in particular uses of the language, including: the amount of shared knowledge between those involved in the communication, a focus on addressing 'insiders', production under time pressure, and the number of recurrent situations in life that require conventionalised language.

The evidence for the storage of multiword units as single choices is growing (Arnon and Snider, 2010; Conklin and Schmitt, 2008; Ellis et al., 2008; Jiang and Nekrasova, 2007; Siyanova and Schmitt, 2007) and there is a growing set of tools and procedures to investigate this (see especially Schmitt, 2004).

Martinez and Murphy (2011) argue that because some multiword units are at least partially opaque (it is not clear how the meanings of the parts make up the meaning of the whole), knowledge of the meaning of these multiword units is important for language use, that is, we need to regard certain multiword units (probably a large number) as items that have to be known in their own right and regarded as part of the vocabulary knowledge needed to use the language.

Language knowledge thus includes multiword units stored as formulaic sequences.

Nature of language

In several papers Ellis and colleagues (Ellis, 2001; Ellis et al., 2008; Ellis and Schmidt, 1997) argue that a lot of language learning can be accounted for by associations between sequentially observed language items, that is, without the need to refer to underlying rules. The major factor affecting this learning by association is frequency of meeting with instances of language use (the power law of practice). By having chunks of language in long-term memory, language reception and language production are made more efficient.

Sinclair (1987) describes two models of the way words occur in a text.

1. The *open-choice principle* sees language text as a series of choices where the only limitation on choice is grammaticalness.
2. The *idiom principle* sees much greater constraints and limitations. The choice of one word to begin to express an idea has a strongly limiting effect on what the following word choices can be. A sentence beginning *Would it be convenient ...* has to a large extent limited choices of what follows. As well as limitations based on the nature of the world, and choice of register, the strongly collocational knowledge of language means that some phrases and clauses offer little or no opportunity for variation.

Because a large amount of language follows the idiom principle, multiword units are an important learning goal.

Nature of language use

Pawley and Syder (1983) consider that the best explanation of how language users can choose the most appropriate ways to say things from a large range of possible options (nativelike selection), and can produce language fluently (nativelike fluency) is that units of language of clause length or longer are stored as chunks in the memory. They suggest that this explanation means that most words are stored many times, once as an individual word and numerous times in larger stored chunks.

The 'puzzle' of nativelike selection is that by applying grammar rules it is possible to create many grammatically correct ways of saying the same thing. However only a small number of these would sound nativelike. For example, all the following are grammatically correct, although not all are nativelike.

> It wasn't me,   it was someone else
> it was the other one.
> it was another person.
> it was a different person.

The 'puzzle' of nativelike fluency is that we can only encode one clause at a time when speaking and we usually need to do so without hesitations in the middle of the clause. Most of the language we use consists of familiar combinations. Only a small amount is entirely new.

Support for this position comes from a longitudinal study comparing learners of French as a second language before and after residence abroad. Towell et al. (1996) concluded that the observed increase in fluency was the result of proceduralisation of knowledge. This proceduralisation was the result of learners storing memorised sequences. Towell et al. reached this conclusion by observing that mean length of run (number of successive syllables unbroken by a pause) was the most important temporal variable contributing to the difference between pre- and post-test performance, and by analysing the qualitative changes in some transcripts.

Pawley and Syder (1983) argue that memorised clauses and clause sequences make up a large percentage of the fluent stretches of speech heard in everyday conversation (p. 208). Pawley and Syder distinguish 'memorised sequences' from 'lexicalised sentence stems'. Lexicalised sentence stems are not totally predictable from their parts. They behave as a minimal unit for syntactic purposes, and they are a social institution (a conventional label for a conventional concept). There are degrees of lexicalisation. 'Memorised sequences' are transparent, regularly formed clauses.

Lexicalised sentence stems and memorised sequences are the building blocks of fluent speech. Pawley and Syder (p. 215) consider that by far the largest part of an English speaker's lexicon consists of complex lexical items including several hundred thousand lexicalised sentence stems. It is worth stressing that Pawley and Syder are talking about clause length units; however, their arguments also apply to two- or three-word phrasal multiword units (Tremblay et al., 2011; see Wray, 2002 and 2008, for a detailed discussion of the importance of formulaic sequences in language use). Laufer and Waldman (2011) present evidence from a corpus of learner writing showing much less use of verb–noun collocations by learners of English than by native speakers. When looking at different proficiency levels of the learners, there was a noted persistence of collocational error. The nature of language use necessitates collocational knowledge.

How can we identify and count multiword units?

We have seen that multiword units are important in language knowledge and use, and if we want to evaluate their effects and take a systematic approach to learning them, we need to be able to identify them.

There are three major related approaches to doing this, using criteria that are based on form, meaning and storage. (1) Form-based approaches to the identification of multiword units primarily use frequency of co-occurrence of the words making up each multiword unit along with the other form-based criteria of adjacency, grammatical well-formedness, grammatical variation and lexical variation. (2) Meaning-based approaches consider how clearly the meanings of the parts make up the meaning of the whole, that is, the degree of compositionality of the multiword unit. (3) Storage-based approaches consider evidence that the multiword unit is stored in the brain as a whole unit, or in Wray's terms, that they are morpheme-equivalent units.

Let us now look in detail at each of these three approaches, considering the criteria they use and the problems associated with the various criteria.

Form-based approaches

Form-based approaches to the identification of multiword units typically use corpus-based searches. A common procedure is to use a computer program that searches the corpus to find frequently co-occurring words (see, for example, Cheng et al., 2006). If the corpus is small, a minimal frequency level of two occurrences might be used, but clearly a large corpus and a higher frequency cut-off point is preferable. Because words differ greatly in their frequency of occurrence (there are high-frequency words and low-frequency words), a formula may be used to adjust for this. If such a formula was not used, then only multiword units combining high-frequency words would be at the top of any list, even if a particular low-frequency word, such as *gibbous* only ever occurred with the same collocate, *moon*, every time it occurred. The mutual information index (Manning and Schuetze, 1999) is an example of such a formula. It is calculated by working out the likelihood of two words occurring together by chance, using their individual frequencies compared with their actual frequency of co-occurrence. Its advantage is that it shows words that are strongly collocated, for example, *gibbous moon*. Its disadvantage is that multiword units with a high mutual information index may be rather infrequent. Note, however, that defining multi-word units as being made up of words that habitually co-occur (Firth, 1957: 14) is ambiguous enough to include both frequent mul-tiword units, and multiword items with a high mutual information index or its equivalent.

From a learning perspective, frequency of occurrence is important because learners need to get the best return for the learning they do, that is, they need to learn items that they will meet often and be able to use often, before they move on to learning less frequent items. Arnon and Snider (2010) found evidence for learners' sensitivity to the frequency of multiword phrases at various frequency levels even when the frequency of the constituent items was controlled for. Arnon and Snider's research supports the position that each meeting with a mul-tiword unit adds to the familiarity of that item.

If frequency of co-occurrence was the only formal criterion used for deciding if words were multiword units, then multiword units like *of the*, *in the* and *is one of the* would be at the top of the list. Clearly, additional criteria are needed to ensure that the multiword units found are items that could sensibly be learned and accessed as whole units, or that make sense when analysing the communicative function of text (Biber et al., 2004). Nation and Webb (2011: 177) describe a range of choices that can be made (see Table 12.1). Note that most of the choices in Table 12.1 involve one option that requires a lot of individual decision-making by the researcher and the other option allows computer-based processing. Typically, the laborious manual processing will give a more valid result and this needs to be weighed against the much more expedient nature of computer-based processing.

The paper by Cheng et al. (2008), on meaning shift units discovered using the ConcGram program, underlines the importance of seeing multiword units not as frozen and adjacent co-occurrences of words, but as co-occurrences of words that can vary in their distance from each other, in their order in the multiword unit, in their grammatical form, and in their accompanying words. However, a multiword unit typically has semantic prosody, semantic preference, colligation restrictions and a canonical form. A single lexical choice is not necessarily an unvarying set of adjacent words.

To understand how a multiword unit may be a 'single choice' and yet may be variable and not arbitrary, it is helpful to use the analogy of a journey: once you decide to go somewhere, in many cases the main places that you will pass through have already been determined, because there may be only one or very few routes to that place. However, along the way you can stop at a shop, make a minor detour or enliven the journey in some way by talking to a friend or looking at the scenery. The route is determined, but the journeys can be different. Similarly, as Stubbs (2009) shows, if you want to use the multiword unit *low ebb* to express the idea of things being in a comparatively bad state, you have chosen the main points on your route (*low* and *ebb*) but you can vary it as appropriate in a variety of acceptable ways:

> at its lowest ebb
> reached a low ebb
> their lowest ebb
> at a particularly low ebb

A 'single choice' is thus not necessarily just the choice of a fixed phrase, but is the choice of the major points which can be accompanied by appropriate additions and restrictions.

It is important to realise that it is the limitations of the software that is used and the desire to gather data as efficiently as possible with a minimum of manual checking that lead many researchers to adopt criteria for gathering and counting multiword units that do not comfortably stand up to close scrutiny from the perspective of validity. Such studies do provide interesting and informative data, but they also provide a necessarily restricted view of what is being investigated.

Table 12.1 shows the main factors to be considered when setting up criteria to do form-based searching for multiword units. Note that in each pair of choices there is one which requires a large amount of manual checking and classification, and another which allows most of the work to be done by the computer.

Because the meanings of the words that go to make up multiword units contribute to the meaning of the multiword units (even though some are partially opaque), it would be misleading to combine counts of single words and multiword units. Until we know more about the learning burden of multiword units it may be safer to do separate counts and analyses of vocabulary load, but consider both when assessing the difficulty of texts.

Table 12.1 *Form-based factors affecting counting the frequency of multiword units (from Nation and Webb, 2011: 177)*

Form-based factors	Cautions
1. Adjacency / discontinuity Words in the multiword unit can occur right next to each other or be separated by a word or words not in the multiword unit. *by and large; serve sb right*	If you count items that are not adjacent, you need to be especially careful that the items are in fact part of a multiword unit.
2. Grammatically fixed / grammatically variable A multiword unit can be counted as a fixed form which is unchanging, or the components in the multiword unit can occur together in a variety of grammatical and affixed forms. *to and fro; pulling your leg*	If you count variable items, you need to search using a variety of search words and combinations of words.
3. Grammatically structured / grammatically incomplete A multiword unit can be a complete grammatical unit, such as a sentence, a sentence subject, a predicate, an adverbial group etc., or it can be grammatically incomplete. *on the other hand; on the basis of*	If you count grammatically structured items, you need to have clear criteria describing what is and what is not grammatically structured.
4. Lexically variable / lexically invariable Counting multiword units can include some substitutable words of related or similar meaning, or it can contain items that cannot be replaced by others. *once a week; as well as*	If you count multiword units that allow substitution, you need to examine a lot of data manually to make sure you are including and counting acceptable substitutions.
5. Number of components A multiword unit must contain at least two words. Some counting is done with a limit on the number of words in the multiword units, some counting has no limit.	If you count multiword units with no limit on the number of units, it becomes even more important to check that they meet other criteria for being a multiword unit.

Meaning-based approaches

Some definitions of multiword unit include a criterion relating to how clearly the meaning of the parts of the multiword unit are related to the meaning of multiword unit. For example, the meanings of *nice* and *person* are closely related to the meaning of the multiword unit *nice person*. On the other hand, the meaning of *kill two birds with one stone*, or *as well*, is not readily apparent from the meaning of the parts. Using the criteria of compositionality (whether the parts make up the whole) and figurativeness (whether a figurative interpretation needs to be applied instead of a literal interpretation), it is possible to rate items on at least a three-point scale: (1) core idioms where the meaning of the parts has no obvious connection to the meaning of the whole; (2) figuratives where a figurative interpretation needs to be applied; and (3) literals where the meaning of the parts largely provides the meaning of the whole (Grant and Bauer, 2004; see Figure 12.1).

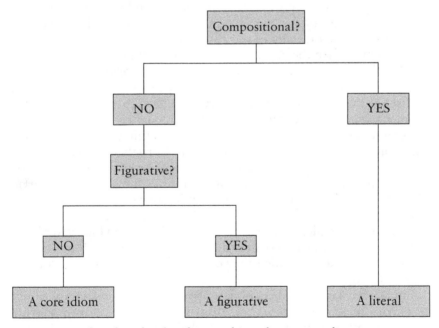

Figure 12.1 A flowchart for classifying multiword units according to transparency

These categories could be doubled by applying the third criterion of word-for-word parallel in the learners' L1. It is unlikely that there would be parallel core idioms in two languages, although it is possible. The likelihood of parallel L1–L2 figuratives is much higher, as is the likelihood of parallel L1–L2 literals. For productive purposes at least, literals without an L1 parallel would need to be learned. Evidence shows that the multiword units which do not have L1 parallels require more processing time and cause more difficulty for learners (Wolter and Gyllstad, 2011; Yamashita and Jiang, 2010). Here are some examples.

Core idioms	Figuratives	Literals
pull the other one *trip the light fantastic* *as well as*	*a bone of contention* *a stumbling block* *out of the blue*	*you know* *I think (that)* *at the moment*

Core idioms. The classification of multiword units according to meaning is closely related to the ease of interpreting and learning their meaning. Core idioms need to be learned as whole units. At one time, core idioms were figuratives, but the history of the relationship between the literal and figurative meaning has been lost. Although there are theories about where *kick the bucket* and *cats and dogs* (as in *raining cats and dogs*) came from, there is now no obvious relationship between the meaning of the parts and the meaning of the whole. Surprisingly, when the criteria of compositionality and figurativeness are strictly applied, there are only just over 100 core idioms in English. Table 12.2 lists the most frequent ones with their frequency in the British National Corpus (Grant, 2005). A few core idioms are very frequent, but most occur with a very low frequency.

Figuratives. Figuratives have a literal meaning and a figurative meaning. Probably the most helpful way to learn them is to relate their literal meaning to their figurative meaning. For example, how is *toe the line* (follow orders) related to its literal meaning of soldiers lining up along a line? How is the literal meaning of *put the cat among the pigeons* related to its figurative sense of 'create a stir'?

Boers and his colleagues (see, for example, Boers and Lindstromberg, 2009) have extensively researched the effect of using such multiword units and the ways in which they can be learned and we will look at these later in this chapter.

English has large numbers of figuratives and they make up the bulk of entries in idiom dictionaries. In a way, figuratives are not truly idioms because the literal meaning of their parts can be related to the figurative sense of the whole. The ease of interpreting figuratives is partly related to the existence or nonexistence of similar items in the learners' first language. Bortfeld (2003) presents evidence that it is possible to classify figuratives on a three-point scale of analysability. Here is an example of multiword units describing insanity translated from Latvian (p. 13).

Normally analysable	Abnormally analysable	Unanalysable
when all five senses are not at home	*to come off one's hinges*	*to turn into a Swede*

Note that what Bortfield classifies as the unanalysable example is not a core idiom, as it is possible to see a relationship between the literal and figurative meaning, but it may require explanation.

Table 12.2 *The most frequent core idioms with their frequency of occurrence in the British National Corpus*

as well (as)	30,400	*so long!*	24
by and large	487	*eat your heart out*	23
so and so	327	*not hold a candle to*	23
such and such	196	*off the wall*	22
out of hand	141	*pull the other one*	19
take the piss	137	*trip the light fantastic*	18
and what have you	136	*cut a dash*	18
serve sb right	101	*to a T*	18
take sb to task	92	*by and by*	17
red herring	87	*push the boat out*	16
(be) beside yourself	72	*gird your loins*	16
out and out	72	*hell for leather*	15
take the mickey	71	*cock a hoop*	15
at loggerheads	63	*Bob's your uncle*	14
pull sb's leg	60	*chew the fat*	14
touch and go	53	*cold turkey*	14
the Big Apple	52	*kick the bucket*	13
cut no ice with sb	50	*the cat's whiskers*	13
come a cropper	49	*give sb the bird*	13
put your foot in it	48	*(be) all in*	13
an axe to grind	47	*a French letter*	12
make no bones about it	44	*not cut the mustard*	12
a piece of cake	43	*odds and sods*	12
a white elephant	43	*like the clappers*	12
(all) of a piece	38	*Beat it!*	12
Uncle Sam	35	*butter wouldn't melt in sb's mouth*	11
and what not	33	*sweet Fanny Adams*	10
go by the boards	32	*to boot*	10

Literals. Literals, the third meaning category in Grant and Bauer's (2004) classification, include multiword units where the meanings of the parts are closely related to the meaning of the whole. Because of the transparency of this relationship, some researchers may be reluctant to call them multiword units, but literals can differ in difficulty for second language learners according to whether there is a word-for-word parallel expression in the learners' first language. *Strong tea* is a literal, but in Korean the equivalent is *thick tea*. Similarly, *take a vacation* may be expressed using a different verb from *take* in the learners' first language. This has led some people to suggest that there is an arbitrariness to such multiword units – you just have to learn that it is said that way. Liu (2010), however, in an insightful article, shows that the words in what may seem to be arbitrary multiword units are in fact behaving with grammatical and semantic consistency with their use in other multiword units. When *strong* is used with *tea*, it refers to the taste or smell of the tea. When *powerful* is used with *tea*, it refers to the effect of the tea. This is consistent with the use of *powerful* when applied to cars and other things. A *strong* car is a solidly built one. The multiword unit *strong tea* is not an arbitrary one but is consistent with its core meaning.

This consistency can best be seen with a concordance program (AntConc, Monopro, WordSmith Tools or www.lextutor.ca) which shows a range of uses of the component words, and thus an underlying grammatical and semantic regularity in their use.

According to Cheng et al. (2008: 237), Sinclair sees multiword units as taking on a life of their own which makes any relationship to other occurrences of their constituents irrelevant;

[w]hen a co-occurrence, such as 'hard+work', is deemed to be significant, the instances of co-occurrence of 'hard' and 'work' are no longer separate or separable linguistic entities, and their behaviour is entirely accounted for in the membership of the new unit.

This is an extreme view and seems to be taken from the viewpoint of text construction or language use rather than the teaching and learning of vocabulary. Clearly, as Liu (2010) has shown, the vast majority of multiword units can usefully be seen as consisting of words that are fulfilling their usual syntactic and semantic roles in ways that are consistent with their occurrence in other multiword units or one-off uses. There is no doubt that multiword units take on a life of their own, but the words that make them up are part of that life (see Partington, 2004: 462).

Martinez and Murphy (2011) argue that multiword units play a very large role in the comprehension of texts because (a) there are many of them, (b) many are very frequent, (c) many are not completely compositional, and (d) learners are often not aware that they have not understood them. Their study compared pairs of texts written with the same words but contrasting in the presence of potentially difficult multiword units. They found large differences in comprehension, with the texts with less transparent multiword units being more difficult. With the multiword unit texts learners tended much more to overestimate how much they understood, showing that they were not aware of misunderstanding the multiword units.

Nesselhauf (2003), working with advanced German-speaking learners of English, found a very strong influence of the L1 both on correct and incorrect use of multiword units. This should be viewed positively, because the learners are working on the assumption that the parts make up the whole in some systematic way and this fits with Liu's (2010) view that the occurrence of the members of multiword units are consistent with their overall use. However, Nesselhauf found a reasonably high rate of error with multiword units suggesting that it takes a long time to develop good intuitions about the meaning and use of individual words and thus about how they can go together.

Storage-based approaches

Researchers are interested in discovering if some multiword units are stored in memory as whole units, what determines which multiword units are stored, and how such storage affects language use and language learning (see Schmitt, 2004, for the classic collection of such studies). Because such storage is a psychological phenomenon, corpus data does not provide sufficient proof, and classification by meaning is also not sufficient, as items in all three categories of core idioms, figuratives and literals are not fixed in their form. The core idiom *pull someone's leg* can take numerous forms: *you're pulling my leg, my leg was being pulled, just giving your leg a gentle tug* and so on, suggesting that something much more flexible than the storage of a fixed unit is happening in this case. Wray (2008: Chapter 8) has an excellent discussion of the pitfalls and criteria in identifying formulaic material, considering factors of frequency, phonology, form, idiosyncrasies, spelling and intuition.

Martinez and Schmitt (2012) used the criteria of frequency, meaningfulness and relative non-compositionality to identify and count what they called 'phrasal expressions'. They began with a computer-based n-gram (2-, 3- and 4-item strings) search for co-occurring words and then worked through the resulting list using a set of pre-determined criteria. Their goal was to identify phrases that were likely to be processed as if they were single words (morpheme equivalent units). This is a highly intuitive judgement, but was guided by more objective criteria such as the presence of a one-word L1 or L2 equivalent for the phrase, for example *put up with* (tolerate) or *used to* (solla, in Spanish), some degree of semantic non-compositionality where the parts do not readily relate to the meaning of the whole, some lack of a word-for-word equivalent form in a variety of L1s, and whether a change in grammar resulted in a different meaning, as in *no doubt* (adverbial) 'certainly' versus *no doubt* (noun). Not all the criteria needed to be met as they were essentially ways of confirming the intuitive judgement of whether the phrase was a morpheme equivalent unit. Their goal was to identify frequent phrasal expressions that 'might pose some difficulty for a learner on a receptive level'. The resulting 505-item list was thus not purely a frequency list, but a frequency-based list of potentially difficult phrasal expressions. The frequency figures were based on the British National Corpus with a minimum frequency cut-off of 787 occurrences which is equal to the cut-off point for the most frequent 5,000 word families in the British National Corpus. A lot of the items on the list were polysemous, but their inclusion depended on the less compositional of their senses and their frequency was based not on the total occurrences of all senses but on the least compositional sense. So, the frequency of *at first* is based on its adverbial use (*at first, it seemed difficult*) not its adjectival use (*at first sight*).

Although n-grams based on adjacent word forms were the initial unit of analysis, there was an attempt to bring items with a variable internal component together. That is, *shake one's head* includes a range of personal pronouns in place of *one's*, and includes *shakes, shook, shaking* and *shaken* as well as *shake*. Almost 98% of the words making up the very useful list of 505 phrases were from the first 2,000 words of English – a frequent multiword unit necessarily contains frequent words.

Because of the amount of intuition involved in the decision-making, and because of the need to use a range of criteria that are often only partially met, it is easy to criticise the reliability of such a study. However, the lists resulting from such studies and the insights gained into the nature of formulaic sequences are invaluable. Studies like this one, those in the Schmitt (2004) collection and in Wray (2008) ask important, brave questions whose answers truly move our knowledge of the field forward.

There are good arguments why some multiword units need special attention, largely because of their partial or complete non-compositionality. These include core idioms (*as well, by and large*), figuratives (*get the green light, down to earth*) and literals which are partially opaque (*sweep aside, about time*). It would also be useful to analyse texts for the effect of these on the texts' vocabulary load (Martinez and Murphy, 2011).

Researchers are also interested in the functions of multiword units. The work of Hyland (2008), Biber et al. (2004) and Biber and Conrad

(2009) shows that an important function of some multiword units is to organise discourse. Hyland (2008) uses the major functional categories of research-oriented, text-oriented and participant-oriented to classify the four-item multiword units in his study. Bardovi-Harlig (2009; 2010) has looked at the roles multiword units (conventional expressions) play in use of the language and their receptive and productive knowledge by learners. She has found that receptive understanding typically precedes productive use, and there are likely to be a variety of reasons why learners lack knowledge of them and underuse them. To test receptive knowledge she used self-rating and for productive knowledge a discourse completion test.

We have looked at the three major approaches to identifying and counting multiword units, and have briefly looked at the Martinez and Schmitt (2012) study which resulted in a list of multiword units that could form the basis for a teaching programme. Let us now look at some other studies which had the goal of creating a list of multiword units.

Where can we find lists of multiword units?

It is useful to have well-made lists of multiword units to work from when teaching and designing courses. Koprowski's (2005) analysis of three coursebooks showed that the multiword units they presented were a rather mixed bag of frequent and infrequent items. Koprowski interprets this as a result of an unprincipled approach by the course designers to choosing what multiword units to include. Of the 822 multiword units found in the three coursebooks, only seven occurred in any two of the coursebooks and none occurred in all three.

Gardner and Davies (2007) used the tagged British National Corpus to find the occurrences of lexical verbs followed by adverbial particles (not necessarily adjacent). The unit of counting for the verbs was the lemma (base and inflected forms). They used WordNet (http://wordnet.princeton.edu/) to distinguish different senses of the phrasal verbs. In line with other frequency-based corpus studies, they found a small proportion of the lemmas accounted for a very large proportion of the occurrences (tokens), and that where forms had several functions, one function tended to dominate. Of the occurrences of *out* 97% were as an adverbial particle, whereas only 0.5% of the occurrences of *under* were. A small number of lexical verbs accounted for a large proportion of the occurrences of phrasal verbs. Gardner and Davies' study provides very useful lists that can guide the teaching of phrasal verbs and the design of coursebooks. Frequency data such as this provides an essential basis for the effective planning of courses and for the deliberate teaching and learning of language items.

Ellis et al. (2008) and Simpson-Vlach and Ellis (2010) describe the rationale and validation of criteria for creating an *Academic Formulas List* of multiword units of relevance in English for Academic Purposes courses. Although frequency of occurrence has a major effect on learning, it is eventually the internal coherence of a multiword unit (measured by the mutual information, or MI, index in their study) that ensures what is stored and used as coherent wholes. They used a weighted combination of frequency and mutual information when creating their Academic Formulas List. In spite of this the list does contain items which are not grammatically well structured. The findings of the study suggested frequency of occurrence needs to be combined with the criterion of grammatical well-structuredness (Shin and Nation, 2008) when choosing multiword units for teaching and deliberate learning.

Biber et al. (2004) looked at the frequent contiguous four-item multiword units in spoken and written academic text. The two criteria used were frequency of occurrence (a minimum of 40 times per one million running words) and the length of the units (four words). The use of the four-word criterion ensured that each unit would contain at least one content word. The resulting lists show the discourse-organising nature of many multiword units and are a very useful resource for the design of English for Academic Purposes courses.

Shin (2009; Shin and Nation, 2008) also used carefully applied form-based criteria to find the most frequent multiword units in spoken English. The criteria included frequency, grammatical well-formedness, and the need for all parts of the multiword unit to occur in the 2000 most frequent English words. The members of the multiword unit did not have to be immediately adjacent to each other. Multiword units with the same form but different meanings were distinguished (*looking up* = improving; *looking up* = searching for a reference). As with the Martinez and Schmitt study, applying the criteria involved a lot of laborious, painstaking work. The study found almost 4,700 multiword units; 308 of these multiword units were frequent enough to occur in the most frequent 2,000 words of English.

A much smaller but also immediately useful list is one created by Nation and Crabbe (1991) for absolute beginners wishing to learn a small survival vocabulary for foreign travel. Rather than a frequency count, the list was the result of interviewing people who had spent about a month living in a non-English-speaking country and who had learned a little of the language. The 120 items in the list includes phrases like *Good morning, Thank you, How much does that cost?, Where is the toilet?* and *I am ill*. The items can be deliberately learned in around three to four hours of study (preferably spread over several days to get spaced repetition) and allow learners to be able to communicate on a very basic level as soon as they arrive in the country where the language is spoken. It has been translated into 14 languages and can be found in the *Vocabulary Resource Book* on Paul Nation's website.

Grant (2005) did an exhaustive count of core idioms using idiom dictionaries, horoscopes, academic texts about idioms and television programmes as sources for the items. The frequency of the various forms was counted in the British National Corpus. The resulting list contained 106 items, only a very few of which deserve deliberate attention by a teacher (see Table 9.2).

Liu (2003), in a study of three corpora, used a list of multiword units found by using idiom and phrasal verb dictionaries. He found plenty of scope for improvement in the ways such dictionaries choose items for inclusion and in the information they provide in each entry.

There are other lists of multiword units with their frequencies, but the multiword units are not ranked in frequency order, making them more difficult to use for deliberate teaching and learning.

What is the range of ways to teach and learn multiword units?

Frequent multiword units need to be learned across the four strands of meaning-focused input, meaning-focused output, language-focused learning and fluency development. There is now plenty of evidence that multiword units, especially those containing known parts, can be learned incidentally through meeting them in context. Incidental learning is helped by repetition (Durrant and Schmitt, 2010; Sonbul and Schmitt, 2013; Webb, 2007; Webb and Chang, 2013), with more repetitions leading to a greater likelihood of learning. Webb and Chang (2013) used reading while listening as the form of input with four different measures of collocation knowledge.

If deliberate attention is directed towards multiword units through enhancement (underlining, bolding, colour, glossing) or through decontextualisation, the chances of learning are much greater (Sonbul and Schmitt, 2013). Explicit teaching is also effective (Boers et al., 2004a; Chan and Liou, 2005; Webb and Kagimoto, 2009). Let us now look at each of the four strands in turn, seeing how they can contribute to the learning of multiword units.

Learning multiword units through meaning-focused input

There is evidence (Kurnia, 2003) that learners can pick up multiword units incidentally through reading, and it is even more likely that such incidental learning occurs through listening. The most frequent multi-word units are made from even more frequent words and so typically the learning burden of multiword units is light because they will mostly contain known parts which are used in ways that are consistent with their other uses. Bogaards (2001) compared learning a new single word form and its meaning with learning the idiomatic meaning of a multiword unit containing known words. Learning the multiword units was easier (11.7 out of 14) than the single words (10.3 out of 14), both in immediate and delayed post-tests. However there was a big drop in the delayed post-test scores three weeks later to 4.3 out of 14 for the multiword units, and 2.6 out of 14 for the single words, showing that long-term retention of a multiword unit with known parts is by no means assured after one meeting.

As with all incidental message-focused learning, quantity of contact with the language will be a major factor affecting the quantity of learning. It is thus reasonable to expect the learning of multiword units to be one of the effects of an extensive reading programme. Such language contact should also be a major opportunity to develop skill in interpreting figurative expressions.

The condition for learning multiword units through listening is helped because the spoken language makes more frequent use of multi-word units than written texts do (Shin, 2009). It would be worth deliberately learning a small number of high-frequency core idioms, like *as well (as), of course, by and large, so and so, such and such, out of hand, and what have you* (Grant, 2005), so that they do not cause a problem while reading or listening.

Establishing multiword units through meaning-focused output

The quickest way to develop early spoken skill in a language is to memorise useful, relevant sentences and multiword units. Palmer (1925) suggested that the most fundamental guiding principle for the student of conversation should be 'Memorise perfectly the largest number of common and useful word-groups' (p. 187). For Palmer, word-groups included whole sentences.

Wray (2004; 2008: Chapter 12) looked at a learner of Welsh's memorisation of word groups required to carry out a set task (a cooking lesson). She found that:

1. Memorisation of multiword units resulted in the learner successfully carrying out the task. Wray notes, 'to the extent that our daily lives do feature a small set of recurring social "scripts", one can

imagine that, armed with a couple of dozen, she might actually be able to pass herself off as linguistically competent quite a lot of the time' (2008: 151).

2. There was attrition after the completion of the task, but several months later (five and nine months) a lot of learning remained.
3. Errors typical of an early learner of Welsh did occur, showing that analysis was taking place even though it was not needed.
4. Items with related but differing forms tended to interfere with each other.

Working with advanced learners of English, Wray (Fitzpatrick and Wray, 2006; Wray, 2008: Chapter 13) found a wide range of ability in memorising and recalling memorised material.

The survival vocabulary (Nation and Crabbe, 1991) mentioned earlier is a very useful first set of word groups to memorise to prepare for speaking.

Language-focused learning of multiword units

Exercises that deliberately focus on multiword units are very effective in resulting in both receptive and productive knowledge of multiword units. Webb and Kagimoto (2009) compared the receptive learning task of understanding glossed sentences with the productive learning task of writing in the multiword units in blanks in sentences where a small degree of choice was required. Both activities resulted in large amounts of learning as measured by receptive tests (around 18 out of 24) and productive tests (around 8 out of 24), and the differences in effect between the two tasks were small.

There are five main focuses for deliberate learning: (1) encouraging noticing; (2) rote learning; (3) the use of mnemonics; (4) seeing patterns; and (5) strategy development.

Encouraging noticing. There is a range of ways of deliberately drawing attention to multiword units. One involves dividing up texts into chunks, which can occur across all four skills. There is a set of activities related to dictation (Nation, 1991) where learners have to hold spoken or written chunks in their working memory before they reproduce them in spoken or written form. These activities include 'read-and-look-up' (West, 1960: 12), 'delayed copying' (Hill, 1969) and 'delayed repetition'.

As preparation for these activities, learners can practise dividing up written text into chunks and discussing the best places to make the divisions. For learners who see attention to grammar as an essential part of a course, this discussion can be a useful way of satisfying that expectation. However, research by Boers et al. (2007) suggests that deliberate practice in identifying chunks in one text does not transfer well to other texts.

Another way to encourage noticing is to get the learners to do multi-word unit exercises. Learners can brainstorm in groups or practice matching multiword units using grids or matching exercises such as this one: A word in the numbered list has to be matched with a word in the accompanying list so that they make a collocation, for example, *commercial investment* or *commercial vehicle*. A word in the numbered list can match with several in the accompanying list.

1 commercial 2 agricultural 3 redundant 4 public 5 inaccessible 6 structural 7 legal 8 isolated

area opinion economy company travellers vehicle patient linguist building term implement machinery miners alterations country information community meeting mineral words facts region claim library surplus television investment features.

Brown (1974) describes a range of such activities. Most of them have a test-like nature which requires learners to draw on previous knowledge. There is some value in making this knowledge explicit and such activities can do this. Not enough research has been done on the effectiveness of such activities and it would be worth looking at their effect and what makes them work. Learners tend to be far too cautious in their use of collocates (Channell, 1981), although this may be proficiency related (Kellerman, 1985). Boers and Lindstromberg (2009: 128–32) are justifiably critical of multiword unit-matching activities which provide no guidance in doing the matching, and suggest providing hints based on source domain, alliteration and other formal clues, and providing a spaced sequence of exercises on the same multiword units starting from the most guided to eventually unsupported gap filling. Drawing attention to multiword units in intensive reading is also a good way of helping learners see that they do not understand what they think they understand (Martinez and Murphy, 2011). Comprehension questions that focus on the understanding of tricky multiword units would be particularly useful.

Rote learning of multiword units. The guidelines for the rote learning of multiword units are no different from those for the rote learning of individual words. Multiword units can be most effectively memorised by applying the same learning guidelines as for isolated words. These are:

1. Write each multiword unit on a small card with its L1 translation on the other side so that there has to be active retrieval of its form or meaning.

2. Repeat the multiword unit aloud while memorising it.
3. Space the repetitions.
4. Use mnemonic tricks as suggested by Boers and colleagues (see below), put the multiword unit in a sentence, visualise examples of the meaning of the multiword unit and analyse the parts of the multiword unit. This increases the quality of the mental processing and helps learning.
5. Don't learn multiword units with similar words or meanings together. They will interfere with each other.
6. Keep changing the order of the cards to avoid serial learning.

There is no need to have separate packs of cards for multiword units and individual words. Steinel et al. (2007) examined deliberate and productive learning of multiword units as L1–L2 pairs (paired-associate learning). Learning was tested receptively and productively using a recall test. The results were very similar to those found in studies of paired-associate word learning. Productive learning was more difficult than receptive learning. Those who learned productively did better on productive tests. Those who learned vocabulary receptively did better on receptive tests. Imageability had positive effects on learning, and transparency of the multiword unit positively affected only the results of the receptive test. These results show that the effectiveness of word card learning applies not only to single words but also to multiword units and thus the recommendation to use both words and multiword units on word cards is well justified.

There is good reason to believe that Elgort's (2011) finding that the deliberate learning of individual words results in both explicit and implicit knowledge also applies to multiword units. Elgort found that both kinds of knowledge are created by the deliberate learning of single words. Sonbul and Schmitt (2013) looked at implicit and explicit lexical knowledge gained from incidental and deliberate learning of two-item multiword units. While they found strong evidence for the development of explicit knowledge, they found no evidence for implicit gains. Their implicit measure used the first word of the collocation as a prime and the second as the target word and was essentially a measure of productive knowledge. It may be better to use the whole collocation as a prime for a word of related meaning which measures a form of receptive knowledge.

Using mnemonics to learn multiword units. Mnemonic devices can focus on learning the form of a multiword unit, and learning its meaning and making the form–meaning connection. Learning the form of multiword units is helped if the multiword unit has formal features like the following (Boers and Lindstromberg, 2009: 106–7) and if the learners notice them:

- word repetition: *so-and-so, such and such*
- rhyme: *steer clear, fair and square*
- slant rhyme: *in actual fact, last gasp*
- alliteration: *take someone to task, bite the bullet*
- assonance: *red herring, faint praise*
- consonance: *casual acquaintance, further afield*

These all share the characteristic of repetition of some aspect of the form in two or more parts of the multiword unit. The repetition helps make the multiword unit memorable in that the form of one part can trigger the form of the other similar part. Boers and Lindstromberg (2009: 114) estimate that around 20% of multiword units have some kind of formal patterning, with alliteration accounting for well over half of this patterning. Simply drawing learners' attention to the patterning may be enough to help learning (Lindstromberg and Boers, 2008).

Boers and his colleagues have also conducted many experiments and replications on learning the form–meaning connection of multiword units. It is helped by:

- Hypothesising about the origins of figuratives. Where does the expression *show s.o. the ropes* come from? Boers (2001) found a strong learning benefit for learners who thought about the origin of figuratives.
- Hypothesising about the origins of figuratives and then getting explanatory feedback about the literal meaning. Boers et al. (2004b) found a learning benefit of 11% compared with learners who only did a gap-filling task with the figurative. When using a sequence of related learning tasks, as in computer-assisted learning, the sequence of identifying the origin of the figurative, learning its figurative meaning and then doing a gap-filling task was the most effective (Boers et al., 2007; Boers and Lindstromberg, 2009: 89).
- Making students aware of the literal meaning of the figurative and then letting them make the literal-figurative connection themselves.
- Letting the students see pictures showing the literal meaning of the figurative, as for example in *going for the jugular* which can be illustrated by a tiger attacking a wildebeest (Boers et al., 2008; Boers et al., 2009). It was found that the pictures helped the learning of the meaning but not the learning of the form of the figurative. This is a common enough finding and supports Barcroft's (2004) idea that what you focus on is what you learn. If the individual words making up the figurative expression are all well known, then the use of pictures would be helpful. If however the figurative contains an unknown or poorly known word (*I am at the end of my*

tether), then the use of pictures can take attention away from the new word form to learn.

- Learning new words through miming (Lindstromberg and Boers, 2005). Once the words had been learned through miming, learners were able to successfully apply these literal meanings (words like *stumble, dodge, wriggle*) to the interpretation of more metaphoric users (*stumble onto a solution, dodge the difficult questions, wriggle out of one's responsibilities*). In the less successful control group, the learners explored the meaning of the word with no visual (miming) representation.

Boers et al. (2007) looked at the frequency of the source domains of 'informal' figuratives finding that games (*the ball is in your court*) and entertainment (*play to the gallery*) accounted for almost 60% of such idioms, while more 'serious' domains (war and religion) accounted for a much smaller proportion. The seriousness of the domain seems to relate to the formality of the expression.

Boers and Lindstromberg (2009: 89–91) note that it is important to give deliberate attention to figuratives, because they are often not easily guessed through context clues, and sometimes their source domains are not obvious.

The feature that runs through all these ways of helping learners deal with figuratives is that deliberate, analytical attention can make the learning of figuratives substantially easier. This finding fits well with the principles of dealing with vocabulary across the four strands of a course: deliberate attention is not an alternative to incidental learning, but an effective complementary approach.

Looking for patterns in multiword units. Liu (2010) effectively points out that multiword units are not arbitrary, but that the words that make them up are used in ways that are consistent with their usual semantic and syntactic patterning. From the perspective of an L2 learner they may seem arbitrary and unpatterned, because they do not correspond to L1 usage. However, in fact, knowing how the parts are used helps the learning of multiword units. Walker (2011) also shows that most multiword units are explainable in that the linguistic features of the multiword units and the processes that make them such as metaphor are not arbitrary but are consistent with the behaviour of the parts of the multiword unit. It is thus useful to look at multiword units analytically and (1) relate them to the usage of the known words that they contain, and (2) draw attention to the wider usage of any unknown words they contain. This can be done through teacher explanation including carefully designed activities, and through learner discovery through the use of concordancing programs.

Boers and Lindstromberg (2009: 96–105), with some research evidence, propose that conceptual metaphors, such as *up* is good, *down* is bad (Lakoff and Johnson, 1980), provide a means for seeing some systematicity in multiword units such as *put someone down* and *we made up again*. This may be helpful as a mnemonic rather than as a strategy, as research by Malt and Eiter (2004) suggests that figuratives seem to be learned on an instance-by-instance basis.

One of the most widely recommended ways of deliberately developing multiword unit knowledge involves the use of concordances. A concordancer is a computer program that can collect all the examples of a word from a collection of texts (a corpus) and can display, sort and to some degree analyse them. Typically, a concordancer displays the examples with at least a line of context. This list is called a concordance:

... you're made redundant through no	[[fault]]	of your own ...
... well that's not the benefit's	[[fault]]	it's not, it's their fault ...
... weren't we just but it's all our	[[fault]]	to be fair ...
... and it's not necessarily the parents'	[[fault]]	...
... well now that's a that's a	[[fault]]	of the measurement er er criteria ...
... because of the grading system that's a	[[fault]]	there ...
... it's not a	[[fault]]	of whether it's internal or external be ...
... seller refuses or fails to repair the	[[fault]]	or takes too long to do it then the ...
might have happened as a result of the	[[fault]]	for example ...

Usually a concordancer can search for two words occurring within a certain distance of each other, for example within three words to the left or right of the main search word. There are web-based concordancers (www.lextutor.ca) and free-standing programs (AntConc, Monopro, WordSmith Tools). As well as a concordancer, a collection of texts is needed in which to search for the examples. Ideally the collection of texts should represent the kind of language uses that learners are expected to use, and should be large enough to get plenty of examples.

What kind of information can the examples in a concordance provide?

1. *Frequency of occurrence.* A concordance can show how often the word occurs in the corpus and how often certain multiword units occur. For example, the word type *boring* occurs 525 times in the Wellington Corpus of Spoken English and its most frequent collocate is *pretty* which occurs in front of it 8 times.

2. *Collocates*. A concordance can be sorted to show the most common collocates of the word. The best concordancers provide this data automatically. Typically two or more items which make up a multi-word unit have a 'canonical form', usually its most frequent multi-word unit of which most other collocates are variants. The variants should be looked at carefully to see how they differ from the most frequent form and to see if there is some kind of patterning amongst the differences which is grammatically based (colligation) or seman-tically based (semantic prosody). This kind of analysis is not always easy to do which suggests that such information could usefully be included in learners' dictionaries or at least dictionaries of multi-word units. If the collocates of different words are being compared, it is useful to look at the shared collocates of the two or more words (these are usually the most frequent collocates) and the characteris-tic collocates which occur only with one of the words. The charac-teristic collocates usually reveal a lot about the differences between the words being compared (Walker, 2011).

3. *Colligation*. In some multiword units there are grammatical catego-ries which typically occur with the node word.

4. *Semantic prosody*. Semantic prosody is the overall functional meaning of the multiword unit, at its simplest, whether it has a positive or negative meaning. Because the purpose of the multiword unit is to express a meaning, semantic prosody 'is the driving force behind the selection of the core and other co-selections comprising the lexical item' (Cheng et al., 2008: 240; see Walker, 2011: 295, for a useful brief discussion).

5. *Semantic preference*. Some words typically collocate with other words sharing a similar semantic feature.

For learners to use concordances in order to improve their writing they require several complex skills. First, they need to learn how to use the concordance program. Second, they need to be able to induce a rule from the concordance examples. Third, they need to be able to apply the results to the production or correction of text. Attempts have been made to automate this by designing a program that finds badly formed multiword units in learners' composition texts by comparison with corpus data and then suggest answers (Chang et al., 2008).

The material required is a concordancer and a relevant corpus. Students generally have positive attitudes to the use of concordances, and there is evidence that learners can usually apply the required skills. It is difficult, however, to decide when to use a concordancer and what headword to use in the search, and to interpret the data, especially when the concordance examples contain unknown vocabulary.

Cobb (1999a) sees concordancing as providing the benefits of learning through input (multiple, contextualised examples) and deliberate learning (conscious attention). Cobb's *Reading with Resources* (www.lextutor.ca) allows learners to hear the word they meet in a text, look it up in an online dictionary, and see several context sentences containing the word either taken from the same text or from a corpus.

Research using corpus-based concordance data has boomed in recent years with focuses on using concordance data to help avoid or correct multiword unit errors in writing (Chang and Sun, 2009; Chang et al., 2008; Shei and Pain, 2000; Sun, 2007; Todd, 2001; Yeh et al., 2007) and improving vocabulary and multiword unit knowledge (Chan and Liou, 2005; Cobb, 1999b; Horst et al., 2005; Kaur and Hegelheimer, 2005; Nesselhauf and Tschichold, 2002; Sun and Wang, 2003; Varley, 2009). Concordancing generally has positive effects on written production and learning (see Chapter 3, pp. 146–7, for more on concordances).

Strategy development. Of the meaning-based categories of multiword units, figuratives are the ones that will benefit the most from an interpretive strategy. Basically, the strategy involves (1) understanding the figurative meaning of the figurative – for example *pass the hat around* means to collect money from an involved group of people; (2) understanding the literal meaning of the figurative – passing a hat around so that people can put money in it; and (3) working out how the literal meaning relates to the figurative meaning (Grant and Bauer, 2004; Grant and Nation, 2006). Boers and Demecheleer (2001) suggest ways of supporting this strategy in order to overcome cross-cultural differences. These include making learners aware of the domain the expression comes from (*let off steam* relates to steam engines), helping learners become familiar with common metaphoric themes (*up* is good, *down* is bad), and alerting them to misleading false friends (*hanging up one's hat* is not the same as *tirer son chapeau à quelqu'un*).

Gaining knowledge of multiword units through fluency development

It is likely that the most effective way of making sure that multiword knowledge plays an important role in language use is through fluency development.

Schmidt (1992) presents a comprehensive survey of a wide range of theories which can be used to explain fluency development. The most accessible theory that describes the development of multiword unit knowledge through fluency development is McLaughlin's (1990) restructuring theory. McLaughlin (p. 113) argues that the restructuring of language knowledge occurs when learners reach a high degree of automatisation through practice. Learners can become fluent through practice at one level of knowledge. The only way they can improve further is to restructure that knowledge, typically into larger chunks. This may slow them down initially, but they will then be able to reach higher levels of fluency because of restructuring. McLaughlin thus sees fluency development playing a central role in the development of multiword unit knowledge.

It seems likely that fluency with multiword units can develop through both, gaining fluency with the multiword unit and in accessing the parts of a multiword unit. It is necessary to make this distinction because, while some multiword units exist in a fixed form, the majority are not frozen but can combine their main parts in a variety of ways.

Evidence for the value of substantial input and repetition for developing multiword unit knowledge comes from a study by Durrant and Schmitt (2010). They showed that adult L2 learners retained information about known words met together in input even though their attention was not deliberately focused on this. Presumably, with larger amounts of input L2 learners would have stronger and greater multiword unit knowledge. This is supported by their previous study (Durrant and Schmitt, 2009) which showed that non-native writers used high-frequency multiword units but underused lower-frequency multiword units with strongly associated components.

Fluency development (see Chapter 3) can encourage the storage of multiword units, and similarly multiword unit knowledge and storage can contribute to fluency (Conklin and Schmitt, 2008; Tremblay et al., 2011). The frequency of multiword units affects the speed with which they are processed, with high-frequency multiword units requiring less processing time. Thus storage of high-frequency multiword units is a contributor to fluency of receptive productive language use. If, as is the case with single words (Elgort, 2011), deliberate learning can contribute to implicit knowledge, then the deliberate learning of multiword units could affect fluency.

In this chapter we have looked at the nature of multiword units and why they are important, making the point that the parts that go to make up multiword units are not arbitrarily combined but are typically filling their normal semantic and grammatical functions. It is thus worth learning multiword units, but it is also worth being analytic during this learning. We can look at multiword units from the viewpoint of their form, their meaning, their storage and their use. When learning multiword units, learners need to have opportunities to learn them across the four strands of a course. Learning through the teaching of multiword units should be only one of a range of opportunities for learning multiword units. It is likely that fluency development activities can be a major source of multiword unit learning.

The area of multiword units is still a very exciting area of study. Improvements in methodology (largely in clarity in defining what is being studied), improvements in technology, and the asking of innovative and brave research questions are all contributing to our knowledge of the nature and importance of multiword units, how multiword units can be taught and learned, and how they contribute to language use.

References

Arnon, I. and Snider, N. (2010). More than words: Frequency effects for multi-word phrases. *Journal of Memory and Language*, **62**, 1, 67–82.

Barcroft, J. (2004). Effects of sentence writing in second language lexical acquisition. *Second Language Research*, **20**, 4, 303–34.

Bardovi-Harlig, K. (2009). Conventional expressions as a pragmalinguistic resource: Recognition and production of conventional expressions in L2 pragmatics. *Language Learning*, **59**, 4, 755–95.

Bardovi-Harlig, K. (2010). Recognition of conventional expressions in L2 pragmatics. *Pragmatics and Language Learning*, **12**, 141–62.

Biber, D. and Conrad, S. (2009). *Register, Genre, and Style*. Cambridge: Cambridge University Press.

Biber, D., Conrad, S. and Cortes, V. (2004). "If you look at ...": Lexical bundles in university teaching and textbooks. *Applied Linguistics*, **25**, 3, 371–405.

Boers, F. (2001). Remembering figurative idioms by hypothesising about their origin. *Prospect*, **16**, 3, 35–43.

Boers, F. and Demecheleer, M. (2001). Measuring the impact of cross-cultural differences on learners' comprehension of imageable idioms. *ELT Journal*, **55**, 3, 255–62.

Boers, F., Demecheleer, M. and Eyckmans, J. (2004a). Cross-cultural variation as a variable in comprehending and remembering figurative idioms. *European Journal of English Studies*, **8**, 3, 375–88.

Boers, F., Demecheleer, M. and Eyckmans, J. (2004b). Etymological elaboration as a strategy for learning idioms. In Bogaards, P. and Laufer, B. (eds.), *Vocabulary in a Second Language: Selection, Acquisition, and Testing* (pp. 53–78). Amsterdam: John Benjamins.

Boers, F., Eyckmans, J. and Stengers, H. (2007). Presenting figurative idioms with a touch of etymology: More than mere mnemonics? *Language Teaching Research*, **11**, 1, 43–62.

Boers, F. and Lindstromberg, S. (2009). *Optimizing a Lexical Approach to Instructed Second Language Acquisition*. Basingstoke: Palgrave Macmillan.

Boers, F., Lindstromberg, S., Littlemore, J., Stengers, H. and Eyckmans, J. (2008). Variables in the mnemonic effectiveness of pictorial elucidation. In Boers, F. and Lindstromberg, S. (eds.), *Cognitive Linguistic Approaches to Teaching Vocabulary and Phraseology* (pp. 189–216). Berlin: Mouton de Gruyter.

Boers, F., Piquer Piriz, A., Stengers, H. and Eyckmans, J. (2009). Does pictorial elucidation foster recollection of idioms? *Language Teaching Research*, **13**, 3, 367–82.

Bogaards, P. (2001). Lexical units and the learning of foreign language vocabulary. *Studies in Second Language Acquisition*, **23**, 321–43.

Bortfeld, H. (2003). Comprehending idioms cross-linguistically. *Experimental Psychology*, **50**, 3, 217–30.

Brown, D. F. (1974). Advanced vocabulary teaching: the problem of collocation. *RELC Journal*, **5**, 2, 1–11.

Chan, T. P. and Liou, H. C. (2005). Effects of web-based concordancing instruction on EFL students' learning of verb-noun collocations. *Computer Assisted Language Learning*, **18**, 231–51.

Chang, W. L. and Sun, Y. C. (2009). Scaffolding and web concordancers as support for language learning. *Computer Assisted Language Learning*, **22**, 4, 283–302.

Chang, Y. C., Chang, J. S., Chen, H. J. and Liou, H. C. (2008). An automatic collocation writing assistant for Taiwanese EFL learners: A case of corpus-based technology. *Computer Assisted Language Learning*, **21**, 3, 283–99.

Channell, J. (1981). Applying semantic theory to vocabulary teaching. *ELT Journal*, **35**, 2, 115–22.

Cheng, W., Greaves, C. and Warren, M. (2006). From n-gram to skipgram to concgram. *International Journal of Corpus Linguistics*, **11**, 1, 411–33.

Cheng, W., Greaves, C., Sinclair, J. and Warren, M. (2008). Uncovering the extent of the phraseological tendency: Towards a systematic analysis of concgrams. *Applied Linguistics*, **30**, 2, 236–52.

Cobb, T. (1999a). Applying constructivism: A test for the learner-as-scientist. *Educational Technology Research & Development*, **47**, 3, 15–33.

Cobb, T. (1999b). Breadth and depth of vocabulary acquisition with hands-on concordancing. *Computer Assisted Language Learning*, **12**, 4, 345–60.

Conklin, K. and Schmitt, N. (2008). Formulaic sequences: Are they processed more quickly than nonformulaic language by native and nonnative speakers? *Applied Linguistics*, **29**, 1, 72–89.

Durrant, P. and Schmitt, N. (2009). To what extent do native and non-native writers make use of collocations? *IRAL*, **47**, 2, 157–77.

Durrant, P. and Schmitt, N. (2010). Adult learners' retention of collocations from exposure. *Second Language Research*, **26**, 2, 163–88.

Elgort, I. (2011). Deliberate learning and vocabulary acquisition in a second language. *Language Learning*, **61**, 2, 367–413.

Ellis, N. C. (2001). Memory for language. In Robinson, P. (ed.), *Cognition and Second Language Instruction* (pp. 33–68). Cambridge: Cambridge University Press.

Ellis, N. C. and Schmidt, R. (1997). Morphology and longer distance dependencies: Laboratory research illuminating the A in SLA. *Studies in Second Language Acquisition*, **19**, 145–71.

Ellis, N., Simpson-Vlach, R. and Maynard, C. (2008). Formulaic language in native and second language speakers: Psycholinguistics, corpus linguistics, and TESOL. *TESOL Quarterly*, **42**, 3, 375–96.

Firth, J. R. (1957). *Papers in Linguistics*. London: Oxford University Press.

Fitzpatrick, T. and Wray, A. (2006). Breaking up is not so hard to do: Individual differences in L2 memorization. *Canadian Modern Language Review*, **63**, 1, 35–57.

Gardner, D. and Davies, M. (2007). Pointing out frequent phrasal verbs: A corpus-based analysis. *TESOL Quarterly*, **41**, 2, 339–59.

Grant, L. (2005). Frequency of 'core idioms' in the British National Corpus (BNC). *International Journal of Corpus Linguistics*, **10**, 4, 429–51.

Grant, L. and Bauer, L. (2004). Criteria for redefining idioms: Are we barking up the wrong tree? *Applied Linguistics*, **25**, 1, 38–61.

Grant, L. and Nation, I. S. P. (2006). How many idioms are there in English? *ITL – International Journal of Applied Linguistics*, **151**, 1–14.

Hill, L. A. (1969). Delayed copying. *ELT Journal*, **23**, 3, 238–9.

Horst, M., Cobb, T. and Nicolae, I. (2005). Expanding academic vocabulary with an interactive on-line database. *Language Learning & Technology*, **9**, 2, 90–110.

Hyland, K. (2008). As can be seen: Lexical bundles and disciplinary variation. *English for Specific Purposes*, **27**, 4–21.

Jiang, H. and Nekrasova, T. M. (2007). The processing of formulaic sequences by second language speakers. *Modern Language Journal*, **91**, 3, 433–45.

Kaur, J. and Hegelheimer, V. (2005). ESL students' use of concordance in the transfer of academic word knowledge: an exploratory study. *Computer Assisted Language Learning*, **18**, 4, 287–310.

Kellerman, E. (1985). If at first you do succeed. In Gass, S. M. and Madden, C. G. (eds.), *Input in Second Language Acquisition* (pp. 345–53). Rowley, MA: Newbury House.

Koprowski, M. (2005). Investigating the usefulness of lexical phrases in contemporary coursebooks. *ELT Journal*, **59**, 4, 322–32.

Kurnia, N. S. (2003). *Retention of Multiword Strings and Meaning Derivation from L2 Reading*. Victoria University of Wellington, Wellington.

Lakoff, G. and Johnson, M. (1980). *Metaphors We Live By*. Chicago: University of Chicago Press.

Laufer, B. and Waldman, T. (2011). Verb-noun collocations in second language writing: A corpus analysis of learners' English. *Language Learning*, **61**, 2, 647–72.

Lewis, M. (1993). *The Lexical Approach*. Hove: Language Teaching Publications.

Lindstromberg, S. and Boers, F. (2005). From movement to metaphor with manner of movement verbs. *Applied Linguistics*, **26**, 2, 241–61.

Lindstromberg, S. and Boers, F. (2008). The mnemonic effect of noticing alliteration in lexical chunks. *Applied Linguistics*, **29**, 2, 200–222.

Liu, D. (2003). The most frequently used spoken American English idioms: A corpus analysis and its implications. *TESOL Quarterly*, **37**, 4, 671–700.

Liu, D. (2010). Going beyond patterns: Involving cognitive analysis in the learning of collocations. *TESOL Quarterly*, **44**, 1, 4–30.

Malt, B. and Eiter, B. (2004). Even with a green card, you can be put out to pasture and still have to work: Non-native intuitions of the transparency of common English idioms. *Memory and Cognition*, **32**, 6, 896–904.

Manning, C. D. and Schuetze, H. (1999). *Foundations of Statistical Natural Language Processing*. Cambridge, MA: MIT Press.

Martinez, R. and Murphy, V. A. (2011). Effect of frequency and idiomaticity on second language reading comprehension. *TESOL Quarterly*, **45**, 2, 267–90.

Martinez, R. and Schmitt, N. (2012). A phrasal expressions list. *Applied Linguistics*, **33**, 3, 299–320.

McLaughlin, B. (1990). Restructuring. *Applied Linguistics*, **11**, 2, 113–28.

Nation, I. S. P. (1991). Dictation, dicto-comp and related techniques. *English Teaching Forum*, **29**, 4, 12–14.

Nation, I. S. P. and Webb, S. (2011). *Researching and Analyzing Vocabulary*. Boston: Heinle Cengage Learning.

Nation, P. and Crabbe, D. (1991). A survival language learning syllabus for foreign travel. *System*, **19**, 3, 191–201.

Nesselhauf, N. (2003). The use of collocations by advanced learners of English and some implications for teaching. *Applied Linguistics*, **24**, 2, 223–42.

Nesselhauf, N. and Tschichold, C. (2002). Collocations in CALL: An investigation of vocabulary-building software for EFL. *Computer Assisted Language Learning*, **15**, 3, 251–79.

Palmer, H. E. (1925). Conversation. In Smith, R. C. (ed.), *The Writings of Harold E. Palmer: An Overview (1999)* (pp. 185–91). Tokyo: Hon-no-Tomosha.

Partington, A. (2004). Review of Reading Concordances by J. Sinclair (2003), London: Longman. *System*, **32**, 459–62.

Pawley, A. and Syder, F. H. (1983). Two puzzles for linguistic theory: Nativelike selection and nativelike fluency. In Richards, J. C. and Schmidt, R. W. (eds.), *Language and Communication* (pp. 191–225). London: Longman.

Schmidt, R. W. (1992). Psychological mechanisms underlying second language fluency. *Studies in Second Language Acquisition*, **14**, 357–85.

Schmitt, N. (ed.). (2004). *Formulaic Sequences*. Amsterdam: John Benjamins.

Shei, C. C. and Pain, H. (2000). An ESL writer's collocational aid. *Computer Assisted Language Learning*, **13**, 2, 167–82.

Shin, D. (2009). *A Collocation Inventory for Beginners: Spoken Collocations of English*. Köln: LAP LAMBERT Academic Publishing.

Shin, D. and Nation, I. S. P. (2008). Beyond single words: The most frequent collocations in spoken English. *ELT Journal*, **62**, 4, 339–48.

Simpson-Vlach, R. and Ellis, N. C. (2010). An academic formulas list: New methods in phraseology research. *Applied Linguistics*, **31**, 4, 487–512.

Sinclair, J. (2004a). New evidence, new priorities, new attitudes. In Sinclair, J. (ed.), *How to Use Corpora in Language Teaching* (pp. 271–99). Amsterdam: John Benjamins.

Sinclair, J. (2004b). *Trust the Text*. London: Routledge.

Sinclair, J. M. (1987). *Looking Up*. London: Collins ELT.

Siyanova-Chanturia, A., Conklin, K. and Schmitt, N. (2011). Adding more fuel to the fire: An eye-tracking study of idiom processing by native and non-native speakers. *Second Language Research*, **27**, 2, 251–72.

Siyanova, A. and Schmitt, N. (2007). Native and nonnative use of multi-word vs. one-word verbs. *IRAL*, **45**, 2, 119–39.

Sonbul S. and Schmitt, N. (2013). Explicit and implicit lexical knowledge: Acquisition of collocations under different input conditions. *Language Learning*, **63**, 1, 121–59.

Steinel, M. P., Hulstijn, J. H. and Steinel, W. (2007). Second language idiom learning in a paired-associate paradigm: Effects of direction of learning, direction of testing, idiom imageability, and idiom transparency. *Studies in Second Language Acquisition*, **29**, 3, 449–84.

Stubbs, M. (2009). The search for units of meaning: Sinclair on empirical semantics. *Applied Linguistics*, **30**, 1, 115–37.

Sun, Y. C. (2007). Learner perceptions of a concordancing tool for academic writing. *Computer Assisted Language Learning*, **20**, 4, 323–43.

Sun, Y. C. and Wang, L. Y. (2003). Concordancers in the EFL classroom: Cognitive approaches and collocation difficulty. *Computer Assisted Language Learning*, **16**, 83–94.

Todd, R. W. (2001). Induction from self-selected concordances and self-correction. *System*, **29**, 1, 91–102.

Towell, R., Hawkins, R. and Bazergui, N. (1996). The development of fluency in advanced learners of French. *Applied Linguistics*, **17**, 1, 84–119.

Tremblay, A., Derwing, B., Libben, G. and Westbury, C. (2011). Processing advantages of lexical bundles: Evidence from self-paced reading tasks. *Language Learning*, **61**, 2, 569–613.

Varley, S. (2009). I'll just look that up in the concordancer: integrating corpus consultation into the language learning environment. *Computer Assisted Language Learning*, **22**, 2, 133–52.

Walker, C. (2011). A corpus-based study of the linguistic features and processes which influence the way collocations are formed: Some implications for the learning of collocations. *TESOL Quarterly*, **45**, 2, 294–312.

Webb, S. (2007). The effects of repetition on vocabulary knowledge. *Applied Linguistics*, **28**, 1, 46–65.

Webb, S. and Chang, A. C.-S. (2013). Incidental learning of collocation. *Language Learning*.

Webb, S. and Kagimoto, E. (2009). The effects of vocabulary learning on collocation and meaning. *TESOL Quarterly*, **43**, 1, 55–77.

West, M. (1960). *Teaching English in Difficult Circumstances*. London: Longman.

Wolter, B. and Gyllstad, H. (2011). Collocational links in the L2 mental lexicon and the influence of L1 intralexical knowledge. *Applied Linguistics*, **32**, 4, 430–49.

Wray, A. (2000). Formulaic sequences in second language teaching: Principles and practice. *Applied Linguistics*, **21**, 4, 463–89.

Wray, A. (2002). *Formulaic Language and the Lexicon*. Cambridge: Cambridge University Press.

Wray, A. (2004). 'Here's one I prepared earlier': Formulaic language learning on television. In Schmitt, N. (ed.), *Formulaic Sequences*. Amsterdam: John Benjamins.

Wray, A. (2008). *Formulaic Language: Pushing the Boundaries*. Oxford: Oxford University Press.

Yamashita, J. and Jiang, N. (2010). L1 influence on the acquisition of L2 collocations: Japanese ESL users and EFL learners acquiring English collocations. *TESOL Quarterly*, **44**, 4, 647–68.

Yeh, Y., Liou, H. C. and Li, Y. H. (2007). Online synonym materials and concordancing for EFL college writing. *Computer Assisted Language Learning*, **20**, 2, 131–52.

13 *Testing vocabulary knowledge and use*

Testing vocabulary is similar to testing in other areas of language knowledge and use. The same criteria of reliability, validity, practicality and washback need to be considered when designing and evaluating vocabulary tests (Nation and Webb, 2011). In some ways testing vocabulary is easier than testing grammatical knowledge or control of discourse because the units to test are more obviously separate. It is not too difficult to identify what a word type is. However, there are problems and issues and we will look at these in this chapter. There is an excellent book devoted solely to vocabulary testing (Read, 2000) and Schmitt's (2010) book on researching vocabulary focuses upon measurement.

Like much of this book, this chapter is organised around questions that teachers typically ask. This means that it is organised rather differently from some other discussions of language testing. This chapter has two major divisions. The first division looks at the purposes of vocabulary tests, covering diagnostic, placement, achievement and proficiency tests. The second division looks at different test formats or item types, answering questions like 'Should choices be given?', 'Should words be tested in context?' and 'How can I measure words that learners don't know well?' This section covers a wide range of vocabulary test formats, along with comments on their design and use.

When deciding which vocabulary test is the best, the test maker has to consider the purpose of the test, the kind of knowledge it will try to measure, and the conditions under which it will be used. After considering these factors the test maker should be able to make a sensible choice from the range of vocabulary test formats, and decide how to make a truly representative sample of words to test, and then at least come close to making the best test.

Purposes of tests

Language tests can be used for a variety of purposes:

1. to find out where learners are experiencing difficulty so that something can be done about it (diagnostic tests). This can also involve looking at how well learners can use vocabulary-learning and coping strategies;
2. to place learners in classes of the right level (placement tests);
3. to see whether a recently studied group of words has been learned (short-term achievement tests);
4. to see whether a course has been successful in teaching particular words (long-term achievement tests); and
5. to see how much vocabulary learners know (proficiency tests).

The major difference between these types of tests for test makers is how to select the vocabulary for the tests. When using the tests, the major difference should be how the results are used. Let us now look at each of these purposes in more detail. Because of its importance for a range of uses on teaching, learning and research, we will take a very detailed look at measuring how much learners know – their vocabulary size.

How can we test to see where learners need help?

A diagnostic test is used so that a teacher or learners can decide what course of action to take. It is important for a teacher to know whether learners have enough vocabulary to do particular tasks. For example, if learners know the 700-word vocabulary of level 2 of the Oxford Bookworms Series, they will be able to read all the books at that level and at lower levels. If learners know the vocabulary of the *General Service List* (West, 1953), then they can read the enormous amount of material written using that vocabulary. For learners who want to do university study, they are also ready to study the words in the *Academic Word List* (see Appendix 1) which builds on the *General Service List*.

The Vocabulary Levels Test is a diagnostic test with four frequency levels and an Academic Word List section. When using the test, the teacher is not particularly interested in the learner's total score on the test, but is first interested in whether the learner knows enough of the high-frequency words at the 2,000-word level. If the learner has a good score at this level and will do academic study in English, then the next point of interest is the learner's score on the Academic Word List section. If they do not intend to do academic study, then the mid-frequency vocabulary measured at the 3,000- and 5,000-word levels is of interest. As we have seen earlier in this book, teachers need to deal with high- and low-frequency words in quite different ways. It is thus very important to know where learners are in their vocabulary knowledge so that an appropriate vocabulary-learning programme can be designed.

Usually it is not possible to test all the words within a particular group. Even a vocabulary test with 100 items is a long test. When we make a test we have to be very careful in selecting the items for the test so that the items we choose are good representatives of our total list of words. For example, if we wish to make a test of the words in the *General Service List*, we have to choose between 60 and 100 words which will be used to represent the 2,000 headwords in the list. First we must exclude all the words that we cannot easily test, for example *a*, *the*, *of* and *be*. In fact, the test will be easier to make if we test only nouns, verbs, adjectives and adverbs. Decisions like this will depend on the type of test item we will use. If the learners are to translate the tested words we may be able to test words that we could not test with a monolingual test. If we are using pictures instead of synonyms or definitions, then the words we can test will be an even smaller group. If we used only pictures, our list of test items would not be a good representation of the total list because it would consist mainly of concrete nouns. Thus our test would not be a good one.

Second, after we have excluded the words we cannot test, we must find a good way of choosing the test items from the words that are left. The best way is to number them and choose every 10th word if this will give us enough words for the test.

One test of the *General Service List* (Barnard, 1961) included almost every testable word in the list. The only exclusions were a few words which were needed to make simple contexts for the tested words. The following items are taken from the test. The learners had to translate the italicised word into their first language.

I cannot say much about his *character*.
Her *idea* is a very good one.
I want to hear only the *facts*.

The test was divided into several parts and different learners sat different parts. The aim of the test was to find which words in the *General Service List* were known and which were not known. The test was used in India (Barnard, 1961) and Indonesia (Quinn, 1968). Barnard found that entrants to university knew 1,500 of the words in the *General Service List*, Quinn found that a similar Indonesian group knew 1,200 words.

The Vocabulary Levels Test was originally designed as a diagnostic test to see what level of vocabulary learners needed to be focusing on – high-frequency words, academic vocabulary or low-frequency vocabulary. Thus, learners' scores on particular levels are far more important than their total score on the test. The test has worked well, largely because of the quality of the *General Service List* and the *Academic Word List* on which two of its levels were based. Because both the original version (Nation, 1983) and the revised version (Schmitt et al., 2001) used the Thorndike and Lorge (1944) word lists for the 3,000-, 5,000- and 10,000-word levels, the test suffers from the limitations of this list. The major weakness is that the unit of counting in Thorndike and Lorge was the lemma (a word and its inflected forms) although this was not clearly defined in the counting. A more appropriate unit for a test of receptive knowledge is the word family (Bauer and Nation, 1993). When the Thorndike and Lorge list is analysed according to word families, it contains much less than 30,000 words and probably less than 20,000. Because of this, the 3,000, 5,000 and 10,000 levels in the Vocabulary Levels Test do not correspond to the 3,000, 5,000 and 10,000 in the more recent British National Corpus lists which are based on word families. Although this is not an overly serious issue regarding the interpretation of the results of the test, it would be good to have a version that used lists based on the same unit of counting, the word family, at all levels of the test. A revised test might also distinguish knowledge of mid-frequency vocabulary from low-frequency vocabulary as these two large groups of words benefit from different kinds of attention. Nation (2002) and Schmitt et al. (2001) provide guidance on interpreting the results of the Vocabulary Levels Test.

There is a need for diagnostic tests of the major vocabulary learning strategies: guessing from context, using word parts, direct learning and dictionary use. Diagnostic tests need to be designed so that it is easy to interpret their results and to relate this interpretation to action.

How can we measure if learners have control of the important vocabulary learning strategies?

Just as we can distinguish between declarative and procedural knowledge of vocabulary – what does the learner know compared with what can the learner do –, it is possible to distinguish between declarative and procedural knowledge of vocabulary-learning strategies. These strategies include guessing from context, direct learning of vocabulary, mnemonic techniques including the use of word parts and dictionary use.

The declarative/procedural distinction is particularly important for vocabulary-learning strategies because teachers tend to spend insufficient time on helping learners become fluent and comfortable with the strategies. As a result, the strategies may be known, but not used. Learners may need to change their knowledge, attitudes and awareness in order to truly make the learning become their own. Adopting a vocabulary-learning strategy involves all these changes.

It is possible to measure declarative knowledge of a strategy by directly testing explicit knowledge of the subskills of the strategy. For example, with guessing from context, learners can be tested on their skill at working out the part of speech of an unknown word in context, doing the 'What does what?' activity on the unknown word, determining the conjunction relationships between the clause containing the unknown word and adjoining clauses, and breaking the word into its component affixes and stem.

To measure procedural knowledge, it is necessary to look at the result of strategy use, usually while the learners' attention is directed towards some other goal such as comprehension of a text or doing a piece of writing. Table 13.1 looks at possibilities for testing declarative and procedural knowledge of vocabulary-learning strategies. Tests need to be developed in all these areas.

How can we test vocabulary to place learners in classes at the right level?

The Yes/No test is an attractive option as a placement test because it is quick to administer, is easily computerised for speedy marking, can contain many items thus increasing reliability, and is easy to make. Meara's *Eurocentres Vocabulary Size Test* (Meara and Buxton, 1987; Meara and Jones, 1987) was designed originally for placement purposes. Fairclough (2011) trialled such a test with learners of Spanish and found it worked well and correlated well with the other measures of language proficiency. A good range of vocabulary from lower frequency levels is needed to avoid a ceiling effect with higher proficiency learners. Harrington and Carey (2009), investigating the use of a Yes/No placement test, found that it correlated highly with the listening, grammar and writing parts of the placement battery. They concluded that because vocabulary is such a central part of language knowledge and because of the high correlations with other tests, the Yes/No test could be a useful part of a placement test battery.

A vocabulary size measure like the Vocabulary Size Test or its bilingual versions, can be a very useful placement tool.

Table 13.1 *Testing declarative and procedural knowledge of the important vocabulary learning strategies*

Strategy	Testing declarative knowledge: What learners can do	Testing procedural knowledge: What learners actually do
Guessing from context	*Subskills* • Test recognition of part of speech • Test use of 'What does what?' • Test application of conjunction relationships • Test word analysis skills *Integration* • Get the learner to think aloud while guessing	• Use sensitive multiple-choice items to test incidental learning from guessing from context • Use a guessing from context test (Sasao, 2013)
Direct vocabulary learning	*Subskills* • Test steps of keyword technique • Test knowledge of direct learning principles *Integration* • Observe the learner doing direct vocabulary learning and question the learner or get the learner to think aloud	• Set the learner a direct vocabulary-learning task and measure the speed and amount of learning (Tinkham, 1989) • Get the learner to retrospect
Using word parts	*Subskills* • Test knowledge of frequent word parts • Test word analysis skills • Test re-wording skills (redefine the word using the meaning of the parts)	• Set a piece of learning as a part of a larger task • Measure the learning. Get the learner to retrospect

Integration
- Get the learner to think aloud while learning analysable complex words

Subskills
- Test knowledge of types of information available in a dictionary
- Test knowledge of a search procedure

Integration
- Test speed and accuracy at finding certain pieces of information in a dictionary

Dictionary use

- Observe dictionary use during a reading comprehension task
- Determine the success of the dictionary use. Get the learner to retrospect

How can we test whether a small group of words in a course has been learned?

Short-term achievement tests are made up of words that learners have been studying, usually within the last week or two. Thus, the words that go into a short-term achievement test come from the course material. The results of such a test do not tell you how many words the learners know in the language, or what vocabulary they should be working on – the results tell the teacher and learners how successful their recent study has been.

Short-term achievement tests need to be easy to make (because they might not be used again), easy to mark (because learners need to know quickly how well they have done) and fair (they should relate to what was studied in a predictable way, and should not expect too much for a short learning time). Here is a sample of a test that meets most of these criteria: The learners know that each week they will be tested on twenty words. They can choose ten of these themselves, words they have worked on in the preceding week. They write these words one under the other on a sheet of paper with their name at the top. Learners hand their pieces of paper to the teacher a day before the test. The teacher looks at each list of words and writes a letter next to each word – if the teacher writes *S* next to a word, the learner has to write a sentence using that word; if the teacher writes *C*, the learner has to write three collocates for the word; if the teacher writes *M*, the learner has to give the meaning of the word; and if the teacher writes *F*, the learner has to write down other members of the word family. Thus learners individually choose words to be tested on but they do not know how the teacher will test each word. The other ten words in the test are provided by the teacher and are the same for everyone in the class.

Other useful item types for short-term tests include translation, matching completion in sentence contexts and true/false items.

Short-term achievement tests are often used to encourage learning, and the washback effect of such tests can be very strong. Nation and Moir (2008) found that many learners studied for the weekly vocabulary test in ways that they knew were not useful for them in the long term, so these tests need to be used with care.

How can we test whether the total vocabulary of the course has been learned?

A short-term achievement test can try to test most of the words that have been studied in the preceding week. A long-term achievement test has to be based on a sample of the words that have been studied. Such a test is usually given at the end of a course, but in long courses there may be a mid-course test.

When choosing the words for a long-term achievement test, the teacher needs to consider what the results of the test will be used for. Most commonly they are used to evaluate the students' learning and to help give them a grade for their work on the course. The results may also be used to evaluate the course to see how well it has done what it set out to do.

The words selected for a long-term vocabulary achievement test should come from the words covered in the course and should represent these in a reasonable way. For example, a certain number of words could be chosen from each week of lessons or each unit of work. The way the words are tested should reflect the goals of the course and the way they were taught. If the course aimed largely at expanding reading vocabulary, then written receptive test items using sentence contexts may be most appropriate and fair.

Achievement tests may also involve seeing how learners can use the vocabulary they have learned. This may involve vocabulary testing combined with reading and listening tests, for example, where vocabulary in the reading and listening texts is tested along with comprehension of those texts.

How can we measure native speakers' and non-native speakers' total vocabulary size?

The vocabulary size of native speakers of English is of interest to language teachers because it provides one kind of goal for learners of English as a second or foreign language. It is a particularly compelling goal when second language learners are in the same English-speaking educational system as native speakers.

There has been a recent revival of interest in the vocabulary size of native speakers of English largely as a result of interest in how children's vocabularies grow and the role of direct teaching and incidental learning in this growth.

There are two major methods of measuring vocabulary size. One is based on sampling from a dictionary and the other is based on a corpus or a frequency list derived from a corpus. The dictionary-based method involves choosing a dictionary that is large enough to contain all the words that learners might know. A representative sample of words is taken from the dictionary and the learners are tested on those words. The proportion of words known in the sample is then converted to the proportion likely to be known in the whole dictionary.

So, if the sample consisted of one out of every 100 words in the dictionary, the learners' scores on the test based on the sample would be multiplied by 100 to get the total vocabulary size. Historically this method has been the most popular way of measuring the vocabulary size of native speakers, but is full of many serious methodological traps. Goulden et al. (1990) and D'Anna et al. (1991) are examples of this method.

The corpus-based method can be applied in two ways. One way is to collect a corpus of language used by a person or group of people and see how many words it consists of. This will not give a measure of total vocabulary size because any corpus is likely to represent only part of a language user's vocabulary. Estimates of Shakespeare's vocabulary (based on his plays and poems) and Schonell et al.'s (1956) study are of this type. Nagy and Anderson's (1984) study was similarly based on a frequency list derived from a corpus of texts used in schools in the United States (Carroll et al., 1971). Hart and Risley (1995) used a corpus-based method, but their study was fatally flawed because they tried to measure vocabulary growth using unequally sized samples and did not have independent measures of the amount of input and vocabulary growth (see Nation and Webb, 2011: 197–200, for a detailed critique).

None of these corpus-based studies involved testing. It is, however, possible to sample from frequency counts based on a corpus to make a test. Typically the sampling involves arranging the vocabulary into frequency-based groups – the most frequent 1,000 words, the second 1,000 most frequent words, and so on – and sampling from each frequency group. Meara and Jones' (1990) *Eurocentres Vocabulary Size Test 10KA* is of this type. Typically 1,000-word levels are used. There is no special reason for this beyond seeming neat and tidy. Ideally the levels should correspond to the purpose for making and using the lists. An important purpose may be to set learning goals, and as native speakers seem to learn around 1,000 word families a year, lists of 1,000 words may be an appropriate division. If learning goals were more modest then 500-word lists would be more sensible.

The *Vocabulary Size Test* (Nation and Beglar, 2007) is also based on sampling from word lists. The vocabulary lists are word family lists developed from the British National Corpus and now include data from the Corpus of Contemporary American English (COCA). The *Vocabulary Size Test* now exists in several versions and measures vocabulary knowledge up to the fourteenth 1,000-word level and the twentieth 1,000-word level. The 14,000 test contains 140 multiple-choice items, 10 at each 1,000-word-family level. The parallel versions of the 20,000 *Vocabulary Size Test* have five items at each

1,000-word-family level up to the twentieth 1,000. A detailed description of the test is available from Paul Nation's website. The *Vocabulary Size Test* is a measure of written receptive vocabulary size. In order to answer the items, the test takers have to have a moderately developed idea of the meaning of the word. This is likely to make it a slightly more difficult test than the Vocabulary Levels Test (Schmitt et al., 2001), because the correct answer and the distractors usually share elements of meaning.

The choices were all written using a restricted vocabulary. For the first and second 1,000 sample, only words from the first 1,000 of West's (1953) *General Service List* were used. As far as possible, the words in the definitions were of higher frequency than the item being defined, but for the highest frequency items, this was not always possible, for example, there was no possibility for defining *time* except with words of lower frequency (e.g. *hours*). For words in samples from the 3,000 level upwards, the defining words were drawn from the first 2,000 of West's *General Service List*.

Bilingual versions are available in Chinese, Japanese, Russian and Vietnamese. Bilingual tests are more suitable measures for low proficiency learners (Elgort, 2013). Here is a sample item from the monolingual version and the corresponding item from the Chinese bilingual version.

1. soldier: He is a **soldier.**   1. soldier: He is a **soldier.**

    a. person in a business   a. 商人

    b. student   b. 学生

    c. person who uses metal   c. 金属工艺制造者

    d. person in the army   d. 士兵

A good vocabulary test has the following features, and Beglar's (2010) examination of the *Vocabulary Size Test* showed that it fulfils these criteria:

1. It can be used with learners with a very wide range of proficiency levels.
2. It measures what it is supposed to measure and does not measure other things. Beglar found that the test was very clearly measuring a single factor (presumably written receptive vocabulary knowledge) and other factors played a very minor role in performance on the test.
3. It behaves as we would expect it to behave, distinguishing between learners of different proficiency levels, having a range of item difficulties related to the frequency level of the tested words, and

clearly distinguishing several different levels of vocabulary knowledge so that learners' vocabulary growth over time could be measured.

4. It performs consistently even though circumstances change. In Beglar's trialling of the test, these changes included comparing the performance of male subjects with female subjects, comparing 70-item versions of the test with the 140-item version, and comparing learners of various proficiency levels. Rasch reliability measures were around .96.

5. It is easy to score and interpret the scores.

6. The items in the test are clear and unambiguous.

7. It can be administered in efficient ways with learners sitting only five words per 1,000 word level.

The test seems to work well because it covers a very wide range of frequency levels, it includes a large number of items (even half of this number would work well), the items have been very carefully designed and made, and the test is designed to measure just one kind of vocabulary knowledge. A reduced form of the test should contain five items from each 1,000 level rather than cutting the later frequency levels from the test, because even learners with relatively low vocabulary sizes still know some low-frequency words (Nguyen and Nation, 2011), often because they are loan words or cognates or because of specialist interests. Many young native speakers know the very low-frequency names of dinosaurs, for example!

Users of the test need to be clear about what the test is measuring and not measuring. It is measuring written receptive vocabulary knowledge, that is, the vocabulary knowledge required for reading. It is not measuring listening vocabulary size, or the vocabulary knowledge needed for speaking and writing. It is also not a measure of reading skill, because although vocabulary size is a critical factor in reading, it is only a part of the reading skill.

Because there are ten items at each 1,000-word level, each item in the test represents 100 word families. If a test taker got every item correct, then it is assumed that this person knows the most frequent 14,000 word families of English. A test taker's score needs to be multiplied by 100 to get their total vocabulary size up to the fourteenth 1,000-word-family level. If a reduced version of the test was used, then if only five items per level were included, the score would need to be multiplied by 200 to get total vocabulary size.

Because the test is a measure of *receptive* vocabulary size, a test taker's score provides little indication of how well these words could be used in speaking and writing.

Initial studies using the test indicate that undergraduate non-native speakers successfully coping with study at an English speaking university have a vocabulary of around 5,000–6,000 word families. Non-native speaking PhD students have around a 9,000-word vocabulary. Unpublished studies of native speakers using the test version going up to the twentieth 1,000 level show that 13-year-olds have a vocabulary size of around 10,000 words, with considerable variation between different learners at the same age.

Biemiller and Slonim (2001) found a growth in root word vocabulary of just under 1,000 word families per year for the native speakers from infancy to Grade 5 (one-year-old to 11 years old). Actual average vocabulary sizes were around 3,000 word families at Grade 1; 5,000–6,000 at Grades 2 and 3; 7,000–8,000 at Grades 4 and 5; and 8,000–9,000 at Grade 6 where learners are around 12 years old.

These figures fit very well with our own current research where 13-year-olds have a vocabulary size of around 10,000 word families.

The tests that Biemiller and Slonim use require learners to provide a meaning for a word presented in a non-defining sentence: 'John got his *math* work done quickly.' What does *math* mean? For younger learners the tests are administered one-to-one (Biemiller, 2005: 227). If a learner's response to an item shows some kind of knowledge of the word, it is scored as correct. Biemiller suspects that multiple-choice tests may overestimate children's *effective* vocabulary because they can be answered with partial knowledge, although his own tests also accept partial knowledge as a satisfactory response. It means that when interpreting the results of interview and multiple-choice tests, we need to be cautious in interpreting the scores.

Biemiller's main findings are as follows:

1. Words are required in a roughly predictable sequence. The frequency of words in a written corpus is not a good predictor of the likelihood of a word being known. Oral frequency may be a better predictor. Biemiller's (2010) book, *Words Worth Teaching*, provides data for the order in which words are likely to be learned, and thus can be the basis for a vocabulary-teaching programme. Studies of the Vocabulary Size Test have shown a rough pattern of decrease in scores from the higher to the lower frequency levels (Beglar, 2010; Elgort, 2013; Nguyen and Nation, 2011).
2. Children of the same age or grade level vary greatly in their vocabulary size.
3. Direct teaching plays an important role in root word vocabulary growth and some learners do not learn a lot from reading.

4. Direct teaching of vocabulary, in oral contexts for young learners, can make a significant contribution to vocabulary growth and can help bridge gaps in proficiency. Given that the average daily rate of vocabulary growth is less than three words per day, teaching can feasibly have a noticeable effect (Biemiller and Slonim, 2001: 506).

Early dictionary-based studies of vocabulary size (Seashore and Eckerson, 1940, and related studies by Smith, 1941; Templin, 1957; and Diller, 1978) suffered from serious methodological flaws (Lorge and Chall, 1963). Thorndike (1924) had been aware of these problems and had suggested solutions, but his paper was published in a collection that was not readily accessible and thus remained unknown to generations of researchers in this area who committed the errors that he warned against. Lorge and Chall, and Nation (1993b) review the situation. The flaws related to the basic questions in measuring vocabulary size:

1. What is counted as a word?
2. How do we choose what words to test?
3. How do we measure if learners know a word?

There is now a good understanding of most of the issues involved in the estimation of vocabulary size, although Miller and Wakefield (1993: 167) note that trying to answer the question 'How many words does a person know?' is much more difficult than asking the question.

Although there is an awareness of the issues related to the three questions, there is by no means a consensus on how they are best answered. However, recent studies of vocabulary size, both dictionary-based and frequency-based, usually deal explicitly with the issues and generally make it clear how they have answered the questions. Let us now look at each of the three questions to get a feeling for what is involved.

What is counted as a word?

This fundamental question relates to an even more fundamental question: 'What is involved in knowing a word?', which we looked at in Chapter 2. Does knowing a word include knowing its closely related derived and inflected forms? Does knowing *agree* involve knowing *agrees*, *agreeing* and *agreed*? Does *agree* also include *agreement*, *disagree* and *agreeable*? Should the unit of counting be the word type (that is, *agree* and *agrees* are counted as different words)? Is it the lemma (*agree* and *agrees* are counted as one word but *agreement* is a different word)? Is it the word family (*agrees*, *agreeing*, *agreed*, *agreement*, *disagree* are counted as the same word)? For good reasons, most counts aimed at learners of English count some form of word family. What is included in a word family needs to be clearly and explicitly described. Some counts unwisely rely on dictionary makers' division of words into dictionary entries. More consistent, well-justified criteria are needed. Bauer and Nation's (1993) study of word families was an attempt to bring some level of standardisation to this issue.

Another important issue in what is counted as a word is what is considered to be a word and what is not. For example, are proper nouns like *Jane* and *Jim* included in the count or excluded? Are alternate spellings (*labor* versus *labour*) counted? Are foreign words (*perestroika*) counted? Once again decisions need to be made and criteria described and justified as they have a direct effect on the results of any counting.

How do we choose the words to test?

Choosing words to test is a sampling problem and has been the major source of weakness in studies of vocabulary size based on dictionaries (Lorge and Chall, 1963; Nation, 1993b; Thorndike, 1924). In essence, the source of the problem is this: in a dictionary, high-frequency words have more entries per word and each entry takes more space than the entries for low-frequency words. If a spaced sampling method is used to choose words (the first word on every tenth page, for example), then there will be more high-frequency words in the sample than there should be. If the sample contains too many high-frequency words, then learners' vocabulary size will be overestimated because high-frequency words are more likely to be known than low-frequency words. This sampling problem has occurred in many studies (Diller, 1978; Seashore and Eckerson, 1940) and has resulted in very inflated figures. Nation (1993b) describes procedures to avoid the problem – it is avoided when frequency lists are used in the corpus-based approach.

How do we measure if learners know a word?

Tests of vocabulary can differ greatly in the amount of knowledge of each word that they require. Some test formats, like translation tests, require strong knowledge of the words, while others, like multiple-choice tests with distractors which are not closely related in meaning, give credit for partial knowledge. The difficulty of the test format can have a strong influence on the number of words that learners get correct and thus influence the measurement of their vocabulary size. The test format used needs to be clearly described and justified according to the construct of vocabulary knowledge that the researcher is interested in.

Dictionary-based studies of the vocabulary size of native speakers

Recent estimates of young adult university graduates (D'Anna et al., 1991; Goulden et al., 1990) indicate that native speakers have a smaller vocabulary size than earlier estimates have shown (Seashore and Eckerson, 1940; Diller, 1978). Seashore and Eckerson's study, for example, estimated that, on average, college students knew over 58,000 basic words and over 155,000 basic and derived words. The Goulden et al. and D'Anna et al. studies, however, suggest basic word vocabularies of less than 20,000 words.

In a very carefully designed study that took account of the methodological issues involved in measuring vocabulary size, Anglin (1993) investigated the vocabulary size of 6-, 8- and 10-year-old native speakers of English. Anglin distinguished word types in *Webster's Third New International Dictionary* according to their morphological characteristics and looked at the following categories: root words (like *happy, define*); inflected words (like *running, sourer*); derived words (like *happiness, redefine*); literal compounds whose meaning can be interpreted from their parts (like *birthday, live-born*); and idioms whose meaning cannot be correctly constructed from their parts (like *dead heat* and *red herring*). The derived words were distinguished from root words using the criterion of whether the words were **psychologically basic** or not, psychologically basic words being those for which there are separate entries in long-term memory (Anglin, 1993: 25) and which could not be decoded through morphological problem solving. In most but not all cases, the root of a derived word seems to have been a free form. The distinction between psychologically basic words and words which were potentially knowable through morphological problem solving was very important in Anglin's study because he wanted to distinguish vocabulary growth through learning new words from vocabulary growth through mastering the morphological systems of English.

Anglin's (1993) research, which we looked at in Chapter 9, suggests that multiple-choice may be more sensitive than an interview in eliciting knowledge of the meaning of a word. Anglin classified the interviews in his experiment according to whether learners overtly used morphological analysis procedures to successfully arrive at the meanings of words. This estimation is equivocal as Anglin points out because learners may not have displayed morphological analysis procedures even though they were using them, or may have displayed such procedures as a kind of informed hindsight even though they originally learned the particular derivational word as an unanalysed item. Nonetheless, Anglin's approach is important, because studies like Goulden et al. (1990) tacitly assume that words classified as derived (i.e., involving derivational affixes) will be learned as members of a word family centred around a root word. For many derived words this may not be so – they may be learned as unanalysed 'psychologically basic words'. Sinclair's (1991) idiom principle suggests that different forms behave in different ways, certainly in terms of collocation and, as a result, possibly also in terms of their meaning. We can look at words with derivational affixes as members of a word family closely related to the root word, and we can look at words with derivational affixes as independent words which differ in many respects from other words that have a formal morphological link with them. It is not difficult to find examples in Anglin's items to support both viewpoints. *Treelet* (a small tree) shares many of the features of its root *tree*, including part of speech, overlapping meaning (*tree* is the superordinate of the hyponym *treelet*) and possibly similar collocates. *Soaking* (very wet) as an adjective, as in 'I'm absolutely soaking', differs in important ways from its root word *soak*. It is a different part of speech, it has different collocates, it requires some grammatical gymnastics to relate its meaning to *soak* (something is soaking wet because it has been soaked with water), and it is likely to be represented by words not related to the translation of *soak* in the learner's first language. However, the relationship between *soak* and *soaking* is not a chance relationship. They are related items, and this relationship can affect learning and storage.

Given these cautions, Anglin attempted to calculate how many psychologically basic words native speaking 6-, 8- and 10-year-old children know. This will be a higher figure than the number of root words and idioms they know because it includes derived words and literal compounds which did not show evidence of morphological problem solving in his research.

In Table 13.2, 'words showing no evidence of morphological problem solving' include root words and some derived words. 'Total words of all types' includes all root words, inflected words, literal compounds and idioms. For psychologically basic words these represent learning rates for native speakers between one and a half and six years old of 3.26 words per day, between six and eight years old of 6.63 words per day, and between eight and ten years old of 12.13 words per day.

Table 13.2 *Estimated vocabulary size of children at three grade levels for root words and psychologically basic words (from Anglin, 1993)*

Types of words	6-year-olds	8-year-olds	10-year-olds
Root words	3,092	4,582	7,532
Words showing no evidence of morphological problem solving	6,173	11,094	19,830
Total words of all types	10,398	19,412	39,994

Anglin's measures agree with those by Biemiller and colleagues and with our own research on young native speakers' vocabulary size. The rough rule of thumb is an increase of about 1,000 word families a year with total vocabulary size for most children and teenagers being a couple of years behind their chronological age in terms of thousands of word families.

Corpus-based studies of native speakers

Corpus-based studies draw on language in use. If the corpus is large enough, the resulting word list will probably provide a good representation of the high-frequency words of the language, but it is likely to not include many of the low-frequency words. This is not a major issue if the aim is not to measure total vocabulary size, but to measure knowledge of high- and mid-frequency vocabulary. It is also not a major issue if the test is to be used with non-native speakers of limited proficiency. Let us look first at studies that did not attempt to measure native speakers' vocabulary size but looked at how much vocabulary might be needed or met in spoken and written language use.

Schonell et al. (1956) carried out a frequency count of the oral vocabulary of the Australian worker. The data was collected from unrehearsed conversations by surreptitious recording of speech in public places, recording conversations at work and through interviews, and totalled 512,647 running words. The count excluded profanity, blasphemy and proper nouns (p. 44) which given the contexts in which it was recorded, may have resulted in a lot of exclusions. No indication is given of how many items were of those types. Table 13.3 overleaf details the number of items in the count.

The most frequent 1,007 word families (head words) included 5,916 types, and covered 94% of the tokens. 755 of the most frequent 1,007 word families appeared in the most frequent 1,000 words of the

Table 13.3 *Words and number of occurrences in the Schonell et al. count*

Items	Number of occurrences	Comments
Tokens	512,647	*to* + infinitive was counted as one item
Types	12,611	Homonyms were distinguished
Lemmas	6,616	Includes comparative and superlative; homonyms were distinguished
Word families	4,539	Includes inflections, derivatives and compound words

General Service List (West, 1953). About a third of the remaining 245 words appeared in West's second 1,000. This lack of a complete overlap is not surprising. The *GSL* is based on a count of written English while Schonell et al. counted spoken English. The Schonell et al. count has a deliberately restricted focus on the informal, collo-quial language of unskilled and semi-skilled workers, and as such it has its own special vocabulary relating to speech (*hurray, Mum*), work (*boss*) and Australia (*bloke, creek, pub*).

There are now several frequency counts of a wide variety of kinds of written English. The one million running word corpora modelled on the *Brown* corpus (Kučera and Francis, 1967) each typically contain around 40,000–50,000 word types. The *American Heritage Word Frequency Book* of Carroll et al. (1971) is a count of a 5,088,721 running word corpus of a wide variety of texts used in a range of subject areas from Grades 3 to 9 inclusive in schools in the United States. It contains a maximum of 86,741 word types but this included capitalised words as different types. Nagy and Anderson (1984), using a detailed study of a sample from this list, set out to calculate the number of words in printed school English. They did this in a two-step procedure. First, they took a representative 7,260-word type sample from Carroll et al.'s corpus and carefully classified the word types in the sample into word families. Second, they used the results of this analysis to predict from a lognormal model used by Carroll et al. (1971: xxi–xl) the number of word families in the *whole* population of printed school English, not just that included in the *American Heritage* count. Nagy and Anderson did not claim that this is the number of words that native speakers at school will know, but it is the number of words that they could meet. They carefully distinguished derived forms of words that were very closely related in meaning to the base word from derived forms that were best treated as different words because they were not clearly related in meaning to the base word. Nagy and Anderson calculated that printed school English contains 88,533 distinct word families. These word families contain members that are all closely related in meaning. In addition, there are around 90,000 proper names. In Chapter 9 (Table 9.2), the typical membership of a word family from Nagy and Anderson's study is shown. The size of word families (on average almost five closely related members) stresses the importance of word-building knowledge in dealing with words. Nagy and Anderson (1984: 317–19) note that their estimate of the number of words in printed school English fits reasonably well with calculations of entries in *Webster's Third New International Dictionary* (Gove, 1963). They also estimated that about half the words in printed school English would occur roughly once in a billion words of text. Many of these words are useful however. Their low frequency may reflect their technical nature and therefore limited range.

These corpus-based studies show the importance of high-frequency and mid-frequency vocabulary in text coverage. They also confirm that vocabulary size estimates for native speakers of English which are in the high tens of thousands and hundreds of thousands of words are faulty and impossible estimates. They also confirm that there is a very large number of low-frequency words that any one native speaker is unlikely to know.

The receptive and productive vocabulary size of non-native speakers

Laufer (1998) compared the amount of passive and active vocabulary in 16-year-old Grade 11 learners and 17-year-old Grade 12 learners using three quite different types of tests: passive vocabulary was measured by using the levels test (Nation, 1983, 1990); active vocabulary was measured by using the *Productive Levels Test* (Laufer and Nation, 1999) and the *Lexical Frequency Profile* (Laufer and Nation, 1995). Because Laufer used very different test formats, she was comparing more than active and passive knowledge and thus was careful in her report to mark this by using the terms *passive, controlled active* and *free active*. Her study showed passive vocabulary being larger than controlled active vocabulary and the size difference between them increasing with learners who were one year older. There were significant correlations of .67 for the 16-year-olds and .78 for the 17-year-olds between passive and controlled active vocabulary size.

In a later study, Laufer and Paribakht (1998) used the same three measures to look at ESL and EFL learners. Once again they found significant and substantial correlations between receptive and productive vocabulary size (.72 for ESL, and .89 for EFL).

Waring (1997b) used the same levels tests (passive and controlled active) as Laufer, with the addition of a 1,000-word level. Waring found that learners always scored higher on the receptive test than the controlled productive test with the difference in receptive and productive scores increasing at the lower frequency levels of the tests, that is, as learners' vocabulary increases, their receptive vocabulary is increasingly larger than their productive vocabulary. Learners with larger vocabulary sizes and learners with low vocabulary sizes did not differ greatly from each other in the relative proportion of receptive and productive vocabulary.

The following conclusions can be drawn from these three studies:

- Learners' receptive vocabulary size is greater than their productive vocabulary size.
- The ratio of receptive vocabulary to productive is not constant.
- As learners' vocabulary increases the proportion of receptive vocabulary becomes greater, that is, the gap between receptive and productive vocabulary becomes greater at the lower frequency levels.
- A large proportion of the high-frequency vocabulary is known both receptively and productively.
- Increases in vocabulary size as measured by direct measures of vocabulary (decontextualised vocabulary tests) are not necessarily reflected in an increase in vocabulary in use (proportion of low-frequency words used in writing a composition).

These findings indicate that although the various kinds of vocabulary knowledge are clearly related to each other, they develop in different ways. This probably reinforces the idea that a well-balanced language course has to provide for learning across the four strands of meaning-focused input (listening and reading), language-focused learning (the direct study and teaching of vocabulary), meaning-focused output (speaking and writing) and fluency development – so that there is a wide range of varied opportunities for vocabulary development.

Laufer's (1998) study suggests that vocabulary growth may proceed in different ways for ESL and EFL learners. Laufer found that intermediate and advanced EFL learners' active (productive) vocabulary size was closer to their passive (receptive) vocabulary size than was the case with ESL learners. It seemed that the language-focused instruction (direct teaching and direct learning) typical of many EFL courses may account for these learners' close passive/active scores. ESL learners, however, had large passive vocabularies which could be accounted for by the large amount of input they get. This passive knowledge does not seem to transfer readily to active use. Milton (2009) provides a range of data on the vocabulary size of non-native speakers.

Umbel et al. (1992) examined Spanish–English bilinguals' receptive vocabulary knowledge in both languages. They found that learners who spoke both English and Spanish at home scored more highly than those who spoke only Spanish. It seems that learning two languages at once does not harm receptive language development in the first language, and it helps gain higher performance in the majority language (p. 1012). Umbel et al. also found that while there was a large overlap of knowledge of translation equivalents in both languages, there was still a significant difference in items known only in one language. To truly estimate a learner's vocabulary size these non-overlapping words would have to be added together.

What kind of vocabulary test item is the best?

There are many different kinds of vocabulary test items. The following set of examples covers many that are typically used in vocabulary tests. A sensitive test is one that gives credit for partial knowledge, or allows partial knowledge to be used when answering (Nagy et al., 1985); for example, a multiple-choice test (meaning recognition) is typically more sensitive than a translation test (meaning recall).

A 1,000-word level true/false test (Nation, 1993a)

Write T if a sentence is true. Write N if it is not true. Write X if you do not understand the sentence.

1. We cut time into minutes, hours and days.   ___
2. Some children call their mother Mama.   ___
3. All the world is under water.   ___
4. When you keep asking, you ask once.   ___

A vocabulary depth test (Read, 1995)

Choose four words that go with the test word. Choose at least one from each of the two boxes.

Sudden

beautiful	quick	change	doctor
surprising	thirsty	noise	school

A definition completion test (Read, 1995)

Choose one word from the list on the right to complete the sentence. Do not use the same word twice.

faint
1. A journey straight to a place is _____   acute
2. An illness that is very serious is _____   common
3. A river that is very wide is _____   bare
4. Part of your body that is not covered by any clothes is ____   alien
5. Something that happens often is ____   broad
direct

A sensitive multiple-choice test (Joe, 1998)

Circle the choice that gives the meaning of the underlined word.
   <u>chronic</u> means   a. lasting for a long time
                          b. dissatisfied
                          c. to greatly decrease
                          d. effective and harmless
                          e. don't know

A translation test (Nurweni and Read, 1999)

Translate the underlined words into your first language.

1. You can see how the town has <u>developed</u>.   _____
2. I cannot say much about his <u>character</u>.   _____
3. Her <u>idea</u> is a very good one.   _____
4. I want to hear only the <u>facts</u>.   _____

With so many possibilities available, it can be difficult to decide which type to use in a particular test. In general, a good vocabulary test has plenty of items – around 30 is probably a minimum for a reliable test (Beglar and Hunt, 1999); it uses a test item type which requires learners to use the kind of vocabulary knowledge that you want to test; it is easy enough to make, mark, and interpret; and it has a good effect on the learning and teaching that leads up to the test and that follows it.

Vocabulary test item types can differ in many ways: some have choices; some use the first language; some put the word in a sentence context; some require the learner to use the word; some focus on its meaning while others focus on the form of the word, its grammar and collocations, or associations. Table 13.4 overleaf is an adapted version of Table 2.1 which lists what is involved in knowing a word.

Table 13.4 is useful for deciding what aspects of vocabulary knowledge are to be tested, and should help with the first and most important question to ask when testing: 'Why do I want to test?', as well as the next question: 'What do I want to test?' After that, the next questions are: 'How difficult do I want the test to be?' and 'Do I want the test to give credit for partial knowledge or do I want to test if the vocabulary is really well known?' There are several ways of making a test more sensitive to partial knowledge, and we will look at these later in this chapter. A teacher may want vocabulary test items to be easy so that learners are encouraged, so that she can see if learners are progressing in the gradual cumulative learning of particular words, and so that she can see if there are even small amounts of knowledge that can be built on.

The next decision is what item type to use. When the testing goal and the degree of difficulty have been decided, then the choice of item types has been narrowed. The choice of a particular type of item should depend upon the following criteria:

1. Is the knowledge required to answer the item correctly similar to the knowledge that you want to test? If the test is an achievement test, then it should reflect the knowledge taught in the course. Thus, word-building items would not be suitable if the course has not focused on word building at all. Similarly, asking learners to make sentences using words is not suitable if the aim of the course is to develop a reading vocabulary.
2. Is it easy to make enough items to test all the vocabulary you want to test? If the teacher is spending hours on a test that the learners will complete in a short time, something is wrong. For this reason traditional multiple-choice items are often unsuitable.
3. Will the items be easy to mark? If the teacher plans the layout of the test carefully with marking in mind, a great deal of time can be saved. For example, if a matching lexical cloze test is used, typing it double-spaced will allow teachers to make a marking key with holes cut in it to fit over the answer sheets. Similarly, if the place for the learners to write their answers is clearly indicated, marking becomes easier.
4. Will answering the item provide a useful repetition of the vocabulary and perhaps even extend learners' knowledge? It is not usually a good idea for a test item to be an exact repetition of what occurred

Table 13.4 *Aspects of word knowledge for testing*

Form	spoken	R	Can the learner recognise the spoken form of the word?
		P	Can the learner pronounce the word correctly?
	written	R	Can the learner recognise the written form of the word?
		P	Can the learner spell and write the word?
	word parts	R	Can the learner recognise known parts in the word?
		P	Can the learner produce appropriate inflected and derived forms of the word?
Meaning	form and meaning	R	Can the learner recall the appropriate meaning for this word form?
		P	Can the learner produce the appropriate word form to express this meaning?
	concept and referents	R	Can the learner understand a range of uses of the word and its central concept?
		P	Can the learner use the word to refer to a range of items?
	associations	R	Can the learner produce common associations for this word?
		P	Can the learner recall this word when presented with related ideas?
Use	grammatical functions	R	Can the learner recognise correct uses of the word in context?
		P	Can the learner use this word in the correct grammatical patterns?
	collocations	R	Can the learner recognise appropriate collocations?
		P	Can the learner produce the word with appropriate collocations?
	constraints on use (register, frequency …)	R	Can the learner tell if the word is a common, formal, or infrequent word etc.?
		P	Can the learner use the word at appropriate times?

Note: In Column 3, R = receptive knowledge, P = productive knowledge in the course. Using language is a creative activity which involves understanding and using words in new contexts. Unless learners can do this we cannot be sure if useful learning has occurred. When testing knowledge of prefixes, for example, it is a good idea to test the prefixes in unknown words which are made of known parts. Then learners cannot rely solely on memory but have to use their analytic skills. When getting learners to do a matching lexical cloze, the passage should be one the learners have not seen before, even though it is made up of known vocabulary and constructions.

In order to decide between different item types, let us look at research evidence about some of the important features of vocabulary test items.

Is it enough to ask learners if they know the word?

Yes/No or checklist tests have been gaining in popularity since Anderson and Freebody looked at them closely in 1983. Before then, such tests were lists of words that learners responded to by saying whether they knew each word or not (Bear and Odbert, 1941; Campion and Elley, 1971; Diack, 1975). Anderson and Freebody included some nonsense words in the test so that the accuracy of learners' responses could be measured – if a learner says that they know a non-word then they are overstating their vocabulary knowledge. Here is an example of part of such a test from Meara (1989).

Tick the words you know

adviser	_____	*moisten*	_____
ghastly	_____	*patiful*	_____
contord	_____	*profess*	_____
implore	_____	*stourge*	_____
morlorn	_____	*discard*	_____

The learner's score is calculated by subtracting the proportion of non-words said to be known from the number of real words said to be known. Meara and colleagues (Meara, 1990, 1991; Meara and Buxton, 1987; Meara and Jones, 1990) have used this test format extensively with second language learners, finding that the test can be a reliable and practical measure of second language vocabulary knowledge. There are, however, problems with working out how to score the test.

Meara et al. (1992) examined the effect of large numbers of cognates in Yes/No tests. As in previous studies they found correlations of around .65 to .75 between the Yes/No tests and language proficiency tests. Large numbers of cognates (50%) had the effect of making the learners' scores higher than, and significantly different from, scores on a non-cognate version. The report on the experiment does not tell us if 50% of the non-words in the test were also items that looked like cognates. This would be essential if the test was to work properly as the non-words must appear to be like the real words in the test so that the only way of distinguishing real words from non-words is through familiarity with the real words. In a study of vocabulary distractor types, Goodrich (1977) suggests that the use of non-words that are based on real words in multiple-choice tests is not unnecessarily distracting, so the same may be true for Yes/No tests. Certainly, the non-words should appear to be like real unknown words.

Yes/No tests of vocabulary size have been developed as placement tests, that is, to decide what course level a learner should be placed in. The *Eurocentres Vocabulary Size Test* developed by Paul Meara and his colleagues (Meara and Buxton, 1987; Meara and Jones, 1987) is a computerised Yes/No test. Strictly speaking it does not measure total vocabulary size but measures knowledge of the 10,000 most frequent lemmas of English. For most learners of English as a second or foreign language in the intermediate stages of their learning, there is probably little difference between what the test measures and total vocabulary size. The test is extremely efficient, taking just a few minutes to sit, and is scored by computer. In the test, a word appears on the screen and the learner has to respond whether it is a word they know or not. Some of the words are nonsense words and the learner's performance on the nonsense words is used to adjust the score on the real words. Computerised Yes/No tests take very little time to sit, give instant results, and are easy to interpret. Eyckmans (2004) has done substantial research on the test as well as proposing other formats to make up for perceived weaknesses in the classic format.

The biggest reservation most teachers and researchers have with the Yes/No test is that learners do not overtly demonstrate knowledge of the meaning of the tested words (see Nation and Webb, 2011: 295–6, for further discussion).

Should choices be given?

Multiple-choice items are popular because they are easy to mark, and, if the choices are not closely related to each other, they can allow learners to draw on partial knowledge. They also have a degree of respectability because they have been used in standardised tests like TOEFL. Comparison with other item types like translation, asking learners to use the word in a sentence, blank-filling with choices and interview show that it is generally the easiest of the item types for first language learners to answer (Nist and Olejnik, 1995; Paul et al.,

1990). Nist and Olejnik (1995) measured learning from context and dictionary definitions using four different tests for each word: (1) a multiple-choice test of meanings; (2) a multiple-choice test of examples; (3) asking learners to write a sentence to illustrate the word; and (4) sentence completion.

An example of *aberration* would be:

a. having a glass of cold milk with freshly baked cookies
b. going to bed every night at exactly the same time
c. a 16-year-old who didn't want her own brand new car
d. an infant who woke up every four hours to eat.

It would be a _____ for Mike to get an A in his second chemistry course, when he failed the first one.

The multiple-choice tests were the easiest with the average item difficulties for the four tests with college freshmen being (1) .86; (2) .83; (3) .53; and (4) .63 (the lower the score, the greater the difficulty).

Laufer et al. (2004) developed a set of four computerised tests measuring meaning recognition (a multiple-choice test with four choices of the word's meaning); form recognition (a multiple-choice test with four choices of words to match the meaning stem); meaning recall (a translation test from L2 to L1); and form recall (a translation test from L1 to L2). The same words were tested four times, once in each test format. This set of tests, the *Computer Adaptive Test of Size and Strength* (CATSS), not only measured how many words were known, but also how well each word was known, focusing on knowledge of the form–meaning link. The 150 test words were those used in the *Vocabulary Levels Test* (Schmitt et al., 2001), and trialling of the test found that:

- low-frequency words were generally less well known than high-frequency words;
- the order of difficulty (from easiest to most difficult) was meaning recognition, form recognition, meaning recall, form recall – although form and meaning recognition were very similar in terms of difficulty. Laufer and Goldstein (2004), however, found a clear difference between form and meaning recognition, although the difference was still small. Test format (recall/recognition) has a stronger effect on results than the type of knowledge measured (productive/receptive); and
- while there was a relationship between size and strength, this was far from perfect, and it is best to report scores on all subtests rather than combine them into a single score.

Laufer and Goldstein (2004) found very strong implicational scaling for individual words, that is, if a difficult item type is answered correctly for a word (for example active recall), the easier item types will also be answered correctly for that word. The gap between form recall and the next easiest, meaning recall, was very large with the meaning recall scores being anything from one-sixth to one-third of the form recall scores. The gap between meaning recall and form recognition was much smaller, and between form recognition and meaning recognition even smaller. Laufer and Goldstein suggest that a possible reason for a clear distinction between form recognition and meaning recognition may be because their test involved L1 choices, that is, it was a bilingual test compared to the monolingual test used by Laufer et al., (2004). Elgort (2013) found that a bilingual receptive recognition test was around 10% easier than a similar monolingual test. Li (2010) found that bilingual tests gave higher scores than monolingual tests, but the monolingual always preceded the bilingual so there was likely to have been a small order effect in this difference.

Laufer and Goldstein (2004) found correlations from 0.40 to 0.63 between language class grade and the various vocabulary formats, with meaning recall having the highest correlation. The correlations between the vocabulary formats ranged from 0.31 (form recall/meaning recognition) to 0.65.

Nagy et al. (1985) have shown how it is possible to design multiple-choice items of different degrees of difficulty by varying the closeness in meaning between the distractors and the correct answer. The use of multiple-choice can encourage guessing. Paul et al. (1990) interviewed first language learners about the strategies they used to answer particular multiple-choice items classifying them into the following categories:

- *Knowing the answer.* The answer was chosen because learners said they knew it was correct.
- *Association.* The answer was chosen because it could be related in some way to something they knew about the word.
- *Elimination.* The answer was chosen by ruling out the other choices.
- *Position of the options.* The answer was chosen because it was first, last or in the middle.
- *Readability of the options.* The answer was chosen because it was the only one they could read and understand.
- *Guessing.* Learners did not know why they chose an answer or they said they just guessed.

Paul et al. (1990) found that for both high-ability and low-ability readers, over 50% of the answers were chosen because of association. Knowing the answer accounted for 16% of the items for the high-ability group and 8% for the low-ability group. The high-ability group guessed only 8% of the answers (with about a 50% success rate) while the low-ability group guessed 21% of the answers (with a 35% success rate). This indicated that guessing is not a major problem with multiple-choice items and that learners' responses are generally not random but largely driven by some knowledge of the words.

Goodrich (1977) studied eight different distractor types in multiple-choice vocabulary items and found that false synonyms (a word with a similar meaning to one of the meanings of the correct word but which was not correct in the given context) were the most distracting. This reinforces Nagy et al.'s (1985) decision to make items more sensitive by having distractors with a minimal meaning relationship to the correct answer.

An advantage of multiple-choice items is that they can focus on particular meanings of words that have more than one meaning. There seems to be no major disadvantage in using multiple choices except perhaps in the amount of work required to make the items. When they are being made, it is important to be consistent about the closeness of the relationship between the distractors and the correct answers in form and meaning as this has a major effect on the difficulty of the item. Nation and Webb (2011: 285–94) have a detailed discussion of multiple-choice tests.

One way of reducing the amount of work involved in making multiple-choice items is to use a matching format like the Vocabulary Levels Test.

Choose the right word to go with each meaning. Write the number of that word next to its meaning.

1. bench
2. charity   _____ long seat
3. mate   _____ help to the poor
4. jar   _____ part of a country
5. mirror
6. province

This not only reduces the number of distractors that have to be made, but also allows many more items to be tested within the same time. A disadvantage, though not a severe one, of the matching item is that the items tested within the same block can affect each other. Campion and Elley (1971) found that changing the block a word was placed in often resulted in a big change in the number of correct answers for the word. This effect can be reduced by checking items carefully when they are made, pilot-testing the items to see if learners cluster around the same wrong answer, using small blocks (about six choices per block) and following well thought out criteria to guide what meaning and form relationships are not permitted between the correct choices and distractors in a block. The matching format of the *Vocabulary Levels Test*, with distractors drawn from the same rough frequency level, deliberately enables informed guessing. Stewart and White (2011) showed that on average this could lead to an increase of 16–17 points on a 99-item task until over 60% of the words are known, and after this the score increase due to guessing will decrease. The test thus inflates estimates of words known at each level and, combined with the sensitive nature of the test, this suggests that when interpreting the results of the *Vocabulary Levels Test*, we should set a high passing score for satisfactory performance at each level.

Xing and Fulcher (2007) looked at the 5,000-word level of Versions A and B of the *Vocabulary Levels Test* and found that Version B was more difficult because of a few particularly difficult items. Thus an adjusted version of the tests may need to be used if they are used longitudinally, although it would be safer to use the same test because of the difficulty in equating test forms. Paterson (2004) used the *Vocabulary Levels Test* matching item format to make a test of four levels (500; 1,000; 1,500; and 2,000) to test the first 2,000 words of English. The meanings were expressed in the L1 of the learners, Japanese. The trialling showed a ceiling effect, but the test generally performed well. Using first language translations for the meanings makes the test much more sensitive to partial knowledge.

Should translations be used?

Translation is one of a variety of means of conveying meaning that in general is no better or worse than the use of pictures, real objects, definitions, L2 synonyms and so on (see Chapter 3; Nation and Webb, 2011: 271–2). Translation or the use of the first language may be discouraged because of political reasons, because teachers do not know the learners' first language, or because first language use is seen as taking away opportunities for second language practice. However, the use of the first language to convey and test word meaning is very efficient.

The greatest value of the first language in vocabulary testing is that it allows learners to respond to vocabulary items in a way that does not draw on second language knowledge which is not directly relevant to what is being tested. For example, in vocabulary interviews learners may find it difficult to explain the meanings of words using the second language. Creating definitions in a second language is quite a sophisticated skill. When scoring an interview, it may thus be difficult to tell if a learner's shaky performance is because the word was not well known or because the word was known but was difficult to define in the second language.

Research with native speakers of English (Feifel and Lorge, 1950) found significant differences at different age levels for the types of definitions provided for known words. For second language learners, translation provides a much easier means of explaining the meanings of second language words. Elgort (2013) compared bilingual and monolingual versions of the *Vocabulary Size Test* where Russian was used in the bilingual version. There was a small but significant difference, with scores on the bilingual test just over 10% higher than scores on the monolingual test. Not surprisingly, learners gained higher scores on cognates particularly for lower-frequency words. In the bilingual versions of the test, cognates were translated with non-cognate synonyms or definitions. Elgort also found that learners who attempted every item (14% of the test takers) gained higher scores than those who did not. This deserves further research. The use of the first language meaning is like using a simple synonym, whereas the use of a second language definition often involves using a classical definition form involving a relative clause or a reduced relative clause, and reading these requires greater grammatical skill. Several bilingual versions of the *Vocabulary Size Test* are available from Paul Nation's website.

The use of first language translations provides a very useful means of testing vocabulary, both receptively and productively, and in recall and recognition items. The difficulties caused by non-exact correspondence between meanings in L1 and L2 are probably less than the difficulties caused by the lack of correspondence between an L2 definition and the meaning that the definition is trying to convey.

Should words be tested in context?

Words can be tested in isolation –

casualty   a. someone killed or injured
b. noisy and happy celebration
c. being away from other people
d. middle class people

– in sentence contexts –
Each room has its own priv_____ bath and WC.

– or in texts.

In a study designed to evaluate vocabulary test item formats for the *Test of English as a Foreign Language* (TOEFL), Henning (1991) compared eight different multiple-choice item types. Note that because of the enormous number of test papers that have to be marked, the issue of multiple-choice (recognition) or no choices provided (recall) was not even considered. The variables investigated included the following.

1. The amount of contextualisation. The various types of context included isolated words, minimal sentence context, long sentence context, and passage embedded items.

ISOLATED WORDS,   MINIMAL CONTEXT,
MATCHING   MATCHING
   deliberately   He spied on them *deliberately*.
   a. both   a. both
   b. noticeably   b. noticeably
   c. intentionally   c. intentionally
   d. absolutely   d. absolutely

PASSAGE EMBEDDED, MATCHING

In a <u>democratic</u>[1] society suspected persons are presumed innocent until proven guilty. The <u>establishment</u>[2] of guilt is often a difficult task. One consideration is whether or not there remains a <u>reasonable</u>[3] doubt that the suspected persons committed the acts in question. Another consideration is whether or not the acts were committed <u>deliberately</u>[4]. Still another concern is whether or not the acts were <u>premeditated</u>[5].

4. (A) both
  (B) noticeably
  (C) intentionally
  (D) absolutely

MINIMAL CONTEXT, MATCHING, INFERENCING
   He was guilty because he did those things *deliberately*.
   a. both
   b. noticeably
   c. intentionally
   d. absolutely

2. Supply versus matching item types.

MINIMAL CONTEXT, SUPPLY
   He planned the crimes _____.
   a. both
   b. noticeably
   c. intentionally
   d. absolutely

Matching item types were found to be easier than supply item types, were more reliable and had higher criterion-related validity. Supply item types may require the learner to draw on additional syntactic and collocational knowledge and this could affect learners' performance. Isolated word or phrase-matching item types were consistently inferior to matching item types that used complete sentence contexts. The item type with a minimal non-inferencing sentence context was the easiest of all the types examined. The value of context may be to orient the learner to the correct part of speech and by more closely resembling conditions of normal use may encourage normal access to the meaning. Therefore, to provide learners with the greatest chance of showing the vocabulary knowledge they have, it seems appropriate to use matching items with a sentence context. Although items with opportunities for inferencing also performed well, they are measuring other things besides previous vocabulary knowledge and, for estimates of vocabulary size, could be misleading.

The passage-embedded items also performed well but would present practical difficulties in constructing paragraphs for randomly selected items. If, however, an achievement test of vocabulary knowledge were based on themes or units of work, designing such items could be less problematic.

Watanabe (1997) found that testing words in the context in which they occurred in a previously read text resulted in higher scores than when the words were tested in isolation. This suggests that the context had a cuing effect on recall. As Baddeley (1990: 268–70) points out, testing under the same conditions as which the learning occurred results in much better recall than testing under new conditions. In Watanabe's study, the increase by testing in the same context was over 50%.

The disadvantages in using sentence contexts include the extra time required to make an item, and the fewer items that can be tested within the same time. Where multiple-choice or matching are used with a deliberately big difference in meaning between the distractors, then contexts are difficult to devise. This is because each of the distractors would have to be able to fit sensibly within the context sentence. If they did not, the learner could choose the correct answer not by knowing the meaning of the tested word, but by using substitution within the context sentence to eliminate the distractors. For example, let us try to rewrite one of the *Vocabulary Levels Test* blocks using sentence contexts.

1. He saw a *bull.*
2. She was a *champion.*   _____ formal and serious manner
3. He lost his *dignity.*   _____ winner of a sporting event

4. This is like *hell*.   _____ building where valuable objects are
5. She liked the *museum*.   shown
6. This is a good *solution*.

Several of the six choices can be eliminated by substitution, for example, 'She was a *formal and serious manner*', 'He lost his *winner of a sporting event*', and so on.

However, where possible, particularly in receptive recall translation tests, sentence contexts should be used. They are also useful in multiple-choice recognition tests, but care has to be taken that all the choices are feasible within the sentence contexts. They thus may not be suitable for sensitive multiple-choice or sensitive matching items. Much vocabulary testing has made use of largely decontextualised discrete-point tests, but there are clearly arguments for also measuring lexical communicative competence.

Should vocabulary be tested in a communicative context?

The issue of testing in a communicative context is well explored by Read (2000), Read and Chapelle (2001) and Qian (2008). In these discussions, context is much more than an isolated non-defining sentence context as used in the *Vocabulary Size Test*, but is an extended text where interpretation of the words is dependent on the wider context. However, Qian found that both contextualised (passage context) and decontextualised (sentence context) vocabulary tests correlated highly with each other (0.751) and were equally effective predictors of reading comprehension scores.

Discrete-point tests work well (Henning, 1991; Qian and Schedl, 2004; Qian, 2008) both in predicting reading comprehension scores and in measuring vocabulary knowledge, but they are seen as providing negative washback effects, that is, they encourage the decontextualised learning of vocabulary (see Qian, 2008: 3). The belief that decontextualised learning is a negative washback effect does not fit with the research. As we have seen in Chapter 3, decontextualised learning is highly efficient and as Elgort (2011) has shown, helps develop the implicit knowledge that is needed for normal language use. Test batteries should however include tests of contextualised reading and listening skills so that learners are also encouraged to engage in meaning-focused input as a means of learning. In high-stakes tests where learners study directly for the test, discrete-point vocabulary tests could have a negative washback effect in that they encourage learners to spend too much time on deliberate learning. Read's (2000: 138–47; see also Qian, 2008) fascinating history of the vocabulary items in the TOEFL test shows how items that were performing very well as a part of the test were replaced by those of a different format to fit with the prevailing communicative teaching methodology to encourage positive washback on message-focused learning and teaching.

Read and Chapelle (2001) present a different very convincing argument in favour of contextualised vocabulary tests: they do not propose the avoidance of testing words in isolation or single-sentence contexts, but make the point that test design should take account of the *purpose* of the vocabulary test. If inferences based on the vocabulary tests are to be made about the learners' ability to use vocabulary, either receptively or productively, then the test should involve relevant aspects of vocabulary used. If vocabulary tests are to be used for diagnostic or placement purposes, then there is a useful role for testing words in isolation or in single-sentence contexts. Read and Chapelle carefully spell out a range of test purposes and how they affect test design. Read's (2000: 7–13) three dimensions – discrete/embedded, selective/comprehensive and context-independent/context-dependent – are a part of this framework. Read and Chapelle analyse eight different well-known vocabulary tests describing the features of their design and purpose. Table 13.5 overleaf summarises their analysis and adds two more tests, the *Vocabulary Size Test* and the *Word Associates Test*.

This broad view of vocabulary testing is very helpful and has the benefits of making testers consider the purpose of their vocabulary tests and whether the test formats they are using are best suited to their purpose, with the understanding that test purpose includes what they want to measure, how they want to use the test data, and the possible impacts the test may have, for example on washback.

How can depth of knowledge about a word be tested?

As Qian and Schedl (2004: 29) note, there have been many attempts to describe what is involved in knowing a word (Bogaards, 2000; Richards, 1976). These descriptions necessarily fragment knowledge that is all part of a strongly interdependent system. The justifications for this fragmentation typically relate to learning and testing – if we can isolate aspects of vocabulary learning, we may be able to enhance their learning and enable such learning to be tested.

Looking at how well a particular word is known is called measuring *depth* of knowledge which is contrasted with measuring how many words are known (*breadth* of knowledge). Table 13.4 lists various aspects of what is involved in knowing a word. Most people consider that the most important aspect of knowing a word is knowing what it

Table 13.5 *A variety of test formats analysed using Read and Chapelle's (2001) criteria*

Test	Construct	Design features
Vocabulary Levels Test	vocabulary knowledge independent of context of use (trait)	discrete, selective, context-independent
Lexical Frequency Profile	vocabulary knowledge independent of context of use (trait)	discrete, comprehensive, context-dependent
ESL composition profile	ability to use vocabulary and academic writing (interactionalist)	embedded, comprehensive, context-dependent
TOEFL vocabulary items (1995)	ability to cope with vocabulary in reading (interactionalist)	embedded, selective, context-independent
Multiple-choice cloze	ability to cope with vocabulary in reading (interactionalist)	embedded, selective, context-dependent
C-test (Singleton and Little, 1991)	vocabulary knowledge independent of context of use (trait)	discrete, selective, context-dependent
Vocabulary Knowledge Scale	vocabulary knowledge independent of context of use (trait)	discrete, selective, context-independent
Lexical density index	vocabulary knowledge independent of context of use (trait)	discrete, comprehensive, context-independent
Vocabulary Size Test	vocabulary knowledge independent of context of use (trait)	discrete, selective, context-independent
Word Associates Test	vocabulary knowledge independent of context of use (trait)	discrete, selective, context-independent

Note: In Column 3 of the table, *discrete* means focused on vocabulary alone, *embedded* means measured as part of a larger construct, for example, reading; *selective* means focused on particular words; *comprehensive* means all the content words in a text may be considered; *context-independent* means that contextual information is not needed to answer the items; *context-dependent* means that contextual information is needed.

means but, as Table 13.4 indicates, there are many other things to know about a word. As we have seen in Chapter 2, some aspects of word knowledge may not need to be directly learned for a particular word because they are predictable from the first language or from known patterns within the second language.

When we test the different aspects of word knowledge, we may be interested in two things: whether a particular word is well known, and whether learners show awareness of the systematic patterns that lie behind many of the words. For example, when testing spelling, we may be interested in whether learners can spell words like *agree*, *balloon* and *practice*. But we may also be interested in whether learners know when double consonants are needed in words like *swimming*, *occurrence* or *spinner*. Finding out how much learners are aware of underlying regularities involves careful selection of test items to include items that involve a particular rule and items that do not or are exceptions. It also involves interpreting the results of the test by classifying the correct answers and analysing incorrect answers. There is a notable lack of tests that measure patterns underlying vocabulary use.

The following test item types are arranged according to the parts of Table 13.4 which itself is based on aspects of word knowledge (R = receptive knowledge, P = productive knowledge).

- Spoken form
  (R) Word or sentence dictation/hear the word and choose the L1 translation.
  (P) Reading aloud/cued oral recall.

- Written form
  (R) Say these written words/say these regularly spelled nonsense words.
  (P) Word or sentence dictation.

- Word parts
  (R) Break the word into parts/choose or provide the meanings of the parts.
  (P) Provide an affixed form of a known word.

- Form and meaning
  (R) Translate these words into L1/choose the right picture.
  (P) Translate these words into L2.

- Concept and referents
  (R) Translate these underlined words into L1. 'It was a hard frost.'
  (P) Choose the words to translate this L1 word.

- Associations
  (R) Choose the words that you associate with this word.
  (P) Add to this list of associated words.

- Grammatical functions
  (R) Is this sentence correct?
  (P) Use this word in a sentence.

- Collocations
  (R) Is this sentence correct?
  (P) Produce collocations to go with this word.

- Constraints
  (R) Which of these words represent UK use?
  (P) What is the formal word for X?

Different types of tests that focus on the same aspect of knowledge correlate with each other to a reasonable degree, but there is still a substantial amount of difference. Paul et al. (1990) compared the three vocabulary test formats of multiple-choice, interview and Yes/No. They found reasonably high and significant correlations between the interview scores and the Yes/No and multiple-choice scores, ranging from .66 to .81. The correlations show that the three kinds of tests are doing a similar job but that there is enough unshared variance to see each of them as revealing some different aspects of vocabulary knowledge. Nist and Olejnik (1995) compared four different vocabulary tests of the same words, one requiring the native-speaking learners to write an illustrative sentence, another involving sentence completion, and others testing meanings and examples. The correlations between the tests were all less than .7, showing that it is likely that different aspects of vocabulary knowledge of the same words were being tested. This lack of high correlation indicates that we must look at item types carefully to see if they are measuring what we want to measure. One item type cannot replace another without changing what will be measured, even if the same aspect of knowledge is measured. Laufer and Goldstein (2004) found even lower correlations between their four tests testing the same words.

Interviews are often used to test several aspects of a word in the same session. When this is done, a lot of care has to be taken in planning the interview to make sure that the early parts of the interview do not provide answers for the later parts. An advantage of interviews is that they allow the researcher to explore an aspect of knowledge in depth by giving the learner repeated opportunities to answer, if necessary with some guidance. Nagy et al. (1985) describe their interview procedure in detail. Wesche and Paribakht (1996) have done considerable work on their Vocabulary Knowledge Scale which has elements of an interview in that it probes for levels of knowledge but is self-administered as a pencil-and-paper test. Several learners can thus sit the test at the same time. Learners are given a word which they respond to using the following statements.

1. I haven't seen this word before.
2. I have seen this word before, but I don't know what it means.
3. I have seen this word before and I think it means ...
4. I know this word. It means ...
5. I can use this word in a sentence.

Their responses are ranked on this scale:

1. The word is not familiar at all.
2. The word is familiar but its meaning is not known.
3. A correct synonym or translation is given.
4. The word is used with semantic appropriateness in a sentence.
5. The word is used with semantic appropriateness and grammatical accuracy in a sentence.

Both Nagy et al.'s and Wesche and Paribakht's interview procedures mix aspects of knowing a word, particularly recognising its form, knowing its meaning, and being able to use it in a sentence. These different aspects do not fit comfortably into one scale. It is possible to use a word in a sentence, for example, without fully comprehending its meaning. There have been several critiques of the Vocabulary Knowledge Scale, largely focusing on its mixing of scales and the different kinds of evidence required at the various steps on the scale (Bruton, 2009; Nation and Webb, 2011; Schmitt, 2010: 218–21; Waring, 2002). Waring (2002) sees the major problem with the Vocabulary Knowledge Scale and similar scales as more fundamentally related to the construct of vocabulary knowledge, and he suggests that knowledge of a particular word is not incremental in the sense of moving through a series of steps, but is accretive in that we accumulate knowledge about a particular word although not necessarily in a particular order, that is, we need to see word knowledge as consisting of a variety of different states, 'which are functionally independent from a testing perspective, and retain the nominal status of the data' (Waring, 2002: 18).

Anglin's (1993: 112–13) interviews about word meanings show the different roles that interview tests and multiple-choice tests can play, particularly with items where there are literal meanings that are not the required answer (I = interviewer; C = child).

I.   OK. What does the word *twenty questions* mean?

C.   It could mean like questions like things that are asked by people.

I.   Mm-mmm.

C.   *Twenty* might mean that you're asking them twenty questions.

I.   OK. Can you tell me anything more about the word *twenty questions*?

C.   Twenty's a number, and it's the amount of questions you can ask.

I.   Can you use it in a sentence to show me you know what it means?

C.   The teacher asked us twenty questions in the afternoon.
     [*Multiple-choice question answered correctly.*]

I.   Have you ever played that game?

C.   Ya, I just forgot about that.

In an interview, although a learner might pursue a meaning that is on the wrong track, they can choose the wanted answer in a multiple-choice item even when one of the wrong choices is the wrong track they originally pursued.

I.   What does the word *dust bowl* mean?

C.   *Dust bowl?*

I.   Mmm.

C.   Well dust is, like, is like little dirt in the air that it'll, it'll collect on things.

I.   Mmm

C.   Dust. And a bowl is like you eat your cereal out of it.

I.   Mmm

C.   A dust bowl. Wouldn't be dust in a bowl I don't think.

I.   Mmm

C.   So I don't know.

I.   OK. Do you think you might be able to use it in a sentence to show me you know what it means?

C.   No. These ones are getting tougher.
     [*Multiple-choice question answered correctly.*]

Interviews have the value of being a stringent unguided test of knowledge. A disadvantage is that the learners' initial mind-set might stop them from reaching the correct answer. Multiple-choice items also seemed to be more sensitive than the interview in that learners gained higher scores. They also allow a focus on particular meanings.

Multiple-choice items provide answers and so there may be a doubt about whether learners really knew the answer in that detail. However, by providing choices they allow learners to consider responses that they knew but may not have considered in the interview.

When examining how well learners knew recently learned words, Webb (2005; 2007) used ten different measures of each word, looking at knowledge of written form, the form–meaning connection, grammatical functions, collocations and associations. Each of these five aspects had a receptive knowledge and productive knowledge test. Webb was thus able to examine the effects of different learning conditions on various kinds of vocabulary knowledge.

Read's (1993; 2000) Word Associates Format has received considerable attention both from Read himself (1998; 2000) and Qian (1999; 2002) and his associates (Qian and Schedl, 2004). Qian renamed it the Depth of Vocabulary Knowledge Test. Qian and Schedl found that the difficulty levels of the Word Associates Format and a four-item multiple-choice test of the meanings of the same words were about equal. The two vocabulary tests correlated highly with each other (.84) and did a very similar job in predicting scores on a TOEFL reading for basic comprehension measure (Word Associates Format .74, multiple-choice .75). When the comprehension questions were classified into five categories (inference, factual detail, main idea, reference, organisation and logic), it was found that the highest correlation was with factual questions. This agrees with Stahl et al. (1989) who found that vocabulary knowledge was most closely related to the microstructure of the text and literal comprehension.

A concern with the Word Associates Format has been its unusual format (see Read (2000: 178–86) for a frank description of the development of the test format). When setting each item it is necessary to first focus on elements of meaning and then on collocations. This switching from one kind of focus to another is very noticeable when sitting the test. In Qian and Schedl's study however, only ten learners out of 202 did not follow the instructions and chose more than four answers for several items. It takes almost twice as long to sit items in the Word Associates Format compared to a multiple-choice test, but the Word Associates Format involves four times as many points of assessment. Schmitt et al. (2011) conducted a very detailed analysis of the Word Associates Format, and found that test scores in the middle range do not represent lexical knowledge well, but they suggested ways of improving items.

Schoonen and Verhallen (2008) developed a test of depth of word knowledge for young learners of Dutch as a second language that was inspired by the Word Associates Format. The test format however is so different, that it is in effect a very different test. Each item consists of a test word surrounded by six choices (see the figure below from Schoonen and Verhallen, 2008: 219). While all six choices have some kind of semantic relationship to the test word, three of them have stronger relationships then the remaining three. Learners have to draw a line between the test word and each of the three words that *always* go together with the test word.

fruit   monkey

nice   **banana**   (to) slip

peel   yellow

Learners were only given a score if all three (and no less or more than three) lines were drawn between the test word and the three intended choices. The test worked well with the 9- and 11-year-olds who sat it. It correlated strongly with a definition test (.82), had high reliability, distinguished native speakers from non-native speakers, distinguished learners of different L1 backgrounds, distinguished 9-year-olds from 11-year-olds, gave very similar scores on two versions, and was answered according to the instructions by almost all of the learners. The tough marking system (all three intended choices correct) correlated very highly (.96) with a more complicated marking system giving a point for each correct choice.

There is considerable evidence that for young native speakers the concepts of some words develop over a considerable period of time. A striking example of this is with words expressing family relationships, like *brother*, where children can take a long time to learn that adults as well as children can have brothers, and that if you are male and you have a brother then that relationship is reciprocal, that is you are also that person's brother (Clark, 1973).

Another well-researched area is that of prepositions. Young native speakers can take several years to get control of the range of meanings of words like *near*, *between* and *next to* (Durkin et al., 1985).

A very innovative test of productive vocabulary is Lex30 (Meara and Fitzpatrick, 2000). In this test, learners are presented with a list of specially chosen stimulus words from the first 1,000 words of English (not a random sample). Learners have to supply preferably three associated words for each stimulus word. Each word supplied which is beyond the first 1,000 words of English and is not a proper noun, number or function word is awarded one point up to a maximum of 90 for the whole test. The scoring can be done by a computer program. The test correlated highly with a Yes/No measure (.84). Unlike the Productive Vocabulary Levels Test, however, the resulting score does not allow any estimate of the number of words known productively at a particular frequency level. Nevertheless, it is a format deserving of further research.

Fitzpatrick and Clenton (2010) provide a very interesting and well-balanced investigation of Lex30 examining many facets of its validity. Overall Lex30 performed well on a variety of reliability measures and in distinguishing learners longitudinally. The low correlations with other vocabulary tests and between spoken and written forms of the test suggest that Lex30 is measuring an aspect of productive vocabulary knowledge that is at best only partly measured by productive translation tests and the Productive Vocabulary Levels Test. Lex30 is thus best not seen as a more efficient way of measuring productive vocabulary knowledge, but as a different kind of measure, tapping different aspects of productive knowledge.

Bogaards (2000) reports on a study of Meara's (1992) innovative Eurocentres French Tests format. In the test, learners have to decide if two given words have a close relationship with each other or not. Here are some English examples:

    blink: eyes   [ ]
    hoist: petard   [ ]
    iron: agree   [ ]

In the pairs above, the first two show a relationship while the third does not. Bogaards sees potential for such tests for testing depth of vocabulary knowledge with advanced learners of the language. His analysis, however, showed that it is very difficult to make such tests that distinguish native speakers from advanced non-native speakers, and provide predictable results. Bogaards' painstaking analysis of the results of the tests is a model of how new test formats can be examined.

How can we measure words that learners don't know well?

Other ways of putting this question include: 'How can I measure how strongly learners know a word?' and 'How can I make tests that give learners credit for partial knowledge?'

In general, learners get higher scores on recognition (multiple-choice) tests than recall tests. This effect is stronger than the receptive/productive effect (Laufer et al., 2004; Laufer and Goldstein, 2004). Learners will get higher scores on receptive knowledge tests than productive tests. This effect is stronger than the kind of learning effect, for example if items learned receptively are tested receptively compared with being tested productively. Learners will get higher scores on tests that match the kind of learning they have done (Stoddard, 1929; Waring, 1997a). So, if you want to make a test as sensitive as possible (1) use a recognition format; (2) use a receptive test; (3) use non-distracting distractors; and if feasible (4) match the kind of learning to the test format, that is, do receptive learning.

Three important sets of factors affecting difficulty are recognition/recall, reception/production, and imprecise/precise.

A recognition vocabulary item format involves the use of choices:

gendarme   a. policeman
              b. path
              c. finger
              d. chair

A recall item requires the test taker to provide the required form or meaning.

Translate this word into English.
gendarme _____

Recognition items are easier because even with partial knowledge a test taker may be able to make the right choice. The recognition/recall distinction has been a matter of some debate in memory research (Baddeley, 1990: 271–5), but when the distractors are not very close in form or meaning to the target word, then recognition tests are easier than recall tests.

The receptive/productive distinction is well recognised in second language teaching and is sometimes called passive/active (Laufer, 1998; Morgan and Oberdeck, 1930; Stoddard, 1929). Receptive knowledge is that used in listening and reading, and involves going from the form of a word to its meaning, for example:

Translate the italicised word into your first language.
He is a *bold* writer. _____

Productive knowledge is that used in speaking and writing, and involves going from the meaning to the word form, for example:

Translate this word into English.
gendarme _____

Where the test item format is controlled for (Stoddard, 1929) receptive recall is easier than productive recall, irrespective of whether the tested items were learned receptively or productively.

The imprecise/precise distinction relates to the degree of accuracy required in the answer. This can be reflected in the similarity of the choices provided, the degree of prompting, and degree of acceptance of an approximate answer. Items allowing for imprecise knowledge are easier because credit is given for partial knowledge.

In experimental research, it is very useful to test the same word in several different ways. In a study of vocabulary learning from oral retelling of a written text, Joe (1995) used three measures of vocabulary knowledge, each at a different level of difficulty. The measures were all receptive and consisted of (1) an easy multiple-choice measure like Nagy et al.'s (1985); (2) a more demanding multiple-choice measure; and (3) an interview using an adaptation of the Vocabulary Knowledge Scale (Wesche and Paribakht, 1996). By testing each target word with each of these three measures, Joe was able to give a strength of knowledge score for each word by assigning a one-point credit for each of the multiple-choice measures answered correctly for each word and rating knowledge of items in the interview on a 1 to 6 point scale. Scores ranged from 1 to 8 for each word. Joe could then relate strength of knowledge to the degree of creative use that the word received during the retelling activity. Use of an item is creative if its use differs in some way from the input on which it is based. She found that words that had been used more creatively during the retelling intervention were more strongly known than words that were less creatively used. This finding would not have been possible without using a range of vocabulary measures of differing difficulty. Waring and Takaki (2003) also used three measures in their study of incidental vocabulary learning from reading: a recognition measure (which of these words appeared in the text?), a multiple-choice measure and a translation measure.

McKeown et al.'s (1985) study with first language learners shows the importance of using various measures of vocabulary knowledge to pick up effects of different types of vocabulary learning. McKeown et al. compared three learning conditions: traditional (involving the learning of form-meaning connections), rich (involving learning the meanings, sentence completion, context generation, comparing and contrasting words), and extended/rich (involving rich instruction plus learners bringing evidence of having seen, heard or used the word outside class). All three treatment groups performed equally well on a multiple-choice vocabulary test. A fluency of lexical access test measured how quickly learners decided whether a word matched a given meaning. Learners with the extended rich instruction performed at significantly faster speeds than learners in the other two treatments. On an interview test involving the interpretation of a context containing the target word, the extended/rich and rich groups equally outperformed the traditional group. If only one measure of vocabulary knowledge had been used, important differences in the effects of the treatments might not have been revealed (see Nation and Webb, 2011, and Schmitt, 2010, for further discussion of multiple tests).

Table 13.6 *Eight test formats ranked according to three factors affecting difficulty*

Recognition	Receptive	Imprecise	Sensitive multiple choice, for example, *fertiliser* a. growing plants
			    b. medicine
			    c. history
			    d. don't know

		Precise	Non-sensitive multiple choice

	Productive	Imprecise	Sensitive multiple choice, for example. *end or highest point* a. event
			    b. profit
			    c. tip
			    d. copy

		Precise	Non-sensitive multiple choice
Recall	Receptive	Imprecise	Recalling a related meaning Does this word remind you of anything?
		Precise	Meaning recall
	Productive	Imprecise	Cued recall, for example, *an additional part suppl*
		Precise	Form recall

How can we measure how well learners actually use words?

Most of the tests we have looked at so far in this chapter have involved testing vocabulary that learners consciously and deliberately retrieve. They could be described as tests of declarative knowledge of the form–meaning link, that is, knowledge that learners can talk about (*declare*) and describe. Ultimately, what we should be most interested in is procedural knowledge, that is, learners' ability to use words receptively and productively when their focus is on the message that they are receiving or conveying. Recent research using eye movement tracking (Underwood et al., 2004), brain activity measurement (McLaughlin et al., 2004) and lexical priming studies (Barcroft et al., 2011; Elgort, 2011; McDonough and Trofimovich, 2009; Sonbul and Schmitt, 2013; Williams and Cheung, 2011) have been particularly useful, showing that deliberately learned words directly enter implicit knowledge and that small amounts of word learning can occur which is not accessible to traditional direct measures of word knowledge.

Vocabulary learning is not a goal in itself. Vocabulary learning is done to help learners listen, speak, read or write more effectively. When testing vocabulary, it is important to distinguish between how well a word is known and how well a word is used. By doing this, it is possible to investigate learners with listening, speaking, reading or writing problems and see if lack of vocabulary knowledge is a source of these problems. For example, a learner may score poorly on a reading comprehension test. There are many causes that could contribute to the poor performance. By testing learners' vocabulary size or knowledge of the particular words in the reading text, it is possible to begin to see if lack of vocabulary knowledge is playing a part in the poor reading performance. If it is found that the learner does not know a lot of the vocabulary in the text or has a small vocabulary size, then an important cause has been found. If the learner seems to know most of the vocabulary, then that does not exclude vocabulary knowledge as a factor, but it excludes some aspects of vocabulary knowledge.

The Lexical Frequency Profile (LFP) (Laufer and Nation, 1995) is an attempt to measure the amount of vocabulary from different frequency levels used by learners in their composition writing. It is important in applying this measure that learners write the compositions as they would normally, without giving more than usual attention to vocabulary choice. The measure is normally applied using a computer program now called Range (previously called VocabProfile) which compares words in a text with word lists that accompany the program. When the learners' texts are typed into the computer, spelling errors need to be corrected, wrongly used lexical words should be omitted and proper nouns should also be omitted. A learner's lexical frequency profile is the percentage of word types at the high-frequency (2,000-word-family) level, the Academic Word List level and not in those levels. The LFP can be a reliable measure (Laufer and Nation, 1995) which can measure change in language proficiency (Laufer, 1994). It has been used in studies of vocabulary size and growth (Laufer, 1998).

The LFP does not show how well particular words are known, but indicates what use learners are making of words at a particular frequency level. This is useful for diagnostic purposes to see if the vocabulary shown to be known on tests like the Vocabulary Levels Test is actually being used in meaning-focused performance, and there typically is a very big lag.

Vocabulary testing is an important part of a well-designed vocabulary programme and is essential if well-informed decisions are to be made about what vocabulary learners need to focus on and how much they need to learn. Vocabulary testing can also have positive effects on motivation. In this chapter we have looked largely at vocabulary testing related to vocabulary teaching and learning. Vocabulary testing in research on vocabulary is dealt with in other books (Nation and Webb, 2011; Read, 2000; Schmitt, 2010) but draws on many of the ideas that we have looked at in this chapter.

References

Anderson, R. C. and Freebody, P. (1983). Reading comprehension and the assessment and acquisition of word knowledge. In Guthrie, J. (ed.), *Advances in Reading/Language Research* (pp. 231–56).

Anglin, J. M. (1993). Vocabulary development: A morphological analysis. *Monographs of the Society for Research in Child Development Serial No. 238*, 58, 10 Serial No. 238, 1–165.

Baddeley, A. (1990). *Human Memory*. London: Lawrence Erlbaum Associates.

Barcroft, J., Sommers, M. S. and Sunderman, G. (2011). Some costs of fooling mother nature: A priming study on the Keyword Method and the quality of developing L2 lexical representations. In Trofimovich, P. and McDonouhgh, K. (eds.), *Applying Priming Methods to L2 Learning, Teaching and Research: 1* (pp. 49–72). Amsterdam: John Benjamins.

Barnard, H. (1961). A test of P.U.C. students' vocabulary in Chotanagpur. *Bulletin of the Central Institute of English*, 1, 90–100.

Bauer, L. and Nation, I. S. P. (1993). Word families. *International Journal of Lexicography*, 6, 4, 253–79.

Bear, R. M. and Odbert, H. S. (1941). Insight of older pupils into their knowledge of word meanings. *School Review*, 49, 754–60.

Beglar, D. (2010). A Rasch-based validation of the Vocabulary Size Test. *Language Testing*, 27, 1, 101–18.

Beglar, D. and Hunt, A. (1999). Revising and validating the 2000 word level and the university word level vocabulary tests. *Language Testing*, 16, 2, 131–62.

Biemiller, A. (2005). Size and sequence in vocabulary development. In Hiebert, E. H. and Kamil, M. L. (eds.), *Teaching and Learning Vocabulary: Bringing Research into Practice* (pp. 223–42). Mahwah, NJ: Lawrence Erlbaum Associates.

Biemiller, A. (2010). *Words Worth Teaching: Closing the Vocabulary Gap.* Colombus: McGraw-Hill.

Biemiller, A. and Slonim, N. (2001). Estimating root word vocabulary growth in normative and advantaged populations: Evidence for a common sequence of vocabulary acquisition. *Journal of Educational Psychology*, 93, 3, 498–520.

Bogaards, P. (2000). Testing L2 vocabulary knowledge at a high level: The case of the Euralex French Tests. *Applied Linguistics*, 21, 4, 490–516.

Bruton, A. (2009). The Vocabulary Knowledge Scale: A critical analysis. *Language Assessment Quarterly*, 6, 4, 288–97.

Campion, M. E. and Elley, W. B. (1971). *An Academic Vocabulary List.* Wellington: NZCER.

Carroll, J. B., Davies, P. and Richman, B. (1971). *The American Heritage Word Frequency Book.* New York: Houghton Mifflin, Boston American Heritage.

Clark, E. V. (1973). What's in a word? On the child's acquisition of semantics in his L1. In Moore, T. E. (ed.), *Cognitive Development and the Acquisition of Language* (pp. 65–110). New York: Academic Press.

D'Anna, C. A., Zechmeister, E. B. and Hall, J. W. (1991). Toward a meaningful definition of vocabulary size. *Journal of Reading Behavior: A Journal of Literacy*, 23, 1, 109–22.

Diack, H. (1975). *Test Your Own Wordpower.* St. Albans: Paladin.

Diller, K. C. (1978). *The Language Teaching Controversy.* Rowley, MA: Newbury House.

Durkin, K., Crowther, R., Shire, B., Riem, R. and Nash, P. (1985). Polysemy in mathematical and musical education. *Applied Linguistics*, 6, 2, 147–61.

Elgort, I. (2011). Deliberate learning and vocabulary acquisition in a second language. *Language Learning*, 61, 2, 367–413.

Elgort, I. (2013). Effects of L1 definitions and cognate status of test items on the Vocabulary Size Test. *Language Testing*, 30, 2, 253–72. DOI: 10.1177/0265532212459028.

Eyckmans, J. (2004). *Measuring Receptive Vocabulary Size: Reliability and Validity of the yes/no Vocabulary Test for French-speaking Learners of Dutch.* Utrecht: Netherlands Graduate School of Linguistics.

Fairclough, M. (2011). Testing the lexical recognition task with Spanish/English bilinguals. *Language Testing*, 28, 2, 273–97.

Feifel, H. and Lorge, I. (1950). Qualitative differences in the vocabulary responses of children. *Journal of Educational Psychology*, 41, 1, 1–18.

Fitzpatrick, T. and Clenton, J. (2010). The challenge of validation: Assessing the performance of a test of productive vocabulary. *Language Testing*, 27, 4, 537–54.

Goodrich, H. C. (1977). Distractor efficiency in foreign language testing. *TESOL Quarterly*, 11, 1, 69–78.

Goulden, R., Nation, P. and Read, J. (1990). How large can a receptive vocabulary be? *Applied Linguistics*, **11**, 4, 341–63.

Gove, P. B. (ed.). (1963). *Webster's Third New International Dictionary*. Springfield, MA: G. and C. Merriam.

Harrington, M. and Carey, M. (2009). The on-line Yes/No test as a placement tool. *System*, **37**, 614–26.

Hart, B. and Risley, T. R. (1995). *Meaningful Differences in the Everyday Experience of Young American Children*. Baltimore: Paul H. Brookes Publishing.

Henning, G. (1991). *A Study of the Effects of Contextualization and Familiarization on Responses to the TOEFL Vocabulary Test Items*. Princeton, NJ: Educational Testing Service.

Joe, A. (1995). Text-based tasks and incidental vocabulary learning. *Second Language Research*, **11**, 2, 149–58.

Joe, A. (1998). What effects do text-based tasks promoting generation have on incidental vocabulary acquisition? *Applied Linguistics*, **19**, 3, 357–77.

Kučera, H. and Francis, W. N. (1967). *A Computational Analysis of Present-Day American English*. Providence, RI: Brown University Press.

Laufer, B. (1994). The lexical profile of second language writing: Does it change over time? *RELC Journal*, **25**, 2, 21–33.

Laufer, B. (1998). The development of passive and active vocabulary: Same or different? *Applied Linguistics*, **19**, 2, 255–71.

Laufer, B., Elder, C., Hill, K. and Congdon, P. (2004). Size and strength: Do we need both to measure vocabulary knowledge? *Language Testing*, **21**, 2, 202–26.

Laufer, B. and Goldstein, Z. (2004). Testing vocabulary knowledge: Size, strength, and computer adaptiveness. *Language Learning*, **54**, 3, 399–436.

Laufer, B. and Nation, P. (1995). Vocabulary size and use: Lexical richness in L2 written production. *Applied Linguistics*, **16**, 3, 307–22.

Laufer, B. and Nation, P. (1999). A vocabulary size test of controlled productive ability. *Language Testing*, **16**, 1, 36–55.

Laufer, B. and Paribakht, T. S. (1998). The relationship between passive and active vocabularies: Effects of language learning context. *Language Learning*, **48**, 3, 365–91.

Li, J. (2010). Learning vocabulary via computer-assisted scaffolding for text processing. *Computer Assisted Language Learning*, **23**, 3, 253–75.

Lorge, I. and Chall, J. (1963). Estimating the size of vocabularies of children and adults: An analysis of methodological issues. *Journal of Experimental Education*, **32**, 2, 147–57.

McDonough, K. and Trofimovich, P. (2009). *Using Priming Methods in Second Language Research*. New York: Routledge.

McKeown, M. G., Beck, I. L., Omanson, R. G. and Pople, M. T. (1985). Some effects of the nature and frequency of vocabulary instruction on the knowledge and use of words. *Reading Research Quarterly*, **20**, 5, 522–35.

McLaughlin, J., Osterhout, L. and Kim, A. (2004). Neural correlates of second language word learning: Minimal instruction produces rapid change. *Nature Neuroscience*, **7**, 7, 703–4.

Meara, P. (1989). Word power and how to assess it. *SELF*, **1**, 20–24.

Meara, P. (1990). Some notes on the Eurocentres vocabulary tests. *AFinLA Yearbook 1990*, **48**, 103–13.

Meara, P. (1991). Scoring a YES/NO vocabulary test. *Unpublished paper*.

Meara, P. (1992). Vocabulary tests for Dutch as a foreign language. *Unpublished paper*.

Meara, P. and Buxton, B. (1987). An alternative to multiple choice vocabulary tests. *Language Testing*, **4**, 2, 142–51.

Meara, P. and Fitzpatrick, T. (2000). Lex30: An improved method of assessing productive vocabulary in an L2. *System*, **28**, 1, 19–30.

Meara, P. and Jones, G. (1987). Tests of vocabulary size in English as a foreign language. *Polyglot*, **8**, Fiche 1.

Meara, P. and Jones, G. (1990). *Eurocentres Vocabulary Size Test. 10KA*. Zurich: Eurocentres.

Meara, P., Lightbown, P. and Halter, R. H. (1992). The effect of cognates on the applicability of YES/NO vocabulary tests. *Unpublished paper*.

Miller, G. A. and Wakefield, P. C. (1993). Commentary on Anglin's analysis of vocabulary growth. In Anglin, J. M. *Vocabulary Development: A Morphological Analysis*. Monographs of the Society for Research in Child Development Serial No. 238, **58**, 10 Serial No. 238, (pp. 167–75).

Milton, J. (2009). *Measuring Second Language Vocabulary Acquisition*. Bristol: Multilingual Matters.

Morgan, B. Q. and Oberdeck, L. M. (1930). Active and passive vocabulary. In Bagster-Collins, E.W. (ed.), *Studies in Modern Language Teaching 16* (pp. 213–21).

Nagy, W. E. and Anderson, R. C. (1984). How many words are there in printed school English? *Reading Research Quarterly*, **19**, 3, 304–30.

Nagy, W. E., Herman, P. and Anderson, R. C. (1985). Learning words from context. *Reading Research Quarterly*, **20**, 2, 233–53.

Nation, I. S. P. (1983). Testing and teaching vocabulary. *Guidelines*, **5**, 1, 12–25.

Nation, I. S. P. (1990). *Teaching and Learning Vocabulary*. Rowley, MA: Newbury House.

Nation, I. S. P. (1993a). Measuring readiness for simplified material: A test of the first 1,000 words of English. In Tickoo, M. L. (ed.), *Simplification: Theory and Application. RELC Anthology Series No. 31* (pp. 193–203). Singapore: SEAMEO-RELC.

Nation, I. S. P. (1993b). Using dictionaries to estimate vocabulary size: Essential, but rarely followed, procedures. *Language Testing*, **10**, 1, 27–40.

Nation, I. S. P. and Moir, J. (2008). Vocabulary learning and the good language learner. In Griffiths, C. (ed.), *Lessons from Good language Learners* (pp. 159–73). Cambridge: Cambridge University Press.

Nation, I. S. P. and Webb, S. (2011). *Researching and Analyzing Vocabulary*. Boston: Heinle Cengage Learning.

Nation, P. (2002). *Managing Vocabulary Learning*. Singapore: SEAMEO Regional Language Centre.

Nation, P. and Beglar, D. (2007). A vocabulary size test. *The Language Teacher*, **31**, 7, 9–13.

Nguyen, L. T. C. and Nation, I. S. P. (2011). A bilingual vocabulary size test of English for Vietnamese learners. *RELC Journal*, **42**, 1, 86–99.

Nist, S. L. and Olejnik, S. (1995). The role of context and dictionary definitions on varying levels of word knowledge. *Reading Research Quarterly*, **30**, 2, 172–93.

Nurweni, A. and Read, J. (1999). The English vocabulary knowledge of Indonesian university students. *English for Specific Purposes*, **18**, 2, 161–75.

Paterson, A. (2004). The development and trialling of an EFL vocabulary test. *Ehime University Journal of English Education Research*, **3**, 29–49.

Paul, P. V., Stallman, A. C. and O'Rourke, J. P. (1990). Using three test formats to assess good and poor readers' word knowledge. *Technical Report No. 509 Center for the Study of Reading, University of Illinois at Urbana-Champaign.*

Qian, D. (1999). Assessing the roles of depth and breadth of vocabulary knowledge in reading comprehension. *Canadian Modern Language Review*, **56**, 2, 282–307.

Qian, D. (2002). Investigating the relationship between vocabulary knowledge and academic reading performance: an assessment perspective. *Language Learning*, **52**, 3, 513–36.

Qian, D. and Schedl, M. (2004). Evaluation of an in-depth vocabulary knowledge measure for assessing reading performance. *Language Testing*, **21**, 1, 28–52.

Qian, D. D. (2008). From single words to passages: contextual effects on predictive power of vocabulary measures for assessing reading performance. *Language Assessment Quarterly*, **5**, 1, 1–19.

Quinn, G. (1968). *The English Vocabulary of Some Indonesian University Entrants*. Salatiga: IKIP Kristen Satya Watjana.

Read, J. (1993). The development of a new measure of L2 vocabulary knowledge. *Language Testing*, **10**, 3, 355–71.

Read, J. (1995). Refining the word associates format as a measure of depth of vocabulary knowledge. *New Zealand Studies in Applied Linguistics*, **1**, 1–17.

Read, J. (1998). Validating a test to measure depth of vocabulary knowledge. In Kunnan, A. J. (ed.), *Validation in Language Assessment* (pp. 41–60). Mahwah, NJ: Lawrence Erlbaum Associates.

Read, J. (2000). *Assessing Vocabulary*. Cambridge: Cambridge University Press.

Read, J. and Chapelle, C. (2001). A framework for second language vocabulary assessment. *Language Testing*, **18**, 1, 3–32.

Richards, J. C. (1976). The role of vocabulary teaching. *TESOL Quarterly*, **10**, 1, 77–89.

Sasao, Y. (2013). Diagnostic tests of English vocabulary learning proficiency: guessing from context and knowledge of word parts. Unpublished PhD thesis, Victoria University of Wellington, New Zealand.

Schmitt, N. (2010). *Researching Vocabulary: A Vocabulary Research Manual*. Basingstoke: Palgrave Macmillan.

Schmitt, N., Ng, J. W. C. and Garras, J. (2011). The word associates format: Validation evidence. *Language Testing*, **28**, 1, 105–26.

Schmitt, N., Schmitt, D. and Clapham, C. (2001). Developing and exploring the behaviour of two new versions of the Vocabulary Levels Test. *Language Testing*, **18**, 1, 55–88.

Schonell, F. J., Meddleton, I. G. and Shaw, B. A. (1956). *A Study of the Oral Vocabulary of Adults.* Brisbane: University of Queensland Press.

Schoonen, R. and Verhallen, M. (2008). The assessment of deep word knowledge in young first and second language learners. *Language Testing,* 25, 2, 211–36.

Seashore, R. H. and Eckerson, L. D. (1940). The measurement of individual differences in general English vocabularies. *Journal of Educational Psychology,* 31, 14–38.

Sinclair, J. M. (1991). *Corpus, Concordance, Collocation.* Oxford: Oxford University Press.

Singleton, D. and Little, D. (1991). The second language lexicon: some evidence from University-level learners of French and German. *Second Language Research,* 7, 1, 61–81.

Smith, M. K. (1941). Measurement of the size of general English vocabulary through the elementary grades and high school. *Genetic Psychology Monographs,* 24, 311–45.

Sonbul, S. and Schmitt, N. (2013). Explicit and implicit lexical knowledge: Acquisition of collocations under different input conditions. *Language Learning,* 63, 1, 121–59.

Stahl, S. A., Jacobson, M. G., Davis, C. E. and Davis, R. L. (1989). Prior knowledge and difficult vocabulary in the comprehension of unfamiliar text. *Reading Research Quarterly,* 24, 1, 27–43.

Stewart, J. and White, D. A. (2011). Estimating guessing effects on the Vocabulary Levels Test for differing degrees of word knowledge. *TESOL Quarterly,* 45, 2, 370–80.

Stoddard, G. D. (1929). An experiment in verbal learning. *Journal of Educational Psychology,* 20, 7, 452–57.

Templin, M. (1957). *Certain Language Skills in Children: Their Development and Inter-relationships.* Institute of Child Welfare, University of Minnesota Press.

Thorndike, E. L. (1924). The vocabularies of school pupils. In Bell, J. C. (ed.), *Contributions to Education* (pp. 69–76). New York: World Book.

Thorndike, E. L. and Lorge, I. (1944). *The Teacher's Word Book of 30,000 Words.* New York: Teachers College Columbia University.

Tinkham, T. (1989). Rote learning, attitudes, and abilities: A comparison of Japanese and American students. *TESOL Quarterly,* 23, 4, 695–8.

Umbel, V. M., Pearson, B. Z., Fernandez, M. C. and Oller, D. K. (1992). Measuring bilingual children's receptive vocabularies. *Child Development,* 63, 1012–20.

Underwood, G., Schmitt, N. and Galpin, A. (2004). The eyes have it: An eye-movement study into the processing of formulaic sequences. In Schmitt, N. (ed.), *Formulaic Sequences* (pp. 153–72). Amsterdam: John Benjamins.

Waring, R. (1997a). A study of receptive and productive learning from word cards. *Studies in Foreign Languages and Literature* (Notre Dame Seishin University, Okayama), 21, 1, 94–114.

Waring, R. (1997b). A comparison of the receptive and productive vocabulary sizes of some second language learners. *Immaculata* (Notre Dame Seishin University, Okayama), 1, 53–68.

Waring, R. (2002). Scales of vocabulary knowledge in second language vocabulary assessment. *Kiyo* (Occasional papers of Notre Dame Seishin University, Okayama), **26**, 1, 40–54.

Waring, R. and Takaki, M. (2003). At what rate do learners learn and retain new vocabulary from reading a graded reader? *Reading in a Foreign Language*, **15**, 2, 130–63.

Watanabe, Y. (1997). Input, intake and retention: Effects of increased processing on incidental learning of foreign vocabulary. *Studies in Second Language Acquisition*, **19**, 287–307.

Webb, S. (2005). Receptive and productive vocabulary learning: The effects of reading and writing on word knowledge. *Studies in Second Language Acquisition*, **27**, 33–52.

Webb, S. (2007). Learning word pairs and glossed sentences: The effects of a single context on vocabulary knowledge. *Language Teaching Research*, **11**, 1, 63–81.

Wesche, M. and Paribakht, T. S. (1996). Assessing second language vocabulary knowledge: Depth versus breadth. *Canadian Modern Language Review*, **53**, 1, 13–40.

West, M. (1953). *A General Service List of English Words*. London: Longman, Green & Co.

Williams, J. N. and Cheung, A. (2011). Using priming to explore early word learning. In Trofimovich, P. and McDonough, K. (eds.), *Applying Priming Methods to L2 Learning, Teaching and Research: 1* (pp. 73–103). Amsterdam: John Benjamins.

Xing, P. and Fulcher, G. (2007). Reliability assessment for two versions of the Vocabulary Levels test. *System*, **35**, 182–91.

14 *Designing the vocabulary component of a language course*

This chapter draws together many of the ideas discussed in the previous chapters by looking at the points to consider when doing curriculum design on the vocabulary component of a language course. It also describes important vocabulary principles by seeing how learners can be encouraged to take control of their vocabulary learning. This chapter follows a traditional model of curriculum design as displayed in Figure 14.1 (Nation and Macalister, 2010).

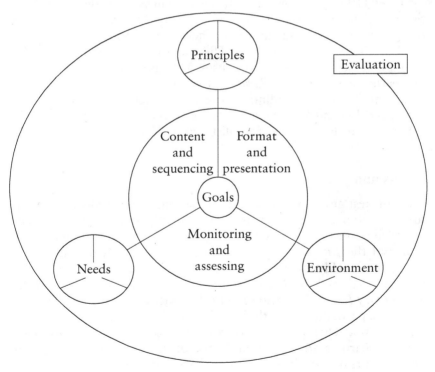

Figure 14.1 A model of curriculum design

Goals

In general, the goals of the vocabulary component of a course will be to increase learners' usable vocabulary size and to help them gain effective control of a range of vocabulary-learning and coping strategies. 'Usable' vocabulary size implies that learners need to not only increase the vocabulary they know but also develop the fluency and skill with which they can use that vocabulary in the relevant language skills of listening, speaking, reading and writing. Similarly, effective control of strategies implies that learners need to not only learn appropriate strategies but also be confident and fluent in their use.

In order to set specific goals, it is essential to know if learners need to focus on high-frequency, academic, technical, mid-frequency or low-frequency words. This is best decided on by diagnostic testing using the *Vocabulary Levels Test*, or by size testing using the *Vocabulary Size Test*, or some similar kind of vocabulary test. Knowing which of these five types of vocabulary to focus on is essential knowledge for course design because high-frequency vocabulary and low-frequency vocabulary need to be dealt with by the teacher in quite different ways.

O'Dell (1997) reviews major movements in syllabus design and particularly the role given to vocabulary. She notes the early lack of attention to vocabulary and the recent increasing attention, largely as a result of the *COBUILD* project. There are however important earlier examples of lexically based syllabuses. Most notable are West's (1932) pioneering *New Method Readers*, the various graded readers series which are in effect reading courses, and Helen Barnard's (1972) *Advanced English Vocabulary* which was very popular in the United States. These all give a central role to vocabulary in syllabus design.

Needs analysis

The quickest and most direct way to determine where learners are in their vocabulary development is to directly test their vocabulary knowledge. Tests like the *Vocabulary Levels Test*, the *Vocabulary Size Test* and the *Eurocentres Vocabulary Size Test* (Meara and Jones, 1987) can quickly indicate whether learners have sufficient control of the essential high-frequency words or not. Interpretation of the *Vocabulary Levels Test* also requires knowledge of learners' language use goals, particularly whether they intend to use English for academic study or not. Direct tests of vocabulary size however do not show whether learners are able to make use of the vocabulary they know, and they do not show learners' control of essential vocabulary-learning strategies like guessing from context, dictionary use and direct

Table 14.1 *Vocabulary needs analysis*

Type of need	Needs analysis tool
Lacks: • What vocabulary do they know? • What strategies can they use?	• Vocabulary knowledge: a vocabulary size test • Vocabulary use: Lexical Frequency Profile, levels dictation • Strategy knowledge: knowledge test • Strategy use: observation of performance
Necessities: • What vocabulary do they need? • What strategies do they need?	• Interview or questionnaire to determine language use goals • Refer to studies of vocabulary size and coverage
Wants: • What vocabulary do they want to learn?	• Use class discussion, an interview, or questionnaire to determine areas of interest

vocabulary learning. If a teacher feels the need for a more detailed knowledge of learners' skill in using vocabulary, it will be necessary to look at things like the Lexical Frequency Profile of their writing (Laufer and Nation, 1995), their skill in reading a series of texts graded according to vocabulary level, their performance on the graded dictation test (Appendix 2), or their skill in communicative speaking tasks, such as role playing relevant speaking tasks like talking to the doctor. Sasao (http://ysasaojp.info) has developed tests of word-building knowledge and skill at guessing from context.

Similarly, essential strategies can be assessed by questioning learners on their knowledge of the strategy, and by observing them using the strategy.

Published studies of the vocabulary size needed to perform certain tasks, such as reading academic texts (Sutarsyah et al., 1994) and taking part in conversation (West, 1956), are a useful source of information about how much and what kind of vocabulary learners may need (Nation, 2006). In order to choose the relevant studies to look at, it may be necessary to question learners on their future plans.

Learners may have specialist areas of interest that they wish to pursue. These may include sport, cultural activities, reading interests, or social activities. Discovering these through class discussion, questionnaires, or interviews can help determine vocabulary needs.

Needs analysis should result in:

- an indication of which type of vocabulary (high-frequency, academic, technical, mid-frequency, low-frequency) needs to be focused on;
- an indication of how much of this type of vocabulary needs to be learned;
- an indication of which strategies need attention;
- an indication of any specialised areas of vocabulary that need attention; and
- knowledge of learners' present areas of strength in vocabulary knowledge and use, and their control of strategies.

Environment analysis

Environment analysis involves discovering features of teachers, learners and the teaching/learning situation which may help or hinder learning. For example, if teachers are well informed about teaching and learning vocabulary, the course designer may not need to provide a lot of detail about the course. If learners are highly motivated and see the relevance of vocabulary learning, then ambitious learning goals could be set. If learners are not highly motivated, then regular vocabulary tests, discussion of vocabulary-learning goals and reward activities may be needed.

Time is often a critical factor in courses; it may be short with much learning to be done. For vocabulary learning, this may mean an emphasis on the direct learning and teaching of vocabulary, or if time is very short, an emphasis on strategies rather than particular words. Learners may favour certain styles of learning. Tinkham (1989) found that Japanese learners tended to have well-developed rote-learning skills, and he suggested that these should be put to good use rather than being neglected in favour of more communicative learning. The result of environment analysis should be a short list of factors that will have a strong effect on the design of the course. Each factor needs to be accompanied by a short description of how it will affect the course. Table 14.2 presents some examples.

Principles of vocabulary teaching

The vocabulary component of a language course should be guided by a set of well-justified principles. These principles should have a major influence on content and sequencing (what vocabulary is focused on and how it is divided into stages), format and presentation (how the

Table 14.2 *Some environment factors and their effects on vocabulary course design*

Environment factor	The effect on the course
Learners • The learners share the same L1. • The learners will do homework.	• Use translation to define words and to test vocabulary knowledge. • Set graded reading and direct vocabulary learning tasks.
Teachers • The teachers do not have much time for marking.	• Use vocabulary exercises with answer keys.
Situation • L1 and L2 share cognate vocabulary. • Computers are available.	• Introduce cognate forms early in the course to get quick vocabulary growth. • Use CALL activities.

vocabulary is taught and learned), and monitoring and assessment (how learning is measured). Table 14.3 lists the most important principles and expresses them as directives. The principles focus on vocabulary teaching on the assumption that learners can be taught and they can teach themselves.

It is worth noting that some teachers and course designers follow principles that go against research findings. These include: 'All vocabulary learning should occur in context'; 'The first language should not be used as a means of presenting the meaning of a word'; 'Vocabulary should be presented in lexical sets'; 'Monolingual dictionaries are preferable to bilingual dictionaries'; 'Most attention should be paid to the first presentation of a word'; and 'Vocabulary learning does not benefit from being planned, but can be determined by the occurrence of words in texts, tasks and themes'. Course designers who follow these principles should read the relevant research and reconsider their position.

Content and sequencing

The principles of content choice and sequencing listed in Table 14.3 and the directives listed with them should guide the choice of what vocabulary is focused on at any particular stage of a course, how it is focused on (words or strategies) and how it is ordered. There are adequate word lists available to act as a basis for choosing the high-frequency and academic words to focus on. Although these lists should be used flexibly, careful thought needs to be given (and preferably

Table 14.3 *Principles of vocabulary teaching*

Content and sequencing
- Use frequency and range of occurrence as ways of deciding what vocabulary to learn and the order in which to learn it.
- Give adequate training in essential vocabulary-learning strategies.
- Give attention to each vocabulary item according to its learning burden.
- Provide opportunity to learn the various aspects of what is involved in knowing a word.
- Avoid interference by presenting vocabulary in normal use rather than in groupings of synonyms, opposites, free associates or lexical sets.
- Deal with high-frequency vocabulary by focusing on the words themselves, and deal with low-frequency vocabulary by focusing on the control of strategies.

Format and presentation
- Make sure that high-frequency target vocabulary occurs in all four strands of meaning-focused input, language-focused learning, meaning-focused output and fluency development.
- Provide opportunity for spaced, repeated, creative retrieval of words to ensure cumulative growth.
- Use depth of processing activities.

Monitoring and assessment
- Test learners to see what vocabulary they need to focus on.
- Use monitoring and assessment to keep learners motivated.
- Encourage and help learners to reflect on their learning.

---

research done) before making substantial changes to them (a substantial change means changing more than 5% of their content).

Within the high-frequency, academic, technical, mid-frequency and low-frequency levels, there are sub-levels that should be considered. For example, the most common 60 words (Sublist 1) of the *Academic Word List* cover 3.6% of the running words in an academic text. The fourth most common 60 words (Sublist 4) cover only 0.9% of the running words. Clearly, it is sensible to give most attention to Sublist 1 and where possible to deal with these words before moving on to other academic words. Similarly, the 2,000 high-frequency words can be divided into the 1,000 most frequent words which cover over 75% of the running words in an academic text, and the second 1,000 most frequent words which cover around 5% to 6% of the running words.

One of the most important decisions concerned with content and sequencing is deciding on the 'unit of analysis' (Long and Crookes, 1992) or **unit of progression** (Nation and Macalister, 2010). The unit of progression is what marks progress through a course. In a grammatically based course the unit of progression is generally grammatical constructions; each new lesson deals with a new construction. In a functionally based course the unit of progression is language functions; each new lesson deals with new functions. The unit of progression need not be a language component. Long and Crookes's advocacy of a task-based syllabus sees integrated language tasks as units of progression, with progress through the course being marked by the increasing coverage of a range of tasks. The course designer needs to decide what unit of language (words, multi-word units, grammar items functions, discourse types), ideas (topics, themes) or language use (situations, tasks) will be used to decide what goes into each lesson or unit, and how the lessons or units will be sequenced.

If vocabulary is used as the unit of progression, then each unit of the course would systematically introduce new vocabulary according to principles such as frequency and range of occurrence. Some courses like Michael West's *New Method Readers* (1960a), Helen Barnard's *Advanced English Vocabulary* (1972), and David and Jane Willis's *COBUILD English Course* (1988) have done this. Such courses generally combine a 'series' and a 'field' approach to selection and sequencing. In a series approach, the items in a course are ordered according to a principle such as frequency of occurrence, complexity or communicative need. In a field approach, a group of items is chosen and then the course covers them in any order that is convenient, eventually checking that all the items in the field are adequately covered. Courses which use vocabulary as the unit of progression tend to break vocabulary lists into manageable fields, each of a few hundred words, according to frequency, which are then covered in an opportunistic way. Graded reader schemes are a very clear example of this approach to sequencing. For example, the excellent Oxford Bookworms series has six levels, ranging from a vocabulary of 400 headwords at Stage 1 to a vocabulary of 2,500 at Stage 6.

Sinclair and Renouf (1988) present the arguments for a lexical syllabus, surprisingly with little reference to West (1953) whose ideas are remarkably similar. Sinclair and Renouf see a lexical syllabus as describing the content and sequencing aspect of course design and being neutral regarding the methodology by which the course will be taught and how it will be assessed. Sinclair and Renouf make the following points:

1. The most important criterion for deciding if and when an item should be included in a syllabus is frequency (range is not mentioned), not just frequency of word forms but also the frequency of the various uses of those forms and their related inflected forms.

Corpus-based research is the most important procedure underlying the specification of the content and sequencing of a syllabus.

2. Because the majority of the most frequent forms are function words, it is necessary to bring in lower-frequency words in the early stages of a course.

3. Care should be taken in introducing lexical sets because this goes against the criterion of frequent use. West (1951) presents similar and more elaborate arguments in his discussion of what he calls 'catenizing'. Further arguments against the presentation of lexical sets as a way of introducing vocabulary can be found in the research of Higa (1963), Tinkham (1993, 1997) and Waring (1997c) which shows the difficulty caused by learning related items together (Nation, 2000).

4. High-frequency words have many meanings but usually some are much more frequent than the rest. It is therefore useful not only to have information about the frequency of word forms, but also about the frequency of their meanings and uses.

Even where vocabulary is not the unit of progression, there needs to be selection and sequencing of vocabulary in some principled way. An important consideration in sequencing the introduction of vocabulary is the avoidance of interference. In general, courses which rely on units of progression like themes or normal language use in texts will easily avoid such interference. Where vocabulary is grouped according to paradigmatic mental associations as in situations or functions, interference will be a problem.

Like the advocates of other units of progression, Sinclair and Renouf (1988) consider that if vocabulary is the unit of progression, then the appropriate grammar will automatically be met in an appropriate proportion (p. 155). That is, it is not really necessary to check the occurrence of other language and content features. Long and Crookes (1992) make similar statements about the use of tasks as the unit of progression. If the tasks are properly chosen then there will be, as a direct result, suitable representation of vocabulary, grammatical features and functions. A more cautious course designer however may wish to check on the representation and occurrences of high-frequency words in courses which are not lexically based, and a list of high-frequency words is a very useful starting point for doing this – computer programs are now available for quickly doing this (see, for example, Range: www.victoria.ac.nz/lals/staff/paul-nation.aspx, VocabProfile: www.lextutor.ca, and AntWordProfiler: www.antlab.sci.waseda.ac.jp/antwordprofiler_index.html).

The outcome of the content and sequencing stage of course design is an ordered list of items that will form part of the learning goals of the course.

Format and presentation

Format and presentation are the most visible aspects of course design and involve the general approach to vocabulary teaching, the selection of the teaching and learning techniques and their arrangement into a lesson plan.

One of the basic ideas in this book is that there is a place for both direct and indirect vocabulary learning. Opportunities for indirect vocabulary learning should occupy much more time in a language-learning course than direct vocabulary-learning activities. This is in fact just another way of saying that contact with language in use should be given more time than decontextualised activities. The range of contextualised activities of course covers the range of the uses of language. As long as suitable conditions for language learning apply, then indirect vocabulary learning can take place.

As far as high-frequency vocabulary is concerned, the most important principle in handling format and presentation is ensuring that the vocabulary occurs across the four strands of meaning-focused input, language-focused learning, meaning-focused output and fluency development. This not only ensures repetition, but provides opportunity for the different conditions of learning to occur which will eventually result in a good depth of knowledge for each high-frequency word. Approximately 25% of the learning time, both inside and outside class, should be given to each of the four strands (Nation, 2007; Nation and Yamamoto, 2011).

Learning through meaning-focused input and output requires around 98% coverage of the running words in the language comprehended or produced (Hu and Nation, 2000). Carver (1994) argues that for native speakers this should be around 99%. This means that in meaning-focused language use, learners should know most of the language they need for a particular task, but a small percentage (1–5%) should be unfamiliar so that there is an opportunity for these items to be learned. If more than 5% of the running words are unknown, then it is likely that there is no longer any meaning-focused learning because so much attention has to be given to language features. This is why simplified material is so important in language curriculum design. Without it, the two strands of meaning-focused input and output will not operate successfully.

Table 14.4 opposite lists the four strands, the general conditions which support learning in each strand, special vocabulary requirements and the activities that put the conditions and requirements into practice. More information on each of the strands can be found in the relevant chapters of this book. For example, Chapter 4 describes learning through spoken meaning-focused output, and Chapters 7 to 11 describe the development of vocabulary strategies that are an important part of language-focused learning.

As a part of format and presentation, a teacher should evaluate the quality of the teaching and learning techniques used to ensure that conditions like repetition, retrieval, creative (generative) use and thoughtful processing occur. If they do not occur, then the techniques should be adapted or replaced. For the teaching and learning of vocabulary strategies, it is fruitful to design mini-syllabuses that will cover all the important aspects of a particular strategy and provide plenty of repetition and practice to ensure that learners have a good chance of gaining fluent control of the strategy. Using a variety of techniques is one way of keeping learners' interest. The outcome of the format and presentation stage of course design is a format for a lesson and an organised, balanced set of teaching and learning procedures.

Monitoring and assessment

A well-designed course monitors the learners' progress and the quality of their learning. It is extremely important that right at the beginning of a course, the teacher and the learners know what vocabulary level they should be focusing on. This is particularly important for teachers because the way in which they deal with high-frequency words is quite different from the way that they should deal with low-frequency words.

It is also useful to test how well learners have fluent control of the various vocabulary-learning strategies. These can be assessed in two complementary ways. One way is to see how well learners understand the strategies, the steps involved in applying them and the knowledge required at each step. Another way is to see how well learners apply the strategies under conditions of normal use. It may also be useful to look at learners' attitude to each strategy – whether they value it, see its usefulness and are willing to apply it. Some studies (Nation and Moir, 2008) have shown that even though learners understand some strategies, they feel that they are not particularly useful for them.

Assessment can be used to look at progress, and it can also be used to encourage learners. Regular short-term achievement tests can help learners focus on vocabulary learning. These need to be carefully

Table 14.4 *The four strands and their application with a focus on vocabulary*

Strand	General conditions	Vocabulary requirements	Activities and techniques
Meaning-focused input	• Focus on the message • Some unfamiliar items • Understanding • Noticing	• 95%+ coverage (preferably 98%) • Skill at guessing from context • Opportunity to negotiate • Incidental defining and attention drawing	• Reading graded readers • Listening to stories • Communication activities
Language-focused learning	• Focus on language items	• Skill in vocabulary learning strategies • Appropriate teacher focus on high-frequency words, and strategies for low-frequency words	• Direct teaching of vocabulary • Direct learning • Intensive reading • Training in vocabulary strategies
Meaning-focused output	• Focus on the message • Some unfamiliar items • Understanding • Noticing	• 95%+ coverage (preferably 98%) • Encouragement to use unfamiliar items • Supportive input	• Communication activities with written input • Prepared writing • Linked skills
Fluency development	• Focus on the message • Little or no unfamiliar language • Pressure to perform faster	• 99%+ coverage • Repetition	• Reading easy graded readers • Repeated reading • Speed reading • Listening to easy input • 4/3/2 • Rehearsed tasks • 10-minute writing • Linked skills

monitored to make sure that the learners are not just going through the motions to satisfy the teacher.

Table 14.5 opposite outlines the main options available for assessing learners' vocabulary knowledge within a course. In the table, placement tests have not been distinguished as a different type of test as their job can be performed by diagnostic or proficiency tests. Chapter 13 looks at vocabulary testing in more detail.

Figure 14.2 shows the sequence of assessment within a course.

Placement testing	Diagnostic testing	Regular short-term tests	End of course achievement test

Figure 14.2 A timeline for vocabulary assessment in a course

Evaluation

Evaluation tries to determine how good a course is. 'Good' can be defined from various viewpoints: good according to the students, good according to a teacher, good according to the curriculum designer, good according to an outside expert, good according to the business manager of a language programme and so on. Each of these people will be interested in different things and will look at different aspects of the course. The business manager will want to see if the course made a profit and if the learners were satisfied enough to recommend the course to others. The learners will think a course is good if they enjoyed the classes and felt they made relevant progress. Evaluation is thus a very broad topic and could involve looking at all parts of the curriculum design process, asking questions such as these:

- Were the goals reached?
- Did the course take account of the important environment factors?
- Were the learners' needs met?

Table 14.6 on p. 582 presents an evaluation schedule that could be used to see if the vocabulary component of a course is getting informed attention.

A useful form of ongoing evaluation that can reshape the course is the careful observation of the learning activities. In Chapter 3 we examined the Involvement Load Hypothesis, Technique Feature Analysis and the four important questions that teachers can ask:

- What are the goals of the activity?
- What psychological conditions are needed to reach that goal?
- What are the signs that the conditions are occurring?
- What are the design features of the activity that make the conditions likely to occur?

Table 14.5 *Options for the assessment of vocabulary in a course*

Type of assessment	Aims of assessment	Available tests, test formats and length of the test	How often and when administered	Content of the test
Diagnostic	• To determine the appropriate vocabulary level to work on • To place students in an appropriate group	• Vocabulary Levels Test • 20–30 minutes	• Once • Beginning of the course	• Vocabulary sampled from frequency levels
Short-term achievement	• To monitor progress • To motivate learners • To guide changes to the course	• A wide variety of easily prepared formats testing a range of aspects of vocabulary knowledge • 10 minutes	• Every week or fortnight throughout the course	• Vocabulary chosen from course materials or by learners
Long-term achievement	• To determine how well and how much vocabulary has been learned in the course • To help plan the next course	• Multiple-choice • Matching • Yes/No • 30–40 minutes	• Twice • Once at the beginning and once at the end	• Vocabulary chosen from the course materials
Proficiency	• To determine vocabulary size • To place students in an appropriate group	• Vocabulary Size Test • EVST • 30–40 minutes	• Once (or twice) • At the end (and beginning)	• Vocabulary sampled from a dictionary or a frequency count

Table 14.6 *Evaluating the vocabulary component of a language programme*

What to look for	How to look for it	How to include it
Does the teacher know what the learners' vocabulary level and needs are?	• Ask the teacher	• Use the levels test • Interview the learners
Is the programme focusing appropriately on the appropriate level of vocabulary?	• Look at what vocabulary or strategies are being taught	• Decide whether the focus is high frequency, academic, or low frequency vocabulary
Is the vocabulary helpfully sequenced?	• Check that opposites, near synonyms, lexical sets are not being presented in the same lesson	• Use texts and normal use to sequence the vocabulary
Are the skill activities designed to help vocabulary learning?	• Look at the written input to the activities • Ask the teacher	• Include and monitor wanted vocabulary in the written input
Is there a suitable proportion of opportunities to develop fluency with known vocabulary?	• Look at the amount of graded reading, listening to stories, free writing and message based speaking	• Use techniques that develop "well-beaten paths" and "rich maps"
Does the presentation of vocabulary help learning?	• Look for deliberate repetition and spacing • Rate the activities for depth of processing	• Develop teaching and revision cycles • Choose a few deep processing techniques to use often
Are the learners excited about their progress?	• Watch the learners doing tasks • Ask the learners	• Set goals • Give feedback on progress • Keep records

Curriculum design can be seen as a continuing process, with adaptations and improvements being made even while the course is being taught. Good curriculum design involves maintaining a balance between the various parts of the curriculum design process, so that important sources of input to the design are not ignored. The use of the eight-part model – goals, needs, environment, principles, content and sequencing, format and presentation, monitoring and assessment, and evaluation – is an attempt to keep that balance by clearly distinguishing the parts to consider.

Let us now, using the curriculum design framework, look at how learners can be encouraged to take responsibility for their own vocabulary learning.

Autonomy and vocabulary learning

Autonomous learners take control and responsibility for their own learning. This does not necessarily mean that they study alone. It is possible to be an autonomous learner in a strongly teacher-led class – by deciding what should be given the greatest attention and effort, what should be looked at again later, how the material presented should be mentally processed, and how interaction with the teacher and others in the class should be carried out. No matter what the teacher does or what the coursebook presents, ultimately it is the learner who does the learning. The more learners are aware of how learning is best carried out, the better the learning is likely to be. Here we will look at the kind of knowledge that a vocabulary learner needs to become autonomous, how that knowledge can be gained, and how autonomy can be fostered or hindered. It is useful to think of autonomy as relying on three factors: attitude, awareness and capability.

1. *Attitude* refers to the need for the learner to want to take control and responsibility for learning. This is one of the hardest aspects of autonomy to develop and yet it is the most crucial. Nation and Moir (2008) found in their study of vocabulary learners that although most of them knew what they should do and knew that what they were doing was not efficient, they were reluctant to make the needed changes. Immediate pressures, the influence of past behaviour and the effect of teacher demands easily overrode the wish to take control of their own learning.
2. *Awareness* is the need for the learner to be conscious of what approaches are being taken, to reflect on their effects and to consider other approaches. Some writers on autonomy consider that all autonomous learning must involve metacognitive awareness (there

is no autonomy without metacognition). In the development of autonomy, reflection is a very powerful tool and this alone may be sufficient to justify seeing metacognitive awareness as an important aspect of autonomy.

3. *Capability* refers to the need for the learner to possess the skills and knowledge to be autonomous in a particular area of study.

The remainder of this chapter discusses the knowledge and skills needed to be an autonomous vocabulary learner. The discussion is organised according to principles of vocabulary learning, for example, the important principle that learners should direct their attention to the high-frequency words of the language. The reason for using such principles as the basis for a discussion of autonomy is that principles provide an opportunity for dialogue about learning, for personal reflection and for a systematic coverage of a field of knowledge. The vocabulary-learning principles will be organised according to the major parts of the syllabus design process, namely: (1) goals; (2) content and sequencing; (3) format and presentation; and (4) monitoring and assessment.

Although a list of principles is provided, to truly encourage autonomy, learners will later need to reflect on these principles on the basis of experience and to confirm, reject, modify or add to them. A similar list of principles for L1 learning can be found in Graves (1987).

The goals of vocabulary learning

Principle 1: Learners should know what vocabulary to learn, what to learn about it, how to learn it, how to put it to use and how to see how well it has been learned and used.

Because this principle represents the goals of vocabulary learning, it is in essence a summary of most of the other vocabulary-learning principles. It includes the three parts of content and sequencing, format and presentation, and monitoring and assessment.

Principle 2: Learners should continue to increase their vocabulary size and enrich the words they already know.

Whereas Principle 1 focuses on the nature of vocabulary learning, Principle 2 focuses on the results.

What should be learned and in what order?

Principle 3: Learners should use word frequency and personal need to determine what vocabulary should be learned.

This principle means that learners should be learning high-frequency words before low-frequency words, except where personal need and interest give importance to what otherwise would be low-frequency words. A learner with academic goals should be focusing on words in the Academic Word List once the general service high-frequency words are known.

Information about word frequency is now readily accessible. The COBUILD Dictionary tags the higher-frequency words of English. It uses a useful system of five frequency bands which allows learners to distinguish high-frequency words from those of moderate and low frequency. The idea of indicating frequency in learners' dictionaries is an excellent one and a major step forward. Longman's Dictionary of Contemporary English and the Macmillan English Dictionary for Advanced Learners also mark the frequency of words. It may be possible, with a little practice and feedback, for learners to develop a feeling for what is high frequency and what is low frequency. This may be easier for speakers of other European languages to do for English vocabulary than for, say, speakers of Asian languages. Eaton's (1940) comparison of English, French, German and Spanish word frequency lists showed very close correspondences between the frequency levels of words referring to similar concepts in the four languages. The major problem in developing an intuitive feel for word frequency comes with synonyms like start, begin, commence. Generally, however, in English there is a tendency for shorter words to be more frequent than longer words, and for words of Anglo-Saxon origin to be more frequent than the morphologically more complex words from French, Latin or Greek. This area of developing learners' intuitions about word frequency is unresearched. However, for the 2,000 high-frequency words and the Academic Word List, teachers can usefully provide lists for learners to use as checklists that they can refer to as a frequency guide.

Hirsh and Nation (1992: 695) found that the more times a word occurred in a novel, the more likely it was to be found in other novels. If learners notice words recurring in their reading, this should suggest to them that the word is worth learning.

There are now computer programs which quickly turn a text into a word frequency list. Learners can get quite excited about the results of this when they see the very high coverage of the text provided by a small number of high-frequency words, and the large number of low-frequency words needed to cover even a small proportion of the text. This visual demonstration can be a useful way of underlining the importance of the high-frequency/low-frequency distinction (see the Frequency program which can be downloaded with the Range program on Paul Nation's website).

McKenzie (1990) suggests that learners should focus on words that they have met before, but which they only partially understand. This has the effect of making sure that the words are not truly low-frequency words but are words that have been repeated and are likely to be met again. Carroll and Mordaunt (1991: 24) suggest that the words chosen for study should not only be partially known but should be ones that the learners can think of themselves using soon. McKenzie, and Carroll and Mordaunt, drawing on Pauk (1984), call these words 'frontier words' because they are on the boundary or frontier of the learner's present vocabulary knowledge.

Principle 4: Learners should be aware of what is involved in knowing a word and should be able to find that information about particular words.

Knowing a word involves knowing a wide range of features. At the most basic this involves being familiar with the written and spoken forms of the word and being able to associate a meaning with those forms. While this kind of knowledge is critically important, it is only a part of what is involved in knowing a word. Other kinds of knowledge include: being able to use it grammatically correctly in a sentence with suitable collocations; being able to interpret and create other members of its word family by using inflectional and derivational affixes; being aware of restrictions on the use of the word for cultural, geographical, stylistic or register reasons; and being aware of the range of meanings and associations the word has. For some words, much of this knowledge will be highly predictable from knowledge of the learners' first language and their knowledge of the subsystems of English. For other words, there will be a lot of new learning.

Learners need to be aware of the different things there are to know about a word. This awareness needs to be based on some organised system so that learners can easily remember what to look for and can easily check for gaps in their knowledge. One system is to use the diagram outlined in Table 2.1 in Chapter 2 on what is involved in knowing a word. This has the advantage of having a simple three-part division with each successive part being more elaborate. It can be used as a means of recording information about words. The 'word spider' (McComish, 1990) uses similar divisions.

Learners can be alerted to the importance of this range of information about words by feedback on errors they make in vocabulary use, by reporting to others on new words they have met (Mhone, 1988) and by comparing information on L2 words with the corresponding L1 word. In order to gather this information for themselves, learners need to become skilful and critical in their dictionary use, and need to be able to gather information from seeing words in context. This use of context to gain information on grammar, collocation and derivatives could make use of computer-based concordance searches (Descamps, 1992; McKay, 1980; Stevens, 1991). Developing skill in gathering this kind of information can begin as a co-operative activity in groups. The group discussion and analysis can act as a conscious-ness-raising activity (Ellis, 1992) encouraging reflection and metacog-nitive awareness of what is involved in knowing a word.

Principle 5: Learners should be familiar with the generalisable lan-guage systems that lie behind vocabulary use.

In spite of the irregularity of many aspects of language use, there are regular patterns that can be used to help comprehend and produce language. These patterns exist at all levels – orthographic, phonologi-cal, morphological, collocational, grammatical and discourse. Because knowledge of these patterns allows learners to comprehend and produce language that they have not met in that exact form before, these patterns are much more important than the exceptions and deserve more attention from the teacher and learner. Here are some examples of patterns that affect vocabulary use.

- *Spelling*. The rule governing free and checked vowels affects a lot of English spelling, including the doubling of consonants and the use of final silent e. Let us illustrate the rule using the written vowel i. The free pronunciation of i is /ai/, the checked pronunciation is /i/. The free pronunciation usually occurs in the following pattern (C = consonant, V = vowel):

  iCV   (the vowel may be final silent e)   dine
  dining

  The checked pronunciation usually occurs in the following patterns:

  iC   (where C is the final letter in a word)   din
  iCCV   dinner
  spinning

Note that when -ing is added to spin, the n is doubled so that i can keep its checked pronunciation.

The rule governing free and checked vowels only applies to stressed syllables. Not only i, but also a, e, o and u have free and checked pro-nunciations and follow the same rule. See Nation (2009: Appendix 1) for a list of sound-spelling correspondences).

- *Pronunciation*. There is a grammar of sounds that describes the order and sounds that can occur in consonant clusters in English. For example, /spr/ is a permitted initial cluster, while /srp/ is not.

- *Word building.* There is a small group of very frequent, regular affixes which can be used to create new words (Bauer and Nation, 1993). These include -able, -er, -ish, -less, -ly, -ness, -th, -y, non-, un-.
- *Collocation.* Sinclair's (1991) corpus-based studies of collocation show that there are general descriptions that can be used to characterise the collocates of a particular word. For example, set about typically refers to 'a subsidiary aim within a grander design. 'We set about X in order, ultimately to achieve Y' " (p. 76).

In some cases, learners can gain information about these patterns through reading descriptions of them, for example in grammar books written for learners of English. In other cases, they will need to rely on explanation from a teacher. The most important requirement is the awareness that there are patterns and an interest in looking for the patterns. This awareness and interest can often be stimulated by activities which use data in the form of examples which have to be classified or analysed. Many of the consciousness-raising activities described by Ellis (1992) are like this. Learners also need to know which books containing descriptions of English are the most useful and accessible for them, and need to gain skill and confidence in using them. When learners meet a new word, they should reflect on the ways it is similar to the words they already know. This reflection need not be restricted to the second language, but should also involve comparison with the first language. Many learners expect that English courses will teach them grammar and other descriptive aspects of the language, and they feel somewhat cheated if a course does not do this. This perceived need can be usefully satisfied by encouraging learners to discover the frequent regular patterns that lie behind language use.

Learning procedures

Principle 6: Learners should know how to make the most effective use of direct, decontextualised learning procedures.

There has been a very large amount of research on the effectiveness of direct decontextualised learning of vocabulary, even though many teachers and writers about language learning have negative attitudes towards it. As the only kind of vocabulary learning, it is insufficient, but when it is used along with message-focused incidental learning it can be extremely effective.

There are several sub-principles that can guide this kind of learning. These can be a very useful starting point for reflection on the effectiveness of the sub-principles themselves, because learners can easily carry out simple experiments on themselves by applying and not applying the sub-principles to their learning, and comparing the results. Carrying out and discussing these little experiments in class is a first step to personal reflection on learning.

Research on vocabulary learning provides useful indications of how learning from vocabulary cards can be done most effectively (see Chapter 11).

1. Retrieve rather than recognise.
2. Use appropriately sized groups of cards.
3. Space the repetitions.
4. Repeat the words aloud or to yourself.
5. Process the words thoughtfully.
6. Avoid interference.
7. Avoid a serial learning effect.
8. Use context where this helps.

Because there are several sub-principles, it is worth giving plenty of time to developing an understanding of them and observing them in action. This can be done in several ways.

- Learners trial a principle and report on it to the class.
- Learners observe others learning and comment on what they see, and interview the learners.
- Learners organise simple experiments with one group applying a principle and the other group deliberately not applying it. For example, one group can learn unrelated words and another learns closely related words. Or, one group learns with cards and the other learns from a printed list.
- Learners report on successful and unsuccessful learning.
- Learners are tested on their understanding and application of the principles.

Learners may be aware of principles and yet not apply them. Counselling and class discussion needs to examine the causes of this and see what can be done.

Principle 7: Vocabulary learning needs to operate across the four strands of meaning-focused input, language-focused learning, meaning-focused output, and fluency development.

There is a feeling among some teachers that focusing on vocabulary and grammar out of context is detrimental to learning. The research evidence does not support this feeling, and in addition it reflects a view that there is only one way to do things. It is much more effective to see the many approaches to learning as being complementary to each other, each bringing different strengths that together can provide balanced support for learning.

One way of dividing up the approaches is to distinguish them on the basis of the conditions for learning that they set up. Table 14.7 opposite outlines these approaches.

In terms of vocabulary learning, a well-balanced vocabulary course has a roughly equal proportion of time given to each of these four strands. This can be expressed as four sub-principles. Nation and Yamamoto (2011) show how the four strands can be applied to learning without a teacher. Nation (2011) describes his ideal vocabulary course where the four strands are the major organising principle.

1. Learners need to have the opportunity to meet and learn vocabulary incidentally through meaning-focused listening and through extensive reading of material at a suitable level of difficulty.
2. This means that autonomous learners need to know ways to obtain comprehensible input: interacting with learners at a level roughly similar to theirs; interacting with native speakers who are sensitive to their level of knowledge of the language; preparing for communicative activity before it occurs; and choosing reading and listening material that suits their level of knowledge.
3. Learners need to be able to effectively choose and learn vocabulary using word cards and other decontextualised ways of learning.
4. Here decontextualised means that the vocabulary learning is not occurring in normal use, but is deliberately focused on words as part of the language system. The focus is directed towards their spelling, pronunciation, grammar, meaning, use and so on, and the linguistic rules that lie behind those parts of the language systems.
5. Learners need to be encouraged – and have the opportunity – to use vocabulary in speaking and writing where their major focus is on communicating messages.
6. Having to produce vocabulary to achieve communicative goals helps learners stretch their knowledge of words and become aware of gaps in their knowledge. It helps them gain control of the aspects of productive knowledge that differ from the knowledge required for receptive use. Autonomous learners need to be brave enough to seek out opportunities for speaking and writing, and need to know how to use those situations to set up the conditions that can lead to successful learning.
7. Learners need to have the chance to use known vocabulary both receptively and productively under conditions that help them increase the fluency with which they can access and use that vocabulary.

Table 14.7 *The four strands of a language course*

Strand	Conditions for learning	Example activities
Meaning-focused input	• Focus on the message. • Include a small number of unfamiliar items. • Draw attention to the new items.	• Extensive graded reading • Listening to stories • Working with familiar content
Language-focused learning	• Focus on language features (vocabulary, structures …). • Do deliberate repeated retrieval of the items.	• Learning from word cards • Grammar exercises • Read difficult text
Meaning-focused output	• Focus on the message. • Include a small number of new items.	• Communication activities • Research and write
Fluency development	• Focus on the message. • Work with completely familiar material. • Work at a higher than normal speed. • Do a large quantity of language use.	• Repeated reading • Repeated speaking on familiar topics • Graded reading

Learners not only need to know vocabulary, they need to be able to use it fluently. Decontextualised learning can rapidly increase vocabulary size, but message-focused language use with very easy language and easy communicative demands is needed to achieve fluency. In addition, there needs to be some pressure on the learners or some encouragement to perform at a faster than normal speed.

It is not too difficult for learners to arrange their own fluency activities. In reading, learners can work through a speed reading course which has strict vocabulary control, read graded readers at a level below their normal comfort level of reading, and reread the same material several times. While doing this learners need to be aware that their goal is to increase speed. They should also reflect on how the language unit that they give attention to changes as fluency develops. From having to become fluent at decoding individual letters (particularly if the English writing system differs from that of the first language), they next move to the speedy recognition of words, and then to the anticipation of phrases.

Learners can take control of the development of their writing fluency by writing on very easy topics, by writing on closely related topics, and by writing on the same topic several times. They can also write on topics that they have already read about and discussed, and on topics that relate closely to their own training and experience.

Learners can assume control of their listening and speaking fluency development by: setting up repeated opportunities to do the same kind of speaking; getting a teacher or friend to give them repeated practice with important words, phrases and sentences (numbers, dates, greetings and polite phrases, description of yourself, your job, your recent experiences, your country etc.); and rehearsal just before speaking. It is usually not too difficult to anticipate the things that learners will need to talk about most often, and with the help of a teacher or friend these can be written out, checked for correctness, and then memorised and rehearsed to a high degree of fluency. The items in Nation and Crabbe's (1991) survival syllabus provide a useful starting point.

It is not easy to gain a suitable balance across the four strands of a language course. Learners need to make sure that the vocabulary that has been deliberately studied is also used for meaningful communication wherever possible and is brought to a suitable level of fluency. Similarly, vocabulary development through extensive reading needs to be stabilised and enriched through the deliberate study of words, affixes, and lexical sets.

Checking learning

Principle 8: Learners should be aware of and excited by their progress in vocabulary learning.

It is often difficult for learners to realise that they are making progress in language learning. Learning a language is a long-term task which is often marked by frustration and disappointment when successful communication does not occur. Learners need to find ways of monitoring their progress and should use these when they feel the need for encouragement. There are several ways in which learners can take control of this in their vocabulary learning.

1. Keeping a record of how many words have been learned. There are several ways of doing this. One method is to keep a record of the packs of vocabulary cards that have been used for direct study. If the words already learned are kept in packs of 50, this becomes an easy task. Looking back over these familiar words can give a feeling of achievement. Another way to keep a record of quantity is to look through a dictionary and see how many words per page are known. If a frequency graded list is available, this can be used as a self-administered test to chart progress.
2. Keeping a record of how quickly learning can occur. For example, after making a pack of 50 vocabulary cards to study, learners could record how much time and how many repetitions are needed to learn 80% or more of the words in the pack. The results will be surprising.
3. Making a list of situations and topics where the second language is used, and ticking these off as a certain degree of success is achieved. Table 14.8 overleaf contains a sample list.

   Using such a list makes learning more goal directed, and breaks down a big task into smaller short-term goals. The list can also be used for a record of fluency development. An item can be ticked off when the needed vocabulary and phrases are known, and it can be ticked off again when the knowledge of these words and phrases are known to a high degree of fluency. For example, when buying stamps at the Post Office it is possible to know all the necessary numbers and words. Further learning, however, is needed to quickly understand the numbers when the clerk tells you how much the stamps cost and to deal with unexpected questions. This can be practised and success noted.
4. Recording examples of their language use at regular intervals. These examples may be tape recordings or videos of performance, examples of written work, or texts read and understood. Looking back over earlier performance can provide reassurance that progress has been

Table 14.8 *A checklist of common situations*

1. Giving information about yourself and your family
    * name
    * address
    * phone
    * partner and family
    * length of residence
    * origin
    * job
    * age

2. Asking others for similar information

3. Meeting people
    * greetings
    * talking about the weather
    * inviting for a meal etc.
    * telling the time and day
    * saying what you like
    * saying you are sorry
    * joining a club

4. Going shopping
    * finding goods
    * asking for a quantity
    * understanding prices

5. Using important services
    * post office
    * bank
    * public telephone
    * police
    * garage

6. Asking how to get to places

7. Telling others directions
    * directions
    * distance and time
    * using public transport

8. Taking care of your health
    * contacting a doctor
    * reporting illness
    * describing previous illness and medical conditions
    * calling emergency services

9. Describing your home, town and country

10. Asking others for similar information
- house/flat and furniture
- features of the town
- features of your country

11. Describing your job

12. Asking others about their job
- job
- place
- conditions
- travelling to work

13. Finding out how to get a job
- kind of job
- where to look
- what to do

14. Finding food and drink
- getting attention
- using a menu
- ordering a meal
- offering food
- praising the food
- finding a toilet
- giving thanks

15. Taking part in sport and entertainment
- saying when you are free
- buying tickets
- say what you like and do not like doing

made. If a course book is used, then going back over very early lessons that once were difficult can give a feeling of progress. A further way of charting progress is to ask a native speaker friend to act as a monitor of progress by evaluating language use at regular intervals.

The principles outlined here have been focused on vocabulary, but they clearly apply more widely. Learners should be encouraged to reflect on these principles both for their vocabulary learning and any other kind of learning that they are engaged in. Appreciating the breadth of application of the principles is a useful step towards valuing the principles and coming to a deeper understanding of them. Taking personal control of learning is a challenge. It is a challenge to the learner to gain the attitude, awareness and capability required for control. It is also a challenge for the teacher to help foster these three requirements while stepping back from control.

References

Barnard, H. (1972). *Advanced English Vocabulary*. Rowley, MA: Newbury House.

Bauer, L. and Nation, I. S. P. (1993). Word families. *International Journal of Lexicography*, **6**, 4, 253–79.

Carroll, M. C. and Mordaunt, O. G. (1991). The frontier method of vocabulary practice. *TESOL Journal*, **1**, 1, 23–6.

Carver, R. P. (1994). Percentage of unknown vocabulary words in text as a function of the relative difficulty of the text: implications for instruction. *Journal of Reading Behavior*, **26**, 4, 413–37.

Descamps, J. L. (1992). Towards classroom concordancing. In Arnaud, P. J. L. and Bejoint, H. (eds.), *Vocabulary and Applied Linguistics* (pp. 167–81). London: Macmillan.

Eaton, H. S. (1940). *An English-French-German-Spanish Word Frequency Dictionary*. New York: Dover Publications.

Ellis, R. (1992). Grammar teaching: Practice or consciousness-raising. In Ellis, R. (ed.), *Second Language Acquisition and Second Language Pedagogy*. Clevedon, Avon: Multilingual Matters.

Graves, M. F. (1987). The roles of instruction in fostering vocabulary development. In McKeown, M. and Curtis, M. (eds.), *The Nature of Vocabulary Acquisition* (pp. 165–84). Mahwah, NJ: Lawrence Erlbaum Associates.

Higa, M. (1963). Interference effects of intralist word relationships in verbal learning. *Journal of Verbal Learning and Verbal Behavior*, **2**, 170–75.

Hirsh, D. and Nation, P. (1992). What vocabulary size is needed to read unsimplified texts for pleasure? *Reading in a Foreign Language*, **8**, 2, 689–96.

Hu, M. and Nation, I. S. P. (2000). Vocabulary density and reading comprehension. *Reading in a Foreign Language*, **13**, 1, 403–30.

Laufer, B. and Nation, P. (1995). Vocabulary size and use: Lexical richness in L2 written production. *Applied Linguistics*, **16**, 3, 307–22.

Long, M. H. and Crookes, G. (1992). Three approaches to task-based syllabus design. *TESOL Quarterly*, **26**, 1, 27–56.

McComish, J. (1990). The word spider: A technique for academic vocabulary learning in curriculum areas. *Guidelines*, **12**, 1, 26–36.

McKay, S. L. (1980). Developing vocabulary materials with a computer corpus. *RELC Journal*, **11**, 2, 77–87.

McKenzie, M. (1990). Letting lexis come from the learner: A word in the hand is worth two in the bush. *English Teaching Forum*, **28**, 1, 13–16.

Meara, P. and Jones, G. (1987). Tests of vocabulary size in English as a foreign language. *Polyglot*, **8**, Fiche 1.

Mhone, Y. W. (1988). "... It's My Word, Teacher!" *English Teaching Forum*, **26**, 2, 48–51.

Nation, I. S. P. (2000). Learning vocabulary in lexical sets: Dangers and guidelines. *TESOL Journal*, **9**, 2, 6–10.

Nation, I. S. P. (2006). How large a vocabulary is needed for reading and listening? *Canadian Modern Language Review*, **63**, 1, 59–82.

Nation, I. S. P. (2007). The four strands. *Innovation in Language Learning and Teaching*, **1**, 1, 1–12.

Nation, I. S. P. (2009). *Teaching ESL/EFL Reading and Writing*. New York: Routledge.

Nation, I. S. P. (2011). My ideal vocabulary teaching course. In Macalister, J. and Nation, I. S. P. (eds.), *Case Studies in Language Curriculum Design* (pp. 49–62). New York: Routledge.

Nation, I. S. P. and Macalister, J. (2010). *Language Curriculum Design*. New York: Routledge.

Nation, I. S. P. and Moir, J. (2008). Vocabulary learning and the good language learner. In Griffiths, C. (ed.), *Lessons from Good language Learners* (pp. 159–73). Cambridge: Cambridge University Press.

Nation, I. S. P. and Yamamoto, A. (2011). Applying the four strands to language learning. *International Journal of Innovation in English Language Teaching and Research*, **1**, 2, 1–15.

Nation, P. and Crabbe, D. (1991). A survival language learning syllabus for foreign travel. *System*, **19**, 3, 191–201.

O'Dell, F. (1997). Incorporating vocabulary into the syllabus. In Schmitt, N. and McCarthy, M. (eds.), *Vocabulary: Description, Acquisition and Pedagogy* (pp. 258–78). Cambridge: Cambridge University Press.

Pauk, W. (1984). *How to Study in College*. Boston: Houghton Mifflin.

Sinclair, J. M. (1991). *Corpus, Concordance, Collocation*. Oxford: Oxford University Press.

Sinclair, J. M. and Renouf, A. (1988). A lexical syllabus for language learning. In Carter, R. and McCarthy, M. (eds.), *Vocabulary and Language Teaching* (pp. 140–60). London: Longman.

Stevens, V. (1991). Classroom concordancing: Vocabulary materials derived from relevant, authentic text. *English for Specific Purposes*, **10**, 35–46.

Sutarsyah, C., Nation, P. and Kennedy, G. (1994). How useful is EAP vocabulary for ESP? A corpus based study. *RELC Journal*, **25**, 2, 34–50.

Tinkham, T. (1989). Rote learning, attitudes, and abilities: A comparison of Japanese and American students. *TESOL Quarterly*, **23**, 4, 695–8.

Tinkham, T. (1993). The effect of semantic clustering on the learning of second language vocabulary. *System*, **21**, 3, 371–80.

Tinkham, T. (1997). The effects of semantic and thematic clustering on the learning of second language vocabulary. *Second Language Research*, **13**, 2, 138–63.

Waring, R. (1997c). The negative effects of learning words in semantic sets: A replication. *System*, **25**, 2, 261–74.

West, M. (1932). *New Method Readers*. Standard edition. London: Longman.

West, M. (1951). Catenizing. *ELT Journal*, **5**, 6, 147–51.

West, M. (1953). *A General Service List of English Words*. London: Longman, Green & Co.

West, M. (1956). In the classroom: 2: The problem of pupil talking time. *ELT Journal*, **10**, 2, 71–3.

Appendices

1. Headwords of the Academic Word List

This list contains the headwords of the families in the *Academic Word List*. The numbers indicate the sublist of the *Academic Word List*. For example, *abandon* and its family members are in Sublist 8 of the *Academic Word List*. Sublist 1 contains the most frequent words and Sublist 10 the least frequent. The list comes from Coxhead (2000).

abandon	8	amend	5	automate	8
abstract	6	analogy	9	available	1
academy	5	analyse	1	aware	5
access	4	annual	4	behalf	9
accommodate	9	anticipate	9	benefit	1
accompany	8	apparent	4	bias	8
accumulate	8	append	8	bond	6
accurate	6	appreciate	8	brief	6
achieve	2	approach	1	bulk	9
acknowledge	6	appropriate	2	capable	6
acquire	2	approximate	4	capacity	5
adapt	7	arbitrary	8	category	2
adequate	4	area	1	cease	9
adjacent	10	aspect	2	challenge	5
adjust	5	assemble	10	channel	7
administer	2	assess	1	chapter	2
adult	7	assign	6	chart	8
advocate	7	assist	2	chemical	7
affect	2	assume	1	circumstance	3
aggregate	6	assure	9	cite	6
aid	7	attach	6	civil	4
albeit	10	attain	9	clarify	8
allocate	6	attitude	4	classic	7
alter	5	attribute	4	clause	5
alternative	3	author	6	code	4
ambiguous	8	authority	1	coherent	9

598

coincide	9	contrast	4	distort	9
collapse	10	contribute	3	distribute	1
colleague	10	controversy	9	diverse	6
commence	9	convene	3	document	3
comment	3	converse	9	domain	6
commission	2	convert	7	domestic	4
commit	4	convince	10	dominate	3
commodity	8	cooperate	6	draft	5
communicate	4	coordinate	3	drama	8
community	2	core	3	duration	9
compatible	9	corporate	3	dynamic	7
compensate	3	correspond	3	economy	1
compile	10	couple	7	edit	6
complement	8	create	1	element	2
complex	2	credit	2	eliminate	7
component	3	criteria	3	emerge	4
compound	5	crucial	8	emphasis	3
comprehensive	7	culture	2	empirical	7
comprise	7	currency	8	enable	5
compute	2	cycle	4	encounter	10
conceive	10	data	1	energy	5
concentrate	4	debate	4	enforce	5
concept	1	decade	7	enhance	6
conclude	2	decline	5	enormous	10
concurrent	9	deduce	3	ensure	3
conduct	2	define	1	entity	5
confer	4	definite	7	environment	1
confine	9	demonstrate	3	equate	2
confirm	7	denote	8	equip	7
conflict	5	deny	7	equivalent	5
conform	8	depress	10	erode	9
consent	3	derive	1	error	4
consequent	2	design	2	establish	1
considerable	3	despite	4	estate	6
consist	1	detect	8	estimate	1
constant	3	deviate	8	ethic	9
constitute	1	device	9	ethnic	4
constrain	3	devote	9	evaluate	2
construct	2	differentiate	7	eventual	8
consult	5	dimension	4	evident	1
consume	2	diminish	9	evolve	5
contact	5	discrete	5	exceed	6
contemporary	8	discriminate	6	exclude	3
context	1	displace	8	exhibit	8
contract	1	display	6	expand	5
contradict	8	dispose	7	expert	6
contrary	7	distinct	2	explicit	6

exploit	8	impact	2	isolate	7
export	1	implement	4	issue	1
expose	5	implicate	4	item	2
external	5	implicit	8	job	4
extract	7	imply	3	journal	2
facilitate	5	impose	4	justify	3
factor	1	incentive	6	label	4
feature	2	incidence	6	labour	1
federal	6	incline	10	layer	3
fee	6	income	1	lecture	6
file	7	incorporate	6	legal	1
final	2	index	6	legislate	1
finance	1	indicate	1	levy	10
finite	7	individual	1	liberal	5
flexible	6	induce	8	licence	5
fluctuate	8	inevitable	8	likewise	10
focus	2	infer	7	link	3
format	9	infrastructure	8	locate	3
formula	1	inherent	9	logic	5
forthcoming	10	inhibit	6	maintain	2
found	9	initial	3	major	1
foundation	7	initiate	6	manipulate	8
framework	3	injure	2	manual	9
function	1	innovate	7	margin	5
fund	3	input	6	mature	9
fundamental	5	insert	7	maximise	3
furthermore	6	insight	9	mechanism	4
gender	6	inspect	8	media	7
generate	5	instance	3	mediate	9
generation	5	institute	2	medical	5
globe	7	instruct	6	medium	9
goal	4	integral	9	mental	5
grade	7	integrate	4	method	1
grant	4	integrity	10	migrate	6
guarantee	7	intelligence	6	military	9
guideline	8	intense	8	minimal	9
hence	4	interact	3	minimise	8
hierarchy	7	intermediate	9	minimum	6
highlight	8	internal	4	ministry	6
hypothesis	4	interpret	1	minor	3
identical	7	interval	6	mode	7
identify	1	intervene	7	modify	5
ideology	7	intrinsic	10	monitor	5
ignorance	6	invest	2	motive	6
illustrate	3	investigate	4	mutual	9
image	5	invoke	10	negate	3
immigrate	3	involve	1	network	5

neutral	6	precede	6	rely	3
nevertheless	6	precise	5	remove	3
nonetheless	10	predict	4	require	1
norm	9	predominant	8	research	1
normal	2	preliminary	9	reside	2
notion	5	presume	6	resolve	4
notwithstanding	10	previous	2	resource	2
nuclear	8	primary	2	respond	1
objective	5	prime	5	restore	8
obtain	2	principal	4	restrain	9
obvious	4	principle	1	restrict	2
occupy	4	prior	4	retain	4
occur	1	priority	7	reveal	6
odd	10	proceed	1	revenue	5
offset	8	process	1	reverse	7
ongoing	10	professional	4	revise	8
option	4	prohibit	7	revolution	9
orient	5	project	4	rigid	9
outcome	3	promote	4	role	1
output	4	proportion	3	route	9
overall	4	prospect	8	scenario	9
overlap	9	protocol	9	schedule	8
overseas	6	psychology	5	scheme	3
panel	10	publication	7	scope	6
paradigm	7	publish	3	section	1
paragraph	8	purchase	2	sector	1
parallel	4	pursue	5	secure	2
parameter	4	qualitative	9	seek	2
participate	2	quote	7	select	2
partner	3	radical	8	sequence	3
passive	9	random	8	series	4
perceive	2	range	2	sex	3
percent	1	ratio	5	shift	3
period	1	rational	6	significant	1
persist	10	react	3	similar	1
perspective	5	recover	6	simulate	7
phase	4	refine	9	site	2
phenomenon	7	regime	4	so-called	10
philosophy	3	region	2	sole	7
physical	3	register	3	somewhat	7
plus	8	regulate	2	source	1
policy	1	reinforce	8	specific	1
portion	9	reject	5	specify	3
pose	10	relax	9	sphere	9
positive	2	release	7	stable	5
potential	2	relevant	2	statistic	4
practitioner	8	reluctance	10	status	4

straightforward	10	team	9	undergo	10
strategy	2	technical	3	underlie	6
stress	4	technique	3	undertake	4
structure	1	technology	3	uniform	8
style	5	temporary	9	unify	9
submit	7	tense	8	unique	7
subordinate	9	terminate	8	utilise	6
subsequent	4	text	2	valid	3
subsidy	6	theme	8	vary	1
substitute	5	theory	1	vehicle	8
successor	7	thereby	8	version	5
sufficient	3	thesis	7	via	8
sum	4	topic	7	violate	9
summary	4	trace	6	virtual	8
supplement	9	tradition	2	visible	7
survey	2	transfer	2	vision	9
survive	7	transform	6	visual	8
suspend	9	transit	5	volume	3
sustain	5	transmit	7	voluntary	7
symbol	5	transport	6	welfare	5
tape	6	trend	5	whereas	5
target	5	trigger	9	whereby	10
task	3	ultimate	7	widespread	8

2. Vocabulary levels dictation test

An account of the making and validation of equivalent forms of this test along with how to use and mark the test can be found in Fountain and Nation (2000).

INTRODUCTION

The <u>demand</u> for <u>food</u>/<u>becomes</u> <u>more</u> <u>important</u>/as the <u>number</u> of <u>people</u> in the <u>world</u>/<u>continues</u> to <u>increase</u>. /

PARAGRAPH 1:

The <u>duty</u> to <u>care</u>/for the <u>members</u> of a <u>society</u>/<u>lies</u> with those who <u>control</u> it,/but <u>sometimes</u> <u>governments</u>/<u>refuse</u> to <u>deal</u> with this <u>problem</u>/in a <u>wise way</u>,/and <u>fail</u> to <u>provide</u> <u>enough</u> to <u>eat</u>./When this <u>occurs</u> many <u>ordinary</u> people <u>suffer</u>. /

PARAGRAPH 2:

Often their <u>economic</u> <u>situation</u>/does not <u>permit</u> them to <u>create</u>/ a <u>system</u> of <u>regular</u> <u>supply</u>./When food is <u>scarce</u>,/the <u>pattern</u> of <u>distribution</u>/is <u>generally</u> not <u>uniform</u>./In some <u>areas</u> <u>production</u>/is <u>sufficient</u> to <u>satisfy</u> the needs of the <u>population</u>./In others <u>pockets</u> of <u>poverty</u> <u>exist</u>. /

PARAGRAPH 3:

Using as their <u>basis</u> the <u>research</u> of <u>experts</u>/to discover the <u>factors</u>/in the <u>previous</u> <u>failures</u> to <u>prevent</u> <u>starving</u>,/those in <u>positions</u> of <u>leadership</u>/should <u>institute</u> <u>reforms</u>./Unless <u>ancient</u> <u>traditions</u> of <u>administration</u> are <u>overthrown</u>/the <u>existence</u> of the coming <u>generations</u> of <u>mankind</u>/will be <u>threatened</u>. /

PARAGRAPH 4:

Though it is <u>reasonable</u> to <u>presume</u> that a <u>reduction</u> of <u>consumption</u>/could be <u>recommended</u> in <u>regions</u> of <u>prosperity</u>,/if this was <u>enforced</u> it would meet <u>opposition</u>/with thousands <u>rebelling</u>/in their <u>determination</u> to <u>maintain</u> their <u>independence</u>/from those <u>politicians</u> <u>dictating</u> to them./The <u>selection</u> of a <u>differently</u> <u>devised</u> <u>procedure</u>/would be <u>essential</u>. /

3. Function words

This list of function words includes 320 word types and 161 word families. Most of the words occur in the most frequent 2,000 words of English and these are unmarked in the following list. The words in **bold** type are in the *Academic Word List* (Coxhead, 2000), and the words in *italics* are mid-frequency words (except for the low-frequency words *thrice* and *whither*) which are not in the *General Service List* (West, 1953) or the *Academic Word List*.

again ago almost already also always anywhere back else even ever everywhere far **hence** here *hither* how however near nearby nearly never not now nowhere often only quite rather sometimes somewhere soon still then thence there therefore *thither* thus today tomorrow too underneath very when *whence* where *whither* why yes yesterday yet

Auxiliary verbs (including contractions)

am are aren't be been being can can't could couldn't did didn't do does doesn't doing done don't get gets getting got had hadn't has hasn't have haven't having he'd he'll he's I'd I'll I'm is isn't it's I've may might must mustn't ought oughtn't shall shan't she'd she'll she's should shouldn't that's they'd they'll they're was wasn't we'd we'll were we're weren't we've will won't would wouldn't you'd you'll you're you've

Prepositions/conjunctions (one category since there is some overlap)

about above after along although among and around as at before below beneath beside between beyond but by down during except for from if in into near nor of off on or out over round since so than that though through till to towards under unless until up **whereas** while with within without

Determiners/pronouns (omitting archaic thou, thee, etc.)

a all an another any anybody anything both each either enough every everybody everyone everything few fewer he her hers herself him himself his I it its itself less many me mine more most much my myself neither no nobody none no one nothing other others our ours ourselves she some somebody someone something such that the their theirs them themselves these they this those us we what which who whom whose you your yours yourself yourselves

Numbers

billion billionth eight eighteen eighteenth eighth eightieth eighty eleven eleventh fifteen fifteenth fifth fiftieth fifty first five fortieth forty four fourteen fourteenth fourth hundred hundredth last million millionth next nine nineteen nineteenth ninetieth ninety ninth once one second seven seventeen seventeenth seventh seventieth seventy six sixteen sixteenth sixth sixtieth sixty ten tenth third thirteen thirteenth thirtieth thirty thousand thousandth three *thrice* twelfth twelve twentieth twenty twice two

References

Coxhead, A. (2000). A new academic word list. *TESOL Quarterly*, **34**, 2, 213–38.

Fountain, R. L. and Nation, I. S. P. (2000). A vocabulary-based graded dictation test. *RELC Journal*, **31**, 2, 29–44.

West, M. (1953). *A General Service List of English Words*. London: Longman, Green & Co.

Subject index

606

Author index

Because of the large number of citations of the leading vocabulary researchers, not all of their citations in the text are recorded in the following list.

Author index 615

Chujo, K. 305, 321
Chun, D. M. 239, 244, 247, 278, 285, 418, 433
Chung, M. 5, 8, 31, 41, 212, 260–261, 278, 294, 304–305, 310, 319, 321
Churchill, E. 368, 382
Clahsen, H. 11, 42
Clapham, C. 43, 324, 566
Clark, C. H. 104, 159,
Clark, E. V., 556, 563
Clarke, D. F. 369, 375–376, 382, 419, 433
Clenton, J. 557, 563
Coady, J. 155, 220, 287, 376, 383–384, 386
Cobb, T. 36–39, 41, 146–147, 153, 211–213, 239, 266, 278–280, 283–284, 288, 384, 469, 506, 509–510
Cohen, A. D. 143, 153, 289, 292, 294, 321, 419, 435
Coll, J. F. 148, 153, 345
Collins, L. 35, 41, 270, 280
Collins, M. F. 169, 199,
Combs, C. 155
Congdon, P. 564
Conklin, K. 482, 507, 509, 511
Conrad, S. 162, 199, 494, 508
Cook, J. M. 42, 353, 382
Corson, D. J. 47–48, 52, 86, 263, 271, 278, 300, 302, 308, 314–315, 321, 407, 411
Cortes, V. 508
Cot, M. 473
Cowan, J. R. 289, 291, 296, 305, 321
Coxhead, A. 6, 8, 19, 38, 41, 264, 270, 278, 289–291, 295, 297, 321
Coyle, G. 382
Crabbe, D. 39, 42, 181, 201, 496, 499, 511
Craik, F. I. M. 384, 462, 473
Cramer, S. 260, 278
Cripwell, K. 252, 278
Crookall, D. 438, 476
Crookes, G. 156, 574–576
Crossley, S. A. 210, 266–267, 278
Crothers, E. 439, 449, 457, 473
Crow, J. T. 46, 51, 86
Cruse, D. A. 81, 86
Cumming, G. 423, 433

Cummins, J. 162–164, 199
Cunningham, J. W. 292, 321
Cziko, G. A. 364, 382

D'Anna, C. A. 43, 92, 153, 523, 529, 563
Daller, H. 266, 278
Daneman, M. 364, 368, 382
Daulton, F. E. 13, 41, 74, 86, 410, 412
Davies, F. 312, 323,
Davies, M. 19, 41, 297, 495, 510, 56
Davies, P. 411, 563
Davis, C. E. 286, 567
Davis, J. N. 242, 245–246, 278
Davis, M. H. 412, 453, 473,
Davis, R. L. 286, 567
Day, R. R. 17, 158, 167,199, 219, 248, 256, 278, 356, 382, 416–417, 435
de Bot, K. 61–62, 86, 355, 383
de Glopper, K. 119, 159, 286, 355, 369–370, 383, 387
de Groot, A. M. B. 45, 87–88, 114, 122, 153, 156, 439, 446, 448, 456, 467, 473, 475
de Jong, N. 142, 153, 192, 199, 216, 278
de la Fuente, M. J. 173, 175, 179, 200
De Ridder, I.105, 153, 240, 242, 246, 279
Deconinck, J. 113–114, 153
Decoo, W. 160
Deese, J. 80, 87
deHaan, J. 148, 153, 176, 200
DeKeyser, R. M. 51, 87
Dempster, F. N. 452, 460–461, 473
Deno, S. L. 448, 473
Derewianka, B. 312, 322
Descamps, J. L. 146, 154, 587
Desrochers, A. 121, 157, 464, 473
Deweerdt, J. 224, 284
Diack, H. 539, 563
Dickinson, D. 476
Dieter, J. N. 459, 477
Diller, K. C. 13, 41, 527–529, 563
Dixon, R. 363–364, 384, 411
Dobinson, T. 180, 200
Dong, Q. 148, 159
Donkaewbua, S. 41, 153, 166, 199, 277, 382
Dordick, M. 267, 279